Mental Handicap

Mental Handicap

A multi-disciplinary approach

EDITED BY MICHAEL CRAFT
JOAN BICKNELL AND SHEILA HOLLINS

Baillière Tindall London Philadelphia Toronto
Mexico City Rio de Janeiro Sydney Tokyo Hong Kong

Baillière Tindall   1 St Anne's Road
W. B. Saunders   Eastbourne, East Sussex BN21 3UN, England

West Washington Square
Philadelphia, PA 19105, USA

1 Goldthorne Avenue
Toronto, Ontario M8Z 5T9, Canada

Apartado 26370 – Cedro 512
Mexico 4, DF Mexico

Rua Evaristo da Veiga 55,20° andar
Rio de Janeiro – RJ, Brazil

ABP Australia Ltd, 44–50 Waterloo Road
North Ryde, NSW 2113, Australia

Ichibancho Central Building, 22–1 Ichibancho
Chiyoda-ku, Tokyo 102, Japan

10/fl, Inter-Continental Plaza, 94 Granville Road
Tsim Sha Tsui East, Kowloon, Hong Kong

First published 1985

Typeset by Macmillan India Ltd, Bangalore
Printed in Great Britain at the Bath Press, Avon

British Library Cataloguing in Publication Data

Mental handicap: a multi-disciplinary approach.
   1. Mentally handicapped—Care and treatment
   I. Craft, Michael   II. Bicknell, Joan
   III. Hollins, Sheila
   362.3'8   HV3004

ISBN 0 7020 1085 5

Contents

Part 4   Education

Part 5   Intervention

Contributors

BERENDEAN ANSTICE
Head Occupational Therapist, Oxfordshire Mental Handicap Service, The Slade Hospital, Headington, Oxford OX3 7JH.

AARON H. ARMFIELD
Professor, Special Education Department, University of Nebraska at Omaha, Omaha, NB 68182, USA.

MICHAEL BARAITSER
Consultant Clinical Geneticist, The Hospital for Sick Children, Great Ormond Street, London WC1N 3JH.

IAN BERRY
Principal Clinical Psychologist, Broughton Hospital, Broughton, Chester.

PAUL BERRY
Reader, The Fred and Eleanor Schonell Educational Research Centre, University of Queensland, St Lucia, Queensland 4067, Australia.

JOAN BICKNELL
Professor of the Psychiatry of Mental Handicap, Department of Psychiatry, St George's Hospital Medical School, Jenner Wing, Cranmer Terrace, London SW17 0RE.

BRENDA L. G. BLYTHE
Superintendent Physiotherapist, Botleys Park Hospital, Guildford Road, Chertsey, Surrey KT16 0QA.

ROSEMARY BOWDEN
District Occupational Therapist, Rivermead Rehabilitation Centre, Abingdon Road, Oxford.

JOHN CORBETT
Physician, Hilda Lewis House, Bethlem Royal and Maudsley Hospital, 579 Wickham Road, Shirley, Croydon, Surrey CR0 8DR.

ANN CRAFT
Health Education Project, School of Education, University of Bath, Claverton Down, Bath, Avon BA2 7AY.

MICHAEL CRAFT
Mental Health Clinic, 121 Ferny Avenue, Surfers Paradise, Queensland 4217, Australia; *formerly* Consultant Psychiatrist, Bryn-y-Neuadd Hospital, Llanfairfechan, Wales.

CLIFF C. CUNNINGHAM
Senior Lecturer, Hester Adrian Research Centre, University of Manchester, Manchester M13 9PL.

HILTON DAVIS
Senior Lecturer in Clinical Psychology, London Hospital Medical College, Turner Street, London E1 2AD.

SALLY DAY
District Dietitian, Wandsworth Health Authority, St George's Hospital, Dorcas House, Blackshaw Road, London.

PETER GILBERT
Team Leader, Social Services Department, The Forest Hospital, 78 Crawley Road, Horsham, West Sussex RH12 4HN.

LARRY O. GOSTIN
Senior Fellow in Health Law, Harvard University School of Public Health/Medical School, Department of Health Policy and Management, 677 Huntington Avenue, Boston, MA 02115, USA; *formerly* General Secretary, National Council for Civil Liberties, 21 Tabard Street, London SE1 4LA.

BARRY GRAY
Senior Lecturer, Department of Nursing and Social Service, Dorset Institute of Higher Education, Wallisdown, Poole, Dorset BH12 5BB.

MATTHEW GRIFFITHS
Advisor for Education, Training and Employment, MENCAP, 123 Golden Lane, London EC1Y 0RT; *formerly* Advisory Lecturer for Students with Special Needs in Further Education, Inner London Education Authority.

PETER S. HARPER
Professor and Consultant in Medical Genetics, Department of Medicine, Welsh National School of Medicine, Heath Park, Cardiff CF4 4XN.

JOHN HERSOV
Tutor, Adult Education Training Unit, City Lit Centre for Adult Studies, Stukeley Street, Drury Lane, London EC2B 5LJ; Consultant in the field of self-advocacy work.

SHEILA HOLLINS
Senior Lecturer and Honorary Consultant in the Psychiatry of Mental Handicap, Department of Psychiatry, St George's Hospital Medical School, Jenner Wing, Cranmer Terrace, London SW17 0RE.

GWILYM HOSKING
Consultant Paediatric Neurologist, The Ryegate Centre, The Children's Hospital, Tapton Crescent Road, Sheffield S10 5DD.

MALCOLM L. JOHNSON
Professor of Health and Social Welfare and Director, Department of Health and Social Welfare, The Open University, Walton Hall, Milton Keynes MK7 6AA.

ISRAEL KOLVIN
Professor of Child and Adolescent Psychiatry, Nuffield Psychology and Psychiatry Unit, Fleming Memorial Hospital, Great North Road, Newcastle upon Tyne NE2 3AX.

DAVID NORRIS
Senior Lecturer, Department of Nursing and Social Service, Dorset Institute of Higher Education, Wallisdown Road, Wallisdown, Poole, Dorset BH12 5BB.

MAUREEN OSWIN
Research Officer, Thomas Coram Research Unit, 41 Brunswick Square, London WC1N 1AZ.

JOHN PATTEN
Consultant Neurologist, Department of Neurology, Royal Surrey County Hospital,
Farnham Road, Guildford, Surrey.

JACQUES PELLETIER
Executive Vice-President, Canadian Association for the Mentally Retarded, Kinsmen
NIMR Building, York University Campus, 4700 Keele Street, Downsview, Ontario
M3J 1P3, Canada.

SIR DESMOND POND
Formerly Professor of Psychiatry at the University of London and President of the Royal
College of Psychiatrists; *formerly* Chief Scientist to the Department of Health and Social
Security, Alexander Fleming House, Elephant and Castle, London SE1 6BY.

ANDREW H. REID
Consultant Psychiatrist, Royal Dundee Liff Hospital, Dundee DD2 5NF.

DIANE RICHLER
Director, National Institute on Mental Retardation, Kinsmen NIMR Building, York
University Campus, 4700 Keele Street, Downsview, Ontario M3J 1P3, Canada.

MARK ROBERTS
Headmaster, Rectory Paddock School, Main Road, St Paul's Cray, Orpington, Kent.

OLIVER RUSSELL
Consultant Senior Lecturer in Mental Health, Department of Mental Health, University of
Bristol, 41 St Michael's Hill, Bristol, Avon BS2 8DZ.

PHILIPPA RUSSELL
Senior Officer, Voluntary Council for Handicapped Children, 8 Wakley Street,
London EC1V 7QE.

DAVID T. SINES
Director of Nursing Services, Winchester Health Authority, Friars Gate Medical Centre,
Winchester, Hampshire SO23 8EF.

P. SLOPER
Hester Adrian Research Centre, University of Manchester, Manchester M13 9PL.

DAVID TOWELL
Fellow in Health Policy and Development, King's Fund College, 2 Palace Court, London
W2 4HS.

MARGARET WALKER
Chief Research Speech Therapist, Section of the Psychiatry of Mental Handicap, St
George's Hospital Medical School, Jenner Wing, Cranmer Terrace, London SW17 0RE.

PETER M. WILCOCK
District Clinical Psychologist, Winchester Health Authority, Friars Gate Medical Centre,
Winchester, Hampshire SO23 8EF.

JANET WYATT
Adult Education Training Unit, The City Lit Centre for Adult Studies, Stukeley Street,
Drury Lane, London EC2B 5LJ.

PART 1
AN OVERVIEW

Chapter 1
Introduction and Overview

JOAN BICKNELL

I'm not made of a different kind,
I don't want to be left behind,
I want to join with the others out there,
Answer me world with your love and care
And let me join in the playing.

Sir John Betjeman

This book is the successor to Tredgold's textbook, one of the classic medical textbooks on intellectual handicap since the beginning of this century. That book reflected throughout its life the mental handicap service at the time each edition was published, and although we have attempted to do the same the replacement of the medical model by the multi-disciplinary approach has caused us to produce an entirely new book. However, the three present editors pay homage to one of the great men in the early care of people with mental handicap, a man who combined compassion and scientific study for the good of those he served.

In the past a textbook on mental handicap was expected to meet the needs of the doctor working in a service which was essentially institution based. It was assumed that the person with the mental handicap was sick and was better off in an institution where first doctors and nurses, and later the professions supplementary to medicine, created the lifestyle. These institutions were essentially for all ages, giving a cradle-to-grave service intended to replicate an English village or self-sufficient colony. Admission was frequently for negative reasons: because the family could not cope, or the child was too dependent or too disturbed; rarely had that child the opportunity for a full investigation by a child-centred service. Occasionally, the admission was based on the assumption that the lifestyle in the institution was more appropriate than that which could be created in the home. This even applied to staff, as this 1930 advertisement indicates: 'Nurse required at the Royal — Institution. Piano player or gardener preferred.'

Segregated in hospitals or colonies, doctors had the responsibility for the diagnosis of the cause of mental handicap, which became an increasing interest for the psychiatrists in these places; they developed expertise in biochemistry, neuropathology and genetics.

The training of such psychiatrists was often isolated, with little emphasis placed on acquiring the skills of the general psychiatrist. Instead, they were expected to acquire a detailed knowledge of the aetiology of mental handicap, the management of additional disorders, such as epilepsy and cerebral palsy, and managerial skills so that they could become benevolent maintainers and superintendents of institutions.

There is little doubt that in those days, with a non-existent or embryonic welfare state and with society's disparaging attitude to mentally handicapped people, many who lived in institutions were saved from the much worse fate of an unsupported community existence.

But times have changed. No longer is the doctor in the mental handicap service expected or indeed able to be fully appraised of the many conditions that cause intellectual handicap. Today this is the role of the obstetrician, with the techniques of antenatal diagnosis, the neonatologist, with a vast array of technological resources, the cytogeneticist, the biochemist, the developmental paediatrician and the genetic counsellor. The psychiatrist can now expect that most mentally handicapped children will have been fully investigated prior to referral to him, or can be referred by him for that purpose. Of course, he must still be aware of aetiological factors in what is commonly a multiply handicapped individual. He needs to understand the stresses of a family who find that their child has a recessive disorder: another child may be a carrier, so a knowledge of genetics is essential in the attempt to support that family in their grief. In this book aetiology is discussed in broad overview in Chapters 10, 11 and 12.

Following aetiological diagnosis, the mental

3

handicap service of the 1980s uses the community rather than the institution as the basis for support and treatment, with both the consciousness that people with mental handicap have the right to ordinary lives and the awareness of their vulnerability unless their ordinary and special needs are also met. The matrix of care into which our various skills are directed is considered so important by the editors that the first chapters of this book are devoted to an outline of the current state of services in this country (Chapters 2 to 5), while Chapter 6 gives a parallel picture for North America.

For those who live in the community ordinary general health care should be as readily available as it is for those who are not handicapped: for those still living in long-stay hospitals there is a likelihood of increasing interest from those doctors who also serve the general population (Chapter 34). The role of the psychiatrist is therefore likely to become more clearly focused on the families and individuals for whom handicap is a major burden, resulting in undue stress, behaviour disorders, psychiatric illnesses and avoidable misery (Chapters 13, 14, 28 and 33).

Living in the community requires far greater skills, more sophisticated standards of behaviour and a greater knowledge of social mores than are needed for institutional life, and results in exposure to the stresses of adverse life events. The inevitable maturation of the child to adulthood brings sexual challenges which cannot be overlooked in the community as they probably were in the long-stay hospitals. As the rights of mentally handicapped people are being championed so must opportunities for learning be provided, so that people with mental handicap acquire skills, through continuing and appropriate education, to acknowledge and make use of these rights.

The chapters in the fourth section of the book give a comprehensive account of education from pre-school times to adulthood both here and in the United States. The current Education Acts enable and indeed give the right for mentally handicapped children to be educated until their late teens. With the developing enthusiasm for further education and adult education, with current concepts such as 'mainstreaming' being debated and practised, and with the rapid increase in the use of high technology in education, education is an important and exciting area of growth in the services for mentally handicapped people.

Education for social competence must be broadly based. Chapters 16 and 17 deal with two important topics in community living; these are sexuality and

interpersonal relationships and the mentally handicapped person's experience of loss and bereavement. Chapter 8 outlines the current state of the law in this country, the preceding chapter examines the link between low intelligence and delinquency, and Chapter 36 deals with the management of aggression.

This book, therefore, reflects the changing emphasis in philosophy within the services for mentally handicapped people, the clarification of the role of the psychiatrist, the involvement of other doctors in health care provision and the dissolution of the traditional medical model. These services are now built round a multi-disciplinary team described in outline in Chapter 24, with the contributions of individual professions presented in more detail in Chapters 25 to 32 – nursing, social work, psychology, psychiatry, speech therapy, physiotherapy, occupational therapy and the role of voluntary organizations. All those who work with mentally handicapped people and their families will benefit by reading Chapter 15 on the art of counselling.

Those who espouse the teamwork model will be the first to confess that it is not easy, and that good teamwork requires commitment and loyalty from each member irrespective of individual professional skills. Yet, if it is acknowledged that the many and various needs of a person with mental handicap can only be met by a team of helpers that will be different at each point in his life, then the need for effective teamwork is a challenge that cannot be ignored.

This is therefore a multi-disciplinary text for all professions involved in the care of people with mental handicap. It is hoped that the postgraduate or post-diploma student of any profession involved at some point in this caring service will find it stimulating and possibly provocative. Many readers will probably select first the contribution from their own colleague to compare, criticize and possibly use the contents of that chapter as a personal checklist, but it is from our increase in knowledge of the skills and relevance of other team members, with a more sympathetic understanding of their role, that the book can be of most value to all professionals, and ultimately to those whom we aim to serve.

Services for mentally handicapped people may be analysed according to the model that is predominantly espoused. The *medical* model, where the handicapped person is seen as sick, applies only to the few who still need hospital care. The social *deviancy* model, where efforts are made to provide segregation and security, applies to even fewer. The *developmental* model, which emphasizes the disparity between the mental and chronological age, is certainly useful, but there is the risk that the more mature needs of the profoundly handicapped adult may be forgotten.

The *warehousing* model reminds us of the time when it was assumed that mentally handicapped people could, and indeed should, be merely contained and 'stored' safely, safeguarded against interference with society – a grim reminder of the origins of some of our present day services. The *horticultural* model assumes that with good premises and equipment mentally handicapped people will feed themselves cheaply and 'flourish' with little in the way of teaching, guidance and support. Yet, those who manage services know that the greatest challenge lies in the maintenance of a good service when the initial burst of enthusiasm and goodwill is over.

Finally, two models – *normalization* as a philosophy and goal, and *multi-disciplinary teamwork* as the process whereby that goal is reached – are those that run throughout this book. They link the various chapters into a united response to the needs and rights of the person with mental handicap.

If there are two omissions from this book then one is a contribution by a handicapped person and another by a parent. Perhaps the latter is partially covered by the fact that several of the contributors have experience of a handicapped person in their families and their writing has been consciously influenced by this. The first omission can be put right by including the dictation of Stephen who was removed from institutional care at $2\frac{1}{2}$ years old and has led a full life in the community despite cerebral palsy, epilepsy and a severe mental handicap. He tells his own story as follows (Hung and Binh are Vietnamese friends):

The Lodge is my Home

I am Stephen Humphreys. I am twenty-one. I live in the Lodge. I have been here for two years. Before I came here I went to Halliwick where Hung goes. I used to look after six tortoises. I looked after three guinea-pigs and one frog. I had to clean the guinea-pigs and tortoises. We go to a pottery class, add money and go to the post office. When I first went there Mr Browning, the headmaster, took us all to the Hall and said to me, 'I hope you like it here'. I left when I was nineteen.

I have got a friend: her name is Auntie Joan. And Diane met me at Auntie's house and she said to me how would I like to come here at Christmas and try it out? I stayed in a room in the house. I didn't settle in quickly, but at the end I did. I liked Nicole because she was fun. I went back to school after Christmas holidays and Jane, the physio, told me how to ride my bike. She told me she was leaving one day and when I saw Mr Browning he said that I

was going to leave too. To come here. I was very pleased. I asked my Auntie before if I could come here, and she chattered to Diane. And I came here.

I came to the Lodge and Nicole looked after me. They kept on talking about Michael and I didn't know who he was. But now he comes and stays at the Lodge for short stays and I like him very much. He is a very great joker!

Andrew used to take me on the bus to Cranstock, where I work – to show me the route. I now go on my own. I make bricks for starting fires, lighters for starting cigarettes, and we do car numbers – sorting them out into piles – and our friend Trevor takes them to Woking. I was shy when I first went there but now know what it is like and have made lots of friends.

In the Lodge Sue and Cheryl live with me. I have two cats – Sarah and Blackie – and a fish and Michelle, the tortoise. I help Matilda, the goat. I go to Phab Club in Woking and the Catholic club where I go to church. I used to go by minibus every week but now I go on the bus on my own. I like going on the bus by myself.

Sue (who looks after me) used to come with me to the post office in Camberley on a Thursday to get my money. We used to go by bus. I now go on my own on the bus after work and cash my money every Thursday.

I am doing my Duke of Edinburgh [award]. I have done a Care of Animals course. I am going on an expedition and if possible I shall go horse-riding for the sport part. I do bird-watching with my binoculars, see different birds and write them down in my book. That is also for my Duke of Edinburgh [award]. I am doing the bronze award.

Every two weeks I have got confirmation classes at church. We learn how to be a Catholic. I also go to special Masses for confirmation. I take the bread up for the service.

I feed the cats, lay the table for breakfast and clear away the things afterward. In the evening I make sandwiches for work. I choose my clothes for work. I go to the hairdresser's on my own when I think my hair needs cutting. I clean the tortoises out and look after them with Binh. I give Matilda her food each day. I watch TV in the Lodge, and I enjoy listening to my tapes on my tape-recorder. I make toast. I made bread with Nicole. I made cakes and a pizza with Sue, and Cornish pasties. I go up to Heatherside if I want something. I bought a battery for my torch. I post my letters at the post box near Prior Road and Heatherside.

I used to visit my Mum and Dad in Mitcham. Now I can't, because they have gone to Canada to stay. I ring my brother. I ring him up and visit him. He has been to visit me and I have been to visit him. Gary is coming again in June. My Granny has come to see Blackie, who used to live with her.

I like football, and my friend Paul (who works in the house) takes me to see Aldershot play at home. I am going this Saturday. I keep in touch with Nicole and I am going to see her in London on the nineteenth [May]. I did my sponsored walk in Hyde Park on Monday with my Phab club. I met Jimmy Saville.

I wouldn't say the Lodge is home as the home with my Mum and Dad, but the Lodge is *my home*.'

Stephen was lucky. He experienced a wide range of ordinary and special services that enabled him to live an ordinary life.

After much thought a medical student at St George's Hospital Medical School defined a person with mental handicap as 'a person who through developmental intellectual handicap requires special services to lead an ordinary life'. This book is about special services and ordinary lives.

Chapter 2
The Organization of Services
Towards Greater Cooperation:
Patterns of Support and Care

OLIVER RUSSELL

During the past thirty years there has been a substantial shift in our understanding of the ways in which resources can most effectively be used to meet the needs of people with mental handicap. The change in our approach to the organization of services has been made possible by a more informed understanding of the role played by members of the family supporting and caring for a mentally handicapped person, by a rediscovery of the processes whereby people with developmental disabilities can learn new skills and acquire greater degrees of independence, and by a shift in social attitudes to the rights of disabled and handicapped people.

In this chapter I shall explore how changes in the planning and organization of services have reflected new ways of structuring care and support. These structures themselves reflect both changes in the theory and philosophy of those working with handicapped people and developments in methods of intervention and support. Examples of current practice will be used to illustrate different styles and methods of working.

WHY SERVICES ARE CHANGING

The social system through which resources and personal support are made available to people with mental handicap is diffuse and complex. Some parts of the system can be readily identified because their specialized function is clear for all to see. Other parts are less visible. The system can be divided into three constituent parts:

1 The financial benefits provided by central government in the form of supplementary benefit payments, attendance allowances and mobility allowances form a crucial part of the household budget for most mentally handicapped people and their families. The quality of life for individuals and their families may be critically determined by the availability of an adequate level of benefit. Recent experiences reported by mentally handicapped people who have been discharged from hospital into minimum-support group homes suggests that they may frequently experience severe hardship because of the low levels of benefit received.

2 The second strand is the informal support provided by the network of neighbours, family and friends. This support system may be difficult to quantify, but for most mentally handicapped people living in the community it is this informal network which sustains them and enables them to become socially integrated into their local neighbourhood.

3 The statutory and voluntary agencies provide the third strand of the system. Social workers, home care assistants and community nurses can probably be most useful when they build on the support being given by family, neighbours and friends. Schools, training centres, hostels and hospitals also form part of this third strand.

This social system which sustains mentally handicapped people is passing through a period of transition. The long-established framework of institutional support is being dismantled before alternative community-based services have been developed. As a consequence of these changes staff working in the institutions feel insecure and uncertain in their role. As investment by the health service and social service departments in the fabric of hostels, hospitals and other residential services declines, so the social security system plays an increasingly important role in maintaining and supporting people. Special rates of supplementary benefit are now available to support severely mentally handicapped people living in ordinary houses and in homes run by voluntary and private agencies.

Although the shift of resources from hospital care to community care has been advocated for many years the realization that large hospitals may soon actually be closing their doors has come as a surprise to many. In his 1970 Reith Lectures, Donald Schon showed how similar transitions have affected other types of social and business systems in Western Europe and North America (Schon, 1971). He described how social systems rarely move smoothly from one state of their culture to another. He observed that 'something old must come apart in order for something new to come together'. For individuals working in the system there is no clear grasp of what is to come, only a clear picture of what has been lost. The dismemberment of a system based largely on custodial care in large institutions must inevitably cause anguish for those who were committed to that system. The loss of professional identity, uncertainties about a future role and doubts about the viability of planned alternative systems of care may combine to generate resentment and fear.

In his analysis of the process of transition Schon argues that change can only rarely be attributed to a single cause. Change usually comes about as a consequence of the interplay between key elements of the system which is in the process of transition. He suggests that those elements comprise the structure of the system, the technology which it employs and the theory and philosophy which guide it. The *structure* is made up of the sets of roles and relationships among the individual members of the system. The *theory* concerns the views held within the social system about its purposes, operation, environment and future. The structure and theory in turn influence the prevailing *technology*.

The elements of structure, theory and technology provide an appropriate framework for our discussion of the process of change in the organization of services for mentally handicapped people.

THE STRUCTURE OF SERVICES

Until the mid-1950s the organization of services providing care and support for mentally handicapped people was dominated by large institutions. The hierarchical structure within these institutions provided a kind of stability but did not easily accommodate change. Because the institutions had a virtual monopoly of services, the roles and relationships of those working with handicapped people were largely conditioned by the institutional model of custodial care.

Outside the institutions the mental health departments of the local authorities provided occupation and support for those mentally handicapped people who lived at home with their families. Mentally handicapped children came under the same provision, as they were considered to be ineducable and were excluded from the education system.

The need for change in that structure was confirmed by the report of the 1957 Royal Commission on the Mental Health Services, which recommended an extension of community care. However, little happened to alter the status quo until 1969, when the report of the Ely Hospital enquiry triggered off the changes which led to the White Paper *Better Services for the Mentally Handicapped* (DHSS, 1971).

When we explore the contemporary structure of services we find that other influences have begun to make a significant impact on the kinds of care and support received by mentally handicapped people. The following examples illustrate the new pressures being brought to bear.

1 The legislation which brought mentally handicapped children into the educational system (Education (Handicapped Children) Act 1971) has now been in operation long enough for us to see the first generation of children leave school after twelve or thirteen years of full-time education. The parents of these children are vocal in their demands for a wider range of options for their teenage children and for a bigger say in what those options will be.
2 In the course of the past decade parents have forged powerful links with professionals, especially in the field of education. These working partnerships between parents and professionals are now a potent force in the shaping of services (Mittler and Mittler, 1983).
3 Alliances between like-minded parents and professionals have led to the establishment of new and more powerful pressure groups. Common concern about the inadequacies of services has led to demands for the reform and restructuring of many parts of the health and local authority services.
4 The introduction of improved cash benefits, such as attendance allowances, mobility allowances and supplementary benefit payments, has provided the opportunity for the purchase of additional support and service.

5 An awareness that profits could be made from the provision of residential services has attracted private investment. Government legislation has encouraged the private entrepreneur, and the state monopoly of residential services is beginning to be eroded. How far these challenges from the private sector will promote better standards and how far they may lead to competition for the same limited resources remains to be seen.

6 Partnerships between health authorities and local authorities have been encouraged by the provision of extra finance for schemes which are jointly managed. Without joint finance many of the most innovative developments in community care would never have been launched.

The structure of the social system which supports handicapped people is likely to change under the influence of these pressures. The pace of that change and the direction it takes will not only be determined by local circumstances and the availability of resources of money and manpower, but most importantly, by the skill and competence of local managers.

THE THEORY AND PHILOSOPHY WHICH UNDERPIN THE ORGANIZATION OF CARE

The pressure for change in the organization of services which emerged in the mid-1950s was informed in part by the results of psychological research. Up until that time it had been assumed that people who were in need of care had irremediable defects in their intellectual functioning and were incapable of benefiting from education or training. A minority who were capable of sheltered employment were absorbed into menial jobs in the institutions.

In the early 1950s researchers demonstrated that so-called 'ineducable' people had the potential to acquire new skills and learn new tasks (Tizard and O'Connor, 1952; Clarke and Clarke, 1954; O'Connor and Tizard, 1954). The 'irremediable defects' were capable of improvement even if the learning difficulties could not be fully overcome. Although mentally handicapped children were slow in their intellectual development, their potential for learning continued into adulthood.

Subsequent reasearch confirmed and extended these findings, and legislation providing full-time education for all handicapped children created the opportunity to convert theory into practice.

Further acknowledgement of the impact of psychological research is to be found in the field of adult education. Mentally handicapped adults now participate in programmes of activity which encourage them to continue their education beyond school. Social education centres focus much time and attention on advancing the social and educational skills of their students.

Following on from the discovery that mentally handicapped people may have an unrealized potential for development has come a growing conviction that many services not only fail to enhance the potential skills of their clients, but may actually devalue them by treating them as less than fully human or by relating to them as children. The principles of normalization (Wolfensberger, 1980; O'Brien and Tyne, 1981) concern the ways in which a service uses culturally valued means to enable people to cope and behave in culturally appropriate and valued ways. Normalization workshops have been held in many parts of the country and the influence of normalization principles can be found in services in most parts of the United Kingdom.

Agreement about an overall philosophy of care is less of a problem than it was. The difficulties of translating the agreed philosophy into practice form the most difficult stumbling block for a service in transition.

THEORY INTO PRACTICE – THE TECHNOLOGY OF THE SERVICE

Services for people with mental handicap are labour-intensive. Staffing levels have gradually increased over the course of the past decade in both day services and residential services, but it has become clear that high staff/client ratios will not by themselves bring about change in the quality of the service offered to the users. Staff must be provided with a structure within which to serve the needs of their clients; they must be taught specific skills and they must be supported and given the motivation to work effectively.

The psychological discoveries of the 1950s found their first practical application in the Brooklands Residential Unit (Tizard, 1964). In this experiment an opportunity was provided for sixteen mentally handicapped children to be cared for outside the traditional hospital setting. An attempt was made to modify the behaviour and to develop the potential of these children in a child-centred environment which was both secure and challenging. The children were divided into family groups, and staff were encouraged to adopt a developmental approach to the children in their care. Specific techniques were evolved to deal with the problems of dressing, eating, washing and toileting. A daily programme, which combined consistency with variety, was established. Special attention was paid to language development and communication.

In reviewing the outcome of the study Tizard concluded that neither nursing training nor the training of teachers for mentally handicapped children could be regarded as a suitable preparation for work in such a setting. In his view insufficient attention was paid in staff training to child development as a subject and to the practical instruction given to the staff in the actual day-to-day techniques of child management. The small size of the unit brought great benefits but the 'technology' was inadequate.

The establishment of small, locally based units in Wessex during the 1960s and 1970s provided further opportunities to explore the kinds of skill needed by residential staff. The Health Care Evaluation Research Team (HCERT) devised ways of clarifying what direct-care staff actually do within the residential settings in which they work. The research team were interested in comparing the performances of staff in the experimental locally based hospital units, which the Wessex Region had developed, with the performances of those working in traditional hospital wards. The researchers found that it was necessary, both in observing and describing these performances, to be highly specific in what they recorded. They distinguished between performance statements and 'fuzzies'. A performance statement is one that includes a precise description of what will be done, together with criteria by which one can tell whether or not it has been done. A 'fuzzy' is an ambiguous statement which describes what people do or are expected to do, but in a vague and imprecise way (Felce et al., 1977).

The Bereweeke Skill Teaching System (Mansell et al., 1979) is a technology which was developed out of this research. The teaching system is designed to be run by the front-line staff in a residential facility, with the back-up and support of an administrator who monitors how well the system is working. Staff are provided with detailed individual teaching programmes, each covering one weekly step towards a long-term goal for their client. The system works on a weekly basis, with new activity charts being written on the same day each week. The provision of handbooks, workshop manuals and checklists enables the system to be quickly and effectively introduced into new settings.

Many recently established community services have invested substantial amounts of time in training direct-care staff for the tasks which they will be required to undertake. The challenges of supporting severely disabled and profoundly handicapped people in ordinary housing has focused attention on the need for more sophisticated approaches to staff training (Shearer, 1983; Ward, 1984, 1985).

At NIMROD, the comprehensive community-based service in Cardiff, procedural guides have been developed to help staff in converting policy into practice. Twenty-seven procedural guides have been written covering four categories of activity: domestic routines in the running of the houses, administrative routines, procedures for the teaching of new skills and guidelines for reviewing the progress of clients.

Another useful method of helping staff to plan for the needs of individual clients is the Individual Programme Plan. The IPP is a written programme of intervention and action drawn up by people who are regularly involved with an individual client. Specific objectives are set and ways of attaining these goals are agreed among all those working with the client. The plan outlines the steps which the client can take in each area of development and specifies the support which will be needed (Blunden, 1980; King's Fund Centre, 1980).

MENTALLY HANDICAPPED PEOPLE WITH SPECIAL NEEDS

Perhaps the most difficult challenge for both hospital and community-based staff is presented by people who have a profound mental or physical handicap or a severe auditory or visual disability or have major behavioural problems. Such people have complex needs and demand highly sophisticated management if they are to achieve their potential for functional independence. They are often excluded from adult training centres or day centres, and families may have to cope without help for up to 24 hours a day. Staff in the back wards of mental handicap hospitals may similarly face intolerable difficulties in coping with the intense demand placed on them. In the management of this group the translation of theory into practice is still at a very early stage. A recent study (DHSS, 1984) has provided a valuable overview of work currently taking place with this group of clients. The report emphasizes the need for each day to be carefully structured to provide an enjoyable learning experience and to provide time for both group work and one-to-one work with clients. The advantages of the Room Management Scheme (Porterfield and Blunden, 1981; Mansell et al., 1982) are described. This technique was first introduced into a special needs unit in South Wales and has proved to be a valuable way of making better use of limited staffing resources.

The use of specially designed play materials and custom-built toys is another recently developed means of engaging those in whom a serious degree of behavioural disturbance complicates their handicap. An evaluation of this type of intervention is being undertaken to establish how it can best be used (Caldwell and Russell, 1984).

NEW PATTERNS OF ORGANIZATION

Every generation attempts to devise ways of solving the pressing human and social problems which it faces. Those who established the Poor Law institutions in the 1830s were attempting to meet the needs of their time. Those who built the 'colonies' for mentally handicapped people at the beginning of this century were meeting a contemporary need. Most organizations have an inertia which sustains them and enables them to survive long after the need for their services has passed. There is frequently a mismatch between what an organization or institution offers and what the clients actually need.

Perhaps because today's services have been built upon the heritage of the past, the rivalries of past generations continue to impede working relationships. Jealousy between those working in the National Health Service and in the local authorities about the allocation of resources ensures that the divisions of the past are perpetuated in the present.

The structure of services for people with mental handicap is changing. Hospitals and adult training centres are gradually being replaced by smaller units of management in which services are arranged more flexibly and more in tune with the needs of individuals. This change in structure has created the opportunities for the development of novel methods of teaching and engagement. These new ways of working have been informed and nourished by research and by significant changes in the attitudes of staff to the tasks which they face. The new technology has evolved to meet the needs of new patterns of organization.

Bringing about change and devising new patterns or organization depends not only on the injection of new ideas but on a willingness to accept new organizational structures. The health service, the local authorities and agencies in the voluntary and private sector share responsibility for the provision of services to people with mental handicap. Education, residential care, day services and support services are provided within a loose framework, which is often poorly coordinated. New patterns of organization have become possible as a consequence of initiatives taken by both public and private bodies.

PLANNING A COMPREHENSIVE SERVICE

The organization of services should, in an ideal world, be constructed so that each handicapped person can have access to the range of resources which he or she is likely to require, have the personal support necessary to enable him or her to benefit from these resources and through this support have the opportunity to enjoy life as a valued member of a local community. An effective pattern of services is one which allows the handicapped person to share the patterns of life and conditions of everyday living which are valued in our society.

The Jay Committee (1979) outlined a model of care which provides a picture of what services in the future could and should look like. Intrinsic to this model are five service principles:

1 Mentally handicapped people should use normal services wherever possible.
2 Existing networks of community support should be strengthened by professional services and not supplanted by them.
3 Specialized services or organizations for mentally handicapped people should be provided only to the extent that they can demonstrably meet or are likely to meet additional needs that cannot be met by the general services.
4 There should be a 'life plan' for every individual mentally handicapped person so that coordination and continuity of care may be achieved.
5 There should be someone to intercede on behalf of mentally handicapped people to enable them to obtain appropriate services.

The report of the Jay Committee was published at an opportune moment. Financial constraints inhibited the development of local authority services and, although the building of adult training centres continued, the building of new hostels had virtually come to a halt. Health authorities had become increasingly perplexed about how to promote joint planning with local authorities and, apart from an expansion in the numbers of community mental handicap nurses (Hall and Russell, 1984), there had been little real progress in the initiation and development of new services since the reorganization of the National Health Service in 1974.

By enunciating the principles around which new services might be planned, the report of the Jay Committee facilitated the development of a range of options for meeting local needs. The publication of *An Ordinary Life* (King's Fund Centre, 1980), the Guy's Health District plan (Guy's Health District, 1981) and the handbook on local services published by the British Institute of Mental Handicap (Simon, 1981) provided much of the stimulus for the initiation of change in the organization of local services.

Where does effective planning begin?

There was a time when planning meant taking a DHSS norm for the number of beds or day centre places required per thousand population and then multiplying that figure by the size of the catchment population. Indeed, some regional planning continues to use these yardsticks. We can now appreciate that such an approach to planning merely perpetuates the past.

Glennerster (1983) argues that the generation of alternative futures must be the first task of the planning team. Because the alternative modes of care and support are changing so rapidly new ways of thinking about the spectrum of services need to be generated.

Guidance from the centre

The Department of Health and Social Security has a management role and a monitoring role in relation to mental handicap services. The management role is expressed via the regional health authorities and through white papers and other documents detailing government policy. The monitoring role is exercised by the Social Work Advisory Service, by the regional liaison officers and by the National Development Team for Mentally Handicapped People.

Until 1980 the National Development Group also provided an important focus for the generation and discussion of new ideas for the organization of services. The pamphlets produced by the NDG stimulated much local discussion and created a climate for change.

A review paper *Mental Handicap: Progress, Problems and Priorities* (DHSS, 1980) provided an overview of the developments which had occurred during the 1970s. The paper, however, gave little guidance to those planning services in the 1980s apart from encouraging authorities to develop local services and warning of the potentially disruptive effects of having a single mental handicap service.

The guidance from the National Development Team (NDT) was much more direct (Development Team for the Mentally Handicapped, 1982). The NDT pressed the view that each health district should provide its own locally based service. The NDT saw the community mental handicap team as the focus of that service. In health districts which had no residential services the team advocated that community units should be established to provide a local resource for residential care, both short-term and long-term, and some day care. The visits of the NDT provided an opportunity for local authority and health service managers to review their progress but they were not obliged to take up the advice offered. It is difficult to assess whether the NDT has had any significant impact on the pattern of developing services. Although many authorities have established community mental handicap teams and community units, others have chosen to develop their local services according to different models.

The most fundamental changes brought about by central government in the pattern of services have come about through the joint financing arrangements. In the consultative paper *Care in the Community* (DHSS, 1981) the government outlined ways in which they intended that authorities might use resources to achieve more care in the community. Subsequent circulars have reaffirmed the government's intention to promote more community-based care by the transfer of resources from the health service into local authority provision.

After a decade and a half of commitment to the establishment of locally based services there is surprisingly little evidence that central government has been able to achieve much real change in the pattern of organization of care. The large institutions have been reduced in size, more adult training centres have been built and more community mental handicap nurses have been employed, but the pattern of services remains essentially the same. The split between those provided by the local authorities and those provided by the health service remains. Joint plans are beginning to be made but there is little sign of any true partnership emerging (House of Commons, 1985).

Initiatives by regional health authorities

Within the National Health Service regional health authorities have responsibility for strategic planning. Some regions (Wessex for example) have pioneered new patterns of organization for the residential care of mentally handicapped people and have had the results systematically evaluated (Felce et al., 1977). Other regions have sought to establish new patterns of organization that involve the local authorities. The North Western Regional Health Authority (1982) has produced an outline for a 'model district service'. This report challenges the assumption that the health service should provide for the more dependent adults and the social services for those who are less dependent. It proposes that a local service can only be effective if both partners jointly provide for the full range of handicapped people. The report proposes changes in day services so that adult training centres can become resource centres and part of a network of community services. Such a network would include further education colleges, courses in social skills and survival skills, vocational training programmes, work enclave schemes and leisure schemes. With regard to residential services the report adopts the model of a local service pioneered by the Eastern Nebraska Community Office of Retardation (ENCOR) and elaborated in a British context by the Ordinary Life Working Party (King's Fund Centre, 1980).

Partnerships at a county level

The implementation of change at a county level depends on close collaboration between a county council and the matching district health authorities. Kent County Council and Kent Health Authority (1981) pioneered the development of the 'single service partnership'. The document in which the partnership was outlined laid particular emphasis on the role of the community mental handicap team in coordinating existing services and in advising on facilities required in the future. One of the most radical and innovative suggestions in an earlier edition of the partnership document was that the health authority and the local authority social services department should pool their revenue resources for mentally handicapped people, and use the partnership as a means of redeploying funds to where they would be most effectively used. In the final version this proposal had to be withdrawn.

In Newcastle upon Tyne a 'Mental Handicap Management Partnership' has been set up between the health authority, the social services department of the local authority, parents and voluntary organizations. The significant element in the Newcastle plan is that parents are involved in the joint planning and management of services. Like the Kent plan the Newcastle proposals make the community mental handicap team the focus for work in the community (Newcastle City Council and Newcastle Area Health Authority, 1981).

The most sophisticated approach to joint development of services at a county level is taking place in South Glamorgan. NIMROD is a community-based service meeting the needs of a defined population in the west of Cardiff. A long-term evaluation of this jointly managed service is in progress (Humphreys et al., 1984).

Voluntary agencies and charitable trusts

Unlike government departments and local authorities, voluntary agencies have complete discretion about how they exercise their influence. Because they do not have responsibility for the whole range of services they can focus attention on particular issues. In the mental handicap field Barnardo's have pioneered residential services for children based on the ENCOR model. The Cheshire Foundation have explored new ways of developing family support services as well as providing opportunities for mentally handicapped children to move into ordinary housing. The Joseph Rowntree Memorial Trust has taken on responsibility for administering the Family Fund, which provides financial benefit and support to thousands of handicapped children and their families. The Trust has more recently become engaged in the sponsorship of research and development and has focused its energies particularly on housing, occupation and care. The evaluation of the Wells Road Service in Bristol (Ward, 1984) and the evaluation of community mental handicap teams in Nottinghamshire are two examples of research sponsored by the Trust which will have implications for the pattern of services in the future.

Other voluntary organizations, like the King's Fund Centre, have played a key role in the dissemination of new ideas. *An Ordinary Life* (King's Fund Centre, 1980) has been followed by other reports and project papers which have reviewed the development of community-based services (Ward, 1982) and the training of staff to work in local services based on ordinary housing (Shearer, 1983).

Professional organizations and the voice of pressure groups

The Royal College of Psychiatrists (1983) has suggested that no single form of provision can meet the needs of the entire range of mentally handicapped people. The College believes that a wide variety of services is required because of the enormous range of handicaps and disabilities in those being served. It advocates that there should be small locally based specialized units which act as resource centres for the catchment area population. Depending on the prevalence of a particular disability the specialized unit might be needed on a district or regional basis. The specialized services would include inpatient facilities for short-term and long-term care, day services, including outpatient clinics, community nursing, family therapy and consultancy services for those working in social services and education.

Other professionals have argued that it is possible to provide services for *all* mentally handicapped people in the community, including profoundly multiply handicapped and behaviourally disturbed people, and that the key feature in the pattern of any service is the staff, their skills and the way they work, not the buildings or units in which they are accommodated (Russell, 1985).

The Campaign for Mentally Handicapped People (CMH) has been the most active and articulate of the pressure groups calling for a change in the organization of services. Working closely with its sister organization CMHERA (CMH Education and Research Association) it has run normalization workshops for groups of staff and managers in many parts of the country. The introduction of the PASS (Program Analysis of Service Systems) evaluation system has provided a structure within which new patterns of service organization can be assessed and existing services evaluated (Wolfensberger, 1980).

THE NEXT STEPS

Comprehensive community-based services are still in their infancy. They will need to be carefully nurtured if they are to survive and flourish. The next steps which have to be taken can be clearly identified (IDC, 1984). Implementation of change will depend not only on the availability of adequate financial resources but also on the recruitment of staff who have the energy and vision to translate theory into practice.

REFERENCES

Blunden R (1980) *Individual Plans for Mentally Handicapped People: A Draft Procedural Guide*. Cardiff: Mental Handicap in Wales – Applied Research Unit.

Caldwell PA & Russell O (1984) *Reaching Out – Techniques for Engagement with Severely Disturbed and Profoundly Mentally Handicapped Adolescents and Young People*. Unpublished report to the Mental Health Foundation.

Clarke ADB & Clarke AM (1954) Cognitive changes in the feeble-minded. *British Journal of Psychology* **45**: 173–179.

Development Team for the Mentally Handicapped (1982) *3rd Report (1979–1981)* London: HMSO.

DHSS (Department of Health and Social Security) (1971) *Better Services for the Mentally Handicapped*. Cmnd. 4683. London: HMSO.

DHSS (Department of Health and Social Security) (1980) *Mental Handicap: Progress, Problems and Priorities*. London: DHSS.

DHSS (Department of Health and Social Security) (1981) *Care in the Community: A Consultative Document on Moving Resources for Care in England*. London: DHSS.

DHSS (Department of Health and Social Security) (1984) *Helping Mentally Handicapped People with Special Problems – Report of a DHSS Study Team*. London: DHSS.

Felce D, Kushlick A, Lunt B & Powell E (1977) *Evaluation of Locally Based Hospital Units for the Mentally Handicapped in Wessex*. Winchester: Health Care Evaluation Research Team.

Glennerster H (1983) *Planning for Priority Groups*. Oxford: Martin Robertson.

Guy's Health District (1981) *Development Group for Services for Mentally Handicapped People: Report to the District Management Team*. London: Guy's Hospital.

Hall V & Russell O (1985) Community mental handicap nurses: the birth, growth and development of an idea. In Sines D & Bicknell J (eds) *Caring for Mentally Handicapped People in the Community*. London: Harper & Row.

House of Commons (1985) *Social Services Committee Report on Community Care*. London: HMSO.

Humphreys S, Lowe K, McLaughnin S & Blunden R (1984) Long term evaluation of services for mentally handicapped people in Cardiff: annual report for 1983. Cardiff: Mental Handicap in Wales Applied Research Unit.

IDC (Independent Development Council for People with Mental Handicap) (1984) *Next Steps*. London: Independent Development Council.

Jay Committee (1979) *Report of the Committee of Enquiry into Mental Handicap Nursing and Care*. Cmnd. 7468. London: HMSO.

Kent County Council and Kent Health Authority (1981) *Mental Handicap: A Single Service Partnership* 2nd ed. Maidstone: Kent County Council and Kent Health Authority.

King's Fund Centre (1980) *An Ordinary Life: Comprehensive Locally Based Residential Services for Mentally Handicapped People*. London: King's Fund Centre.

Mansell J, Felce D, Flight C & Jenkins J (1979) *The Bereweeke Skill-teaching System: Programme Writer's Handbook*. Winchester: Health Care Evaluation Research Team.

Mansell J, Felce D, De Kock U & Jenkins J (1982) Increasing purposeful activity of severely and profoundly mentally handicapped adults. *Behavioural Research and Therapy 20*: 593–604.

Mittler P & Mittler H (1983) Partnership with parents: an overview. In Mittler P & McConachie H (eds) *Parents, Professionals and Mentally Handicapped People – Approaches to Partnerships*. London: Croom Helm.

Newcastle City Council and Newcastle Area Health Authority (1981) *Mentally Handicapped People and their Families:*

Blueprint for a Local Service. Newcastle, England: Newcastle Area Health Authority.

North Western Regional Health Authority (NWRHA) (1982) *Services for People who are Mentally Handicapped: A Model District Service*. Manchester: NWRHA.

O'Brien J & Tyne A (1981) *The Principle of Normalisation: A Foundation for Effective Services*. London: Campaign for Mentally Handicapped People.

O'Connor N & Tizard J (1954) A survey of patients in twelve mental deficiency institutions. *British Medical Journal i:* 16–20.

Porterfield J & Blunden R (1981) Establishing activity periods in day settings for profoundly handicapped adults: a replication study. *Journal of Practical Approaches to Developmental Handicap 5:* 10–17.

Royal College of Psychiatrists (1983) Mental handicap services – the future. *Bulletin of the Royal College of Psychiatrists 7:* 131–134.

Russell O (1985) *Mental Handicap*. Edinburgh: Churchill Livingstone.

Schon D (1971) *Beyond the Stable State*. London: Temple Smith.

Shearer A (ed) (1983) *An Ordinary Life: Issues and Strategies for Training Staff for Community Mental Handicap Services*. London: King's Fund Centre.

Simon G (ed) (1981) *Local Services for Mentally Handicapped People: The Community Team, the Community Unit and the Role and Function of the Community Nurse, Social Worker and some other Members of the CMHT*. Kidderminster: British Institute of Mental Handicap.

Tizard J (1964) *Community Services for the Mentally Handicapped*. London: Oxford University Press.

Tizard J & O'Connor N (1952) The occupational adaptation of high grade defectives. *Lancet ii:* 620.

Ward L (1982) *People First: Developing Services in the Community for People with Mental Handicap*. London: King's Fund Centre.

Ward L (1984) *Planning for People: Developing a Local Service for People with Mental Handicap: 1. Recruiting and Training Staff*. London: King's Fund Centre.

Ward L (1985) Training staff for 'An ordinary life' – experiences in a community service in South Bristol. *British Journal of Mental Subnormality* (in press).

Wolfensberger W (1980) The definition of normalisation – update problems, disagreements and misunderstandings. In Flynn RJ & Nitsch KE (eds) *Normalization, Social Integration and Community Services*. Baltimore: University Park Press.

Chapter 3
Residential Needs and Services

DAVID TOWELL

'Be it ever so humble, there's no place like home.' So say the words of an old song. Like other popular sayings, this phrase captures something of significance to us all – the fundamental importance of *home* in our lives. The Oxford English Dictionary suggests why this should be so. Home is 'the place of one's dwelling or nurturing, with the conditions, circumstances and feelings which naturally and properly attach to it'. It is 'the seat of domestic life and interests'. It is 'a place to which one properly belongs, in which one's affections centre, or where one finds refuge, rest or satisfaction'. Reflecting on our own experiences it is clear that home and home-life meet a wide range of essential human needs. Home is typically the place where we eat, sleep and wash. It provides shelter and security. It offers opportunities for privacy (for example, in making love) and freedom (for instance, in our choice of leisure activities). Home is where the relationships which provide us with friendship and affection are often sustained. It is these relationships which help us make links with the wider networks of people described by the terms 'neighbourhood' and 'community'. Home is also therefore important to our personal identities – defining our place in the world and our sense of personal worth. Finally, home is one place where we learn and grow as people.

These needs are important to *all* of us. In addition, people with mental handicap are likely to have in varying degrees further needs which should be fulfilled within the context of their home life. Most obviously, precisely because of their handicap, they may need assistance in activities which otherwise might be undertaken unaided (like dressing) or help in coping with special problems (like physical disability). They are also likely to require relatively intensive education in the knowledge and skills necessary for everyday life.

The aim of a residential service is to meet these needs: to provide a home and home-life for people who cannot find these independently. It requires two kinds of resources. The first kind are material: the buildings in which people live and the furniture necessary to make them comfortable. The second kind are even more important: the people who staff the service and bring to it their home-making skills. Their tasks include both 'doing' and 'teaching': they assist their clients where necessary in carrying out the activities of daily living and teach them skills required for greater independence. Through their personal relationships with residents, they also foster the distinctive climate of friendship, support and mutual respect which we associate with a good home.

This chapter comes in the first section of this book for three main reasons. First, residential services are of fundamental significance to the quality of life open to people with mental handicap, and to their identities and status in the community. Accordingly, in developing comprehensive local services, particular attention should be given to the residential component of provision. Decisions on this front will have widespread ramifications for how other elements of provision are organized and delivered. Second, the prominence given to residential services provides an overdue corrective to common practice in the past, which has neglected home-making as a service in itself but rather made it a subsidiary feature of more specialized services like therapy and training. In this situation, home-life, for example in mental handicap hospitals, has often been of very poor quality (Tyne, 1978). Third, the arguments of this chapter are part of a wider challenge to traditional thinking in which a description of disability ('mental handicap') has been elevated into a label ('the mentally handicapped') which characterizes whole groups of people. Such thinking readily leads to a view of people with mental handicap as basically different from the rest of us, and to segregated services which confirm this

15

difference (Shearer, 1981b). The starting point for this chapter is that a home and home-life are things we all need although some people with mental handicap require assistance to cope successfully in a home of their own.

PREVAILING TYPES OF PROVISION

In the United Kingdom, as in many other countries, there have until recently been only two places in which people with mental handicap have usually lived: the family home or a large institution. In the most recent government review of mental handicap policies (DHSS, 1980), which gives figures relating to England in 1977, over 70% of more severely incapacitated children and 40% of adults (aged 16–44 years) with severe handicap were living in their parental home. Of the remainder, 35 per 100 000 population under 16 years old were living in hospital (this figure has since declined sharply) and 20 per 100 000 in local authority and other residential homes. Of those aged 16 years or over 125 per 100 000 were living in hospitals and 33 per 100 000 in local authority and other provision. In England there are still (in 1984) well over 35 000 adults with varying degrees of handicap living in large hospitals.

The last twenty years, however, have seen considerable expansion in a third type of residential provision through rather smaller and more local hospital, hostel or 'community' units. A pioneer was the Wessex Regional Hospital Board which in the late 1960s adopted a policy of establishing 25-place locally based hospital units both for children and for adults with severe mental handicap (Kushlick, 1980). As the statistics above suggest, there has been growth too in local-authority hostel provision, typically for people with lesser degrees of handicap. Quite recently many health authorities have made plans to build multipurpose community units (DTMH, 1978), often containing about 24 residential places.

In the UK the last decade has also seen a variety of innovations by public and voluntary agencies which provide the antecedents for a fourth type of provision. Following ordinary child-care practice, some children with mental handicap requiring an alternative to the parental home have been fostered. A similar approach has been adopted in the 'family placement' of adults. Drawing on the example offered by psychiatric services, there have been experiments in providing 'group homes' for small numbers of adults (perhaps three to five) with

limited external staff support. Reflecting arrangements designed to secure more independent living for people with physical disabilities (Shearer, 1982), there has been modest growth too in schemes which seek to combine ordinary housing and care.

These piecemeal innovations have paralleled larger-scale developments in other countries, notably Sweden (Grunewald, 1983), Canada (Neufeldt, 1983) and the United States, explicitly based on the principle of *normalization* (O'Brien and Tyne, 1981). Particularly influential in the British context has been the working model of comprehensive service provision offered by ENCOR, the Eastern Nebraska Community Office of Retardation (Thomas et al., 1978). Learning from these developments, a coherent philosophy on which to design residential services has been advanced nationally by the Committee of Enquiry into Mental Handicap Nursing and Care (Jay Committee, 1979) and has since received widespread endorsement. This new 'model of care' has been reflected in regional development strategies, notably in Wales (Welsh Office, 1983) and the North-West (North Western Regional Health Authority, 1982), and is increasingly reflected in local services at the 'leading edge' of current provision (Shearer, 1985).

Through its *An Ordinary Life* programme, my own organization, the King's Fund Centre, has played an important role in supporting these British initiatives. Over the past five years we have worked with policy-makers, professionals and consumer representatives to clarify ideas and identify practical steps required to establish comprehensive local residential services for people with all kinds of mental handicap. We have produced a series of reports addressing key issues arising in these endeavours, so far examining service design for adults and children, staff training, related employment and day services, the wider context of community care and leading examples of current provision (Gathercole, 1984; King's Fund Centre, 1982; Shearer, 1981a, 1983, 1985; Ward, 1982, 1984). Drawing on this work, the rest of this chapter focuses attention on experience of this fourth type of residential provision – based on the principles of *An Ordinary Life*.

AN ORDINARY LIFE: PRINCIPLES INTO PRACTICE

The *An Ordinary Life* programme was launched with the aspiration to see people with mental handicap 'in the mainstream of life, living in ordinary houses in ordinary streets, with the same range of choices as any citizen, and mixing as equals with the other, and mostly not handicapped members of their own community'. Like all visions of future services, this aspiration reflects principles which must be made explicit if they are to be used in service design and evaluation. These principles include the following.

1 People with mental handicap have the same human value as anyone else and the same human rights.
2 More specifically, *all* people with mental handicap have a right to live like others within the community and where necessary are entitled to the extra help which will enable them to do so.
3 People with mental handicap are developing human beings and services should assist them towards the greatest possible independence.
4 People with mental handicap should be involved as far as possible in decisions which affect their own lives.
5 Services should therefore affirm and enhance the dignity, self-respect and individuality of people with mental handicap; they are people first and mentally handicapped second.
6 Services should support the social networks which people with mental handicap have already established and thus contribute to continuity in personal relationships.
7 Services should be local, accessible and comprehensive.
8 Existing general services available to the rest of the community (like ordinary housing) should be used, rather than separate specialist services, wherever possible.

How can these eight principles be translated into practice?

For children

Children with mental handicap, like other children, should be expected wherever possible to live in their parental home. Among younger children this is typically the case even for those with severe handicap and problem behaviour. However, there is considerable evidence (Bayley, 1973; Wilkin, 1979) of families (especially mothers) in many localities making great efforts to sustain this situation with little support either from neighbours or from professional services. What is possible therefore depends both on parental willingness and the services available. Parents of young children need information, the opportunity to share experiences with other parents, and support from professionals, for

example, in the form of early introduction to home teaching schemes. As the children grow, they need nursery schools, play facilities and holiday opportunities. Many parents also need respite either in the form of 'sitting in' and 'care attendant' services (Inskip, 1981) or through short-term care of the child by placement with other families (Oswin, 1984).

Even where these and more specialist support services are available, there are some children who need an alternative to the family home. Others, currently growing up, for example, in large institutions, require more suitable placements. Each locality has to provide services carefully designed to meet the needs of individual children. Following the principles set out above, the two main kinds of provision are likely to involve either living with another family (through long-term fostering or adoption) or living with a small group of other children with mental handicap in staffed housing near to their own family.

Shearer (1981a) has reviewed the growing British experience of these options, especially for children with severe handicap. Both local authority social services departments and, on their behalf, specialist placement agencies can arrange fostering and adoption with people who should of course be appropriately housed and receive the full range of support services and welfare benefits. The largest provider of residential services for children with mental handicap in Britain is a charity, Barnardo's, which has pioneered the creation of dispersed networks of staffed houses (Kendall, 1983). This approach has also been adopted in schemes designed to bring children out of mental handicap hospitals, as in the NHS project in Northumberland where three rented council houses each provide a home for three or four local children supported by care staff (King's Fund Centre, 1984; Northumberland Area Health Authority, 1981).

In a variety of similar projects (Shearer, 1981a) children and young people, some with severe behavioural, sensory or physical difficulties, are also living more ordinary lives. For a *very small* number of these children (some of whom have been further handicapped by the absence or inappropriateness of past provision) experience suggests that support in ordinary houses will only be possible through especially well designed and intensively staffed services.

For adults

If children with mental handicap grow up in ordinary houses in their own community, they should have the opportunity to continue this form of home-life as adults. Where young adults live in their parental (or substitute family) home, they should have the opportunity, like other adults, to move with appropriate preparation to a home of their own. Applying the eight principles above, a comprehensive residential service for adults aims to provide a flexible range of housing and support options which meet individual client needs in ways designed to help each person live as full a life as possible in the locality of their choosing.

A variety of ordinary housing (some adapted for people with physical handicap) is required, dispersed throughout the community, together with a wide range of support services. Ideally, each local catchment area should include the following options:

1 continuing residence, where both client and parents choose this, in the *parental home*, but with domiciliary support and other services available as necessary;
2 placement in *another family home* in a way analogous to fostering schemes for children (see Gathercole, 1981b);
3 a *staffed home*, where up to three or four people with mental handicap live in a house with continuing staff support appropriate to their needs (see Ward, 1983);
4 a *co-residence arrangement*, where one or more people with handicap share a flat or house with

one or more other people who offer support as part of the deal (see Mansell, 1977);
5 a *group home*, where two or more people with handicap share their own flat or house, possibly with volunteer or visiting staff support (see Gathercole 1981a; Malin, 1984);
6 *independent housing* or flats available in the same way as housing for those without handicaps to people who can manage domestic life unassisted or with visiting support only (see Shearer, 1982).

A comprehensive residential service integrates these options into a system that is responsive to individual needs and where it is usually staff rather than residents who move as the need for support in particular homes changes. A good example is provided by the 'Wells Road Service' (Bristol and Weston Health Authority, 1983). In part of Bristol, residential services on this pattern are being developed for a total population of 35 000, among whom 77 adults with severe mental handicap have been identified, together with 40 others who originate from the locality but currently live in institutions elsewhere. A constellation of dispersed homes is being established to meet the requirements of this population (schematically illustrated in Figure 3.1).

In this service the office provides a contact point and administrative centre for the whole scheme. It is a base for the service coordinator, psychologist and community staff who support people in their own or

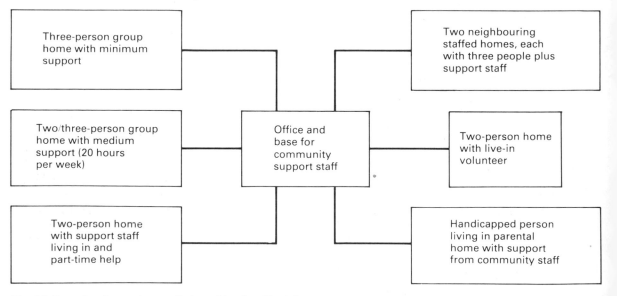

Fig. 3.1 Part of a dispersed constellation of local residential options in the 'Wells Road Service', Bristol (Bristol and Weston Health Authority, 1983).

parental homes. The first two staffed homes offer residential support to a total of six adults with severe mental handicap and in the early days of the scheme provided for assessment and initial training of new clients moving into the local service.

KEY ISSUES IN LOCAL SERVICE DEVELOPMENT

While these examples show what can be achieved, the tasks involved in developing local services are far from straightforward. There is space here only to note the main issues (referencing other sources for more detailed discussion).

Establishing commitment to basic principles

The starting point for developing good services is clarification of the principles which inform service design (Jay Committee, 1979; O'Brien and Tyne, 1981). As *An Ordinary Life* argues (King's Fund Centre, 1982) a coherent set of principles provides a basis for mobilizing the support of local people who will be influential in securing progress and ensuring that opportunities for service development are systematically exploited (see also Harlow CMH/CVS, 1981; North Western Regional Health Authority, 1982).

Planning comprehensive services

The planning process is concerned with converting these principles into detailed strategies for developing comprehensive local services. Arrangements are required which bring the relevant health, local authority and voluntary organizations into partnership (National Development Group, 1976; Newcastle City Council and Area Health Authority, 1981) and encourage widespread participation of people with an interest in future services. Planners have to define catchment areas for local services and identify the needs of the people to be served (King's Fund Centre, 1982). Residential services have to be planned together with other elements of a comprehensive service (IDC, 1982; Welsh Office, 1978; Guy's Health District, 1981).

Acquiring appropriate housing

In Britain housing for people with mental handicap can be rented from public housing authorities or private landlords, provided by housing associations, or purchased in the private market by the statutory authorities. Ordinary housing provision (including flats and bedsitting rooms) is required, selected to meet the requirements of individual clients and adapted (for example to accommodate physical handicap) as necessary (Centre on Environment for the Handicapped, 1981; Heginbotham, 1981, 1983).

Staffing the residential service

The most important investment is the staff: home-makers who 'do' and 'teach' and managers who provide the framework for these activities (Tyne, 1982). A local service needs to recruit and retain people with appropriate attitudes and relevant experiences, develop staff skills in home-making tasks and encourage commitment to the principles on which the service is based (Ward, 1984).

Financing the service

The 'capital' costs of housing can be met through the public housing authorities, housing associations (whose government grants also permit some contribution to staffing), from health and social services budgets and occasionally through voluntary contributions (MENCAP, 1982). Staff costs can be met by health authorities, social services or the reallocation processes designed to foster 'care in the community' (DHSS, 1983). Social security payments to clients can contribute to rent and running costs. Comprehensive local services require funding from a variety of these sources in order to achieve 'cost dispersal' (Heginbotham, 1983).

Operational policies and management arrangements

A vital aspect of planning is the production of operational policies which define in detail how the residential service is intended to be run (Felce et al., 1977). Management arrangements are required which foster coordination between this and other elements of the local service, and ensure implementation of the operational policies. Managerial tasks include recruitment and training of staff, their deployment to meet changing client needs, and continuing support for front-line staff in maintaining standards and avoiding isolation (McKnight, 1980).

Staff training

The definition of roles and the training of staff to perform those roles are essential for the success of new services. Partly because of weaknesses in the statutory training arrangements, innovative services must invest heavily in tailor-made training and development programmes. This includes training for senior staff in setting up local services (South East Thames Regional Health Authority, 1983) and opportunities for these and other staff to explore the values underlying operational policies as well as to improve their specific skills (Shearer, 1983).

Individual programme planning

A fundamental requirement for effective delivery of services is the individual programme plan (IPP) (Blunden, 1981) – a written statement of each client's strengths and needs, the specific goals being pursued and the programme of intervention through which these goals are to be achieved. The IPP is established and reviewed regularly through consultation among the people usually involved with each client, with participation of the client and relatives. It is the basis for organizing daily activities so as to create learning opportunities in the home environment and elsewhere. The IPP is particularly important in ensuring a consistent and individualized approach to serving people with profound or special needs (Firth and Firth, 1982; North Western Regional Health Authority, 1983).

Using community resources

Community-based residential services provide the opportunity for people with mental handicap to participate in local life through contact with neighbours and use of amenities available to other people. There is evidence of negative attitudes, at least among a minority of the public, to people with mental handicap moving into a neighbourhood (Locker et al., 1979), although these attitudes may change as familiarity weakens traditional stereotypes (McKnight, 1980). A further task for staff is to promote social integration within the local community.

Quality assurance and advocacy

Even well-designed services require mechanisms which sustain the quality of provision and highlight any need for improvements. Management includes the positive monitoring (Houts and Scott, 1975) necessary to provide staff with constructive feedback about how well services are meeting explicit goals and standards. There are also benefits in encouraging external monitoring, for example by consumer representatives (Wolfensberger, 1977). Among the tools available, PASS (Program Analysis of Service Systems) (Wolfensberger and Glenn, 1975) is particularly useful in assessing the consistency of services with the normalization principle (see Chapter 4).

MAKING CHOICES AND MOVING FORWARD

In most parts of Britain there remain major deficiencies in services available to people with mental handicap and in public-sector resources allocated to meet their needs. Local people face important choices in deciding how best to change this situation. This chapter has examined an emerging model of residential provision, which aims to meet the needs of *all* people with mental handicap through ordinary housing in the community. This approach will typically be in competition with other proposals, most commonly – particularly in relation to people with severe handicap – the model of the small institution with perhaps 24 'beds'.

In deciding between the alternatives, five key questions need to be considered:

1 How far does the proposed option reflect the values and principles which local people believe should inform service design?
2 To what extent will proposed services meet the preferences of consumers in so far as these can be determined?
3 What does operational experience and research evidence suggest about the effectiveness of particular services in providing high quality of life and promoting individual development of clients?
4 In achieving required levels of effectiveness, what are the relative costs incurred by different types of provision?
5 How well can the different options adapt to new ideas and changing needs as local services develop?

This chapter has made clear the principles upon which *An Ordinary Life* services are built. Such services are consistent with expressions of preference by people with mental handicap, and although some parents may have initial doubts (McKnight, 1980), there is evidence of increasingly positive views among families where this option can be seen in practice. British experience of providing these services is still limited although reports from the pioneering areas are largely encouraging. Evaluative research is now under way. Early results from Wessex show that 'substantial improvements in the quality of life of severely and profoundly mentally handicapped adults can be brought about by moving them from institutional settings to those which are smaller, based in the community, equipped as autonomously functioning houses and staffed by a single category of care staff who have been given specific training on behavioural principles of teaching and interaction' (Felce, 1983). It can indeed be argued that only *An Ordinary Life* services are likely to achieve an adequate level of effectiveness, while available evidence (North Western Regional Health Authority, 1982) suggests that the public sector costs of well-staffed institutions and services based on ordinary housing are broadly comparable. It is also apparent that the more a service avoids investment in specialist buildings, the more likely it is to prove flexible to changing demands.

Even where the choice among different options for a residential service has been made, however, there are still major challenges in making progress. Resource constraints, policy ambiguities, organizational complexities and diffuseness in professional leadership all constitute problems for local service development (Towell, 1982). At a time of retrenchment in public expenditure, there is tension between providing alternative community-based services for people living in the large institutions and offering appropriate services to the larger numbers of people still living in their parental homes (IDC, 1981). In both situations professionals will have to work sensitively with parents in planning moves for their offspring. The traditional allocation of resources for mental handicap services can lead to the paradox of the National Health Service assuming the functions of other public agencies, for example in providing housing. Experience in the United States (Landesman-Dwyer, 1981) also suggests that unless the development of community-based services is managed with considerable skill, the whole enterprise may lead to disillusionment and conflict.

Nevertheless, bold strategies are emerging to confront these challenges. The government's 'Care in the Community' initiative (DHSS, 1983) is providing financial arrangements which promote the relocation of services based in large institutions. In Wales, the government has gone further, in adopting a clear strategy for local authority leadership in implementing new patterns of provision (Welsh Office, 1983). Among English regions, the North Western Regional Health Authority (1982, 1983) had been at the forefront in promoting genuinely community-based services, while South

East Thames Regional Health Authority (see Glennerster and Korman, 1983) has given particular attention to how existing large institutions can be made redundant.

These large-scale strategies can only work when combined with the local initiative required from professionals and others to build coalitions for progress among the interested parties and seize any opportunities available to implement change (King's Fund Centre, 1982; IDC, 1984). At the end of the day, whether people with mental handicap are offered good services in their own communities will depend on the enthusiasm and skill of local people and their success in mobilizing political support.

REFERENCES

Bayley M (1973) *Mental Handicap and Community-care – A Study of Mentally Handicapped People in Sheffield*. London: Routledge & Kegan Paul.
Blunden R (1981) *Individual Plans for Mentally Handicapped People: A Procedural Guide*. Cardiff: Mental Handicap in Wales: Applied Research Unit.
Bristol and Weston Health Authority (1983) *The Wells Road Project: Operational Policy*. Bristol: Bristol and Weston Health Authority.
Centre on Environment for the Handicapped (CEH) (1981) *Housing Projects for Mentally Handicapped People*. Seminar Report. London: CEH.
DHSS (Department of Health and Social Security) (1980) *Mental Handicap: Progress, Problems and Priorities. A Review of Mental Handicap Services in England since the 1971 White Paper 'Better Services for the Mentally Handicapped'*. London: DHSS.
DHSS (Department of Health and Social Security) (1983) *Care in the Community and Joint Finance*. Circular HC83(6), London: DHSS.
DTMH (Development Team for the Mentally Handicapped) (1978) *First Report: 1976–7*. London: HMSO.
Felce D, Kushlick A, Lunt B & Powell E (1977) *Detailed Rules for the Setting-up and Maintenance of Locally-based Hospital Units for the Mentally Handicapped in Wessex*. Winchester: Health Care Evaluation Research Team.
Felce D (1983) *Observing the Activity of Severely and Profoundly Mentally Handicapped Adults and their Staff in Residential Facilities of Different Sizes* Winchester: Health Care Evaluation Research Team.
Firth M & Firth H (1982) *Mentally Handicapped People with Special Needs*. Discussion Paper. London: King's Fund Centre.
Gathercole C (1981a) *Residential Alternatives for Adults who are Mentally Handicapped. 2. Group Homes – Staffed and Unstaffed*. Kidderminster: British Institute of Mental Handicap.
Gathercole C (1981b) *Residential Alternatives for Adults who are Mentally Handicapped. 3. Family Placements*. Kidderminster: British Institute of Mental Handicap.
Gathercole C (ed) (1984) *An Ordinary Working Life: Vocational Services for People with Mental Handicap*. Project Paper. London: King's Fund Centre.

Glennerster H & Korman N (1983) *Darenth Park Project: Regional Strategic Planning*. London: London School of Economics, Department of Social Administration.

Grunewald K (1983) Sweden: community living for mentally retarded adults. In Jones G & Tutt N (eds) *A Way of Life for the Handicapped*. London: Residential Care Association.

Guy's Health District (1981) *Development Group for Services for Mentally Handicapped People: Report to the District Management Team*. London: Guy's Health District.

Harlow CMH/CVS (Harlow Campaign for Mentally Handicapped People and Harlow Council for Voluntary Services) (1981) *An Ordinary Life in Harlow: Report of a Working Party set up to Explore Ways of Providing Locally Based Services for the Whole Range of those Citizens of Harlow who are Mentally Handicapped*. Harlow CMH/CVS.

Heginbotham C (1981) *Housing Projects for Mentally Handicapped People*. London: Centre on Environment for the Handicapped.

Heginbotham C (1983) *Promoting Residential Services for Mentally Handicapped People*. London: Centre on Environment for the Handicapped.

Houts P & Scott R (1975) *How to Catch your Staff Doing Something Right*. Hershey, Pennsylvania: Hershey Medical Center.

IDC (Independent Development Council for People with Mental Handicap) (1981) *Response to Care in the Community: A DHSS Consultative Document on Moving Resources for Care in England*. London: IDC.

IDC (Independent Development Council for People with Mental Handicap) (1982) *Elements of a Comprehensive Local Service for People with Mental Handicap*. London: IDC.

IDC (Independent Development Council for People with Mental Handicap) (1984) *Next Steps: An Independent Review of Progress, Problems and Priorities in the Development of Services for People With Mental Handicap*. London: IDC.

Inskip H (1981) *Family Support Services for Physically and Mentally Handicapped People in their own Homes*. London: Bedford Square Press (for the Leonard Cheshire Foundation).

Jay Committee (1979) *Report of the Committee of Enquiry into Mental Handicap Nursing and Care* (Chairman: Peggy Jay) Cmnd. 7468. London: HMSO.

Kendall A (1983) England: services to mentally handicapped children and their families. In Jones G & Tutt N (eds) *A Way of Life for the Handicapped*. London: Residential Care Association.

King's Fund Centre (KFC) (1982) *An Ordinary Life: Comprehensive Locally-based Residential Services for Mentally Handicapped People*. KFC Project Paper 24, revised edition. London: King's Fund Centre.

King's Fund Centre (1984) *Progress in Bringing Mentally Handicapped Children out of Hospital*. Conference Report. London: King's Fund Centre.

Kushlick A (ed) (1980) *Evaluation of Alternative Residential Facilities for the Severely Mentally Handicapped in Wessex*. Advances in Behaviour Research and Therapy, Vol. 3, No.1.

Landesman-Dwyer S (1981) Living in the community. *American Journal of Mental Deficiency 86(3)*: 223–234.

Locker D, Rao B & Weddell JM (1979) Public acceptance of community care for the mentally handicapped. *Apex 7(2)*: 44–46.

Malin N (1984) *Group Homes for Mentally Handicapped People*. London: HMSO.

Mansell J (1977) CUSS: a student project at University College, Cardiff. In Wyn Jones A (ed) *Involvement of the Client, the Family and the Community*. Report of the 1977 Spring Conference, Taunton, National Society for Mentally Handicapped Children, SW Region.

McKnight D (1980) *Residential Care Research Review: A Review of Published Literature on the Viability of Small Residential Units for Mentally Handicapped People, and Factors Involved in the Development of Non-institutional Care*. London: Thomas Coram Research Unit.

MENCAP (Royal Society for Mentally Handicapped Children and Adults) (1982) *The MENCAP Homes Foundation: A Plan for Development of Residential Services for Mentally Handicapped People*. London: MENCAP.

National Development Group for the Mentally Handicapped (NDG) (1976) *Mental Handicap: Planning Together*. NDG Pamphlet 1. London: NDG.

Neufeldt A (1983) Canada: Canada's ComServ plan – a nation-wide strategy of service development. In Jones G & Tutt N (eds) *A Way of Life for the Handicapped*. London: Residential Care Association.

Newcastle City Council and Area Health Authority (1981) *Mentally Handicapped People and their Families: A Blueprint for a Local Service*. Newcastle: Newcastle City Council and Area Health Authority.

Northumberland Area Health Authority (1981) *NHS Residential Accommodation For Mentally Handicapped People: Operational Policy*. Morpeth: Northumberland Area Health Authority.

North Western Regional Health Authority (NWRHA) (1982) *Services for People who are Mentally Handicapped: A Model District Service*. Manchester: NWRHA.

North Western Regional Health Authority (NWRHA) (1983) *Services for People who are Mentally Handicapped: Services for People with Additonal Special Needs*. Manchester: NWRHA.

O'Brien J & Tyne A (1981) *The Principle of Normalisation: A Foundation for Effective Services*. London: Campaign for the Mentally Handicapped.

Oswin M (1984) *'They Keep Going Away': A Critical Study of Short-term Residential Care Services for Children who are Mentally Handicapped*. London: King Edward's Hospital Fund for London.

Shearer A (1981a) *Bringing Mentally Handicapped Children out of Hospital*. King's Fund Centre Project Paper No.30. London: King's Fund Centre.

Shearer A (1981b) *Disability: Whose Handicap?* Oxford: Blackwell.

Shearer A (1982) *Living Independently*. London: Centre on Environment for the Handicapped and 'King Edward's Hospital Fund for London.

Shearer A (ed) (1983) *An Ordinary Life: Issues and Strategies for Training Staff for Community Mental Handicap Services*. King's Fund Centre Project Paper No. 42. London: King's Fund Centre.

Shearer A (1985) *The Leading Edge: Community-based Services for People with Mental Handicap*. London: Campaign for the Mentally Handicapped and King's Fund Centre.

South East Thames Regional Health Authority (SETRHA) (1983) *Developing Staffed Housing for Mentally Handicapped People*. Croydon: SETRHA.

Thomas D, Firth H & Kendall A (1978) *ENCOR – A Way Ahead*. London: Campaign for Mentally Handicapped People.

Towell D (1982) Developing mental handicap services in an

English county: lessons from an action research strategy. *Hospital and Health Services Review*. January: pp. 9–13, February: pp. 40–43.

Tyne A (1978) *Looking at Life . . . In a Hospital, Hostel, Home or Unit*. London: Campaign for Mentally Handicapped People.

Tyne A (1982) *Staffing and Supporting a Residential Service*. London: Campaign for Mentally Handicapped People.

Ward L (1982) *People First: Developing Services In The Community For People With Mental Handicap*. King's Fund Centre Project Paper No.37. London: King's Fund Centre.

Ward L (1983) An ordinary life. *Community Care*, November 10, pp. 16–19.

Ward L (1984) *Planning for People*. London: King's Fund Centre.

Welsh Office (1978) *NIMROD: Report of a Joint Working Party on the Provision of a Community-based Mental Handicap Service in South Glamorgan*. Cardiff: Welsh Office.

Welsh Office (1983) *All–Wales Strategy for the Development of Services for Mentally Handicapped People*. Cardiff: Welsh Office.

Wilkin D (1979) *Caring for the Mentally Handicapped Child*. London: Croom Helm.

Wolfensberger W & Glenn L (1975) *PASS: Program Analysis of Service Systems*, 3rd ed. Toronto: National Institute on Mental Retardation.

Wolfensberger W (1977) *A Multi-component Advocacy and Protection Scheme*. Toronto: Canadian Association for the Mentally Retarded.

Chapter 4
Evaluation of Residential Provision

PAUL BERRY

As we have seen in the previous chapter contemporary patterns of residential provision may vary considerably between and within countries, and even today a wide range of facilities may be observed. These include services like hospital care as well as the more favoured community and home-based programmes.

In spite of this wide range of services, there is much consistency within each category in different countries. While a 'farm residence' in the tropics of Northern Queensland will not look like a family group home in Alaska or the suburbs of Cardiff in the United Kingdom, the similarities far outweigh the differences.

The overriding and essential element, however, in any residential service is the way in which it meets the developmental needs of its clients. It is clearly important, therefore, that the efficiency of all the different kinds of residential settings be evaluated. The relative assets and deficiencies of a residential programme have to be evaluated in terms of how they meet the needs of the clients. There is little doubt that smaller home-like establishments can improve the learning and social development of the clients. The emphasis on changes in adaptive behaviour as a result of changing environments is evident from many studies, both historical and contemporary. The experiments of Skeels (1966), based on earlier research (Skeels and Dye, 1939), and more recently of Tizard (1964), all suggest that 'sterile' environments have a deleterious effect upon behaviour. Very recent studies have indicated that even in people with very severe handicaps adaptive behaviour can be fostered, to conform to societal mores and allow them greater freedom to enjoy community living. Together with the radical change in the basis of residential services from one of institutional segregation to one of community-based living in the least restrictive environment, this emphasizes even more the need for careful monitor-

ing and specially trained staff to undertake such evaluation of services.

DEFINITION AND LEVELS OF ASSESSMENT IN THE EVALUATION OF SERVICES

Evaluation in this context may be described as the systematic process of measuring the relative efficiency of a residential service in attaining its defined objectives. An appropriate evaluation will be able to answer a number of questions concerned with how well a service system or programme is achieving its aims. Continuing evaluation is essential for successful monitoring of service provision and for developing better services which are more informed, streamlined and suited to the particular needs of the clients in the programme. In many respects, as will be seen, evaluation has its roots in individual assessment.

Assessment is seen to be the foundation stone of intervention: without appropriate assessment, intervention programmes and hence the facilities in which they are implemented have no systematic basis and their effectiveness will be undermined. Hence, assessment of client skills and progress is an integral component of the evaluation of services.

As with residential provision, there are a number of levels of evaluation, ranging from basic to very broad levels. Figure 4.1 gives a diagrammatic analysis of four levels. It will be noted that at each level the appropriate components of services are described. Interaction between each level is emphasized and it is important to consider the points at which communication and information dissemination are adequate or inadequate.

The first level, the level of individuals within the system, is the basic level of analysis. Unless it can be demonstrated that a programme within a facility

Type of evaluation

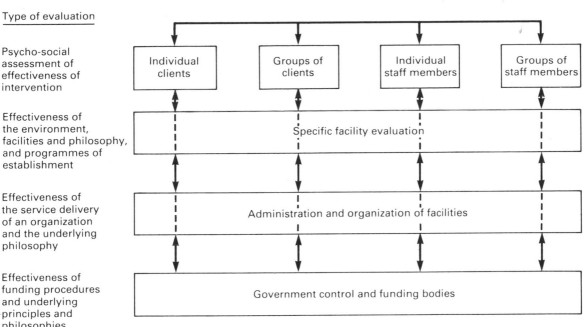

Fig. 4.1 The evaluation of services for the handicapped: levels of evaluation. From Berry et al. (1977), with kind permission of the authors and the Australian Department of Social Security.

actually produces systematic and effective change and development in the psycho-social characteristics of people with mental handicap, the basic foundations of the programme require analysis, especially in the area of staff practice and training. The aim of this level of evaluation should be to enhance the programme through better staff training and a better curriculum for the clients.

At the second level the specific role of the facility is investigated. This evaluation considers the establishment as a facilitator of the aims and objectives of the organization under which it is administered. This level evaluates such factors as buildings and fitments, the construction of curricula, the ways in which staff are recruited and trained and the provision of a comprehensive service for the clients.

Evaluation of the organization, the third level, relates the philosophies and procedures of an agency's administration (whether this be a government or voluntary organization) to the actualization of the programme. It also investigates the degree to which the administrators, at this level, are effective as change-agents in the system of service delivery.

Finally, at the fourth level, the funding bodies, particularly government departments of health and social security, and voluntary organizations, are evaluated. Such issues as the extent to which they are able to control and direct the philosophies of the organization towards a comprehensive set of services for the handicapped are explored. The issues of adequate funding, appropriate use of resources and top-level political decisions relating to policies of service provision are part of this legal level of evaluation.

It is important then to establish a comprehensive and coherent policy from government or agency to client level within the context of a country or region's specific social system. This four-tiered basis of evaluation may be difficult to implement, but given appropriate resources and cooperation from all those involved both in providing and in receiving services it should be attainable.

INSTRUMENTS AND PROCEDURES IN EVALUATION

For a comprehensive evaluation of services each aspect of the service offered needs to be analysed. Although a wide variety of phychological assessment techniques are available for the evaluation of learning in people with mental handicap, there is some evidence that they are not optimally employed in the development of the majority of programmes. In addition, residential programmes may often not be seen as having a place in the development of clients, so those involved may not generally appreciate the programmes being evaluated in terms of client development.

Individual evaluation

At the individual or first level (client or staff) many assessment instruments are available for immediate use by residential staff. For example, a residence may wish to evaluate the effectiveness of a programme to develop communication skills. Before-and-after measures can be effected in a number of ways. A checklist approach could be undertaken, such as that devised by Kellett (1976). This technique does not require specialist training, and measures four different aspects of language: comprehension, production, articulation and gesture. The development of personal social skills can be measured by devices such as the Progress Assessment Chart (Gunzburg, 1963), or that of the Wessex Health Care Evaluation Research Team (National Development Group for the Mentally Handicapped, 1977). The latter technique covers aspects of development important for performance in residential settings, such as toileting and walking skills, through to language, defects in vision, hearing and speech, as well as basic reading, writing and number abilities. Also included in this questionnaire is a brief analysis of behaviour problems. The form can be completed very quickly by residential workers and can be useful in the initial evaluation of clients.

An important recent project on the development and evaluation of services for the mentally handicapped is the NIMROD (New Ideas for the care of Mentally Retarded People in Ordinary Dwellings) (1976–1983) project in South Wales. This project fulfils the main requirements of the principles of normalization in that a fully integrated series of residential facilities has been planned in the community. Support services are provided to ensure that there are individual programmes for each client, and the clients themselves (as consumers) play an important part in the development of the service. The NIMROD team has constructed a number of instruments for the analysis of client improvement and to enable optimum individual programmes to be created. The instruments include:

1 A disability assessment schedule: to assess degrees of problems in specific areas (for example, mobility, behaviour, vision, hearing, communication).
2 An adaptive behaviour scale: to assess the specific skills involved in community living (for example, economic activity, vocational activity, responsibility, socialization).
3 'Pathways to Independence' checklist: where an interviewee who knows a client well assesses development in domestic skills, freedom of movement, and community living skills.
4 Consumer satisfaction schedule: to evaluate to what extent a client or his advocate have used the service and how satisfactory they have found it.

The schedules and reports of the NIMROD team are published by and available from the Mental Handicap in Wales Applied Research Unit, University of Wales, Welsh National School of Medicine, Cardiff, Wales UK. They are important documents for the monitoring of a new community service for persons with handicaps.

Facility evaluation

At the second level, that of facility evaluation, a number of particular methods which are currently available will be described. These include *Program Analysis of Service Systems* (PASS) (Wolfensberger and Glenn, 1975), and a programme produced by the Joint Commission on Accreditation of Hospitals (1973) in the USA. In addition, the use of the 'Delphi' technique in evaluation will be discussed and examples of the National Development Group checklist of standards presented.

Program Analysis of Service Systems (PASS)

PASS is a procedure for the objective measurement of the quality of a wide range of human management service projects, systems and agencies. It is based on a number of ideological or value systems. The most important of these is the principle of normalization. From this are derived practical implications for service delivery.

The procedure is equally applicable to small and large institutions and facilities, whether they are based on education, medical, welfare or other practices. It is also applicable to the evaluation of community services and attitudes – in fact, to virtually all we think and do in relation to the handicapped.

Wolfensberger (1972) has discussed in depth the principle of normalization as a rationale for human management. Briefly, this principle calls for the use of 'means which are as culturally normative as possible, in order to establish and/or maintain personal behaviours and characteristics (in a potentially deviant person) which are as culturally normative as possible'.

The PASS system evolved from the identification of certain needs in evaluation services, and as an evaluation procedure is claimed to meet all of these needs. Thus the purposes of PASS are:

1 To provide a quantitative analysis of the quality and adequacy of human services.
2 To identify how programmes are related to the principle of normalization.
3 To enable continuous or repeated assessment of services.
4 To enable comparative studies in evaluation of services.
5 To provide a system of accreditation of services with the objective of providing appropriate funds for continuation and/or development of programmes.
6 To provide service personnel with a teaching tool related to the normalization principle to the extent that services could be continuously evaluated by staff in respect of these defined criteria.
7 In evaluation, to provide a specification of whether 'the right to treatment' is being met.

Wolfensberger and Glenn (1975) have fully described the mechanics of administering PASS and analysing the results obtained. An example, however, of the item of 'normalization' may also serve to clarify the system. This is outlined briefly in Table 4.1 and illustrates the nature and scope of the programme ratings in that area. The broad bases of the ratings in the table are as follows:

A.1 *Proximity.* The physical distance of the facility from population centres, with reference to social integration (for example, are shops, services and hotels nearby?)
A.2 *Access.* The lack of physical barriers to access to the facility, with transportation (trains, bus services etc.) a key factor.
A.3 *Physical context.* The proximity of the facility to resources such as community facilities.
A.4 *Size or dispersal.* The size of the facility and of the community, with reference to the number of persons with disabilities in the location of the facility and the ability of the location to assimilate them (large institutional settings are non-normalizing; family

Table 4.1 An example of the structure of the PASS system (Wolfensberger and Glenn, 1975)

Item area
Normalization
Items
A Physical integration
B Social integration
Sub-items and ratings
A Physical integration
1 Proximity (i)
2 Access (ii)
3 Physical context (iii)
4 Size or dispersal (iv)
B Social integration
1 Socially integrative interpretations
a Programme and facility labels (v)
b Building perception (vi)
2 Socially integrative programme structures
a Deviant staff contact (vii)
b Other deviant contact (viii)
c Socially integrative social opportunities (ix)

group homes are generally of the right size for integration).
B.1.a *Programme and facility labels.* Are they appropriate and not detrimental? Do they give a perception of non-deviance? (For example, a label like 'Subnormal Children's Welfare Association' implies deviancy in clients.)
B.1.b *Building perception.* The past and present use of the buildings; general appearance, non-prominence (for example, buildings once used for a special purpose such as a nursing home may have deviant implications if recycled as a residence for the mentally handicapped).
B.2.a *Deviant staff contact.* The percentage of habilitated staff employed (it is considered non-normalizing to allow disabled staff to be employed in establishments for the handicapped).
B.2.b *Other deviant contact.* The amount of contact by 'clients' with other persons with handicaps.
B.2.c *Socially integrative social opportunities.* The opportunity for the clients to interact or engage in 'normative' activities with other members of the community (for example, recreational and social experiences in local clubs, and further or higher educational activities).

Full descriptions of each of the 50 items of PASS are given in the PASS manual.

It should be noted that the expression of the normalization principle in PASS is based on rating areas which were judged by the authors to be important reflections of normalization in service delivery. Likewise, the weighting given to each rating is also a judgement of the authors.

Evaluations using PASS are carried out by a team of four assessors, each independently evaluating the agency or facility. Data is gathered from ratings based on familiarization through written descriptions, interviews and site visits. A total score for each facility, which can range from -947 to $+1000$ using the Wolfensberger and Glenn procedure, is based on the average ratings of the four assessors over the 50 items in the analysis, but comparison between programmes on all 50 areas of the evaluation is possible. This has the advantage of identifying the extent to which programmes vary as well as highlighting strengths and weaknesses.

A study comparing 36 facilities (including residential, vocational and educational establishments) was undertaken by Berry et al. (1977) and Andrews and Berry (1978). This study indicated the degree to which programmes may have many individual characteristics and is a useful guide to persons undertaking PASS evaluations.

Standards for Community Agencies Serving Persons with Mental Retardation and other Developmental Disabilities

The Joint Commission on Accreditation of Hospitals (1973) in the USA has developed a very detailed survey questionnaire for evaluating standards for residential facilities for the handicapped. This procedure also invokes the principle of normalization, as indicated by the following statement: 'The essential requirements for a normalized environment include a physical environment that is as home-like as possible, and in which residents can be divided into small groups, for which specific direct-care staff are responsible, so that there can be individualized attention to the developmental needs of residents, rather than merely large-group or mass care routines.'

This process of accreditation has five main aspects, which are given in Table 4.2. It is important to distinguish between accreditation and evaluation. The difference lies in the object of the exercise: *evaluation* attempts to identify how well a facility is functioning, whereas *accreditation* aims at licensing a facility which has achieved at least minimal standards.

Table 4.2 Process of accreditation for residential facilities for the handicapped: requirements and number of standards (Joint Commission on Accreditation of Hospitals, 1973)

Requirements		Number of standards
I	Provision of active habilitation programming to each resident	
	A General requirements	20
	B Interdisciplinary process	17
	C Evaluation and programme planning	48
	D Management of programme delivery	8
	E Resident training	23
	F Behaviour management	27
	G Attention to resident health needs	64
	H Habilitation services	42
	I Staff training and consultation	14
	J Staffing	24
	K Documentation	21
	L Facilities and equipment	12
II	Provision of services within a normalized and normalizing environment	
	A General normalization	20
	B Community integration	11
	C Integration of multihandicapped	7
	D Rhythm of life	10
	E Physical environment	24
III	Assurance of the rights of residents and their families	
	A General rights-assurance	13
	B Rights of residents	43
	C Rights of families	18
IV	Effective administrative practices	
	A General administration	39
	B Communication	5
	C Records	19
	D Research	8
V	Maintenance of a safe and sanitary environment	70
	Total	607

The process of accreditation is two-fold. First, the facility is sent copies of the questionnaire, which are completed by the appropriate officer(s) of the establishment. These are then returned to the Commission with any other documentation which may be required. The Commission then conducts a site survey and its surveyors observe very closely whether the programme actually pertains to the needs of the clients. Then either the programme is formally granted accreditation or the facility is provided with a report which indicates how it can improve its programme to the level of the standards laid down by the Commission.

Although the Commission's approach to accreditation and evaluation is time-consuming as well as very intricate, it aims to provide consumers of the services offered with a precise statement of the adequacy of the services, and in addition the facility itself is given evidence of its accountability to the people it aims to serve. Recent extensions of this system have resulted in a further accreditation manual by the Accreditation Council for Mentally Retarded and other Developmentally Delayed Disabled Persons (AC-MRDD) (1978) on 'Standards for Services for Developmentally Disabled Individuals'. In addition, the Commission on Accreditation of Rehabilitation Facilities (CARF) (1978) have produced the Standards Manual for Rehabilitation Facilities. While both manuals have standards relevant to residential facilities, they have broader implications for general services for the disabled and will not therefore be discussed in detail here.

The Delphi technique

In many ways evaluation is directed to future practices and policies, and involves judgements about these. In recent years research directed towards the development of judgements about future policies and events has made considerable use of the Delphi technique. A comprehensive review of the development and potential use of this procedure was recently published by McGaw et al. (1976). When they compiled the material reported, McGaw and his associates had been involved in a study which looked at the future of teacher education in Australia. Another useful review is available in Schipper and Kenowitz (1976).

The Delphi technique was originally used for forecasting in such areas as industry and defence. As such it had been employed to forecast technological change. Recently, however, its use has been extended to educational and social areas, and evidence suggests that it is a promising procedure in these areas. There seems to be little doubt as to its potential value in looking ahead in the areas of rehabilitation and services for the handicapped.

The technique systematically processes individual judgements about problems and issues to give a useful consensus concerning desired ends. This consensus can be reached without bias if the procedure is conducted without the formation of groups, and with anonymity of the participants. In this way the technique, generally employing a number of rounds (usually three) in which the judgements of the participants are sought, can be used to predict future patterns of services, based on the expectations and knowledge of individuals associated with the field under study.

The Delphi technique is, thus, seen to be a useful tool in future developments in the residential evaluation sphere. To date a number of evaluation procedures available at the facility level have been based on their authors' judgements about desirable standards and future characteristics of services. A more adequate way of deriving these is to sample the opinions and judgements of a wide range of users, administrators and professional workers, and use the results of such a study as the basis for evaluation instruments.

A large-scale Delphi study has been undertaken in Australia (Elkins et al., 1980). Almost 400 'experts' from all over Australia, including people from health, education and welfare departments as well as parents of handicapped people and handicapped people themselves, took part in the study. While it is impossible to summarize briefly all of the findings of this study (some 1700 statements were generated in round 1) there were several important trends, most of which clearly indicated a move towards the principles of normalization, even though some important events were not seen to be able to be implemented until the 1990s. Some important trends were:

1 means-test-free pensions;
2 free transport and legally enforced access;
3 legislation for the adoption of a bill of rights for the disabled;
4 residential provision in the community with appropriate support (to parents or to the disabled themselves depending upon circumstances);
5 better, and comprehensive, educational facilities, including more appropriate assessment techniques;
6 improved staff training at all levels of services, especially in-service training schemes.

This study emphasized future trends as recognized by those involved with the handicapped and the handicapped themselves and highlights the need for the analysis of services within a broad context. While in this chapter the aim is to point out some of the basic techniques for the evaluation of residential provision, accommodation for the handicapped must be seen in the contexts of other health, educational, vocational and welfare facilities. In many respects the Delphi technique allows a broadly based analysis of future trends within which any specific service type may be considered.

Checklist of Standards –
National Development Group

A further example of a checklist of standards for the improvement of quality of services for people with mental handicap has been devised by the National Development Group for the Mentally Handicapped (1980) for the UK Department of Health and Social Security. The checklist aims at (a) identifying strengths, weaknesses and gaps in existing services, (b) improving existing services, (c) providing a baseline for measuring progress, (d) providing a means for developing new services, and (e) educating staff. The underlying principle governing the checklist is that 'mentally handicapped people are entitled to the same range and quality of services as are available to other citizens, and to services designed to meet their special needs. Services for children should recognize their distinctive needs' (p. x). Then there are four further principles, each one with a series of standards in a number of sections. Each standard, in question form, must be answered and signed by the person filling out the form. It is suggested, for educational purposes, that teams be involved in completing the standards. The four sub-principles are as follows:

Principle 1. The services provided to a person with mental handicap, whatever his ability, should be based on interdisciplinary assessment of his individual needs and a training plan designed to meet them. Such plans should be regularly reviewed and revised.

Principle 2. Services should be available to help families look after a person with mental handicap at home and to enable adults to live in homes of their own if they wish.

Principle 3. People with mental handicap require day and residential services that promote their development and independence.

Principle 4. Services should be jointly planned and delivered by health and local authorities in partnership with voluntary organizations and those directly providing the services. The needs of clients and their families are the prime consideration.

Altogether there are 224 standards in the various areas. Once again, this is a useful, comprehensive and readily available tool for use in programme evaluation and up-grading, especially in the area of residential services. An important element to note in this system is that it may be undertaken by key workers and groups of personnel involved in services; no special training is required to undertake the exercise.

Schonell Evaluation and Accreditation Procedure (SEAP)

A final method of evaluating residential services will be mentioned briefly. This system, developed in Australia for the federal Department of Social Security under a national scheme aimed at the upgrading of services for the disabled, has three main components (Andrews et al., 1983). In the first component each facility to be evaluated fills in a form comprising extremely open-ended questions about the general aims and objectives of the service, together with questions on the size of the establishment, staff/client characteristics and the activities of the facility designed to implement the stated aims and objectives. The second component is a site visit by a team of three – a public servant from the Department of Social Security who has special knowledge of the region in which the service operates, a person selected because of expertise in the field (such as a parent with a child in a residence other than the one being evaluated or a manager or director of a residence in another area or organization) and, thirdly, an academic specialist in the general area of disability. The team has 12 guidelines to bear in mind during the visit; these range from the staffing parameters to the general economic aspects of the facility. The team meets and interviews staff, clients and management bodies concerned with the facility. The final stage is based upon a report drafted by one of the team and discussed with each team member. The draft report is in turn commented upon by the staff and management of the facility itself. In the final report both long- and short-term objectives for the development of the service are enumerated, as well as recommendations in each of the 12 guideline areas where necessary. Thus the system is built upon a principle of dialogue between a team whose members have various skills and expertise in the area and the facility itself which actively seeks development guidelines from an outside body. A handbook which includes a description of the procedure and several examples of reports is available from the Department of Social Security in Canberra (Andrews et al., 1983).

CONCLUSION

The evaluation procedures outlined have been considered only in the context of residential provision. These techniques and methods, however, do have implications for other services for people with intellectual disability since the principles of normalization as well as general community standards are applicable to educational, vocational and welfare facilities. For example, the four principles outlined by the National Development Group in Great Britain and mentioned earlier in this chapter should have a pervasive influence on service provision in general, as should, for example, the principles of normalization.

In addition the question of 'who should evaluate' must be faced. In a way, all evaluation in any context is somewhat stressful, be it a test of car driving skills or of professional competence. Generally there are not easy answers to the question of who should evaluate residential services. Whether the evaluation team or group comprises members outside or inside the residence or voluntary or government body, or whether it comprises residential staff, parents, paramedical professionals and clients is somewhat determined by the nature of the evaluation exercise. In some cases a key member of the team may be an architect or town planner; in other cases it may be a teacher or psychologist. In our own research, we have found a team of three comprising a public servant, an academic and a concerned and experienced person (for example, a parent, residential care officer, psychologist or social worker) to be useful. In such a team many different skills and values are an aid in the task of deciding how well a facility is providing for the needs of clients. One major consideration, however, is that whoever is chosen to undertake an evaluation must be given open access to staff, clients, their families and records. Without such access to information it will not be possible to make an accurate assessment or to make positive and realistic suggestions for improvement. Evaluation of services should not be seen as a threatening exercise but one of cooperation for the overall up-grading of a service. Without such a spirit of cooperation for the general good of clients the outcomes would probably be considerably limited in effectiveness and implementation. Hence, whoever is chosen to act on an evaluation team, there must be an atmosphere of cooperation and mutual respect.

Quite clearly no residential service is adequate without some kind of analysis, whether it be self-analysis or by an outside body. As lifestyles change and community attitudes and influences gradually awaken towards the acceptance of disabled people in the neighbourhood and community at large, there is an even greater need to monitor new residential provision. The fact that there is general agreement among 'experts' that people with handicaps should both live in and have an active, useful part in society to the greatest degree possible, should not make professionals complacent about the difficulties in making a residential service system based on these ideas work. Staff training seems to be a universal problem, and not until appropriate salaries and working conditions are determined will the field attract the most suitable applicants. Too often the best residential-care officers are lost to other professions because of such factors. At the legislative level, too, further developments will play their part in upgrading and changing services. Acts such as the Dependent Adults Act 1980 of Alberta will have important ramifications for services as well as for staff and the community at large.

As lifestyles change and as the number of disabled people generally is on the increase, there will be more and more pressure placed on governments and organizations to provide suitable residential provision in the community. Together with far-sighted and skilled policy-makers and highly trained personnel such services can be provided. Evaluation plays a critical role in ensuring that all those involved in residential services, at both client and service-provider levels, can articulate their needs and desires. While no one method for the evaluation of residential services is perfect, those described in this chapter indicate the variety of instruments available to undertake programme monitoring and up-grading exercises. Without regular review of residential services it is impossible to cater for the needs of disabled clients and their advocates.

REFERENCES

Accreditation Council for Services for Mentally Retarded and other Developmentally Disabled Persons (AC-MRDD) (1978) *Standards for Services for Developmentally Disabled Individuals.* Chicago: Joint Commission on Accreditation of Hospitals.

Andrews RJ & Berry PB (1978) The evaluation of services for the handicapped: promoting community living. *International Journal of Rehabilitation Research 1(4)*: 451–461.

Andrews RJ, Elkins J & Berry PB (1983) *Evaluation, Standards and Accreditation of Government-subsidized Services for Handicapped People: Schonell Evaluation and Accreditation Procedure (SEAP).* Canberra: Department of Social Security.

Berry P, Andrews RJ & Elkins J (1977) *An Evaluative Study of Educational, Vocational and Residential Programmes for the Moderately to Severely Mentally Handicapped in Three States.* Research report to the Department of Social Security, Canberra.

Commission on Accreditation of Rehabilitation Facilities (CARF) (1978) *Standards Manual for Rehabilitation Facilities.* Chicago: CARF.

Dependent Adults Act 1980 Government of the Province of Alberta, Canada.

Elkins J, Andrews RJ, Berry PB & Wells B (1980) *The Future of Services for Handicapped Persons in Australia.* St Lucia; Queensland: Fred and Eleanor Schonell Educational Research Centre.

Gunzburg H (1963) *Progress Assessment Chart (PAC) (Form I, Form II).* London: National Association for Mental Health.

Joint Commission on Accreditation of Hospitals (1973) *Standards for Community Agencies Serving Persons with Mental Retardation and other Developmental Disabilities.* Chicago: Joint Commission on Accreditation of Hospitals.

Kellett B (1976) An initial survey of the language of ESN(S) children in Manchester: the results of a teachers' workshop. In Berry P (ed) *Language and Communication in the Mentally Handicapped.* London: Edward Arnold.

McGaw B, Browne RK & Rees P (1976) Delphi in education: review and assessment. *Australian Journal of Education 20(1):* 59–76.

National Development Group for the Mentally Handicapped (NDG) (1977) *Mentally Handicapped Children: A Plan for Action.* NDG Pamphlet 2. London: Department of Health and Social Security.

National Development Group for the Mentally Handicapped (NDG) (1980) *Improving the Quality of Services for Mentally Handicapped People: A Checklist of Standards.* London: NDG.

NIMROD (New Ideas for the Care of the Mentally Retarded in Ordinary Dwellings) (1976–1983) Cardiff: Mental Handicap in Wales Applied Research Unit.

Schipper WV & Kenowitz LA (1976) Special education of exceptional children 1976–2000. *Journal of Special Education 10(4):* 401–413.

Skeels HM (1966) Adult status of children with contrasting early life experiences: a follow-up study. *Monograph for the Society of Research in Child Development 31(105):* 3.

Skeels HM & Dye HB (1939) A study of the effects of differential stimulation on mentally retarded children. *Proceedings of the American Association of Mental Deficiency 44:* 114–136

Tizard J (1964) *Community Services for the Mentally Handicapped.* Oxford: Oxford University Press.

Wolfensberger W (1972) *The Principle of Normalization in Human Services.* Toronto: National Institute on Mental Retardation.

Wolfensberger W & Glenn L (1975) *Program Analysis of Service Systems: A System for the Quantitative Evaluation of Human Services,* 3rd edn. Toronto: National Institute on Mental Retardation.

Chapter 5
Social Policy and Service Development

MALCOLM JOHNSON

Social policy is a term which has vagueness about it. How is it created? By whom? What does it look like? What effect does it have? In all the best fairy stories kings made policies (on matters of gravity like the slaying of dragons and the search for worthy husbands for beautiful princesses) and these were immediately carried out by faithful servants and obedient populations. In the real world of politics and people these simplistic and autocratic models are inoperable. Even the most determined and powerful government will often fail to exert its will. So it is something of a curiosity to be able to report that in the field of mental handicap in Britain there is, at the time of writing, a remarkable consensus about what should be done. It constitutes an agreed social policy.

At its most basic, social policy might be said to be the declared intention of the incumbent government about any matter of social concern. Health, social welfare, housing and income maintenance are the main sub-fields. Clearly then, any policy about the care and support of mentally handicapped people comes within this definition, for it cuts across all the items in the list. Traditionally, policy for all handicapped and vulnerable people has been about what to do *for* and *to* them. The assumption has been that such people are unable to live in ordinary society or to make any contribution to it. Not surprisingly, the resulting solution to the problems presented by unproductive and dependent sections of the populace has been to institutionalize them. This has had the dual benefit of ensuring that society at large was protected from – usually imaginary – dangers and of providing a relatively cheap way of meeting a moral obligation.

It is easy to be wiser than those who preceded us and to assume that they all suffered from a mixture of mean-mindedness, ignorance and insensitivity. In reality the original notion of an asylum was one which was based on Christian love and charity. Those who sought help from the Church were offered shelter from the elements and from the pressures of the world. It was a compound of failed idealism and the pressure of numbers which produced the wretched institutionalism of the Victorian era, as Kathleen Jones describes in her history of the mental health services (Jones, 1955). During the last century, the social policy for all those who suffered any kind of mental impairment (mental handicap was seen as a form of mental illness) was to gather them together in large hospitals as far removed from towns and cities as was possible. Various kinds of logic justified their exclusion from ordinary communities. Amongst these was a genuine belief that it was better for those who became patients and inmates.

This set of beliefs about the worth and needs of mentally ill and handicapped people was also reflected in provision for old and physically handicapped people (Townsend, 1962). Together they provided the foundation for a policy which saw custodial containment as a necessary and desirable objective. Social policy, in modern democracies, usually involves a common understanding of what needs to be done, to which governments give executive strength. There are exceptions to this generalization, such as the abolition of hanging and the legalization of male homosexuality, both against public opinion, but it is broadly true to say that firm intention and action more often results when agreement exists.

Within the field of mental handicap we have another variation on the theme. In the late 1970s, informed opinion moved steadily towards the belief that mentally handicapped people are harmed by institutional living and should live ordinary lives in ordinary houses, rather than be incarcerated. Alas, public opinion cannot be said to have moved in parallel with the professionals, the voluntary bodies and the parents. It is largely on this partial agreement and the prospects of its widespread implementation that I focus in this chapter.

CHANGING PATTERNS

Until very recently the numbers and age-structure of the population of mentally handicapped people remained fairly constant, owing to the high incidence of deaths in the early months of life and to the limited life-expectancy of those who survived. Better knowledge about the conditions associated with handicap, better preventive services and improved medical and surgical procedures in the early stages of life mean that the chances of survival for children with handicaps both physical and mental are greatly enhanced. Similarly, the higher standard of care and medical treatment has extended the average life-span of mentally handicapped people so that it now approaches that of the rest of the population. Together these factors have produced what is believed to be a significant increase in numbers and extended adulthood in a way which presents society with a new set of problems. The report of the Committee on Child Health Services *Fit for the Future* (Court Committee, 1976) was unable to provide detailed figures but concluded '... the number of retarded children may decline with advances in prevention and treatment and if fewer children were born to older women' (para. 14.75), indicating that the present increases are likely to fall off and not create a permanent growth in numbers.

Reliable statistics on mental handicap are not available because of the difficulties of definition, and those in common currency are now a little out of date. None the less, the Jay Committee (1979) found it had to rely on figures published in the 1971 White Paper *Better Services for the Mentally Handicapped* (DHSS, 1971), which suggests they are the latest available. They give an estimate of 120 000 severely mentally handicapped people (that is, below IQ 50) in England and Wales, of whom about 50 000 were children. Studies of prevalence suggest that there are between 2.95 and 5.81 severely mentally handicapped children per 1000 population. The Department of Health and Social Security in their review of mental handicap services since 1971 (published in December 1980) have worked on a general prevalence figure of 3.2 per 1000 population, which suggests a current total in the region of 148 000 severely mentally handicapped

children and adults. At the time of the 1971 White Paper, more than ten years after the 1959 Mental Health Act, half of this group remained in hospital; the movement into the community has been slow. Adults formed the overwhelming part of the hospital residents, with children making up only about 12% of the whole.

Information about age distribution is very inadequate, but the 1971 White Paper provides evidence indicative of an ageing population. In 1954 there were 5500 people over the age of 55 in hospital units for the mentally subnormal. This figure had risen to 11 200 by 1963 and to 13 850 by 1969. As people in this group get older the likelihood of institutional living increases greatly, so whilst these figures are by no means complete they can act as a fairly reliable guide to the changing shape of the age-structure. This has considerable implications for a field which so far has been overwhelmingly child-centred. However, the present numbers of those who have reached old age are small and it will be the end of the century and after before the expanded cohorts reach this stage, when they will cause considerable problems for health and social services.

THE FORMATION OF SOCIAL POLICY

In the latter years of the 1970s a number of government committees of enquiry have reported on subjects related to or specifically focused on mental handicap. The Court Committee's 1976 report on child health services recommended the establishment of district handicap teams, incorporating medical, nursing and social work personnel into hospital-linked domiciliary services. These proposals have been widely adopted throughout the National Health Service, but the patterns and practices vary a great deal. Some commentators assert that in most places the hospital still exerts too much influence and that the district handicap teams have so far failed to provide sufficient support in the community to make any significant difference to the numbers remaining in institutional settings.

The Warnock Committee (1978), which examined education for handicapped children and young people, concluded very firmly that much needs to be done by way of further integration of handicapped children into ordinary schools. It also drew attention to the cocooning effect of the special schools, which provide stimulation and expectations which often have little relationship to life after school age. The Warnock Committee recommended a curriculum more geared to the world of work and further efforts to finding ways of utilizing the demonstrable talents of handicapped school leavers. If properly executed these recommendations could make much heavier demands on the rest of the community than do the current special school arrangements.

More comprehensive than either of these documents is the report of the Jay Committee (1979) on mental handicap nursing and care. Despite the dissent of some of its members the report comes out very strongly in favour of community care provision and the rapid run-down of the larger hospital units. In recommending the shift from hospital to community the report observes that the tasks and therefore the training of caring staff will need to change radically – from an essentially nursing model to one more akin to residential social work with special emphasis on mental handicap. At first it was given a cool reception by the government, not least because it had considerable cost implications. It also faced strong opposition from the nursing profession. However, in the subsequent period the general philosophy and approach has gained wide acceptance. Many health and local authorities have begun to discuss and implement various forms of community-based alternatives to institutional provision.

The Secretary of State for Social Services made a clear commitment to clarify policy on mental handicap in *Care in the Community* (DHSS, 1981). In it he broadly endorsed the sort of developments outlined by the Jay Committee. Earlier and more detailed indication of this is found in his foreword to *Mental Handicap: Progress, Problems and Priorities* (DHSS, 1980), in which he says, 'I strongly endorse the final conclusion – that we need to build a pattern of local services and that for this the basic principles of the 1971 White Paper hold good. These principles have recently been re-stated in the Model of Care set out in the Report of the Committee chaired by Mrs Peggy Jay.'

It is clear that the debate about mental handicap policy has reached a point of broad consensus about the desirability of creating non-institutional arrangements in the community for those now in hospitals whose needs are not primarily medical. In practical terms this means that the great bulk of the present and prospective residents of mental handicap hospitals should in the foreseeable future be transferred to smaller, community-based forms of accommodation, or be maintained in the family home. In these places, the living arrangements will be designed to reflect the physical and social needs of those who will occupy them. Support will be provided according to the degree of mental (and physical) handicap through a social model of care, supplemented where required by medical and nursing services.

Such a model implies the eventual abandonment of the mental handicap hospitals as we have known them. In their place a wide variety of forms of care and potential development will need to emerge. It also means a massive transfer of resources, manpower and responsibility from one statutory authority to another – a transfer which even in fortunate times would prove difficult and technically complex, as well as costly. So, if radical change is to come about so that this conception of mental handicap care can become a reality, attention needs to be given to the active encouragement of the necessary structural change, as well as to innovation and the creation of alternative provision.

INTO THE COMMUNITY

An excellent policy analysis and implementation manual for comprehensive locally based residential services for mentally handicapped people has been provided by the King's Fund Centre 'Ordinary Life' group (King's Fund Centre, 1980a). It sets out plainly and convincingly how the lives of even the most severely impaired can be 'normalized' and given independence with dignity. A full account is given of tried and evaluated experiments such as the ENCOR schemes in Eastern Nabraska (Thomas et al., 1978). Core and cluster living arrangements developed there are offered as a viable model and extensive guidance is given on how to set up residential arrangements of this type. The whole tenor of the group's work is of liberation for mentally handicapped people. Its aim is to have the maximum number of people in their own (not family) homes – ordinary houses in ordinary neighbourhoods. (These matters are dealt with at greater length in Chapter 3.)

The focus on normalization, a concept developed by Wolfensberger (1972), is set against the repressiveness and the lack of creativity and dignity in present-day institutions. Such a radical shift in thinking, policy and practice faces so many obstacles that it is not surprising that its advocates give most of their attention to unblocking the paths which need to be made through statutory agencies and professional staff. At this early stage of development, normalization is seen as something which will be achieved by enlightening professionals, enabling handicapped people to live an ordinary life. Even so passionate an advocate as Alan Tyne concentrates on *service* provision (O'Brien and Tyne, 1981). Yet once people are placed in ordinary housing schemes, much of the success of the venture relies on the reception given to the new residents by neighbours, local shopkeepers, publicans, cinemas and others. Considerable attention has been given to voluntary support, but very little exists in print which engages with informal and neighbourhood acceptance and nurture. Whilst the direction of effort towards other objectives is understandable, the neglect of community responses is a glaring omission, especially in the light of hostile reactions to normalized housing schemes and holiday arrangements.

Mental handicap policy probably represents the most radical and coherent thrust for positive change to be found on the UK scene. The working agreement about how de-institutionalization should occur is far in advance, both in clarity and conviction, of anything to be found in the case of any other group in need of care. Yet the history of previous responses, which in turn reflect traditional patterns of containment and care, leave mental handicap research, policy analysis and practice with little knowledge of informal care. Some of the reasons have already been indicated, but others arise out of the way organized voluntary and self-help initiatives have stepped into the 'community' slot. Because public misunderstanding of mental handicap has given rise to fear as well as distaste for what is outside the normal range, those concerned have insulated themselves from open society whilst advocating normalization.

What can the community offer?

In a most thorough and valuable literature review of community services for people with mental handicap, Ward (1982) provides a sound guide to knowledge and issues. From it we can observe an elaborate structure of voluntary services both to carers (almost exclusively parents) and their charges. This arises directly out of the parents' and relatives' organizations which have grown up in recent decades to support hospital residents and those at home. MENCAP, the largest voluntary agency in this field, is essentially a parents' body. Despite strong encouragement from its national officers for the membership to embrace normalization principles, many still feel unable to shed their understandable customary protective role (St John Brooks, 1982; Thomas et al., 1980). Instead they

seek more direct services, the extension of 'respite' care (Oswin, 1981) and the development of self-help groups.

Characteristic of the expressed requirements of parents who are carers is the growth of short-term residential placements of the sort started in Leeds (Crosby et al., 1978) and Somerset (Crine, 1981) and the Crossroads Care Attendant Scheme (King's Fund Centre, 1980b). The Crossroads scheme provides paid attendants in the family home to provide relief to parents from the constant pressure of their task. The other side of this coin is an increasing willingness to take part in self-help groups.

In the mid-1970s Maurice and Doreen Collins created Kith and Kids out of the sheer frustration of seeing their daughter isolated from other children and in danger of living in a ghetto of mental handicap (Collins and Collins, 1976). The meetings provide social contact, mutual help, and mixing of handicapped with non-handicapped in a wide range of pre-planned activities. In her evaluation of Kith and Kids, Pugh (1981) observes the groups giving not only reciprocal service and experience, but a realization that there are others who share their situation. This perhaps also explains the more recent success of Contact A Family, which has expanded rapidly from its original small group in Wandsworth started by Noreen Miller, then a community social worker, now director of the national organization.

In recognition of the greater longevity of people with mental handicaps, new strategies are being developed to take account of those who outlive their parents and continue into later life. Again the responses are formal rather than informal. On current evidence few siblings will take handicapped brothers or sisters into their own households. So, with the growing disenchantment with institutional provision, MENCAP have devised the Homes Foundation to enable parents to ensure the future care of their children. The scheme involves the donation of houses and other gifts in return for appropriate residential and support arrangements after the parents' death.

Why then does a zeal for enabling independence coexist with a professional service ethic in mental handicap? The short answer is because there has never been an informal caring aspect to public care in the traditional mould. Where families have failed in the past hospitals have been the agency most ready to take on the load. Glendinning's (1983) detailed study of 17 families containing disabled children supplies powerful evidence of the continuation of the help and emotional support they receive from their own families: 'None had a great deal of regular, frequent, practical help. Relatives' own family commitments or grandparents' advancing age meant that some parents just did not expect any help.' In concluding that section of the book the author writes, 'The general impression from these families is that there is little close involvement of relatives in the daily grind of caring for their disabled child.'

Both Bayley (1973) and Wilkin (1979) in earlier studies had shown that care was available in these circumstances, but in particular limited forms. Glendinning (1983) reaffirms and refines their views by showing that family support was most likely to come in the form of babysitting. More substantial aid tended to be reserved for crises. In recognition of this, parents often chose not to make other claims on the time of relatives, for fear it might jeopardize their 'safety net'.

Assistance from neighbours and friends might have been expected on the basis of general studies of neighbouring, even taking into account the strategic nature of what Abrams et al. (1980) call the new neighbourhoodism. Glendinning (1983) finds that '. . few of the 17 families had regular or substantial help from neighbours with, for example, shopping, babysitting, or looking after children during the day.' Little wonder she called her book *Unshared Care.* But mitigating the low level of direct assistance it was evident that both family and neighbours gave valuable emotional support to parents, which provided an important – if non-instrumental – boost in carrying out the care tasks. This phenomenon was observed in chapter 2 in other contexts and is one which deserves more careful study in assessing the contribution of informal carers.

In the light of public attitude changes towards mental handicap and the new extension of volunteer and self-help contributions, there is a limited case for expecting that informal care in this field will grow. For the time being, parents will continue to carry their burdens alone with the help of professionals.

POLICY AND PRACTICE

It has already been observed that policy tends to arise out of working agreement, following a period of debate and innovation. In the case of mental handicap the development of new practices, particularly outside institutions, has been rich and varied. Moreover, it has been initiated by a wide variety of individuals, from doctors, psychologists and nurses through to social workers, horticulturists, relatives, friends and voluntary bodies. Until after the Second World War, services were largely directed by medical staff, who continued to believe that 'idiots' and 'imbeciles' were constitutionally incapable of being educated or trained. Indeed the eugenic belief, developed at the turn of the century, continued to dominate medical opinion for some decades.

Tredgold (1908) provides authoritative accounts of the fixed and negative view adopted by medical science in the early years of this century. In this view mental deficiency was a genetically determined and unchangeable condition. In consequence segregated living in colonies was advocated – a practice which received warm commendation from the Wood Committee (1929), especially where the mix of 'high-grades' and 'low-grades' provided a balance of workers and more dependent people. Not until the researches of Tizard and O'Connor (1952) and the Clarkes (1953) challenged the notion of fixed intelligence did service innovation begin to accelerate.

Just as earlier research had produced the segregation of mentally handicapped people, it later provided the base for a liberalization which focused upon the capacity for personal growth and skill development. In the first phase attention remained within the institutional setting, and largely concerned itself with rudimentary education and useful physical labour. The medical model, without its eugenic overtones, continued to be the frame of reference for care. Yet by the 1960s, Jack Tizard (1964) and then Albert Kushlick (1968) were advocating small residential units of 20 to 40 people which were not hospital-orientated.

Despite the increasing accumulation of evidence that mental handicap was not an illness and required little or no medical attention (unless associated with other conditions), and that hospitals were inappropriate forms of residential care, the traditional beliefs lingered on. In the 1971 White Paper which heralded the run down of mental handicap hospitals (DHSS, 1971) it continued to be assumed that 40% would remain living there – a view strongly challenged then and since.

Led by research, public policy moved cautiously towards a community-based service. At first it gave most attention to children, providing services for parents to ensure continued living at home. Professor Brimblecombe's Honeylands Centre in Exeter offered a mix of medical, counselling and social support from a hospital base. Special education also expanded, providing a form of environment and instruction which the Warnock Committee (1978) was later to condemn roundly. For adults, both those who lived in the parental home and many who were in public care, work was seen as a normalizing influence. Provision was made through adult training centres (ATCs), which went through an expansionary period during the 1970s, only to suffer the same fate as the special schools by the end of the decade. David Lane's 1980 study indicated that up to 95% of those with Down's syndrome could be employed in open, but supported work, whereas many ATC instructors would claim that this would be true for only a handful of their charges.

The shift in thinking towards normalization and to ordinary living has already been noted. In its present form, liberal thinking sets no uncommon limits on the opportunities and civil rights of mentally handicapped people and advocates that these be provided through enabling support systems rather than through the controlling and custodial methods which derived from the medical model.

CONCLUSIONS

In this necessarily selective review it has been possible to observe the trends in social policy moving from common prejudice and medical caution to openness and liberation for the mentally handicapped person. These developments have not been peculiar to those whose handicap is intellectual. Others – the old, the mentally ill and the physically handicapped – have also gained some benefit from the relaxation of attitudes. Similarly, the current anti-institutionalism occurs across all 'client' groups. In all cases the movement has been composed of the challenging of myths through research, the willingness of far-sighted individuals and groups to develop innovative forms of services and the co-operation of government – local and national – to reinforce and legitimise the proven advances.

Because it is a circumscribed problem involving a relatively small section of the population (compared with ten million over retirement age), mental handicap policy is now moving beyond the stage of consensus into national implementation. In Wales, for example, the Welsh Office, in its All-Wales Strategy for Mental Handicap, has set out to close all its mental handicap hospitals. During the five years 1984–1989 £27 million has been earmarked for this transition to the community. So now we can speak of there being an *active* policy which has government support and special funding.

Yet even in these favourable circumstances there are dangers. The history of social policy is littered with failed initiatives of this kind where ministers have tried valiantly to deliver a submerged group from its Cinderella status. Four Secretaries of State for Social Services – Enoch Powell, Richard Crossman, Barbara Castle and Sir Keith Joseph – all made similar attempts during the past 25 years. In their cases, it was to a large extent professional greed and manipulation which diverted the funds to other (somehow related) activities. Not only could this happen again, but also there are structural pitfalls within the system.

Progress so far has been created almost exclusively by professionals – doctors, psychologists, nurses and social workers – with the aid of voluntary bodies. With thoughtful enthusiastic advocates, this has taken the vanguard of mental handicapped adults into ordinary living. In the next 'mass' phase there could easily be a rush of inferior schemes which will result in a scatter of mini-institutions isolated on housing estates. This danger is amplified by the lack of an informal care network into which the vulnerable residents could be placed. So if the new partnership which is now in vogue (Mittler and McConachie, 1983) is to work for the benefit of mentally handicapped people, it will be essential for all the policy elements to be in harmony: money and enthusiasm, experience has shown, are not enough.

REFERENCES

Abrams P et al. (1980) Social change, social networks and neighbourhood care. *Social Work Service*, 22 February.

Bayley M (1973) *Mental Handicap and Community Care.* London: Routledge & Kegan Paul.

Clarke ADB & Clarke AM (1953) How constant is the IQ? *Lancet ii*: 877.

Collins M & Collins D (1976) *Kith and Kids – Self-help for Families of the Handicapped.* London: Souvenir Press.

Court Committee (1976) *Fit for the Future: Report of the Committee on Child Health Services* (Department of Health and Social Security and Department of Education and Science). London: HMSO.

Crine A (1981) Partnership with parents – a real alternative to hospital. *Mind Out 51*: July.

Crosby I, Runciman M & Naylor D (1978) 'Time off for parents.' *Social Work Today*, June.

DHSS (Department of Health and Social Security) (1971) *Better Services for the Mentally Handicapped.* Cmnd. 4683. London: HMSO.

DHSS (Department of Health and Social Security) (1980) *Mental Handicap: Progress, Problems and Priorities.* London: DHSS.

DHSS (Department of Health and Social Security) (1981) *Care in the Community*. London: DHSS.

Glendinning C (1983) *Unshared Care: Parents and their Disabled Children*. London: Routledge & Kegan Paul.

Jay Committee (1979) *Report of the Committee of Enquiry into Mental Handicap Nursing and Care*. Cmnd. 7468. London: HMSO.

Jones K (1955) *Law, Lunacy and Conscience, 1744–1845*. London: Routledge & Kegan Paul.

King's Fund Centre (1980a) *An Ordinary Life: Comprehensive Locally Based Residential Services for Mentally Handicapped People*. London: King's Fund Centre.

King's Fund Centre (1980b) *Stress and the Caring Relative: Crossroads Schemes for Mentally Handicapped People*. London: King's Fund Centre.

Kushlick A (1968) Care of the mentally subnormal. *Lancet ii*: 1196.

Lane D (1980) *The Work Needs of Mentally Handicapped Adults*. London: Disability Alliance.

Mittler P & McConachie H (eds) (1983) *Parents, Professionals and Mentally Handicapped People: Approaches to Partnership*. London: Croom Helm.

O'Brien J & Tyne A (1981) *The Principle of Normalisation: A Foundation For Effective Services*. London: Campaign for the Mentally Handicapped.

Oswin M (1981) *Issues and Principles in the Development of Short-term Care for Mentally Handicapped Children*. London: King's Fund Centre.

Pugh G (1981) *Parents as Partners*. London: National Children's Bureau.

St John Brooks C (1982) Passing on the burden. *New Society*, 25 February.

Thomas D, Firth H & Kendall A (1978) *ENCOR – A Way Ahead*. London: Campaign for the Mentally Handicapped.

Thomas DA, Smith PS & Smith LJ (1980) Consulting the consumers. *Health and Social Services Journal*, 15 February.

Tizard J (1964) *Community Services for the Mentally Handicapped*. London: Oxford University Press.

Tizard J & O'Connor N (1952) The occupational adaptation of high-grade defectives. *Lancet ii*: 620

Townsend P (1962) *The Last Refuge: A Survey of Residential Institutions and Homes for the Aged in England and Wales*. London: Routledge & Kegan Paul.

Tredgold A F (1908) *A Textbook of Mental Deficiency (Amentia)*. London: Baillière, Tindall & Cox.

Ward L (1982) *People First: Developing Services in the Community for People with Mental Handicap (A Literature Review)*. Project Paper No. 37, London: King's Fund Centre.

Warnock Committee (1978) *Special Education Needs: Report of the Committee of Enquiry into the Education of Handicapped Children and Young People*. Cmnd. 7212. London: HMSO.

Wilkin D (1979) *Caring for the Mentally Handicapped Child*. London: Croom Helm.

Wolfensberger W (1972) *The Principles of Normalisation in Human Services*, Toronto: National Institute on Mental Retardation.

Wood Committee (1929) *Report of the Committee on Mental Deficiency*. London: HMSO.

Chapter 6
Service Delivery Patterns in North America: Trends and Challenges

DIANE RICHLER AND JACQUES PELLETIER

North American society has undergone many changes in the last ten years. One such change concerns people who are handicapped: they are now visible. The presence of people who are handicapped is still a somewhat new but increasingly common phenomenon, as people who have a handicap go to school, travel to work, do their shopping, or take advantage of a warm spring day. People with visible handicaps make regular appearances in the public media, either as the subject of human interest stories or, increasingly, as members of the public at large. They are present on television, sometimes as the focus of attention, but more often, especially in educational children's programming, as another integral part of the community.

The visibility of people with handicaps in North American society is an indication of other underlying changes and trends in society. The most significant of these is an increased recognition of the rights of people who are handicapped to be full participants in their communities, and the responsibilities of communities to make such participation a reality for people regardless of the severity of their handicap.

This chapter will examine trends in the way supports are being provided to people with mental handicaps in order to foster this participation. It will identify some of the innovative thinking, some models for service provision, and challenges for the future. The chapter is not a quantitative review of service delivery patterns; rather, it is a personal reflection on trends, challenges and the current mood in North America.

HOW PEOPLE RECEIVE SUPPORTS

Living at home with one's family

When barraged by the hundreds of articles written monthly on the theme of living arrangements for mentally handicapped individuals, when reviewing public accounts of how governments invest their funds earmarked for mental retardation, or reading newspaper accounts about endless public debates on the future of various facilities, it is difficult to maintain the recognition that most mentally handicapped persons in North America, especially children and young adults, live at home with their families. This has always been true throughout the history of service development in North America, and in fact the proportion of people with a mental handicap living with their families is increasing.

A few factors can help to explain this phenomenon. One of them is a growing public awareness that the most important needs of a child, regardless of handicap, are for the emotional and human supports that are available only within a normal family life. It has increasingly been recognized that forcing people who are handicapped to live together in large groups, away from society, simply does not make any sense at any level of analysis: such facilities are expensive and are inappropriate places for people to live, learn, grow or be happy. Government policies have increasingly reflected this trend in North America, and in many jurisdictions it is now virtually impossible for most mentally handicapped children, especially at a young age, to be admitted to a large facility. At the same time, many governments have encouraged the emergence of a variety of family support services that usually include family counselling, in-home infant stimulation programmes, pre-school services, parent training, family relief programmes, and various forms of physical support programmes. The combination of these two trends – that is, a growing demystification of institutions and the creation of family support programmes – has led to a basic change in public opinion so that people increasingly support the view that handicapped people regardless of the degree of handicap, belong in their communities, living with their families. This in turn has led to an increased availability of public or generic services which continue to reinforce families' capabilities to cope with the requirements of their handicapped member. This trend is further reinforced by a growing body of professionals, especially medical practitioners and social workers, who believe that the presence of a handicapped child in the family does not usually pose any danger to that family if appropriate supports are provided. Where in the past it was common practice for professionals to counsel institutional placement, increasingly parents are being encouraged to keep their handicapped child at home. While formerly most handicapped children remaining with their families were mildly handicapped, the recent trend in this area has been for children with even severe and possibly very significant handicaps to remain at home.

The emergence of a new breed of families – those with a member who has a severe or significant mental and/or physical handicap – is bringing forward a growing demand for more extensive and comprehensive family and individual support services. Other factors are emerging. Many parents who have received sound counselling and stable family supports, and who have seen their handicapped children grow up with their siblings and peers, are demanding different services than those traditionally available in the school and vocational system. Parents and mentally handicapped individuals are increasingly expecting and demanding integrated services. The special school, the special class, is becoming less and less acceptable where a child has had the benefit of intensive early stimulation and has always been included within the mainstream of family and community life.

In the past, mentally handicapped children who lived with their parents tended to continue living with them much longer than the average offspring. In fact, many have stayed with their families until the parents died or until they were unable for health reasons to manage. Such is often the pattern today. However, where in the past institutionalization was often the only option after parents could no longer cope, this is no longer being viewed as an acceptable destiny. More and more middle-aged parents are beginning to lobby for services outside their families for mentally handicapped adults reaching their thirties and forties. Parents' concerns are to avoid crises as parents get older and also to ensure that their children can survive them in conditions that

are at least as good as those that they have been accustomed to at home. This usually means living arrangements in the home communities. There is also a growing lobby of younger parents who are working on the notion that a young adult, whether handicapped or not, will usually leave his family when he reaches his twenties. These parents insist that social service agencies make available living arrangements for their children once they reach adulthood.

A further concern of such parents who are thinking towards the future is for a guardianship or protective service arrangement that would not only meet the legal and financial needs of handicapped offspring, but more importantly would guarantee a continuity of personal relationship after the death of parents. If community life is to be secure and meaningful, this element of on-going advocacy for the handicapped individual and on-going personal relationships will have to be resolved.

All families who have kept their mentally handicapped child at home with them will admit that life was often a challenge, that it was often hard, and that the other children in the family did suffer at times. Most will add, however, that the problems and challenges strengthened both the family as a whole and the members as individuals, that the benefits far outweighed the losses, and that the non-handicapped children learned and became better people because of their handicapped sibling. There are exceptions; there will always be failures. But there is a growing recognition that the failures are the exceptions, confirming the rule.

Living outside the natural family

Where do people with mental handicaps live, if not with their families? Many, when they reach adulthood, will live independently and integrate into the mainstream of society. Others live in segregated facilities in groups of eight or more, while others live in a variety of funded living arrangements that range from individual arrangements for children in foster homes or apartments for adults to group homes.

It should not be forgotten that institutional populations in the United States reached a peak of 190 000 in 1971, and by 1981 had decreased by to approximately 130 000 (Janicki et al., 1982). Similarly, in Canada there were approximately 24 000 people with a mental handicap living in institutions for 50 or more in 1981 (National Institute on Mental Retardation, 1982). From 1971 there was a 900% increase in group home places across the United States to a total of 58 000 places by 1981 (Janicki et al., 1982). Similarly, in the same period approximately 5000 group home places were developed in Canada (National Institution on Mental Retardation, 1982). Individualized residential places have only recently become an accepted form of publicly supported accommodation support, and it has been estimated that about 10 000 such places exist in the United States (Janicki et al., 1982). In Canada the number of such funding arrangements is negligible; however, they are extremely significant in terms of the models which they present and their empirical evidence of the potential to support people to live very individualized lives. In general, the institutional model, though far from extinct, has been condemned by serious policy-makers, while community-based alternatives have become increasingly feasible and desirable. Fewer and fewer people are deemed by any programmers to require institutions, and in fact a growing number of professionals, policy-makers, families and politicians are beginning to adopt the view that no handicapped person requires an institution: people who have a handicap require varied and flexible degrees of support, and none need to be grouped excessively in order to receive such support.

This general acceptance of how people should be served has resulted in two concurrent processes: one that is broadly described as de-institutionalization and the other described as community-based service development. Currently, the process of de-institutionalization – the emptying of institutions – has met with varying degrees of success and has created problems as well as new opportunities. In many cases, the process of developing community-based services has been directly linked to the people coming out of institutions, and this has sometimes been to the detriment of handicapped people already living in the community. At other times, rapid closure of institutions has often resulted either in the dumping of people in the community without proper supports or in the transfer of people from large institutions to smaller nursing homes and community back wards, often privately operated and poorly monitored. In other instances, the transfer of people from institutions to community services in large numbers has meant a transfer of institutional cultures and in fact little difference in quality of life between a larger setting and a smaller one. Many times, the process has meant that those who were less handicapped left the institution leaving those with more severe handicaps behind, and making it even more difficult for them to

leave. This 'horizontal' approach to deinstitutionalization is being slowly abandoned in favour of an approach which is more 'vertical' in nature. In other words, people with varying degrees of needs or levels of handicap are being brought out at the same time. This approach not only forces agencies to plan more systematically around the needs of individuals, but also eliminates the phenomenon described above, where institutions become permanent homes for the most severely handicapped.

Governments are increasingly aware that institutional closures are complex processes which require adequate planning. Poorly prepared plans result in improper community placements and services. They also inevitably result in labour conflicts and controversy with parents and often the community at large. On the other hand, well planned programmes based on individuals and their needs have permitted many hundreds to leave institutions with proper support to live better lives in the community.

In North America this movement to shift from publicly funded large institutions to community-based services in the past ten years has seen a virtual explosion in community service developments, even though the economic recession and recent conservative government policies have slowed down this process. For all their promises, however, institutional closures, decreases in institutionalized populations, and increases in community infrastructures, have yet to make a major difference in a number of jurisdictions in many parts of North America. In ten years, the net decrease in the number of people with a mental handicap living in institutions is negligible in Canada and in several American states (McHale, 1980; McWhorter, 1984). Even more significant is the fact that disproportionate amounts of budgets are spent on the maintenance of institutions as compared with the development of community services and family support programmes. The transformation of North American services for mentally handicapped persons, especially residential services, has yet to be done.

Furthermore, the community services and particularly the residential services, which have mushroomed and spread across North America during the past 15 to 20 years, offer a very large disparity in quality. The group home model, which to many seemed such an innovation in the early 1970s, is now coming under severe criticism for many of the same reasons that larger institutions have been condemned in the past, particularly the inability of services which are organized to serve groups of people to meet individual needs adequately at the same time. The most radical advances in thinking about new service models have arisen out of a frustration with trying to fit unique individuals into existing services which may meet only part of the individual's needs, and a desire to tailor-make services to suit the individual. Throughout the 1970s, there was a general acceptance of a model of a continuum of services which extended from those which provided a high degree of support and usually segregation to those which offered clients a minimal level of support and virtual independence. It was assumed that as people's needs changed, they would move along the continuum of services. For example, it was felt that an individual leaving an institution would have to move into a fairly structured group home setting. As the person gained new skills, he might then move into a less structured group home setting; as he became able to meet most of his needs he might move into a supervised apartment and possibly eventually move on to live independently. The new approaches to individualization totally reject the underlying assumption that as a person's needs change so should his place of residence. Rather, implicit in the newer models is the commitment to the concept that a person has a right to his or her own home, and that it is the supports to the person in that home that must be adjusted as needs change. In this model, a person can easily move from a very restricted institutional setting into an apartment, town house or small home with one or two friends who may or may not also have handicaps. Whatever supports are needed by the person can be provided in the home, and as new skills are acquired and independence gained, the supports can be gradually withdrawn, or new supports can be provided if need be. In the old model, the group homes and their structure remained constant and the handicapped individual moved in and out. In the newer models, people who are handicapped can establish a home with a sense of permanence, though the supports that the individual receives in his home may change continuously.

Where people learn

Until after the Second World War children with a mental handicap were systematically excluded from the school system. In the late 1940s, throughout the 1950s and even into the 1960s, the first community education programmes were often begun by local associations for the mentally retarded and were usually in the form of private segregated schools.

Although most such schools have since been absorbed by the public school system, throughout the 1970s segregation was still the norm. However, passage of Public Law 94–142 in the United States has made appropriate public education a right of all children labelled as retarded. School boards are now obliged not only to educate children with special needs, but to do so in an appropriate manner, and there are appeal procedures for parents when arrangements are unsatisfactory. In Canada, whilst there is no universal federal legislation, individual provinces are beginning to take steps in the same direction.

Whilst the norm continues to be a pattern of segregation, there are many innovative programmes demonstrating that when children who are handicapped, and even those with the most severe handicaps, are educated in the same classroom as their age peers benefits accrue to all children in the class. Because of the newness and small number of such programmes, they are still perceived as experimental, and there are few examples of system-wide educational programmes of such a nature. The most notable is the Madison School District in Wisconsin, where there are students graduating from secondary school who have been integrated for their entire school careers. The success of the Madison programme in terms of the benefits to handicapped and non-handicapped students alike, has made this school district a focus for North American educators and a model which is being studied, adapted, and implemented to varying degrees all over the continent.

Vocational training and earning a living

The last decade has seen a virtual explosion of innovation and thinking in terms of where people with mental handicaps live and go to school. This upbeat mood and general feeling of optimism has not yet penetrated the traditional vocational service systems; they continue to be a living relic of the past, usually condemning people with mental handicaps to years of repetitive and boring piecework in segregated and unstimulating environments.

It must be underlined that the current bleak vocational outlook must be blamed not on problems inherent in the people with mental handicap but rather on the ways in which supports or non-supports have been provided to them.

Technologies have been developed since the 1970s which demonstrate that people with severe and profound impairments are capable of productive activity (Bellamy and Snyder, 1979). Others have demonstrated that people can move directly from sheltered workshops into the workforce with the right kinds of support (Shelton and Lipton, 1983).

There appear to be two major reasons for the current lack of development in the field of vocational training and employment. First, many of the innovations in the education system are still taking place at the primary level, and few people with mental handicaps are yet graduating from secondary schools adequately prepared to take their place in the workforce. Secondly, most of the public assistance programmes available to adults who are mentally handicapped are tied to a service model centred around the sheltered workshops. There is little room for experimentation and gradual transition from public assistance to competitive employment because under current structures as soon as a person starts to earn any significant amount of money, even if it is not equal to the full benefits received under social assistance, those social assistance benefits are withdrawn. This has made service deliverers and families hesitant about jeopardizing existing supports when future job security is not guaranteed.

We are only just beginning to witness significant discomfort amongst parents, advocates and service providers with the segregated workshops as the prime options for young adults who have lived the beginning of their lives as full members of their communities and who expect to be able to continue this pattern in their adult lives. Whilst still not as strong and clearly defined as the lobby for better family support services and better educational opportunities, the lobby for change at the vocational and employment levels is growing. One can predict that the present segregated social welfare models of work will come under increasing attack and public scrutiny in the next few years.

Recreation and leisure

As in other service areas, most recreation and leisure activities for people labelled mentally handicapped were initially developed by local associations for the mentally retarded and began as segregated programmes. These included bowling leagues, floor hockey leagues, swimming clubs, dances and summer camps. In the 1970s, with the increased public recognition and willingness to meet the needs of handicapped citizens, many generic recreation agencies and municipal recreation departments assumed the responsibility to provide services for people who are handicapped, but usually these have continued to be segregated programmes. Such recreational opportunities are available in most cities, but a recent survey of Canadian programmes has indicated a dramatic lack of recreational services in rural areas (Lyons, 1981). The Special Olympics programme sponsored by the Kennedy family in the United States and by the Foster Foundation in Canada provides an opportunity for many handicapped people to engage in physical activity and sports and to compete at regional, national and international levels. However, there is an increased recognition of the need to take a fresh look at recreation programming and overcome the attitudes amongst professionals who have been trained for segregation. Newer models, such as the leisure-buddy programme, which is widely practised across Canada, provide an opportunity for volunteers to help persons who are handicapped make use of the regular leisure and recreation opportunities of their communities. Similarly, adults who are mentally handicapped are being helped to take responsibility for planning and going on ordinary vacations, within their budgets, while receiving as much or as little support as necessary.

How services are organized

Roeher (1979) outlined a model for organizing systems of services at a regional level which has been advocated by the Canadian Association for the Mentally Retarded since 1971 under the name ComServ (Comprehensive Community Service Systems). A review of this process (Pelletier and Richler, 1982) has indentified several major lessons which are instructive in order to maximize the benefits of current and future planning efforts. In brief there are four crucial issues to be considered in the organization of service systems.

Regionalization. There must be a well-defined service region in which there is legislative backing for the provision of services. There must be regional coordination whereby a regional body is empowered to establish objectives, develop and operate a service system and the region must be a viable size, with a large enough population to warrant, afford, organize and manage a service system that answers the widest possible variety of individual needs and yet is not so complex that it becomes cumbersome to manage; and finally, it must offer comprehensiveness in terms of being able to meet a wide variety of individual needs.

Operation of service systems. Managers must learn to coordinate existing generic or special services around individual needs rather than continuing old management styles which involved running special services.

Community participation and control, advocacy and monitoring. There must be built-in mechanisms assuring community involvement in regional service systems and advocacy and monitoring at all levels within the structure.

Ideology. The critical element in all service systems is an inherent belief and commitment to a recognition of the value and rights of people who are handicapped, and a rigorous attempt to develop supports which will both foster continual growth and development and maximize full participation in the community.

While these issues have been identified, debated, and widely accepted their implementation is in its infancy. A critical element is the role of governments at the provincial and state levels; these have traditionally controlled mental retardation programming through control of large state-run institutions, and are attempting to develop community models with the same degree of state control. The voluntary sector, represented primarily by associations for the mentally retarded in Canada and associations for retarded citizens in the United States, is involved in an on-going process of negotiation with the respective provincial or state governments in order to determine the balance between citizen control and state control in the development and administration of community service systems.

SOME ISSUES INFLUENCING CHANGE

The first part of this chapter dealt with how people with mental handicaps in North America currently tend to receive services. This next section will examine three broad issues which are having a major impact in the way supports are being planned, evaluated and implemented. These issues are human rights, serving people with complex needs in the community, and the volunteer movement and self-advocacy.

Human rights

In December 1971 the United Nations General Assembly adopted the Declaration on the Rights of Mentally Retarded Persons which proclaimed that ' . . . the mentally retarded person has to the maximum degree of feasibility, the same rights as other human beings'. Since the mid-1970s courts in both the United States and Canada have been testing-grounds to determine the meaning of the word 'feasibility', and to test the limits of federal, state and provincial legislation in extending equal rights to people with handicaps.

Litigation on the human-rights front has tended to focus on two main issues: right to medical treatment, which is often equivalent to a right to life, and right to personal freedom and a decent place to live.

On neither of these issues have decisions been totally consistent, but even where decisions in courts have been contradictory, it is important to examine the nature of cases which are being brought to the highest courts in the land.

In the United States, two of the most recent, and well publicized, cases have had opposite conclusions. In the case of Baby Jane Doe, born in New York state in October 1983 with multiple neural tube defects, it was found that her parents had the right to opt for conservative medical treatment rather than surgery which could correct her spina bifida and hydrocephalus and significantly increase her life expectancy. The New York Court of Appeals held that the intrusion of a totally unrelated person, with no knowledge of the infant or her condition or treatment, invaded the parents' privacy, and could not supersede parental decision in this case (Steinbock, 1984). Conversely, in California, in the case of Phillip Becker, whose natural parents refused permission for their son's recommended heart surgery, a couple who had become close to Phillip were granted guardianship and eventually the surgery was performed (Annas, 1982). In Canada, the Supreme Court of British Columbia decided in favour of Stephen Dawson, a six-year-old with hydrocephalus, and against his parents, who refused permission for surgery to replace their son's shunt, surgery without which he would have died (*In re Dawson*, 1983).

Another type of litigation is exemplified in the case of Justin Clark, a young man in Ontario who challenged his parents in court in order to prove that he was mentally competent and could decide to leave the institution where he had been living in order to share a home with friends in Ottawa (*In re Clark*, 1982). Legislation in the United States has not only permitted individuals to challenge institutional placement, but has permitted class action suits, such as the most noteworthy Pennhurst decision whereby the State of Pennsylvania was ordered to provide suitable and individualized living arrangements for institution residents in the community (Human Services Research Institute, 1980; Bradley and Conroy, 1983; MPDLR, 1984).

What has been remarkable about all of the cases mentioned above has been the amount of interest they have generated in the media and among the public at large. Regardless of the final court decision, the presence in the courts of law of people who have a mental handicap has brought the rights of handicapped persons to the public consciousness, and this fact, as much if not more than the actual court decisions, is producing an increasing respect for handicapped persons. Some of that respect is based on a healthy fear of the consequences of contravening the law, but much more is based on issues regarding the value of the lives of people who are handicapped, which have never been adequately considered in the public mind before.

People with complex needs

In the early 1970s the ENCOR project in Nebraska was noteworthy not only for its aggressive development of community services for people who had been institutionalized for decades, but also for its rejection of all of the then current assumptions about the developmental potential of children born with multiple handicaps. The first ENCOR service for children with complex needs, originally called the Developmental Maximation Unit, was housed in a general hospital in order to allay the fears of parents and service providers alike. However, those directly involved in the care of the children felt from the beginning that the medical supports provided a security blanket for staff, but were not really essential for good care and healthy development of the children. This is not to minimize the complications in the conditions of the children: many were very ill, and some died. However, the aggressive programmatic intervention of doctors, physiotherapists, occupational and speech therapists and educators had a profound impact on most of the children and most developed in ways which greatly surpassed any previous expectations for them.

In recent years, across North America, there has been a more widespread focus on people who have sometimes been described as 'medically complex', 'multi-handicapped', 'behaviourally disordered' or 'severely or profoundly handicapped'. As indicated above, the advent of additional family supports has meant that fewer and fewer children born with complex needs are being removed from their families at birth, and as the child grows and takes its rightful place within the family models of service once considered inevitable for children with such needs are being rejected by parents who expect more. These are the parents who are securing aggressive early-intervention programmes for their children, and who are seeing them, one at a time, integrated into regular classroom settings with their peers. These examples are still limited, but each one has a snowball effect in its community. When parents whose child is only moderately handicapped see a child with much more complex needs integrated into the school system, they start to have a higher expectation for their own child, and new demands are made of the system. Because children and adults with very complex needs often do require very particular kinds of supports, including technical aids for positioning, medical technology, expert programming, and so on, it has often been around the situations of people with such needs that the concept of planning for the individual has become articulated and well understood. These concepts, once practised in a community, have then been broadened to include other people whose needs may be less complex, but for whom the individual planning approach is equally applicable.

The volunteer movement and self-advocacy

To a great extent, the history of services for people with a mental handicap in North America has been the history of the associations for the mentally retarded, started and continued largely by parents. In the late 1970s and especially in the early 1980s a new element has entered the picture: people with a mental handicap are beginning to speak for themselves. What began as a social club of workshop trainees has grown to a movement which is having a profound effect on the mental retardation movement. The early American groups called themselves 'People First', and many local and provincial Canadian counterparts have adopted the same name. While there is still no national or international movement that is having an organized effect on service development, it is clear in many communities and in many states and provinces that people with a handicap are beginning to be listened to with a new respect. It has been difficult for parents and volunteer-run associations to learn how to accommodate handicapped members without being patronizing or condescending and while allowing meaningful opportunities for participation. There has had to be patience and understanding on both sides, but in jurisdictions which have made real attempts to provide a voice to people with a handicap mechanisms are being found and the messages of people who live with a handicap are being heeded. In Canada, one of the current controversies is the pain and unhappiness expressed by people with a mental handicap about the label 'mental retardation', which is currently used in Canada and which is in fact contained in the name of the national voluntary organization, the Canadian Association for the Mentally Retarded. Consumers have lobbied vigorously at the local, provincial and national level in an attempt to have the name of the organization changed in a way that will remove this label from the people who feel most hurt by it. The jury is still out, but there is a conscious effort within the Association to adopt a new name which will not offend the very people whom it is the supposed intention of the Association to serve.

THE FUTURE

The 1970s were a period of 'boom' for the field of mental retardation in North America. Economic prosperity happily coincided with a change in perception about how to meet the needs of handicapped people, and massive investments were made in new community services. The creation of some community services created a pressure for more as increasing numbers of parents, advocates and professionals became convinced of the potential of people with a mental handicap to benefit from and contribute to community life. The economic recession of the early 1980s has forced many governments, planners, service providers and advocates alike to look at what now appears to have been almost unbridled spending in the past decade and to face the harsh reality that if new services are still desired, old ones will have to be forfeited to free the necessary funding. For many, this means simply that we cannot afford both an institutional system and a good community system, and that the institutional system must be sacrificed to provide funds for the community. Many vested interests see a different scenario: continue to maintain the institution and at the same time fund a mediocre community system. As long as their view prevails — and, despite rhetoric to the contrary, most state and provincial governments appear to endorse it (Richler, 1981; Flynn and Nitsch, 1980) — the community system will be unable to achieve a satisfactory level of comprehensiveness or excellence.

REFERENCES

Annas GJ (1982) A wonderful case and an irrational tragedy: the Phillip Becker case continues. *Hastings Center Report 12 (1)*: 25–26.

Bellamy GT & Snyder S (1979) *Vocational Habilitation of Severely Retarded Adults: A Direct Service Technology.* Baltimore: University Park Press.

Bellamy GT, Rose H, Wilson DJ & Clarke JY (1982) Strategies for vocational preparation. In Wilcox B & Bellamy GT (eds.) *Design of High School Programs for Severely Handicapped Students.* Baltimore: Paul H Brooks.

Bellamy GT, Rhodes LE, Bourbeau PE & Mank DM (1985) *Mental Retardation Services in Sheltered Workshops and Day Activity Programs: Consumer Outcomes and Policy Alternatives.* University of Oregon (in preparation).

Bracewell D & Milligan K (1983) Thousand Cranes School: building a dream. *Mental Retardation 33(4)*: 26–30.

Bradley VJ & Conroy JW (1983) *Third Year Comprehensive Report of the Pennhurst Longitudinal Study.* Philadelphia: Temple University Developmental Disabilities Centre.

In re Clark (1982) Ontario, Ministry of the Attorney-General, County Court of the County of Lanark (Action No. (CC)M 1608) Judge John Matheson, *Judgment with Reasons in the Matter of Justin Clark.* November 25, 1982.

In re Dawson (1983) British Columbia, Ministry of the Attorney-General, Supreme Court of British Columbia (No. C831628 and No. 830797, Vancouver Registry) *Oral Reasons for Judgment of the Honourable Mr Justice McKenzie in the Matter of Stephen Dawson.* March 18, 1983.

Flynn RJ & Nitsch KE (eds.) (1980) *Normalization, Social Integration and Community Services.* p. 365. Baltimore: University Park Press.

Forest M (1984) The emperor is naked: the truth about educational integration. *Canadian Journal on Mental Retardation 34(1)*: 24–28.

Green-McGowan K & Kovacs M (1984) Twenty-four-hour planning for persons with complex needs. *Canadian Journal on Mental Retardation 34(1)*: 3–11.

Human Services Research Institute (HSRI) (1980) *Longitudinal Study of the Court–Ordered Deinstitutionalization of Pennhurst,* p.1. Washington DC: HSRI.

Hutchison P (1983) *Curriculum Guidelines for Canadian Colleges and Universities: Leisure and Disabled Persons.* Ottawa: Canadian Parks/Recreation Association.

Janicki MP, Mayeda T & Epple WA (1982) *A Report on the Availability of Group Homes for Persons with Mental Retardation in the United States.* Alexandria, Virginia: National Association of State Mental Retardation Program Directors.

Lord J (1983) Reflections on a decade of integration. *Journal of Leisurability 10(4)*: 4–11.

Lutfiyya Z (1984) A unique camping trip to the Rockies. *The Canadian Journal on Mental Retardation 34(1)*: 16–21.

Lyons RF (1981) *Analysis of Service Delivery to Special Populations by Municipal Recreation Departments in Canada.* Ottawa: Fitness and Amateur Sport Branch, Government of Canada.

McHale J (1980) Mental retardation and the future. In Plog SC & Santamour MB (eds.) *The Year 2000 and Mental Retardation.* New York: Plenum Press.

McWhorter A (1984) *Service Delivery Patterns in North America: An Overview of Change* (unpublished).

MPDLR (Mental and Physical Disability Law Reporter) (1984) High Court remands *Pennhurst.* MPDLR, January-February, 1984, 8:1, p. 7.

National Institute on Mental Retardation (1982) *Experimenting with Social Change: An Interpretive History of the Southern Alberta ComServ Project*. Downsview, Ontario: National Institute on Mental Retardation.

National Institute on Mental Retardation (1983) *Breaking Through* (film). Toronto: National Institute on Mental Retardation.

Ontario, Ministry of the Attorney-General, County Court of the County of Lanark (Action No. (CC)M 1608) Judge John Matheson, *Judgment with Reasons in the Matter of Justin Clark*. November 25, 1982.

Pelletier J & Richler D (1982) *Major Issues in Community Living for Mentally Handicapped Persons: Reflections on the Canadian Experience*. Downsview, Ontario: National Institute on Mental Retardation.

Richler D (1981) A decade of change: how far have we come? *Mental Retardation 31 (2):* 35–43.

Rioux M & Crawford C (1982) *Choices: The Community Living Society: New Methods of Responding to the Individual with a Handicap*. Vancouver: Community Living Society.

Roeher GA (1979) Services for the mentally retarded in North America. In Craft M (ed.) *Tredgold's mental retardation*, 12th edn. London: Baillière Tindall.

Savage HS (1984) *Justice for Some: A Discussion Book on Law for People with Mental Handicaps and their Friends*. Downsview, Ontario: National Institute on Mental Retardation.

Shelton C & Lipton R (1983) An alternative employment model. *Canadian Journal on Mental Retardation 33(2):* 12–16, 42.

Steinbock B (1984) Baby Jane Doe in the courts. *The Hastings Centre Report 14(1):* 13–19.

Wolfensberger W (1972) *The Principle of Normalization in Human Services*. Toronto: National Institute on Mental Retardation.

Wolfensberger W (1975) *The Origin and Nature of our Institutional Models*. p. 28. Syracuse: Human Policy Press.

PART 2
THE LAW

Chapter 7
Low Intelligence and Delinquency

MICHAEL CRAFT

HISTORICAL BACKGROUND

Poor conditions of child-rearing have always been known to be associated with both educational retardation and criminality. At the beginning of the century Alfred Binet developed his intelligence test to try to distinguish between feeble-minded criminals with an IQ of less than 70 and those above IQ 70. Yet by 1916 Terman (who with Merrill constructed the Terman Merrill IQ test) was so convinced of the close association of low intelligence and crime that he wrote: 'There is no investigator who denies the fearful role played by mental deficiency in the production of vice, crime and delinquency. Not all criminals are feeble-minded, but all feeble-minded are at least a potential criminal. That every feeble-minded woman is a potential prostitute would hardly be disputed by anybody.'

The attempt to treat such people by doctors using hospitals led to the English Mental Deficiency Act 1913, its subsequent amendment in 1927 to include moral defectives, and the usage of the term 'psychopathic disorder' in the 1959 Mental Health Act. Since those times, large-scale investigations have teased out the differing results of childhood deprivation, the deprivative factors which lie behind the causation of many of the mentally handicapped with IQ 50–70 (see Chapter 9) and the paucity of crime associated with those who are truly mentally handicapped. This chapter reviews the current situation.

Surveys of offenders

Woodward's 1954 review on the role of low intelligence in delinquency was a landmark review to that date, and still makes good reading. Table 7.1 gives her analysis of research reports into IQ testing of various criminal populations. Defining as she did

Table 7.1 Proportion of convicts found to be feeble-minded (Woodward, 1954).

Years	Number of studies	Percentage feeble-minded in median survey	Percentage feeble-minded: range
1910–14	50	51	1.96
1915–19	142	28	1.82
1920–24	104	21	1.69
1925–28	46	20	2.58

those under IQ 70 as feeble-minded, she shows that the proportion of the convicted who were found to be under IQ 70 decreases with the refinement of intelligence tests (Table 7.2). The results of early tests depended mainly on educational prowess, whereas later tests measured practical abilities rather than the acquired education so often lacking in deprived adolescents. Gittens (1951), who tested 1000 recidivist schoolboys using the Wechsler test, found an average IQ of 92, which was much higher than the earliest tests. He found a mere 3% in all under IQ 70, which is the same as the proportion of the general population scoring under IQ 70 on Wechsler tests. Woodward concluded in 1954: 'All these lines of evidence therefore, indicate that the eight IQ points by which delinquents differ from the general population norm are entirely attributable to the depressive effect on the test score constellation of factors which differentiate delinquents from the general population. In other words there would be no difference in intelligence between delinquent and non-delinquent groups matched for all the cultural variables* '. . . . Over a period of 40 years the

---

* For a detailed analysis concerned with crime, cultural factors, genetic endowment and the sex chromosome anomalies, see Craft and Craft, 1984.

Table 7.2 Mean IQ of convicted prisoners (Woodward, 1954).

Date	Number tested	Test used	Mean IQ	IQ < 70	Source of sample	Investigators
1931	200	1916 Stanford Binet	71	34	Institution	Sayder
1931	401	Not stated		5.9*	Institution	
1931	300	1916 Stanford Binet	82†	18.65	Institution	
1933	602	1916 Stanford Binet	79.34		Court	McClure
1934	979	1916 Stanford Binet		13.4	Court	Gluecks
1934	3584	1916 Stanford Binet	82.2	13.9	Court	Rogers & Austin
1935	699	Otis Group Test	87.96	10.0	Institution	Land & Witty
1937	152	Otis SA test 14 year norm	75.5		Institution	Moore
1937	21 studies		82.4		Institution	Owen
1939	1731	Revised Stanford Binet	84.45		Court	Mann & Mann
1945	463	Revised Stanford Binet and Kulhmann Anderson	86.74	10.4	Court and others	Kvataccus
1947	300	1916 Stanford Binet	86.7		Court	Merrill
1947	500	Revised Stanford Binet	92.5	11.6	Court	Merrill
1950	500	Wechsler	92.28	4.2	Institution	Gluecks
1952	1000	Wechsler	9.2		Approved school	Gittens

* Percentage feeble-minded: not based on test alone.
† Median IQ.

extent to which the test results underestimate the intelligence of delinquents in America has gradually decreased. Beginning in the defective range, the test results of delinquent groups have steadily approached the average, and this change is paralleled by improvements in tests and methods of sampling.' Woodward also quotes Eleanor Glueck's work on 1000 juvenile delinquents in Boston, which was concerned with deprivative factors of upbringing. At that time Glueck (1935) interpreted her data as 'flowing from the mental deficiency of the delinquents themselves and from the sub stream of delinquency in their families.' Nowadays one would talk in terms of deprived and poverty-stricken parents bringing up deprived and poverty-stricken children or a cycle of deprivation.

From America there are three interesting surveys which highlight the difficulties in assessing intelligence quotients of criminals. To illustrate the pitfalls let us analyse the survey by Brown and Courtless (1968). They carried out a postal survey of offenders 'incarcerated in penal correctional institutions in the United States'. As they say, there is still no precise knowledge of what the total number might be on any day, for many states do not make returns from county jails, police cells and lock-ups. Thus, postal replies could neither be random nor complete. They had questionnaires concerning

217 280 inmates on 13 December 1963; IQ scores had been performed on 90 477 of these. 'We found there was a rather bewildering array of tests used by the institutions to measure intelligence', they say. Testers ranged from officers to fellow inmates; tests were sometimes done during the shock of incarceration after arrest, and sometimes in the long-term penal unit. They found that 1.6% of the surveyed population (1454) had IQ scores below 55, yet among these there was no pre-trial psychological or psychiatric examination for 78%, competence to stand trial was not questioned among 92%, no appeal was made among 88%. All of this attests more to the lack of interest taken in such people than to their severe retardation. In Britain an IQ score under 55 usually applies to a retardate who is illiterate and unable to travel alone, yet in this American sample, most had committed burglary, and some were capable of fraud or forgery!

In 1973 Tarjan and his colleagues analysed the literature on mentally handicapped offenders, and were impressed with the variation between different US states in numbers scoring under IQ 70. They found that among offender populations the proportion ranged from 2.6% in states with few black people (Idaho, Montana and Nevada) to 24.3% in southern states like Alabama and 39.6%

in Georgia. They thought that the differences arose from very considerable differences in literacy between predominantly black populations in the south, and better educated whites in the north.

The best recent survey is by MacEachron (1979). In a comprehensive analysis of test results from US states, she found that prevalence of retardation tended to be higher when all offenders in the state took an intelligence test than when only a proportion of the offenders were tested. The point here is that if only those who look as though they are retarded are selected for testing, many quiet retardates may be missed. Turning to the type of intelligence test used, MacEachron notes that testers in Georgia found that the prevalence would drop by eight percentage points merely because the type of test was changed. In Texas the same convicted population gave a prevalence varying from 7% to 23% on four different tests. The variation depended as much on the type of test used as on the type of tester and the circumstances used. Because of all this, MacEachron decided to concentrate her research on two states, Maine and Massachusetts, to contrast a state such as Maine which tested all criminals with Massachusetts, where 'some unknown proportion had received intelligence testing either within the penal system or before entering the system'. She also rated legal variables such as severity of sentence and type of offence, 14 pre-trial social variables, and a number of post-trial variables which are not our concern, but which do show how far the legal system is biased in favour of conviction and lengthy incarceration for the retardate in Massachusetts as elsewhere in the standard adversary system.

Her detailed analysis showed that the prevalence rate for mentally retarded offenders in a state like Maine uniformly testing all offenders was higher, at 2.3% than in a state which tested only some of the offenders like Massachusetts, where the prevalence was 0.6%. She also notes, 'The one important source of variability in prison prevalence rates is the method used to determine who is enumerated as retarded,' and that properly standardized scores show results much closer to the known population rate than ordinary test scores. She concludes, 'The prevalence rate of mentally retarded adult male offenders is only slightly higher than the prevalence rate of retarded male adults in the general population.' She decided that her results 'indicate that there is little empirical support for a conceptual linkage between retardation and criminality'. She made a further analysis between the group of mental retardates scoring under IQ 70 on standar-

dized tests and those labelled 'borderline intelligence', with IQ 70–84 on the same test. This analysis attempted to sort out the difference in the degree of deprivation of upbringing between the two groups, but she found that 'the social and legal profile of retarded offenders is similar to offenders of borderline intelligence. . . . Multivariate results indicate that social and legal characteristics predict offense severity and that social and legal characteristics separately predict sentence length and past recidivism. From a theoretical perspective these results indicate that the social and legal variables are more germane to the problem of being an offender than his intelligence.' In other words, she found that it was not innate intelligence which lay behind the retardate breaking the law, but his aggression or inadequacy, and his homelessness, recidivist upbringing or lack of social support. She reaches sad conclusions about the prospect of rehabilitation for the retardate either in prison or afterwards; the few resources for further education in prison are most likely to be commandeered by the most able.

In England and Wales, as in American states, it is rare to have an intelligence test result enshrined in law describing mental handicap. Even in the latest Mental Health Act of 1983 the English and Welsh definition of 'mental impairment' does not cite an intelligence test. Indeed, as we have seen, unless details were given as to the type of test, who tested and its circumstances, such results would be little better than the current definition superseded. Thus, all the best known surveys of offences among 'the subnormal' population in England, as defined under the 1959 Act, include a substantial proportion of people labelled 'subnormal' yet over IQ 70. Walker and McCabe (1973) analysed hospital orders made under Sections 60 and 65 of the 1959 Act by courts in England and Wales from April 1963 to April 1964. There were 1332 hospital and guardianship orders made during this year, of which 330 (26%) were for subnormality. Next to the schizophrenics, this was the largest diagnostic group, and Walker and McCabe found that most were admitted for acquisitive offences committed after leaving the sheltered protection of school between the ages of 15 and 20. They say their youth 'was particularly striking in the case of females, of which 38% were in this age group. Nevertheless, what is surprising is not so much this concentration – which is simply the result of emerging from the shelter and control of the family and the school – as the fact that so few are committed by compulsory procedures which do not involve the courts. The explanation may be that their behaviour, unlike that of schizophrenics or depressive patients, is seldom such that it is seen by doctors as endangering the "health and safety" of themselves or others. Certainly we have seen that subnormals do not often commit serious personal violence, although we have also seen that they are responsible for more than their share of arson and sexual offences, both of which can do considerable harm.' Other surveys have also found that arson and sexual offences are common to subnormals, and yet, throwing doubt on how many of their group were under IQ 70, Walker and McCabe found that 'Some of them had not even been in special schools [for the retarded]. . . . Indeed, out of all our subnormals, 93 had been educated at secondary modern schools or the equivalent. . . .one man and one woman were said to have attended technical colleges [of further education]. . . . The pattern is reasonably consistent with the hypothesis that for the most part our subnormals are near the ill-defined borderline that separates the incompetents who are cared for in subnormality hospitals from those who have to fend for themselves in the community. In these cases it is only when there is trouble with the law, and the problem of disposal arises, that admission to hospital apears as a solution,' with, of course, the need to label these community inadequates as subnormal, whatever their IQ. Walker and McCabe were unable to analyse IQ assessments, because replies to this section of their questionnaire were so poor (McCabe, personal communication). They also carried out a follow-up of offender-patients extending over two years after the original hospital order was made. 673 of a total of 1160 offender-patients surveyed had been discharged or absconded, and 23 of these were re-convicted. Of the 350 'subnormals' surveyed, five had been re-convicted for sexual offences during this two-year period. Their analysis was also interesting in providing a comparison of what percentage of offender-patients on hospital orders in different parts of the country were labelled subnormal. South West England labelled 55%, whilst 'Wales, nearly all of whose rates are low, has exceptionally small percentages for both schizophrenia and subnormality; the reason may be the over-representation of psychopaths due to the attractions of Dr Craft's unit for them in North Wales.' The impact of specialized units and differential labelling practice could hardly be better put!

In 1983 the number of hospital orders made as 'subnormal' was lower than for many years, and this is likely to remain so for 'mental impairment' under the 1983 Mental Health Act. A large proportion of such orders are to the special hospitals of Rampton and Moss Side. Parker (1974) provides an analysis of intelligence tests in these hospitals. At the date of her 1970 survey Rampton and Moss Side held 1398 males and females, of whom 12% were mentally ill, 26% were psychopathic, 37% were subnormal, 24% were severely subnormal and the remainder were unclassified. Only 43% had IQ results available. 'For the purposes of classification persons with intelligence quotients below 50 are usually considered to be severely subnormal and those with quotients between 50 and under 70 are designated subnormal. As shown in Table 21 [of Parker's report] only 31% of the severely subnormal patients had intelligence quotients falling below 50, and 59% of the group fell in the 50 to 70 subnormal range. Three per cent had intelligence quotients of over 80. Nearly half (46%) of the subnormal patients met the criteria of an intelligence quotient of at least 50 but under 70; 16% had intelligence quotients of over 80.' Adding up, 60% of the severely subnormal and 54% of the subnormal had IQs above the normally accepted levels, one even scoring above IQ 100, probably resulting from recovery from his considerable deprivation (Craft, 1958). Of course, courts welcome a hospital disposal for many dull inadequates and as Fowles (1977) says, 'The surprising fact is that the majority of medical evidence is accepted without question, and indeed the courts do trust the experts. Their enthusiasm for psychiatry in a court of law can be quite startling at times.' The literature is full of analyses showing the high proportion of sexual offences occurring among those labelled 'subnormal' at court. As the above analysis shows, it is probable that at least some of those labelled 'subnormal' at court are so labelled because of a circular argument: because sexual offences were known to be common in the subnormal, dullards with sexual offences were so labelled at court. Indeed, some mental deficiency hospitals accumulated large numbers of such offenders and ran special programmes for them (Craft, 1958). Nowadays, such programmes and health education can be carried out in the community.

THE PROFESSIONAL AND THE MENTALLY HANDICAPPED CLIENT AT LAW

The professional advising the mentally handicapped person who has offended needs to know what opportunities the law affords for the mentally handicapped, and these are dealt with in Chapter 8. Briefly, there are three possible categories. Firstly, a person who is technically severely mentally impaired may be found 'unfit to plead', which makes him, under the Criminal Procedure (Insanity) Act 1964, subject to an order with restrictions. Secondly, if he is medically examined and found mentally impaired a court can make an order under Section 37 or Section 41 of the Mental Health Act 1983. It may make an order either with or without recording conviction. Thirdly, the court may use ordinary penal means, such as probation, with or without making a condition of psychiatric treatment, either in or out of a hospital. The professional, from his own assessment of his client's abilities, can initiate action towards one or other of the above categories. For instance, for the many offenders who are mildly mentally handicapped (IQ 60 to 75) the last category is greatly preferable to the earlier two, however difficult a client may find it to communicate with professional advisers, who he technically has to 'instruct'. In the event, what measure is pursued, often depends on the practical availability of treatment or training facilities in the locality, together with an assessment as to whether the court is likely to demand a residential placement for the protection of the public against any offences being committed.

At least in the UK, there have recently been other changes in practice, which protect the genuinely mentally handicapped person (under IQ 70). Following a Home Office circular, which advised police enquiries to take special precautions with the known mentally handicapped, Crown Court judges have excluded as inadmissable a number of confessions by people known to be mentally handicapped which were extracted by police. In my practice these include a confession made after six hours in a small darkened cell (Swansea, 1979), another after a mentally handicapped youth of 22 attending an adult training centre was arrested at midnight from his bed at home, and interrogated for four hours, having allegedly buggered a nine-year-old neighbour (Cardiff Crown Court, 1980), and the well-known case in 1977 in which a known ESN(M) youth had been induced to confess, after many hours of interrogation on his own, to the murder of Confait, a transvestite, and to arson. As a result, police interrogating known mentally handicapped persons can be asked to have a professional present, and to conduct the interrogation during daylight hours. If this is not complied with, and a confession is produced in court at a later date, an adjournment

can be requested in order to produce medical evidence on the suggestability of the client, the admissability of the evidence and the reliability of the interrogation.

The social worker or probation officer asked to produce a report may indeed have crucial data to guide the court. Apart from objective data such as home support and day occupation, both before the offence and afterwards, both professionals are entitled to give their own opinions as to the likely effect of measures available to protect the client from further offending or to protect the public from further offences for the court to take into consideration, either in mitigating the current offence or in improving future outlook. Medical evidence itself may be crucial, and it is important to advise the court as to the likely outcome of treatment. Once more, the court will expect objective data of the individual's mental capacity and abnormalities following examination, but the doctor is allowed much further leeway as to the professional opinion expressed. In addition, the doctor may have access to residential facilities either on a temporary or longer-term basis, which may greatly please the court by lessening risk of further offence and improving the chances of 'maturation', whilst the powerful new drugs available offer even greater possibilities for change.

TREATMENT AND TRAINING

The amount of research and documentary evidence to support the effect of behaviour conditioning or re-training of the mentally handicapped is now very large. In the United Kingdom most areas now have a staff of clinical psychologists employed either by the local health authority or by the social services department. These are available to guide on re-training manoeuvres. Like most children, most mentally handicapped people are very susceptible to reward and reproof, detailed elsewhere, as 'positive reinforcement' and 'negative reinforcement' respectively. In regard to sexual offences, these are considered elsewhere, but a short case example may suffice here:

John, an 18-year-old severely handicapped with Down's syndrome, had discovered the pleasures of erection and exposure. The product of a divorced home with mother's attention elsewhere, he discovered the immediate and satisfying attention given him after street exposure. He even fondled a small girl. Convicted, and given probation outside and re-training in an adult training centre (ATC), he speedily grew out of this manoeuvre. The re-training consisted of simple counselling (which in basic English can be surprisingly effective, both with normal infants of two, and those with a mental age down to two), reward by praise and with sweets for going to the toilet with an erection, and zipping his flies up; verbal reproof and 'time out' in the corridor for exposure at the ATC. His mother was also counselled and understood.

In retrospect, if the consultant had been asked to write an effective letter to the police at an early stage, the court case would have been withdrawn.

At other times, residential placement may be necessary, particularly where a mentally handicapped person not only has intellectual retardation, but also a disturbed personality. Where a major offence occurs, such as buggery with boys, or arson, the public might need to be protected by hospitalization, but, as MacEachron (1979) and Parker (1974) point out in their analyses, there are substantial disadvantages to securing a hospital order for one's client. Few psychiatric hospitals are keen to accept Section 3 (court) orders: for most such patients probation with a condition of treatment is preferred. There is also the risk of a restriction order without limit of time added by the Crown Court. The effect of the latter is to prevent discharge from hospital until the Home Office is satisfied that community placement is safe, which in the nature of things is extremely difficult to achieve in the absence of any resources being available from the Home Office. Such patients are therefore usually forwarded to the special hospitals, with the difficulties for parole, transfer or discharge enumerated above, sometimes for decades of time.

For most mentally handicapped offenders, the courts will usually accept a psychiatric probation order which contains a requirement of inpatient residence and treatment in a psychiatric facility for anything up to three years, specified in the order made. A condition of residence can be made to any place, including home, but the court needs to be satisfied that the individual is receiving proper care to improve his mental condition, and that the public is protected from further offence by this manoeuvre.

As the literature reviewed above makes clear, and one's personal practice verifies, the prevalence of offenders among the mentally handicapped is little more than in the general population. The type and severity of offence are also similar. Thus, the vast majority of offences are situational in character, and to do with petty theft, breaking into known premises, or trivial sexual offences committed in the course of maturation. Among the mentally handicapped, as among the general population, the really serious offences usually take place only against a background of strong family upset; with both groups these can be to some extent predicted in advance from their career at school and after, or are the result of strong provocation. There are two sets of offences unlikely to occur among the mentally handicapped by definition: firstly, the range of motoring offences and, secondly, the crime which needs long-term planning and execution.

Treatment is mainly devoted towards an improvement of the existing situation, the prevention of further damage or sexual upset, and the occupying of time while maturation either takes place or can be accelerated by counselling on simple lines by parent or professional. Actual psychiatric treatment, in the sense of psychotherapy, psychoanalysis or group psychotherapy, is rarely done well by psychiatrists, and often ineffective because of differences in cultural mores and verbal expertise. The mentally handicapped are usually better able to relate to trainers and care assistants, who are closely involved with their needs. Thus the professional, whether he be social worker, psychologist, psychiatrist or other university graduate, often finds it more effective to work through everyday care staff, and to counsel and advise staff rather than patients in what is to be done.

Electro-convulsive treatment, psycho-surgery and electro-narcosis rarely, if ever, have any part in the treatment of the mentally handicapped. Some mentally handicapped do get depressed and, like normal people, commit offences; others commit offences in the course of a personality upset, and with these anti-depressants or tranquillizers both may play their part. Occasionally, a depot injection of a tranquillizer to last one month is effective in a patient who objects to oral medication, but if he is as resistive as this, it is likely that residential admission will also be needed. For sexual offenders, an anti-testosterone drug may be useful on a daily basis to reduce sexual desire and drive, and this may be useful for a year or two during a late adolescent stage before maturation is complete. The mentally handicapped are often delayed in sexual as well as emotional maturation, so that medication can prove particularly effective with them. With the implied prognosis that the opportunity for further offences is reduced and that maturation is on its way, courts are likely to be reassured about the mentally handicapped offender. For the mentally handicapped boy or girl who is sexually offending, a course of sexual education and counselling is appropriate, together with the use of contraceptives for protection from the consequences of otherwise normal desires.

The field of sexual counselling for mentally handicapped offenders and sex education for those who have not offended is a rapidly developing one, and the interested reader is referred to more detail in Chapter 16 and elsewhere (Craft and Craft, 1983).

REFERENCES

Brown BS & Courtless TF (1968) The mentally retarded offender. In Allan RC, Forster LZ & Rubin JG (eds) *Readings in Law and Psychiatry*. Baltimore: Johns Hopkins University Press.

Craft MJ (1958) *Mental Disorder in the Defective*. Starcross: Royal Institution.

Craft A & Craft M (1983) *Sex Education and Counselling for Mentally Handicapped People*. Tunbridge Wells: Costello Press.

Craft M & Craft A (1984) *Mentally Abnormal Offenders*. London: Baillière Tindall.

Dell S (1980) *The Transfer of Special Hospital Patients to National Health Service Hospitals*. Special Hospital Research Report 16. London: DHSS.

Fowles MW (1977) Sexual offenders in Rampton. In Gunn J (ed) *Sex Offenders: A Symposium*. Special Hospital Research Report 14. London: DHSS.

Gittens J (1951) *Approved School Boys*. London: HMSO.

Glueck ET (1935) Mental retardation and juvenile delinquency. *Mental Hygiene 19*: 549–572.

MacEachron AE (1979) Mentally retarded offenders: prevalence and characteristics. *American Journal of Mental Deficiency 84(2)*: 165–176.

Parker E (1974) *Survey of Incapacity Association with Mental Handicap at Rampton and Moss Side Special Hospitals*. Special Hospital Research Report 11. London: DHSS.

Robertson G (1981) The extent and pattern of crime among mentally handicapped offenders. *Apex 9*: 100–103.

Tarjan C, Wright SW, Eyman RK & Keeran CW (1973) Natural history of mental retardation: some aspects of epidemiology. *American Journal of Mental Deficiency 77*: 369–379.

Terman L (1916) *The Measurement of Intelligence*. Boston: Houghton.

Walker N & McCabe S (1973) *Crime and Insanity in England, Vol 2*. Edinburgh: Edinburgh University Press.

Woodward M (1954) The role of low intelligence in delinquency. *British Journal of Delinquency 5*: 281–303.

Chapter 8
The Law Relating to Mental Handicap in England and Wales

LARRY O. GOSTIN

There are approximately 110 000 severely mentally handicapped people in England and more than 350 000 with mild mental handicap. There are nearly 60 000 in residential care, 47 000 in hospitals (78 % of these patients had been resident for five years or more) and over 10 000 in lodgings, foster homes and similar accommodation (DHSS, 1976b).

These mentally handicapped people have been designated a priority group for expenditure in the health and social services sector. The intended aims are to ensure that they have a satisfying environment (which should, as far as possible, be within the general community) and to provide education, social stimulation and purposeful occupation and employment so as to develop and exercise skills to their full potential (DHSS, 1976b, 1981, 1983).

Despite the broad aims of government there are thousands of mentally handicapped individuals who are arbitrarily excluded from essential services and financial assistance (MIND, 1977). Others are deprived of liberty and rights of citizenship solely on the basis of their handicaps (Gostin, 1975).

Increasingly, mentally handicapped people and their familes are turning to the law for redress (*In re D*, 1975). This chapter examines the impact of law on issues which have previously been considered as within the exclusive domain of the medical profession. Here only a brief account of the law relating to mental disorder can be provided: for a full account a reference text is available (Gostin, 1985), together with a practical guide to the Mental Health Act 1983 (Gostin, 1983).

THE LEGISLATIVE FRAMEWORK FOR MENTALLY HANDICAPPED PEOPLE IN HOSPITAL: THE MENTAL HEALTH ACT 1983
Informal admission: mental handicap hospitals and alternatives

The Royal Commission on the Law Relating to Mental Illness and Mental Deficiency (1957) con-

sidered that whenever possible a mentally handicapped person should be admitted to hospital without formality of any kind. Section 131 of the Mental Health Act 1983 implements this recommendation and authorizes admission to a mental handicap hospital on the same basis as admission to a general hospital. The patient need not sign an application form or obtain a medical recommendation, and there is no statutory requirement of a fixed notice of intention to leave.

The mentally handicapped person is often incapable of understanding the implications of hospital admission and of giving consent. Section 131 of the Act does not require his consent, but only that he should not positively object. Accordingly, admission is not on a 'voluntary' basis but on a 'nonvolitional' or 'informal' basis.

For a proposed patient below the age of 16 a request for informal admission must be made by the parent or guardian. If a parent wants a child to be informally admitted, and a hospital will take him, no legal authority will accept the child's inability or refusal to consent as sufficient to bar admission.

In 1978, 98 % of the 15 813 admissions to mental handicap hospitals and units in England were arranged informally. In that year 41 % of all admissions were of children under the age of 15: 3232 were under the age of 10 (DHSS, 1983). (Statistics for hospital admission are now computed separately for England and Wales: see Welsh Office (1978).)

International disquiet has been occasioned by the extensive use of informal admission into hospital without appropriate safeguards. A mentally handicapped person is normally unable to give a meaningful consent to admission or to subsequent decisions taken on his behalf. Further, the parent or guardian may not always take decisions which are fully in the best interests of the child. Various efforts have been made to resolve this problem. For example, the Swedish Mental Retardation Service has advised county directors that infants and pre-school children should not be cared for in institutional settings, except for some specific physical condition. Where such a mentally handicapped child's own family proves unable to manage, care is provided in some 'other family home'. This position has now been buttressed by the recent Swedish law which provides a publicly paid spokesman for every vulnerable mentally handicapped person. This measure allows these spokesmen to question closed care provisions where normal settings would suffice (Herr and Gostin, 1975).

In the United States the Constitution requires some 'due process' prior to the admission of non-consenting minors to mental handicap institutions. The British government, on the other hand, does not recognize a legal component in the resolution of this problem and has thus dissociated itself from the American position. There is apprehension that the use of procedural safeguards in the absence of a coherent national policy on the provision of community accommodation and care will result in hardship for mentally handicapped people. Care in a hospital ward is sometimes considered more humane than homelessness or neglect in the community.

The approach of the British government is to revise substantially the role of the hospital services within a projected period of 15 to 20 years. Currently, a considerable part of the function of mental handicap hospitals is to provide long-term residential accommodation. The government estimates that between one-half and one-third of the residents of these hospitals could be relocated in the community if appropriate housing were available Hansard, 1976; DHSS, 1980). Its response is to reduce the number of in-patient beds by a half over the projected period. The only patients to be eligible for long-term placements will be those who require constant nursing care under specialist supervision, for example patients with severe physical disability or serious behaviour disorder (DHSS and Welsh Office, 1971; DHSS, 1976b, 1980). There is also to be a corresponding increase in community housing and fostering arrangements; augmented education, occupation and training services are to be available in the community or in existing hospitals on an out-patient or day-patient basis.

Compulsory admission to hospital

Mental disorder is broadly defined in Section 1 of the 1983 Act as mental illness, severe mental impairment, mental impairment, psychopathic disorder and 'any other disorder or disability of mind'. Two of these – mental illness and severe mental impairment – might be regarded as major disorders, mental impairment and psychopathic disorder being minor disorders. Significant legal consequences flow from this distinction.

Mental impairment is defined in Section 1(2) as a state of arrested or incomplete development of mind (not amounting to severe mental impairment) which includes significant impairment of intelligence and social functioning and is associated with abnormally aggressive or seriously irresponsible conduct. The term *severe mental impairment* is defined in exactly the same way, except that it encompasses 'severe' (as opposed to 'significant') impairment of intelligence and social functioning. The legal difference between 'significant' and 'severe' is by no means clear, reflecting only a subtle difference in emphasis.

Changes from the 1959 Act

The term *subnormality*, which was used in the Mental Health Act 1959, has been replaced by *mental impairment* in the new Act, but this does not mean that mental handicap has been removed from the scope of mental health legislation. The general definition of mental disorder still refers to 'arrested or incomplete development of mind', and this can be taken to encompass mental handicap. Thus, wherever the generic term *mental disorder* is used in health or social services legislation it includes mental handicap. Mentally handicapped people will still be eligible for all services specified in legislation, including priority housing, care and after-care. They will also continue to be liable to be detained for assessment for up to 28 days under Section 2 of the Act and for up to 72 hours in an emergency admission under Section 4 if appropriate (see below). They may also be subject to the jurisdiction of the Court of Protection.

In legal terms, however, the effect of the 1983 Mental Health Act will be to remove the great majority of mentally handicapped people from the scope of those provisions which require that a person must be suffering from one of the four specific categories of mental disorder. Therefore mentally handicapped people will not be subject to compulsory admission to hospital for treatment, reception into guardianship, admission under a hospital order (with or without restrictions), or an order or transfer direction with the same effect as a hospital order *unless* their condition is associated with *abnormally aggressive* or *seriously irresponsible* conduct.

For the purposes of the law and of hospital records, the great majority of mentally handicapped people should be legally classified as suffering from *arrested or incomplete development of mind*. For medical or nursing purposes, however, and in common language, the term *mentally handicapped* should be retained. Only if a mentally handicapped person is dangerous or seriously irresponsible in his conduct should he be classified as mentally impaired.

To sum up, mentally handicapped people can no longer be compulsorily admitted to hospital for long periods unless they exhibit seriously irresponsible or abnormally aggressive behaviour. For most other purposes, however, they are still subject to the provisions of the Mental Health Act and related legislation.

Admission for assessment in case of emergency (Section 4)

In any case of urgent necessity a mentally handicapped person may be admitted for emergency observation under Section 4 of the Mental Health Act, on the basis of one medical recommendation, preferably by a medical practitioner who has some previous acquaintance with the patient; this is normally his general practitioner. In addition, an application must be made by an approved social worker, or by the nearest relative as defined in Section 26 of the Act. The authority to detain expires after 72 hours from the time of admission unless a second medical recommendation is obtained within that period to satisfy Section 2 (see below).

There was a great deal of concern over the use of emergency admissions under the 1959 Act. Under that Act, nearly one-quarter of all applications for civil (as opposed to criminal) admissions to mental handicap hospitals purported to be of 'urgent necessity'. Conceptually, one would not have expected that intellectual retardation itself would require emergency intervention in quite so high a proportion of cases. There was also substantial empirical evidence which suggested that the emergency admission procedures had been misused (Barton and Haider, 1966).

The ease of emergency application under the 1959 Act, along with its extensive and improper use, had resulted in disquiet expressed by government agencies throughout the years (Ministry of Health, 1967; Hospital Advisory Service, 1975; DHSS, 1976a). In response to these criticisms, the 1983 Act made three significant changes: the period within which the applicant must have seen the patient was reduced from three days to 24 hours, the period within which the patient must be admitted to hospital following the medical examination or application (whichever is earlier) was also reduced from three days to 24 hours, and the application has to be made by the *nearest* relative, as opposed to any relative.

Admission for assessment (Section 2)

A person may be compulsorily admitted to hospital for assessment for 28 days under Section 2 of the Act on the grounds that he is suffering from a mental disorder which warrants his detention in hospital for assessment and that he *ought* to be so detained in the interests of his own health or safety or for the protection of others.

An application under Section 2 must be made by the nearest relative or by an approved social worker. The application must be founded upon the recommendations of two medical practitioners, one of whom must be approved by the Secretary of State for Social Services as having special experience in the diagnosis or treatment of mental disorder. The recommendations must be signed on or before the date of the application, and must be given by practitioners who have personally examined the patient either together or at an interval of not more than five days (Mental Health Act 1983 Section 12). The purpose behind an admission for assessment is that the patient can be taken to hospital for assessment to be followed by medical treatment for a limited period. A patient admitted for assessment can be treated compulsorily in accordance with Part IV of the Mental Health Act. For the first time since 1959 a patient admitted for assessment for up to 28 days can apply to a mental health review tribunal; he can apply at any time within the first 14 days of admission (Gostin et al., 1984).

Admission for treatment (Section 3)

A person may be compulsorily admitted to hospital under Section 3 for treatment for a period not exceeding six months on the grounds that he is suffering from a mental disorder which warrants his detention for medical treatment, and that it is necessary for his health or safety or for the protection of others that he should be detained. The application for admission has to be made by the nearest relative or by an approved social worker.

and must be supported by two medical recommendations in the same way as an application for assessment under Section 2.

Section 3 requires a specific diagnosis to be made. If a person is classified as suffering from one of the minor disorders (for example mental impairment) he can be compulsorily admitted only if 'treatment is likely to alleviate or prevent a deterioration in his condition'. However, this 'treatability' requirement does not apply to the major disorders (severe mental impairment and mental illness). The authority to detain under Section 3 may be renewed for one further period of six months, and for subsequent periods of one year. The renewal is effected by the responsible medical officer, who must furnish a report to the hospital managers in accordance with Section 2 of the Act.

A patient may apply for a mental health review tribunal within six months, following his admission under Section 3. He may also apply at any time during each period of renewal. The nearest relative may apply on behalf of the patient up to twelve months after admission, and in any subsequent period of twelve months. The nearest relative may also exercise a 'discharge order'. However, the Act gives the responsible medical officer the right to override this if, in his opinion, the patient poses a danger to himself or others. This in turn gives the relative an augmented right to apply for a tribunal within 28 days following the doctor's decision to override the discharge order (see Mental Health Act 1983, Sections 23 and 25; Gostin et al., 1984).

Mental health review tribunals are independent bodies with the power to discharge patients. They consist of a lawyer (the chairman), a medical member (a consultant psychiatrist) and a lay member.

The primary criticism of the tribunal under the 1959 Act was that the patient must have taken the initiative to apply before its jurisdiction could be invoked. Empirical research had shown that only about 12% of those eligible to apply for tribunals actually exercised their right (Gostin, 1975).

The kind of patient who is likely to spend much of his hospital time making detailed arragements for his tribunal is not necessarily the kind of patient who needs to be heard. It may well be, for example, that a mentally handicapped person who has been in hospital for five years and whose case has been overlooked should have his case reviewed. He may not be aware that he has a right to a tribunal, or he may be too submissive and unassertive to interrupt his daily routine in order to apply. Such a person neither takes the initiative to apply for a tribunal

nor has the capacity to question the judgement of professionals and family members who may take decisions which affect his life. Yet he may be precisely the kind of patient whom the tribunal may want to hear from. To overcome this, the new Mental Health Act provides for automatic references to tribunals: if the patient does not have a tribunal hearing within the first six months of detention his case must be referred to the tribunal by the hospital managers. After this, if a patient does not have a tribunal hearing in any period of three years (one year for a child aged 16 or under) the managers must automatically refer the case again.

Guardianship (Section 7)

The procedure and criteria for reception into guardianship under Section 7 of the Act are in most respects the same as for an admission to hospital for treatment under Section 3. The duration of the guardianship order and the right to apply to a mental health review tribunal are also the same as for an admission for treatment. However, the patient under guardianship must be aged 16 or older.

The person named as guardian may be either a local authority social services department or any person accepted by the authority. The guardian has the following specific powers: to require the patient to reside in a specified place, to require the patient to attend for medical treatment, occupation, education or training and to require access to the patient to be given by a doctor or recognized social worker. Despite these powers, it is clear that the guardianship patient cannot be forced to receive treatment against his will.

The number of mentally handicapped people under statutory guardianship in England and Wales dropped from 1132 in 1960 to 134 in 1974 (DHSS, 1976a). Apparently, it is no longer regarded as appropriate to the needs of the people involved. One reason for this may have been the emphasis of this form of guardianship on supervision and control. A feasible alternative could be provided by a facilitative guardianship, emphasizing the positive aspects of guidance, help and advice. The facilitator guardian already operates in Sweden. He has responsibility for supporting the mentally handicapped person in taking major decisions, in obtaining a fair share of resources, and in obtaining the most appropriate (for example, the least restrictive) service.

Powers of courts to order hospital admission or guardianship (Section 37)

In pursuance of Section 37 of the Act a court may authorize a person's admission to a specified mental handicap hospital or place him under the guardianship of the local authority social services department. The effect of a Section 37 order is virtually equivalent to an admission for treatment under Section 3 or a civil guardianship order under Section 7 of the Act. The essential difference is that the nearest relative cannot exercise a discharge order in respect of a Section 37 patient.

The following conditions must be fulfilled if a hospital or guardianship order is to be made. First, the person must have been convicted of an imprisonable offence. A magistrate's court may make a hospital or guardianship order in respect of a severely mentally impaired person without recording a conviction if satisfied that he committed the act or made the omission charged. Secondly, the court must be satisfied, on the written or oral evidence of two medical practitioners, that the offender is suffering from a mental disorder of a nature or degree which warrants his detention in hospital or admission into guardianship. Thirdly, the court must be of the opinion, considering all the circumstances, including the nature of the offences and character and antecedents of the offender, and the other methods of dealing with him, that the most suitable method of disposing of the case is a Section 37 order. Finally, a hospital order cannot be made unless the admission of the offender to the hospital specified in the order has been arranged; he must be admitted to that hospital within 28 days from the date on which the order is made. In practice, this means that the court must be satisfied that the hospital specified in the order is willing to accept the offender. If the offender is thought to be dangerous, the order may specify a special (maximum security) hospital such as Broadmoor, Rampton, Moss Side or Park Lane: otherwise he will normally be admitted to an ordinary national health service hospital in his home area.

In making a hospital order, the court is placing the patient in the hands of doctors, and is nominally forgoing the imposition of punishment. Therefore, unless the order is coupled with a restriction order under Section 41, the court and Home Office relinquish control over the patient; either the responsible medical officer (RMO) or the mental health review tribunal (MHRT) can discharge the patient at any time.

Hospital orders with restrictions (Section 41)

A Crown (superior) Court may consider, having regard to the nature of the offence, the antecedents of the offender and the risk of his committing further offences if set at large, that it is necessary for the protection of the public from serious harm, to also make an order under Section 41 of the Act. This restricts the offender's discharge from hospital. The restriction order may be either without limit of time or for a specified period. Less than 5% of all restriction orders are made with a specified limit of time.

A person admitted to hospital with special restrictions under Section 41 is not subject to the civil provisions of the Act (Part I), relating to the duration, renewal and expiration of the authority for the compulsory detention of patients. This means that neither the RMO nor the hospital managers have the power to grant a leave of absence, a transfer to another hospital or a discharge without the consent of the Home Secretary.

Under the 1959 Act, the mental health review tribunal had no power over a restricted patient and no authority to discharge him. It could only *advise* the Home Secretary in the exercise of his discretionary powers. The patient or his representative was not informed of the tribunal's recommendation. Further, the Home Secretary did not give reasons and there was no appeal against his decision. In the years 1970 to 1975 the Home Secretary rejected the tribunals' recommendations for discharge in 40% of all cases (Gostin, 1977).

International remedies. The European Commission for Human Rights reviewed the lawfulness of a restriction order under Article 5(4) of the European Convention on Human Rights (*X* v. *United Kingdom*, 1981). Article 5(4) states, 'Everyone who is deprived of his liberty by arrest or detention shall be entitled to take proceedings whereby the lawfulness of his detention shall be decided speedily by a court and his release ordered if the detention is not lawful.' The issue before the Commission was whether the patients (detained for periods disproportionate to the gravity of their offences) were provided with a periodic judicial review of the lawfulness of their detention.

The Commission held that a restriction order was in contravention of Article 5(4) because the patient did not have periodic access to a court of law (Gostin, 1982). The European Court of Human Rights upheld the Commission's decision. As a result, the 1983 Act gives a restricted patient the right to apply to a tribunal between six and twelve months after the order and during each subsequent period of one year. The tribunal has the full power to discharge the patient either absolutely or subject to conditions.

The patient's right to refuse treatment

Informal patients in mental handicap hospitals (or their guardians) can legally refuse to consent to treatment. They have the same remedy against receiving treatment to which they do not consent as do patients in any other kind of hospital: they have a common-law right to sue for assault.

Generally, an action for assault will be successful if the patient has been treated without his (or his guardian's) informed legal consent. However, treatment can be given without consent in the case of urgent necessity, for example when the patient has become unconscious. The professional carrying out the treatment would then defend himself on the grounds that he acted in good faith and in the best interests of the patient, and that urgent necessity made it impracticable to seek consent. Indeed, if the professional had not treated the patient in such circumstances, he might have been liable in an action for negligence.

The general right of the informal patient to refuse treatment may be infringed through the threat of a compulsory order, loss of privileges or other sanctions. It may also be infringed if the patient or his guardian is inadequately informed of the purpose or side-effects of the treatment, or of his legal right to withhold consent.

The state of law as regards the compulsory patient was not as clear under the 1959 Act despite representations by the Department of Health and Social Security that detained patients could not legally refuse treatment.

Part IV of the Mental Health Act 1983 comprehensively regulates when a detained patient can be treated against his will; the following step-by-step guide to Part IV may be helpful (see Gostin, 1983, 1985).

Step 1: Identify the legal status of the patient

As a general rule, patients compulsorily admitted to hospital for up to 28 days or longer come within the scope of Part IV of the Act; informal patients, patients detained for up to 72 hours and guardianship patients do not. If the provisions of Part IV do not apply the patient has the same legal rights as a patient receiving treatment for a physical disorder and, generally speaking, he can refuse treatment.

(Remember that *all* patients for whom psycho-surgery or sex-hormone implant treatment is proposed come within the scope of Part IV.)

Step 2: Identify the treatment

Category 1: psycho-surgery and sex-hormone implant treatment.

Category 2: medication after it has been administered for three months, and electro-convulsive therapy.

Category 3: any other treatment for mental disorder administered under the direction of the RMO. (For non-psychiatric treatments, the common-law rules apply; treatment for mental disorder includes nursing.)

Step 3: Apply the safeguards according to the category of treatment

Category 1: (i) *consent*, the validity of which must be confirmed by a certificate signed by three people appointed by the Mental Health Act Commission (MHAC) (only one a doctor); **and**

(ii) a *second opinion* as to the appropriateness of the treatment from a doctor appointed by the MHAC;

(iii) before giving the second opinion the doctor must *consult* with two other people on the therapeutic team, one a nurse and the other neither a nurse nor a doctor.

Category 2: (i) *consent*, the validity of which must be confirmed by a certificate signed by the RMO or a doctor appointed by the MHAC; **or**

(ii) a *second opinion* as to the appropriateness of the treatment from a doctor appointed by the MHAC;

(iii) before giving the second opinion the doctor must *consult* with two other people on the therapeutic team, one a nurse and the other neither a nurse nor a doctor.

Category 3: The patient can be treated without consent or a second opinion.

Mental handicap: in or out of the Act?

The question arises whether mental handicap should be covered by the Mental Health Act at all.

The inclusion of mental handicap in the Act is primarily criticized for implicitly equating it with forms of psychiatric incapacity such as mental illness and psychopathic disorder. The premise of the Act is that psychiatric illness may cause antisocial behaviour. The 'illness' can be cured and the behaviour corrected through compulsory hospitalization.

Whatever the merits of this model in relation to the psychiatrically ill, it appears to be inapplicable to the handicapped. Mental handicap does not of itself result in disruptive or antisocial behaviour. The factors which may warrant the detention of a mentally handicapped person are more usually attributable to a concomitant psychiatric disorder than to intellectual retardation and diminished social competence. Moreover, uncomplicated intellectual deficit by the time of adulthood is not usually susceptible to medical treatment. Simple deficit is likely to result from genetic factors or prenatal or postnatal damage influencing the ability to learn and reason. By adulthood it is not so much likely to be 'curable' in a health context in the same sense as an illness, as open to improvement by education, training and social care. This hardly warrants compulsory hospital admission.

The language of the Mental Health Act 1959 indicates that mental handicap was forced into a legislative straightjacket which really applied to the psychiatrically ill. The Act presupposes that the handicap, having intially manifested itself, will cease to exist after a period in hospital. Thus an important criterion for the discharge of a Section 3 patient is that he no longer suffers from mental handicap (Mental Health Act 1959, Section 72). Similarly, a person can be admitted to hospital under Sections 2 or 4 purely on the basis of a developmental disability. The question that should be asked is what needs of a mentally handicapped person are met by detaining him for 72 hours or 28 days. Medical intervention as a measure of crisis intervention, or for a short period of assessment, is based less on intellectual handicap, but more upon a supervening disability, that is a behaviour or personality disorder. Admission could therefore be accomplished without including mental handicap within the jurisdiction of the Act.

The opposing view is that the need for compulsory admission arises because of an impairment in an individual's reason and judgement or his appreciation of the effect of his behaviour on himself or others. The impairment of judgement may render the person unable to care for himself in the community or may lead to behaviour which is offensive to other people. It would be difficult to deny that mental handicap could not, in any circumstances, have such an effect.

These issues were resolved by the introduction of the term 'mental impairment' in the 1983 Act. A mentally handicapped person cannot be admitted for a long period unless he is aggressive or socially irresponsible. However, any mentally handicapped person can be compulsorily admitted for 28 days or less if the criteria are met.

The question to be asked is whether it would be appropriate to authorize the detention of an individual solely because of his inability to lead an independent life in the community, or simply because he is 'socially irresponsible'. If this were the legislative standard, it might unfairly include the severely physically handicapped, the aged, the chronically infirm, and so forth. So too, the question should be asked whether the intolerance of the community towards non-conforming or irresponsible behaviour not amounting to dangerous behaviour would be an over-broad criterion for compulsory admission to hospital.

THE LEGISLATIVE FRAMEWORK FOR MEETING THE NEEDS OF THE MENTALLY HANDICAPPED IN THE COMMUNITY

Legislation in England and Wales places great emphasis on the deficits in a person's intellectual capacity and the need for custodial care. In this way, the law may neglect the everyday needs of mentally handicapped people. What are the needs of these people? What is the legal framework available to ensure that these needs are met? Are there any procedures available to the handicapped person when government arbitrarily fails to meet a basic human requirement?

The basic needs of any human being – including the handicapped – are for a home, food, medical care, education and training, marital and sexual expression and, if necessary, protection from harm. Unlike the United States, Great Britain does not have a written constitution on which these rights can be based. Rather, each element of a handicapped person's life-needs is dealt with through a number of fragmented statutory and administrative provisions. An exposition of the rights of a mentally handicapped person to the fulfilment of some of his basic life-needs follows. These and other rights, including the right of access to the courts, to correspond by post, to drive a motor vehicle and to vote, are described elsewhere by the author (Gostin, 1985).

The need for a home

Department of Health and Social Security figures on reasons for admission show that substantial numbers of people enter mental handicap hospitals and other specialist facilities primarily for domiciliary and social reasons. The institution, therefore, has a distinct 'hotel' or 'asylum' function, providing lodgings for vulnerable people with no home. Existing legislation has the effect of encouraging local government to adopt such an approach, in which fundamental 'housing' needs are obscured by a need for 'care'. In the following section the relevant provisions under health and social services legislation are explained; most mentally handicapped people who have no-one to care for them either find their way into hospital or into medium-sized establishments built in accordance with these provisions. Thereafter, ordinary housing legislation is explained; a case is made for more general use of these provisions for the benefit of handicapped people (see Tyne, 1976, 1977).

Residential provision under health and social service legislation

Most of the special residential care legislation in England and Wales is derived from the National Assistance Act 1948. Section 21(1) of that Act places a duty on local social services departments to provide 'residential accommodation for persons who by reason of age, infirmity or any other circumstances are in need of care and attention which is not otherwise available to them'. Subsection (2) specifies that in the exercise of this duty departments should provide accommodation of various descriptions suited to the needs of the individual (see DHSS, 1974b).

A further but relatively less used provision is contained in Section 29 of the 1948 Act, which empowers local authority social services departments to 'make arrangements for the welfare of persons who are blind, deaf or dumb, and other persons who are substantially and permanently handicapped by illness, injury or congenital deformity'.

National Assistance Act accommodation is not directly referrable to the ordinary housing needs of mentally handicapped people, although some clearly will benefit (for example, the aged or those with accompanying physical disabilities).

Domiciliary provision arranged in pursuance of Section 21 is principally used for old people or the temporarily homeless, while provision under Section 29 is associated with workshop places for disabled people of various descriptions.

The National Health Service Act 1977 is more directly applicable to mentally handicapped people, although the point should be reiterated that it, like other health service legislation, is principally designed for the physically or psychiatrically ill. Section 21(1) of that Act lays down that '. . . a local authority shall, with the approval of the Secretary of State, and to such extent as he may direct, make arrangements for . . . the prevention of illness and for the after care of persons who have been so suffering.' 'Illness' is defined in the National Health Service Act to include 'mental disorder'. This provision had been implemented by Local Authority Circular 19/74 (DHSS, 1974c) which *directs* social services departments to provide residential accommodation for mentally disordered people ordinarily resident in their areas. This would include residential homes, hostels, group homes, minimum-support facilities or other appropriate accommodation. An important domiciliary arrangement made under this provision is the standard mental handicap hostel with 24 beds.

The foregoing is concerned with special residential provision for mentally handicapped people. This is directly related to a person's need for care, which is provided in moderately-sized segregated accommodation. This may not accord with the needs of mentally handicapped people for their own homes – ensuring a sense of identification, privacy and freedom from the stigma and regimentation associated with specialist facilities.

General housing legislation does offer mentally handicapped people some opportunity for ordinary housing, but they have been regarded in the past as 'in need of care and attention', even if their handicaps have been relatively mild. This operates to exclude them from housing legislation and make them eligible for special residential care legislation.

General housing legislation

The Housing Act 1957 requires local housing departments to consider the needs of their area and to prepare schemes for providing housing to meet these needs. They are empowered under this Act, and under the Housing Act 1974, to provide a range of accommodation which would be suitable for many mentally handicapped people, including single dwellings, bedsitters and hostels.

The Housing (Homeless Persons) Act, which came into force on 1 December 1977, is a potentially important development for mentally handicapped people. The Act imposes a duty on housing departments to provide accommodation for homeless people with a priority need. Section 2 of the Act specifically states that a mentally handicapped person and his family are in such need.

The joint circular on homelessness (DoE, 1974; DHSS, 1974a) suggests that what may be described as the 'hidden homeless' is not a recognized category. These people, who remain in institutional care only because there is no alternative provision in the community, do not meet the standard of being 'literally without shelter or likely to lose in the immediate future what shelter they may have'. Thus, if mental handicap hospitals sought to discharge the 'hidden homeless' would they be entitled to assistance under the 1977 Act? (For a discussion, see Gostin, 1985.)

Cost-effectiveness

In 1977 MIND (the National Campaign for Mental Health), in its evidence to the Royal Commission on the National Health Service, produced a cost–benefit analysis of the various forms of accommodation for mentally handicapped people: hospitals, medium-sized hostels, small housing units designed to cope with highly dependent children ('Wessex units') and ordinary lodgings, foster homes and unsupervised group homes (MIND, 1977).

The 'hotel' function of mental handicap hospitals cost in the region of £90 per in-patient per week, exclusive of interest charges on capital loans. This was considerably higher than the average cost of maintaining a mentally handicapped person in a local authority staffed hostel which stood at £33 per week. Other less restrictive domiciliary arrangements were even less expensive. The single exception was the 'Wessex units', where the revenue costs were comparable with those of conventional hospitals. However, it was concluded that these units were more cost-effective as they took a higher proportion of severely handicapped children. It was also shown that the capital costs of these units were less than those of mental handicap hospitals.

The need for education

The Education Act 1944

The Education Act 1944 (Section 8) requires every local education authority in England and Wales to ensure that there are sufficient schools in their areas to provide full-time primary and secondary education to all children between the ages of five and sixteen. The schools are not deemed to be sufficient for the purposes of the Act '. . . unless they are sufficient in number, character and equipment to afford for all pupils opportunities for education offering such variety of instruction and training as may be desirable in view of their different ages, abilities and aptitudes . . . including practical instruction and training appropriate to their respective needs'.

In addition to the statutory duties placed on the local education authority, there is a duty imposed on the parents of every child of compulsory school age to ensure that their child receives education, 'either by regular attendance at school or otherwise' (Section 36).

The standard of education which the local authority and the parent must arrange for each child is 'full-time education suitable to [his or her] requirements' (Sections 8 and 36).

These general legal provisions apply to all children, whether or not they suffer from a mental or physical handicap. However, special considerations apply to the education of handicapped children.

The background to the Education Act 1981

Transfer of responsibilities to local education authorities. The Education Act 1944 allowed local education authorities to avoid their responsibilities for providing education to severely mentally handicapped children. Section 57 laid a duty on authorities to ascertain which children in their areas were 'unsuitable for education at school'. Such children were generally regarded as ineducable and their treatment, care and training were the responsibility of local health authorities.

Local health authorities lost the power to provide training for mentally handicapped children under Section 1 of the Education (Handicapped Children) Act 1970; the duty to provide education, together with staff and premises, was transferred to local education authorities. Some 400 new special schools were formed from previous training centres, special-care units and hospital provision. The present duty placed upon local education authorities is to ascertain the children in their areas requiring special education and to make appropriate provision. The Department of Education and Science clarified the 1970 Act by stating that 'no child within the age limits for education . . . will be outside the scope of the educational system'.

Classification of children. The 1944 Act provided for education authorities to identify any child needing special education by classifying him into one of the categories of handicap defined by the Secretary of State. These formal categories included educationally subnormal (ESN) pupils – those 'who, by reason of limited ability or other conditions resulting in educational retardation, require some specialised form of education wholly or partly in substitution for the education normally given in ordinary schools'. In practice, two broad groupings emerged within the educationally subnormal category: moderate – ESN(M) – and severe – ESN(S).

Integration. Section 10 of the Education Act 1976 required local education authorities to arrange for the special education of all handicapped pupils to be given in ordinary schools, except where this was incompatible with efficient instruction in the schools or involved unreasonable expenditure. The provision, however, was never implemented by the Secretary of State for Education and Science. The case for integrated education is that the handicapped person is entitled to education within a normal school environment, reflecting the normal diversity and problems in society, in order to prepare for participation and integration within the community. Integration is also thought to be beneficial for non-handicapped pupils to help them overcome their inhibitions and lack of knowledge about handicapped people, and to provide early experience in relating to handicapped pupils as people first.

The Warnock Report. The Committee of Enquiry into the Education of Handicapped Children and Young People (chairman: Mary Warnock) reported in 1978. It recommended that the planning of services should be based upon the assumption that one in five children at some time in their school career will require some form of special educational provision. This would considerably widen the scope of those for whom special education could be provided.

The Committee considered that the statutory classification of handicapped pupils provided an indelible and inflexible label which unnecessarily stigmatized the child, and drew a sharp distinction between handicapped and non-handicapped children. Its central recommendation, therefore, was that special education should be conceived in terms of children with 'special educational needs' calling for 'special educational provision', rather than of defined categories of handicap. The term 'children with learning disabilities' should be used to describe mentally handicapped people and those with education difficulties.

Categorization of handicaps brought with it the safeguard that the special education of the child so identified was ensured. The Warnock Committee, therefore, recommended a system of recording the need for special education provision for those children who, based on a detailed profile of their needs prepared by a multidisciplinary team, are judged to require special educational provision not generally available in ordinary schools.

The new legal framework

Implementation of the Warnock Report. The Warnock Report was followed by a White Paper in 1980 and the Education Act 1981; most of the provisions of the Act came into force on 1 April 1983. The 1981 Act follows the broad framework of the Warnock Report. It provides that special educational provision should be on the basis of the special educational needs of children rather than for specific categories of handicap (s. 1). This is estimated to cover some 20% of the school population, for whom planning for special education is usually left to the school in which they are enrolled. The local education authority must, however, identify a more limited category of children with special educational needs which call for the local education authority to determine the special educational provision that should be made for them (s. 4). It is this limited category, estimated to be some 2% of the child population, where the authority has a duty to make formal assessment and to maintain statements of the child's special educational needs, specifying the educational provision to be made to meet those needs (ss. 5–8). In connection with assessments and statements, parents are to be given the right to be informed at every stage and to appeal in various ways, including to the Secretary of State (ss. 8, 9). The Act also states, for the first time in implemented legislation, the general principle that the education of children with special needs should take place in ordinary schools, alongside other children. This duty applies to all children, regardless of the severity of their disability. However, the general integration principle is subject to certain conditions.

Enforcement machinery

The statutory duties placed upon local education authorities by the Education Act 1944 may be enforced by the Secretary of State for Education and Science in accordance with Section 99 of that Act. Under Section 99 any interested person may make a complaint to the Secretary of State that a particular local authority has failed to discharge its duties to provide education to a mentally handicapped child. However, the Secretary of State has given indiscriminate approval to local authorities under Section 56 to educate children 'otherwise than at school'. In these circumstances, it is perhaps unrealistic to expect him to hold a particular authority in default under Section 99. The more important legal question is whether a court of law will be prepared to review the discretion of the Secretary of State in holding under Section 99 that the local authority was not in default of its duties.

The issue was first presented to the courts in *Watt* v. *Kesteven County Council* (1955), where a parent applied for an order of *mandamus* to compel a local education authority to carry out its duties to educate his mentally handicapped child. The application was rejected by the Court of Appeal. Lord Denning said: 'I would not like to say that there can be no cases under the Act, in which an action would lie, but I do not think an action lies in this case. It is plain to me that the duty under Section 8 (to make schools available) can only be enforced by the Minister under Section 99 of the Act and not by action at law.'

This dictum was quoted with approval in *Wood* v. *Ealing Borough Council* (1967). The earlier case of *Passmore* v. *Oswaldtwistle UDC* (1898) laid down the general rule that where an Act provides its own administrative machinery for enforcement of any duties in the Act (as does Section 99), that constitutes grounds for refusing *mandamus*. However, it is of significance that, in the above cases, the administrative machinery had not been tried; if an applicant first used the administrative procedures available, and failing that, applied for *mandamus*, the court might be more amenable.

An illustrative case study

Dwight Francis was classified as educationally subnormal and sent to Northgate ESN school. He was suspended from school because the headmaster found him a disturbing influence and difficult to control. Since then he has been living at home with his parents, and has received no proper education. The Northamptonshire Education Authority (NEA) has approached 27 schools, but none has accepted Dwight. The NEA also discussed the possibilities of home tuition but, according to the Francis family, no tutors have ever come to the house to teach Dwight. Thus, in the past five years, Dwight has not received the education to which he is entitled by law.

In response to a Section 99 complaint filed by MIND, the Secretary of State held that the NEA was not in default of its duties because blanket approval under Section 56 had been given by the Department of Education and Science, and because the NEA made reasonable attempts to find a place for Dwight during the last five years.

Dwight subsequently became 16 years of age and the NEA maintained that it no longer had a statutory responsibility to provide education, as Dwight was beyond school age. A request was made on behalf of the parents in pursuance of Sections 18 and 114 of the Education Act 1944 to provide education until the age of 19. This request had the effect of extending the legal obligation of the NEA to provide appropriate education.

If a court was to decide to examine the substantive issues in Dwight's case, there are many questions which would be explored. For example:

1 What is the standard of education which a local authority must provide in order to fulfil its statutory duties?
2 Is it sufficient to provide a mentally handicapped child with an unfulfilled promise of home tuition and short-term residential assessments?
3 If a child attends a day centre, training school or mental handicap hospital, can the Secretary of State or the court examine the curriculum in order to assess whether 'full-time' and 'suitable' education is provided?
4 Can the local education authority discharge its duties by making reasonable attempts to arrange for education? Or must it ensure that there is a sufficient range of alternatives to meet the needs of all kinds of children, regardless of the severity of the handicap?

In sum, the mentally handicapped child's basic need for education is adequately provided for under the law. The pitfalls, however, are deep and occur largely as a result of improper government implementation of the legislation. The immediate future of handicapped children under the education system is, in the final analysis, dependent on the will and power of the judiciary to intervene.

The need for marital, sexual and other social expression

The rights to marry, to bear children, and to sexuality, sociability and privacy, are central to the life of physically and mentally handicapped people. The law lays down certain boundaries which cannot be transgressed. The circumstances in which the mentally handicapped are cared for in practice frequently impose further restrictions on the exercise of such rights.

Marriage and divorce

There is nothing in English law to prevent a mentally handicapped person from going through the ceremony of marriage, provided none of the usual impediments apply (for example, consanguinity or age) and no objection is raised, as below. The granting of a marriage licence is discretionary, and an intended marriage may be prevented by voicing dissent to the publication of banns or entering a caveat against the issue of a common or special licence. If a caveat is entered, the licence cannot be issued until the caveat is withdrawn or alternatively until a judge certifies that it ought not to obstruct the granting of the licence. Thus, it is possible for a third party, if he feels the marriage to be misguided, to prevent or substantially impede the ceremony.

People detained under a section of the Mental Health Act 1983 will require leave from their responsible medical officer to attend the ceremony. (A person detained with restrictions under Sections 37/41 of the Mental Health Act will require the consent of the Home Secretary.) Special hospital patients have been given the right to marry within the confines of the hospital.

The fact that one or both of the partners to the marriage is severely mentally handicapped may give grounds for obtaining a decree of nullity or divorce. Under Section 12 of the Matrimonial Causes Act 1973 a marriage is voidable where either party did not validly consent to it in consequence of unsoundness of mind. The court is not concerned with any general definition of unsoundness. It will ask whether at the date of the marriage the person was capable of understanding the nature of the marriage and the obligations and responsibilities which it involved (*Estate of Park* 1953). The contract of marriage is a simple one, which does not require a high degree of intelligence to comprehend, and, therefore, there is a strong presumption, *prima facie*, that the consent is valid. Mere backwardness or impaired intelligence is not enough to void an otherwise legal marriage.

A marriage is also voidable under Section 12 if at the time of the marriage either party, though capable of giving a valid consent, was suffering (whether continuously or intermittently) from a mental disorder within the meaning of the Mental Health Act 1983 of such a kind or to such an extent as to be unfitted for marriage. Here, the court will ask whether the person is capable of living in a married state and of carrying out the ordinary duties of marriage (*Bennett* v. *Bennett* 1969). A voidable marriage is one which the parties may choose to continue or to have dissolved within the first three years. It is not a nullity from the beginning as is a void marriage.

The sole ground for divorce is the irretrievable breakdown of the marriage. However, it must be established that the reason for the breakdown comes within one of five categories, which can be loosely summarized as adultery, unreasonable behaviour, desertion, two years separation with consent of the respondent and five years separation without the respondent's consent. (Matrimonial Causes Act 1973, Sections 1 and 2.)

In practice, there may be important obstacles to the marriage of mentally handicapped people. There are, for example, financial and social problems in finding a home and paid employment, both essential for building a family unit. Objections may also be raised by parents and staff who, having devoted kindness and care to the individual since infancy, may consider him unsuitable for an adult institution like marriage. Yet marriages come in many forms and mentally handicapped people are no less capable of expressing love and commitment than 'normal' members of the community.

Freedom of sexual expression

Mentally handicapped people are seen by the law as being particularly vulnerable to exploitation in the area of their sexuality. It is an offence for a man to have unlawful (extramarital) intercourse with a severely mentally handicapped woman. It is also an offence for a man on the staff or employed by a hospital or mental nursing home to have unlawful sexual intercourse with a woman receiving treatment for other forms of mental disorder (including mild mental handicap) in that hospital or home (Mental Health Act 1959, Sections 127 and 128;* see also Sexual Offences Act 1967, Section 1). In both of these offences it is a defence for a man charged to prove he did not know and had no reason to suspect that the person was mentally handicapped.

It is interesting to note that these offences can only be committed by a man and that the law does

---

* These sections of the 1959 Act are still in force. The intention is to place them in other appropriate legislation when the opportunity arises.

not consider it possible that patients require protection from the sexual advances of a woman, whether or not in a position of responsibility over them.

Clearly, to the extent that mentally handicapped people may be more suggestible and less able to protect themselves from the advances of those who are ill-intentioned or may seriously harm them, the law needs to provide safeguards. However, in so doing, there is a danger that mentally handicapped people may be deprived of the pleasure and affection that sexual expression brings. The question to be asked is whether the proper balance has been struck between protection against exploitation and ordinary enjoyment of sexual expression (see MIND, 1983).

LEADS FOR THE FUTURE

Legislative reform must begin with recognition that the needs of mentally handicapped people are the same as those of all citizens together with some special needs associated with their handicaps. The 'general need' services are those which are legally mandated for all members of the community: housing, education, medical care and social services. Each service is provided by the appropriate department of national or local government. Under current law, mentally handicapped people are sometimes denied equal access to these statutory services, simply on the basis of their disabilities. Instead, a comprehensive, if sometimes substandard (MIND, 1977), service is provided in a segregated facility – either a hospital or a medium-sized hostel. A more humane and normal alternative is to provide a complete community-support system based on ordinary residential housing; legal authorization for the support services already exists in large measure. Delivery of primary medical care is available through a general practitioner under ordinary national health service legislation. Under these provisions, medical requirements may be clearly identified and dealt with by appropriate specialist referrals or by admission to a general hospital, when the need arises. There is also a statutory right to home nursing services for those with chronic physical development or behavioural disabilities. So too, education can normally be provided in ordinary schools, and social support and training in day-care facilities.

Mentally handicapped people also require special services, not readily available under ordinary welfare legislation. The first objective should be to strengthen the families of mentally handicapped people by providing practical, material and advisory assistance (Bayley, 1973). Families may need a good laundry service, respite from total care, meals-on-wheels, advice on welfare benefits and professional assistance in ensuring that their full and fair entitlement is received, aids to daily living and, in the case of multiply handicapped children, adaptations to premises or rehousing. Social services departments are authorized to provide these special services, but accord them a low priority because there are no mandatory duties within existing law. Legislative changes giving mentally handicapped people and their families an enforceable right to these services would provide a foundation for building a viable community alternative to institutional care. In addition, a 'mentorship', or citizen's advocate, programme, similar to the Swedish model described earlier, would enable mentally handicapped people to take full advantage of existing and proposed services.

There are also medical (prevention and early detection), paramedical (speech therapy, physiotherapy and chiropody) and psychological services which are particularly relevant to the needs of mentally handicapped people (DHSS and Welsh Office, 1971). These should be more readily available in the community according to individual needs, and may also require special legislative and financial arrangements for proper implementation.

The needs of a child

The analysis suggested above can be simply illustrated by examining a fairly standard response by local authority social services departments to mentally handicapped children in the community. The professional gives primary attention to the child's disability, not to his normal emotional needs. He is referred to as 'mentally handicapped', and a social response is formed on that basis. In some ways, parents seem to manage better than professionals because they see the person as a child, not solely as a disabled individual.

What would a social worker do if a 'normal' child and his or her family were unable to cope? The answer is that the social worker would provide support to ensure that the child had, as far as possible, a natural healthy development. All children have material needs for a home, education and medical care; they also have emotional needs for love, warmth, attention and friendship. These are accomplished by professional, practical and financial support and assistance for the family. If the family situation is irretrievable, other alternatives are examined, such as fostering. This is the preferred caring response to a child in need. However, the response may be wholly different in the case of a developmentally disabled child who requires special attention. This child, although not medically ill, may be channelled into a health care system, where he may spend his childhood days within the confines of a hospital ward, in an isolated institution attended, *inter alia*, by doctors and nurses; his friends may be limited to those with physical and mental handicaps equivalent to, or more severe than, his own.

Admission to a hospital setting, which may heighten a child's disabilities, is virtually always on an informal basis. Accordingly, there is no statutory review of the propriety of admission or of the consequences of long-term residence, the legal and social fiction being that the placement is made with the meaningful consent and in the best interests of the child. The proposals made in this chapter (see also Gostin, 1975) reflect the belief that the state cannot look after the interests of mentally handicapped children and adults by applying a standard lower than that which it applies to other people who are dependent or in need of care.

CASES

Bennett v. *Bennett* (1969)a All E.R. 539.
Estate of Park (1953)1 All E.R. 1411.
In re D (a minor), Times Law Report, Sept 18 1975.
Passmore v. *Oswaldtwistle UDC* (1898) A.C. 387.
Watt v. *Kesteven County Council* (1955)1 Q.B. 408.
Wood v. *Ealing Borough Council* (1967) Ch. 354.
X v. *United Kingdom*, European Commission for Human Rights; application no. 6998/75. European Court of Human Rights, judgment given 5 November 1981.

STATUTES

Education Act 1944. London: HMSO.
Education Act 1976. London: HMSO.
Education Act 1981. London: HMSO.
Education (Handicapped Children) Act 1970. London: HMSO.
Health Services and Public Health Act 1968. London: HMSO.
Housing Act 1957. London: HMSO.
Housing Act 1974. London: HMSO.
Housing (Homeless Persons) Act 1977. London: HMSO.
Matrimonial Causes Act 1973. London: HMSO.
Mental Health Act 1959. London: HMSO.
Mental Health (Amendment) Act 1982. London: HMSO.
Mental Health Act 1983. London: HMSO.
National Assistance Act 1948. London: HMSO.
National Health Service Act 1977. London: HMSO.
Sexual Offences Act 1967. London: HMSO.

BOOKS, ARTICLES AND ADMINISTRATIVE REGULATIONS

Ashworth A & Gostin L (1984) Mentally disordered offenders and the sentencing process. *Criminal Law Review* [1984] pp. 195–212.
Barton R & Haider I (1966) Unnecessary compulsory admission to a psychiatric hospital. *Med Sci and Law* 6, 3, 147.
Bayley M (1973) *Mental Handicap and Community Care: A Study of Mentally Handicapped People in Sheffield*. London: Routledge & Kegan Paul.
DES (Department of Education and Science) (1970) Circular 15/170. London: HMSO.
DES (Department of Education and Science) (1975) *Statistics of Education*, Vol 1. p. 54. London: HMSO.
DHSS (Department of Health and Social Security) (1974a) Circular 4/74. London: HMSO.
DHSS (Department of Health and Social Security) (1974b) Circular 13/74. London: HMSO.
DHSS (Department of Health and Social Security) (1974c) Circular 19/74. London: HMSO.
DHSS (Department of Health and Social Security) (1976a) *A Review of the Mental Health Act 1959*. London: HMSO.
DHSS (Department of Health and Social Security) (1976b) *Priorities for Health and Personal Social Services in England: A Consultative Document*. London: HMSO.
DHSS (Department of Health and Social Security) (1978) *Inpatient Statistics from the Mental Health Enquiry for England 1975*. Statistical and Research Report Series No. 17. London: HMSO.
DHSS (Department of Health and Social Security) (1980) *Mental Handicap: Progress, Problems and Priorities*. London: DHSS.
DHSS (Department of Health and Social Security) (1981) *Care in Action: A Handbook of Policies and Priorities for the Health and Personal Social Services in England*. London: HMSO.
DHSS (Department of Health and Social Services) (1983) *Health Care and its Costs*. pp. 19–22. London: HMSO.
DHSS (Department of Health and Social Security) & Welsh Office (1971) *Better Services for the Mentally Handicapped*. Cmnd. 4683. London: HMSO.
DHSS (Department of Health and Social Security) & Welsh Office (1977) *The facilities and services of mental illness and mental handicap hospitals in England and Wales* (1975), Table 18. Statistical and Research Report Series No 19. London: HMSO.
DoE (Department of the Environment) (1974) Circular 18/74. London: HMSO.
Gostin L (1975) *A Human Condition: The Mental Health Act from 1959 to 1975. Observations, Analysis and Proposals for Reform, Vol. 1*. London: National Association for Mental Health. (MIND).
Gostin L (1977) *A Human Condition: The Law Relating to Mentally Abnormal Offenders, Vol 2*. London: National Association for Mental Health (MIND).
Gostin L (1982) Human rights, judicial review and the mentally disordered offender. *Criminal Law Review* [1982] pp. 779–891.
Gostin L (1983) *A Practical Guide to Mental Health Law*. London: National Association for Mental Health (MIND).
Gostin L (1985) *Mental Health Services and the Law*. London: Shaw.

Gostin L, Rassaby E & Buchan A (1984) *Mental Health: Tribunal Procedure*. London: Oyez Longman.

Hansard (1976) Written parliamentary answer by Dr David Owen, Minister of State for Health (15 January 1976).

Herr S & Gostin L (1975) Volunteering handicapped children for institutions. *Oxford Medical School Gazette, 27(2)* (Michaelmas term): 86.

Hospital Advisory Service (1975) *Annual Report for 1974*. London: HMSO.

MIND (National Association for Mental Health) (1977) *Evidence to the Royal Commission on the National Health Service with Regard to Services for Mentally Handicapped People*. London: MIND.

MIND (National Association for Mental Health) (1983) *Getting Together: Sexual and Social Expression of Mentally Handicapped People*. London: MIND.

Ministry of Education (1950) *Manual of Guidance – Special Services*. London: HMSO.

Ministry of Health (1967) *Annual Report for 1966*. London: HMSO.

Royal Commission on the Law Relating to Mental Illness and Mental Deficiency (1957) Report. London: HMSO.

Tyne A (1976) Residential provision for mentally handicapped adults. *Social Work Today 7:* 163–164.

Tyne A (1977) Mental handicap, housing need and the law. *Housing Monthly* (June): 7–11.

Warnock Committee (1978) *Special Educational Needs: Report of the Committee of Enquiry into the Education of Handicapped Children and Young People. Cmnd. 7212*. London: HMSO.

Welsh Office (1978) *Statistics of Psychiatric Hospitals and Units in Wales: 1975 and 1976*. London: HMSO.

WHO (World Health Organization) (1978) *The Law and Mental Health: Harmonizing Objectives. Guiding Principles based on an International Survey* Curran WJ & Harding TW (eds). Geneva: WHO.

PART 3
THE PERSON
WITH MENTAL HANDICAP

Chapter 9
Classification, Criteria, Epidemiology and Causation

MICHAEL CRAFT

Man needs to organize his knowledge, and labelling plays an essential part in this. There are fashions in labelling, particularly where the subject rouses strong emotion, as with mentally and multiply handicapped people, and the generally accepted labels change from time to time.

CLASSIFICATION IN MENTAL DISORDER

Man has always known the difference between those retarded from birth and those temporarily affected by madness. The Bible makes this clear in discussing those temporarily 'possessed by spirits'. In Greek the term *idiot* means a private person, while the term *lunatic* is derived from the Latin word *luna* (moon) and was applied to those believed to have been affected by the waxing and waning of the moon. In England a statute of Edward I distinguished between those who were 'born fools' and those temporarily mad, principally for guidance in disposition of their property. For the poor in Western Europe care was provided by the Catholic Church, and the word *cretin*, a corruption of the French word *chrétien* (Christian), is a reminder of those times. The word *mongol* has a similarly interesting derivation. Mongols were believed by Down, the first European to describe the condition, to be ethnic throwbacks, for until 1944, when Stalin returned the Crimean Tartars to Central Asia, there had been groups of ethnic mongols throughout central Europe, reminders of previous conquests. Cretins and mongols have now been relabelled as sufferers from hypothyroidism and Down's syndrome respectively, although the latter will be found described in this book under its latest label, chromosome 21 trisomy.

The terms *idiocy* and *lunacy* have long histories and give rise to similar words in most European languages today. The eighteenth-century French

writer Jean Jacques Rousseau introduced the concept of the noble savage, a simple person unsullied by civilization, and by the end of the century the French physician Itard had published a book explaining his attempts to civilize such a noble savage, Victor. It is still not clear whether Victor was autistic, retarded or deprived, but Itard stimulated much nineteenth-century work with the mentally disordered.

In France Binet emphasized the importance of work and occupation for the retarded, and Sequin took this one stage back in writing on the need for early education. We shall see these arguments in modern guise in this book: research has shown the importance of starting to educate Down's syndrome subjects in their first year of life (Chapter 18).

In the United States first Benjamin Rush, and then Howe, underlined the importance of accurate diagnosis and labelling of mentally disordered patients. Rush in particular showed what a substantial part environmental deprivation could play in causing retardation in childhood and in exacerbating the effect of non-progressive genetic misendowments.

In Victorian Britain retardation was seen as a medical matter. Later Victorian humanists introduced compulsory education with the Education Act of 1870; universal education made clear that there were groups slow to profit, and the 1899 Act distinguished 'defective' and 'epileptic' children who had special needs. The need for refuge and asylum in a system of residential care was reflected by the 1866 Idiots Act, which clarified the special residential needs of idiots and imbeciles (as opposed to lunatics, who were provided for under a separate Lunacy Act of 1890). In most languages the term *idiot* has kept its meaning over the centuries, applying to one who needs special care from birth. The widely used term *imbecile* was applied to the less retarded, ambulant person who nevertheless from birth needed special supervision and occupation. These terms were recently changed, with labels given by the 1968 World Health Organization Expert Committee, to *profound* (IQ 0–20), *severe* (IQ 20–35) and *moderate* (IQ 35–50) respectively (Table 9.1).

In the nineteenth century there was a worldwide movement towards the provision of asylums for the needy defective as well as the insane, the poor, and the social misfits or inadequates. This arose partly from an attempt to do better than previous generations, partly from a desire to order the unordered and unlabelled, and partly from the wish to banish those who offended the sight. The Victorians were good at both ordering the masses and labelling those with needs. In addition to idiots and imbeciles further educational labels were needed for the *educable imbecile* and the *feeble-minded*. In France the latter were called *morons*, and at the turn of the century Alfred Binet devised the first IQ tests to help distinguish between those who could be educated and thus be enabled to become partly self-supporting and those who could not. In Britain one-third of the army recruits for the Boer War were found unfit to serve, a great shock to the government and the ruling classes. As often happens in Britain, a royal commission was set up in 1904 to investigate the problem. Many of its recommend-

ations were included in the 1913 Mental Deficiency Act. This advised segregation of 'the feeble-minded' on eugenic grounds, with voluntary and compulsory admission to *colonies*, keeping the sexes apart to reduce the number of their defective progeny, with which it was thought the State was having to cope. Fashions had changed again by the time this Act became generally operational in Britain after the First World War: the provisions for voluntary admission to institutions were forgotten and only compulsory provisions were applied from 1918 to 1957. Much grief and suffering resulted from strict application of the rules. For instance, a woman of average intelligence in receipt of unemployment allowance who had an illegitimate child could be certified as a defective, and many were (Craft, 1959). By the time fashions had changed again in the 1960s some hundreds of such women had spent many years in colonies before release.

Yet the Victorian systems of labelling and of order were intended to protect the individual defective from exploitation and society from depredation. At the turn of the century Binet's IQ tests apparently showed most convicts and prostitutes to be illiterate and thus 'feeble-minded', whilst case histories of improvident families such as the Kallikaks and Jukes read like a roll-call of detrimental

Table 9.1 World Health Organization (1968) classification of the mentally handicapped.

1968 WHO terms and standard deviations from population mean*	IQ	Old terms	Other terms	1983 Mental Health Act terms[†]	Proportion per thousand general population
Profound Over 5.3 s.d.	0–20	Idiot	Low-grade	Severe mental impairment[†]	0.5
Severe 4.3–5.3 s.d.	20–35	Imbecile	Medium-grade		3.0
Moderate 3.3–4.3 s.d.	35–50				
Mild 2.0–3.3 s.d.	50–70 or 75	Feeble minded or moron	High-grade	Mentally impaired[†] (and/or psychopathic)[†]	20–30

* Meeting in 1968, the World Health Organization Expert Committee proposed these IQ limits for the different gradations of mental defect, assuming a mean of 100 and a standard deviation of 15 points. It emphasized that IQs were not exact measurements and should not be regarded as sole criteria and that in practice groups overlapped. Both this committee and others subsequently, on the International Classification of Disease, opposed the term 'borderline mentally retarded' for the IQ group 68–85 (16% of the general population) and this has been deleted.

† These terms are not synonymous with earlier UK legal terms. For action under the 1983 Act there must be a degree of behavioural disorder as well as intellectual impairment.

Darwinian natural selection. Sarason and Doris (1969) quote Fernald: 'The feeble-minded are a parasitic predatory class, never capable of self-support or of managing their own affairs. The great majority ultimately become public charges in some form.' As Sarason and Doris make clear in their excellent historical discussion on the subject, most countries rapidly followed the British model and established medical asylums for such people under the care of the profession which had taken the earliest and liveliest interest. Within these asylums, colonies or hospitals, conditioning factors were at work. Most were unlocked and placed emphasis on work and self-sufficiency, having a graduated system of rewards and staged release towards licence and freedom. This behaviour reinforcement over a few years was very effective with *morally defective* or what later came to be known as the *subnormal and psychopathic*, for it often represented the first ordered educational experience in a disordered childhood. There were legal checks upon the system, as potential patients had to be 'subject to be dealt with' and certifiable as mentally defective, whilst the periodic recertifications had to be signed by a magistrate. This system still operates in some countries. In the last resort, absconding from under-staffed institutions was relatively easy, and there was a selective staff disinclination to hunt too hard for those who were too aggressive, too difficult or too intelligent. Absconders disappeared within their native slums.

The use of labels

Labels, and classifications generally, are used to clarify human thought and possible action. The labelling of one group by another may be the result of reason or action and both have played their part in the nomenclature of mentally handicapped people.

Legal labels were the first attempt to bring order into confusion, as we have seen, principally to clarify medieval disposition of property in the Middle Ages. The idiot needed his property under permanent care as he would not have the lucid intervals of the lunatic during which he could think logically for himself. Despite the modern tolerance of handicapped people such labels are still needed, and in most countries an initial medico-legal label, authenticated by a registered professional, is required before benefits can be obtained. These legal labels are further discussed in Chapter 8.

Medical labels or diagnoses can now be made during the first days of life for the profoundly affected and, if disorder is suspected before birth, tests can be made in utero. As other chapters show, this is increasingly a field where intervention or treatment can avoid or reverse otherwise severe retardation. Thus efficient labelling here can lead to highly effective early treatment of metabolic anomalies such as the amino acid disorders.

Educational labels may depend initially on the results of medical labelling, and one of the defects of the latter is that few doctors, and fewer books, spell out the consequences of earlier medical diagnoses.

Administrative labels. It is a truism to say that administrators only act when they are provided with a label to serve as authorization. Yet it is important to note that the labelling or classification process is important for a government or organization, allowing a particular machinery to operate to the advantage of the individual. For example, to be termed *mentally handicapped* once invited permanent residential placement. It now indicates the many community social needs that have to be met. There has arisen a cadre of professionals and social workers to meet these needs, with their own labels and classifications, which will be described later in this chapter.

Social labels reflect community ethos. The 8000-strong American Hutterite community removed the responsibility of Christian baptism from mentally handicapped children. Absolved from this responsibility handicapped adults move among the community in a state of permanent childhood, loved and reproved by all, and not required to work or keep a family (Eaton and Weil, 1955).

Research classification. The more accurate the label the more accurate the action possible and expected. Doctor can communicate with teacher; American can communicate with Australian. The 'true' Down's syndrome subject with 47 chromosomes can be distinguished from an identical looking mosaic, genetically with the potential to be a professional but whose expectations might otherwise be geared low. The child with muscular atrophy can be classified as either recoverable or degenerative, with implications for appropriate management. For administrators, research may clarify whether Down's syndrome subjects are everywhere living longer, with the important deductions about residential care that follow from this.

Classifications in mental handicap

Whilst it is relatively simple to separate most varieties of mental illness from mental handicap, it is by no means easy to distinguish between the mentally handicapped needing special education during childhood (the mild) and those needing care for most of their life (the moderate). Those permanently incapacitated throughout life (the severe and the profound) are the most obvious.

Early classifications were not much concerned with nuances, for if a person was certified as defective this was a long-term label. The label could be applied to a wide variety of people who misbehaved socially, providing they were 'subject to be dealt with' under the 1913 Mental Deficiency Act. One of six criteria had to be satisfied: these included placement for the person's own safety, being on unemployment benefit, and being convicted by a court.

Pathological/subcultural classification

One of the best-known early classifications was that proposed by Tredgold into primary and secondary amentia (Tredgold, 1952). By primary he meant constitutional, that is genetic, chromosomal or innate, and by secondary he referred to that damage occurring to the fetus, at childbirth or from infection in infancy. In timing, he referred to antenatal, natal and postnatal causes. This classification was later used by Lewis (1933) as the basis of his pathological/subcultural dichotomy, and by Penrose (1963), who pointed out that at IQ 38 the two groups separated neatly, the pathological group being mainly below, and the subcultural above, this marker. In 1962 Penrose noted an interesting shift in viewpoint over the century. Early writers, including Tredgold, thought that genetic factors played the major part in aetiology for the milder defective and damaged 'germ plasm' the major part for the severe. Now it is believed that inheritance of recessive genes (such as those for phenylketonuria and galactosaemia) and chromosomal anomalies such as that causing Down's syndrome cause most of the severe handicaps, with environmental deprivations playing the major part in causation of milder handicap. Clarke (1969) reminds us that even in the subculture group, with environmentally caused handicap, almost half the contribution to the handicap may be supplied by normal genetic variation.

The classification used in this book follows the above traditions. Pathological (or following Tredgold, primary) causes are discussed first, in Chapter 11, dealing with *chromosomal anomalies*, and Chapter 10, on primary *genetic disorders* and their management, whilst environmental causes of damage are discussed in several chapters. However, most retardation is not monocausal. There is multiple as well as mental handicap. In the past the major handicap has often been environmental, that is, lack of stimulation, the wrong stimulation, or even negative stimulation due to community ostracism, banishment within sheltered villages, or plain institutionalization. When protein deprivation is included, it has been calculated that most of the 100 million mentally handicapped people in the world are moderately to severely retarded because of environmental deprivation. The latter part of this book is concerned with methods of improving management and environment so that the potentialities of the individual may best be fulfilled.

CRITERIA OF MENTAL HANDICAP

Social criteria have always been principal boundary markers for mental handicap, but unfortunately they are also the most vague and most open to chance. Particularly for the mild and moderately handicapped, entirely random elements may operate, such as the local unemployment level. Many in this category can manage in the community for long periods until an unexpected illness, or the demands of children or unemployment cause the collapse of their adjustment.

Some guidelines have been established, especially for severely handicapped people. They depend on three main criteria: low intelligence, low achievement at peer-group level and low standard of behaviour.

Low intelligence

The early enthusiasm for delineating mental handicap by the use of intelligence tests waxed and has now waned. At one time intelligence tests were used by some American states as the principal criteria in assessing mental deficiency. The argument about their use and abuse has raged through many books and the interested reader is referred to Clarke and Clarke (1974) for a general discussion. The following summary outlines the assets and defects of intelligence tests.

1. Binet's earlier IQ tests depended heavily on education to understand the nature of the ques-

tions. Where the deprived had had little or no education, as was the case with many convicts and prostitutes, they scored low. Thus American negroes and Indians were found generally to score low, many being in the defective range, although it was clear that the prowess of many outside the test situation was of a high order. This bias diminished with the development of non-verbal IQ tests and comprehensive education, but remains greatest for those most in need of careful assessment, that is delinquent retarded adolescents about to have their liberty removed.

2. It has now been shown that growth in intelligence is not steady for everyone, and is particularly variable in the growth spurts in individuals at puberty, when compared with their age peer groups. In adolescence the stresses of school or work throw up more candidates for the label 'mentally handicapped'.

3. Because of differences in standardization between tests, the same IQ figure does not necessarily have the same significance from test to test. This could be overcome by using standard deviations (see Table 9.1) but this concept is less popular than IQ scores for those working in the assessment field.

4. Even with a well standardized IQ test there will be variations in score from day to day and week to week. These can be between tester and tester, or with variations in health, mood and distractions at interview. Whilst these considerations may cause differences of only a few points each, the result is vitally important if an arbitrary figure of IQ 70 or 75 is set as the demarcation between two very different placements.

Individual achievements compared with those of peer groups

Since it was in childhood that individuals could be excluded from state schools on grounds of mental deficiency – and this is still so in some states in Australia – the criterion of individual achievements compared with those of the peer group deserves a mention. For deprived youngsters this can be a 'Catch 22' situation of double indignity, for owing to lack of tuition they fail to meet the criterion which would have allowed them access to tuition.

Social behaviour

Social behaviour, the vaguest criterion, has always been the most important. Standards of behaviour outlining what is unacceptable will vary between classes in a community as well as between communities, and may apply to some of the mentally ill, sex deviants, the armed forces, the inadequate and the reforming eccentrics. The Soviet Union has been accused of labelling social misfits as both mentally ill and mentally handicapped from time to time to suit the political climate.

Among the most explicit accounts of social misbehaviour as a criterion of mental deficiency was that evolved from the 1913 English Mental Deficiency Act which nowhere discussed low intelligence, but always 'arrested or incomplete development of mind', throughout its various amendments up to repeal in 1959. Consider this comment from the British Medical Association and the Magistrates' Association in 1947: 'The concept of mind is wider than intellect, and . . . mental defect (that is, deficiency of mind) is not the same thing as intellectual deficiency, although it includes it.' The Board of Control (1954) went further: 'We regard the present definitions as enabling medical practitioners to certify mentally defective patients on the ground that they have characteristics from early youth which make them antisocial, although their intelligence might be quite normal.' In the same year O'Connor and Tizard (1954) showed in a 5 % survey of some 12 000 inpatients that the *average* IQ of younger adult feeble-minded defectives in southeast England was just over IQ 70. For some years after about a quarter of institutionalized defectives in England were between IQ 70 and 100. Many textbooks supported this viewpoint strongly. In 1952 Tredgold wrote: 'An arrested development of any process or department of mind, provided it resulted in social incapacity, constitutes mental deficiency.' However, fashions in England changed in the 1970s and whilst it remained perfectly legal to treat such patients with an IQ in the average range informally or compulsorily (as psychopathic) in a hospital administratively run for mentally handicapped people, it became uncommon to find many above IQ 70. Fashions differ in different communities, and some still believe the mental handicap hospital to be an effective system for treating personality disordered delinquents.

The American Association of Mental Deficiency criteria

Social behaviour and other criteria were discussed at length by a widely based committee of experts set up by the American Association of Mental Deficiency to propose definitions. The resulting manual (Heber, 1959) started with the following statement, and then evolved an interdisciplinary concept of retardation intended to serve as a new basis for interstate statistical comparisons: 'Mental retardation refers to subaverage general intellectual functioning which originates during the development period and is associated with impairment in one or more of the following: (1) maturation, (2) learning, and (3) social adjustment.'

The manual defines *subaverage* as more than one standard deviation below the population mean for the age groups concerned, *intellectual functioning* in terms of 'objective tests', *developmental period* as childhood to 16 years, *maturation* in terms of rate of attainment of self-help skills, *learning ability* as the acquisition of achievements during school years, and *social adjustment* in terms of ability to maintain oneself in adult life in community living, employment and conformity to accepted standards. The manual repeatedly emphasizes mental retardation as a label denoting *current* functioning of the individual, without necessarily auguring permanent arrest.

A variation on this is the multidiscipline diagnosis, including, for example, anatomic data (i.e. site of damage), psychological assessment (i.e. current skills), assessment of social, home-support and work level, and sexual developmental level and orientation, and assessment of behaviour, including psychiatric abnormality, if any.

EPIDEMIOLOGY

Kushlick's criteria

Kushlick (1961) and his associates (Kushlick and Cox, 1968; Kushlick and Blunden, 1974) have carried out important surveys in England using IQ 50 as the cut-off point for severe subnormality and IQ 70 as the cut-off for mild subnormality (Table 9.2). IQ 50 is a useful point, for, as Tizard (1958) noted, follow-up studies show that only 10 % to 20 % of those below IQ 50 are capable in adult life of becoming economically independent, whereas most of those above IQ 50 are capable of deletion from a mental handicap register on grounds of no longer needing help (Kushlick, 1961). In the discussion to follow World Health Organization terms of *severely*, *moderately*, and *mildly retarded* are used.

In the Aarhus surveys of 1962 and 1970 Bernsen (1977) found that his second survey was more comprehensive than the first because the first depended on medical 'registration' of severe mental handicap, whereas the second was an intensive community survey.

IQ 50 is a widely recognized cut-off point, and numerous international studies suggest a prevalence for the severely and moderately subnormal (IQ 0–50) of about 3.7 per 1000 of the general population (Table 9.2).

Table 9.2 Prevalence of subjects with IQ 0–50 in age-groups where all are likely to be known.

	Age group	IQ under 50 (per thousand)	Down's syndrome (per thousand)
England and Wales 1926–9 (Lewis, 1929)			
Urban	7–14	3.71	0.34
Rural		5.61	NK
Baltimore 1936 (Lemkau et al., 1943)	10–14	3.3	NK
Onondaga County 1953 (Onondaga Survey, 1955)	5–17	3.6	NK
Rural Sweden 1959 (Akesson, 1961)	All ages	5.8	0.03
Middlesex 1960 (Goodman & Tizard, 1962)	7–14	3.45	1.14
Salford 1961 (Kushlick, 1961)	15–19	3.62	0.90
Aarhus 1962 (Bernsen, 1977)	0–14	2.55	NK
Aberdeen 1962 (Birch et al., 1970)	8–10	3.7	NK
Northern Ireland 1962 (Scally & MacKay, 1964)	15–19	4.7	1.45
Edinburgh 1962–4 (Drillien et al., 1966)	$7\frac{1}{2}$–$14\frac{1}{2}$	5.0	1.8
Wessex 1963 (Kushlick & Cox, 1968)			
County boroughs	15–19	3.54	1.15
Counties	15–19	3.84	1.18
Camberwell 1967 (Wing, 1971)	5–14	3.89	0.90
Aarhus (Bernsen, 1977)	0–14	3.38	NK
Oxfordshire (Elliott et al., 1981)	5–16	3.90	1.03

It will be seen that more recent surveys are very similar in the rates found. Inspection of the results shows that in early surveys less than a quarter, but more recently nearer a third, of those under IQ 50 are Down's syndrome subjects, who now tend to live longer. In Kushlick's Wessex survey 10% of these subjects scored over IQ 50, probably being translocation, phenotypes, and mosaics rather than true trisomy.

Possession of an IQ under 50 was a severe disadvantage to subjects in all the countries under survey. Tizard's follow-up studies (Tizard, 1958) showed 90% to be permanently dependent, and the remaining 10% was likely to contain many, for reasons given earlier in the discussion, who would later score much higher than IQ 50. Earlier surveys in England suggested that most of those under IQ 50 would eventually be admitted to hospital accommodation, but this is no longer true. Social services in most parts of the world are developing group homes able to care for most if not all the range of disabilities once cared for only in parallel systems of accommodation under regional or state hospital authorities.

Kushlick's surveys

In their surveys in Salford and Wessex Kushlick and his associates (Kushlick, 1961; Kushlick and Cox, 1968) used the practical criteria of being continent, ambulant and having severe behaviour disorder to rate the degree of care needed by handicapped people. Continence and ambulance were easy enough to define but behaviour disorder not so, as would be expected. Nevertheless, a surprising degree of agreement was obtained on this last criterion from care personnel.

Despite most of the children being incontinent and non-ambulant throughout childhood the majority were cared for at home. By age group 15–19, 71% of those under IQ 50 had become continent, ambulant and were without severe behaviour disorder, and this proportion continued to rise with age, owing to both the higher death rate among the severely physically handicapped, and the tendency for behaviour disorders to improve with the years. Yet Kushlick's early surveys (1961, 1968) showed that of those over 16 an increasing proportion arrived in hospital as the years advanced.

Kushlick's Wessex survey of 1963 showed not only that two-thirds of those severely mentally handicapped (SMH) adults who were continent, ambulant and free from behaviour disorder were in residential institutions (mainly hospital), but also that 86% of the mildly mentally handicapped (MMH) (IQ 50–70) were in residential institutions too. The original survey also showed that among both the SMH and MMH groups the vast majority were able to feed, wash and dress themselves. The results showed that hospitals care for a considerable proportion of people who lack serious disability.

Recent mental handicap registers

The Camberwell Psychiatric Register was established by the MRC Social Psychiatry Unit, based at the Maudsley Hospital, London. It estimated mental illness and retardation prevalence rates for an inner London district population of 172 070. The prevalence rates for children are given in Table 9.2 and those for adults in Table 9.3. The latter analyses service usage as of 31 December 1968, an important element in epidemiological surveys for administrative planning. It will be seen that although the prevalence of severe and mild adult mental handicap at 2.35% is less than that found for children, this is an *administrative* prevalence, that is people known to service agencies.

The Oxfordshire mental handicap register (Elliott et al., 1981) was set up in 1976 as a joint health, social services and education project. Family doctors, health visitors and 'the more usual sources' report handicapped people to the registry; the 'entry criteria are less strict than other registers'. The register is used for joint planning and service needs; 'it is likely that nearly all children who are moderately or severely handicapped are identified at an early age'. Unlike the Aarhus survey (see above) the Oxford register does seem to show a prevalence approaching the 3.0 per thousand expected in the community. Out of the 2027 located in a population of 550 000, 539 were still in hospital (Table 9.4).

The British government's 1971 planning document 'Better Services for the Mentally Handicapped' advised that hospital inpatients without treatment need should be discharged to community placements, and many have been. The Oxfordshire survey shows how the hospital population has changed as a result. Whereas in the 1960s surveys Kushlick found two-thirds of his hospital population continent, ambulant and without behaviour disorder, the Oxford survey showed a similar proportion of the handicapped in hospitals, but 54% were incontinent, non-ambulant or had behaviour disorder, and 59% of the rest were severely physically handicapped. In other words, over the 20 years between Kushlick's original hospital surveys and

Table 9.3 Numbers of mildly and severely retarded adolescents and adults in Camberwell, London in the care of the various mental retardation services on 31 December 1968 (numbers and age-specific rates per 1000).

	Adolescents 16–24		Adults 25–64		Elderly 65+		Total 16+	
	Number	Rate	Number	Rate	Number	Rate	Number	Rate
At home and not attending day or residential centre	*	*	*	*	*	*	*	*
Adult training centre								
Living at home	53	2.21	24	0.28	0	—	77	0.59
Living in local hostel	4	0.16	0	—	0	—	4	0.03
Long-term care homes (run by voluntary or private bodies)	8	0.33	9	0.10	3	0.15	20	0.15
Area mental retardation hospitals	28	1.17	127	1.46	26	1.31	181	1.38
Psychiatric hospitals	2	0.08	15	0.17	9	0.45	26	0.20
Total	95	3.95	175	2.01	38	1.91	308	2.35

* Not known

Table 9.4 Grade of mental handicap and place of residence.

	Community			Hospital		
	Age < 20	Age > 20	Total (%)	Age < 20	Age > 20	Total (%)
ESN(M)	102	295	397 (36)	2	71	73 (14)
ESN(S)	318	274	592 (53)	52	314	366 (76)
Other (e.g. mental illness and handicap)	9	108	117 (11)	4	77	81 (16)
Total graded	429	677	1106 (100)	58	462	520 (100)
Handicap not stated	85	297	382	3	16	19
Total			1488			539

Data from Elliott et al. (1981).

the 1981 Oxford survey, the total hospital population had only declined slowly. The greatest changes were in the types of patient: in 1981 there were far more aged patients, most had severe physical handicap and there were fewer with behaviour disorders. It is likely that these findings are true of most areas in developed countries.

CAUSATION

Causation of severe and moderate handicap (IQ 0–50)

Surveys in Western countries (Lemkau et al., 1943; Penrose, 1938; Sabagh et al., 1959; Saenger, 1960) have shown very clearly that parents of severely and moderately handicapped children come from all social classes, and cases are scattered throughout the general population. The chromosomal anomalies and genetic misendowments contributing to these cases of handicap are described in Chapters 10 and 11. Other cases are caused by trauma or infection at birth or thereafter; some of the causes are discussed in Chapter 12. An increasing proportion of severely handicapped children can, as a result of recent research, have an *anatomical* diagnosis applied to them, as the Oxford survey showed (Table 9.5). The proportion without diagnosis is 34.5%, whilst the proportion of cases due to 'cultural familial' causes is 1%.

Table 9.5 Diagnosis of causation in 450 severely handicapped children aged 3–16 years (percentages).

	Percentage
Down's syndrome or other chromosomal anomaly	26.5
Non-chromosomal abnormalities of central nervous system	9.0
Cerebral palsy	6.5
Birth injury	2.0
Infective, postinfective, or immunological causes	2.0
Nutritional or metabolic causes	2.0
Psychiatric syndromes	4.0
Cerebral anoxia	1.5
Cultural–familial causes	1.0
Heredofamilial degenerative diseases of central nervous system	1.5
Epilepsy	1.0
Recognized syndromes of unknown aetiology	1.5
Other conditions	3.0
Subnormality (not elsewhere classified)	4.0
No known cause	34.5
	100.00

Data from Elliott et al. (1981).

Whilst the basic *anatomical* cause, whether chromosomal trisomy, recessive genetic phenylketonuria or birth anoxia, may set restrictions on the total acquisition of ability, the actual *rate of achievement* will depend on psychological variables such as quality of home care, availability of special education or institutionalization. These aspects are discussed in detail in other sections of the book, but it is important to emphasize that considerable secondary retardation can occur as a result of over-protection as well as because of poor facilities. Eaton and Weil's (1955) survey of 51 mentally handicapped people in the 8000-strong American Hutterite community, where every individual is entitled as of right to be loved by every other in the community, showed that all 51 adults had a job of some sort, all managed at least some self-care and none were in hospital. Kibbutz communities in Israel show similar results. The incidence of genetic abnormalities in the community gene pool is similar in most communities, but the degree of psychological retardation or, to put it another way, the rate of advance, can be very different, and depends on the quality of tuition and community care. The problem is made worse by the difficulty facing the expert in accurately assessing progress in young handicapped people. There is a need to ensure good care of the most handicapped people, because many will do sur-

prisingly well. For instance Illingworth (1961), Professor of Child Health at Sheffield, followed up 122 infants under 12 months of age for whom he had made a confident diagnosis of mental subnormality excluding Down's syndrome, hypothyroidism or hydrocephalus. Thirty died under the age of six, many with severe brain pathology. Of 87 of the remainder who could be traced there were six with IQ 100 and over, three with IQ 90–99, nine with IQ 80–89, eight with IQ 70–79, ten with IQ 50–69 and 51 with IQ 0–50. Thus there were 36 with IQ of 50 or over and 26 were not intellectually mentally handicapped. Furthermore, the hypothyroid and hydrocephalic subjects would nowadays be treated, whilst the Down's subject could respond to special tuition (see Chapter 18). There are now many studies on retardation resulting from unstimulating environments; in extreme cases the patients have been called deprivation dwarfs (see, for example, Silver and Finkelstein, 1977). It is important to realize that mild retardation can occur in the over-protective home, as well as in an ill-staffed hostel or hospital. The classic Brooklands experiment was carried out by Tizard (1964), who transferred a group of imbecile children from hospital, matched for relevant factors with a group of children who stayed behind in hospital. The transferred group had much play and close verbal and practical stimulation from adults who grew to love them, and they improved markedly in verbal IQ compared with the control group. Other research studies have confirmed these findings and emphasized that it is not the number of staff but their deployment which is crucial. The handicapped child at home may actually have fewer hours per week with adults than the institutional child, but the face-to-face time and its quality will be quite different.

Causation of mild handicap (IQ 50–70)

Clinical studies have shown that, whereas, for instance, Birch et al. (1970) could find clear evidence of central nervous system impairment in all except one of a group of 100 severely mentally handicapped children, less than one-third of children with IQ 50–75 had such damage. A pathological study by Crome (1960) showed that 267 out of 272 brains sectioned by him in a hospital for severe and moderately handicapped children had 'definite abnormality'. Most surveys show that only a small proportion of the mildly handicapped (IQ 50–70) have central nervous system abnormality, and much more importantly that mental handicap in the absence of central nervous system abnormality occurs mainly among the lower social classes. In other words, there is now evidence that it is rare for a child in a higher social class to have an IQ less than 80 unless he has one of the pathological syndromes outlined later.

The evidence is compelling. Birch (1970), in the Aberdeen survey, showed the incidence of mental handicap among children in the lowest social class to be nearly nine times that in the top two classes. Also from Scotland, the Mental Health Survey of 1947 noted that fathers in their top social class had no non-pathological children scoring less than IQ 86, whilst lowest class fathers had 26 % scoring under IQ 86. Stein and Susser (1963) confirmed this in an analysis of referrals to a child health service for 'backwardness'. Not only did schools serving 'aspirant' (higher social class) families refer fewer children for backwardness (8.7/1000) than 'demotic' (of the people) schools for working-class areas (25/1000), but at the 11-plus intelligence examination the schools serving the higher social class had only 0.9 % scoring IQ 50−79, whilst 10 % of all pupils from working-class areas scored in this range. In this area of survey, Salford, education is compulsory and state-provided, and the writers were able to show a gradation between these figures according to district. They also checked private schools to ensure that retardates had not been preferentially streamed there. In a further examination of 106 severely retarded children, the seven who came from 'aspirant' families all had clinical abnormalities; of the 50 who came from 'demotic' families 30 were clinically normal.

It is now possible to conclude from the evidence that whilst *moderate* and *severe* mental handicap (IQ 0−50) is due mainly to chromosomal anomalies, severe rare genetic misendowments and brain damage, only a small proportion of cases of *mild* mental handicap (IQ 50−70) are caused in this way. Most mildly retarded individuals without central nervous system signs, biochemical abnormality or sense deprivation occur among the working classes and it is rare to find a clinically normal retardate under IQ 86 among the professional classes.

This has profound implications when one comes to consider a general theory of genetic endowment.

Genetic endowment and mental handicap

The contribution of dominant and recessive genes and chromosome anomalies to severe handicap is well known. Indeed, there is no known example of chromosome anomaly increasing potential; all such anomalies reduce mental and physical ability, usually to a profound degree. Down's syndrome (21 trisomy) is a perfect example of too many (genetic) cooks spoiling the final human broth.

Some cases of mild mental handicap are caused by single genes of high import, as with muscular dystrophy, but since the research by Roberts et al. (1938) it has been generally agreed that above IQ 50 the general population nears a normal distribution in respect of intelligence as for other bodily characteristics. Roberts and his colleagues built upon earlier work to show that large-scale IQ tests among children produced results in accord with a normal distribution down to IQ 50, beyond which there was an *excess* presumably due to pathological variants. They postulated that intelligence above IQ 50 was the result of multiple factors, particularly additive genes. The theory has been widely accepted and supported by subsequent work, although, as O'Connor and Tizard (1956) pointed out, IQ tests have been generally framed to fit this theory rather than the other way about.

At about the same time Penrose (1938) showed that relatives of severely handicapped people tended to have normal intelligence, whereas relatives of the mildly handicapped tended to have low IQs in proportion to the closeness of relationship. This could support common environmental − or deprivative − as well as genetic factors among the lower social classes. Later Penrose (1963) reviewed the evidence that the additive genetic theory was supported by closeness of relatives to the mildly subnormal, and stated that this theory depended on random mating in the general population. Research has shown that this does not apply, for like tends to marry like. University graduates marry graduates, unskilled workers other unskilled workers. Apart from intelligence, other human characteristics believed to be governed by additive genes, such as height, also tend to be assortative. Assortative mating would tend to exacerbate the tendency for low IQ to occur in lower classes.

It is clear that a theory of multiple genetic causation cannot explain all the IQ differences between individuals. The environmental contribution is also considerable, as Susser and Watson (1962) pointed out, and genetic factors cannot explain the comparative rarity of mild mentally handicapped children among professional classes. Applying statistics to a theory of multiple genetic endowment gives a greater number of cases expected than are actually found. In addition, unskilled workers have proportionately more mildly handicapped children than do skilled workers of similar IQ, and one has to hypothesize that children with the same genetic potential rise to a higher level of achievement with the second group than the first, presumably because of the environmental improvement resulting from their parental handling.

The most comprehensive analysis of IQ status of parents and children is provided by a population survey from the Minnesota Institute of Human Genetics, looking at records for 7778 children (Reed and Reed, 1965). In the 89 instances where both parents had IQs under 70, nearly 40% of the children were also educationally retarded (although the average IQ of the children was 74). Where only one parent had an IQ below 70, 15% of the children were retarded (54% had IQs above 90). Of the 7035 with neither parent retarded, 1% were mentally handicapped. Surveying their data, they calculated that for a mentally handicapped person under IQ 70 the expectation for one of their children also consistently to score under IQ 70 was 17.1%. Reed and Anderson (1973) constructed a model which predicted that some 17% of mentally handicapped children in any generation would have been produced by the retarded, the remaining 83%, produced by parents of normal IQ, having retardation resulting from abnormal mutations, recessive genes and other chance pre- and postnatal factors. Other, more recent studies are less impressive.

Low birth-weight is a further factor associated with mild mental handicap. Drillien (1961) showed that among all classes the mean IQ among children with birth-weight less than 1.6 kg (3.5 lb) is less than the mean IQ of those with birth-weight above this. Craft (1967), reviewing studies to that date, noted that as with height (mentioned earlier) birth-weights of children correlated with maternal shortness, which itself correlated with social class. In other words the incidence of 'premature' babies (below 2.5 kg/5.5 lb) rises from social class I to V, as does the incidence of perinatal mortality and of morbidity. There is a concatenation of adverse factors behind the association of low IQ children, with low birth-weight, low social class and small mothers. Among many others, Birch et al. (1970) also found mild handicap in Scotland to be associated with poor houses, big families and congestion.

Minimal brain damage has been suggested, notably by Lilienfeld and Pasamanick (1955), as an important component in the association between low IQ and low social class. The idea has generated much work and many reviews. It is perfectly true that both perinatal morbidity and mortality are greater in the lower social classes than in the higher classes and that this holds good for most Western countries. Since minimal brain damage is by definition associated with few if any central nervous system signs and little or no demonstrable brain pathology, it is by definition hard to prove or disprove this claim, or to use it for treatment purposes.

Communication defects as a cause of mental handicap

The incidence of blindness, deafness and mutism has always been high among populations of mentally handicapped people, and it is well known that memory deficits retard the development of children who later show quite normal intelligence. Luria (1963) has pointed out the importance of language to the rate of advancement of achievement in children. In later books he showed that lacks in communication with others lead to lack in mental activity, understanding and self-help skills. Using monozygotic twins, he taught one of the pair to speak faster than the other, and showed how language may speed up the rate of acquisition of skills in children. Other works have related the usage of language to class. For instance, on average a working class family has a smaller vocabulary, a larger family and less verbal contact between adults and children than a professional family. The latter is likely to have a greater wealth of verbal and written material about the house, with which to stimulate the children, and to use schools where classes are smaller and teachers stay longer. The natural development of Luria's teaching and his behavioural approach with its emphasis on early language development and the wealth of stimulating material needed to maximize rate of development in those with limited genetic potential may be followed in Chapter 18.

ESTIMATIONS OF FUTURE TRENDS IN NUMBERS OF HANDICAPPED PEOPLE

A variety of surveys have suggested that the incidence of moderate and severe mental handicap (IQ 0–50) in the general population lies between 3.3/1000 (Lemkau et al., 1943) and 5.8/1000 (Akesson, 1961) (see Table 9.2). High figures, such as the latter, for rural areas probably reflect the findings for those under 14 years, whose subsequent work-holding and community success bore little relation to the early prognoses. Most recent surveys give results between 3.8 and 3.5/1000 for the post-school-age group.

From these surveys over the decades one cannot immediately deduce whether the prevalence is rising or falling. Even when examining the proportion of Down's syndrome subjects within these surveys deductions are not straightforward. The incidence of Down's syndrome is 1 per 550 live births and 90 % are IQ 0–50. In surveys in the 1960s the prevalence ranged between 0.9/1000 (Kushlick, 1961) to 1.8/1000, in Edinburgh (Scally and Mackay, 1964) (see Table 9.2). This evidence and the knowledge that better methods of medical care are now available, underlines the increasing longevity and thus prevalence of the Down's group. Because the total prevalence of the IQ 0–50 group has not changed much over the years – for example, it was 3.71/1000 in urban England and Wales in 1926–9 (Lewis, 1929), 3.45/1000 in Middlesex in 1960 (Goodman and Tizard, 1962) and 3.54/1000 in Wessex in 1963 (Kushlick and Cox, 1968) – one could conclude that the proportion of non-Down's-syndrome severely handicapped people (IQ 0–50) must have fallen. Lewis' figures showed a high incidence among rural children, but this fell substantially in the 15 to 19 age group, and it seems that he included a number of children who either improved or were mislabelled (Lewis, 1929). It is possible that part of the improvement was due to recovery from minor brain damage or infections (ear infections were common in rural areas) or even to overcoming communication difficulties, for his highest rates came from Cardigan, Wales, where Welsh was the first language. At all events, the prevalence rate in age group 15 to 19 probably gives a truer picture.

More recently Stein and Susser (1971) considered changes in prevalence. They concluded that prevalence was increasing slightly, owing to longevity of Down's syndrome subjects, and that there was only a slight decrease in incidence of all other types. Kushlick and Cox (1968) agree, analysing mortality rates for a 4½-year period using Wessex data. These suggested an increase in the more able and a static prevalence of the less able (profound) handicapped in the IQ 0–50 group. For the mildly handicapped (IQ 50–70) it is much harder to estimate change, for numbers and incidence depend so much on environmental variables. As Illingworth (1961) and others have found, it is difficult indeed to predict the later ability of infants found to be mentally handicapped, although the predictive value of being under IQ 50 for children aged 7–14 is fairly good. In contrast, the evidence shows that children of IQ 50–70 are responding to a variety of environmental deprivations and many make good social and work adjustments after leaving school. Indeed, where

groups of these children have been tested in adult years, their IQ test results have commonly risen, a sizeable proportion being beyond IQ 80 and by no means intellectually handicapped. That they may still have degrees of personality or social handicap has been shown by Gibbens (1963), who found boys from low-status homes to be much more likely to be convicted and institutionalized than those from high-status homes.

The general view used to be that the mildly handicapped tended to produce large families of dull, if not problem, children, and therefore were best placed in segregated colonies. The theory behind this view has now been teased out into component parts, and for mildly handicapped people where marriage with birth control is concerned might be thought to have swung full circle to advocacy of marriage in Sweden and elsewhere, as Chapter 16 reports. Since it is perfectly true that larger families were common among the poor, two surveys of intelligence among 11-year-old Scottish children are relevant (Scottish Council for Research in Education, 1949). These surveys were analysed to examine whether national intelligence was being adversely affected by large families born to low-status parents. In 1932 76 498 children were found to have a mean test score of 34.5 (s.d. 15.5), compared with a mean of 36.7 (s.d. 16.1) for 70 805 children in 1947. It was felt that this small increase was due principally to improved tuition for low scorers. In other words, it was possible to effect an improvement with these Scottish children by improving one of the environmental variables. The importance of low birth-weight, large families and poor adult language contact may be currently being influenced by better obstetric facilities, falling birth rate and television respectively.

Kushlick (1961) made an attempt to measure the number of mildly mentally handicapped people produced by the Salford community. He estimated the prevalence for the years 1948 and 1961 and found little difference. In addition, the annual figures produced by the Department of Health and Social Security show a substantial decline in the proportion of the mildly mentally handicapped who were in hospital. This has more than halved from the figure of 52 % in 1954, and continues to fall. It is probable that this reflects a number of changes, including the increase in facilities for day work for this group in the community, the increase in hostel and boarding-house beds and the pressure on hospitals not to admit 'social problems'. Such figures do not represent the prevalence of the mildly mentally handicapped throughout the whole community. It is likely that the numbers of the mildly handicapped in hospital will continue to fall as measures to deal with such people by hospitalization fall increasingly out of favour. Unfortunately, this policy, humane on many counts, leads to a dearth of residential facilities for the difficult person from an overcrowded, poor home, once scoring IQ 50–70 but now an adult scoring IQ 70–90, in social difficulties in an increasingly automated society, which does not need his work. Craft et al. (1975) in 'Lost Souls' suggest that sheltered villages on a voluntary basis might help.

SUMMARY AND CONCLUSIONS

It will be seen from this chapter that there have always been mentally handicapped people in our society. Not only are their handicaps commonly multiple, but so also is the causation. Research means that one can be far more clear as to causation of handicap now than before, and it has become important as a guide to treatment.

Profound, severe, and moderately handicapped people (IQ 0–50) make up 3.5–4/1000 of the general population in most developed countries. Causation is multiple. *Chromosomal anomalies* such as Down's syndrome are responsible for over a third of the mentally handicapped in these categories; their condition cannot be reversed after birth, although modern methods of tuition help many to reach a higher level of adult achievement than formerly, and enable many to be independent with supervision. *Genetic anomalies* such as phenylketonuria are increasingly open to treatment. *Neonatal and postnatal damage and infection* are preventable and treatable to a large extent. The effect of these variables is that the total incidence of these (IQ 0–50) is static, although the proportion with Down's syndrome within this group is rising. The proportion who, as they get older, become ambulant, continent and without severe behaviour disorder is also rising. The obvious deduction is that the proportion of this group who need to be in hospitals is falling.

The mildly handicapped (IQ 50–70) are ten or more times commoner in incidence, and causation rarely involves the pathological factors responsible for the IQ 0–50 group. Mild handicap rarely occurs among the higher social classes, and it results from predominantly environmental and to a lesser degree multiple and additive genetic factors. In underdeveloped countries protein malnutrition and other deprivative variables are believed to raise the number of those affected. In developed countries there is evidence that special remedial education programmes decrease the incidence.

The mildly handicapped, IQ 50–70, and others above this intellectual level, whose primary problems are lack of work in an automated society, lack of adequate places to live or lack of controlling social influences, and who may be labelled 'behaviourally disordered', have been little discussed in this chapter. Some of their particular problems are discussed elsewhere – psychiatric problems in Chapter 28, social problems in Chapter 26. The political and economic aspects of planning are beyond the scope of a book such as this.

BIBLIOGRAPHY

Akesson H (1961) *Epidemiology and Genetics of Mental Deficiency in a Southern Swedish Population.* Sweden: University of Uppsala.

Bernsen AH (1977) Severe mental retardation among children in a Danish urban area. In Mittler P (ed) *Research to Practice in Mental Retardation. Vol 1.* Baltimore: University Park Press.

Birch HG, Richardson SA, Baird D, Horobin C & Illsley R (1970) *Mental Subnormality in the Community: A Clinical and Epidemiological Study.* Baltimore: Williams & Wilkins.

Board of Control (1954) *Memorandum of Evidence before the Royal Commission on the Law relating to Mental Illness and Mental Deficiency.* (Ministry of Health). London: HMSO.

British Medical Association and Magistrates' Association (1947) *Interpretation of Definitions in the Mental Deficiency Act, 1927.* London: British Medical Association.

Clarke ADB (1969) *Recent Advances in the Study of Subnormality*, 2nd edn. London: National Association for Mental Health.

Clarke AM & Clarke ADB (1974) *Mental Deficiency*, 3rd edn. London: Methuen.

Craft MJ (1959) Personality disorder and dullness. *Lancet, i:* 856.

Craft MJ (1967) *Patterns of Care for the Subnormal.* Oxford: Pergamon.

Craft A & Craft M (1981) Sexuality and mental handicap: A Review. *British Journal of Psychiatry 139:* 494–505.

Craft MJ, Elliott JR & Sime DA (eds) (1975) *Lost Souls: Services for Mentally Abnormal Offenders.* Mental Handicap Papers 7. London: King's Fund Centre.

Crome L (1960) The brain and mental retardation. *British Medical Journal i:* 897–900.

Drillien CM (1961) A longitudinal survey of the growth of prematurely and maturely born children. Part VII. *Archives of Disease in Childhood 36:* 233–240.

Eaton JW & Weil RJ (1955) *Culture and Mental Disorders.* Glencoe, Illinois: Free Press.

Elliott D, Jackson JM & Graves JP (1981) Oxfordshire mental handicap register. *British Medical Journal 282:* 789.

Gibbens TCN (1963) *Psychiatric Studies of Borstal Lads.* Oxford: Oxford University Press.

Goodman N & Tizard J (1962) Prevalence of imbecility and idiocy among children. *British Medical Journal i:* 216–219.

Heber R (1959) *Manual on Terminology and Classification in Mental Retardation.* American Association of Mental Deficiency.

Illingworth RS (1961) The predictive value of developmental tests in the first year, with special reference to the diagnosis of mental subnormality. *Journal of Child Psychology and Psychiatry 2:* 210–215.

Klineberg O (1940) *Negro Intelligence and Selective Migration.* New York: Columbia University Press.

Kushlick A (1961) Subnormality in Salford. In Susser MW & Kushlick A (eds) *A Report on the Mental Health Services in the City of Salford for the Year 1960.* Salford: Salford Health Department.

Kushlick A & Blunden R (1974) The epidemiology of mental subnormality. In Clarke AM and Clarke ADB (eds) *Mental Deficiency*, 3rd edn. London: Methuen.

Kushlick A & Cox G (1968) Planning services for the subnormal in Wessex. In Wing JK & Bransby BR (eds) *Psychiatric Case Registers.* DHSS Statistical Report Series 8. London: HMSO.

Lemkau P, Tietze C & Cooper M (1943) Mental-hygiene problems in an urban district. Fourth paper. *Mental Hygiene 27:* 279–295.

Lewis EO (1929) *The Report of the Mental Deficiency Committee, Being a Joint Committee of the Board of Education and Board of Control: Part IV – Report on an Investigation into the Incidence of Mental Deficiency in Six Areas, 1925–27.* London: HMSO.

Lewis EO (1933) Types of mental deficiency and their social significance. *Journal of Mental Science 79:* 298–304.

Lilienfeld AM & Pasamanick B (1955) Association of maternal and fetal factors with development of mental deficiency. Relationship to maternal age, birth order, previous reproductive loss and degree of mental deficiency. *American Journal of Mental Deficiency 60:* 557–569.

Luria AR (1963) *The Mentally Retarded Child.* Oxford: Pergamon.

O'Connor N & Tizard J (1954) A survey of patients in twelve mental deficiency institutions. *British Medical Journal i:* 16–18.

Onondaga County Survey (1955) A special census of suspected referred mental retardation. *Community Mental Health Research.* New York State Dept of Mental Hygiene Report.

Penrose LS (1938) *A Clinical and Genetic Study of 1280 Cases of Mental Defect (Colchester Survey).* Special Report Series, Medical Research Council 229. London: HMSO.

Penrose LS (1962) Biological aspects. *Proceedings of the London Conference of the Scientific Study of Mental Deficiency I:* 11–18.

Penrose LS (1963) *The Biology of Mental Defect*, 3rd edn. London: Sidgwick and Jackson.

Reed SC & Anderson VE (1973) Effects of changing sexuality on the gene pool. In de la Cruz & LaVeck GD (eds) *Human Sexuality and the Mentally Retarded.* London: Butterworth.

Reed EW & Reed SC (1965) *Mental Retardation: A Family Study.* Philadelphia: Saunders.

Roberts JAF, Norman RM & Griffiths R (1938) Studies on a child population: IV. The form of the lower end of the frequency distribution of Stanford Binet intelligence quotients and the fall of low intelligence quotients with advancing age. *Annals of Eugenics 8:* 319–336.

Sabagh G, Dingman HF, Tarjan G & Wright SW (1959) Social class and ethnic status of patients admitted to a state hospital for the retarded. *Pacific Sociological Review 2:* 76–80.

Saenger GS (1960) *Factors Influencing the Institutionalization of Mentally Retarded Individuals in New York City.* Report to the New York Interdepartmental Health Resources Board.

Sarason SB & Doris J (1969) *Psychological Problems in Mental Deficiency*, 4th edn. New York: Harper & Row.

Scally BG & Mackay DN (1964) Mental subnormality and its prevalence in Northern Ireland. *Acta Psychiatrica Scandinavica 40:* 203–211.

Scottish Council for Research in Education (1949) *The Trend of Scottish Intelligence.* London: University of London.

Silver HK & Finkelstein M (1977) Deprivation dwarfism. *Journal of Pediatrics 70:* 317–324.

Stein Z & Susser M (1963) The social distribution of mental retardation. *American Journal of Mental Deficiency 67:* 811–821.

Stein Z & Susser M (1971) Changes over time in the incidence and prevalence of mental retardation. In Helimuth J (ed) *Exceptional Infants, Vol 2: Studies of Abnormalities.* New York: Brunner/Mazel.

Susser MW & Watson W (1962) *Sociology in Medicine.* Oxford: Oxford University Press.

Tizard J (1958) Longitudinal and follow-up studies. In Clarke AM & Clarke ADB (eds) *Mental Deficiency: The Changing Outlook*, 1st edn. London: Methuen.

Tizard J (1964) *Community Services for the Mentally Handicapped.* Oxford: Oxford University Press.

Tredgold AF (1952) *Mental Deficiency*, 8th edn. London: Baillière Tindall.

Wechsler D (1958) *The Measurement and Appraisal of Human Intelligence.* Baltimore.

Wing L (1971) Severely retarded children in a London area: prevalence and provision of services. *Journal of Psychological Medicine i:* 405–415.

Wing L, Corbett J, Pool D, Wollen W & Yeates S (1977) Services for mentally retarded children and adults. In Wing JK & Hailey AM (eds) *Evaluating a Community Psychiatric Service.* London: Oxford University Press.

World Health Organization (1968) *Organization of Services for the Mentally Retarded.* 15th Report of the WHO Expert Committee on Mental Health. World Health Organization Technical Reports Series 302.

Chapter 10
Primary Genetic Disorders

PETER S. HARPER & MICHAEL CRAFT

General Aspects

PETER S. HARPER

Genetic factors are of major importance in almost all forms of mental retardation, but it is only in a minority of cases that one can identify a specific disorder with a recognizable genetic basis. Increasing understanding at a clinical, genetic and biochemical level has steadily enlarged the number of disorders in this group and enabled a specific cause to be given in many instances that would previously have been termed 'non-specific' mental retardation.

In some of these disorders the existence of a unique clinical syndrome is clear, but the genetic basis appears slight or obscure; in a small but important number a recognizable abnormality of chromosome morphology can be found. In the majority there is no visible chromosome defect, but the condition can be attributed to the action of a major gene whose pattern of transmission follows Mendelian inheritance.

It is this last group which is emphasized in this chapter. Not only does it contain numerous clinically distinctive disorders in which mental retardation is a prominent feature, but it is the group in which practical preventive and therapeutic measures have their greatest scope, and in which our depth of understanding is greatest.

The recognition that Mendelian inheritance is operating in a particular form of mental retardation is of considerable theoretical as well as practical importance, for it makes it certain not only that the disorder is a specific entity, but also that it is ultimately the result of a unique biochemical abnormality, almost certainly in the primary structure of a specific protein coded by a specific portion of genetic material. Study can then be directed towards identifying the complex chain of events connecting this basic defect with the end result of the clinical and pathological features. The degree to which this understanding has been achieved varies greatly from condition to condition, and it is possible to recognize a number of stages, summarized here:

1 Identification of a specific clinical syndrome.
2 Recognition of a specific mode of Mendelian inheritance.
3 Discovery of an underlying metabolic abnormality.
4 Identification of the specific enzyme or other protein that is absent or defective.
5 Identification of the gene itself and of the precise nature of the changes in the nucleic acid sequence.
6 Replacement of the defective gene product.

The mucopolysaccharidoses provide an illustration of the different stages and of how rapidly our knowledge may evolve. Stage 1 was represented by the recognition of a clinical syndrome of facial and bony dysmorphic features, together with visceral involvement and progressive neurodegeneration, and was taken further by the realization that individual clinical entities existed within this group. In stage 2 it was realised not only that Mendelian inheritance was acting, but also that one form (type II, the Hunter syndrome) followed X-linked recessive inheritance, while others were inherited in an autosomal recessive manner. In stage 3 characteristic changes in mucopolysaccharide excretion were identified, along with the storage of partly degraded mucopolysaccharide molecules in the tissues, while in stage 4, only recently achieved, specific deficiencies of individual lysosomal enzymes were identified, corresponding in general with the clinical and biochemical groups already defined. Although stage 5 has not been reached, our existing knowledge already allows accurate preventive measures such as genetic counselling, carrier detection and prenatal diagnosis, while attempts are in progress to realise stage 6 with the use of bone marrow transplantation. In successful cases this restores enzyme levels to normal and may arrest the physical progress of the disorder, though the effects on mental development remain to be seen.

THE BASIS OF MENDELIAN INHERITANCE

The majority of primary genetic disorders causing mental retardation have not had all six stages of elucidation, and indeed the grounds for a genetic basis of some of the specific disorders considered later in this chapter are tenuous, but the rapid changes for some disorders provide a challenge both to improve the level of understanding of others, and to identify new entities whose existence is at present not clearly defined.

Autosomal recessive inheritance

Most of the disorders for which a clear biochemical basis has been identified show an autosomal recessive inheritance (Table 10.1), and most of these have proved to be enzymatic defects. This arises from two factors: firstly, our understanding of non-enzymatic proteins of cells under direct genetic control is poor in comparison with our knowledge of specific enzymatic processes; secondly, the great majority of enzymes can be reduced to a level of well under half the original amount or activity without harmful result, so that the heterozygote for an enzymatic disorder, where enzyme activity is generally around half the normal level, will be clinically normal. By definition, therefore, such disorders will be recessively inherited; the heterozygous carriers will show minimal or no abnormalities, and may require special investigations for their identification.

Genetic counselling for families in which an autosomal recessive disorder has occurred is important and relatively straightforward. There will be a 1-in-4 risk of future sibs of an affected individual being similarly affected, but since both parents have to transmit an abnormal gene the risk will be small for the children of healthy sibs, or if a parent remarries. Consanguinity (marriage between close relatives) is a particular feature of rare autosomal recessive disorders and should always be specifically inquired for.

Perhaps the commonest error in the genetic evaluation of autosomal recessive disorders is failure to appreciate that absence of other affected families is the rule rather than the exception. It is essential for the genetic basis of such isolated cases to be recognized early and for the parents to be advised of the risk of recurrence and how this may be prevented.

Autosomal dominant inheritance

This mode of inheritance is also responsible for a number of specific disorders causing mental retardation (Table 10.2), but in contrast to autosomal recessive disorders, we rarely have an indication of the underlying metabolic basis.

The few dominantly inherited enzyme defects known, such as the porphyrias, are related to pathways which are unusually critical and sensitive in their regulation. Some others are thought to result from mutations in structural molecules of cell membranes and other components, and others to specific failures of regulatory processes in development, but in most instances we simply do not know.

Recognition of autosomal dominant inheritance is essential for appropriate genetic counselling; affected individuals have a 50 % chance of transmitting the disorder to a child of either sex, but the children of healthy individuals should not be at risk. It is especially important to recognize the mildly affected parents in such variable disorders as tuberous sclerosis, myotonic dystrophy and Treacher Collins syndrome. The birth of a severely affected child may be the first indication for such parents to be examined. Where both parents are truly unaffected there has probably been a new mutation,

Table 10.1 Autosomal recessive disorders associated with mental retardation.

Ataxia telangiectasia
Canavan's disease (spongy degeneration of white matter)
Carpenter's acrocephalopolysyndactyly
Galactosaemia
Homocystinuria
Laurence–Moon–Biedl–Bardet syndrome
Marinesco–Sjögren syndrome
Microcephaly (severe form)
Mucopolysaccharidoses (types I, III)
Neurolipidoses (including Tay–Sachs, Gaucher's,
   metachromatic leucodystrophy and numerous others)
Phenylketonuria
Seckel syndrome
Sjögren–Larsson syndrome
Wilson's disease
Xeroderma pigmentosum

Table 10.2 Autosomal dominant disorders associated with mental retardation.

Apert's syndrome
Huntington's chorea (juvenile cases)
Mandibulofacial dysostosis (not constant)
Myotonic dystrophy (particularly early onset and congenital
   cases)
Neurofibromatosis (not constant)
Tuberous sclerosis (epiloia)

---

and recurrence in future children is not to be expected; in uniformly severe conditions where reproduction is rare (for instance Apert's syndrome) such sporadic cases may form the majority.

X-linked inheritance

The specific chromosomes on which are located the genes controlling the various Mendelian forms of mental retardation have for the most part not been identified, but in the case of the X chromosome the pattern of inheritance itself provides this information. There are in fact numerous X-linked disorders accompanied by mental retardation, and some are listed in Table 10.3.

Of particular interest has been the recognition of an X-linked form of mental retardation associated with a fragile site at the end of the long arm of the X chromosome. This disorder, discussed more fully in Chapter 11, is now recognized to be relatively common, and to account for many of the clearly X-linked families previously classified as 'Martin–Bell' or 'Renpenning' non-specific mental retardation. Macro-orchidism is a specific feature in adult males. There undoubtedly remain, however, other undetermined causes for the overall excess of males with mental retardation.

In the classical pattern of X-linked recessive inheritance, only males are affected, but the disorder may be transmitted by healthy carrier females. If an affected male does reproduce, all his daughters will be carriers.

Most of the problems of genetic counselling in X-linked disorders arise from the variability of expression shown by the heterozygous carriers. In some disorders (for example, fragile X syndrome) a proportion of females are overtly affected; more

commonly there is a milder degree of expression. At the other extreme, some women known to be carriers on genetic grounds cannot be identified as affected even with the most sophisticated of tests. It is in this situation that the use of DNA techniques, not influenced by gene expression, is going to be of the greatest use (see below).

INBORN ERRORS OF METABOLISM

Although documentation of dominantly inherited abnormalities has in most cases not passed the descriptive stage in terms of clinical recognition and pathology, a wide variety of types of metabolic defect have now been identified in recessively inherited disorders, allowing a classification within the broad framework of the term 'inborn error of metabolism'. Table 10.4 summarizes the main groups, which are rapidly becoming subdivided as knowledge increases. At present the disorders causing mental retardation fall principally into groups 1 and 2, probably because the normal processes of groups 3 and 4 as occurring in the brain are very little understood.

Although this classification provides a useful framework for the consideration of inborn errors of metabolism, many disorders either overlap or do not accurately fit a specific group. Phenylketonuria, one of the most extensively studied of inborn errors, may be used as an example. The most important clinical finding in untreated phenylketonuria is mental retardation, but pathological studies have shown no macroscopic or microscopic features which are diagnostic of phenylketonuria, reduction in brain weight being the most constant finding. A raised blood phenylalanine level has itself been shown to have toxic effects in animals, inhibiting a number of key brain enzymes and reducing myelin formation. However, there is also accumulation of a

Table 10.3 X-linked disorders associated with mental retardation.

Albright's hereditary osteodystrophy
Anhidrotic ectodermal dysplasia (occasional)
Cerebral sclerosis with Addison's disease
Cerebral sclerosis, Pelizaeus–Merzbacher type
Duchenne muscular dystrophy (not constant)
Fragile X chromosome syndrome
Hunter's syndrome (mucopolysaccharidosis II)
Incontinentia pigmenti (male lethal, X-linked dominant)
Lesch–Nyhan syndrome
Lowe's oculocerebrorenal syndrome
Menkes' syndrome
Norrie's disease
Orofaciodigital syndrome (male lethal, X-linked dominant)
X-linked aqueduct stenosis
X-linked 'non-specific' mental retardation without fragile X

Table 10.4 Classification of inborn errors of metabolism.

1 Classical 'Garrodian' inborn error with specific block in a metabolic pathway causing
  (a) accumulation of precursors, e.g. phenylketonuria.
  (b) deficiency of products, e.g. adrenogenital syndrome due to 21-hydroxylase defect, with cortisol deficiency.

2 Storage disease, due to specific lysosomal enzyme defects, e.g. mucopolysaccharidoses, Tay–Sachs disease.

3 Defects of membrane transport processes, e.g. cystinuria, Hartnup disease.

4 Defects of specific non-enzymic proteins, e.g. haemoglobinopathies.

number of metabolites of phenylalanine and deficiency of other substances normally derived from tyrosine, and it remains possible that the cerebral changes in phenylketonuria may be related to deficiency of these factors as well as to phenylalanine accumulation.

Phenylketonuria illustrates another cardinal feature of inborn errors of metabolism, that of heterogeneity. Although the great majority of patients have a deficiency of phenylalanine hydroxylase as the brain defect, cases have been described in which the enzymatic abnormality has been of either phenylalanine transaminase or dihydropteridine reductase. In addition, transient and partial deficiencies of phenylalanine hydroxylase itself have been described, producing the various hyperphenylalaninaemic syndromes that require distinction from classical phenylketonuria.

Genetic heterogeneity has proved to be an almost universal feature of those inherited disorders whose metabolic basis is well understood, and is likely to be responsible for much of the clinical variation seen in the many conditions for which we do not yet understand the metabolic basis. There is a fundamental difference between heterogeneity produced by alleles at the same genetic locus, where the biochemical defect is likely to be the same, and heterogeneity due to genes at different loci, which implies that the types are both biochemically and genetically distinct, even though producing a similar clinical picture.

The second group of inborn errors of metabolism which makes a major contribution to the genetic causes of mental retardation is the group of storage diseases. This group is characterized by the defective breakdown of macromolecules such as glycoproteins, mucopolysaccharides and complex lipids, which accumulate within neural and other cells, with slowly progressive deterioration in function as a result. The nature of the stored material can be identified both histochemically and by more specific biochemical studies, and electron microscopy shows the accumulated substances to be located in the lysosomes. Specific deficiencies of a variety of lysosomal enzymes are now recognized as the primary cause, and a major factor in our understanding of this group has been the discovery that the entire group of lysosomal enzymes is expressed in generalized cells such as the cultured skin fibroblast, the white blood cell and the cultured amniotic cell. This has not only made diagnosis feasible without the need for taking samples of cerebral tissue, but has also allowed techniques of prenatal diagnosis and carrier detection to be evolved and to play a major role in prevention of these disorders.

THERAPY

Although the possibility for treatment of most genetic forms of mental retardation remains slim, it is becoming feasible in a growing number, making their accurate and early diagnosis even more important. Table 10.5 summarizes some of the approaches used, which range from the well-established to some that are still entirely experimental.

Where a specific product is missing, the logical aim is to attempt to replace it, a task which is frequently difficult, even when the product is known and available. One of the simplest and most satisfactory examples of this approach is thyroxine therapy for congenital hypothyroidism; here the product is readily available, can be taken orally, and

Table 10.5 Approaches to therapy in genetic causes of mental retardation.

Approach	Example
Replacement of deficient product	Thyroxine in congenital hypothyroidism
Avoidance of harmful or excessive product	Low phenylalanine diet in phenylketonuria
Stimulation of enzyme activity by cofactor	Pyridoxine in homocystinuria
Direct administration of deficient enzyme	Experimental at present (lysosomal disorders)
Replacement of enzyme-producing cells	Marrow or thymic transplant in immune deficiencies; marrow transplant in mucopolysaccharidoses (still under evaluation)
Correction or replacement of defective genetic material	Various experimental 'genetic engineering' approaches

has a therapeutic effect on cerebral development related directly to the age at which treatment is started.

Where the clinical features of the disease are due to accumulation of an intermediate product, dietary treatment may allow this to be avoided. Phenylketonuria again provides an excellent example, with phenylalanine restriction allowing near-normal blood phenylalanine levels and brain development. The use of a low-protein diet in organic acid disorders such as methylmalonic aciduria is a similar, though less successful example, as is the avoidance of milk products in galactosaemia.

In those disorders with a defined enzymatic basis it may be possible to increase enzyme activity by the use of suitable cofactors. The use of vitamin B_6 (pyridoxine) and vitamin B_{12} in the responsive forms of homocystinuria and methylmalonic aciduria respectively provide examples of this approach. It is important to realize in this respect that a small amount of extra enzyme activity may produce a dramatic clinical effect, and that the aim need not be to restore a normal level of enzyme activity. Direct replacement of deficient enzymes has so far been much less satisfactory owing to rapid breakdown and failure to reach the main site of action, even when administered by injection and when encapsulated in various particulate forms. This approach has been used particularly for the lysosomal enzyme deficiencies, particularly the lipidoses and mucopolysaccharidoses, in which it is hoped that the enzyme will reach the appropriate site by direct ingestion by the lysosomes. So far, however, the effects have not proved sufficiently satisfactory for this approach to be used in clinical practice.

A somewhat different approach to enzyme replacement has been the use of living tissue to provide enzymatic activity. Although the use of marrow and thymic transplants in certain immune deficiencies provides a precedent for this, the field of mental retardation is less encouraging. Trials are in progress to evaluate the use of bone marrow transplants in patients with mucopolysaccharidoses, but careful objective and long-term assessment of results will be essential before this can be regarded as therapy rather than experiment.

It is likely that even more fundamental approaches to therapy will be undertaken in the near future, with the possibility of replacement of the actual genetic material itself rather than the enzymic product. New techniques of cell hybridization and gene transfer, along with the development of recombinant DNA techniques (see below), are all making this a practical possibility in the not too distant future. This rapid development gives extra importance for the identification of specific genetic disorders within the residue of non-specific mental retardation.

RECOMBINANT DNA TECHNIQUES IN THE STUDY OF MENTAL RETARDATION

The past five years have seen the development of a number of techniques that allow direct analysis of genes, as opposed to indirect study through their products. The methods broadly involve (a) the breakdown of human DNA into short sequences by specific enzymes – *restriction enzymes*, (b) the incorporation of specific sequences into bacterial or viral DNA, which allows multiplication of the human DNA sequence – *gene cloning*, and (c) the use of radiolabelled human DNA sequences – *DNA probes* – to identify their counterparts in diagnostic samples from patients with genetic disorders.

It is now clear that the variety of changes seen at the enzyme level in inherited metabolic disorders is found to an even greater degree at the gene level, with some cases (a minority) due to actual deletion of all or part of the gene, while other cases result from lesser rearrangements or changes in specific DNA sequences.

At present we know most about those disorders, such as the thalassaemias, which are well understood at the protein level, but specific gene probes have been identified already for such disorders as phenylketonuria and Lesch–Nyhan syndrome; others are likely to follow rapidly.

The use of these techniques is not confined to those genetic disorders whose metabolic basis is well understood, since the same approach is being used to map the genes for individual disorders to specific chromosomes by exploiting a wealth of inherited variation at the DNA level. These *DNA sequence polymorphisms* can be used as markers to establish genetic linkage for a disease, even when nothing is known about its cause. Such markers have already been established for such major disorders as Duchenne and Becker muscular dystrophies and for Huntington's chorea; they offer the possibility of accurate carrier detection and also of prenatal diagnosis, since DNA changes can be detected from samples taken in the first trimester of pregnancy, using chorion biopsy (see below).

It is likely that further work in this area will uncover an entire series of new specific causes for mental retardation in the same way as did the introduction of cytogenetic techniques. An example of this possibility is seen in the discovery that deletion of DNA in the region of the alpha globin gene (previously not known to be associated with mental retardation in any way) may occur in some individuals whose mental retardation had been classified as 'non-specific' and of unknown cause. As more detailed study of other regions of DNA progresses, it is likely that comparable examples will be found and that yet more patients will prove to have a specific and identifiable cause for their problems.

PREVENTIVE MEASURES

There are now few genetic causes of mental retardation for which effective preventive measures do not exist, though the most appropriate strategy will vary between different disorders, as well as between different families with the same disorder. Where effective treatment exists, the emphasis is likely to be on early detection and therapy, while for those disorders with serious effect but no satisfactory treatment, early prenatal diagnosis and termination of an affected pregnancy is the usual course. In all cases, recognition of the possible risk *before conception*, with appropriate genetic counselling and associated investigations, is desirable.

In Figure 10.1 the main available preventive measures are summarized, seen against the time-scale of development. It is clear that measures designed to prevent conception of an affected individual, such as genetic counselling and carrier detection tests, will only be effective if undertaken before a pregnancy occurs; preferably, they will be done before any affected child is born into the family. Genetic counselling and the risks for the various patterns of Mendelian inheritance have been mentioned briefly earlier in this chapter; more

details are given in the bibliography. It is essential that other tests are considered in the light of this and of the overall estimate of risk that genetic counselling identifies.

Carrier detection is particularly valuable in those disorders showing X-linked recessive inheritance, such as the Hunter syndrome, Duchenne dystrophy and the Lesch–Nyhan syndrome. Unfortunately, this is also the group where results are most variable, owing to the variability of X chromosome inactivation in the carrier females, and in most X-linked disorders there is a proportion of carriers that are difficult, even impossible, to distinguish from normal unless tests can be carried out on tissue derived from single cells, such as hair bulbs, or by DNA techniques.

Carrier detection is of less general importance in autosomal recessive disorders except for the small number where the gene is at high frequency, for it is only here that the risks of a known carrier marrying another carrier become appreciable in the absence of consanguinity. Identification of carriers is feasible for a number of the lysosomal enzyme deficiencies, and an excellent example of its application is provided by the lipidosis Tay–Sachs disease, where population screening of Ashkenazi Jewish communities in America has allowed identification of those married couples where both members are carriers and thus at risk of having an affected child. The availability of prenatal diagnosis increases the efficacy of this approach.

Autosomal dominant disorders of late onset or variable severity provide another group in which carrier detection is of considerable importance. Asymptomatic individuals with myotonic dystrophy may require electromyography or slit-lamp examination for lens opacities, while skull X-ray or computerized tomography of the parents of a child with tuberous sclerosis may show the case to be a transmitted one rather than a new mutation.

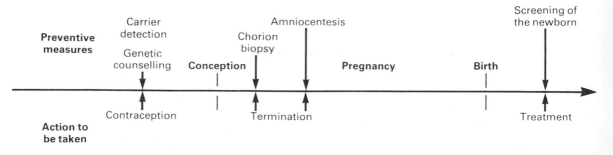

Fig. 10.1 Preventive measures in inherited disease.

Even when pre-conceptual measures have failed to prevent conception of a high-risk pregnancy, intrauterine diagnosis may make it possible to offer selective termination of an affected pregnancy. The technique of amniocentesis is the principal approach used at present, though the development of ultrasound and methods of fetal blood sampling has greatly extended the range of disorders for which prenatal diagnosis is possible. Although some disorders can be diagnosed from study of the amniotic fluid itself (for example, organic acidurias and some mucopolysaccharidoses), most intrauterine diagnoses are dependent on the use of cultured amniotic cells. Table 10.6 lists some of the genetic causes of

Table 10.6 Prenatal diagnosis of inherited metabolic disorders causing mental retardation (autosomal recessive inheritance unless indicated).

Disorder	Usual enzyme deficiency	Comments
Adrenoleukodystrophy	Long-chain fatty acid defect	
Argininosuccinic aciduria	Argininosuccinase	Argininosuccinic acid also raised in amniotic fluid
Citrullinaemia	Argininosuccinate synthetase	
Farber's disease	Ceramidase	
Fucosidosis	α-L-Fucidase	
Gaucher's disease	Glucocerebrosidase	Heterogeneous
Generalized gangliosidosis	β-Galactosidase	
Glutaric aciduria	Glutaryl (CoA dehydrogenase)	
Glycogenosis type II (Pompe's disease)	α-1, 4-Glucosidase	Heterogeneous
Homocystinuria	Cystathionine synthetase	Heterogeneous
Hyperammonaemia, X-linked	Ornithine carbamyl transferase	X-linked; variable expression in female. Detection by fetal liver biopsy
'I' cell disease (mucolipidosis II)	? Lysosomal membrane defect	Increase in multiple lysosomal enzymes
Krabbe's disease	β-Galactosidase	
Lesch−Nyhan syndrome	Hypoxanthine−guanine phosphoribosyl transferase	X-linked recessive. Heterogeneous
Mannosidase	α-Mannosidase	
Maple syrup urine disease	α-Ketoacid decarboxylase	
Menkes' disease	Defective copper metabolism	X-linked. Abnormal copper uptake
Metachromatic leukodystrophy	Arylsulphatase A	Heterogeneous
Methylmalonic aciduria	Methylmalonyl CoA mutase	Methylmalonic acid detectable in amniotic fluid. May be treatable in utero. Heterogeneous.
Mucopolysaccharidosis I (Hurler's syndrome)	α-L-Iduronidase	Mucopolysaccharidosis IS (Scheie's syndrome) has same enzyme deficient. Amniotic fluid mucopolysaccharidase levels useful in types I, II and III
Mucopolysaccharidosis II (Hunter's syndrome)	Iduronate sulphatase	X-linked; enzymatic diagnosis possible from amniotic fluid as well as cells
Mucopolysaccharidosis IIIA (Sanfilippo A syndrome)	Heparan sulphate sulphatase	
Mucopolysaccharidosis IIIB (Sanfilippo B syndrome)	α-N-Acetyl-hexosaminidase	Carrier detection feasible on serum
Niemann−Pick disease	Sphingomyelinase	Heterogeneous
Phenylketonuria (classic)	Phenylalanine hydroxylase	Treatable. DNA probe applicable to some families
Phenylketonuria (dihydropteridine reductase type)	As indicated	Severe and difficult to treat
Propionic acidaemia	Propionyl-CoA-carboxylase	Also directly detectable from amniotic fluid
Refsum's disease	Phytanic acid oxidase	Possible. Not actually confirmed
Sandhoff's disease	β-N-Acetyl hexosaminidase (A and B)	
Tay−Sachs disease	β-N-Acetyl hexosaminidase A	Carrier detection and high-risk population screening feasible
Wolman's disease	Acid lipase	

mental retardation for which prenatal diagnosis is feasible.

The possibility of prenatal diagnosis is not limited to those disorders for which a specific biochemical basis has been found. For chromosomal defects, discussed fully elsewhere, the karyotype of cultured amniotic cells allows intrauterine detection, while structural defects accompanied by open lesions, notably neural tube defects, can now be detected by the increased level of alphafetoprotein that occurs in the amniotic fluid as a consequence of leakage from fetal tissues. It is now also feasible to detect directly those disorders showing obvious limb abnormalities, such as the acrocephaly–syndactyly group, by means of a fine flexible amnioscope, though this procedure still carries a significant risk of inducing abortion.

A major development now coming into use is chorion biopsy sampling performed transcervically by a fine suction catheter during the first trimester (9–11 weeks) of pregnancy. These samples can be used to study DNA and chromosomes, as well as specific enzymes.

Fetal sexing is also possible. The reliability and pregnancy loss rate associated with this procedure is still being assessed, but the fact that the technique can only be performed prior to 12 weeks of pregnancy makes it imperative that all couples at high risk are aware of the need to seek advice *immediately* a pregnancy is recognized. It is unlikely that this approach will replace amniocentesis for routine chromosome studies in the near future.

FURTHER READING

Baraitser M (1983) *The Genetics of Neurological Disorders.* Oxford: Oxford University Press.

Harper PS (1984) *Practical Genetic Counselling*, 2nd edn. (1984) Bristol: John Wright.

McKusick VA (1983) *Mendelian Inheritance in Man*, 6th edn. Baltimore: Johns Hopkins University Press (An accurate, detailed and regularly updated compendium of information on genetic disorders and an invaluable source of references.)

Penrose LS (1972) *Biology of Mental Defect*, 4th edn. London: Sidgwick & Jackson. (Still an outstanding contribution to the subject, written from the viewpoint of the worker in mental handicap.)

Slater E & Cowie V (1975) *The Genetics of Mental Disorders.* Oxford: Oxford University Press.

Stanbury JB, Wyngaarden JB & Fredrickson DS (eds) (1982) *The Metabolic Basis of Inherited Disease*, 5th edn. New York: McGraw Hill. (The most comprehensive source of detailed information on inborn errors of metabolism.)

Weatherall DJ (1984) *New Genetics and Clinical Practice.* (A brief and readable account of the clinical implications of the new DNA techniques.)

Specific Genetic Disorders

MICHAEL CRAFT & PETER S. HARPER

METABOLIC DISORDERS

Argininosuccinic aciduria

Genetics. Autosomal recessive. Prenatal diagnosis feasible on amniotic fluid cells.

Clinical features. Scanty, thin, friable hair in all parts, microscopically showing many transverse fractures, arginine being an essential constituent of hair. Marked enlargement of the liver. There seem to be two types of this condition. In the first there is relatively normal development during the first year with rapid deterioration in the second and third; in the second type there is 'failure to thrive' following birth, with poor feeding, hepatomegaly, abdominal distension and CNS deterioration with epilepsy. Patients with the milder type may have few hair abnormalities and reach adult life. It may result from usage of alternative metabolic pathways or less susceptible target organs.

CNS features. Almost all surviving patients are markedly retarded, many have epilepsy and some have cerebellar ataxia. Most of those with the severe form die within a few days of birth, after milk ingestion.

Treatment and outcome. The missing enzyme acts in the Krebs–Henseleit cycle of ammonia detoxication; thus there is a marked rise in blood ammonia level after protein ingestion. On reduced protein intake there is improvement and life is prolonged to adulthood. Adequate arginine is needed to restore the hair to normal (Brenton et al., 1974).

Morbid anatomy. The brain shows widespread oedema and spongiform change (Crome and France, 1971).

Diagnosis. Argininosuccinic acid is raised in the red cells, plasma, CNS and urine.

BIBLIOGRAPHY

Allan JD, Cusworth DC, Dent CE & Wilson VK (1958) A disease, probably hereditary, characterized by severe mental deficiency and a constant gross abnormality of amino acid metabolism. *Lancet i:* 182–187.

Brenton DP, Cusworth DC, Hartley S, Lumley S & Kuzemko JA (1974) Argininosuccinic aciduria: clinical, metabolic, and dietary study. *Journal of Mental Deficiency Research 18:* 1–7.

Crome L & France NE (1971) The pathological findings in argininosuccinic aciduria. *Journal of Mental Deficiency Research 15:* 266–270.

Aspartylglucosaminuria

Genetics. Autosomal recessive. Heterozygous carriers can be assayed by using skin fibroblasts (Autio, 1974). Prenatal diagnosis is feasible.

Clinical features. Believed to be due to defective production and activity of *N*-aspartyl-6-glucosaminidase (AADGase). As in mannosidosis there is a gargoyle-like face, progressive psychomotor retardation, a 'failure to thrive' and diffuse skeletal change. There is an excess of glycoprotein residues in the urine, and intracellular storage of glycoprotein residues.

Further testing. Urine shows excess glycoprotein.

Treatment and outcome. The results of treatment are quite variable (see Autio et al., 1974).

BIBLIOGRAPHY

Autio S (1972) Aspartylglycosaminuria: analysis of 34 patients. *Journal of Mental Deficiency Research*. Monograph 1.
Autio S, Aula P & Manto U (1974) Cultured skin fibroblasts in disorders of glycoprotein catabolism and cell disease. *Developmental Medicine and Child Neurology 16:* 376–378.
Jenner FA & Pollitt RJ (1967) Large quantities of AADG in the urine of mentally retarded siblings. *Biochemical Journal 103:* 48.

Galactosaemia

Frequency. Estimated at one per 70 000 live births (Schwartz et al., 1961). One per 30 000 live births in the United Kingdom (Lee, 1972).

Genetics. Autosomal recessive. The classical form is due to lack of galactose-1-phosphate uridyl transferase with inability to break down galactose-1-phosphate. Prenatal diagnosis using amniotic fluid cells is feasible but of questionable value.

Clinical features. During the first few weeks of life there is 'failure to thrive' and development of cataracts. Fatal overwhelming septicaemia is frequent in the neonatal period. All untreated infants develop enlargement of the liver, and about one-third develop ascites and splenomegaly. There is jaundice in about half during the first few weeks of life, anaemia, and occasionally thrombosis from sepsis of the feet.

CNS features. Lethargy and hypotonia are common. Epilepsy is rare, and there is progressive mental retardation.

Morbid anatomy. In affected infants the liver cells show damage repair, which in older patients develops into a picture like cirrhosis.

Further investigations. There is increased serum and urine galactose, with the red blood cells showing increased galactose-1-phosphate, but specific assay for transferase activity should be done on all suspected cases. The serum glucose level may later drop, with signs of hypoglycaemia. As a result of later kidney damage, there may be proteinuria.

Treatment. This consists of removal of dietary galactose, as a result of which there should be improvement and recovery, although the cataracts may not totally regress and may need needling. If diagnosis is late there is a high death rate, and some continue with mental retardation. In a follow-up of 60 affected children Lee (1972) found a marked shift towards dullness; 16% had residual visual difficulty, mainly cataracts; 25% had speech impairment. In some areas all infants are screened by testing urine for galactose or by enzyme assay on cord blood.

Differential diagnosis. Rubella causes cataracts and enlargement of the spleen and liver, but the urine is clear and serum galactose normal. In galactokinase deficiency galactose also accumulates, but cataract is the only abnormality and mental retardation does not occur.

Of the other related genetic abnormalities the Duarte variety appears to be without symptoms or signs of illness, although the homozygotes have a moderate reduction in levels of transferase activity, and red blood cell galactose-1-phosphate is increased as in classical galactosaemia. The heterozygotes also show no clinical features of the illness.

BIBLIOGRAPHY

Donnell GN, Bergren WR & Cleland RS (1960) Galactosemia. *Pediatric Clinics of North America 7:* 315–332.
Lee DH (1972) Psychological aspects of galactosemia. *Journal of Mental Deficiency Research 16:* 173–191.
Schwartz V, Wells AR, Holzel A & Komrower GM (1961) A study of the genetics of galactosemia. *Annals of Human Genetics 25:* 179–188.
Segal S, Blair A & Roth H (1965) The metabolism of galactose by patients with congenital galactosemia. *American Journal of Medicine 38:* 62–70.

Gaucher's disease (cerebroside lipidosis)

Numbers. There are at least three types of Gaucher's disease – the abdominal, the cerebral and the infantile forms – whose separation depends on the main site of deposition of glucocerebroside in sensitive target organs; the adult abdominal form commonly shows hypersplenism without neurological features. In all, over 1000 patients have been reported (Fredrickson and Sloan, 1972).

Genetics. Autosomal recessive. It thus occurs in males and females with particularly high incidence in Jewish populations. The different clinical forms all have the same enzymatic defect; since each 'breeds true' within a family there are probably several alleles at the same locus. Prenatal diagnosis is feasible using cultured amniotic fluid cells.

Clinical features (see also Chapter 12). Infants with this disease usually develop hepatomegaly and splenomegaly in the first few months, with deterioration of mental function in the cerebral type. In this type there is hypertonicity, squint and deterioration of the cranial nerves with difficulty in swallowing.

Morbid anatomy. Typically the lymph nodes, liver, spleen and bone marrow develop the Gaucher cell, which is large and whose cytoplasm appears like crumpled paper owing to accumulation of lipid. The CNS shows progressive cellular fall-out.

Further investigations. There is a deficiency of the glucocerebroside-cleaving enzyme β-glucosidase, which can be demonstrated in white blood cells and skin fibroblasts. The serum acid phosphatase is high, and this provides a useful preliminary test.

Treatment. Severe cases die in infancy; milder types may survive to adult life. Splenectomy has been helpful; replacement of glucocerebrosidase has been attempted (Brady et al., 1974) with equivocal results.

Differential diagnosis. Niemann–Pick disease shows CNS deterioration with hepatosplenomegaly but the infant is hypotonic and has a macular cherry-red spot. The mucopolysaccharidoses show characteristic long-bone X-ray changes.

BIBLIOGRAPHY

Brady RO, Pentchev PG, Gal AE, Hibberd SR & Dekeban AS (1974) Replacement therapy with purified glucocerebro-sidase in Gaucher's disease. *New England Journal of Medicine 291:* 989–993.
Fredrickson DS & Sloan HR (1972) Glucosyl ceramide lipidoses: Gaucher's disease. In Stanbury JB, Wyngaarden JB & Fredrickson DS (eds) *The Metabolic Basis of Inherited Disease*, 3rd edn. New York: McGraw-Hill.
Sengers RCA, Lamers KJB, Bakkeren JAJ, Schretlen ED & Trijbels JMF (1975) Infantile Gaucher's disease: gluco-cerebroside deficiency in peripheral blood leucocytes and cultivated fibroblasts. *Neuropadiatrie 6:* 377–382.

Hartnup disease

Genetics. Autosomal recessive. The heterozygous state is not yet detectable. The enzyme defect causes inability to prevent loss of monoamino monocarboxylic acids across the renal tubules and intestinal mucosa. The result is a massive loss of all amino acids, resulting in pellagra.

Clinical features. There is a pellagra-type rash after exposure to sunlight, coincident attacks of cerebellar ataxia, and mental changes with variable retardation and emotional instability. The changes depend on the amount of protein consumed, and lead on to dementia in later life. Some 20% of children are said to show steady retardation.

Further investigation. The diagnosis is established by the pattern of urine amino acids, measured by paper or ion-exchange chromatography.

Treatment. Oral nicotinamide (50 to 200 mg per day) together with a high-protein diet is effective (Jepson, 1972).

BIBLIOGRAPHY

Baron DN, Dent CE, Harris H, Hart EW & Jepson JB (1956) Hereditary pellagra-like skin rash with temporary cerebellar ataxia, constant renal amino aciduria, and other bizarre biochemical features. *Lancet ii:* 421.
Jepson JB (1972) Hartnup disease. In Stanbury JB, Wyngaarden JB & Fredrickson DS (eds) *The Metabolic Basis of Inherited Disease*, 3rd edn. New York: McGraw-Hill.
Levy HL, Madigan PM & Shih VE (1972) Massachusetts Metabolic Disorders Screening Program. 1. Technics and results of urine screening. *Pediatrics 49(6):* 825–836.

Hepatolenticular degeneration (Wilson's disease)

History. Described by Kinnier Wilson in 1912 in a classic monograph, *Progressive Lenticular Degeneration*.

Genetics. Autosomal recessive trait, for deficiency of serum caeruloplasmin. The precise enzymatic defect remains unknown.

Clinical features. The disease is due to copper accumulation, mainly in the liver. When the level in the liver reaches values of 500–2000 mg/kg dry weight, after several years, the liver cells die and copper is released to the serum and deposited elsewhere, in particular in the basal ganglia and cornea, where the rusty brown ring is called the Kayser–Fleischer ring. The accumulation in the kidneys damages the proximal renal tubules.

The serum protein caeruloplasmin is deficient. It is normally responsible for binding about 95% of the copper in the serum. Five per cent is carried by albumin, and this fraction is increased in Wilson's disease. Copper is easily dissociated from albumin by the kidneys and therefore causes damage here. The result is an overall decrease in serum copper.

The disease is manifest between the ages of 6 and 20, and occasionally as late as over 40 years of age. The presentation is very variable, depending on the organ most damaged at first. Thus mental retardation, kidney, anaemia or liver failure are possible presentations. Usually the liver first gives rise to symptoms, with a clinical picture resembling chronic active hepatitis.

Treatment. Two types are effective. Potassium sulphate 20 mg three times daily prevents the absorption of copper by rendering it insoluble in the diet. The treatment is usually given for up to 12 months; no side-effects have been observed.

The copper-chelating agent D-penicillamine causes mobilization of copper from the tissues and therefore its excretion. 500 mg is given orally three times daily for the subject's lifetime. Sensitivity does occur. Treatment can be very effective and compatible with normal life (Cartwright, 1974).

Diagnosis. Kayser–Fleischer rings, cirrhosis of the liver and basal ganglia disease are a distinctive triad. For diagnosis the serum copper should be less than 80 mg per 100 ml, the serum caeruloplasmin less than 20 mg per 100 ml, and a urinary excretion of over 100 mg of copper in 24 hours is expected.

BIBLIOGRAPHY

Bearn AG (1972) Wilson's disease. In Stanbury JB, Wyngaarden JB & Fredrickson DS (eds) *The Metabolic Basis of Inherited Disease*, 3rd edn. New York: McGraw-Hill .

Cartwright G (1974) Hepatolenticular degeneration (Wilson's disease). In Wintrobe MW, Thorn GW, Adams RD, Braunwald E, Isselbacher KJ & Petersdorf RG (eds) *Harrison's Principles of Internal Medicine*, 7th edn. New York: McGraw-Hill.

Histidinaemia

Genetics. Autosomal recessive. Deficiency of histidine A-deaminase (histidase) results in increased histidine in blood and urine, increased excretion of the imidazolepyruvate group, and high blood and urine alanine. Histidase is detectable in epithelial cells but not in fibroblasts; prenatal diagnosis is not feasible.

Clinical features. There is a 'failure to thrive' without any particular system other than speech being affected. Since the original surveys took place in mental handicap hospitals, it is uncertain how far the association with speech defects is general or specific to histidinaemia. The results of mass screening of newborns suggest that the majority of affected individuals are entirely normal, and the need for treatment is not proven.

CNS features. Later surveys have shown that about a third of the affected individuals are said to be retarded (La Du, 1972). Epilepsy and cerebellar ataxia are reported for some 20% of reported cases.

Further investigation. Urine amino acid chromatography shows increased histidine and alanine content. Increased imidazolepyruvic acid will give a positive ferric chloride test (green or green-blue) to the urine. Urocanic acid is absent in urine and sweat; skin biopsy shows absent histidase activity.

Treatment. Reduction of protein intake in the diet has been recommended (La Du, 1972). Histidine is an amino acid essential for growth, so keeping to less than 6 mg/100 ml is difficult (Holmgren et al., 1974).

BIBLIOGRAPHY

Holmgren G, Hambraeus L & Le Chateau P (1974) Histidinemia and 'normohistidinemic histidinuria'. *Acta paediatrica (Stockholm)* 63: 220.
La Du BN (1972) Histidinemia. In Stanbury JB, Wyngaarden JB & Fredrickson DS (eds) *The Metabolic Basis of Inherited Disease*, 3rd edn. New York: McGraw-Hill.
Levy HL, Madigan PM & Shih VE (1972) Massachusetts Metabolic Disorders Screening Program. 1. Technics and results of urine screening. *Pediatrics* 49(6): 825–837.

Sabater J, Ferre M, Puliol M & Maya A (1976) Histidinuria: a renal and intestinal histidine transport deficiency found in two mentally retarded children. *Clinical Genetics 9:* 117–124.

Homocystinuria

Genetics. Autosomal recessive. Most of those affected have reduced or absent cystathionine synthetase, an enzyme in the pathway converting methionine to cystine which can be detected in cultured skin fibroblasts. Heterozygotes (parents) have a decreased activity of this enzyme, which is only shown up in the decreased clearance of plasma methionine following heavy loading. Pyridoxine can be effective in treatment, but since not all those affected respond to pyridoxine, the precise mechanism of the chemical derangement is unclear. A small number of patients have different enzymatic defects, and since prenatal diagnosis of the classical type is feasible it is important to establish an enzymatic diagnosis.

Clinical features. Only 50–60 % of patients develop the pronounced features of dislocated lens in the eye, malar flush, osteoporosis, infarcts and mental retardation. While infants are normal at birth, there is 'failure to thrive' some months later. The disease is slower in onset than maple syrup disease. The limbs are long and slender, the joints are stiff, the palate is narrow and the mouth and teeth are crowded. There is a marked thrombotic tendency.

Treatment and outcome. For the affected, pyridoxine (250–500 milligrams per day) is variably effective (Kang et al., 1970). A diet low in methionine (20–40 milligrams per kilogram body weight per day) supplemented by L-cystine has also been tried, and has produced improvement.

Differential diagnosis. Marfan's syndrome is similar, but has no malar flush, joint stiffness, retardation or positive urinary nitroprusside test for homocystine.

BIBLIOGRAPHY

Field CHB, Carson NAJ, Cusworth DC, Dent CE & Neill DW (1962) Homocystinuria: a new disorder of metabolism. Abstracts of the *International Congress of Pediatrics, Lisbon.* p. 274.
Gerritsen T, Vaughan JG & Waisman HA (1962) The identification of homocystine in the urine. *Biochemical and biophysical Research Communications 2:* 493–496.

Kang ES, Byers RK & Gerald PS (1970) Homocystinuria: response to pyridoxine. *Neurology (Minneapolis) 20:* 503–507.

Lesch–Nyhan syndrome (hyperuricaemia with choreo-athetosis)

Genetics. X-linked recessive. Prenatal diagnosis has been achieved (Demars et al., 1969). There is deficient activity of the enzyme hypoxanthine–guanine phosphoribosyl transferase (HGPRT). It is easiest to consider this as a rare sub-type of gout in which the target organs in the basal ganglia are unduly sensitive to hyperuricaemia, resulting in choreo-athetosis. Gout itself consists of hyperuricaemia due to hereditary endowment when it starts young and to environmental factors (dietary) when it starts later, or due to kidney and other organ failures; it acts mainly on joints, as sensitive target organs, and to a lesser extent the CNS (Wyngaarden and Kelly, 1976).

Clinical features. The face is normal, but in severe cases lip-biting in early childhood causes scarring and loss of tissue. There may be gouty tophi containing uric acid on the tips of ears. There may be gouty arthritis of the joints and the ends of fingers may be bitten.

CNS features. Most reported patients have been severely retarded but the less affected can show symptoms in adolescence or adult life, with torsion spasm, spastic paresis and developing athetosis, with involuntary movements of limbs and trunk. The deep reflexes are hyperactive and the plantars are extensor. There may be speech difficulties. There are two striking features of the disease: the compulsion to self-mutilation and the torsion spasms, particularly of neck muscles.

Further investigation. There is a deficiency of HGPRT in the brain, liver, red blood cells and amniotic cells, so prenatal diagnosis is possible. The urinary uric acid is raised, as is its ratio to creatine. The blood uric acid is also usually raised. Gouty tophi may be seen and there may be urinary stones containing uric acid. The syndrome seems the most severe of a range of rare genetically endowed deficiencies of the enzyme, which in adults may result in gout, with milder neurological abnormalities or even none at all.

Treatment. Allopurinol is effective in lowering blood uric acid by blocking its synthesis, but has not been proved to help the behavioural abnormalities. Addition of adenine to the diet may be useful (van der Zee et al., 1970).

Differential diagnosis. Other causes of chorea and involuntary movement do not have the biochemical abnormality or the clinical features of gout.

BIBLIOGRAPHY

Demars R, Santo G & Felix JS (1969) Lesch–Nyhan mutation. *Science 164:* 1303–1305.
Lesch M & Nyhan WL (1964) A familial disorder of uric acid metabolism and central nervous system function. *American Journal of Medicine 36:* 561–570.
Seegmiller JE (1976) Lesch-Nyhan syndrome and its variants. *Archives of Human Genetics 6:* 75–163.
van der Zee SPM, Lommen EJP, Trijbels JMF & Schretlen EDAM (1970) The influence of adenine on the clinical features and purine metabolism in the Lesch–Nyhan syndrome. *Acta Paediatrica (Stockholm) 59:* 259–264.
Wyngaarden JB & Kelly WN (1976) *Gout and Hyperuricaemia.* New York: Grune & Stratton.

Menkes' syndrome (kinky-hair disease, steel-hair syndrome)

Genetics. X-linked recessive, therefore occurring in males only. A homologous X-linked gene has been described in the mouse. Both in man and in mouse the disorder is due to a defect in copper metabolism. Prenatal diagnosis is likely to become feasible.

Clinical features. A high-arched palate and micrognathia are reported. The hair is thin, kinky and has a wiry feel to it like steel wool. All parts of the body have the same abnormality and the hair fades in colour during infancy, so that it may become quite white, stiff and lustreless. There is a 'failure to thrive' with epilepsy, myoclonus and development of spasticity, nystagmus and retardation. By the age of three weight starts to decrease and retardation is profound with little spontaneous movement. Death follows.

Morbid anatomy. The hair shows fractures and is variable in diameter. Microscopically it can be seen to be twisted around its long axis. There is atrophy of the brain.

Investigations. Biochemical studies (O'Brien and Sampson, 1966) show low brain docosahexaenoic acid on biopsy, but now low serum copper and caeruloplasmin are held to be diagnostic, with an inability to absorb copper from the intestine (Dekaban et al., 1976).

Treatment and outcome. Intravenous copper has been used, but the degree of success is unclear (Gordon, 1974; Garnica et al., 1977).

Diagnosis. Twisty curly hair is common in the population, but kinky hair has a particular look and feel, as well as specific associated abnormalities. Argininosuccinic aciduria has abnormal hair but also has the abnormal metabolite in the urine.

BIBLIOGRAPHY

Dekaban AS, Aamodt R, Rumble F, Johnston GS & O'Reilly S (1976) Kinky hair disease: study of copper metabolism with use of ^{67}Cu. *Archives of Neurology (Chicago) 32:* 672–675.
Garnica AD, Frias JL & Rennert OM (1977) Menkes kinky-hair syndrome, is it a treatable disorder? *Clinical Genetics 11:* 154–161.
Gordon N (1974) Menkes kinky hair (steely-hair) syndrome. *Developmental Medicine and Child Neurology 16:* 827.
Menkes J, Alter M, Steigleder GK, Weakley DR & Sung JH (1962) A sex-linked recessive disorder with retardation of growth, peculiar hair and focal cerebral and cerebellar degeneration. *Pediatrics 29:* 764–769.
O'Brien JS & Sampson EL (1966) Kinky hair disease. II. Biochemical studies. *Journal of Neuropathology and Experimental Neurology 25:* 523–530.

Muscular dystrophy – Duchenne type (progressive muscular weakness)

Frequency. 1 in 3500 live male births in most European populations, making it the commonest childhood muscular dystrophy.

Genetics. X-linked recessive and thus practically confined to males, though very rare instances of a closely similar disorder have been recorded in girls. Heterozygous female carriers may show minor degrees of muscle weakness. About one-third of cases are the result of new mutations. Detection of the majority of carrier females is feasible because there is slight elevation of serum creatine kinase (CK), but performance and interpretation of the test requires great caution and an experienced laboratory, as well as consideration of the full genetic data, if serious errors are to be avoided. Serum CK is greatly raised in affected males.

Clinical features. Affected children are normal at birth. Most present with motor delay or waddling gait at two to four years, with signs of proximal weakness at hip and shoulder girdles and pseudo-hypertrophy of calf muscles. Many children are mentally normal, but there is clear evidence of a downward shift of IQ overall (Dubowitz, 1965) and some are seriously mentally retarded, with mental retardation as the presenting feature. Progressive muscle weakness results in death, usually between 15 and 25 years of age. Confirmation of the diagnosis can be obtained by measurement of serum CK, electromyography and muscle biopsy (only worthwhile if facilities exist for expert preparation and interpretation). The late-onset X-linked (Becker) form of muscular dystrophy follows a more benign course and is more rarely associated with mental deterioration. Particular care must be taken to distinguish this and other dystrophies from the Duchenne type in view of the different prognosis and, in some cases, inheritance.

Treatment and prevention. No specific treatment exists, but families require much support. Accurate assessment of mental capacity is important in view of the eventually severe physical disability. All close female relatives should be carefully checked for carrier status. In pregnancies of carriers fetal sexing followed by termination of male pregnancies is feasible, but there is no means of prenatal diagnosis at present.

BIBLIOGRAPHY

Dubowitz V (1965) Intellectual impairment in muscular dystrophy. *Archives of Disease in Childhood 40:* 296–301.

Mucopolysaccharidoses

Clinical, genetic and biochemical classification allows recognition of at least seven varieties of mucopolysaccharidosis, in addition to allied disorders such as mucolipidoses. All are inherited as autosomal recessive disorders except for type II (Hunter syndrome), which is X-linked and confined to males. Each type results from a specific deficiency of one of the lysosomal enzymes involved in breakdown of mucopolysaccharides, though in some cases different enzyme defects cause an identical clinical picture (type IIIA and B), while in others different clinical syndromes (IH and IS) share the same enzyme defect. Type IS (Scheie) is associated with normal intelligence, the enzyme defect not affecting the brain.

Common features of those forms showing mental retardation are coarse facial features ('gargoyle-like'), characteristic bony X-ray changes, hepatosplenomegaly and evidence of mucopolysaccharide accumulation in tissues. Prenatal diagnosis is feasible using cultured amniotic cells and amniotic fluid mucopolysaccharide levels. Treatment has been attempted with bone marrow transplants, but remains experimental.

Hurler's syndrome (type IH)

Affected children are normal at birth, but show slowed development, hepatosplenomegaly, corneal clouding, progressive facial coarsening, dwarfing, joint contractures and frequent deafness. Increased urinary mucopolysaccharides and X-ray changes in the spine (beaking of lumbar vertebrae), skull (J-shaped sella) and hands (short carpal bones) will confirm the diagnosis of a mucopolysaccharidosis. Presence of corneal clouding will exclude type II, and mental retardation will exclude type VI. In type III physical abnormalities are generally less marked.

A progressive downhill course is usual, with severe mental impairment and death by the age of ten.

Hunter's syndrome (type II)

Physical abnormalities appear later than in Hurler's syndrome; there is a more benign course and moderate to minimal mental retardation. Absence of corneal clouding distinguishes this type from types I and VI. Survival into adult life is common, but cardiac involvement is commonly fatal. The X-linked inheritance puts asymptomatic female relatives at risk of having affected sons. Carrier detection is feasible using enzyme levels in hair bulbs and serum. Pregnancies at risk can be monitored by fetal sexing and specific biochemical studies.

Sanfilippo syndrome (types IIIA and IIIB)

Types A and B are clinically indistinguishable phenotypes, with a different enzyme subtype responsible for each. Physical abnormalities are slight in comparison with other forms, but progressive mental deterioration commonly requires hospitalisation. Hepatosplenomegaly, mildly suspicious facial and X-ray changes and increased mucopolysaccharide excretion suggest the diagnosis. Corneal clouding is absent.

Phenylketonuria (PKU)

History. In 1934 Fölling first described defective patients who excreted phenylpyruvic acid, whilst in 1953 Jervis showed that this was due to an inability to metabolize phenylalanine.

Frequency. This is commonly around 1 in 14 000 births, but in the United Kingdom varies from 1 in 5000 (Northern Ireland) to less than 1 in 20 000 (South-East England). It is particularly common in some gypsy groups.

Genetics. Autosomal recessive. Heterozygotes are clinically normal, but can be detected by phenylalanine loading tests. The reasons for the high gene frequency are uncertain; evidence as to reproductive advantage of heterozygotes is conflicting. Most classical cases result from deficiency of the liver enzyme phenylalanine hydroxylase, which is responsible for conversion of phenylalanine to tyrosine. Partial or transient deficiency of this enzyme may produce hyperphenylalaninaemic states detected by screening but without clinical effects. Rare cases result from deficiency of related enzymes (for example, phenylalanine transaminase or dihydropteridine reductase). Heterozygous carriers can usually be identified by being given a high-phenylalanine protein diet, which causes a temporary raised plasma phenylalanine (Westwood and Raine, 1975). A specific gene probe now exists for the enzyme, and this may be useful in heterozygote detection and possibly prenatal diagnosis.

Clinical features. Patients, especially those who have been treated, are often normal. Half the untreated become microcephalic. A light colour of the skin and iris develops. Eczema occurs in about a third of those untreated. The patient's hair is lighter than that of other members of the patient's family.

CNS features. Untreated individuals rarely develop beyond an IQ of 20. They may learn to walk but only a quarter are able to talk. Epilepsy is common.

Diagnosis. All infants in Britain and in many other countries are screened in the postnatal period, using a microbiological (Guthrie) or biochemical phenylalanine estimation on capillary blood. Before starting treatment, confirmation of the diagnosis is required by finding a blood phenylalanine level greater than 20 mg/dl, and the presence of phenylpyruvic acid and its metabolites in the urine. In symptomatic children suspected of being affected a positive ferric chloride or Phenistix test, followed by urine chromatography, are useful preliminary tests. In tyrosinaemia, a raised phenylalanine level may occur in the urine but is accompanied by much increased tyrosine. The diet has to be controlled with much care for it is easy to cause neurological damage with variation in diet even up to seven to ten years old. Despite this, a minimum of phenylalanine is essential for the diet, making proper control difficult. Too little phenylalanine leads to weight loss, eczema, feeding difficulties and poor development; too much leads to mental retardation, microcephaly and growth retardation. With successful treatment affected individuals are now beginning to reproduce. While the risk of phenylketonuria in the offspring is small, affected females may have brain-damaged children as a result of transplacental passage of phenylalanine, and will require strict dietary control in pregnancy. Similar cases have resulted from reproduction by the rare untreated women who are only mildy retarded.

Treatment. A synthetic phenylalanine diet with sufficient added phenylalanine to supply nutritional requirements allows normal or near normal physical and mental development, if started before the age of two months and controlled well by regular blood phenylalanine measurement. Although dietary control in later childhood need not be so strict there is no general agreement as to when it should be stopped.

BIBLIOGRAPHY

Brown ES & Warner R (1976) Mental development of phenylketonuric children on or off diet after age of six. *Psychological Medicine 6:* 287–296.
Knox WE (1972) Phenylketonuria. In Stanbury JB, Wyngaarden JB & Fredrickson DS (eds) *The Metabolic Basis of Inherited Disease*, 3rd edn. New York: McGraw-Hill.
Westwood A & Raine DN (1975) Heterozygote detection in phenylketonuria. *Journal of Medical Genetics 12:* 327–333.
Woolf LI, McBean MS, Woolf FM & Cahalane SF (1975) Phenylketonuria as a balanced polymorphism: the nature of the heterozygote advantage. *Annals of Human Genetics 38(4):* 461–469.

Xeroderma pigmentosum

Genetics. Autosomal recessive. Prenatal diagnosis is possible (Regan et al., 1971) using thymidine incorporation into ultraviolet-exposed amniotic cells. Recognition of the failure of DNA repair following damage by ultraviolet light has led to identification of several distinct types, and further heterogeneity is likely to be shown in the future.

Clinical features. What appear to be freckles occur on exposure to light in infancy, and over the years become more pronounced with more sun. They fuse and extend over several centimetres in length and width. The centres atrophy, become white and develop pedunculated growths. In adult life they become cancerous and bleed. Eyes become photophobic and shed excessive tears and the eyelid may atrophy. There may be corneal ulceration. Genitals may be underdeveloped.

CNS features. In one study half were severely handicapped, others were microcephalic, spastic and had ataxia (El-Hefnawi et al., 1967).

Morbid anatomy. The skin is grossly atrophic.

Further investigation. The group of endonuclease enzymes, essential for repair of skin and replication of DNA, are deficient. Following exposure to ultraviolet light or intradermal injection of tritiated thymidine there is a lack of DNA synthesis in a skin biopsy.

Treatment and outcome. Exposure to sunlight is deleterious and thus to be avoided. Ultraviolet barrier creams should be used. Cancers should be excised where feasible.

Differential diagnosis. Xeroderma pigmentosum needs to be distinguished from the basal cell multiple naevus syndrome, which occurs in people of normal intelligence and does not cause such extensive areas of atrophy of the skin. Xeroderma pigmentosum is the first of a now rapidly growing group of genetic disorders of DNA repair, and it is of interest that mental retardation is a common feature of many of these disorders (for example Fanconi's anaemia, ataxia telangiectasia and Cockayne dwarfism).

BIBLIOGRAPHY

El-Hefnawi H, Gawad MSA & Rasheed A (1967) Neuropsychiatric manifestations in xeroderma pigmentosum. *Gazette of the Egyptian Society of Dermatology and Venereology 2:* 6–22.
Epstein WI, Fukuyama K & Epstein JH (1969) Early defects of ultraviolet light on DNA synthesis in human skin in vitro. *Archives of Dermatology 100:* 84–89.
Holton JB & Ireland JT (eds) (1975) *Inborn Errors of Skin, Hair and Connective Tissue.* Lancaster: Medical and Technical Publishing. (Review of skin anomalies.)
Regan JD, Setlow RB, Kaback NM, Howell RR, Klein E & Burgess G (1971) Xeroderma pigmentosum: a rapid sensitive method for prenatal diagnosis. *Science 174:* 147–150.

DYSMORPHIC SYNDROMES

Cornelia de Lange's syndrome

History. This was described by Cornelia de Lange in 1933. It has been reported from most countries.

Frequency. One in 40 000 (Berg et al., 1970).

Genetics. Most cases are sporadic, but affected siblings have been reported. The empiric recurrence rate is not over 5 %. Early reports of a chromosomal abnormality have not been confirmed.

Clinical features. Microcephaly and excess facial hair may be noted at birth, together with a downward and outward slanting of eyes and mouth. There may be eye anomalies such as ptosis, nystagmus and microphthalmia; the ears are often small. The palate is often narrow with irregular teeth. The genitals are underdeveloped in both males and females.

Characteristically the limbs are highly abnormal with small hands and feet, inability to extend each limb fully, and gross anomalies of hands or feet consisting of absent digits or any variety of syndactyly and clinodactyly.

Birth weight is usually low and height is below the third percentile.

CNS features. All patients are reported retarded, often severely so. Some have epilepsy; others are spastic. The deep tendon reflexes are usually excessive.

Morbid anatomy. Congenital heart defects are common, as are abnormalities of the brain of very varied extent.

Further investigations. The limb X-rays may be highly abnormal, with various defects of bone.

Treatment and outcome. This depends on the degree of abnormality. If there are gross defects of the mouth and palate, aspiration pneumonia is common.

Differential diagnosis. Other causes of microcephaly and dwarfism and the Rubinstein–Taybi syndrome (see later), must be considered.

BIBLIOGRAPHY

Beck B (1976) Epidemiology of Cornelia de Lange's syndrome. *Acta Paediatrica (Stockholm) 65:* 631–638.
Berg JM, McCreary BD, Ridler MAC & Smith GF (1970) *The de Lange Syndrome,* p. 127. Oxford: Pergamon.
McArthur RG & Edwards JH (1967) De Lange syndrome: report of 20 cases. *Canadian Medical Association Journal 96:* 1185–1198.

Craniosynostosis syndromes (Apert's, Chotzen's, Pfeiffer's and Carpenter's)

History. In 1901 Carpenter first reported two sisters with acrocephaly (tower skull), but Apert described the most common variant in 1906. A number of other syndromes with acrocephaly and syndactyly have since been reported by different authors; most of these disorders appear to be constant within families and to represent distinct genetic syndromes. Acrocephaly may occur as an isolated abnormality, or with fusion of digits (acrocephalosyndactyly), or with extra digits in addition to fusion (acrocephalopolysyndactyly).

Genetics. Most types of acrocephalosyndactyly are autosomal dominant, and occur equally among men and women. With Apert's syndrome (type I) there is often severe mental handicap, and therefore lack of reproduction, so it is assumed that many cases are fresh mutants. Increased paternal age in isolated cases has been documented. With the milder types there have been a number of instances of passage from parent to child along classical dominant Mendelian lines. Carpenter's syndrome is likely to be autosomal recessive as it has been reported in siblings born to healthy parents.

It is important in advising parents to recognize that mental retardation is only usual in the Apert and Carpenter forms, and even in Apert's syndrome is often absent. Corrective surgery is important for cosmetic reasons but it is doubtful whether it is required for or helps brain growth.

Classification

For full details of the classification of this group of diseases see the reviews of Temtamy and McKusick (1969) and McKusick (1982). The main forms to be considered are as follows:

Group A: Acrocephalosyndactyly
Apert's syndrome (type I): a milder form (type II) has been distinguished, but it may be part of the same disorder.
Chotzen's syndrome (type III): here both syndactyly and the cranial abnormality are partial.
Pfeiffer's syndrome (type VI): the digital abnormalities, particularly of the thumb, are specific.

Group B: Acrocephaly with polysyndactyly (Carpenter's syndrome).

Group C: Craniosynostosis without limb abnormalities.

Acrocephalosyndactyly type I (Apert's syndrome)

Clinical features. In 1906 Apert described the high wide forehead and flattened occiput with the apex at the anterior fontanelle which is characteristic of acrocephaly. The mid-face bones are poorly developed, causing apparent prominence of the nose, chin and eyes, although these are really normal in size. The face is often assymetrical and the eyes are wide apart and protuberant and have a downward slant. Apert's syndrome is the most severe and most common type of craniosynostosis, many hundreds of cases being reported.

The palate is usually high and may be cleft; the teeth are often irregular. In type I all digits in the hand and foot are fused by skin, and sometimes the bone, cartilage and nails are also fused.

CNS features. Because of common premature closure of cranial sutures there may be an increase in intracranial pressure, with dilated ventricles and atrophy of brain tissue. Craniectomy has been used to relieve pressure, but the relationship between surgery and subsequent mental outcome remains uncertain.

Acrocephalosyndactyly type III (Chotzen's syndrome)

Clinical features. This has milder features of acrocephaly and only soft-tissue syndactyly. The forehead is wide and flat, the eyes are far apart and there is a pronounced nose and chin, as in type I. Ptosis is common and the teeth are poorly developed.

Syndactyly of fingers extends only to the soft tissues.

CNS features. Intelligence is usually normal. In some families the inheritance from parent to child makes clear the autosomal dominant inheritance.

Acrocephalosyndactyly type VI (Pfeiffer's syndrome)

Clinical features. In Pfeiffer's syndrome the high skull of acrocephaly is present, together with wide eyes which protrude and a prominent chin. As in the other types of acrocephalosyndactyly the teeth are poorly developed and there is a high palate. The main features are spade-shaped thumbs and great toes; the thumbs and great toes also have marked medial deviation. Syndactyly is least common, affecting soft tissues only. Occasionally there is decreased movement of elbows.

*Acrocephaly with polysyndactyly
(Carpenter's syndrome)*

Clinical features. Carpenter's syndrome has a high skull with early widespread cranial synostoses; there is relative microcephaly and diminution of intelligence. The face is flat but there is underdevelopment of the chin in this variety. There may be epicanthic folds and corneal opacities. All reported examples have hypogenitalism, polydactyly of feet, and soft tissue syndactyly, often of the third and fourth fingers of the hand.

BIBLIOGRAPHY

Blank CE (1960) Apert's syndrome (a type of acrocephalo-syndactyly): observations on a British series of 39 cases. *Annals of Human Genetics 24:* 151–164.
McKusick VA (1982) *Mendelian Inheritance in Man.* Baltimore: Johns Hopkins University Press.
Temtamy S & McKusick VA (1969) Synopsis of hand malformations with particular emphasis on genetic factors. In Berzoma D (ed) *Clinical Delineation of Birth Defects, Vol. 3.* New York: National Foundation.

Dwarfism

Three major classes can be recognized among the numerous causes of dwarfism:

1 Primary dysplasias of bone, generally associated with disproportionate dwarfism. In most such dysplasias intelligence is normal.
2 Endocrine disorders, in particular deficiency of growth hormone and hypothyroidism.
3 Low-birth-weight dwarfism, in which a primary failure of somatic growth is part of a variety of syndromes, some chromosomal, some genetic (such as Cornelia de Lange's syndrome), and others environmental or nutritional and poorly understood. Mental retardation is a frequent accompaniment of many of these conditions.

Hallermann–Streiff syndrome (oculomandibulodyscephaly)

Genetics. The genetics are uncertain, but affected siblings have been described. Siblings and monozygotic twins have been affected occasionally but most cases are isolated.

Clinical features. The cranial sutures and both fontanelles remain open, in one case for 20 years (Falls and Schull, 1960). As a result the forehead and sides of the skull appear prominent, although the circumference is almost average, all enlargement taking place upwards. The facial bones appear hypoplastic and the nose is small and beaked. The mouth and chin are hypoplastic and receding; the ears are low set. Hair is thin and sparse. The eyes are often small, with cataracts in 90% of cases. Nystagmus and squint are common. The mouth is small and the teeth appear early; often some are absent. The temperomandibular joints may be stiff. The skin over the face may be thin, with many visible blood vessels.

The testes and penis are small, and occasionally the testes are absent.

CNS features. There is no excess CSF pressure, and only a third or possibly less, are retarded (Suzuki et al., 1970).

Treatment. There is no specific treatment.

Further tests. X-rays show wide sutures and hypoplastic face and mandible.

Differential diagnosis. This syndrome is to be distinguished from Cockayne's dwarfism, with light-sensitive skin, from Treacher Collins syndrome, in which ear anomalies are more extreme, and from craniocleidodysostosis, in which mental deficit is uncommon.

BIBLIOGRAPHY

Falls HF & Schull WJ (1960) Hallermann–Streiff syndrome. *Archives of Ophthalmology (Chicago) 63:* 409–420.
Suzuki Y, Fuju T & Fukuyama Y (1970) Hallermann–Streiff syndrome. *Developmental Medicine and Child Neurology 12:* 496–506.

Incontinentia pigmenti (Bloch–Sulzberger syndrome)

Genetics. Almost all cases are females, so it is probably an X-linked dominant that is lethal in the male.

Clinical features. The infant is normal at birth, but in the first few months develops pruritic bullae which develop into pustules. These are variable in extent, eventually being replaced by fibrotic and hyperkeratotic areas, which are the second stage of the abnormality. Once the crusts have gone, the third stage – dermal fibrosis – occurs. All three stages take a variable time, up to several years

There is a degree of fading, with atrophic areas as the result in adolescence. The teeth are irregular, the nails are poorly developed, and microcephaly may occur, with variable eye abnormalities affecting up to a third of patients. These vary from corneal opacities, cataracts and squints to masses in the posterior chamber.

CNS features. In one review one-third had retardation, microcephaly, spastic paresis and epilepsy.

Morbid anatomy. The bullae contain eosinophilic extravasations and the skin has increased histamine content. Hyperkeratosis distinguishes the second stage, while the epidermis is atrophied in the third.

Further investigation. Eosinophilia, affecting up to 50% of white blood cells, is the cardinal feature.

Treatment and outcome. Supportive measures are indicated, and a favourable outcome is probable. By adolescence bullae are few, and it is the atrophic skin which needs life-long care.

BIBLIOGRAPHY

Asboe-Hansen G (1968) Incontinentia pigmenti: bullous keratogenous and pigmentary dermatitis with blood eosinophilia in newborn girls. *Cutis 4:* 1341–1344.
Carney RG & Carney EG (1970) Incontinentia pigmenti. *Archives of Dermatology 102:* 157–162.

Laurence–Moon–Biedl–Bardet syndrome

Genetics. Autosomal recessive. Both sexes are affected.

Clinical features. The most common features are retinal degeneration with macular involvement, optic atrophy, cataracts, hypogonadism and digit abnormalities. Polydactyly of feet or hands is common and may include each limb. Obesity is usual and present mainly on the trunk.

CNS effects. Most patients are mentally retarded, usually of mild degree.

Further investigation. Urinary gonadotropins are diminished.

Treatment and outcome. This syndrome is compatible with average length of life. No specific treatment is indicated.

Differential diagnosis. In the Alstrom syndrome retinitis pigmentosa, obesity and diabetes are associated with nerve deafness. Some of the skeletal features are also found in Carpenter's syndrome, but this lacks retinal dystrophy, and the facial features are acrocephalic.

BIBLIOGRAPHY

Bell J (1958) The Laurence–Moon syndrome. In *The Treasury of Human Inheritance, Vol. 5,* Part 3, pp. 51–69. Cambridge: Cambridge University Press.
Koepp P (1975) Laurence–Moon–Biedl syndrome associated with diabetes insipidus neurohormonalis. *European Journal of Paediatrics 121:* 59–62.
Moini AR, Emamy H & Asadian A (1975) The Laurence–Moon–Biedl syndrome. *Clinical Pediatrics 14(9):* 812–815.

Mandibulofacial dystosis (Treacher Collins syndrome)

Genetics. Autosomal dominant. The expression of the gene varies greatly within a family, so a mildly affected parent may have a severely affected child.

Clinical features. The eyes slant downwards and outwards and there is underdevelopment of the malar and zygoma areas so that the child has a pinched-in look in the centre of its face. The eyes may have colobomas, and the normal nose and mouth appear large. About half of affected patients have underdeveloped ears, which may be entirely absent, leaving a simple hole for the external auditory meatus. The teeth are irregular and crowded, with a cleft lip course in some patients.

CNS features. Most are of average intelligence but a substantial number are retarded. The external ear anomalies may be associated with inner ear anomalies causing deafness.

Further investigation. Skull X-rays show underdevelopment of the central skull bones and the maxilla, zygoma, mandible and middle ear bones.

Treatment and outcome. Any hearing loss should be remedied; cosmetic surgery has been used with effect.

Differential diagnosis. The Goldenhar syndrome shows occasional association with mental retardation, but has specific physical abnormalities, including conjunctival dermoid tumours. A variety of genetic syndromes cause abnormalities of the ears and eyes which must be distinguished from this syndrome.

BIBLIOGRAPHY

Rogers BO (1964). Berry–Treacher Collins syndrome: a review of 200 cases. *British Journal of Plastic Surgery (17):* 109–137.

Noonan's syndrome (Turner-like syndrome)

History. Described by Noonan and Ehmke (1963). The disorder shares some features with Turner's syndrome, occurring in both males and females as mental retardation, skeletal abnormalities, webbing of neck, short stature and ptosis, without chromosomal abnormality.

Genetics. Although some families with an autosomal dominant inheritance have been described, abnormalities among relatives may be mild or minimal, and many cases are isolated. No visible chromosome abnormality has been found even with modern banding techniques.

Clinical features. Hypertelorism, ptosis and slanted eyes are common. Some have a webbed neck, others a deformity of the lower sternum. The murmur and right ventricular hypertrophy of pulmonary stenosis may be found. Genital underdevelopment with cryptorchidism is common in males. There may be scoliosis and kyphosis. Females may also be underdeveloped sexually, with delayed puberty.

CNS features. Most patients have been reported as retarded.

Morbid anatomy. A variety of congenital cardiac abnormalities have been reported, the most common being pulmonary stenosis.

Investigations. Chromosome studies will exclude Turner (XO) syndrome. No biochemical abnormalities have been found.

Treatment and outcome. The syndrome is compatible with good life expectation.

Differential diagnosis. Turner's syndrome is differentiated by the chromosomal typing and only occurs in females; patients with Turner's syndrome are usually mentally normal and have gross sexual immaturity.

BIBLIOGRAPHY

Noonan JA & Ehmke DA (1963) Associated noncardiac malformations in children with congenital heart disease. *Journal of Pediatrics 63:* 468–470.

Orofaciodigital syndrome

Genetics. Patients are almost always females, so it is probably a dominant X-linked trait that is lethal for males, or possibly a sex-limited autosomal dominant.

Clinical features. Characteristically there is a midline cleft of the upper lip with large nasal bridge and medial canthi displaced laterally. The forehead is prominent and the mid-face appears flattened. The mouth is highly abnormal, with lateral incisors often absent, the tip of the tongue split into two or three parts, a pronounced frenulum, a cleft palate and split soft palate with bands and clefts to the side of the mouth. The fingers and toes may show syndactyly, polydactyly or clinodactyly.

CNS features. Mild subnormality affects up to one-half of the series reported (Gorlin and Psaume, 1962).

Morbid anatomy. The tongue may show haematomas.

Further investigation. The skull X-ray may show a poorly developed mandible. There may be irregularities of the bones of the hands and feet.

Differential diagnosis. This syndrome is distinctive, although the Mohr syndrome has a bifid nasal tip, bifid great toe and hearing loss; however, it occurs in males as well as females.

BIBLIOGRAPHY

Dodge JA & Kemohan DC (1967) Oral–facial–digital syndrome. *Archives of Disease in Childhood 42:* 214–219.
Gorlin RJ & Psaume J (1962) Orodigitofacial dystosis – a new syndrome. A study of 22 cases. *Journal of Pediatrics 61:* 520–530.
Papillon-Leage & Psaume J (1954) Une malformation héréditaire de la muqueuse buccale, brides et freins anormaux: généralités. *Revue de Stomatologie et Chirurgie Maxillofaciale 55:* 209–227.

Prader–Willi syndrome

History. Described by Prader, Labhart and Willi in 1956.

Genetics. Most cases are sporadic, but affected sibs have been recorded. Specific abnormalities in chromosome 15 have been recognized in a proportion of cases.

Clinical features. Excessive fat in the head and face, open mouth, thick saliva and extreme dental caries are reported. Males have a small penis and undescended testes. Females have small external genitalia and amenorrhoea. Patients are grossly obese; the hands and feet appear small, below lines of fat, and their skin is thick. Height is slightly below average in childhood; overeating leads to overweight in adult life.

CNS features. Muscular hypotonia, delayed milestones, poor speech, broad walking and amiable disposition are reported. Most are moderately retarded.

Morbid anatomy. There have been few autopsies and the real abnormality is testicular atrophy.

Further investigation. Some have mild diabetes, which responds to insulin and tolbutamide (Sareen et al., 1975). Chromosomes should be studied carefully.

Treatment. This consists of antidiabetic agents for the diabetes, and diet for the obesity. Lifespan is good, but limited by obesity.

Differential diagnosis. The Laurence–Moon–Beidl–Bardet syndrome shows similar features but has polydactyly and retinal degeneration.

BIBLIOGRAPHY

Dunn HG (1968) The Prader–Labhart–Willi syndrome: review of the literature and report of nine cases. *Acta paediatrica (Stockholm) Supplement 186:* 1–38.
Prader A, Labhart A & Willi H (1956) Ein Syndrom von Adipositas, Kleinwuchs, Kryptorchimus und Oligophrenie nach myatonieartigem Zustand im Neugeborenalter. *Schweizerische Medizinische Wochenschrift 86:* 1260–1261.
Sareen C, Ruvalcaba RHA & Kelley VC (1975) Some aspects of carbohydrate metabolism in Prader–Willi syndrome. *Journal of Mental Deficiency Research 19:* 113–120.

Rubinstein–Taybi syndrome (abnormal facies, broad thumbs and toes)

History. Rubinstein and Taybi (1963) described this as consisting of facial abnormality, broad thumbs and toes and retardation.

Genetics. Usually sporadic, with no evidence of a genetic basis.

Clinical features. The head has variable features, some patients being microcephalic and others having hypertelorism. The eyes are set normally but have a downward and outward slant; there may be a beaked nose, ptosis, cataracts and squints. The palate is often high and the teeth irregular. The broad thumbs and big toes are most characteristic, but other digits are often broad, with flat wide nails. The thumb or great toe may also be deviated radially. Some patients have excessive dark hair.

CNS features. All are said to be mentally retarded with epilepsy in one quarter. The tendon reflexes appear to be variable.

Morbid anatomy. Defects of the heart have been noted in several autopsies. The corpus callosum has been totally absent in some.

Further investigation. Skull X-rays may show delay in closure of the anterior fontanelle. The phalanges are broad. There is a characteristic dermatoglyphic pattern.

Treatment and outcome. The syndrome is compatible with adult life.

Differential diagnosis. Other causes of combined digital and facial abnormalities should be considered.

BIBLIOGRAPHY

Marshall RE & Smith DW (1970) Frontodigital syndrome: a dominantly inherited disorder with normal intelligence. *Journal of Pediatrics 77:* 129–133.
Naveh Y & Friedman A (1976) A case of Rubenstein–Tabyi. *Clinical Pediatrics 15:* 779–783.
Rubinstein JH & Taybi H (1963) Broad thumbs and toes and facial abnormalities. *American Journal of Diseases of Children 105:* 588–608.
Rubinstein JH (1969) *The Broad Thumb Syndrome–Progress Report 1968.* Birth Defects: Original Article Series 5, No. 2, pp. 25–41. Baltimore: Williams & Wilkins.

Seckel's syndrome (bird-headed dwarfism)

History. This was first described by Seckel (1960).

Genetics. Probably autosomal recessive (see Frijns and van den Berg, 1976).

Clinical features. Microcephaly is the main feature, with a pronounced nose but small chin and forehead. The palate is narrow and high, with hypoplastic molar area and absent teeth. The ears are small and simple. Numerous skeletal anomalies – curvature of the fingers, syndactyly of the toes and dislocations of various joints – have been reported. Hypogonadism with cryptorchidism is common. Height and weight are low at birth and remain so.

CNS features. Most patients are retarded, with intelligence up to IQ 80.

Morbid anatomy. The brain is underdeveloped.

Further investigation. The bones are immature for their chronological age, but no specific abnormalities have been identified.

Treatment and outcome. This condition is compatible with a normal lifespan.

Differential diagnosis. Other types of dwarfism and microcephaly must be considered.

BIBLIOGRAPHY

Frijns JP & van den Berg HEH (1976) Bird-headed dwarfism. *Acta Paediatrica Belgica 29:* 121–122.
Lambotte C, Dony G & Bonnet F (1976) Seckel syndrome: bird-headed dwarfism. *Acta Paediatrica Belgica 29:* 79–82.
Seckel HPG (1960) Bird-headed dwarfs. Basel: Karger; Springfield, Illinois: Charles C. Thomas.

Sturge–Weber syndrome

Genetics. Unusually sporadic.

Clinical features. The infant presents with capillary haemangioma (the port-wine stain or naevus) over the affected half of the face at birth, usually in one or more of the distributions of the fifth nerve. The colour lessens with adolescence, but the skin may become dry. The capillary haemangioma may also affect the anterior chamber of the eye, causing glaucoma. There may be associated angioma in the mouth and nose, with early eruptions of teeth on the affected side.

CNS features. Epilepsy may be frequent, of grand mal type, and associated with status epilepticus. The degree of retardation is very variable: in one series only half were retarded (Peterman et al., 1958).

Morbid anatomy. Haemangioma of the skin and the meninges is the main defect. The size of the abnormality on the meninges is associated with the degree of retardation and epilepsy. There may be calcification of the fibrous overgrowth with age. Atrophy of the affected area of the brain follows.

Further investigation. There is specific skull X-ray evidence of calcification on the same side as the naevus. The EEG may show decreased amplitude on the affected side, with epileptic spike and wave abnormality.

Treatment and outcome. Removal of intracranial angioma has benefited some with severe epilepsy. Effective anti-epileptic medication is possible.

Differential diagnosis. The extent of the facial naevus is not indicative of the size of the abnormality inside the skull. Intracranial calcification is also seen in other conditions such as intracranial prenatal infections and tuberous sclerosis.

BIBLIOGRAPHY

Alexander GL & Norman RM (1960) The Sturge–Weber syndrome. Bristol: John Wright.
Boltshauser E, Wilson J & Hoare RD (1976) Sturge–Weber syndrome with bilateral intracranial calcification. *Journal of Neurology, Neurosurgery and Psychiatry 39:* 429–435.
Peterman AF, Hayles AB, Docherty MB & Love JG (1958) Sturge–Weber disease: clinical study of 35 cases. *Journal of the American Medical Association 167:* 2169–2176.

CENTRAL NERVOUS SYSTEM DISORDERS

Batten's disease (juvenile amaurotic idiocy, ceroid-lipofuscinosis)

There is lipid accumulation in cells, but no sphingolipid accumulation. This is possibly a result of deficiency in the peroxidase enzyme group.

Genetics. Autosomal recessive.

Clinical features and CNS effects. Eye degeneration is among the first abnormalities: there is central vision impairment, narrowing of the retinal vessels and optic disc pallor. Next, peripheral vision deteriorates, and yellow pigmented areas appear in the retinal periphery. Later, there is optic atrophy, with thin arteries, and finally the abnormality covers the entire retina. Dementia advances quickly in younger patients and more slowly in older patients; and Sjögren's (1931) series emotional instability was the main feature of oncoming dementia. Later there is spasticity, extensor plantar responses, deep tendon jerks and cerebellar ataxia. Epilepsy has been noted.

Morbid anatomy. The grey matter is thin, with reduced cells and atrophy.

Further investigation. Lipid accumulation with vacuoles may be seen in white blood cells. Ganglion cells in the rectum may also show characteristic lipid accumulation.

Treatment. The age of death is variable, as the many investigators have noted, and vitamin E has been successfully used to delay deterioration (Nelson, 1974). Anti-epileptic, dopaminergic and other symptomatic drugs are needed.

Differential diagnosis. Tay–Sachs disease, GM_1 gangliosidosis, Niemann–Pick disease and other lipid accumulations must be considered. Diagnosis depends on the laboratory analysis but rectal biopsy of ganglion cells is preferable to brain biopsy (Nelson, 1974).

BIBLIOGRAPHY

Batten FE (1903) Cerebral degeneration with symmetrical changes in the maculae in two members of a family. *Transactions of the Ophthalmological Society of the United Kingdom 23:* 386–390.
Bielschowsky M (1913) Über spätinfantiler familiärer amaurotischer Idiotie mit Kleinhirnsymptomen. *Deutsche Zeitschrift für Nervenheilkunde 50:* 7–29.
Kufs H (1925) Über einer Spätform der amaurotischen Idiotie und ihren heredofamiliären Grundlagen. *Zeitschrift für die gesante Neurologie und Psychiatrie 95:* 169–188.
Malone MJ (1976) The cerebral lipidoses. *Pediatric Clinics of North America 23:* 303–326.
Motulsky AG (1976) Current concepts in genetics: the genetic hyperlipidemias. *New England Journal of Medicine 294:* 823–827.
Nelson JS (1974) Rectal biopsy in the diagnosis of paediatric neurological disorders. *Developmental Medicine and Child Neurology 16:* 830–831.
Sjögren T (1931) Die juvenile amaurotische Idiotie. *Hereditas 14:* 197–426.
Spielmeyer W (1905) Weitere Mitteilung über eine besondere Form von familiärer amaurotischer Idiotie. *Neurologisches Zentralblatt 24:* 1131–1132.
Swaiman KF & Wright FS (eds) (1975) *The Practice of Pediatric Neurology.* St. Louis: Mosby. (A good review.)
Vogt H (1909) Familiärer amaurotischer Idiotie, histologische und histopathologische Studien. *Archiv für Kinderheilkunde 51:* 1–35.

Congenital blindness

A variety of syndromes exist in which congenital blindness may be associated with mental retar-dation. Some of these are clearly environmental in origin (for example rubella syndrome), in some the aetiology is unknown, and others follow Mendelian inheritance. The visual defect may be the result of numerous ocular abnormalities, and some of the major syndromes considered to be genetic in origin are considered below.

Norrie's disease

Clinical features. There is little if any vision from birth. White vascularized masses behind clear lenses appear at birth or shortly afterwards and the globes become shrunken. Short fingers have been reported in two families. Deafness is fairly common, but it is mild and hearing aids are effective.

CNS features. In a series of 35, 20 were mentally retarded, 9 severely so (Warburg, 1968). Warburg showed that the retinal abnormalities and hearing loss were primary and other features, possibly including environmental retardation, emotional in-stability and violence, appeared to be secondary. The hearing loss was said to be due to cochlear degeneration.

Morbid anatomy. Rods and cones are absent.

Further testing. No biochemical abnormality has yet been found.

Treatment and outcome. Apart from environmental stimulation, hearing aids are the most effective help.

Differential diagnosis. Retrolental fibroplasia, retinoblastoma and glaucoma (Abbassi et al., 1968) must be considered.

BIBLIOGRAPHY

Anophthalmos
Joseph R (1975) A pedigree of anophthalmos. *British Journal of Ophthalmology 41:* 541–543.

Congenital glaucoma
Abbassi R, Lowe CU & Calcagno PL (1968) Oculo-cerebro-renal syndrome: a review. *American Journal of Diseases of Children 115:* 145–168.

Norrie's disease
Warburg M (1968) Norrie's disease. *Journal of Mental Deficiency Research 12:* 247–251.

Other conditions

Cyclopia (one central forehead eye), ethmocephaly (rudimentary eyes and a central nasal proboscis) and cebocephaly (as ethmocephaly but with the proboscis at the side) are found with multiple anomalies among stillbirths.

Microphthalmos

This heterogeneous condition is commonly associated with mental retardation; the causes are well reviewed by Warburg (1971).

BIBLIOGRAPHY

Warburg M (1971) The heterogeneity of microphthalmia in the mentally retarded. *Birth Defects. Original Articles Series 7(3):* 136–154.

Hallervorden–Spatz syndrome

Genetics. Autosomal recessive.

Clinical picture. There is an accumulation of pigmented material containing iron in the basal ganglia of the brain, producing brownish discoloration. The result is an abnormality in muscle tone and movement with choreo-athetosis in late childhood or adolescence. Finally there is cerebellar ataxia, myoclonus and an adult picture similar to Parkinsonism, with slurred speech and retardation.

Further investigation. Serum iron and transferrin are normal. Hepatolenticular degeneration produces Kayser–Fleischer corneal rings and deficient serum caeruloplasmin. There are no specific laboratory tests.

Treatment and outcome. Death is usually ten years after onset. Chelating agents have been ineffective. Levodopa is effective symptomatically (Richardson and Adams, 1974).

BIBLIOGRAPHY

Richardson EP & Adams RD (1974) Degenerative diseases of the nervous system. In Wintrobe MW, Thorn GW, Adams RD, Braunwald E, Isselbacher KJ & Petersdorf RG (eds) *Harrison's Principles of Internal Medicine*, 7th edn. New York: McGraw-Hill.

Hereditary ataxias

The hereditary ataxias are a heterogeneous and poorly delineated group of genetic disorders gener-

ally associated with normal intelligence. Ataxias in which mental retardation may occur include ataxia telangiectasia, Refsum's syndrome and Hallervorden–Spatz syndrome.

BIBLIOGRAPHY

Harding AE (1984) *Hereditary Ataxias and Related Disorders.* Edinburgh: Churchill Livingstone.

Other progressive ataxias

There are several syndromes in this group which appear in particular families and have not yet been fully evaluated.

Type 1 (Pelizaeus–Merzbacher)

Genetics. Autosomal recessive and X-linked recessive inheritance have been cited, but there is probably more than one interrelated syndrome.

Clinical features. Patients are normal at birth, but thereafter nystagmus, ataxia and spasticity appear. Extensor plantar responses, increased deep tendon reflexes, intention tremors and hearing loss develop over the infant months, with severe spasticity in legs and arms causing immobility by three to six years of age. Dementias, seizures and finally swallowing difficulty precede death. There are gross deformities.

Morbid anatomy. There is widespread loss of myelin.

Treatment and outcome. Most patients die by the age of six.

Type 2 (Marinesco–Sjögren)

Genetics. Autosomal recessive.

Clinical features. During infancy microcephaly, bilateral cataracts, dwarfism, mental retardation and cerebellar ataxia develop slowly; these features are fully developed by the age of five. Most learn to walk and may be able to speak and feed themselves, but some develop considerable spinal deformities needing surgery (Hensinger and McEwan, 1976).

The tendon reflexes are variable and muscle weakness may be a feature. Sensation is normal.

Morbid anatomy. Cerebellar atrophy is the main feature on post-mortem examination.

Treatment and outcome. Removal of cataracts is effective; other symptoms are treated with drugs.

BIBLIOGRAPHY

Type 1
Pelizaeus F (1885) Über eine eigenthümliche Form spastischer Lähmung mit Cerebralerscheinungen auf hereditärer Grundlage (multiple Sklerose). *Archiv für Psychiatrie und Nervenkrankheiten 16:* 698–710.

Type 2
Hensinger RN & McEwan D (1976) Spinal deformity associated with hereditable neurological conditions. *Journal of Bone and Joint Surgery 58A:* 13–24.
Marinesco G, Dragonesco S & Vasiliu D (1931) Nouvelle maladie familiale caractérisée par une cataracte congénitale et un arrêt du développement somato-neuro-psychique. *Encéphale 26:* 97–109.
Neuhauser G, Wiffler C & Optiz JM (1976) Familial spastic paraplegia with distal muscle wasting in the old order Amish. *Clinical Genetics 9:* 315–323.
Sjögren T (1950) Hereditary congenital spinocerebellar ataxia accompanied by congenital cataract and oligophrenia. *Confinia Neurologica 10:* 293–308.
Whyte MP & Dekaban AS (1976) Familial cerebellar degeneration. *Developmental Medicine and Child Neurology 18:* 373–380.
Zee DS, Cogan DG, Robinson DA & Engel WK (1976) Ocular motor abnormalities in hereditary cerebellar ataxia. *Brain 99:* 207–34.

Sjögren–Larsson syndrome (ichthyosis with spasticity and mental retardation)

Genetics. Autosomal recessive.

Clinical features. Although first reported in Sweden this is now known to occur throughout the world. There is ichthyosis of the trunk, extremities and neck, particularly in the underarm and popliteal fossae. The palms are hyperkeratotic. There are variations in different parts of the world as to the dryness of skin and ichthyosis, but most of those affected have difficulty in sweating. The hair is usually unaffected, but it may be thin. Nails are normal. There is macular degeneration of the retina in about a quarter of the cases. Dwarfism is frequent.

CNS effects. Most are severely retarded with spastic legs and hyperactive deep reflexes. Some are epileptic.

Further investigation. No biochemical abnormalities have been reported.

Treatment. This is symptomatic. Life expectation is near-normal.

Differential diagnosis. This syndrome is to be distinguished from Refsum's syndrome, in which there is behaviour disorder, low–average intelligence, peripheral neuropathy, and retinal degeneration. Phytanic acid excess in the serum confirms Refsum's syndrome.

BIBLIOGRAPHY

Sjögren T & Larsson R (1957) Oligophrenia in combination with congenital ichthyosis and spastic disorders: a clinical and genetic study. *Acta psychiatrica Scandinavica 32* (Suppl. 113): 1–112.

Myotonic dystrophy (dystrophia myotonica, Steinert's disease)

Genetics. Autosomal dominant. Both sexes are equally affected, but there is extreme variability in severity, mode of presentation and age at onset. In severe childhood cases it is almost invariably maternally transmitted. It is linked to secretor and Lutheran blood group loci on chromosome 19.

Clinical features. In adult life most patients present with muscle weakness, stiffness, cataract or related symptoms. Characteristic signs include facial weakness, ptosis and distal limb weakness, with myotonia of grip and on percussion of the thenar muscles. Cataract and testicular atrophy are frequent. Most asymptomatic gene carriers can be detected by slit-lamp search for lens opacities and electromyography. Many affected adults show mild to moderate mental deterioration with marked lethargy and somnolence. Affected children are frequently mentally retarded and may have no muscle symptoms. Myotonia may be slight and in infancy absent, but this frequently overlooked condition has a characteristic facial appearance due to jaw weakness and facial diplegia (Harper, 1979). No definite biochemical defect is known; serum creatine kinase is generally normal.

Treatment and prevention. Cataract may require surgery. General anaesthesia should be undertaken with care because of increased sensitivity to normal doses of many agents. Careful family study usually shows other affected members, and there is a 50% risk of offspring having the condition. Linkage with the secretor locus can be used in some families to predict affected individuals prenatally (Harper, 1979).

BIBLIOGRAPHY

Harper PS (1979) Myotonic Dystrophy. Philadelphia: W. B. Saunders.

Neurofibromatosis (von Recklinghausen's disease)

Genetics. Autosomal dominant.

Clinical features. The infant may present at birth with pale or light brown patches on the trunk or café-au-lait spots on the facial skin; the latter are diagnostic. Both increase steadily during childhood and adolescence and are quite distinctive. Axillary freckles are said to be pathognomonic. Skin tumours occur in adolescence; these consist of firm nodules of a few millimetres in size. They may be pedunculated or subcutaneous.

CNS features. About a third of patients are mentally retarded, and some develop gliomas of the cranial nerves, affecting function. Gliomas are common upon the auditory nerve, where they cause deafness.

Morbid anatomy. The tumours are neurofibromas or schwannomas, but the café-au-lait patches are due to accumulation of melanosomes in the Malpighian cells. Intracranial tumours may interfere with brain function or develop into glioblastomas.

Treatment and outcome. Little treatment is effective apart from removal of tumours, if they are unsightly or malignant.

Diagnosis. In general a child from an affected family who has more than six café-au-lait spots is likely to develop this disease. It has to be distinguished from Albright's syndrome of fibrous hyperplasia, but this also has bone cysts and normal intelligence.

BIBLIOGRAPHY

Crowe FW, Schull WJ & Neel JV (1956) *A Clinical, Pathological and Genetic Study of Multiple Neurofibromatosis.* Springfield, Illinois: Charles C. Thomas.
Fienman NL & Yakovac WC (1970) Neurofibromatosis in childhood. *Journal of Pediatrics 76:* 339–346.

Tuberous sclerosis (epiloia)

Frequency. This is said to be one per 20 000 to 40 000 live births in the USA. The triad of epilepsy, retardation and sebaceous adenoma has long been known.

Genetics. Autosomal dominant. Zaremba (1968) calculated one-third, and Penrose (1972) one-half, of cases to arise by fresh mutations, but parents must be carefully examined before fresh mutation can be accepted as a cause.

Clinical features. Normal at birth, the infant develops macules of variable size over the trunk, and flesh-coloured nodules on the face and elsewhere by five years of age. The classical butterfly rash of the face is most marked by adolescence, when it may be large and indurated. There may be fibromas underneath the nails and up to half of patients may develop retinal nodules. There are small white raised flioses. Less frequent are nodules in the conjunctiva and cataracts.

CNS features. In one series one-third were of average intelligence and two-thirds retarded. Most have epilepsy in infancy, which decreases with adolescence. Cerebral astrocytomas are not uncommon (Galant et al., 1976).

Morbid anatomy. There are smooth white hamartomas which may be in any part of the brain. In one series rhabdomyomas of the heart caused one-third of the deaths. Kidney hamartomas may be quite large and may interfere with function.

Special investigation. Skull X-rays often show calcifications in adult life in the basal ganglia, their incidence increases with age. Computed tomography may prove helpful in detecting intracranial lesions. The EEG is usually abnormal and may show specific abnormalities in infancy.

Treatment and outcome. The degree of retardation is said to vary with the number of abnormalities, as over one-third are of average intelligence and show few abnormalities. Removal of skin lesions may help appearance, and internal tumours, which are common and which interfere with function, may need removal (Galant et al., 1976). Life expectation varies with severity of lesions.

Differential diagnosis. Skull X-ray calcification may be seen in intracranial infections such as herpesvirus, rubella and toxoplasmosis as well as in the Sturge–Weber syndrome.

BIBLIOGRAPHY

Galant SP, Fowler GW, Amin L, Davis R & Fish CH (1976) Immunological status in tuberous sclerosis. *Developmental Medicine and Child Neurology 18:* 503–511.
Pampiglione G & Maynahan EJ (1976) The tuberous sclerosis syndrome: clinical and EEG studies in 100 children. *Journal of Neurology, Neurosurgery and Psychiatry 39:* 666–673.
Paulson GW & Lyle CB (1966) Tuberous sclerosis. *Developmental Medicine and Child Neurology 8:* 571–586.
Penrose LS (1972) *The Biology of Mental Defect*, 4th edn. London: Sidgwick & Jackson.
Rundle AT & Atkin J (1976) Serum X2 macroglobulin levels in tuberous sclerosis. *Journal of Mental Deficiency Research 20:* 231–236.
Zaremba J (1968) Tuberous sclerosis: a clinical and genetic investigation. *Journal of Mental Deficiency Research 12:* 63–80.

Chapter 11
Chromosomal Abnormalities

MICHAEL BARAITSER

Live-birth figures give little indication of the frequency of chromosomal abnormalities as a whole. Indeed, as the vast majority of embryos with chromosomal defects do not reach term, the total can only be evaluated if all pregnancies are investigated.

On average one-third of abortions will be found to have a chromosomal abnormality, and even this figure is probably an underestimate as many early miscarriages remain undetected. The evidence suggests that the earlier the rejection of the products of pregnancy the higher is the proportion of abnormalities and that the figures might reach 50 % if all abortions were examined. Although most fetuses with chromosomal abnormalities are rejected, the proportion that reach term is still significant. The importance of major loss or addition of chromosomal material (this excludes some alterations in the X and Y sex chromosomes) is the association with major congenital malformation. Most live-born children with a structural chromosome abnormality involving an autosome will be mentally handicapped (autosomes are the 44 chromosomes other than the XX or XY pair). Prevention rather than treatment is a realistic goal. At present secondary prevention, that is termination of pregnancy after amniocentesis, is the main approach. Unfortunately primary prevention – an attempt to influence the cause of the abnormality – has had little impact. Even the aetiology of non-disjunction (the failure of chromosomes to separate) in Down's syndrome is not understood. Not all changes of structure are harmful. There are some regions on the chromosomes where variation in the population is frequent and changes need not have clinical importance. For instance, an elongation of the dark heterochromatic area on the long arm of chromosome 1 adjacent to the centromere can occur in the population or within families without consequence. These heterochromatic areas probably contain little genetic material of importance. Other normal variation can be seen in chromosomes 16 and 9, where secondary constrictions near the centromere are common in the population. The laboratory report might call these 'familial polymorphisms'. The same applies to the presence of satellites on some of the small chromosomes. In general, the cytogenetic laboratory will advise about the significance of the observed changes. It is often helpful to look at parental chromosomes before finally evaluating the importance of minor changes.

MENTAL RETARDATION AND CHROMOSOME ABNORMALITIES

In institutions for people with mental handicap 20 % will have a significant chromosomal abnormality. Down's syndrome makes the major contribution to this figure and is responsible for 12 % of the total. Fragile site X-linked mental retardation with the marker X chromosome is second in importance to Down's syndrome, and contributes 6 %. Other autosomal abnormalities are much less frequent and account for fewer than 1 % of patients. On a population basis the frequency of Down's syndrome is much higher as many more patients are cared for in the community. About one-third of all severe mental retardation will be accounted for by Down's syndrome and possibly one-sixth by X-linked fragile site mental retardation. It should be noted that these are prevalence figures. If the birth frequency of chromosomal abnormalities is assessed, then 1 in 200 children is born with a significant abnormality. Many of these children do not survive the first few years of life. The likelihood of chromosomal abnormalities increases in those infants with developmental delay and three or more congenital abnormalities. Even if Down's syndrome is excluded, 21 % of this group will have a chromosomal abnormality. These figures are much higher than expected, but the early demise of a large proportion of these patients accounts for their small representation in populations of people with mental handicap.

KARYOTYPING

All children with either developmental delay or mental handicap should have a chromosome analysis performed. Previously it had been the practice to karyotype only those who had, in addition, dysmorphic features, but this policy is now known to be insufficient. The dysmorphic features are often subtle and the sex chromosome abnormality would be undetected.

In most laboratories chromosome 'banding' is performed as a routine. Indeed, with the accumulation of evidence that even small deletions can be significant, the examination is incomplete without banding. Giemsa or G banding has been in existence for more than 10 years and this is still the most frequent method employed. The laboratory will usually decide whether extra methodology is needed; for instance, T-telomere banding can be used if the terminal part of the chromosome needs better visualization. For fragile site mental retardation special handling is required. The laboratory needs to be warned if this diagnosis is being contemplated in a male and there is a clinical likelihood of finding a fragile site on the X chromosome. They might grow the cells in a folic-acid-deficient medium by adding 5-fluorodeoxyuridine (FUdR). Parents will be anxious to hear the result of chromosome analysis; they should be warned that on average the results take about four weeks before they are ready for communication.

Prophase banding

Special handling of the chromosomes is indicated in those situations where a small deletion is known to cause a specific syndrome. For instance, in Prader Willi syndrome (see Chapter 10) a small interstitial deletion in the long arm of chromosome 15 is found in half of the patients. The laboratory needs to be requested to look specifically at a particular area.

Material needed for the karyotype

Blood

The karyotype is performed on white blood cells. Most laboratories will provide their own tubes with the appropriate amount of heparin. For adults 5 ml of blood is usually sufficient; for children half that

will suffice. Skin and other tissues are occasionally used, especially when mosaicism is being sought in various organs. Buccal smears are now performed much less frequently than before and most clinicians will omit requesting the procedure and ask for a full chromosome analysis.

Trophoblast culture

The late diagnosis of Down's syndrome that results when amniocentesis is the method of obtaining fetal cells for culture is unfortunate. Recently chorion biopsy is being tried; with this method fetal material becomes available for culture at 8–9 weeks. The safety of the procedure is yet to be established but the prospects seem good.

Amniocentesis

Prenatal diagnosis of the chromosomal abnormalities can be achieved by sampling amniotic fluid cells at 16 weeks and performing a karyotype on the fetal cells. There are two problems about this approach. One is the lateness of the termination if the fetus is found to have a significant abnormality. The results of the test are seldom to hand before 18 weeks of pregnancy and the termination is less acceptable to many women at this stage than it would be if the test could be performed by the eighth to tenth week. The other problem is the small risk of the test causing a miscarriage. This risk is, in good obstetric hands, about 1 % and is usually accepted as a small risk.

Despite these two minor reservations amniocentesis has led to the whole approach of secondary prevention of the birth of children with chromosomal abnormalities.

Terminology

All clinicians will need to familiarize themselves with the terminology used by cytogeneticists on the karyotype report. Table 11.1 shows some of the more frequent abbreviations that are used.

ABNORMALITIES OF STRUCTURE

Deletions

These occur when chromosomal breakage takes place and a fragment is lost. These fragments can be small regions from the end (terminal deletions) or areas in the middle (interstitial deletions).

Table 11.1 Karyotype nomenclature

46, XY	A male with the normal 23 pairs of chromosomes. The autosomes are numbered in descending order of size. The long arm of the chromosome is designated as q, the short arm as p. Points on the chromosome are designated by numbers; these refer to the Giemsa bands.
+	after the number indicates extra material, but not an extra whole chromosome, e.g. 4p+ (extra material on a short arm of chromosome 4).
+	before the number indicates a whole extra chromosome, e.g. +21 (Down's syndrome).
−	after the number indicates a loss of material, e.g. 4p− (loss of part of the short arm of chromosome number 4.
t	translocation (written before parenthesis). A second parenthesis designates the break point.
:	indicates the chromosome break
::	indicates a break and rejoin
ter	terminal end of chromosome, e.g. 13qter (the terminal portion of the long arm of chromosome 13).
r	ring
inv	inversion
del	deletion

Examples

46, XX del(4) (p12)	Deletion in the short arm of chromosome 4 at band p12.
46, XX del(4) (qter-q12)	Deletion in chromosome 4, from the end of the long arm to band 12 on the long arm.
46, XY t(14q21q)	A translocation has occurred between the long arms of chromosomes 14 and 21. No breakpoints are specified.
46, XX t(1; 9) (p13q23)	The translocation involves the short arm of chromosome 1 and the long arm of chromosome 9; the breakpoints are indicated.
46, XX inv(9) (p21q31)	An inversion involving the long arm of 9 between p21 and q31.
46, XY r(18)	A ring of chromosome 18. Breakpoints not given.
46, XY del(13) (q11 :: q22)	Interstitial deletion between the bands indicated by the ::

Partial trisomies

Here there is an extra piece of chromosome, be it part of or the whole of the short or long arm of any chromosome.

Ring chromosomes

When deletions take place at both ends of the chromosome the 'sticky' ends can join to form a ring. This, in most instances, amounts to a deletion of one of the arms.

Inversions

These occur when chromosome breakage is followed by the reinsertion of the material the wrong way round. If this involves the centromere it is called a pericentric inversion, and if not, a paracentric inversion. The significance of these inversions has not been conclusively established. Possibly only large inversions are important. When present both parental karyotypes should be checked. If one parent carries the inversion then this would be good evidence that it is not causally related to the mental retardation in the offspring.

Isochromosomes

Normally at meiosis the centromere divides lengthwise and the chromatids move to the opposite poles of the cell. If the division takes place across the centromere, the resulting chromosomes might consist of two long or two short arms. These are isochromosomes.

Translocations

Definition. Normally at the first meiotic cell division homologous chromosomes ('like' chromosomes) pair and exchange material. Where exchange takes place between non-homologous chromosomes, a translocation occurs.

Frequency. Balanced rearrangements occur with a minimum frequency of 1 in 250 couples in the general population. Most people with these rearrangements are only detected after the birth of a child with an unbalanced translocation. Balanced rearrangements should not cause any phenotypic change as no material is lost or gained, only exchanged.

Reciprocal translocations. Where an exchange of material takes place between non-homologous chromosomes – that is one of the pair receives material and the other donates material – there is a reciprocal exchange or reciprocal translocation.

Robertsonian translocations. This is the result of pairing between two non-homologous acrocentric chromosomes. Acrocentrics are short chromosomes with the centromere near one end, leaving very little genetic material on the short arm. For instance, a Robertsonian translocation between two number 21 chromosomes results in 45 chromosomes, with the two 21s having joined their short arms – one riding over the other. In balanced reciprocal translocations the chromosome number remains at 46.

In some instances the additional piece of material cannot be identified. For example, a mentally handicapped child with extra material on say, chromosome 1, has a partial trisomy but there is no certainty about the identification of the extra material. If a parent is a balanced translocation carrier and has part of, say, chromosome 6 attached to the end of chromosome 1, then the child under discussion will have partial trisomy 6. Many rearrangements are de novo and examination of the parental chromosomes will not provide an answer to the origin of the extra material.

CHROMOSOME 21 TRISOMY
(47 + 21, Down's syndrome, mongolism)

History. First reported by Down in 1866. Lejeune et al. (1959) first identified the extra chromosome in the 21 position.

Clinical features. The skull is brachycephalic in shape, with, in particular, a flattened occiput. The face is characteristic, having upward slanting eyes, simple ears, and an often-open mouth with a protruding, horizontally fissured tongue. The eyes have Brushfield spots, which are a collection of white patches on the edge of the iris (in 70% of cases), and poor development of the iris itself (in about 50%). Half have congenital heart lesions, mainly ventricular septal defects, atrioventricular canal defect, atrial septal defect or patent ductus arteriosus. A short thick neck is seen, but no webbing; the nipples are often small. Umbilical hernias are common. Genitalia are usually underdeveloped. Males are usually sterile; females can reproduce but have rarely done so. Hands and feet are short and broad, and characteristically there is a wide space between the thumb and second digit. Hypotonia is usual; joints are often hyper-retractile. The fifth finger is usually small and bent inwards (clinodactyly).

Dermatoglyphics. A simple simian palm, with one transverse crease, distal displacement of the triradius, ulnar loops on digit two or radial loops on fourth and fifth fingers, is suggestive. The skin generally is dry and often cyanotic with scanty hair follicles everywhere. Palm-prints and sole-prints have been intensively used in comparing 21 trisomy with mosaics and parents. Mosaics and parents of mosaics occupy an intermediate position between trisomy 21 and normal controls. For a detailed discussion of the latest system of classification see Loesch (1974).

CNS features. Most subjects have an IQ below 50. The 10% of Down's syndrome patients who are above IQ 50 are often mosaics, that is, nondisjunction has occurred at the first mitotic division or a later stage of embryonic development so that only one-half, one-quarter or fewer of all cells have the 21 trisomy anomaly. Subjects usually have marked hypotonia. Coordination is poor and a cerebellar deficit may be noted. Final personality development may be immature, and emotional tantrums during childhood are frequent. In adulthood most are noted for a happy, amiable and tractable disposition, conscientious at work and undemanding at home. Degrees of deafness used to be common, probably due to untreated upper respiratory infections.

Frequency. The frequency is about 1 in 660 overall (Ratcliffe et al., 1970). See Table 11.2 for figures related to maternal age above 35 years.

Three ways in which the Down's phenotype is produced

About 95% are trisomies which occur as a result of a failure of a parent's number 21 chromosomes to separate at the first or second meiotic cell division, mosaicism accounts for 2–3% and unbalanced translocations account for about 4%.

Mosaicism

In this situation the non-disjunction occurs after meiosis, mostly in the first few mitotic cell divisions. In this way two populations of cells result, only one of which will be trisomic. There is usually a relationship between the ratio of trisomic to normal cells and the phenotypic expression of Down's syndrome, but the ratios might differ in the different tissues that are sampled and the ratios can change with age (the trisomic cell line might be selected against). In those rare instances of familial Down's syndrome in which neither parent is a translocation carrier it is likely that parental mosaicism could explain the occurrence in sibs. The affected child would have inherited the trisomic cell line and have the full Down's syndrome phenotype. Mosaicism itself is rarely passed on: either the children will be normal or they will have Down's syndrome. It should also be noted that mosaicism should not be suggested in all families with two affected children. There appears to be a 'familial chromosomal stickiness' which could account for the occasional recurrence.

Translocations

Unbalanced translocations account for about 4% of all Down's syndrome children. A study from Copenhagen, Mikkelsen et al. (1976) found a figure of 6.2% but this might reflect the younger maternal age in their study as translocations are more common in the category of Down's syndrome unassociated with increased maternal age.

D-G translocations. Just over half the translocations in which a chromosome 21 is involved are associated with a D group chromosome. This is a group of acrocentric chromosomes (those with the centromeres near the end) numbered 13, 14 and 15 (the G group comprises 21, 22 and the Y chromosome). In just over half the patients where there is an unbalanced translocation involving this group the translocation will have arisen de novo and neither parent will be a carrier. In just under half, a parent will be observed to carry a balanced translocation. Amniocentesis and antenatal diagnosis should be offered in both of these situations but the risks of recurrence are higher if a parent is a carrier. Theoretically, a carrier parent could have a normal child, a child with a balanced translocation who would be phenotypically normal, a child with Down's syndrome and a miscarriage due to a monosomy 21. This gives a risk of one in three of a live-born child with Down's syndrome. In practice the risks are much lower than this as a large proportion of the abnormal fetuses will abort. A risk of 10% if the mother is a carrier and 2% if the father is a carrier are reasonable risk figures for counselling.

G-G translocations. The group as a whole contributes 40% to translocation Down's syndrome and can be subdivided into 22-21 and 21-21 translocations.

Risks are less well established for balanced carriers of *22-21 translocations* but there is less difference between risks to carrier mothers and risks to carrier fathers than with D-G translocations. The majority arise de novo and only 6–8% come from carrier parents. Current practice is to offer mothers an amniocentesis after a child with a 22-21 translocation.

If one parent is a carrier of a *21-21 translocation* the risk of recurrence is 100%. The fetus which survives can only be trisomic; that is, it will inherit the two united 21's from the translocation carrier and another 21 from the other partner and therefore have Down's syndrome. The alternative is a non-viable fetus which inherits the single chromosome 21 from the non-carrier and is monosomic. Genetic counselling will be confined to an explanation of the chromosomal anomaly, and alternative methods for having a child should be discussed. These will include fostering, adoption and possibly ovum implantation if the mother carries the translocation and artificial insemination by donor if the father carries it.

The changing incidence of Down's syndrome

Down's syndrome occurs with a frequency of 1.5 per 1000 live-births. There is evidence of a change in frequency over the past 20 years. A study from Liverpool by Owens et al. (1983) shows that the expected frequency of 1.6 per 1000 in the 1960s dropped to 1.09 per 1000 in the late 1970s. This change has been confirmed by studies elsewhere. The reason for the drop differs from area to area. In Liverpool over this period the mean maternal age fell from 36.7 years in 1961 to 29.0 in 1979. Consequently, the fall in incidence could be explained by the corresponding decline in the maternal age (see Table 11.2). In the Liverpool area prenatal diagnosis had been instigated in 1969. By 1974 only 2.37% of women over 35 had an amniocentesis. By 1979 the uptake rate was 16.37%. At this rate, prenatal diagnosis has had little effect on the overall incidence.

In London there has been a slightly better uptake but the response has been poor in general. 48% of women over 40 had an amniocentesis. In rural United States, only 5–6% had the test. The reasons are variable. Late booking played a role but many women are not offered the test and some obstetricians have never offered it. The highest uptake in the USA was 33.6% in New York City. In Denmark it was much higher: in the county of Vejle, 80–85% of women over 35 were examined in

Table 11.2 Frequency of Down's syndrome at amniocentesis and among live births.

Maternal age	Amniocentesis (per 1000) (European figures)	Live births (per 1000) (South Glamorgan)
35	4.5	4.91
36	4.9	5.84
37	7.7	6.93
38	9.1	8.24
39	13.2	9.78
40	12.0	11.62
41	23.4	13.80
42	33.3	16.39
43	17.8	19.47
44	55.9	23.13

1979–80. Even here selective termination was not thought to be the chief factor in the decline in incidence of Down's syndrome. The greatest impact was made with women over 35 not wanting to continue with any pregnancy and making use of legal abortion.

Two studies have suggested an increase in the frequency of Down's syndrome between the ages of 35 and 39. The reason for this increase is unknown. It is now questioned whether even 35 years as a cut-off point for amniocentesis is too high and whether it should not be lowered to 30. It is likely that the solution to this problem lies in another type of test being developed – either trophoblast sampling or a simple method for obtaining fetal cells from mother's blood.

Paternal non-disjunction

It is now evident that not all the errors of separation of the pair of number 21 chromosomes are of maternal origin. Indeed, pooled data show that in 20–30 % of cases paternal meiotic non-disjunction is the cause. Whereas paternal non-disjunction can occur during meiosis I or II, maternal meiosis I errors are still the most frequent cause. The role of age in the paternal nondisjunction is uncertain. Very few fathers in the series of Mattei et al. (1979) were above 50 and if father's age plays any role at all, it is small. Maternal age might even be operating as a factor in Down's syndrome caused by paternal non-disjunction in that the failure to abort trisomic fetuses spontaneously might be age-related: the older the mother the less efficient might be her mechanism for aborting trisomic fetuses. It might be that only a proportion of Down's syndrome occurs in this way.

Longevity and mortality

Penrose (1949) calculated that the life expectancy for children with Down's syndrome born in 1929 was nine years. By 1961 it had risen to 18.3 years and now the average life-span is 35 years. Vulnerability to infection, congenital heart defects, leukaemia and Alzheimer's disease are the main causes of death. About 20 % of the Down's syndrome population are living beyond 50.

Medical problems

Ocular anomalies are common in Down's syndrome. The most important are keratoconus and cataract, as both may lead to blindness. The incidence of these conditions is 4–8 %.

Dementia

The two main causes for this are hypothyroidism and Alzheimer's disease. In the older population of Down's syndrome (over 40 years old) hypothyroidism may occur with a frequency of 13.54 % (Korsager et al., 1978). As this, in contrast to Alzheimer's disease, is reversible it should be excluded before making a clinical diagnosis of Alzheimer's disease.

Alzheimer's disease (or presenile dementia) is characterized clinically by progressive loss of memory and the development of long tract signs in people between 40 and 60. Most patients die within five to ten years. The condition has a prevalence of about 70 per 100 000. Pathologically, the typical lesions found are argyrophilic plaques and neurofibrillary tangles.

The association between Alzheimer's disease and Down's syndrome is well-established. If the brains of patients with Down's syndrome dying from various complications are examined at post-mortem nearly all of those over 40 will have histological evidence of Alzheimer's disease (Thase, 1982). This intriguing finding has not been explained.

Much less certain is the association of Alzheimer's disease and Down's syndrome occurring in different members of the same family. Heston (1977) found a fivefold increase in first- and second-degree relatives of a cohort of patients with Alzheimer's disease, but this has not been everyone's experience (Whalley et al., 1982).

Counselling

The period after the birth of a baby with Down's syndrome is a fraught time for the parents and the doctor. Parents want to be told as soon as the diagnosis is suspected. In one survey most medical attendants were found to be understanding, informative and helpful, but 25% of parents were dissatisfied because they were told too late. Only 27% were told when their spouse was present. Anger and frustration is often directed towards the physician in charge, who will need to absorb this but at the same time will need to help parents make a sensible decision. Those who recommend institutionalization will not help 'bonding' and decisions will have to take the needs of the child and the parents into account. Genetic counselling follows some weeks or even months later (see Chapter 15). The recurrence risk is 1% plus an age-related risk for mothers over 35 (Table 11.2).

Primary prevention

This might only be achieved when the primary cause of non-disjunction is better understood. The 'stale ovum' theory, which implies that the ovum at the maternal age of 40 has been subjected to 20 years more environmental influence than the ovum when the mother is aged 20 is still attractive, but little progress has been made in identifying the environmental factors responsible (maternal exposure to radiation and maternal thyroid antibodies are possibilities). Other possibilities include the low parental coital rates at the time of conception. Delayed fertilization results in a longer stay of the ovum in the Fallopian tube. Intercoital intervals are difficult to evaluate retrospectively. Some prospective studies have failed to confirm the relationship between low coital rates and Down's syndrome but it remains a possibility.

SEX-LINKED MENTAL RETARDATION DUE TO A FRAGILE SITE ON THE X CHROMOSOME

There is a preponderance of males with severe mental retardation. Some of the sex difference was considered to be due to X-linked syndromes but previously only families with several affected males could be recognized as having an X-linked syndrome. Single cases could not be assigned to that group because no specific tests were available. More recently, the whole field of X-linked mental retardation has been revolutionized by the discovery that one form, now called Martin–Bell or Gillian Turner syndrome, is due to a detectable chromosomal abnormality. First reported by Lubs in 1969, many males have now been shown to have what appears to be a fragile site on the X chromosome. Autism has been commented on as one of the behavioural manifestations of fragile-X mental retardation, although the validity of this latter observation has yet to be tested on larger populations.

Frequency

It seems likely that fragile-site X-linked mental retardation will account for between one-third and one-half of families with non-specific X-linked mental retardation. In an unselected series of 96 severely mentally retarded boys (Blomquist et al., 1982) 6% were found to have the fragile sites. Thus the chance that any severely mentally retarded boy will be found to have this type of chromosomal abnormality is 1 in 16. On a general population basis it might be so common that 0.5 per 1000 males will have X-linked fragile site mental retardation, making it second only to Down's syndrome in importance. The fragile site has been localized to the long arm of the X chromosome, involving the q27 or q28 bands. These are near to the end of the long arm.

Clinical features in males

The degree of retardation varies and IQs of 30 to 60 have been recorded. The males are of normal stature, have a long face, prominent ears and a broad forehead. Microcephaly is not present. Verbal skills are especially affected. Most males have macro-orchidism. It is usually obvious after puberty but not always before. Prior to the discovery of the fragile site, all X-linked mental retardation was called Renpenning's syndrome. In the family originally described by Renpenning, males were short, had abnormal ears, prominent jaws and moderate microcephaly. The family was re-examined by Fox et al. (1980). Nine males had a mean IQ of 30, but one had an IQ of 70. Fragile sites were looked for but not found. The term 'Renpenning's syndrome' should now be reserved for X-linked mental retardation with microcephaly without fragile sites.

Caution

There is evidence of a positive correlation between the degree of retardation and the proportion of fragile sites but there is growing evidence that very rarely allegedly normal males can have the fragile X chromosome. Daker and colleagues (1981) reported this, and subsequently Webb et al. (1981) have shown transmission through a male carrier who had an unusual personality but was not thought to be of low IQ. Neilson et al. (1981) reported similar families. These data have increased the problem of prenatal diagnosis. Whereas the detection of fragile sites in the male fetus has now been achieved, the fact that some males with the fragile site will be of normal intelligence must make decisions more complicated. It should be stressed that at present this would be a rare occurrence.

Female carriers

The identification of female carriers can be difficult. If a woman has an affected son and another affected close male relative, she is an obligate carrier. The same applies if she has two affected sons. Most obligate female carriers are of normal intelligence, but a third are mildly retarded. Evidence suggests a positive correlation between the degree of retardation and the in-vitro expression of the fragile X in carrier females. Carrier detection is also made difficult because it is now well documented that the number of fragile sites decreases with increasing age. The reason for this is unclear.

Prenatal diagnosis

Obligate carriers have a 50% chance of having an affected son and the same risk of having a carrier daughter. There is a 30% risk that the carrier daughter might be mildly intellectually slow. If the mother is identified after one affected son and there is no family history then she is a possible carrier. If her chromosomes are normal this does not totally exclude carrier status. Fetal sex determination followed by the termination of all males has been adopted and follows the strategy used in other X-linked conditions such as Duchenne muscular dystrophy. Fetal blood sampling has been used in order to obtain a sample for the detection of fragile sites in the male fetus, but the test has a 5% risk of setting up a miscarriage. Detection in fibroblasts from amniotic fluid has now been achieved by using FUdR. In this way it is possible that affected males can be detected in utero and this would obviate the difficulty in detecting obligate carrier women. A short communication from LeJeune (1982) has caused a stir amongst those caring for children with X-linked fragile-site mental retardation. He has claimed that by treating patients with folic acid supplement these children have shown improvement in their autistic patterns of behaviour. This remains to be confirmed.

OTHER CHROMOSOMAL ABNORMALITIES

Chromosome 18 trisomy
(Edwards' syndrome)

Prominent occiput, small chin, low set ears, severe mental retardation (see Figure 11.1). Reported by Edwards et al. (1960).

Numbers and frequency. Some 200 have been reported. The frequency is 1 in 3500 live births in North America.

Clinical features. Severe microcephaly is rare. There is a pronounced occiput, hypertelorism, epicanthic folds, ptosis of eyelids and a small chin. Microphthalmos is noted in one-third (Taylor, 1968). Cataracts and opacities of the cornea are common. The ears are small, low-set and maldeveloped. Cleft palate is occasionally present. Congenital heart abnormalities are common — mainly ventricular septal defect or patent ductus arteriosus. Undescended testes are usual. Inguinal hernia is common, as is exomphalos. The hands are distinctive in that the second and fifth fingers are often flexed on the palm, while fingers 3 and 4 overlap them. The thumb is unduly mobile and the nails are poorly developed. The commonest foot deformity is a rocker-bottom, valgus deformity.

Dermatoglyphics. Six to ten low arches and a high axial triradius are characteristic; this combination occurs in only 0.1% of normals.

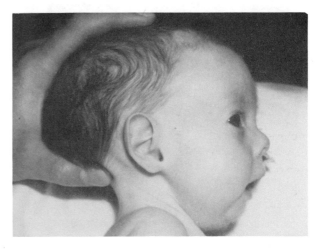

Fig. 11.1 Trisomy 18 (Edwards' syndrome), showing typical head profile. (Courtesy of Dr McDermott and Dr Insley.)

CNS features. All have been markedly retarded, with hypertonia and frequent epilepsy. A child who could be taught to walk was so uncommon that it has been recorded (Abbie, 1976).

Treatment and outcome. One-half survive beyond two months and only 10% beyond the first years of life.

The majority of cases have been de novo full trisomy 18, with a much smaller number of translocations than found in trisomy 13. Recurrence risks are small (less than 1%). Amniocentesis is indicated because there is a small increased recurrence risk of Down's syndrome.

Chromosome 13 trisomy
(Patau's syndrome)

Microcephaly, severe facial defects, infantile death (see Figure 11.2). Described by Patau et al. (1960). *Numbers*: Over 200 have been described.

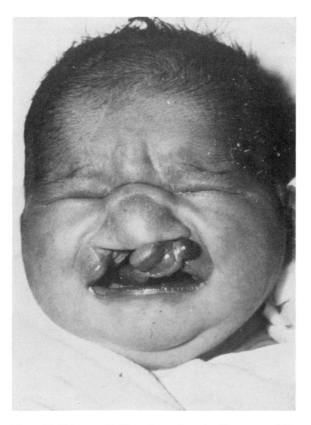

Fig. 11.2 Trisomy 13 (Patau's syndrome). (Courtesy of Dr McDermott and Dr Insley.)

Clinical features. Most infants are microcephalic, with a sloping forehead, and have severe bilateral cleft lip, hypertelorism and a small chin. Some have absent or small eyes with cataracts and iris colobomas. Most have simple or small ears. Half have cleft palate as well as the cleft lip. Shortness of the neck is common. 80% have congenital heart defects: ventricular septal defect and patent ductus are common and dextroposition occurs occasionally. Renal anomalies are also present. Hernias are frequent, as are undescended testes. Half the females have had abnormal uteri. Post-axial polydactyly is a cardinal feature; some have fused fingers or toes.

Dermatoglyphics. 25% have more than three arches in finger patterns, 81% a high triradius, and 58% a simian crease.

CNS features. All reported are severely retarded, some with marked hypertonia and myoclonic spasms. Holoprosencephaly is frequent.

Treatment and outcome. Magenis et al. (1968) showed that only half of 221 patients lived beyond one month, over half the remainder died before three months, and only 5% survived beyond three years of age.

Differential diagnosis. Some of the features are found in the Meckel–Gruber syndrome but these infants often have an encephalocele, and all have cystic dysplastic kidneys. Hypertelorism, cleft palate and cleft lip are found in the 4p— syndrome.

Genetics. Mosaics (normal/13 trisomy) occur; they have fewer signs. Parents need to be told that the birth incidence is 1 in 5000 but that recurrence risks are small. If the patient has an unbalanced translocation, parental examination is necessary. If a parent shows a balanced translocation, the recurrence rate is high enough to warrant amniocentesis. There is a suggestion that the risk of Down's syndrome might be increased after trisomy 13 – and most geneticists would offer amniocentesis. Translocation occurs in 14–20% of cases, whereas mosaicism is present in 6–9%.

Chromosome 4p— (deletion of the short arm)

Wolf-Hirschhorn syndrome

Clinical features. There is mental and growth retardation, microcephaly, 'Greek warrior helmet' forehead and nose (because of the large glabella and the parallel edges of the nose), downturned 'carp' mouth, cleft lip and palate, short philtrum, pre-auricular ear tags, hypospadias and heart defects. It has been found on more than one occasion that the deletion can be small enough to be missed on initial cytogenetic examination. If the clinician is suspicious of the diagnosis he should direct the laboratory to look carefully at the short arm of chromosome 4.

Chromosome 18q− (partial deletion of long arm)

Clinical features. Most are microcephalic, with deep-set eyes, flattened maxillae and mid-face, prominent mandible, broad forehead and downward slanting angles of the mouth. Eyes are usually normal. Simple external ears occur, with a narrow external canal. There are underdeveloped genitalia and undescended testes. Fingers are long and tapering with extra dimples over the major joints. The thumbs can be 'fingerized'. All reported persons have moderate to severe retardation. 40% have congenital heart lesions.

Diagnosis. Chromosome analysis is essential. In approximately 10% of cases a parent was a translocation carrier; the rest have been de novo deletions (80%) or translocations (10%).

Chromosome 5p− (deletion of short arm)

(in a female 46, XX 5p− , cri du chat syndrome). Frequency 1 per 45 000 live births (Niebuhr, 1978).

Clinical features. The head is microcephalic and the face is round, with a high forehead, markedly alert eyes slanted down, with broad epicanthic folds, flat nasal bridge in the newborn and a small chin. Eye defects are common (such as squint and defects of the iris). Ears are simple and set low. The cat-like cry is distinctive in the newborn; it is high in note like the wailing of a cat. 15% have congenital heart anomalies, mainly ventricular or atrial septal defects or a patent ductus arteriosus. All those reported have been severely retarded. Epilepsy is uncommon.

Diagnosis. Neither the cry nor the facial features are diagnostic. A karyotype is the only important diagnostic test. Parental translocation accounts for 10% of cases; if such a parental cause is found, an amniocentesis should be offered for all subsequent pregnancies.

9p trisomy

This is characterized by small stature, severe mental retardation, microcephaly, deep-set eyes, anti-mongoloid slant, bulbous nose, and short fingers and toes with dystrophic nails.

Treatment and outcome. Between 5% and 10% of cases die in early childhood.

SEX CHROMOSOME ABNORMALITIES

Frequency. 1 in 365 live male births; 1 in 661 live female births.

Clinical features

Ideas about the clinical relevance of many of these conditions has changed since prospective investigations have shown that mental retardation is not as prominent a feature of most sex chromosome aneuploidies as had previously been thought.

Mental retardation

In general the XO female will be of normal intelligence, but in those with multiple X chromosomes (more than two) there is an increased risk of mental retardation. Many of those with sex-chromosome abnormalities are mosaics: there are, in other words, two or more cell lines. For instance, 10% of males with the Klinefelter phenotype are mosaics.

Risks to offspring

These will vary according to the category: XO females will be infertile (except for mosaics), whereas XXX females can reproduce. Theoretically, one would expect that half the offspring of the latter group would have sex chromosome anomaly, but in practice, where the offspring have been examined, 90% are normal. Klinefelter males will be infertile but the same is not true for XYY males: their testicular histology and spermatogenesis are often normal.

XO: Turner's syndrome

Mental retardation is not a feature of Turner's syndrome, so any child with severe mental retardation whose chromosomes have an XO constitution will have another reason for the retardation. There might be minor selective defects in perceptual organization and spatial abilities. In general XO females score in the low-average range on performance tests, whereas verbal scores are above average.

There are no differences between patients and controls on verbal comprehension.

XXX: triple X

The frequency is 1 in 1000 live female births.

Unlike XXY and XYY males, where the proportion believed to have severe mental handicap has fallen as more population figures have become available, about 14% of those aged 4–8 will have an IQ 10–25 points below expected; a few will have IQs less than 70. No specific congenital malformations are associated with triple-X females. Fertility ranges from normal to those who have streak gonads and are infertile. Girls do tend to be tall, and in a prospective study most were above the 50th percentile at six years old (Ratcliffe et al., 1979).

XXXXX: penta-X syndrome

Besides severe mental retardation the main dysmorphic features are hypertelorism, epicanthus, mongoloid eye slant and congenital heart defects. About half are microcephalic. None of the features are specific and do not in general help to make a clinical diagnosis. Radio-ulnar synostosis occurs in one-third of patients, and this is perhaps the only feature which is unusual enough for the clinician to contemplate the diagnosis. It is interesting to note that there are facial similarities between the Penta-X and the XXXXY syndromes.

XXXXY

The main features are pre- and post-natal growth delay, mental retardation, hypertelorism, epicanthus, upward eye slant, low-set ears and small penis or testes. Radio-ulnar synostosis and epiphyseal dysplasia are frequently present. Mental retardation is often severe, with an eventual IQ between 20 and 25.

XXY: Klinefelter's syndrome

This was first reported by Klinefelter et al. (1942) in an adolescent male. It occurs in approximately 1 in 1000 live male births.

Clinical features. Since the advent of prospective studies it has become evident that the typical features of Klinefelter syndrome do not occur until puberty and indeed may never occur. In a review by Simpson et al. (1982) of males with the XXY genotype, 18% had one or more major congenital abnormalities, but in general these were remediable malformations – cleft palate was the most frequent.

Height distribution was unremarkable below three years old. Later the legs tend to be long and arm-span exceeds height. In the 63 children studied to date there were fewer below the 25th percentile than expected. More than a half had delayed speech development. The statistical distribution of intelligence was skewed to the left, with one-third having IQs below 90. Poor verbal skills were mainly responsible for this. Psychiatric problems occur more frequently than in the general population, 50–75% developed breast enlargement, and breast cancer occurs 20 times more frequently than in normal males (from Simpson et al., 1982).

Penis length is normal to moderately short. Testes are often normal until puberty but thereafter are small and firm. Other medical problems include hypostatic ulcers on the legs, mitral valve prolapse and pulmonary disease.

XYY

This is found in 1 in 1000 live births.

In Ratcliffe et al.'s Edinburgh study (1979) all children were at or above the 50th percentile for height by the age of four years. Language delay occurred in 5 out of 13 cases. IQs were within the 70–90 range and were rarely below 70.

The intense dispute about the validity of the original observation that males with XYY were over-represented in institutions has been temporarily settled. Angry disbelief has changed to acceptance of a small but real difference. The frequency of XYY males in maximum security prisons compared with the frequency in a newborn population is 2% versus 0.1%. This represents a 20-fold increase over the newborn figure. However, the original postulate of serious aggression has not been substantiated. The types of crime committed are probably no different from those committed by XY males. In one double-blind study of 28 patients selected from a group of young conscripts undergoing compulsory medical check-ups all 28 could be correctly assigned to the XYY group because of impulsivity when faced with an emotional stimulus (Noël et al., 1974).

REFERENCES

Abbie M (1976) Unusual development of motor skills in a child with trisomy 18. *Developmental Medicine and Child Neurology 18:* 85–89.

Alberman E, Berry AC & Polani PE (1979) Planning an amniocentesis service for Down syndrome. *Lancet i:* 50.

Blomquist HK, Gustavson K-H, Holmgren G, Nordenson I & Sweins A (1982) Fragile site X chromosomes and X-linked mental retardation in severely retarded boys in a northern Swedish county. A prevalence study. *Clinical Genetics 21:* 209–214.

Coco R & Penchaszadeh VB (1982) Cytogenetic findings in 200 children with mental retardation and multiple congenital anomalies of unknown cause. *American Journal of Medical Genetics 12:* 155–173.

Daker MG, Chidiac P, Fear CN & Berry AC (1981) Fragile X in a normal male: a cautionary tale. *Lancet i:* 780.

Edwards JH, Harnden D, Cameron A, Crosse V & Wolff O (1960) A new trisomic syndrome. *Lancet i:* 787–789.

Fox P, Fox D & Gerrard JW (1980) X-linked mental retardation: Renpenning revisited. *American Journal of Medical Genetics 7:* 491–495.

de Grouchy J, Royer P, Salmon C & Lamy M (1964) Délétion partielle des bras longs du chromosome 18. *Pathologie Biologie (Paris) 12:* 579–82.

Heston LL (1977) Alzheimer's disease, trisomy 21 and myeloproliferative disorders: associations suggesting a genetic diathesis. *Science 196:* 322–323.

Klinefelter HF, Reifenstein EC & Albright F (1942) Gynaecomastia, aspermatogenesis without A-Leydigism and increased excretion of follicle-stimulating hormone. *Journal of Clinical Endocrinology 2:* 615–627.

Korsager S, Chatham EM & Kristensen HP (1978) Thyroid function tests in adults with Down's syndrome. *Acta Endocrinologica 88:* 48.

LeJeune J (1982) Is the fragile X syndrome amenable to treatment? *Lancet i:* 273–4.

LeJeune J, Gauthier M & Turpin R (1959) Etudes des chromosomes somatiques de neuf enfants mongoliens. *Comptes Rendus des Seances de l'Academie des Sciences D 248:* 1721–1722.

LeJeune J, Lafourcade J, Berger R, Vialette J, Boeswillwand M, Seringe P & Turpin R (1963) Trois cas de délétion partielle du bras court d'un chromosome r. *Comptes Rendus des Seances de l'Academie des Sciences D 257:* 3098–3102.

Loesch D (1974) Dermatoglyphics characteristics of 21 trisomy mosaicism in relation to the fully developed syndrome and normality. *Journal of Mental Deficiency Research 18:* 209–269.

Magenis RE, Hecht R & Mulham S (1968) Trisomy 13 (D_1) syndrome. Studies on parental age, sex ratio, and survival. *Journal of Pediatrics 73:* 222–228.

Mattei JF, Ayme MGS & Giraud F (1979) Origins of the extra chromosome in trisomy 21. *Human Genetics 46:* 107–110.

Mikkelsen M, Fische G, Stene J, Stene E & Petersen E (1976) Incidence study of Down's syndrome in Copenhagen 1960–1971: with chromosome investigation. *Annals of Human Genetics 40:* 177–82.

Niebuhr E (1978) The cri du chat syndrome. Epidemiology, cytogenetics and clinical features. *Human Genetics 44:* 227–275.

Neilson KB, Tommerup N, Poulsen H & Mikkelsen M (1981) X-linked mental retardation with fragile X. A pedigree showing transmission by apparently unaffected males and partial expression in female carriers. *Human Genetics 59:* 23–24.

Noël B, Duport JR, Revil O, Dussuyer I & Quack B (1974) The XYY syndrome: reality or myth? *Clinical Genetics 5:* 387–394.

Owens JR, Harris F, Walker S, McAllister E & West L (1983) The incidence of Down's syndrome over a 19-year period with special reference to maternal age. *Journal of Medical Genetics 20(2):* 90–93.

Patau K, Smith DW, Therman E, Inhorn SL & Wagner HP (1960) Multiple congenital anomaly caused by an extra autosome. *Lancet i:* 790–793.

Penrose LS (1949) The incidence of mongolism in the general population. *Journal of Mental Science 9:* 10.

Ratcliffe SG, Stewart AL, Melville MM & Jacobs PA (1970) Chromosome studies on 3500 newborn male infants. *Lancet i:* 121–122.

Ratcliffe SG, Axworthy D & Ginsborg A (1979) The Edinburgh study of growth and development in children with sex chromosome abnormalities. *Birth Defects: Original Article Series, XV(I):* 243–260.

Renpenning H, Gerrard JW, Zaleski WA & Tabata T (1962) Familial sex-linked mental retardation. *Canadian Medical Association Journal 87:* 954–956.

Simpson JL, Golbus MS, Martin AO & Sarto GE (1982) Chapter 10 of *Genetics in Obstetrics and Gynaecology*. p 157. New York: Grune & Stratton.

Sutherland GR, Clisby SR, Bloor G & Carter RF (1979) Down's syndrome in South Australia. *Medical Journal of Australia 2:* 58–61.

Taylor AI (1968) Autosomal trisomy syndromes. A detailed study of 27 cases of Patau syndrome. *Journal of Medical Genetics 5:* 227–252.

Thase ME (1982) Longevity and mortality in Down's syndrome. *Journal of Mental Deficiency Research 26:* 177–192.

Webb GC, Rogers JG, Pitt DB, Halliday J & Theobald T (1981) Transmission of fragile X (q27) site from a male. *Lancet ii:* 1231–1232.

Whalley LJ, Carothers AD, De Mey AD, Collyers R & Frackiewicz S (1982) A study of familial factors in Alzheimer's disease. *British Journal of Psychiatry 140:* 249–256.

Young ID, Williams EM & Newcombe, RG (1980) Down syndrome and maternal age in South Glamorgan. *Journal of Medical Genetics 17:* 433–436.

BOOK REFERENCE

de Grouchy J & Turleau C (1977) *Clinical Atlas of Human Chromosomes*. New York & Chichester: Wiley. (This is by far the best book for the clinician: it deals with all the recognizable abnormalities with pictures of the chromosomal abnormalities and the phenotypic appearance. There is a short section on the nomenclature used by the cytogenetic laboratory.)

Chapter 12
Some Conditions Seen by the Paediatric Neurologist

GWILYM HOSKING

Conditions that may be associated with major developmental disabilities (including intellectual impairment) may be acquired through exogenous influences in the pre-natal, peri-natal or post-natal periods of life or as a result of a genetic disorder inherited either as a chromosomal defect (Chapter 11), as a single gene defect or as a genetic abnormality modified by known or unknown environmental effects (Chapter 10). The range of causative possibilities is wide. This chapter will attempt to review this wide field and discuss some of these conditions, in particular those that are not clearly genetic or chromosomal. It will not be a comprehensive view, but more specific, as paediatric textbooks have already undertaken this task and readers will be referred to these.

This chapter will describe and discuss cerebral palsy, neural tube abnormalities (spina bifida), developmental abnormalities due to infections or toxins and the clinical features of some of the neurodegenerative disorders.

CEREBRAL PALSY

Cerebral palsy is defined as a group of disorders characterized by abnormal movement and muscle tone due to defects of or damage to the brain during early life. The condition is not progressive, but it invariably alters in character as the child becomes older.

Causation

In approximately 20% no cause can be identified. Strong relationships nevertheless exist with a number of adverse pre-natal and peri-natal events, the latter being from the onset of labour to the age of one week.

In approximately 75% of children with cerebral palsy the cause is likely to be pre- or peri-natal. Of the pre-natal factors a high proportion will be in the late pre-natal period; this contrasts with the causation of severe intellectual impairment.

Amongst the early pre-natal factors may be included some congenital brain malformations, a small proportion of which may be genetically determined, early intrauterine infections and threatened abortions. Late pre-natal factors may include maternal illness, specific complications of pregnancy such as toxaemia, a failure of growth of the fetus (intrauterine growth retardation), ante-partum haemorrhage and intrauterine infection. Difficulties in labour, resuscitation at birth and acute problems immediately after birth may be associated subsequently with cerebral palsy.

There is a strong association, although difficult to quantify, between low birth-weight and the subsequent development of cerebral palsy. This is seen in particular when the infant is of very low birth-weight (less than 1500 g), especially if that infant is both premature and light for gestational age. Some estimates have suggested that 10% of such very low birth-weight babies will ultimately develop cerebral palsy, particularly if they are small for gestational age.

The post-natal factors, that is those active one week or later after the birth, relevant to the development of cerebral palsy constitute approximately 15% of identifiable factors. Central nervous system infections and inflammation, trauma (including non-accidental injury), thrombo-embolic episodes (strokes) – a risk for children with severe cyanotic heart disease – are examples.

Incidence

Estimates of incidence vary greatly from country to country. Some decrease has been noted in several countries over the last few decades, for example in

Sweden. In Britain the combined incidence is probably around 2.2 per thousand. The spastic diplegic and dyskinetic forms of cerebral palsy have declined in European countries. Dyskinetic cerebral palsy has a strong association with severe jaundice in the perinatal period; this may go on to produce kernicterus and still presents as a major problem in many developing countries.

Clinical features

The classification of cerebral palsy is based upon the nature and distribution of the major motor deficits or abnormalities. The spastic forms of cerebral palsy are the most common and include hemiplegia, diplegia and quadriplegia. The other varieties reflect differing types of motor abnormality and include ataxic, hypotonic and dyskinetic forms. All of these will briefly be described here. In any one child the classification of the particular form of cerebral palsy only reflects the most prominent aspect of his disorder.

Hemiplegia. This is the commonest form of cerebral palsy. The motor deficit involves one side of the body – the hand and arm more than the leg. In 50% no definite cause may be identified. The earliest signs of hemiplegia may be either abnormal fisting or lack of use of the affected hand. The onset of walking will be delayed and when it occurs there is a tendency for the leg to be rotated inwards to varying degrees and a tendency to walk on the toes on the affected side (where shoe wear will be excessive). In some the affected arm and leg will be smaller, especially if the hemiplegia is severe.

Contractures (tightening and lack of movement) of joints may occur at the elbow, wrist, thumb, ankle and spine (scoliosis).

Quadriparesis. Alternative terms used for this variety of cerebral palsy are double hemiplegia and tetraplegia. All four limbs are affected, the arms more than the legs, with one side being more involved than the other. This is probably the most severe form of cerebral palsy, although there is great variation between one child and another. Intense irritability in early infancy is common and usually there have been problems at or around the time of birth. Intellectual impairment, epilepsy, and oral dysfunction affecting feeding and later language are common. Contractures occur, particularly at the hips, which may dislocate.

Spastic diplegia (sometimes still referred to as Little's disease). This was the commonest form of cerebral palsy seen in European countries but is now much less common. A strong association exists between this variety of cerebral palsy and the infant being premature and light for gestational age. Postnatal factors do not feature. These children are initially hypotonic (floppy) but later show spasticity in their legs. Sitting and walking are delayed. The spasticity of the muscles in the legs is such that they will often be held closely together, and if it is particularly severe they may cross over – so-called scissoring. While classically the upper limbs are described as being unaffected, it is very common to find a mild impairment of function. Intelligence is generally normal. Contractures of ankles, knees and hips occur.

Ataxic diplegia (ataxia: an impairment of coordination). This is common in low-birth-weight babies who have sustained an intra-ventricular haemorrhage of the brain in the peri-natal period. This variety of cerebral palsy may be genetically determined. Hypotonia is present but improves with age, although locomotion is usually delayed. As the child gets older and starts to grasp with his hands a tremor is noticeable. Walking is with a broad-based stamping gait. Spasticity is not a feature.

Ataxic cerebral palsy. This may be genetically determined. The principal features will include hypotonia and delayed motor development, a coarse tremor of the head and hands and marked instability of sitting and standing.

Dyskinetic cerebral palsy. The characteristic features are irregular, involuntary and bizarre movements, frequently associated with fluctuation of muscle tone from hypotonia to hypertonia. The term 'choreo-athetoid' cerebral palsy is often employed. Severe jaundice causing 'kernicterus' is a well described cause but severe birth asphyxia is more common now in Europe.

Initially an infant with dyskinetic cerebral palsy is hypotonic, and it is only in the second or third year of life that the characteristic bizarre movements and rapid and sudden changes in the tone of muscles become apparent. Usually the different abnormalities described here will be present in the same child.

'Athetosis' is typically a slow writhing movement affecting the smaller muscle groups (distal) as well as the larger muscle groups nearer to the trunk (proximal), and this will be induced by passive or active movements. 'Chorea', by contrast, is characterized by rapid jerking movements seen again both in distal and in proximal muscles. 'Dystonia', often triggered by voluntary movement or the activity of the abnormally persisting so-called primitive reflexes, induces sudden and often severe alterations in posture due to increase in the tone of the various muscle groups. Dystonic posturings may involve any number of muscle groups from the limbs to the trunk and also the oral muscles, rendering speech almost impossible.

Even in the presence of major physical disabilities and the absence of speech and expressive language the majority are of normal or near-normal intelligence.

Mixed cerebral palsy. Some children, particularly when very young, may have features suggestive of several forms of cerebral palsy. Later, as they mature, the pattern may evolve to become more characteristic of one of the forms described.

Non-motor problems associated with cerebral palsy

In meeting the needs of a child with cerebral palsy it is vital to recognize that even in some with a mild physical disability there may be significant coexisting non-motor deficits, and these may be of great importance in relation to the child's development.

Vision and hearing. There is a high incidence of squints, refractive disorders and poor vision in children with cerebral palsy. Various degrees and types of hearing loss are common, particularly in those with dyskinetic cerebral palsy – especially if the cause was severe perinatal jaundice.

Alteration in sensation and perception. Abnormalities of sensation, although rare, are sometimes found in the affected hands of children with a hemiplegia. More common is a disordered total perception of the affected side, leading to neglect and a reluctance to involve the upper limb in activity.

Learning difficulties. A great number of perceptual deficits may exist in children with cerebral palsy. These will be relevant to daily activities and educational performance. Early and careful psychometric evaluation is vital.

Intelligence. Low intelligence is common amongst those whose physical deficits are severe. Severe intellectual impairment is very commonly seen with quadriparetic cerebral palsy.

Epilepsy. Nearly one-half of all children with cerebral palsy have epilepsy, particularly those with the hemiplegic or quadriparetic forms.

Emotional disorders. Emotional disorders and behavioural problems are common whether the cerebral palsy is severe or mild. For the mildly affected child attending an ordinary neighbourhood school this may become a significant problem as the limitations imposed by the disability infringe more and more on his academic and recreational activities.

Management

The complex nature of the cerebral palsy group of disorders demands a team approach that starts from the point of comprehensive assessment. The clinical nature of cerebral palsy will vary with age and maturity and therefore demands the willingness and the ability for continuous assessment from the team.

Physiotherapy (see also Chapter 30). In cerebral palsy there may be a period of abnormal retention of primary automatic reflexes and a delay in the acquisition of secondary automatic reflexes. Coupled with this there will be disordered patterns of voluntary movements, balance and muscle tone. Early diagnosis may be beneficial by enabling early stimulation with a variety of sensory inputs.

Many differing forms of therapy exist. In Britain probably the most widely used is the 'neurodevelopmental therapy' linked with the name of Bobath. The main feature of this approach is a functional assessment of the child's neurological involvement and an understanding of abnormal movements and tone, thereby allowing the therapist to inhibit the abnormal, to facilitate the normal and ultimately to improve functional abilities. The approach employed is one which is based upon the normal development of movement and balance reactions which occur as the child matures neurologically.

Occupational therapy (see also Chapter 31). The occupational therapist's responsibility in general terms is to evaluate the child's disability in relation to his environment, offering practical support and advice to parents and teachers and other care workers. The encouragement of skills to overcome or diminish the effects of the disability will be combined with the provision of appropriate aids to assist with the various aspects of daily living; these include feeding, seating, toileting and dressing.

Speech therapy (see also Chapter 29). A speech therapist has two major areas of responsibility in relation to children with cerebral palsy: the early development of oral function and the acquisition of a language for communication.

Significant feeding difficulties occur in many children with severe cerebral palsy owing to abnormal sensitivity inducing strong reflex actions, a small spastic tongue or poorly coordinated swallowing mechanisms. Many of these children will eventually have severe dysarthria (incoordination of speech production). Immaturity in chewing patterns may be at the root of many feeding problems.

Communicative ability may be impaired because speech is virtually unintelligible. If this is so, a non-verbal communication system may have to be considered. As modern technology is applied to developing more advanced communication systems the opportunities for such handicapped children continue to improve.

Orthopaedic surgery. Orthopaedic surveillance is important. Surgical release of short spastic muscles and the release of contractures around joints may, if carried out after a careful evaluation, be highly beneficial to function. But decisions to operate have to be undertaken with the greatest of care.

Drug therapy. A number of drugs have been used in the treatment of patients with severe spasticity. Diazepam (Valium) may help relieve spasticity, but if often causes drowsiness before it can be effective. Baclofen (Lioresal) appears more effective than diazepam, with a lower incidence of side-effects. Dantrolene sodium (Dantrium) may be effective for reducing spasticity, but it often causes muscle weakness. It may be of value in the non-ambulant child. Whichever drug is used it is vital to monitor the effect on function and not just the reduction in spasticity.

NEURAL TUBE ABNORMALITIES

Of the several varieties of neural tube abnormalities the commonest severe lesion is that which is usually referred to as spina bifida (SB). This is associated with hydrocephalus in a very high proportion, particularly if the SB lesion is in the lumbar or thoracolumbar region.

There are several different varieties of the severe spina bifida cystica lesion, of which the following three are the most common: rachischisis (myeloschisis), in which the neural tube is wide open,

commonly in the thoracolumbar region, with the upper end of the spinal cord opening on to the surface; myelomeningocele, in which the neural tube is covered by a membrane but the spinal cord and nerve roots are outside the vertebral column, and meningocele, in which the lesion consists of meninges and fluid in continuity with the cerebrospinal fluid but containing no neural tissue. The covering is usually intact skin.

Incidence

Within Britain the overall incidence is approximately 2.0–2.5 per thousand births (including stillbirths). There are considerable differences in incidence between different parts of the world and between different regions in Britain.

Genetic factors have some influence in that there is a 10% incidence of positive family histories and a 5% incidence of SB or an encephalocele (see p.133) in the siblings of an affected child and a 10–15% incidence if two siblings have been affected.

The variation in regional incidence and a predisposition towards occurrence in lower socio-economic groups suggests that a major SB lesion is influenced by a combination of environmental factors and a genetic predisposition.

'Selection' for active treatment or nursing care only

Few paediatric centres in the world can have escaped the difficult controversy over active treatment of all children with SB lesions as against a selective policy of treatment for those thought to have a more favourable outlook. The disappointing results of active treatment for all SB children in Sheffield culminated in Lorber suggesting that in the presence of certain unfavourable criteria in the neonatal period nursing care only should be provided (Lorber, 1971). The criteria proposed consisted of the following:

1 Gross paralysis of the legs.
2 Thoracolumbar or thoraco-lumbo-sacral lesions.
3 Kyphosis (acute forward angulation of spine) or scoliosis (lateral curvature or angulation of spine).
4 Hydrocephalus, with a head circumference of 2 cms or more above the 90th percentile.
5 Intracerebral birth injury.
6 Other gross congenital anomalies, such as cyanotic heart disease.

Many centres in addition to Sheffield have followed

Lorber's suggestions, although a number had adopted similar criteria for treatment prior to his definitive publication. While experiences in different centres vary, most of the infants who receive nursing care only do not survive the first year of life.

'Active' management

The back defect is closed within the first few weeks of life. Some degree of hydrocephalus is present in the majority of SB infants at birth but it is clinically significant in only 25%. The drug isosorbide may be used for a short period to control hydrocephalus, but in those that do not settle down or 'arrest' a surgical bypass operation is required – a 'shunt'.

There are a number of shunt systems, but the commonest are the ventriculo-atrial (ventricles of the brain to the right atrium of the heart) and the ventriculo-peritoneal.

With the ventriculo-atrial shunt the two parts of the catheter system are connected via a Holter or similar one-way valve, which is placed near to the mastoid. In the Pudenz system the valve will be located at the end of the lower distal catheter.

With the ventriculo-peritoneal shunt the proximal catheter is similar to that used in the ventriculo-atrial shunt system but is connected to a distal catheter fitted subcutaneously into the peritoneum. A special distal catheter (Raimundi) is sometimes used to prevent blockage by abdominal contents. Whichever system is used it is common practice to place a small reservoir subcutaneously between the proximal and distal catheters. Into this a needle may be subsequently inserted to measure spinal fluid pressure to test the patency of the shunt system, as well as to allow samples of CSF to be obtained for bacteriological study.

Orthopaedic management. The initial optimism that active and multiple operations in the earlier years of life might enable a high proportion of patients to walk independently with or without calipers has not been fully realized.

Complexity of the lower-limb neurological deficit in SB patients coupled with sensory deficits and major joint abnormalities has in more recent years encouraged a conservative approach. If at two years there appear to be reasonable prospects of walking – based not only on physical but intellectual and developmental status – then consideration is given to correcting any lower-limb deformity.

Urinary tract. In the SB child bladder paralysis of one form or another is common, giving rise to a variety of difficulties. In some children regular manual expression of the bladder will achieve moderate continence, but the child may object as he gets older. Drugs can be helpful: either imipramine or propantheline has been used. For boys over the age of five years the use of a penile appliance may be advised. In girls the continuously in-dwelling silastic urinary catheter has achieved continence for many, although the concomitant administration of antibiotics seems essential to prevent infection. Intermittent non-sterile catheterization of the bladder has produced effective continence in some without urinary infection. Such self-catheterization can be undertaken by a number of older girls.

Urinary diversion procedures have been employed but still seem to be associated with significant difficulties.

Bowels. A balance has to be struck between the avoidance of troublesome constipation and the achievement of continence. Constipation may lead on to rectal and colonic inertia and may aggravate bladder emptying. Control of diet, with or without the judicious use of laxatives, is satisfactory for many, although regular suppositories, enemas and even manual evacuation are required for a proportion of SB children.

Problems of management

Shunt complications. While shunts are simple in principle, complications are common. These may include detachment of one catheter from another, blockage of shunts, shunt infection and a renal problem known as 'shunt nephritis'.

Seizures. Nearly one-third of people with shunts have epilepsy, and it would appear that the risk of this is increased by the need for shunt revisions (Hosking, 1974).

Upper limb weakness. In older patients with hydrocephalus symptoms reminiscent of syringomyelia may occur in the upper limbs. This is thought to be a result of the cavitation of the spinal cord due to long-standing increased cerebrospinal fluid pressure.

Intellectual development. Between 40% and 50% of SB children are intellectually impaired, some severely so. Besides this, many will have varying specific learning disorders which require careful psychometric examination in order to meet their educational needs. The somewhat superficial impression of normal intelligence often quoted as the 'cocktail party' personality may well mask an underlying low intellectual capacity.

Visual defects. Concomitant and paralytic squints due to lesions of the 6th nerve following raised intracranial pressure are common. An acute loss of vision may follow an abrupt rise in pressure: although the pressure may subsequently be reduced optic atrophy may develop.

Endocrine dysfunction. Various disorders of hypothalamic function may occur, producing precocious puberty, infantilism or diabetes insipidus, possibly as a consequence of chronic dilatation of the third ventricle of the brain.

Obesity. This is a common problem in children with severe spina bifida and it must be managed by dietary control.

Skin care. The combination of incontinence, the wearing of urinary appliances, orthoses, impaired sensation and lack of movement makes care of the skin particularly difficult in a number of those with spina bifida.

Psychological and psychosexual problems. A high incidence of emotional problems in children who, in spite of often-repeated hospital admissions and surgical procedures, remain physically handicapped would not seem surprising. Many adolescents with SB are frankly depressed and have specific concerns over sexual function. Careful counselling is required in recognizing this aspect of their handicap.

Prevention of spina bifida

Parents and relatives and also the young people with SB should receive genetic counselling.

In many parts of Britain the routine assessment of maternal serum alphafetoprotein in early pregnancy, supplemented by ultrasonic examination and amniocentesis, enables the major neural tube defects to be identified. The possibility of termination of pregnancy has then to be faced; this will be unacceptable for some on religious or moral grounds.

The administration of high doses of vitamin B complex at the time of conception in those who have previously had a child with a major neural tube defect or who are considered to be at risk of having a fetus similarly affected is currently under evalu-

ation. Preliminary results suggest that such periconceptual administration of vitamin B is associated with a significant reduction in the occurrence of a subsequent malformation.

Management of hydrocephalus not related to a myelomeningocele

Management of children who have hydrocephalus not associated with an SB lesion does not differ significantly from management of children with both. This includes hydrocephalus that is apparently idiopathic or secondary to aqueduct stenosis, infection, haemorrhage or trauma.

Encephaloceles

The majority of encephaloceles that are seen in Europe are situated in the occipital region. In some areas of the world anterior and nasal encephaloceles are more commonly seen.

In some the sac that protrudes from the bony defect in the skull (cranium bifidum) will not contain brain tissue whereas in others it will, perhaps to the extent that surgical closure is impossible. Before a decision is taken on resecting an encephalocele it is vital that studies are undertaken to ascertain the contents of the sac. In a number of children with an encephalocele drainage of spinal fluid is compromised and a shunting procedure will be required. Mild to severe intellectual impairment, visual impairment or total cortical blindness and spastic diplegia may develop in some children with this lesion.

INFECTIONS

Intra-uterine infections

Intra-uterine infections may occur with a variety of different organisms and cause severe deficits within the developing nervous system as well as in other body systems. Pre-eminent amongst this group are the organisms toxoplasma, rubella, cytomegalovirus (CMV) and herpes simplex. Together they are often nicknamed the 'ToRCH' infections.

Toxoplasma

60% of the British population have at some time been infected by the protozoan organism *Toxoplasma gondii*. The principal damage is when it infects for the first time a woman in pregnancy, when the organism may cross the placenta. In 45% of cases infection of the fetus occurs, the possibility increasing throughout the duration of pregnancy (Hall, 1983).

Congenital toxoplasmosis will cause chorioretinitis (inflammation and scarring of part of the retina), hydrocephalus or calcification in the brain. Other more widespread signs of infection may also occur, with jaundice and hepatosplenomegaly. Only 10% to 20% of congenitally affected infants have clinically apparent signs at birth. In the others the signs of neurological damage appear months or even years later.

Cytomegalovirus (CMV)

CMV alone may account for up to 10% of cases of intellectual impairment. The major risk to the fetus is when the primary maternal infection occurs during the pregnancy as distinct from a reactivation from a previous infection. When a primary infection occurs during pregnancy it is likely that 5% of fetuses will be affected (Panjvani and Hanshaw, 1981). The vast majority of affected infants will be asymptomatic at the time of birth. Later, microcephaly with intracranial calcification may be noted, together with the early onset of seizures.

Congenital rubella

Thanks partly to active immunization programmes in Britain for schoolgirls the incidence of congenital rubella has significantly declined, although some slight increase has been noted in recent times because of poor immunization uptake.

In those where rubella during pregnancy is symptomatic there is approximately a 50% risk to the fetus; when asymptomatic the risk is about 20%. The state of gestation will also determine the risks to the fetus in terms of severity. If maternal infection occurs during the first 12 weeks the risk might be as high as 80% and as low as 25% by the end of the second trimester (Miller et al., 1982).

It is important to recognize that prolonged follow-up after birth is important if congenital rubella infection is suspected, as deafness may be the only finding and not apparent until later on.

Herpes simplex

Neonatal herpes simplex infection is usually acquired during passage through an infected birth canal. Less commonly trans-placental passage of virus causes intra-uterine infection, or post-natal acquisition of virus causes post-natal illness. Unlike cytomegalovirus infection almost all examples of neonatal herpes simplex infection are symptomatic, often with serious neurological concomitants apparent in the newborn period.

Neonatal meningitis

Neonatal meningitis is always a severe illness. Particularly at risk is the premature infant, in whom the classic signs of meningitis may be absent. The overall mortality is between 30% and 80% and a morbidity of 20% to 50% with gross neurological damage is seen in the survivors. The development of newer and more efficacious antibiotics may serve to improve on these figures.

Meningitis in later childhood

Meningitis of bacterial origin is always a serious illness and delay in diagnosis is likely to affect the mortality and morbidity. For example, in *Haemophilus influenzae* meningitis the mortality is about 20% and in those that survive 30% may have some neurological sequelae, including intellectual impairment.

Tuberculous meningitis may often be insidious in its presentation and by the time diagnosis is made considerable central nervous system damage may already have occurred. The mortality may be 40% and the morbidity in survivors 20%.

Encephalitis in childhood

The encephalitides in childhood may range from relatively mild illness characterized by headache, drowsiness, pyrexia and perhaps neck stiffness to a life-threatening illness with coma, respiratory arrest and significant mortality.

Herpes simplex encephalitis

This usually severe encephalitis is often associated with involvement of the temporal lobes. The use of a new antiviral agent, acyclovir, gives some hope in counteracting what has hitherto been a predominantly highly destructive encephalitic illness.

Japanese B encephalitis

This usually severe encephalitis is relatively common in a number of South East Asian countries. The virus is transmitted by a mosquito. When it occurs in children under the age of ten years the mortality and morbidity with various neurological sequelae are high.

Progressive neurological disease with dementia related to previous virus infection

Sub-acute sclerosing panencephalitis (SSPE)

This is a disorder that appears to be related to a previous measles infection. The onset (at a mean age of eight years) is usually insidious and typically involves personality changes, deterioration in school performance and difficulty with speech. Myoclonus (irregular jerks that are a form of seizure disorder) is common and occurs at regular intervals. Ultimate progression is towards increasing difficulty with myoclonic epilepsy and the development of a spastic quadriparesis. Survival may be for between one and two years or for very much longer, with many patients entering a so-called 'quiescent' or 'burnt-out' phase.

From the laboratory investigations there is evidence of previous measles infection in the cerebrospinal fluid and blood (high measles titre in the CSF with a ratio of $1:10$ between the spinal fluid and plasma, a high level of IgG and abnormalities of the Lange curve). The EEG tends to be diagnostic, with the appearance of regularly recurring periodic complexes.

SSPE appears to occur in all races, although in the United States it is more common in whites than in blacks, the reverse being the case in South Africa. In Israel it is more common in Arabs than in Sephardic Jews and Ashkenazi Jews. In the United States it is more common in rural communities than in urban ones. In all it would appear that the original measles occurred at a particularly early age.

Attempts to treat this progressive disorder have been made with a variety of agents. Currently of interest is the drug methisoprinol (isoprinosine). So far this drug would appear to arrest the progression of the disease in some, and perhaps in a few some improvement has been seen (Anonymous, 1979).

TOXINS

Lead

A wide variety of environmental agents have been called into question in connection with intellectual impairment: not the least of these has been lead. The evidence linking environmental lead, often originating from the exhaust fumes of cars, is still uncertain and controversial (Yule et al., 1981).

In a study undertaken in schoolchildren around the age of six years in two London boroughs, Smith et al. (1983) concluded that a reduction in the body lead burden could not be guaranteed to be accompanied by an improvement in intelligence, educational attainments or behaviour. This conclusion was arrived at after allowance was made for relevant social factors. But it was noted that even when such social factors were taken into account, the children with a higher body lead content did show more difficult behaviour and worse performance on measures of intelligence than the children with lower lead contents. However, in all of these measures the differences did not attain statistical significance.

Alcohol

It has been suggested that maternally ingested alcohol may be the commonest known cause of intellectual impairment after Down's syndrome and the neural tube defects – and the most preventable (Edwards, 1983). The term 'fetal alcohol syndrome' has been coined for the association between dysmorphic features, poor fetal growth and various neurodevelopmental abnormalities. Alcohol ingestion in the early weeks of pregnancy poses the greatest risk to the fetal well-being (Wright et al., 1983).

Maternal phenylketonuria

Untreated maternal phenylketonuria during pregnancy may be associated with microcephaly and other physical and developmental abnormalities (Angeli et al., 1974).

ACCIDENTS

Head injuries are more common in children than in adults and a significant minority sustain a permanent neurological deficit. These may include neuropsychological deficits and epilepsy. Nevertheless, the majority do make a full recovery, even if this may be over many months (Brink et al., 1980; Jackson, 1983). Head injury in children is frequently a consequence of a road traffic accident when the child is a pedestrian or a cyclist. For this reason the widely introduced car seat belt legislation has had little impact on the problem.

Near-drowning will inevitably pose a risk of brain damage. However, the outlook for complete brain recovery for children who nearly drown appears to be good and 95% make a complete recovery. Of those left with a severe neurological deficit – severe mental retardation or a spastic quadriparesis – all were clinically dead at the time of rescue (Pearn, 1977).

Non-accidental injury to children often includes head trauma, either by direct blows to the head or secondary to severe shaking. In a survey of 86 children with cerebral palsy seen in one centre over a twelve-month period Diamond and Jaudes (1983) identified seven children that had been subjected to child abuse. In eight of these cerebral palsy was a result of abuse. These authors drew attention to the already described increased risks of abuse to children with already established cerebral palsy.

ACQUIRED BIOCHEMICAL AND METABOLIC CAUSES

Hypoglycaemia

Low blood sugar in the neonatal period may have a damaging effect upon the brain if unrecognized. Especially at risk are premature and the light-for-dates infants. But, in addition, other older children may be at risk in certain situations, such as during generalized severe illnesses or starvation before operations or mismanaged diabetes.

Other electrolyte disturbances, such as hypo- or hypernatraemia, uraemia and hypocalcaemia, pose risks that may be associated with central nervous system damage.

NEURODEGENERATIVE DISORDERS

Although individually rare, there are a large number of these diseases that give rise to degeneration of the nervous system in childhood, and this is recognized by a loss of previously attained abilities, with, in some cases, the development of epilepsy and other neurological abnormalities. These disorders can be grouped into storage disorders (in which a compound is abnormally stored within the various body tissues) and neurodegenerative disorders without known storage.

Storage disorders

In these disorders there is an abnormal accumulation of a substance within the brain and there may in many also be an accumulation of the same substance in the peripheral nervous tissue, as well as in other organs of the body. In most of these disorders the biochemical fault is at least partially understood and the absence or deficiency of certain enzymes has been recognized. The storage may initially be within the white matter or within the grey matter of the brain. With storage in the white matter the early signs will be of motor dysfunction, whereas with storage in the grey matter the early signs will be social and intellectual dysfunction, frequently with the development of seizures and visual impairment.

Metachromatic leukodystrophy

In this disorder there is an abnormal storage of cerebroside sulphate, with degeneration affecting primarily the white matter in the central and peripheral nervous system. Accumulation takes place preferentially in the dentate nucleus and the basal ganglia. Symmetrical demyelination of the brain (loss of the myelin tissue), spinal cord and peripheral nerves occurs.

Metachromasia in a number of tissues occurs because of the abnormal accumulation of sulphatides, giving rise to a shift in the absorption spectra of certain blue cationic dyes. Thus, after staining with toluidine blue there will be a greeny-brown colour – metachromasia. The cause of this abnormal accumulation of sulphatides is the deficiency of the enzyme cerebroside sulphatase (aryl sulphatase A).

There are several different clinical forms of metachromatic leukodystrophy, but the most common is the late infantile variety, which accounts for 60% of cases. There is also an intermediate or early juvenile form, starting between the ages of four and six years, and a juvenile form, with an onset between six and ten years.

Early development in the late infantile variety appears to be normal, but disturbance of gait due to ataxia appears in the second and third years of life. An alternative clinical presentation may be with progressive spastic paraplegia coupled with striatal signs (Parkinsonian features), difficulty with speech and swallowing and, at a later stage, optic atrophy. The ultimate progression is towards increasing dementia, blindness and often seizures. Tendon reflexes will often be absent owing to the coexistence of a peripheral segmental demyelination. Death occurs in this form between six months and six years after diagnosis.

In the intermediate or early juvenile form the presentation is with gait disorders, with intellectual deterioration and extrapyramidal and cerebellar signs later.

In the juvenile form the presentation may be educational difficulty, behavioural problems and, later, the development of difficulties in gait. In this form progression may be extremely slow.

Metachromatic leukodystrophy has an autosomal recessive pattern of inheritance, and possibilities for antenatal diagnosis exist.

Tay–Sachs disease (G_{M2} gangliosidosis)

In this disorder there is an abnormal storage of the G_{M2} ganglioside, predominantly in the grey matter of the brain, but also in other tissues. This is due to a deficiency of hexosaminidase-A, and in some varieties hexosaminidase-B as well. There are several different clinical forms: the most common is the infantile form (66% of patients in the United Kingdom).

In the infantile variety of Tay–Sachs disease the onset is usually in the first six months of life, with the first sign being an excessive startle reaction to sound (hyperacousia). A cherry-red spot due to the storage of the ganglioside is seen at the macula, and later there is optic atrophy, leading to blindness. There is a loss of intellectual, social and motor developmental milestones coupled with inappropriate laughing and marked hypotonia, eventually leading to a spastic paraplegia. Megaencephaly (an enlargement of brain and head) is a common feature.

In the late infantile variety of Tay–Sachs disease, often known as Sandhoff's disease, the onset will be within the second or third year of life. Presentation will most typically be with an excessive startle response, leading on to psychomotor deterioration, the onset of seizures, the cherry-red spot developing somewhat later, and slight enlargement of the liver. Death from this disease most commonly occurs between four and ten years old.

There is a propensity for infantile Tay–Sachs disease to occur in Ashkanazi Jews, in whom the gene frequency is 1 in 27, contrasting with non-Jews, in whom the frequency is 1 in 380. This gene frequency refers to infantile Tay–Sachs disease only; the various other forms do not seem to have an ethnic bias.

Niemann–Pick disease

In this disorder there is an abnormal storage of sphingomyelin, due to a deficiency of the enzyme sphingomyelinase. There are probably five varieties. 85% of patients are of the type A, infantile, variety. In this the presentation is usually within the first six months of life, with early persistent jaundice and later failure to thrive, feeding difficulties, vomiting and bouts of fever. A protuberant abdomen with marked hepatosplenomegaly develops by the end of the first year of life. Chest X-rays show pulmonary involvement.

In the second half of the first year of life there is increasing hypotonia, sometimes cerebellar signs, and, in about 25% of cases, the development of a cherry-spot as in Tay–Sachs disease. Death is usually before the age of five years.

In the so-called type C – late infantile – variety the clinical picture is similar, but the onset is usually between two and four years.

Gaucher's disease

In the various forms of this disorder there is an abnormal accumulation of cerebroside, due to a deficiency of glucocerebrosidase. There are three principal clinical forms, the most common being the chronic variety, in which there is no apparent central nervous system involvement.

In the acute infantile variety there is a period of normal development up to the age of about four months. There is then an apparent failure to thrive, development of a large abdomen in association with hepatosplenomegaly, and anaemia. Strabismus is common. The deterioration tends to be very rapid, with misery, a whining cry, opisthotonic posturing (acute extensor posturing involving the whole trunk), spasticity and progressive bulbar paresis. Death tends to occur at a very early age – usually by the age of twelve months.

Batten's disease (neuronal ceroid lipofuscinosis)

At present there are known to be at least four clinical forms of Batten's disease, in which there is intraneuronal storage of lipofuscin-like material. The exact enzyme defect is not known but suggestions have been made that it may be a primary metabolic disorder in which there is an inability to metabolize retinoic acid; the storage material seems to be a derivative of this.

The infantile, Santavouri or Finnish, type has its onset at about one year of age, with retardation of mental development, increasing microcephaly, ataxia, visual loss and myoclonic jerks. During the third year the disease enters its quiescent phase. Death occurs most typically at the age of six years.

The late infantile variety (Jansky–Bielschowsky) form has its onset between the ages of eighteen months and four years, with seizures that are increasingly more difficult to control, ataxia, progressive mental deterioration, visual loss and optic atrophy. Death occurs most usually before the age of ten years.

In the juvenile variety (Spielmeyer–Vogt) the onset is most typically between the ages of six and ten years, with progressive visual loss and pigmentary changes and later optic atrophy. The most usual initial diagnosis for these children is retinitis pigmentosa, but it is not long after the onset of visual difficulties that the intellectual development is obviously compromised. At a later stage seizures develop, coupled with ataxia, swallowing difficulties and a spastic quadriplegia. Death occurs at any time between the ages of 15 and 25 years.

The investigation of this group of disorders is complex. In a number of the white blood cells (lymphocytes) there will be vacuolation, particularly in the juvenile variety. In all there will be change in the electroencephalogram. In the infantile variety this takes the form of progressive slowing and diminution in amplitude of the potentials seen on the recordings. In the late infantile form slow photic stimulation will produce very-high-amplitude discharges over the occipital lobes (Pampiglione and Harden, 1973). The electroretinogram (ERG) will be absent in all.

Confirmatory diagnosis has previously been obtained by means of rectal biopsy, in which a chemical staining of neuronal plexi has demonstrated the abnormal storage, but more recent electron-microscopic techniques have been able to show a number of inclusion bodies which are of diagnostic significance in a variety of body tissues.

Neurodegenerative disorders without known storage

In a large number of neurodegenerative disorders in which no storage is identified it is possible to find that degeneration takes place in specific parts of the central and peripheral nervous system. Correct diagnosis will depend upon careful clinical examination of such patients, and on knowledge of this group of disorders.

Leigh's disease (sub-acute necrotizing encephalomyelopathy)

In this condition, which was first described by Denis Leigh (1951), there is a development of dysfunction of the brainstem, spinal cord and sometimes peripheral nerves which has features similar to Wernicke's encephalopathy. In the latter condition there is known to be a deficiency of thiamine and a high level of acetyl-CoA. Elevated levels of the chemicals lactate, pyruvate and alanine are commonly identified in both conditions.

Most typically, Leigh's disease presents in early infancy with swallowing and feeding difficulties, hypotonia, weakness, ataxia, a peripheral neuropathy (impairment in the function of nerves) and an external ophthalmoplegia (an abnormality of eye movement), with a loss of vision and the development of seizures. Clinical features, however, are variable and the clinical course, although towards degeneration, fluctuates.

In more recent years a number of reports have occurred of patients with a clinical picture suggestive of Leigh's disease but in whom have been discovered a number of inborn errors of carbohydrate metabolism (Pincus at al., 1969).

Schilder's disease (diffuse cerebral sclerosis)

In 1912 Schilder described three patients with a demyelinating and progressive disorder which has since been given his name. Unfortunately, confusion over the main characteristics has occurred since then.

There appear to be a variety of demyelinating disorders which may have their onset in childhood. Some of these appear to be familial and include Pelizaeus–Merzbacher and a sudanophilic leukodystrophy associated with adrenal atrophy or dystrophy, Addison–Schilder's disease.

Addison–Schilder's disease appears to be a sex-linked condition with clinical onset between five and eight years. The usual presentation is with gait disturbance followed by intellectual impairment. In a number there is evidence of adrenal dysfunction, with pigmentation and hypotonia. Seizures are common.

In Pelizaeus–Merzbacher disease there will be a clinical onset before the age of three months with roving eye movements, poor head control and progressive cerebellar ataxia. Progression occurs over some years with increasing involuntary movements and mental retardation.

The term Schilder's disease is used by some to describe a condition which does appear to have some association with multiple sclerosis. Typical pathology is a widespread demyelination, particularly on the occipital lobes. The clinical pattern is of a sporadic type, with onset between the ages of five and twelve years. The usual presentation is with mental retardation, the development of seizures, cortical blindness and hemiplegia, which may simulate a space-occupying lesion. A pseudobulbar palsy is common in the later stages of this disorder.

Some have advocated treatment with ACTH as for other patients with demyelinating disorders of central origin.

CONCLUSION

The range of disorders that may be causative or strongly associated with intellectual impairment in childhood is large. Only some of these have been mentioned and reviewed in this chapter. For a more complete discussion reference should be made to the texts listed under 'Further Reading'.

REFERENCES

Angeli E, Denman AR, Harris RF, Kirman BH & Stern J (1974) Maternal phenylketonuria: a family with seven mentally retarded siblings. *Developmental Medicine and Child Neurology 16:* 800–807.

Anonymous (1979) Subacte sclerosing panencephalitides. *British Medical Journal ii:* 1096.

Brink JD, Imow C & Woo-San J (1980) Physical recovery after severe closed head trauma in children and adolescents. *Journal of Paediatrics 97:* 721–727.

Diamond LJ & Jaudes PK (1983) Child abuse in a cerebral palsied population. *Developmental Medicine and Child Neurology 25:* 169–174.

Edwards G (1983) Alcohol and advice to the pregnant woman. *British Medical Journal 286:* 247–248.

Hall SM (1983) Congenital toxoplasmosis in England, Wales and Northern Ireland: some epidemiological problems. *British Medical Journal 287:* 453–455.

Hosking GP (1974) Fits in hydrocephalic children. *Archives of Diseases in Childhood 49:* 633–635.

Jackson RH (1983) Accidents and handicap. *Developmental Medicine and Child Neurology 25:* 656–659.

Leigh D (1951) Subacute necrotizing encephalomyelopathy in an infant. *Journal of Neurology, Neurosurgery and Psychiatry 14:* 216–222.

Lorber J (1971) Results of treatment of myelomeningocele. *Developmental Medicine and Child Neurology 13:* 279–303.

Miller E, Cradock-Wilson JE & Pollack TM (1982) Consequences of confirmed maternal rubella at successive stages of pregnancy. *Lancet ii:* 781–784.

Pampiglione G & Harden A (1973) A neurophysiological identification of a late infantile form of 'neuronal lipidosis'. *Journal of Neurology, Neurosurgery and Psychiatry 36:* 68–74.

Panjvani ZFK & Hanshaw JB (1981) Cytomegalovirus in the perinatal period. *American Journal of Diseases of Children 135:* 56–60.

Pearn JH (1977) Neurological and psychometric studies in children surviving fresh water immersion accidents. *Lancet i:* 7–9.

Pincus JH, Itokawa Y & Cooper JR (1969) Enzyme inhibiting factor in subacute necrotizing encephalomyopathy. *Neurology 19:* 841–845.

Smith M, Delves T, Lansdown R, Clayton B & Graham P (1983) The effects of lead exposure on unborn children: the Institute of Child Health/Southampton Study. *Developmental Medicine and Child Neurology 25:* Supplement 47.

Wright JT, Barrison IG, Lewis IG, MacRae KD, Waterson EJ, Toplis PJ, Gordon MG, Morris NH & Murray-Lyon IM (1983) Alcohol consumption, pregnancy and low birth weight. *Lancet i:* 633–665.

Yule W, Lansdown R, Millar IB & Urbanowicz MA (1981) The relationship between blood lead concentrations, intelligence and attainment in a school population: a pilot study. *Developmental Medicine and Child Neurology 23:* 567–576.

FURTHER READING

Ampola MG (1982) *Metabolic Diseases in Paediatric Practice.* Boston: Little, Brown & Company.

Brett EM (ed) (1983) *Paediatric Neurology.* Edinburgh: Churchill-Livingstone.

Brocklehurst G, Sharrard WJW, Forrest D & Stark G (eds) (1976) *Spina Bifida for the Clinician.* Clinics in Developmental Medicine 57. London: William Heinemann Medical Books.

Eadie MJ & Tyrer JH (1983) *Biochemical Neurology.* Lancaster: MTP.

Finnie NR (1974) *Handling the Young Cerebral Palsied Child at Home,* 2nd edn. London: William Heinemann Medical Books.

Frank JD & Fixsen JA (1980) Spina bifida. *British Journal of Hospital Medicine 24:* 422–436.

Hosking GP (1982) *An Introduction to Paediatric Neurology.* London: Faber & Faber.

Levitt S (1982) *Treatment of Cerebral Palsy and Motor Delay,* 2nd edn. Oxford & London: Blackwell Scientific.

Menkes JH (1980) *Textbook of Child Neurology,* 2nd edn. Philadelphia: Lea & Febiger.

Swaiman KJ & Wright FS (1982) *The Practice of Pediatric Neurology, Vols. I & II,* 2nd edn. St. Louis, Toronto & London: Mosby.

Volpe JJ (1981) *Neurology of the Newborn.* Philadelphia & London: Saunders.

Chapter 13
Families and Handicap

SHEILA HOLLINS

THE IMPACT OF HANDICAP ON THE FAMILY

'Elizabeth starts at her "Special School" next week. A painful experience as we, her parents, are now part of a different world – rather like seeing a poverty-stricken village on the television, and saying from the comfort of our armchairs "poor things" and then finding that we too are poverty-stricken and starving.'

'A handicapped child is a handicapped family'?

This chapter will look at some of the implications of this well-worn phrase, first coined in the early 1970s. My introductory quotation expresses a sense, for Elizabeth's family, of entering a new and restricted world – restricted, that is, from the choice of activities and worldly values of the rest of us. The demands made by a person with a mental handicap in a family may be sufficiently great to obscure the needs and identity of other family members and of the family unit itself. This distortion of identity may be short-lived while the family adjusts to the new member, or it may be a long-term maladjustment, which will deeply affect and alter the lives of the rest of the family. However, having a child with a handicap does not remove the basic differences between one family and another of background, expectations and behaviour.

The family has always been the foundation of our social structure, and although two out of every three marriages in the UK do still survive, the 'typical' nuclear family of two parents and two children is increasingly rare.

Farber (1960) insisted that the main determinant of marital integration in families with a handicapped member was simply the degree of integration achieved prior to the introduction of a handicap; bad marriages may be made worse while good ones withstand the added tension, or strengthen under its influence. We do not have clear evidence that the presence of a handicapped family member increases the rate of marital breakdown, although, in families which have broken up, the stress of 24-hour caring is often given as the precipitating factor. One recent comparison (Friedrich et al., 1983) of stress in families where there was a handicap, and in those without a family member with a handicap, identified four factors which contributed to an increase in stress. These were physical incapacity, parent and family problems, pessimism, and certain characteristics of the people with handicaps themselves. However, in the GLC Spina Bifida Survey, rather surprisingly, parental stress was not shown to be related to the degree of disability. Carr et al. (1983) found that mothers' subjective ratings of ill-health were higher than the controls and were related to higher scores on the Malaise inventory. Wishart et al. (1981) found no evidence of an increase in ill-health in parents who have a child with a handicap compared with parents of normal children. Ferguson and Watt (1980) found that, although mothers of handicapped children reported more family problems than did those of normal children, their scores on the Malaise inventory did not show any significant difference.

Elizabeth's father went on to say, 'I suppose we have been given the same but painful privilege of seeing children the way God sees us – as people to be loved not because of what we can do but because of who we are.' Their Christian faith helps them to come to terms with Elizabeth's disability. However, some families lose their faith, being unable to believe in a God who allows a damaged child to be born.

Characteristically, there are many stages to be worked through before a newly diagnosed child with a handicap is fully accepted and loved.

The bereavement response

More is published now about counselling the parents of handicapped children, and particularly about breaking the bad news (see Chapter 15). Most paediatricians will be aware of the debate about the relative merits of telling the truth in one way or another, and will know of the need for consistent repetition and an openness to questioning. Parents want to be told early, honestly and sympathetically (Carr, 1983), and, in my view, together. This will apply whether the diagnosis of disability or impairment is made at birth or later, as the toddler is seen to be falling behind his peer group in developmental terms, or following an accident later in childhood.

Less familiar is the idea that before parents can fully accept the handicapped or impaired child who is theirs, they must first mourn the loss of the perfect child they had been expecting or who had been changed through illness or accident.

The sense of loss experienced by the family may depend on the extent of the discrepancy between the hoped-for child, and the child born (Solnit and Stark, 1977). A child who is damaged during childhood may be invested with idealized memories to which other siblings cannot match up.

When the diagnosis is made soon after birth there is no time for parents to adjust to the loss of the desired child before they are expected to develop a close and loving relationship with this new child who is damaged. Parents often report overwhelming feelings which interfere with their ability to get on with life. The pattern of this psychic crisis has been seen so often that it has come to be known as the 'bereavement response': it bears marked similarities to the response seen when any other major loss has been experienced. Fox (1977) described the work facing the family as 'an ambivalent conflict between acceptance of the unacceptable and rejection of the clearly real'. The emotional work to be done may be delayed or interrupted because the family is so burdened with the tasks of daily caring, and a pathological adjustment may be made within the family circle (Bicknell, 1983).

Even if acceptance of a severely handicapped infant is achieved, the bereavement response and the whole process of readjustment may be initiated again by the arrival of another developmental stage requiring decisions. Starting or leaving school, for example, may force comparisons with normal siblings or friends of comparable age. This constant readjustment will be facilitated if the initial bereavement response was worked through to a healthy equilibrium. I believe that this dynamic process of working towards acceptance or adjustment must be well under way before a family's energies can be fully harnessed in partnership with their professional advisors.

By looking at different aspects of a family's development, structure and function it may be possible to understand more precisely an individual family's coping abilities or difficulties at any particular time.

THE DEVELOPMENT OF THE FAMILY

This begins before marriage and continues through the arrival of children, their growing up and developing personal relationships outside the family, and their becoming increasingly independent.

The young family

When their first child is born parents have to learn parenting skills which are not innate. In Western society these skills are difficult to learn by imitation because of the isolation of the nuclear family. The desire to nurture is powerful, however, and suggestions that the handicapped fetus or infant is better off dead deny this desire. Even where the fetus has been aborted, or the infant has died, or been admitted to an institution, feelings of guilt and regret are common. Such family secrets may impinge on the dynamics of family relationships later. For example, a mother who had a stillborn baby then learnt for the first time that her own mother's first child had been stillborn. The young bereaved parents were able to benefit from genetic counselling in planning a new pregnancy. Feelings of guilt and blame were brought into the open and resolved. Thus genetic counselling remains an important issue when the handicapped child has been rejected or denied both in current and future generations.

The 'good-enough' mother will aim to be in tune with her child's needs and will achieve this best if she can be in a state of *reverie* – listening and responsive to verbal and non-verbal cues in her child's attempts to communicate with her. Some mothers gain great pleasure from eliciting positive responses from their infants and they seem sensitive to encouraging the most highly developed skills in their infant's repertoire (Blacher and Meyers, 1983). Delayed or distorted cues from a handicapped child may interfere with the development of this early parent–child communication. Other factors which may interfere with the mother's ability to be responsive to her child's cues include high levels of anxiety and feelings of failure. Even with an experienced mother there is a difference between knowing how to develop a nurturing and interactive relationship with a child, and being able to with the child in question. She may put all her energy into her own emotional growth or she may be overwhelmed by time-consuming physical demands and be unable to go shopping or to work or to do the housework until after her child is in bed. She may also have to deal with feelings of humiliation provoked by strangers who stare or complain that her normal-looking child's immature behaviour or her child's abnormal appearance is causing offence.

Often worse is the sheer indifference of neighbours or friends. The resulting isolation may be exaggerated by her husband seeking solace in his work, in alcohol, or with another woman. Once a child with a handicap has arrived in a family, it may be very difficult for that family to establish new social contacts. Voluntary organizations, such as Contact a Family, in England, try to resolve such difficulties by offering opportunities to meet other families who have children with handicaps.

Opportunities to enjoy the same leisure activities as the rest of the community are much more limited: 'the idea of that total social desert that would face our daughter as she grew older began to haunt us . . . there were no friends . . . no invitations . . . we had for some time been feeling like social pariahs in the neighbourhood . . . for Kim, we began to realize this would be the way she lived her whole life' (Collins and Collins, 1976). There is a clear need to help people with mental handicap and their families seek out ordinary leisure activities and use them (Wertheimer, 1983).

Growing up and letting go

This is a slow process for all children. It comes with the acquisition of physical and mental skills and the knowledge that one can cope on one's own. It is learning to disagree with parents and teachers, volubly if necessary. It is having the confidence to stand one's ground in the face of superior age and authority. It is being able to withstand pressure from all those who argue that they know better. And it is being able to earn a living. For the young adult with a handicap, however, leaving school may mean increasing dependency.

The greatest worry of all for parents is about what will happen to their son or daughter when they are dead. There is no absolute guarantee that adequate support and provision will be made for them without parents to fight on their behalf. A 32-year-old man, a year after his mother's sudden death, remained preoccupied with his perception

that nothing would be the same again unless he could go back home and live with his mother.

In learning to let their offspring go, parents have to push them to the limits of their capabilities so that the maximum degree of independence can be achieved. If independent or alternative supported living is established before a forced separation by death, parents' worries are more likely to be relieved. It is sad when grief at the death of a child with a handicap is alleviated by relief that worries about the future have been taken away!

THE STRUCTURE OF THE FAMILY

The family as a group

Where the socio-economic status of a family is low, the crisis of organization tends to be greater. The long-term reactions of siblings are most likely to be related to the burden of care which they will share with their parents. In families of higher social class the so-called 'tragic crisis' due to shattered expectations may be more common, and the siblings' reactions tend to depend on the ability of the family to accept individual limitations. The extent and openness of parental communication about the child's handicap is of major importance for the siblings' understanding. The attitudes the parents express exert a major influence on their other children's acceptance of the child with a handicap, and it seems that this is especially true of middle-class families (Oliver, 1973).

Substitute families

Substitute families require similar networks of support to natural parents if placement of a child with a handicap is to be successful. Alternative homes may be found by fostering, adoption or in ordinary or specialist children's homes. In England, where children are in the care of the local authority, community homes are required to make proper provision for their care, treatment and control, and this includes a six-monthly review of each child's changing needs and plans for the future. Many voluntary homes are not subject to these regulations. The National Children's Bureau recommends that even when parents visit regularly, the child should be received into the voluntary care of the social services department in order that the statutory right to regular review is established. There are many anomalies associated with the admission of children to hospital or local authority care; for example, in National Health Service provision no charge is made for residential care, but the parents of a child who is taken out of hospital into local authority accommodation may suddenly find themselves required to pay a proportion of the cost.

THE FUNCTION OF THE FAMILY

Roles adopted by different family members

The individual family member who has a mental handicap may fulfil a number of roles; these may be adaptive or maladaptive. For example, the youngest child of an older mother who has Down's syndrome himself may in adulthood become the essential companion of a lonely widow, deprived of the chance to develop a life of his own. He may have become the centre of his mother's life as other children have grown up and taken their independence, or he may be the family pet, spoilt by all, allowed what he wants with no limits, his inappropriate behaviour tolerated and excused. He may fulfil an economic role earning his own living, contributing to the household budget or supporting other family workers by doing the household chores. He may become a go-between or a scapegoat where lines of communication within the family have become distorted.

The wider family needs consideration too – not just mother but also father, siblings, grandparents and cousins, together with neighbours and the community. Most have choice about how much involvement in relation to the individual member with a handicap they will have. Some mothers will experience continuous informal caring as a denial of the chance to have a life of their own – something felt more acutely in cultures where emphasis is placed on personal freedom and fulfilment. Some families will cut themselves off from wider family and social contacts. Simeonsson (1981) has described both positive and negative effects on brothers and sisters of children with handicaps. Siblings may decline to bring friends home because they have not owned up to having a brother or sister who is 'different'. Within the family such a sibling may have become idealized, with parental expectations for the child who is damaged being transferred to the healthy sibling. In sensing their parents' disappointment, siblings often carry a heavy burden of responsibility to put things right by trying to be everything their parents ever wanted.

On the other hand, siblings are often happy and well-adjusted, with a greater sense of responsibility and maturity than their peers. The brother or sister with a handicap is usually loved and accepted. Their siblings are more likely to enter a caring profession than children without this personal experience of disability in their own family.

Sometimes brothers and sisters over-identify with the sibling who has the disability, secretly asking themselves how many of the same characteristics they have: 'Am I defective myself in some way?' As they grow older this may change to a fear of having a defective child themselves. It is true that the brother or sister with a handicap will require more time and attention, and he will effectively become the youngest in the family with his needs always coming first. Thus physical demands to deal with household chores or to sit in while parents go out may prove a heavy burden.

As families succeed in keeping their children with mental handicaps out of hospital and as de-institutionalization and community care proceed families may cope without complaining, underneath a 'superficial shell of competence'. It is my opinion that these informal carers are in danger of being 'left to get on with it' at home, unless society gives them more status and more support.

ACCESS TO SERVICES

For many families the realization that facilities readily available to their other children are no longer available to the child with a handicap is a harsh shock; 'special' facilities may not be special or may even be non-existent. The long round of appointment visits for secondary handicaps, such as epilepsy requiring medication, or cerebral palsy requiring mechanical aids and therapies, can be exhausting. Access to health care and habilitation is more difficult where there are multiple handicaps, behavioural problems or social factors compounding the major disability (Manciaux et al., 1981).

Supporting the carers

Increasingly it is being seen and understood that parents must have adequate support of both a practical and an emotional nature to enhance their coping skills, and to avoid 'burn out'.

Adequate social work input can provide a preview of needs and aid access to practical help and services (see Chapter 26).

Counselling (see Chapter 15) is not the sole prerogative of the social worker or psychiatrist.

Provision of practical help at home, not only with the chores but also to allow space and social pursuits for other family members, is difficult for a family to arrange themselves. An extension to the home-help service offered by local authorities in the United Kingdom would achieve this. Accessible transport can make all the difference between enabling a family to take up available services and leaving them in isolation.

Respite care may be offered to give the family a break, but at least as importantly to widen the individual's social horizons. In a family where other social contacts may have become fewer, making relationships outside the nuclear family becomes difficult for all family members. For the individual with a handicap who cannot simply go out to play, social contact has to be organized. Regular care away from home in familiar surroundings on a planned basis, as well as in response to family crisis, will begin to prepare the individual for longer separations in adulthood.

Education is provided from two years until the age of 19 in the United Kingdom, but an increase in day care and leisure activities (with transport available) is needed for holiday periods and for the adult population.

Early intervention programmes may be available; in these, professionals and parents share information as well as practical skills, in order to reach a better understanding of an individual's current needs. This can be a euphemism for providing a pre-packaged programme which does not take into account the wishes and needs of the family at that time. Home-visiting schemes cut out the problems and expenses of travel for parents, but have the disadvantage that they may reinforce a mother's isolation. Parent groups and workshops, on the other hand, strengthen parents solidarity and choice.

Adequate financial support and advice is essential. In Britain the take-up of state financial allowances such as the attendance allowance (a weekly tax-free payment to those over the age of two years who need substantially more assistance than their peers) and the mobility allowance (a weekly allowance for those over the age of five who are unable to walk) is between half and three-quarters of those thought to be eligible.

This catalogue of services is inclined to cast the parents of a person with a handicap in a rather passive role. One of the important developments in recent years has been the recognition of a more active role for parents.

Parents' role in assessment

It is built into the 1981 Education Act that parents have a right to participate in assessment of their own child's special educational needs. For the first time parents have a right to read professional reports about their child. This differs from ordinary parenting: as far as their special child is concerned these parents are to become professionals themselves, but without the training and guidance normally afforded the latter. The structure of service provision, whether health, social services or education, may lead parents to assume that the professionals are the experts, and that their own role is a subsidiary and rather passive one. It is common to give more weight to the opinion of the expert, who sees an individual for a few minutes at times months or years apart, than to the observations of parents, who have 24-hour responsibility for the individual concerned. Parents and other family members will need help if they are to make the most of their opportunities to represent the interests of the individual concerned. The concept of the key worker, who provides a link between the individual and his family and all the agencies involved in delivering care, is a useful one. Such a person, who can be from any of the professions involved, will have a responsibility to improve the access of families to required facilities, to increase choice and to aid the expression of opinions and needs.

For example, if inappropriate help is offered, or the suggested help is unavailable, parents may conclude that decisions affecting their child's future are being made on inadequate grounds. 'Nobody told me anything' really means 'Nobody told me anything that meant anything to me'! If the significance of the expert's diagnosis and prescription is not understood, the anxiety or fear engendered may well generate hostility towards the professionals. Such a breakdown in relationships between the users of the service and the service providers results in loss of hope and bitterness. Re-establishing trust can be a lengthy and difficult process.

THE PROFESSIONAL RESPONSE

The professional response will influence the development of the family's attitudes in the evolution of the disability. The individual's attitudes to himself and to his disability will reflect those of his family and carers and those of the wider community; such attitudes will be important factors in his response to relationship opportunities and to other choices presented to him.

It is worth us all asking ourselves why we chose a career in one of the caring professions. Parents are more dissimilar than they are similar – so are professionals! Parents and professionals are all people with psyches! They will all have emotional reactions to the presence of severe handicap. The emotional response of an adult, whether a professional or a parent, who is faced with the reality of a child with a severe disability, will have more to do with that adult's own perception of the disability than with anything inherent in the child himself. To his perception of a disability each adult will bring past and present experiences and relationships, fears and aspirations. While the professional may have been trained to be scientifically objective, disturbing emotions of revulsion or guilt may interfere with his ability to communicate with a distressed family.

Possible professional responses
  Use of jargon to obscure the truth
  Judgemental attitudes about the parents
  Over-identification with the family
  Denial of the extent of the disability
  Omnipotence in decision-making
  Collusion with the family's response

Examples of the least appropriate responses range from apportionment of blame – 'Why didn't you bring him to the surgery sooner?' – and other judgemental comments, to the use of medical jargon to avoid an acknowledgement of a harsh reality – for example, 'There is probably some cerebral cellular dysfunction and the EEG shows a non-specific abnormality', instead of 'His brain is not developing normally and this means he will be slower to learn than other children.' However the use of labels such as 'developmental delay' or 'slow learning' may appear more acceptable to the parents of a small child than the stark terms 'retarded' or 'mentally handicapped', to accuse the same parents of denial when they ask why he is not catching up by 11 or 12 years seems to reflect professional remoteness.

It is often too hard for the expert to get outside himself and yet to be sufficiently in touch with his own feelings to be able to ask the parents, 'What are *you* worrying about?' without the expectation that he can take the worry away, and still to admit that he does not know all the answers.

What is the professional's task in relation to the family with a handicapped child? At least part of the task is to be aware of, and to help others to be aware of, family adjustments and to enable the parents to achieve psychological growth and thus the possibility of shared decision-making. However, one's own investment in a family's copin[g] bedevilled by a shortfall in service [other hand, an inability of the through bitter experience of bein result in one's offer of practical h..p ...

Parent–professional partnership

This must be based as far as possible on a shared and changing perception of reality. Diagnosis as such plays only a small part in this, although it may be a very useful therapeutic tool which enables other communication to take place. The important distinction to be made both for the parents and for the professionals involved is between each individual's internal and external realities. The external reality as seen by an unbiased observer bears little relation to the reality perceived by parents or siblings, by teachers or therapists, or by the handicapped people themselves. The impact of handicap or serious illness on the internal worlds of family members *and* professionals may be of greater consequence than the diagnosis in planning realistic objectives for an individual child or adult.

The internal world comprises the personal structure of each individual's early relationships and governs present emotional responses. An individual's self-esteem is dependent on the stability of these internalized relationships. For example, someone's perception of his own father as aggressive and rejecting may bear no resemblance to the kindly gentleman known to others. The parent who says he cannot cope is making his own harsh judgement about himself. He sees himself as lacking in skills or personal resources. Such feelings of inadequacy and rejection are dangerous, not just because of the consequences to the child, but because it is for the parent a second failure. Even if we as professionals see parents as less than ideal, nothing is to be gained by sharing this viewpoint with parents, who are only too aware of their own feelings of inadequacy. More positively, we must build on each parent's own style, accepting their own perceptions and drawing on their own unique resources. Even when a substitute family placement has been requested and arranged, every attempt must be made to retain links with the natural family and to encourage participatory management in the care of their child. Such co-operation will be a defence against secondary guilt developing in the parents, and may allow increasing involvement at a later date.

All must help parents and other family members reconcile their internal and external worlds, so as to able to embark on realistic activities and make appropriate decisions for their own situations.

CONCLUSION

I would like to end this chapter with an open letter to professionals working with families from the father of an adolescent who has an intellectual handicap.

Dear Professional,

Could I please give you some advice when you are dealing with people like me:

1 Don't patronize us: we may be ignorant of the technical jargon of your profession, but we're not stupid.
2 Do give us credit for what we know. The time we spend with our children and the depth of our relationship is much greater than you will know. Make use of this: don't discount it or discredit it.
3 Don't let your preconceptions of us, the parents, distract you from the needs of our children; listen to what we say.
4 Do try to give straight answers to our questions: we often worry about our children. Be frank and tell us what you can, even when we don't ask the right questions. We need accurate information to do our job well.
5 Do not be afraid to tell us when you don't have an answer; we realize that everyone's knowledge and experience are limited. Honest uncertainty is preferable to a pretence of expertise.
6 Do, above all, take us into your confidence, so that we can work as equal partners, bringing different skills to the job of providing a better life for our children. We are not a handicapped family: we are a family in which there is a member with a handicap.

Yours sincerely,
The parent of a handicapped child.

SUGGESTED READING

Gath A (1978) *Down's Syndrome and the Family. The Early Years.* London: Academic Press.
Heron A & Myers M (1983) *Intellectual Impairment: The Battle against Handicap.* London: Academic Press.
Kew S (1975) *Handicap and Family Crisis.* London: Pitman Publishing.
Milunsky A (1981) *Coping with Crisis and Handicap.* New York: Plenum Press.
Mittler P & McConachie H (1983) *Parents, Professionals and Mentally Handicapped People: Approaches to Partnership.* London: Croom Helm.

Newell P (1983) *ACE Special Education Handbook: The New Law on Children with Special Needs.* London: Advisory Centre for Education.
Newson E & Hipgrove T (1982) *Getting Through to your Handicapped Child.* Cambridge: Cambridge University Press.
Pless IB & Pinkerton P (1975) *Chronic Childhood Disorder – Promoting Patterns of Adjustment.* London: Henry Kimpton.
Russell P & National Children's Bureau (1983) Parliamentary Social Services Select Committee on Children in Care. Submission from the Voluntary Council for Handicapped Children. London: National Children's Bureau.

REFERENCES

Bicknell J (1983) The psychopathology of handicap. *British Journal of Medical Psychology 56:* 167–178.
Blacher J & Meyers CE (1983) A review of attachment formation and disorder of handicapped children. *American Journal of Mental Deficiency 87(4):* 359–371.
Carr J (1984) Family processes and parent involvement. In Dobbing J (ed) *Scientific Studies in Mental Retardation. Proceedings of the 1st European Symposium.* London: Macmillan.
Carr J, Pearson A & Halliwell M (1983) *The GLC Spina Bifida Survey: Follow-up at 11 and 12 Years.* Information Section, Research & Statistics Branch, ILEA, Addington Street Annex, London SE17UY.
Collins M & Collins D (1976) *Kith and Kids.* London: Souvenir Press.
Farber B (1960) Effects of a severely mentally retarded child on family integration. *Monographs of the Society for Research in Child Development 21(1):* Serial 75.
Ferguson N & Watt J (1980) The mothers of children with special educational needs. *Scottish Educational Review 12(1):* 21–31.
Fox AM (1977) Psychological problems of physically handicapped children. *British Journal of Hospital Medicine 17(5):* 479–490.
Friedrich WN, Greenbezrg MT & Crnic K (1983) A Short-Form of the Questionnaire on Resources and Stress. *American Journal of Mental Deficiency 88(1):* 41–48.
Manciaux M, Salbreux R & Tomkiewicz S (1981) La deficience mentale dans les polyhandicaps de l'enfance. *Archives Francaises de Pediatrie 38:* 627–634.
Oliver BE (1973) The psychiatrist in the assessment and care of young handicapped children. *British Journal of Mental Subnormality 19(1):* 33–37.
Simeonsson RJ (1981) Review: research on handicapped children: sibling relationships. *Child: Care, Health and Development 7:* 153–171.
Solnit AJ & Stark MH (1977) Mourning and the birth of a defective child. In Eissler, Freud, Kris & Solnit (eds.) *Physical Illness and Handicap in Childhood.* pp. 181–194. New Haven, Connecticut: Yale University Press.
Wertheimer A (1983) *Leisure.* London: Campaign for Mentally Handicapped People.
Wishart MC, Bidder RT & Gray OP (1981) Parents' report of family life with a developmentally delayed child. *Child: Care, Health and Development 7/5:* 267–279.

Chapter 14
Childhood Autism

ISRAEL KOLVIN

Strange and bizarre behaviour in young children holds a particular fascination both for professionals and for the lay public. The notion that clusters of such types of behaviour represented psychosis, perhaps different types of psychosis, or perhaps even a unitary psychosis related to adult schizophrenia, slowly began to dawn in the second half of the twentieth century. In the period leading up to the 1950s eponymous labelling of such clusters was rife, but the only label which has stood the test of time is Kanner's (1943) clear and brilliant descriptive account of the behavioural abnormalities of 'infantile autism'. This was the first major leap forward. In due course it was followed by a series of other 'leaps' representing advances in neurology, classification, aetiology and therapy, all of which were underpinned by more modern scientific methods. However, the second major leap forward was when classification and the characteristics of these psychoses were established on a more solid basis, and this has been a central feature of work in this field over the last quarter of a century.

CLASSIFICATION AND DIAGNOSIS

Diagnostic criteria

Kanner (1943) saw the condition as being characterized by three primary features – (a) a profound failure to develop social relationships and an aloneness which he termed 'autism', (b) an obsessional desire for maintaining environmental sameness, represented by a dislike of change (in domestic and personal routines, customary routes and topography) and (c) an onset within the first two years of life – together with secondary features in the sphere of communication, evidence of some circumscribed cognitive potential and abnormalities of motor behaviour. Kolvin's (1971) criteria were broadly similar – in terms of age of onset, a self-isolating pattern of social behaviour, catastrophic reactions to environmental changes and/or stereotyped motor movements. Most authors include as a diagnostic criterion an onset before the age of three years. The exception is Wing (1982b) who continues to argue against age of onset as an essential criterion; however, this may be felt to widen the concept of infantile autism unduly.

As Eisenberg (1957) has pointed out, the specification of criteria for diagnosis is crucial and essential. The hope of a number of workers has been to develop a set of diagnostic criteria based on statistical frequency analysis rather than on clinical impression (see Kolvin et al., 1971c). Rutter's (1974) solution, consisting of identifying discriminants between infantile autism and other child psychiatric disorders, controlled for IQ, sex and age, is essentially similar. He found that there were only three symptoms which were universally present and specific in terms of being significantly more frequent in the autistic group: (a) a profound and general failure to develop social relationships, (b) language retardation and (c) ritualistic or compulsive behaviour. However, as each of these symptoms can occur in the absence of the others, none can be regarded as pathognomonic.

Other workers have developed diagnostic checklists (Rimland, 1968; DeMyer et al., 1971) or screening instruments (Creak, 1964) in an attempt to make diagnosis more objective (Rimland, 1968). Using relatively structured and standardized diagnostic systems and even different systems, collaborators can apparently achieve good agreement on diagnosis (DeMyer, 1971). Although such agreement is considerably reduced when the instruments are used by non-collaborators, nevertheless, such diagnostic systems or instruments are helpful in distinguishing autistic children from other diagnostic groups (DeMyer et al., 1971); however, they are of little use in attempting to distinguish different subgroups of autism.

Nosological issues

The traditional approach to psychiatric classification, used by Kraepelin (1913), was to undertake detailed clinical examination of demonstrable features and, where possible, to study the onset, course and natural history. With the scarcity of aetiological knowledge (Slater and Roth, 1969), the early workers based their classifications on symptomatological or phenomenological criteria, seeking evidence of clustering of features that were thought to have prognostic or predictive utility. In the Anglo-American child psychiatric literature, Kanner proved the master of this descriptive classificatory technique, but he was not alone in this exercise. A wide diversity of psychotic disorders of childhood were conceptualized and were eponymously labelled: for instance, Heller (1954) described his 'dementia infantilis', a condition in which the main feature was a period of regression in behaviour and deterioration in other aspects of functioning; Despert (1951) described a condition in which the behavioural abnormalities were present at birth; another concept which has a continuing fascination is Mahler's (1952) notion of 'symbiotic psychosis', which is chiefly characterized by affectionless clinging. The relationship of these disorders was not evident, particularly as different centres used different terms for the same condition or the same term for different conditions. The most widely advanced hypothesis was that there was a single pathological process. An extension of this hypothesis was that all the varieties of childhood psychoses constituted sub-types of adult schizophrenia.

The advances which heralded order and simplicity in this complex field all relate to classification. The careful and now classic reviews by Eisenberg (1957, 1968) in the United States and by Rutter (1967, 1968) in the United Kingdom pointed to the importance of more precise diagnosis based on demonstrable behavioural symptomatology and logical classification rather than the grouping of disparate conditions under one broad heading. A crucial contribution was the distinction by Anthony (1958a, b; 1962) of the childhood psychoses by the age of onset. This conceptualization highlighted the surprising harmonies and overlaps between named syndromes within age bands, in contrast to the dysharmonies across such bands. However, the nature of the psychoses within these age bands still remained to be defined. Anthony postulated three groups:

1 Those in whom the abnormalities had an early onset, that is up to the age of three years, and a slow chronic course. Included are Kanner's syndrome, Bender's 'pseudodefective' type and Despert's 'no onset' type.
2 Those with onset between three and five years of age and in which there was an acute course followed by regression, including Heller's disease, de Sanctis and Weygandt's dementias, Bender's pseudoneurotic type, Despert's 'acute onset' type, and Mahler's symbiotic psychosis.
3 Finally, those with a late onset and a fluctuating, sub-acute course, including Bender's pseudopsychopathic type.

The systematic empirical validation of the latter classification was undertaken by the Oxford and Newcastle Group (Kolvin, 1971; Kolvin et al., 1971a–e). They divided their psychotic children into three groups according to age of onset (under three, three to five and over five years). They focused on the under-three group (infantile psychotic) and the over-five group (late-onset psychotic) and used modern statistical techniques to provide validation in terms of differences of clinical features and aetiological factors between the two main groups studied.

The second group, those with an onset between three and five years old, has been described as 'disintegrative psychosis' (Rutter, 1972) and is very rare (Makita, 1966; Kolvin et al., 1971e). In this group initial development is normal but is followed by a serious deterioration of speech, language, cognition and behaviour. These children have mostly been found to be suffering from clear-cut organic disorders of varying aetiology and clinical picture (Anthony, 1958a, b, 1962; Rutter, 1968; Kolvin, 1971; Kolvin et al., 1971c).

The Newcastle/Oxford research has elaborated the distinction between infantile and later-onset psychoses, with the latter group showing more features representative of adult schizophrenia. For instance, hallucinations and delusions occur frequently in late-onset psychosis but never in infantile psychosis, even when the patients get older (Rutter, 1968; Kolvin et al., 1971c). On the other hand, gaze avoidance, finger flicking (stereotypies), resistance to change and serious retardation of speech and language are characteristic of infantile psychosis. Second, late-onset psychotics as a group tend to have only moderate intellectual impairment, but the majority of infantile psychotic children have very poor intellectual development (Kolvin et al., 1971b). Third, there is a significantly high rate of schizophrenia in the parents of the late-onset psychotic group, compared with a low rate in the parents of the infantile psychotic group (Kallman and Roth, 1956; Rutter and Lockyer, 1967; Kolvin et al., 1971c). Fourth, there is an excess of parental personality oddities in the late-onset psychotic group (Kolvin et al., 1971a). Finally, there is evidence of an excess of cerebral dysfunction in the infantile psychotic group (Kolvin et al., 1971e). These findings (replicated by Green et al., 1984) provide definitive support for the hypothesis that infantile psychosis bears no relation to late-onset psychosis.

Rutter (1972) has reviewed the evidence distinguishing infantile psychosis from adult-type schizophrenia. A steady course is more typical in autism, while marked remissions and relapses frequently occur in schizophrenia; mental retardation is a common feature of autism but less so with schizophrenia; better visuo-spatial skills, poorer language skills and poorer intelligence are characteristic of autism but not schizophrenia; there is a marked male preponderance in autism but equality of sexes in adult schizophrenia; there is a high frequency of perinatal factors and organic factors in autism (Kolvin, 1971) but not in schizophrenia; there is a high genetic loading in the parents of schizophrenic adults but very low loading in the parents of autists (Kolvin, 1971; Rutter, 1972) and, finally, there is the bipolar distribution of onset of childhood psychosis (Kolvin, 1971) which Rutter (1972) interprets as a discontinuity between autism and schizophrenia. Rutter sees no reason for making any distinction between late-onset psychosis and adult-type schizophrenia and argues for a single disease concept to cover both of these groups. While schizophrenia may begin in later childhood (Kolvin et al., 1971e; Rutter, 1972), this is rare, and, further, it is unusual for schizophrenic symptoms to become overt before the age of seven or eight.

Hypotheses have been advanced, tested and verified that infantile autism (infantile psychosis) differs significantly from primary mental handicap (Rutter, 1966, 1967; Rutter and Lockyer, 1967; DeMyer et al., 1971–1974) and from late-onset psychosis (Kolvin, 1971; Kolvin et al., 1971a–e) and adult-type schizophrenia. There remains the question of the relationship (and the difference) between infantile autism and specific receptive developmental language disorders (dysphasia). While children in the latter group were thought to differ from autistic children, a number of overlapping features, particularly social withdrawal and repetitive activities, have been described which have led to the hypothesis that autism is an extreme variant of such language disorders. This latter hypothesis has been tested by the Maudsley group (Bartak et al., 1975, 1977; Cox et al., 1975) who compared autistic children of normal (non-verbal) intelligence with dysphasic children. Autism proved to be associated with a language deficit which was more extensive in that it spanned several different language modalities such as impairment of inner language, an impaired understanding of written language, and also involved a severe comprehension defect. Furthermore, the language impairment of the autistic group involved deviance in terms of echolalia, pronominal reversal, metaphorical language and inappropriate remarks in addition to linguistic delay. Finally, the autists used the speech they possessed poorly for social communications, whereas the dysphasic children had more impaired articulatory skills, but were better able to communicate, were far less behaviourally disturbed and much more socially mature, particularly as time passed. There is thus evidence that the language defect in autism is qualitatively different and quantitatively more severe than that in dysphasia.

Differential diagnosis

It is helpful to attempt a distinction between those disorders which, while different from infantile autism, may be confused with it and those disorders which may coexist with it. Unfortunately these two categories are not mutually exclusive. First, there are those non-autistic conditions which may have minor 'secondary' autistic features which are not sufficient to suggest an autistic syndrome. These conditions include profound deafness, developmental language disorders, psychosocial deprivation, elective mutism, schizoid personality disorder, organic brain disorders and severe mental handicap. For instance, children with profound mental handicap may have two-way social interactions which are appropriate for their developmental age or such social interactions may be moderately impaired (Wing and Gould, 1979). Second, there are the common coexisting disorders; these include hearing and other sensory defects, mental retardation, organic brain damage and language disorders.

Wing and Gould (1979) have demonstrated a relationship between severity of social interactional impairments and severity of handicap in the areas of language and cognitive ability and also severity of organic impairment. Such findings give rise to the important question of whether there are degrees of autism. This latter notion is of crucial relevance to Asperger's syndrome (1944) which presents clinically as a schizoid-type personality disorder of childhood. Some authorities (Wing, 1981) regard it as a mild variant of autism, while others agree with Asperger that it is a personality trait (Kolvin and Goodyer, 1981).

BEHAVIOUR OF INFANTILE AUTISTIC CHILDREN

Social relationships

The poor relational ability which these children display is most disconcerting and distressing for the parents and relatives. In essence this consists of a maintenance of social distance and aloofness (autism). Autistic children generally avoid contact with people and mix and play very poorly with other children. They show poor ability to initiate or to respond to social overtures: three forms of impaired social interaction have been described – namely aloof, passive and odd (Wing and Gould, 1979) – with aloofness being more characteristic at lower levels of IQ. Autistic children gaze equally little at faces and at objects (O'Connor and Hermelin, 1967; Wing, 1982b). Some think that the tendency of these children to avoid eye contact (gaze avoidance) is part and parcel of the above relational difficulty.

Disorders of communication

Most autistic children have difficulties in the use of verbal and non-verbal methods of communication (Rutter, 1978c). Some remain mute and most have serious delays or abnormalities of speech and symbolic language. The more common abnormalities consist of a tendency to echo or repeat words or phrases, use of meaningless words or phrases, reversal of pronouns and inappropriate use of prepositions and conjunctions, and general immaturity of speech. When it develops, their speech is frequently stereotyped, monotonous and pedantic. In addition, there are difficulties of comprehension and in the use of gestures and imitation. All the above suggest that the underlying disorder is similar to developmental receptive dysphasia. Such children cannot cope with the nuances of communication or the subtleties of humour and often have little appropriate variation in facial expression,

which parallels their poor response to the nuances of humour.

Imagination and purpose in play and behaviour

Especially in the pre-school years, autistic children tend to wander around aimlessly, devoid of the usual constructive and exploratory ventures seen in toddlers, who commonly display considerable curiosity about their environment. In autistic children play tends to be neither creative, imaginative nor constructive; nor do they display pretend play, but rather seem to prefer mechanical or repetitive pursuits. However, some circumscribed symbolic imaginative interests have been described in a small minority of autistic children (Wing et al., 1977).

Ritualistic and compulsive behaviour

Autistic children often insist obsessionally on a particular routine in their daily lives, and their resistance to any change – either of the routine or of objects or people in their environment – creates major management problems. Some children develop a deep attachment to an unusual object, such as a piece of string or a cup, from which they cannot easily be parted. These behaviours have been interpreted as an attempt by the child to create some order and constancy (Kanner, 1943) in a confusing and chaotic world. Kanner considered them to represent a desire to maintain 'sameness' in the environment.

Catastrophic reactions

Autistic children tend to cling to these rituals or compulsions and may react with considerable, 'catastrophic' distress to interruptions of these or other changes in their routine. Nevertheless, such reactions do not always seem to have obvious determinants. Some children are apparently suddenly abnormally distressed by an everyday object, such as a table or a jug, but for other catastrophic reactions there are obvious explanations. The stimuli to which the children react so disastrously appear to be specific to each child; for instance, one may react to reorganization of furniture within the home, another to an unfamiliar route on a journey, and another to a change in a dressing routine.

Motor abnormalities

These are particularly evident when the child is distressed or excited. The most characteristic consists of finger stereotypies and hand-flapping. Facial grimaces, jumping, toe walking, pirouetting and a number of other repetitive activities are seen. Some autistic children are over-active while others may be underactive.

Sensory disorders

One of the conundrums of autism is that these children tend to show a greater response to proximal sensory stimuli than to distal ones: whereas they are likely to ignore aural or visual stimuli they seem to explore the external world by touching, tasting and smelling objects. There are notable exceptions to such general tendencies, in that they are often transiently alert to new, strange noises and appear fascinated by rotatory or pendular movements. Nevertheless, the ignoring of sound stimuli and the failure to respond to startle stimuli often suggests a degree of deafness and it is not always easy to exclude this; often information from parents about the child's response to ordinary domestic auditory stimuli may provide helpful clues. Some autistic children display a dangerous combination of a lack of response to painful stimuli plus fearlessness.

Mood and aggressive behaviour

Rages and tantrums and self-directed aggression are relatively frequent; although most episodes do not appear to have obvious precipitants, many authors speculate that these behaviours may be a reaction, either to frustration following poor ability to communicate or to boredom. Self-destructive behaviour, such as biting of hands, face-slapping and head-banging, generates considerable anxiety in parents.

INTELLECTUAL DEVELOPMENT

The impression of good intellectual potential which was gained by earlier authors was probably based on the attractive physical appearance of autistic children and the special ability of a minority of autists on non-verbal, non-symbolic tasks. A few autistic children show exceptional abilities in circumscribed areas, such as with jigsaw puzzles, or have remarkable memories for numbers or tunes.

Subsequent research has shown that autism is associated with major intellectual deficits, with about half having IQs below 50 and another quarter between 50 and 70 (Rutter and Lockyer, 1967;

Kolvin et al., 1971b). Nevertheless, Rutter and Lockyer point out that autistic children with low IQs have symptoms similar to those with higher IQs and so 'mental subnormality as a concept is insufficient to account for the autism.' Fluctuations (Rutter, 1970) in IQ over time (DeMyer et al., 1974) in autistic children have proved to be similar to those found in normal children. However, there are marked fluctuations on sub-test scores reflecting different types of skills: thus a simple averaging of sub-tests may mask any individual strengths and weaknesses.

EPIDEMIOLOGICAL FACTORS

Prevalence

The work of Lotter (1967) has emphasized the rarity of the condition (that is, 4 per 10 000) when early childhood psychosis is tightly defined. When more widely defined, the rate jumps to 21 per 10 000 (Wing et al., 1976). However, such rates need to be viewed with caution as the nature of this wider group of psychotic children is not yet clear. In addition, such epidemiological rates, even when narrowly defined, are far greater than the so-called administrative rates (numbers in the community who are known to the local services) and hence should be used with caution in planning services, to avoid over-provision.

Sex ratio

There is a high male:female ratio ranging from 3:1 or 4:1 in hospital series (Creak and Ini, 1960; Rutter and Lockyer, 1967; Kolvin et al., 1971d) to 2.9:1 in epidemiological research (Lotter, 1967).

ORIGINS

Social and psychological factors

Previously, it has been commonly assumed that the fundamental determinants of psychiatric disturbance in childhood are parental personality, attitudes and emotional disturbance (Kolvin et al., 1971a). Whereas, with few exceptions (Ritvo et al., 1971), clinical studies have reported that the parents of autistic children came predominantly from the upper social strata and were of above-average intelligence (Creak and Ini, 1960; Rutter et al., 1967; Kolvin et al., 1971c), population surveys have either reported a weaker association (Lotter, 1967) or have not confirmed such findings (Wing, 1980). Nevertheless, such findings have been used to support the notion of an origin for childhood autism in environmental and family factors, one of the earliest environmental explanations being based on descriptions of social formality and lack of warmth of mothers (Kanner, 1943, 1949) and of fathers (Eisenberg, 1957). Such notions soon led to the concept of 'refrigerator parents', who were said to have obsessive and cold personalities, despite these features being relatively common characteristics of the public manners of middle- to upper-class parents.

Unfortunately, the basic premise was not validated before explanations were considered to have been proved: a plethora of similar theories have been advanced, mainly stemming from clinical practice, most of which are totally unacceptable on the grounds of being based on heterogeneous or unduly small samples; nor were objective and reliable measures used to accumulate empirical data upon which a theory could be based (Kolvin et al., 1971a). Finally, not only were some of the theories that were developed incapable of generating testable hypotheses, but also some theorists did not perform the two axiomatic methodological steps of demonstrating a correlation between child and parent variables and of carrying out experimental or observational studies in an attempt to validate a cause–effect relationship; neither did most theorists consider the possibility that the syndrome might have a multifactorial basis.

Modern research has not confirmed the parental personality stereotype, irrespective of the method of assessment. DeMyer et al. (1973) reported that child-care practices of parents of autistic children were similar to those of the parents of matched, normal children. Cox et al., (1975) used objective clinical interviews plus parental self-rating inventories and reported that although mothers of autistic children showed less warmth to their autistic child, this could be attributable to the difficulty of showing warmth to an unresponsive child.

Not only is there no evidence that autism is secondary to abnormal parental personalities or unusual child-rearing practices, but also there is no evidence of a link between extremely depriving environmental circumstances (Rutter, 1972) or faulty conditioning (Ferster, 1961) and infantile autism. It would be difficult to imagine how any of these extreme environmental experiences could give rise to the complex but specific patterns of impairments in such diverse areas as cognitive, perceptual, motor and autonomic functioning (Wing, 1976). Further, even where organic factors have been ruled out, with children of normal intelligence being studied, there is good evidence of a cognitive defect and so 'it seems entirely improbable that the aetiology is entirely psychogenic' (Bartak et al., 1975). The sum total of these studies and reviews provides strong refutation of a psychogenic hypothesis. In addition, there is suggestive evidence (Bell, 1968, 1971; Cox et al., 1975) that some of the parental social reactions may be secondary to the autism and that social isolation, when present in mothers of autists, may follow the onset of the disorder (Kolvin et al., 1971a).

Biological factors

There is a great deal of evidence to suggest that autism may be the final common behavioural expression of a wide variety of organic-cum-developmental influences. First, presumptive evidence of cerebral injury has been obtained from studies of perinatal complications, with particularly high rates being reported in clinical studies (Gittelman and Birch, 1967; Lobascher et al., 1970; Kolvin et al., 1971e), but the evidence from population studies is less impressive (Lotter, 1967; Treffert, 1970). Second, in about half of the cases in the two major hospital series there is evidence of cerebral dysfunction and up to one autistic patient in three in the course of time develops epileptic fits (Rutter et al., 1967; Kolvin et al., 1971e; DeMyer et al., 1973). EEG studies confirm this evidence, with high rates of clear-cut abnormalities (spike or spike and wave activity) (White et al., 1964; Gubbay et al., 1970; Kolvin et al., 1971e; Small, 1975). Other workers have shown an excess of abnormalities of evoked potentials during waking and sleep (Ornitz, 1970; Small, 1971). Epileptic fits are usually associated with lower levels of IQ (Rutter, 1970). Third, certain organic conditions appear to have a close relationship with infantile autism: for instance, it occurs a hundred times more frequently in children whose mothers have had rubella in pregnancy than in the general population (Chess, 1971); it is also associated with previous episodes of infantile spasms (Kolvin et al., 1971e; Taft and Cohen, 1971) and with congenital or profound blindness (Freedman, 1971) and has been described in association with a variety of other specific cerebral organic conditions (Darby, 1976). One group of workers (Hauser et al., 1975) report enlargement of the temporal horn of the left lateral ventricles, with atrophy of the adjacent area of the left medial temporal lobe. But there is doubt about the homogeneity of the sample and there is a suggestion that the cases were highly selected, with heavy loadings of neurological disorder and, indeed, other questions have been raised about methodology (Lancet, 1976). There are also suggestions of involvement of the dominant hemisphere (Hermelin, 1966) and of the non-dominant hemisphere, which is concerned with both comprehension and expression of emotion (Ross and Mesulam, 1979). However, it is unlikely that the lesion would be confined to one or other of the hemispheres.

It is evident that we have little idea what the specific brain dysfunction comprises; however, the diversity of EEG and seizure patterns, which range from focal epilepsy to the widespread disorganization of hypsarrhythmia (Rutter et al., 1967; Kolvin et al., 1971e; Taft and Cohen, 1971), appears to argue against a single underlying homogeneous pathological mechanism. Indeed, on the basis of knowledge available at that time, in 1974 Rutter found it impossible to localize the lesion and favoured the hypothesis of a non-specific syndrome of biological impairment. Nevertheless, a number of unifying theories have been advanced. For instance, Damasio and Maurer (1978) attempted to incriminate dysfunction of a single and yet widely based system consisting of the bilateral neural structures of the mesolimbic cortex. They postulated that autism might be the result of macroscopic or microscopic changes in the above-mentioned target areas or in structures influencing them. Thus, the broadly homogeneous functional aberration of autism might be the result of very different types of structural disorganization. Unfortunately, this theory is so far-ranging that it is incapable of generating more specific testable hypotheses. An allied theory is that multiple neurological deficits do not necessarily imply multiple aetiologies but are dependent on the abnormality impinging on a specific relevant brain centre or centres, such as association areas (Crawley, 1971) or language areas (Wing, 1971). This is a plausible explanation, which could account for the multiple handicaps or impairments of language, perception, motor ability and behaviour described by Wing and Wing (1971): 'a number of different brain functions could be affected by, for example, a single genetic or biochemical abnormality, or anatomical proximity could make different brain centres vulnerable to the same lesion'. Hence, these workers assert that

any condition which produces abnormality or delayed maturation of relevant brain areas could theoretically lead to the impairments of infantile autism.

Other workers have incriminated subcortical dysfunction which directly or indirectly affects the reticular activating system (Des Lauriers and Carlson, 1969) involving either under- or over-arousal (Hutt et al., 1964, 1965) or an imbalance between these systems. However, the empirical evidence advanced in support of these sometimes conflicting theories tends to be rather questionable.

Cognitive factors

As implied above, the pattern of cognitive functioning in autism suggests a specific defect involving language not only in terms of comprehension but also in terms of conceptual skills in thinking (Rutter, 1968, 1974; Rutter et al., 1971). Not only are the earliest signs of language (babbling) deficient (Ricks, 1972), but subsequently there is evidence of impairments in comprehension and in production of language and language modalities, such as gesture (Tubbs, 1966). In addition, there are 'pragmatical deficiencies', which relate to inappropriate use of speech and language in a social context (Frith, 1982). Further, the experimental evidence available implicates an impaired ability to conceptualize and symbolize and to process meaningful and temporally patterned stimuli (Hermelin and O'Connor, 1970; Frith, 1971). Hermelin and Frith (1971) assert that the deficit is central and appears to consist of an inability to encode information in a meaningful way; this results in an autistic child having difficulty in 'making sense of what he sees and hears' (Frith, 1982). Despite their poorer ability in processing meaningful information, autistic children tend to have good rote memory.

It has been suggested that such cognitive defects could impair social interactions (Churchill, 1972), but the problem with this theory is the existence of autistic children who are not cognitively impaired and yet are socially impaired (Frith, 1982). In addition, it is not clear whether the disorder is primarily one of language or whether the language disorder arises from a more widespread cognitive deficit (Rutter, 1974) or more widespread cerebral dysfunction as described above (Damasio and Maurer, 1978).

A related and plausible theory is one that implicates non-specific cerebral dysfunction and suggests that, whatever the pathophysiology, the mechanism involves a learning disorder (DeMyer et al., 1972a) which hinders the acquisition of language (Rutter, 1968; Hermelin, 1971; Wing, 1971). The theory suggests that the learning disorder also hinders the acquisition of certain visuomotor acts such as the imitation of body movements. These disabilities in turn impair the child's ability to establish social relationships with others. Indeed, Churchill (1972) circumscribes the theory by implicating specific anomalies of areas subserving perceptual, sensorimotor and language functions. He suggests that autistic children share, with non-psychotic brain-damaged children, various perceptual–motor deficits, but the essence of the psychotic condition is a central language deficit allied to, but more severe than, that found in children with a dysphasic disorder. In support of this theory is the finding that the abnormality of response by autistic children to sensory stimuli resembles that seen in developmental receptive dysphasia and congenital partial blindness/deafness, particularly when associated with maternal rubella.

Other workers have pointed to the association between impaired interpersonal relationships and impaired imaginative play in autistic children (Rutter, 1978b; Wing and Gould, 1979). Hermelin (1978) suggests, on the basis of her experimental work, that this reflects a deficit in symbolic thought. On the basis of the above-mentioned facts and a presumed social deficit existing in autistic children at a Piagetian 'pre-symbolic level' (Piaget, 1951), Frith (1982) speculates 'that this deficit alone may prevent the development of imaginative play'. She goes on to suggest that normal children are likely to play with toy objects as if they were social objects and this in turn gives rise to pretend play, while autistic children rather treat people as objects. Such a theory takes us back forty years to Kanner's original assertion that a profound social impairment is primary and explanatory of the more widespread disturbances.

Maturational factors

There remain those autistic children with higher IQs with little or no evidence of neurological dysfunction and fewer demonstrable cognitive deficits, whose disorder cannot easily be accounted for by the above theories. Rutter and colleagues (1971) have, in the past, speculated that in these cases autism may be due to a kind of maturational delay which is associated with a physiological developmental language disorder. However, despite its attraction, the support for this hypothesis is reduced by the fact that very few autistic children ever recover completely (Rutter et al., 1971).

Biochemical and genetic factors

Biochemical studies do not suggest an inborn error of metabolism (Guthrie and Wyatt, 1975). Very occasionally, defects have been identified, such as hyperserotonaemia, but there has often been insufficient rigor in the definition of the groups studied and in standardization of the assay procedures, and the findings have seldom been replicated. While the possibility remains that infantile psychosis is aetiologically heterogeneous, such studies have not as yet identified a sub-group which have other features which cluster together in a meaningful way.

Has autism a genetic basis? First, are there genetic links with schizophrenia? When a tight definition of psychosis is applied, in comparison with the general population there is no evidence of excess of schizophrenia in parents of children with early-onset psychosis (Kanner, 1954; Creak and Ini, 1960; Rutter and Lockyer, 1967; Kolvin et al., 1971d); this is in contrast to late-onset psychosis, which appears to be genetically linked to adult schizophrenia (Kallman and Roth, 1956; Kolvin et al., 1971d).

What about other types of genetic causation of autism? Hanson and Gotteman (1982) have reviewed the evidence for a genetic basis. First, they point out that inheritance of autism is not of a simple Mendelian pattern. In addition, no chromosomal abnormalities had been identified (Böök et al., 1963; Wolraich et al., 1970). However, an excess of fragile X marker aberrations has been reported in the male autistic population (Gillberg and Wahlström, 1985), and this appears to be specific to autistic psychoses. Second, if rare mutations were the cause of autism then it is to be expected that neither parents nor siblings would be affected; in fact, while there are no reports of parents of autistic children being autistic, there is a slight excess (i.e. under 0.5%) amongst siblings in the British series (Creak and Ini, 1960; Rutter, 1967; Rutter and Lockyer, 1967; Kolvin et al., 1971d). In addition, none of the other findings fit theoretical expectations for a rare mutation: there is not an equal sex ratio and the identical-twin concordance rate is also low (Folstein and Rutter, 1977); hence a simple dominant mutation theory is unsupportable.

Third, a theory of polygenic inheritance is not supportable: there are no distinctive qualities in the parents, for instance of personality, which would suggest they have a milder version of their child's condition. The sibling rate, though very low, could support a notion of familial clustering, as could the twin concordance, but the latter is equally consistent with an explanation in terms of perinatal brain damage (Hanson and Gotteman, 1982). Finally, as in their twin study, discordance was usually associated with brain damage; Folstein and Rutter (1977) suggest that infantile autism may be determined by a combination of genetic predisposition and brain damage. The one plausible genetic explanation relates to fragile X chromosome anomalies. Jörgenson et al. (1984) suggest these make the child vulnerable to deviant speech/ language development; interaction with different pre- or neonatal brain insults may give rise to one sub-group of autism. However, there is no identifiable genetic basis for most cases of childhood autism.

Mention must be drawn to the personality disorder of childhood originally described by Asperger (1944), comprising gross lack of skills in social diplomacy, associated with a degree of naivety, giving rise to an impairment of social relationships. He considered that this personality variant must be transmitted genetically. Van Krevelen (1971) has postulated that such a personality could be turned into an autistic psychosis by earlier brain damage. However, there remain doubts about the relationship of this disorder to infantile autism (Wolff and Barlow, 1979; Kolvin and Goodyer, 1981).

OUTCOME AND PROGNOSIS

Outcome

The clinical features of infantile autism tend to vary with the age of the child and his stage of development. For instance, in early infancy a characteristic feature is a failure to cuddle; babbling may be absent and there may also be a failure to engage in pre-verbal mother–baby social interactions. In the toddler a prominent feature consists of profound social withdrawal and avoidance of gaze, together with language abnormalities and repetitive activities. This is the peak period for the more florid symptoms of the disorder. Subsequently, many

children continue to have difficulties in interpersonal relationships, particularly outside the home, and this may be because the adults not in regular contact with the child are unaccustomed to interpreting his communications or making allowance for his behaviour.

Older autistic children show an inability to appreciate the nuances in social relationships and have a lack of appreciation of other people's feelings. Often in adolescence there is a real desire for close friendships, but the lack of social skills and appropriate empathy makes these difficult. While most of the other symptoms disappear eventually, it is not uncommon for obsessional and ritualistic symptoms not only to persist, but to expand. When the child attends infant school the prominent features are inactivity, inertia and educational difficulties.

In spite of the modern methods of treatment, the outcome in adolescence and adulthood is mostly poor in terms of intellectual development, overall adjustment and, additionally, work potential in adulthood. Irrespective of whether the sample is drawn from a clinic (Rutter et al., 1967; Kanner, 1971; DeMyer et al., 1973) or epidemiologically based (Lotter, 1974b) the picture of the outcome is roughly the same. While two out of three autistic children remain severely handicapped, one out of four does fair-to-moderately, with some continuing social and relational problems; however, only just over one child in ten (Kanner, 1971) develops adequately in terms of intellect and social adjustment and is able to survive in an unsheltered work situation (Rutter et al., 1967; DeMyer et al., 1973). Even those who improve may show continuing difficulties of relationships and oddities of personality.

Prognosis

The most important prognostic factor is the *testable level of intelligence* (Rutter et al., 1967). Outcome can be envisaged as being closely tied to the degree of associated handicap. For instance, DeMyer and her colleagues have demonstrated that children tend to remain in the same intellectual academic-/work category in which they were initially assigned, rather than improving with time. However, there is an important variation: while the mean IQ of the population of autists remains stable, autists who are rated as having the best potential at initial assessment show considerable gains in verbal IQ with the passage of time (DeMyer et al., 1973).

The following constitutes a useful guide. Those in the lowest bands of intelligence (with IQs below 50), constituting about 40 % of the autistic population, will comprise the majority of those who remain severely handicapped; the next band (with IQs ranging from 50 to 70), constituting about 30 % of the autistic population, contains a high proportion of those who do moderately well; the highest band (with IQs above 70), constituting again about 30 % of the autistic population, comprises the majority of those who develop adequately. In the course of time some movement does occur between bands, but upward movement, while unusual, tends to be confined to adjacent bands. There is therefore little support for the belief that autistic children have latent intelligence (Wing, 1976). Careful psychometric assessment by an experienced child psychologist constitutes a fundamental basis of prognosis and also a useful guide to educational placement. Inter-related with these cognitive factors are *organic* factors; not only is IQ related to severity of cumulative evidence of brain damage (Kolvin et al., 1971e), but so too is prognosis (Gubbay et al., 1970; Small 1975).

The question of the *effects of treatment in relation to IQ* has been studied by DeMyer et al. (1974). Their work suggests that while children with initial IQs above 50 showed a greater increase in IQ than untreated autistic children in the same IQ range, those with IQs below 40 showed no differential effect. Furthermore, after treatment the verbal IQ gains achieved during treatment tended to be maintained in the autists with higher initial IQs but stagnated in the middle groups or were even lost in those in the lower IQ groups.

The next set of important prognostic factors is in the area of *speech, language and communication.* It is well known that an improved prognosis is associated with the development of meaningful speech by the age of five years, but about half do not achieve this. The more communicative the child, or the better developed the speech or language at initial assessment, and the more constructive or symbolic the play (as these reflect inner language), the better the development of conversational speech later (DeMyer et al., 1973). Mutism has a particularly poor prognosis. However, even where speech improves considerably, there are often residual difficulties with speech rhythm, repetitiveness, and with abstract concepts (Rutter et al., 1967; DeMyer et al., 1973).

A poor prognosis is also associated with the severity of psychosis (DeMyer et al., 1973) and a slow rate of losing the more florid autistic symptoms (Kolvin, 1972a). If substantial improvement is to occur it will usually show itself by the age of seven years (Rutter, 1967). The child with a good prognosis is one with a good IQ, little evidence of cerebral dysfunction, early speech and language development, mild symptomatology which he rapidly loses, and who is given appropriate behaviour modification and adequate schooling.

It has been suggested that the origins of the usually reported poor work record are three-fold: poor cognitive development, adverse temperamental features, such as inertia, inactivity and poor concentration, and poor social skills in the work setting (Lotter, 1974b). However, environmental factors, particularly home factors, must play a part and Lotter (1974b) commends the importance of a harmonious home atmosphere.

TREATMENT

The multiplicity and diversity of treatments which have hitherto been used in early childhood autism are an indication of the ineffectiveness of most of them. Further, the previous extravagant claims that were made for many of the approaches subsequently have had to be substantially modified. Such treatments have included electro-convulsive therapy, intensive psychotherapy of the parents and/or the child, high-dosage vitamin supplements, pharmacotherapy, and the Delacato (1974) programme of physical stimulation.

Early diagnosis and counselling

The need for early diagnosis in autism has been questioned. So far, there is no clear-cut evidence that early intervention affects the underlying handicaps or the child's progress. Some UK researchers have reported that younger children respond more rapidly (Hemsley et al., 1978), but some US researchers have denied this (Goldfarb, 1974). However, even if early intervention does not lead to substantial improvement, inadequate systematic stimulation and behavioural training from an early age can actually result in deterioration (Lovaas et al., 1973). Further, early diagnosis is helpful to parents who may have gone through a period of distress and exasperation at their child's behaviour, but who can now more easily understand this behaviour and will want to know more about its causes. It also enables them to seek referral of the child to an appropriate specialist centre with a multi-disciplinary staff who have had wide experience in assessing such children's skills and handicaps. Careful and detailed medical assessment is indicated in all cases.

The child's condition must be described carefully and patiently and explanations and advice will need to be given, preferably with both parents present. The nature of the condition and the implications may be difficult for parents to understand. The clinician must be well-informed and experienced so that he or she is able to give a balanced opinion with due frankness and compassion. There are other important facets to counselling: for instance, it is helpful for the parents to know that there does not appear to be a major genetic component and that autism is not in any way related to schizophrenia; this should help to dissipate anxiety about a genetic predisposition to developing the latter condition. Further, practical advice and support can be given concerning the day-to-day handling, how to stimulate and play with the child, and guidance and direction about general management, education, holiday relief and so on.

Two important components in treatment are counselling in conjunction with the use of parents as 'co-therapists' in home-based treatment programmes (Schopler and Reichler, 1971a, b; Howlin et al., 1973) and the use of parent support associations (Wing, 1981). Finally, it must be stressed here that not only has intensive analytical psychotherapy of parents of autistic children not worked as a cure for autism, on occasion it has been counterproductive. It can generate a deep sense of guilt in parents, implying that their personality has contributed to their child's autism.

Pharmacotherapy

Pharmacotherapy cannot modify the course of severity of the disorder. Further, there is no specific drug treatment for any associated brain damage. Nevertheless, anticonvulsants are useful in the 25–33% of autistic children who suffer from seizure disorders; sedatives and tranquillizers may be useful to allay specific symptoms, such as overactivity or aggressiveness (Wing 1976). Hypnotics may be indicated if sleeplessness becomes a severe problem. Unfortunately, the response to drugs tends to be idiosyncratic and dosage has to be tailored to the individual child.

Operant approaches

The main focus of treatment has now moved to those educational and operant conditioning approaches geared to help the child overcome social, behavioural, educational and linguistic difficulties. However, the optimism engendered by the introduction of operant conditioning has been tempered by subsequent evaluation (Lovaas et al., 1973). As often occurs with new therapeutic techniques, its usefulness has been exaggerated: improvement often may be specific to particular situations, and also transient; it should be considered as one of a range of techniques which must be tailored to the individual child and his or her handicaps. There is evidence that operant techniques work best in conjunction with educational measures as part of a general training approach (Lovaas et al., 1973; Wing, 1976). These basically comprise systematic encouragement of appropriate behaviour and discouragement of inappropriate behaviour using a programme tailored to the individual child. Operant principles can be applied to increase imitative behaviours, to encourage play and to improve self-help skills (Everard, 1976). In adolescence, training in social skills may increase the ability to socialize. Most clinicians have now turned away from using punitive forms of discouragement, partly because therapists dislike them, many questioning the morality of the use of noxious stimuli; in addition, there is little evidence of their long-term effectiveness. However, physical aversive measures have been used as a last resort in those severely handicapped autistic children who are prone to serious self-injury.

Home based approaches

It is well known that autistic children may not generalize skills acquired in one setting, in particular the school, to other settings (Hermelin, 1972; Rincover and Koegel, 1975). This has encouraged involvement of parents in the child's treatment: for instance, a variant of the operant conditioning approach has been developed by Schopler and Reichler (1971a,b), who use the parents' high degree of motivation to help children with learning and the acquisition of practical and social skills. These ideas have been expanded by the Maudsley group (Rutter and Sussenwein, 1971; Howlin et al., 1973) to a home-based approach in association with multiple impact therapy adapted to the needs of the individual child. They focus on social and linguistic development and the removal of maladaptive behaviours, using a range of operant techniques together with appropriate parental counselling. In the treatment programmes the parents are helped either to participate in treatment or to be the main vehicle for carrying this out. These workers report considerable improvement in behaviour, social responsiveness and language abilities.

Special education

Work by the Maudsley group constitutes a landmark in the evaluation of special educational treatment of autistic children (Bartak and Rutter, 1973; Rutter and Bartak, 1973). They report considerable social, behavioural and scholastic gains even with those children with the most marked behavioural disturbance (Rutter and Bartak, 1973). Furthermore, it would appear that greater educational benefits derive from specific teaching in a well-controlled and more structured classroom situation (Rutter and Bartak, 1973). However, it is to be noted that the autists' understanding of what they learn often lags behind the mechanical skills that they achieve. This has important implications for the curriculum: particular emphasis should be given to language comprehension and social skills training. For instance, language training and education should be directed towards helping the autistic child to understand language and not merely the use of words. Operant techniques have been developed for children who have acquired some spoken language. The techniques are geared to helping the child to imitate sounds, expand the use of words and phrases and to couple this with comprehension. Allied to this is the reduction of echolalic and other jargon and inappropriate speech (Sloane and MacAulay, 1968). Attention should also be given to the needs of those 50% of autistic children who do not develop meaningful speech, and to the possibility of training in the use of alternative forms of communication (Deich and Hodges 1977), for instance through imitation, gesture and drawing.

Inevitably, educational approaches need to be wide-ranging and geared to a child's level of development rather than to his chronological age, and therefore must be preceded by careful assessment (Everard, 1976; Jeffree et al., 1977). In addition, there is much evidence to suggest that the tasks with which autistic children are presented must be reduced to small steps which are within their grasp. High staff:pupil ratios are therefore especially important, in that they facilitate attention to curricular details and provide opportunities for staff–child interactions and appropriate interventions.

Residential approaches

As discussed above, improvement in school or hospital units does not necessarily generalize to the home environment unless effective reinforcement is available at home and at a parental level (Lovaas et al., 1973; Rutter and Bartak, 1973). Indeed, the emphasis is now on the importance of extensive parental involvement, which allows parents to maintain or enhance their skills, and consequently the importance of residential management is apparently questioned. (Schopler and Reichler, 1971a, b; Lovaas et al., 1973; Rutter and Bartak, 1973). On the other hand, Menolascino (1973) has argued in favour of a specific residential or milieu setting for fostering relational contacts, for planning and tailoring behaviour modification programmes and, finally, for evaluating the efficacy of education and speech training. In addition, the varying abilities of families to cope with their autistic children must be borne in mind: before the family cracks under the strain, the professional advisers should consider residential placements, usually on a short-term basis.

Mental handicap alone or with autism

There remains the important question of whether the autist who is seriously retarded merits any different treatment from the mentally handicapped child without autism. Rutter and Bartak (1973) point out that autistic children (at least in the preschool and infant school years) are dependent on the active intervention of adults for social and educational progress; mixing with non-autistic children at this age is apparently of no significant benefit to the autist. Nevertheless, for children with an IQ of less than 40 the educational benefits are minimal, despite the best schooling available. However, because most handicapped children can benefit from attempts to educate them (Bartak and Rutter 1973; Lotter 1974b), on humanitarian grounds all children, no matter what their degree of handicap, merit educational help. The evidence therefore is in favour of the view that advocacy on behalf of the brighter autistic child is advocacy on behalf of all autistic children but with resources and facilities appropriate to their potential.

REFERENCES

Anthony EJ (1958a) An etiological approach to the diagnosis of psychosis in childhood. *Review of Psychiatry in Infancy 25:* 89–96.

Anthony EJ (1958b) An experimental approach to the psychopathology of childhood autism. *British Journal of Medical Psychology 21:* 211–225.

Anthony EJ (1962) Low-grade psychosis in childhood. In Richards BW (ed) *Proceedings of the London Conference on the Scientific Study of Mental Deficiency, Vol. 2.* Dagenham: May & Baker.

Asperger H (1944) Die autistischen Psychopathen im Kindesalter. *Archiv für Psychiatrie und Nervenkrankenheiten 117:* 76–137.

Bartak L & Rutter M (1973) Special educational treatment of autistic children: a comparative study: I. design of study and characteristics of units. *Journal of Child Psychology and Psychiatry 14:* 161–179.

Bartak L, Rutter M & Cox A (1975) A comparative study of infantile autism and specific developmental receptive language disorders: I. the children *British Journal of Psychiatry 126:* 127–145.

Bartak L, Rutter M & Cox A (1977) A comparative study of infantile autism and specific developmental receptive language disorders III: discriminant function analysis. *Journal of Autism and Childhood Schizophrenia 6:* 297–302.

Bell RQ (1968) A reinterpretation of the direction of effects in studies of socialisation. *Psychological Review 75:* 81–95.

Bell RQ (1971) Stimulus control of parents or caretaker behaviour by offspring. *Developmental Psychology 4:* 63–72.

Bender L (1947) Childhood schizophrenia: a clinical study of 100 schizophrenic children. *American Journal of Orthopsychiatry 17:* 40–56.

Böök JA, Nichtern S & Gruenberg E (1963) Cytogenetical investigations in childhood schizophrenia. *Acta Psychiatrica Scandinavica 39:* 309.

Chess S (1971) Autism in children with congenital rubella. *Journal of Autism and Childhood Schizophrenia 1:* 33.

Churchill DW (1972) The relation of infantile autism and early childhood schizophrenia to developmental language disorders of childhood. *Journal of Autism and Childhood Schizophrenia 2:* 182–197.

Cox A, Rutter M, Newman S & Bartak L (1975) A comparative study of infantile autism and specific developmental receptive language disorder. II. Parental characteristics. *British Journal of Psychiatry 126:* 146–159.

Crawley CA (1971) Infantile autism – an hypothesis. *Journal of the Irish Medical Association 64:* 335.

Creak EM (1964) Schizophrenic syndrome in childhood: further progress report of a working party. *Developmental Medicine and Child Neurology 4:* 530–535.

Creak EM & Ini S (1960) Families of psychotic children. *Journal of Child Psychology and Psychiatry 1:* 156–175.

Damasio AR & Maurer RG (1978) A neurological model for childhood autism. *Archives of Neurology 35:* 777–786.

Darby JK (1976) Neuropathologic aspects of psychosis in children. *Journal of Autism and Childhood Schizophrenia 6:* 339–352.

Deich R & Hodges P (1977) *Language Without Speech.* London: Souvenir Press.

Delacato CH (1974) *The Ultimate Stranger: The Autistic Child.* New York: Doubleday.

DeMyer MK (1971) Perceptual limitations in autistic children and their relation to social and intellectual deficits. In Rutter M (ed) *Infantile Autism: Concepts, Characteristics and Treatment.* pp. 81–96. London: Churchill.

DeMyer MK, Churchill DW, Pontius W & Gilkey KM (1971) A comparison of five diagnostic systems for childhood schizophrenia and infantile autism. *Journal of Autism and Childhood Schizophrenia 1:* 175.

DeMyer MK, Pontius W, Norton JA, Barton S, Allen J & Steele R (1972a) Parental practices and innate activity in autistic and brain-damage infants. *Journal of Autism and Childhood Schizophrenia 2:* 49–66.

DeMyer MK, Alpern GC, Barton S, DeMyer WE, Churchill DW, Hingten JM, Bryson CQ, Pontius W & Kimberlin C (1972b) Imitation in autistic, early schizophrenic and non-psychotic subnormal children. *Journal of Autism and Childhood Schizophrenia 2:* 264–287.

DeMyer MK, Barton S, DeMyer WE, Norton J, Allen J & Steele R (1973) Prognosis in autism: a follow-up study. *Journal of Autism and Childhood Schizophrenia 3:* 199–246.

DeMyer MK, Barton S, Alpern GD, Kimberlin A, Allen J, Yang E & Steele R (1974) The measured intelligence of autistic children. *Journal of Autism and Childhood Schizophrenia 4:* 42–60.

Des Lauriers AM & Carlson CF (1969) *Your Child is Asleep.* Illinois: Dorsey.

Despert JL (1951) Some considerations relating to the genesis of autistic behaviour in children. *American Journal of Orthopsychiatry 21:* 335.

Eisenberg L (1957) The course of childhood schizophrenia. *Archives of Neurology and Psychiatry 78:* 69–83.

Eisenberg L (1968) Psychotic disorders in childhood. In Cooke RE (ed.) *The Biologic Basis of Paediatric Practice.* New York: McGraw-Hill.

Everard P (ed) (1976) *An Approach to Teaching Autistic Children.* Oxford: Pergamon Press.

Ferster CB (1961) Positive reinforcement and behavioural deficits of autistic children. *Child Development 32:* 437–456.

Folstein S & Rutter M (1977) Infantile autism: a genetic study of 21 twin pairs. *Journal of Child Psychology and Psychiatry 18:* 297–321.

Freedman DA (1971) Congenital and perinatal sensory deprivation: some studies in early development. *American Journal of Psychiatry 127:* 1539–1545.

Frith U (1971) Spontaneous patterns produced by autistic, normal and subnormal children. In Rutter M (ed.) *Infantile Autism: Concepts, Characteristics and Treatment,* pp. 113–131. London: Churchill Livingstone.

Frith U (1982) Psychological abnormalities in early childhood psychoses. In Wing JK & Wing L (eds) *Handbook of Psychiatry 3. Psychoses of Uncertain Aetiology.* pp. 215–221. Cambridge, England: Cambridge University Press.

Gillberg C & Wahlström J (1985) Chromosome abnormalities in infantile autism and other childhood psychoses: a population study of 66 cases. *Developmental Medicine and Child Neurology 27:* 293–304.

Gittelman M & Birch HG (1967) Childhood schizophrenia: intellect, neurological status, perinatal risk, prognosis and family pathology. *Archives of General Psychiatry 17:* 16–25.

Goldfarb W (1974) *Growth and Change of Schizophrenic Children.* New York: Wiley.

Green WH, Campbell M, Hardesty AS et al. (1984) A comparison of schizophrenic and autistic children. *Journal of the American Academy of Child Psychiatry 23:* 399–409.

Gubbay SS, Lobascher W & Kingerlee P (1970) A neurological appraisal of autistic children: results of a Western Australian survey. *Developmental Medicine and Child Neurology 12:* 422–429.

Guthrie RD & Wyatt RJ (1975) Biochemistry and schizophrenia. III. A review of childhood psychosis. *Schizophrenia Bulletin No. 12:* 18–32.

Hanson DR & Gottesman II (1982) The genetics of childhood psychoses. In Wing JK & Wing L (eds) *Handbook of Psychiatry 3. Psychoses of Uncertain Aetiology.* pp. 222–228. Cambridge, England: Cambridge University Press.

Hauser S, Delong GR & Rossman N (1975) Pneumographic findings in the infantile autism syndrome, a correlation with temporal lobe disease. *Brain 98:* 667–688.

Heller T (1954) Dementia infantilis (translated by W. Hulse). *Journal of Nervous and Mental Disease 119:* 471–477.

Hemsley DR, Howling P, Berger M, Hersov L, Holbrooke D, Rutter M & Yule W (1978) Treating autistic children in family context. In Rutter M & Schopler E (eds) *Autism: A Reappraisal of Concepts and Treatment.* pp. 379–411. New York: Plenum Press.

Hermelin B (1966) Psychological research. In Wing L (ed) *Early Childhood Autism,* 1st edn, pp. 159–174. Oxford: Pergamon.

Hermelin B (1971) Rules and language. In Rutter M (ed) *Infantile Autism: Concepts, Characteristics and Treatment,* pp. 98–112. London: Churchill Livingstone.

Hermelin B (1972) Locating events in space and time: experiments with autistic, blind and deaf children. *Journal of Autism and Childhood Schizophrenia 2:* 288–298.

Hermelin B (1978) Images and language. In Rutter M & Schopler E (eds) *Autism: A Reappraisal of Concepts and Treatment.* pp. 141–154. New York: Plenum Press.

Hermelin B & Frith U (1971) Psychological studies of childhood autism. Can autistic children make sense of what they hear? *Journal of Special Education 5:* 1107–1117.

Hermelin B & O'Connor N (1970) *Psychological Experiments with Autistic Children.* Oxford: Pergamon Press.

Howlin PA, Marchant R, Rutter M, Berger M, Hersov L & Yule W (1973) A home-based approach to the treatment of autistic children. *Journal of Autism and Childhood Schizophrenia 3:* 308–336.

Hutt SJ, Hutt C, Lee D & Ounsted C (1964) Arousal and childhood autism. *Nature 204:* 908.

Hutt SJ, Hutt C, Lee D & Ounsted C (1965) A behavioural and electro-encephalographic study of autistic children. *Journal of Psychiatric Research 3:* 181–197.

Jeffree D, McConkey R & Hewson S (1977) *Let Me Play.* London: Souvenir Press.

Jörgenson OS, Nielsen KB, Isager OT & Mouridsen SE (1984) Fragile X chromosome among child psychiatric patients with disturbances of language and social relationships. *Acta Psychiatrica Scandinavica 70:* 510–514.

Kallman FJ & Roth B (1956) Genetic aspects of pre-adolescent schizophrenia. *American Journal of Psychiatry 112:* 599–606.

Kanner L (1943) Autistic disturbances of affective contact. *Nervous Child 2:* 217–250.

Kanner L (1949) Problems of nosology and psychodynamics of early childhood autism. *American Journal of Orthopsychiatry 19:* 416–426.

Kanner L (1954) To what extent is early childhood autism determined by constitutional inadequacies? *Proceedings of the Association for Research in Nervous and Mental Diseases 33:* 378–385.

Kanner L (1971) Follow-up study of eleven autistic children originally reported in 1943. *Journal of Autism and Childhood Schizophrenia 1:* 119–145.

Kolvin I (1971) Studies in the childhood psychoses: I. Diagnostic criteria and classification. *British Journal of Psychiatry 118:* 381–384.

Kolvin I (1972a) Infantile autism or infantile psychoses. *British Medical Journal iii:* 753–755.

Kolvin I (1972b) Late onset psychosis. *British Medical Journal iii:* 816–817.

Kolvin I & Goodyer I (1981) Child Psychiatry. In Granville-Grossman (ed) *Recent Advances in Clinical Psychiatry 4,* pp. 1–24. Edinburgh: Churchill Livingstone.

Kolvin I, Garside R & Kidd J (1971a) Studies in the childhood psychoses: IV. Parental personality and attitude and childhood psychosis. *British Journal of Psychiatry 118:* 403–406.

Kolvin I, Humphreys M & McNay A (1971b) Studies in the childhood psychoses: VI Cognitive factors in childhood psychoses. *British Journal of Psychiatry 118:* 415–420.

Kolvin I, Ounsted C, Humphreys M & McNay A (1971c) Studies in the childhood psychoses: II. The phenomenology of childhood psychoses. *British Journal of Psychiatry 118:* 385–395.

Kolvin I, Ounsted C, Richardson L & Garside RF (1971d) Studies in the childhood psychoses: III. The family and social background and childhood psychoses. *British Journal of Psychiatry 118:* 396–402.

Kolvin I, Ounsted C & Roth M (1971e) Studies in the childhood psychoses: V. Cerebral dysfunction and childhood psychosis. *British Journal of Psychiatry 118:* 407–414.

Kraepelin E (1913) *Psychiatrie,* 8th edn, pp. 297 & 648. Leipzig: Thieme.

Lancet (1976) Neurological foundations of infantile autism. Sept. 11, 668–669.

Lobascher ME, Kingerlee PE & Gubbay SS (1970) Childhood autism: an investigation of aetiological factors in twenty-five cases. *British Journal of Psychiatry 117:* 525–529.

Lockyer L & Rutter M (1969) A five to fifteen year follow-up study of infantile psychosis III. Psychological aspects. *British Journal of Psychiatry 115:* 865–882.

Lotter V (1967) Epidemiology of autistic conditions in young children. II. Some characteristics of the parent and children. *Social Psychiatry 1:* 163–173.

Lotter V (1974a) Factors related to outcome in autistic children. *Journal of Autism and Childhood Schizophrenia 4:* 263–277.

Lotter V (1974b) Social adjustment and placement of autistic children in Middlesex: a follow-up study. *Journal of Autism and Childhood Schizophrenia 4:* 11–32.

Lovaas OI, Koegel R, Simmons JQ & Long JS (1973) Some generalisations and follow-up measures on autistic children in behaviour therapy. *Journal of Applied Behaviour Analysis 6:* 131–165.

Mahler MS (1952) On child psychosis and schizophrenia: autistic and symbiotic infantile psychoses. *Psychoanalytic Study of the Child 7:* 286–305.

Menolascino FJ (1973) Mentally retarded children. *Journal of Autism and Childhood Schizophrenia 3:* 49–64.

Makita K (1966) The age of onset of childhood schizophrenia. *Folia Psychiatrica Neurologica Japonica 20:* 11–121.

O'Connor N & Hermelin B (1967) The selective visual attention of psychotic children. *Journal of Child Psychology and Psychiatry 8:* 167–179.

Ornitz EM (1970) Vestibular dysfunction in schizophrenia and childhood autism. *Comprehensive Psychiatry 11:* 159–173.

Piaget J (1951) *Play, Dreams and Imitation in Childhood.* London: Routledge & Kegan Paul.

Ricks DM (1972) **The Beginning of Vocal Communication in Infants and Autistic Children.** MD Thesis, University of London.

Rimland B (1968) On the objective diagnosis of infantile autism. *Acta Paedopsychiatria 35:* 146–161.

Rincover A & Koegel RL (1975) Setting generality and stimulus control in autistic children. *Journal of Applied Behaviour Analysis 8:* 235–246.

Ritvo ER, Cantwell D, Johnson E, Clements M, Benbrook F, Slagle S, Kelly P & Ritz M (1971) Social class factors in autism. *Journal of Autism and Childhood Schizophrenia 1:* 297–310.

Ross EM & Mesulam MM (1979) Dominant language functions of the right hemisphere? Prosody and emotional gesturing. *Archives of Neurology 36:* 144.

Rutter ML (1965) The influence of organic and emotional factors on the origins, nature and outcome of childhood psychosis. *Developmental Medicine and Child Neurology 7:* 518–528.

Rutter ML (1966) Behavioural and cognitive characteristics. In Wing JK (ed) *Early Childhood Autism,* 1st edn, pp. 51–82. Oxford: Pergamon Press.

Rutter ML (1967) Psychotic disorders in early childhood. In Coppen AJ & Walk A (eds) *Recent Developments in Schizophrenia,* pp. 133–151. Ashford, England: RMPA.

Rutter ML (1968) Concepts of autism; a review of research. *Journal of Child Psychology and Psychiatry 9:* 1–25.

Rutter ML (1970) Autistic children; infancy to adulthood. *Seminars in Psychiatry 2:* 435–450.

Rutter ML (1972) Childhood schizophrenia reconsidered. *Journal of Autism and Childhood Schizophrenia 2:* 315–317.

Rutter ML (1974) The development of infantile autism. *Psychological Medicine 4:* 147–163.

Rutter ML (1978a) Communication deviances and diagnostic differences. In Wynne LC, Cromwell RL & Matthysse S (eds) *The Nature of Schizophrenia: New Approaches to Research and Treatment,* pp. 512–516. New York: Wiley.

Rutter ML (1978b) Language disorder and infantile autism. In Rutter M & Schopler E (eds) *Autism: A Reappraisal of Concepts and Treatment.* New York: Plenum Press.

Rutter M & Bartak L (1973) Special educational treatment of autistic children: a comparative study II. Follow-up findings and implications for services. *Journal of Child Psychology and Psychiatry 1.:* 241–270.

Rutter M & Lockyer L (1967) A five to fifteen year follow-up study of infantile psychosis: I. Description of the sample. *British Journal of Psychiatry, 113:* 1169–1182.

Rutter M & Sussenwein F (1971) A developmental and behavioural approach to the treatment of pre-school autistic children. *Journal of Autism and Childhood Schizophrenia 1:* 376–397.

Rutter ML, Greenfield D & Lockyer L (1967) A five to fifteen year follow-up study of infantile psychosis. II. Social and behavioural outcome. *British Journal of Psychiatry 113:* 1183–1199.

Rutter ML, Bartak L & Newman S (1971) Autism – a central disorder of cognition and language? In Rutter M (ed) *Infantile Autism: Concepts, Characteristics and Treatment,* pp. 148–171. New York: Longman.

Schopler E (1971) Parents of psychotic children as scapegoats. *Journal of Contemporary Psychotherapy 4:* 17.

Schopler E & Reichler RJ (1971a) Developmental therapy by parents with their own autistic child. In Rutter M (ed) *Infantile Autism: Concepts, Characteristics and Treatment,* pp. 206–227. London: Churchill Livingstone.

Schopler E & Reichler RJ (1971b) Parents as cotherapists in the treatment of psychotic children. *Journal of Autism and Childhood Schizophrenia 1:* 87–102.

Slater E & Roth M (1969) *Clinical Psychiatry.* London: Baillière,

Tindall & Cassell.

Sloane HN & MacAuley BD (1968) *Operant Procedures in Remedial Speech and Language Training.* Boston: Houghton Mifflin.

Small JG (1971) Sensory evoked responses of autistic children. In Alpern GD & DeMyer MK (eds) *Infantile Autism,* pp. 224–242, Springfield, Illinois: Charles C. Thomas.

Small JG (1975) EEG and neuropsychological studies of early infantile autism. *Biological Psychiatry 10:* 385–397.

Taft LT & Cohen HJ (1971) Hypsarrhythmia and infantile autism: a clinical report. *Journal of Autism and Childhood Schizophrenia 1:* 327–336.

Treffert DA (1970) Epidemiology of infantile autism. *Archives of General Psychiatry 22:* 431–438.

Tubbs VK (1966) Types of linguistic disability in psychotic children. *Journal of Mental Deficiency Research 10:* 230–240.

Van Krevelen DA (1971) Early infantile autism and autistic psychopathy. *Journal of Autism and Childhood Schizophrenia 1:* 82–86.

White PT, DeMyer W & DeMyer M (1964) EEG abnormalities in early childhood schizophrenia: a double-blind study of psychiatrically disturbed and normal children during promazine sedation. *American Journal of Psychiatry 120:* 950–958.

Wing L (1971) Perceptual and language development in autistic children: a comparative study. In Rutter M (ed) *Infantile Autism: Concepts, Characteristics and Treatment,* pp. 173–197. London: Churchill Livingstone.

Wing L (ed.) (1976) *Early Childhood Autism: Clinical, Educational and Social Aspects,* 2nd edn. Oxford: Pergamon.

Wing L (1980) Childhood autism and social class: a question of selection. *British Journal of Psychiatry 137:* 410–17.

Wing L (1981) Asperger's syndrome. *Psychological Medicine 11:* 115–129.

Wing L (1982a) Development of concepts, classification and relationship to mental retardation. In Wing JK & Wing L (eds) *Handbook of Psychiatry 3. Psychoses of Uncertain Aetiology.* pp. 185–190. Cambridge, England: Cambridge University Press.

Wing L (1982b) Clinical description, diagnoses and differential diagnosis. In Wing JK & Wing L *Handbook of Psychiatry 3. Psychoses of Uncertain Aetiology.* pp. 191–197. England: Cambridge University Press.

Wing L & Gould J (1979) Severe impairments of social interactions and associated abnormalities in children: epidemiology and classification. *Journal of Autism and Developmental Disorders 9:* 11–29.

Wing L and Wing JK (1971) Multiple impairments in early childhood autism. *Journal of Autism and Childhood Schizophrenia 1:* 256–266.

Wing L, Yeates SR, Brierley LM & Gould J (1976) The prevalence of early childhood autism: comparison of administrative and epidemiological studies *Psychological Medicine 6:* 89–100.

Wing L, Gould J, Yeates SR & Brierley LM (1977) Symbolic play in severely mentally retarded and in autistic children *Journal of Child Psychology and Psychiatry 18:* 167–178.

Wolff S & Barlow A (1979) Schizoid personality in childhood: a comparative study of schizoid, autistic and normal children. *Journal of Child Psychology and Psychiatry 20:* 29–46.

Wolraich M, Bzostek B, Neu RL & Gardner L (1970) Lack of chromosome aberrations in autism. *New England Journal of Medicine 283:* 1231.

Chapter 15
Early Parent Counselling

CLIFF C. CUNNINGHAM & HILTON DAVIS

There can be few, if any, professionals associated with handicapped children who have not experienced the frustrated and aggressive outpourings of parents. These criticisms usually fall into three categories: (a) those concerned with information and guidance, including lack of accurate information, being misinformed or denied information and lack of practical guidance, (b) those concerning organizational factors, such as delay in appointments and lack of assistance or access to services, and (c) those related to the characteristics of the professionals, such as lack of sympathy, sensitivity or genuine feelings of concern and inability to communicate. From the professional viewpoint it is not uncommon to assume that such criticism and aggression is inevitable – that it is the irrational and misdirected release of anxiety and guilt at having given birth to a handicapped child. As one physician put it, 'There is no way of breaking bad news without the person hating you for it.' Whilst there may be some truth in this for some parents, such conceptions tend to emphasize expected pathology and maladjustment and fail to explore methods of facilitating positive adaptations.

Several studies on the problem of telling parents the diagnosis of Down's syndrome have reported complaints by parents that they were not told together, in a sensitive way, that they were not told soon enough, that they were told in front of a large number of people and no privacy was available, that the baby was not present, that they were not given any or enough information, and that they had no further support or time to work through their reactions and feelings (e.g. Gayton and Walker, 1974; Pueschel and Murphy, 1976; Cunningham and Sloper, 1977a).

When parents are told later than they would have liked they often feel that they have been 'cheated' or 'fobbed off', that 'there was something to hide' or that they could not be 'trusted with the information'. This can suggest to them that there is a stigma in having such an infant and that professionals are unsure whether they can cope with either the information or the child. If the teller appears unsympathetic, or the infant is not present this can be perceived by parents as the child being unwanted and not valued, especially as they are themselves often reacting to their feelings of possible rejection. Such reactions are hardly conducive to the development of positive feelings towards the child or self-confidence in being able to cope. At this time parents are in a highly aroused emotional state and are often particularly sensitive to events around them: 'I knew something was wrong as soon as he was born. They all looked at each other and went very quiet. Some other people then came in . . . but when I asked was he all right, they said he was fine and not to worry . . . but I know they knew all the time, so why didn't they say something instead of keeping me wondering and worrying all that time.' Thus, many parents report that it was changes in the normal hospital routine or subtle staff reactions that concerned them (Cunningham and Sloper, 1977a).

Recent surveys of the disclosure of diagnosis to parents suggests that there have been improvements (e.g., Springer and Steele, 1980), and the inevitability of expressed dissatisfaction is refuted in a study by Cunningham et al. (1984). A 'model procedure', which included many of the concepts described later in this chapter, was developed based upon parental criticisms and stated needs. All parents receiving the 'model procedure' expressed satisfaction and were characterized by their positive and confident attitude towards services, compared with 42% of a retrospective, and 25% of a contemporary comparison group.

An important feature of this 'model procedure' was that it did not limit itself to the immediate disclosure of the diagnosis, but provided continuity of support from the maternity ward to the home. Too often, even when parents make an apparently good initial adjustment to the diagnosis, professionals fail to see this within a context of change. For example, Cunningham and Sloper (1977b) noted three main phases in the adjustment of parents to the diagnosis of Down's syndrome over the first year. The first period was tagged the 'traumatic phase', and was directly related to achieving a relative adjustment to the disclosure; with considerable individual variation, it covered the first 12 weeks of the infant's life. There then followed a 'euphoric phase', when parents often commented on the normality of the child – how he or she did things like their other children. The beginning of this phase is often signalled by parents noting that they no longer keep seeing the characteristics of Down's syndrome and by changes in the infant, such as the onset of smiling. By ten to twelve months, however, parents began to comment spontaneously about 'seeing the handicap'. Often this occurs when mothers make the typical age and ability comparisons with other children. Quite suddenly the reality of the delay – the handicap – becomes apparent and new adjustments have to be made. With more able Down's syndrome children such realities may not appear until much later; as a consequence, some parents find the adjustment even more difficult.

A related point is that while many professionals are aware of the trauma of the initial disclosure of severely handicapping conditions, far fewer appreciate that parents may have equally strong reactions if additional disabilities are found later. All too often, professionals predict parental reactions from their own interpretation of the relative severity of the condition and their own set of attitudes, beliefs and value judgements. Thus, the diagnosis of mild spasticity or partial visual impairment may be as traumatic to one parent as that of Down's syndrome to another. This is evidenced by the comparative lack of investigation of the effects on parents of disclosure of developmental delay, language delay or special educational needs. In all cases, parents have to reconcile their current perceptions and future expectations of the child with the implications of such information, and may need help in adjusting to the new circumstances.

Thus, parental anger, frustration and criticism of services should not be interpreted merely as an inevitable consequence of their feelings about the child's handicap to which we professionals have little to offer but sympathy, with 'time as the only healer'. It is our contention that an understanding of (a) parental reactions and feelings, (b) the processes by which parents attempt to readjust to the diagnosis, needs and behaviours of their child's condition, (c) the organization and support requirements and (d) the skills of interacting and communicating with parents are a necessity for all professionals who are in contact with families of handicapped children.

In this context, we are not referring to the more specialized counselling approaches required for the minority of parents who suffer severe disruption and depression when discovering that the child has a severe handicapping condition. Indeed, we are arguing that counselling for the majority of parents should not be viewed as the treatment of some mental aberration or pathology. Their reactions should be seen as normal and healthy and they should expect and be given active skilled counselling.

This has a preventive function not only in attempting to reduce current stress but also in predicting possible future difficulties and preparing parents in advance. Thus, it is important to appreciate fully that the counselling and support process begins prior to the diagnosis being given and must be viewed as a long-term, continuous need. The addition of a child with severe handicap to the family is not a transient or remediable event: it is a life-long event which brings a continually changing set of interrelated and interactive needs. The first months after the disclosure of diagnosis should be viewed as a *formative period* when parents are developing new conceptions about the child, themselves, their family and the services.

AIMS OF COUNSELLING

When parents are faced with the diagnosis of a handicapping condition in the child or any new set of events (whether real or imagined) which are unexpected, unfamiliar or perceived as distressing, we generally talk about (a) their reactions, (b) their ability to cope, and (c) the stress put upon them. It is useful to distinguish between *reactions*, such as crying, feelings of anxiety, guilt, anger and helplessness, and *attempts to cope*. Coping refers to the ways parents try to avoid or reduce the stressful consequences of the diagnosis or new set of events. Stress can be seen as the result of an imbalance between the demands that the situation puts on the parents and their resources to meet these demands; the greater the imbalance the greater is the likelihood of stress. From this viewpoint, coping is an attempt to direct one's energies towards solving problems, and the attempted solutions can be seen as coping strategies (see Ray et al., 1982, for a useful schema of such strategies).

The main aim of counselling is the joint identification by parent and professional of (a) the sources of stress, (b) goals or a plan of action to reduce the stress, (c) the available resources, and (d) coping strategies that can be developed to meet these goals. One advantage of this goal-directed approach is that it allows the process to be evaluated and analysed. Thus, if one identifies that lack of information is acting as a stressor then one can evaluate whether the provision of the information (the goal) is instrumental in reducing stress.

A useful categorization of coping resources has been suggested by Folkman and Lazarus (1980). These are (a) the individual parent's physical and emotional well-being at the time of the diagnosis or event and during the adjustment phase, (b) individual ability and past experience in problem-solving (i.e. coping), such as seeking out and understanding information and relating it to their own situation, (c) the support they receive from the family, friends and services – the social network, (d) utilitarian resources, such as financial means and mobility, and (e) their values, beliefs and feelings of self-efficacy and control – this includes attitudes and beliefs about both the infant and themselves.

For each resource category there are complementary stressors (lack of resources), and it is these that become a major focus of services. Indeed, the provision of an early counselling and support service is one factor in the social network resources, and lack of it can be viewed as a potential stressor. However, a number of principles must guide the provision of the resource.

Firstly, the activity of seeking out appropriate coping strategies may itself be a stressor, and only the parent can indicate the amount of strain this places on his or her resources. Thus, the process has to be undertaken with joint appraisal and with the parent largely in control of the timing. For example, parental denial of the diagnosis, or avoidance of situations emphasizing the problem, such as clinics, discussions with professionals or other parents, should be seen as coping strategies. To interpret the parental statement that 'they wished the child was dead' literally may be less useful than to perceive it as an attempt to explore feelings about the child and the effects of the child on the parents' future lives. Similarly, to label the parents as non-accepting or denying the handicap because their perceptions of the child and future expectancies are more favourable than the professional's is far from constructive. It will not only depend on the value judgements and belief systems of professionals and parents but may also reflect the parents' attempt to cope with the diagnosis and is best seen as one step in the process of adjustment.

Secondly, coping will involve both overt strategies, such as seeking information and learning skills to interact with the child, and covert strategies related to more emotionally oriented behaviours aimed at understanding personal feelings and concepts. These are closely linked. Thus, parents usually seek out activities for stimulating the infant's development which can be seen by them as meaningful because they help the child. The discussion of why such activities help the child is therefore necessary, and will also aid the parents' ever-changing conceptions of the child, often leading to self-appraisal of feelings.

Thirdly, and possibly most importantly, counselling has to be aimed at developing parent feelings of confidence, independence and self-control. One of the most commonly reported reactions of parents to early support services or parent workshops (Chapter 18) is that it gave them confidence in themselves. This feeling of self-efficacy or being able to cope is a considerable resource to parents. Unfortunately, too often professionals can place the parent in a dependent role – dependent on the professional for knowledge and direction. Commonly, professionals demonstrate that they are more able to handle the child and make decisions on behalf of the child. Whilst this is sometimes unavoidable, it is more useful to involve the parents in the decision-making process. To do this the information needed in making a decision has to be shared with them, thereby demonstrating that they are trusted and viewed as capable of learning and applying procedures. This is best achieved by identifying and reinforcing their existing skills and building upon them, but not in a didactic or patronizing manner. Dependency is but one dimension of coping. At times, parents will need to reduce stress by relying upon professionals to make decisions and give direction. In the current spirit of equal partnership, the professionals must not abdicate this responsibility. It has, however, to be negotiated with parents and related to the long-term aim of parent independence.

Thus, counselling is concerned with a process of adjustment. The aims are to identify resources and potential stressors and to develop coping strategies. It is a process which takes time and has to be based on mutually agreed and understood plans of action. This requires mutual trust and respect between parent and professional, which is achieved through honest negotiation. The professional must respect parents' beliefs, values and skills. The professional's role is to provide parents with the necessary information and guidance to develop coping strategies without undermining their feelings of self-esteem and confidence. To do this the professional will need (a) insight into the feelings and reactions aroused by a handicapped child, (b) a framework for understanding the process of adjustment, and (c) basic counselling skills.

FEELINGS AND REACTIONS

The presence of a handicapped child will arouse in parents and professionals a range of feelings and reactions. Often parents are surprised at the range and forcefulness of these and many are unsure how normal such reactions are. This uncertainty may cause them to hide their feelings and so one aim of counselling is to enable them to examine their reactions and to appreciate that they are usually far more common than they believe. Since these feelings also influence the way professionals interact and communicate with the child and with the parents, professionals must openly examine their own feelings and reactions as well as trying to understand those of the parent. Many of the reactions will be common both to professionals and to parents and can create an empathy between them. But to be a parent (natural, fostered or adoptive) is to have a unique relationship with the child. Most parents accept a degree of responsibility for the child which would be viewed as unreasonable for the professional. The parents will be the main advocates for the child. As such, they will make what may be seen from the professional viewpoint as unreasonable demands on themselves and the services on behalf of the child. Their feelings of having a handicapped child will often enhance this and need to be understood and appreciated by professionals.

Since such feelings are highly individual and personal, no one can fully understand and appreciate them in another person. Thus, in developing empathy with the parent it is a mistake to assume that one does fully understand. Empathy is the act of trying to see things from the other person's view but knowing that this can never be fully achieved. One has to respect the person's own right to have a set of unique feelings and reactions. This has to be kept in the forefront of one's considerations when applying the frameworks for understanding feelings and reactions described below.

MacKeith (1973) suggested a classification of common feelings, based upon his long experience as a paediatrician, which is increasingly being used for parent and professional counselling (e.g. Cunningham, 1982; Newson and Hipgrave, 1982). The main ones are:

1 Biological reactions: (a) protection of the helpless child; (b) revulsion to the abnormality.
2 Feelings of inadequacy: (a) inadequacy in reproductive ability; (b) inadequacy in rearing the child.
3 Feelings of bereavement, such as grief, anger and shock, associated with not having the expected child.
4 Feelings of embarrassment, particularly when explaining to others about the child and when in public places with the child.
5 Feelings of guilt, for instance guilt at feeling revulsion and rejection or feeling anger and resentment towards the child or feeling inadequate in interacting with the child.

To these we can add:

6 Feelings of fear, for example fear of the future and the uncertainty, fear of their feelings towards the child, and sometimes, in the first months, fear of becoming so attached that if the child has to be placed in a residential facility or may not survive they may not be able to face the situation.

Biological reactions

In using the term 'biological reactions' MacKeith was suggesting that these are fundamental to most people and hence are common to parents and professionals. Few people do not feel protective towards an infant, a child who is ill or one with a visible handicap. Such feelings generally lead the parent towards developing a warm, loving and caring relationship with the child. However, in the case of handicap, such feelings can become too protective. This may result in parents becoming particularly sensitive to any implied suggestion of criticism or negativism towards the child. This can interact with their own feelings of negativism, resentment and anger, which may then be reflected in hostility toward the perceived critic. An overprotective reaction can also produce imbalance within the family, particularly in relation to other children. It can easily become a set pattern in which the development of the handicapped child's independence is prevented and the child is not allowed to take reasonable risks in its exploration of the world. Most children demand this independence, but many handicapped children have to be consistently encouraged to develop it.

Feelings of protectiveness are also involved when parents and professionals consider the effect of the handicap on the family. Many wish to protect their children and relatives from the hurt that they feel and the projected consequences of having a handicapped child in the family. Sometimes parents support their decision not to take the infant home by arguing that the siblings would suffer. This has to be carefully considered. There is much evidence that the presence of a severely handicapped child can have deleterious effects on family functioning. However, such effects are highly variable and relate to the nature of the condition and the family's coping resources. Also, no research has fully examined whether such long-term effects can be avoided if the necessary support and counselling are available. Equally, few analyses have been made of the positive effects of having a handicapped member in the family. If parents do argue that they are protecting the siblings by not taking the infant home, they should be aware that this may make the siblings feel responsible. Older siblings have expressed their difficulty in reconciling their parents' apparent 'rejection' of their brother or sister.

Although revulsion towards abnormality is not uncommon, expressing such feelings is. If there is revulsion, recognition of it may be helpful both for parents and for professionals. An associated reaction is resentment, in which the handicap is resented on behalf of the child and the child is resented for having a handicap and affecting the family. Many years after birth, such feelings can still be present: '. . . deep down, I have never been able to forgive him for the genetic confusion that produced him. The contradiction haunts me . . . ' (Charles Hannam, The Guardian, October 14, 1979). Such feelings can lead to the reaction of rejection, which is a far more subtle set of responses than simply not being able to take the baby home. Many parents have expressed relief that they love the child but reject the handicap. Since the child and his handicap are one, this appears to be a contradiction. Yet, many parents find it does reflect their feelings and others, when told of this, often state that it is a helpful concept.

Thus, parents may oscillate between the contradictory feelings of revulsion and protectiveness and, indeed, it may be the attempt to maintain a balance that produces stress. The presence and strength of such feelings varies between individuals and from time to time within individuals. This can cause strain in the relationship between the child's parents and of course between parents and relatives and professionals. It is often noted, for example, that mothers appear more accepting of the handicapped child than fathers, although objective evidence for this is not yet sufficient. A common explanation is that men have a self-image less able to cope with the reflected loss of self-esteem at having produced an abnormal child. Another explanation that we have found useful for some families is that fathers are more predisposed to feelings of protection for the family whilst mothers, certainly at the time of birth, have strong feelings of protection toward the helpless infant. Obviously, such generalizations are inadequate, but they can offer parents plausible explanations from which to explore a range of alternative explanations so necessary in developing an understanding of their own and each other's feelings. They become a resource in their attempts to cope.

Professionals' own feelings of protection and revulsion and value judgements of the infant influence their work. Parents who have strong feelings of protection and love towards the child often comment on how the professional tended to ignore the infant, 'never even looked at him, let alone picked him up'. To reject is also to avoid and one cannot avoid more obviously than keeping one's distance from another. When being given the diagnosis, many parents comment on the fact that the baby was not even present. In the 'ideal model' referred to earlier, the paediatrician's concern and valuing of the infant was demonstrated in his handling and comments and was an integral part of the procedure.

Protectiveness can also cause bias. Many professionals find it particularly difficult to understand and interact with parents who are apparently rejecting the child. Such parents frequently comment on the professional's sudden change of manner, to that of being matter of fact and cold 'once they felt we were not going to take him home'. Most parents in this situation also appear to feel that the professional judges them as uncaring and unloving people. It is important for professionals to appreciate their feelings and the danger of taking sides. The counsellor's role is to help the parents to make decisions for themselves based upon as full a knowledge of the situation as is available.

Feelings of inadequacy

The extent and frequency of feelings of reproductive inadequacy is poorly understood. The sexual relationship of partners can be affected, often associated with a fear of producing another handicapped child. Obviously information on reproductive risk and cause of the handicapping condition is important at this time. Many parents, particularly if the handicapped child is their first, appear to recognize these feelings after the birth of a subsequent non-handicapped child: 'It wasn't until he was born and we knew he was OK, that I realised how much it meant to me to produce a normal baby'. To reproduce means to produce a copy, and there appears to be a fundamental desire in most human beings to have children and to see them as extensions of themselves. Thus, producing a child who is handicapped can undermine parents' self-esteem and confidence. This again appears to affect fathers more than mothers and can vary according to whether the child is a boy or girl. Not uncommonly, parents and grandparents reproach each other: 'We have not had anything like this in our side of the family.' Siblings can also experience such feelings of family inadequacy in reproduction.

When they arise, such feelings are deep-seated and painful, and are a potential source of conflict in the interactions between family members. Whilst they are often more visible in the first months after the diagnosis, they can surface at later times such as the birth of a non-handicapped baby to a relative or friend and when siblings are teased or questioned about their handicapped brother or sister.

Feelings of inadequacy in rearing the child are common to most parents whether the child is handicapped or not. Will I cope? Am I doing the right things? Am I doing enough? What should I do? They become particularly forceful when parents are faced with a child with a severe handicap for two obvious reasons. Firstly, few parents have any knowledge or experience about the handicap from which to assess their own resources of coping, the child's needs and the methods of helping. Their knowledge of normal children, gained over years of direct and indirect learning, can, at first, be perceived as irrelevant.

Secondly, handicapped children, even with a similar condition like Down's syndrome, display enormous individual variations. Thus, it is difficult and sometimes unwise to generalize knowledge of one individual or even groups to others. There are few occasions when parents can compare their child to others in order to answer such questions as 'Am I doing enough?' or 'Am I doing the right thing?' Yet this is the main procedure used by most parents of non-handicapped children to evaluate their rearing practices. As more information on the range of

abilities, progress and treatment of the handicapped children becomes available, some assistance can be given. However, parents do need regular access to competent professional guidance for this. Professional palliatives such as 'I think the way you cope with him is just wonderful' are of little help. Parents can get this from friends and relatives. Factual discussion of feelings, the child's progress and above all analysis and evaluation of parental attempts to encourage the child's development and the management of the child are required.

As was noted in the introduction, parental concerns of not being able to cope can be very strong in the first months and parents are particularly sensitive to innuendo or suggestions of their inability to cope. They are grateful to professionals who display knowledge and competence and will often pressurize (both overtly and covertly) the professional into situations which encourage dependency. Professionals can easily slip into the pattern of telling parents what to do and when to do it, so shielding them from the complexity and demands of decision-making and seeking out sources for information and support, and of too quickly offering the parents apparent solutions without joint discussion of needs, implications and consequences. However, a danger is that if professional support ceases, parents may not have developed sufficient confidence and coping strategies to continue on their own. Even with continuing support, the hidden danger is that they will not develop self-esteem and will perceive the professional as being in control rather than themselves. It is generally accepted that individuals' responses to stress are greatly influenced by their conception of whether they have control over events. Further, to be dependent on others to perform the parenting role is to reduce the satisfaction gained from being a parent. Many parents who do cope with the enormous demands of having a handicapped child express how much satisfaction this gave them:

'If you had asked me before she was born . . . I would have said there's no way I could cope with a child like—.'

'I learnt so much about myself, and about what friendship and families really mean. I don't think about life the way I used to . . . in fact, just having J . . . in the family has taught us all so much about ourselves. . . .'

Such expressions of self-esteem have to be a goal for all parent counselling. Whilst professionals may gain satisfaction from parents saying 'I couldn't cope without you' or 'I could not have done it without you' this surely must be evaluated as indicating a need for more counselling or a change in counselling strategy.

The extent to which the counsellor takes over the decision-making and responsibility for the child at certain times must be carefully judged. If there is an honest relationship based on mutual respect, this can be achieved through open discussion. However, the counsellor must have a plan of action based on past knowledge of the parent and current coping resources and this will often require questioning about feelings in order to (a) initiate a joint exploration and (b) allow the counsellor to evaluate his or her projected goals. Because parents do not raise issues does not necessarily mean there are none. At the same time, this has to be done in a way that does not suggest to parents that they should have difficulties.

Feelings of inadequacy are associated with uncertainty and lack of self-confidence. Although the effect may be to increase dependency it can also be expressed by reacting defensively when criticized. This affects professionals as well as parents. Being asked for a second opinion or directly questioned about alternative treatments may be perceived as threatening and become manifest in defensiveness. Such responses may reduce the parents' confidence in the services and therefore inhibit their active search for support. Similar results may occur when professionals, as reported by parents, give contradictory advice or criticize other aspects of the service or other professionals. Why they do this is unclear. It can be a professional dilemma in that the evidence to advise on different treatments is not available. But, if so, parents require an objective set of facts concerning the alternatives. More often, however, it appears to relate to the professional's feelings of inadequacy. There appears to be some process in human beings by which the denigration of another raises one's own self-esteem by comparison. But, with few exceptions, it is neither professional nor useful to deny one's own uncertainties to parents. Indeed, sharing such uncertainties has a valuable function in counselling and creating a working partnership. An art of counselling, however, is to do this without, at the same time, denying professional competence. All members of the partnership have to define their areas of competence and knowledge.

Feelings of embarrassment

Feelings of embarrassment are expressed by a whole range of behaviours common to all people. The neighbours, for example, may avoid the parent because they do not know how to deal with the mother; the doctor may be curt or circumlocutory in giving the diagnosis, fidgeting and avoiding eye-contact. Similar behaviours may be common to the siblings, parent or grandparent trying to explain the handicap or the child's behaviour to others. To avoid such feelings one tries to avoid situations which become or are perceived as stressful. In situations when feelings of embarrassment arise, interactions with others can become defiant and aggressive, cutting short discussions which could be embarrassing and stressful. Alternatively, the interaction may begin apologetically, with the implication of having done something wrong. When we do something wrong we generally feel guilty. When we are embarrassed and avoid situations we imply that some stigma is attached .

Many practical strategies can be discussed with parents. After a discussion of feelings, why they arise, and their normality, one may then examine consequences. For example, if others are embarrassed at talking to the parent of the new baby because they are unsure of how to broach the subject, then the parent will have to help them. By working out with the parent how they might react or cope with this situation, they are prepared for future events and reduce the probability of further stress.

Within this, one also includes how to break the news to others, such as siblings and grandparents, and tries to give an insight into their feelings. Taking the baby out on the first occasion can be difficult. Parents need to know why it is important and that the sooner they do it the better. Learning to talk about their child to others and therefore reducing their embarrassment can be helped by interaction with other parents of handicapped children. However, since not all parents want to be introduced to other parents in the first months, they need to decide for themselves when they feel ready.

Feelings of guilt

Feelings of guilt are generally associated with believing that one is directly or indirectly responsible for something which one did not want to happen, or alternatively, not doing something one should have. Having and bringing up children is a major responsibility and seldom proceeds according to hopes and expectations. When the difference between reality and expectations is too big, according to the parents' judgement, parents may ask, 'Is it my fault?' or 'Where did I go wrong?' Thus, feelings of guilt in parents with a handicapped child are as normal as with any child, but enlarged by the situation. For many years too much emphasis has been placed by professionals on the assumption that parents will feel guilty about producing a handicapped child. This is a gross oversimplification and possibly a projection of professionals' feelings of guilt at not being able to avoid the damage to the child, and the pain to the parents, and feeling inadequate to help.

Many parents do not have strong feelings of guilt associated with producing the child, and become upset when it is assumed. However, they do need to know why it happened – why it happened to them. Well-communicated explanations of causes are vital at this time; when these are given few parents will have persistent feelings of guilt. Where no causal explanation is apparent, parents are more likely to continue to ask, 'Why me?' or 'Was it something I did?' Counselling here has to be directed at helping parents to understand that even if such knowledge was available it would not actually change the situation for the child. They need to understand that such questions can debilitate them and that this reduction in their resources could affect the child.

There are, of course, conditions where the parent's action or decision is directly associated with the handicap (for instance, vaccine damage and fetal alcohol syndrome). Again, it is necessary to help parents express and understand their feelings and to explore the consequences, so that they can build up coping strategies for the benefit of the child. One should never underestimate the positive therapeutic effect of doing something which is seen or believed to be beneficial to the child. However, if such actions are largely motivated by feelings of guilt, they can lead to false hopes of making atonement which can lead to an imbalance in family interactions. This can be avoided by an appreciation of feelings and their consequent actions, and the provision of factual information on what to expect as a result.

More common are feelings of guilt related to (a) not doing enough to help the child, particularly if parents are engaged in early intervention programmes, (b) not doing enough for their other children because of the demands of the handicapped child, and (c) being unable to help. Feelings of guilt about not doing enough to help can usually be reduced by detailed explanation of the nature of child development and learning difficulties, an evaluation of progress and the realization that many parents feel that they never do enough. Where there is guilt about the other children one has to evaluate with the parents just what they would be

doing if the handicapped child was not present and precisely what the others are missing. It is then possible to decide on strategies that may produce a more acceptable and fair arrangement. If parents feel guilty at being unable to help – that is, being inadequate – 'I get upset when I go to the Mothers' group . . . they all seem to know what to do and how to help the baby and their babies are doing so well. . . .' it is not very helpful for professionals merely to assure them that they are 'doing very well'. Because of the tremendous heterogeneity in the handicapped population and the difficulties in learning and development that these children present, we are all relatively inadequate. One must accept that some parents are less able than others. However, when a parent expresses feelings of inadequacy, one should not deny them but instead help them to evaluate in what ways they feel inadequate and from this help them decide what knowledge and skills they need to explore. Of course, as with all teaching, one applies the fundamental principle of working from the known to the unknown, building on what is available. In identifying current levels of parent strength this can be reassuring and reduce feelings of guilt associated with inadequacy.

Parents can also feel guilt about their feelings. There is nothing abnormal in such feelings and the way to cope with them is to understand and recognize this. Many parents find that they cope more easily by expressing such feelings with other parents in parent-support groups. Parents are often far more aware than professionals of the way such feelings come and go and the relief that can be gained from discussing them in the safety of others who understand and accept them. Sometimes when parents have expressed such feelings to another person, they may be reluctant to bring them up again 'because they've heard it all before'. This may be particularly so if they perceived the professional as very busy. It is also associated with the parental perception of the professional role; 'no matter how good professionals are, they can never fully understand'. As yet, we know very little about the distinctions between parent and professional roles in counselling, but we should all be very conscious of the fact that the parents' perception of the professional role will largely govern how they behave in interactions. In developing a relationship with parents professionals should give some explanation of their role, what they can and cannot do and negotiate with the parents whether this is useful. Similarly, one aspect of counselling is the provision of information to parents on the role of various professions and services and how they can get what they need from them. Parental satisfaction with services will directly relate to their expectations of the services.

In this respect, one needs to consider how society as a whole treats parents. The child is born and suddenly a whole range of professions are involved. The family and child are subjected to a fairly intense scrutiny and constant visits are arranged to service facilities and at home. Questions can be asked not just about the child but about family relationships, financial resources, other children, support from relatives, friends and neighbours. Even the questions asked by friends and relatives can change in content. Whilst this can often be positive, it can also make parents feel that they are under examination – that their abilities to cope and help the child are being questioned from all sides. To avoid this, counselling and parent support must be as unintrusive as possible. Careful evaluation of the benefits of each visit, and each request, must be weighed against the possibility of additional stress. Again, open discussion with parents, allowing them to control the process as much as possible, is one strategy. But they can only make decisions if they have a clear set of information on possible benefits and disadvantages. The professional has to attempt to provide an honest and objective evaluation of the services offered. Parents are vulnerable and will usually try to give the child every possible advantage. Any treatment which might help will be considered and sought. Without competent professional help, many parents may feel guilty that they are unable to provide the treatments or may overload their resources by trying them all.

Feelings of fear

Being afraid is often associated with uncertainty. We fear what we do not know and this can often lead to avoidance and inaction. Most parents at some time feel apprehensive for their child's future and this is particularly so for handicapped children. Information on future possibilities can help. At the time of the birth some parents are afraid to develop an attachment for the child:

'They said she wouldn't live very long and so I thought it would be better not to get too attached . . . I was afraid that if I grew to love her it would hurt when she went. . . .'

'We thought about bringing him home but felt that we would not be able to put him up for fostering if we needed to. I suppose we were frightened of getting too close to him.'

In the case of the dying baby, the counselling focused on helping the parents to evaluate the likely consequences of adopting the strategy of not getting attached, on defining what they felt were the needs of the infant and themselves and what actions would meet these needs. The mother questioned whether she would be hurt more by the death of the child or by her 'guilt' at not being 'willing to love' the child. The philosophy that the basic needs of infants are food, warmth, loving attention and stimulation was discussed, along with the idea that provision of these was more likely to make each day a 'happy one'. All the other feelings of the parent were also discussed over this period and when the infant died, the mother said: 'I feel very sad but at least I know that while she was with us we did everything we could for her. She was loved and I have many happy memories of the time we splashed together in the bath and played together. Looking back, I think I would have been haunted by feeling guilty if I had not loved her and given her something.' Parents can also fear and be shocked by the power of their feelings toward the child. They can be frightened at ideas of wanting to kill or hurt the child or their anger and aggression to others. Again, a realization that these are common and understandable feelings is helpful.

Feelings of bereavement

We say of the pregnant mother that she is expecting a baby. What are these expectations? Both parents will have built up an image of the hoped-for child based on their own experiences and values. They may have imagined what the child will be like and what he or she will achieve far into the future. They will often have made plans for the child and the future development and structure of the family. They will usually have made some assessment of their responsibilities as parents and considered the implications for their own lifestyle and financial circumstances.

The diagnosis of a handicap destroys these images and plans. It is as though the expected (albeit imagined) child was dead. Hence parents often feel a great sense of loss at this time and may need to grieve. Yet, at the same time, they are faced with a child who has a handicap and they are unlikely to be equipped with sufficient information on the nature and implications of it. What sort of child is this? What does it mean? In a sense they have a void in their knowledge or a stereotyped conception, often fearful, of the condition. To differing degrees they will experience many of the feelings and reactions discussed previously. Invariably, they experience a great sense of shock and often anger: 'Why us?' 'It is unfair'; 'What did we do to deserve this?' At this time they are particularly vulnerable and highly sensitive. Good counselling has to be available and will have long-term consequences.

THE PROCESS OF ADJUSTMENT

We have described all these reactions without emphasizing the function. We have ended with bereavement because the process of adjustment can be seen as similar to the process of grieving. Both involve severe shocks that require the demolition of one model and the construction of a new one. Following the concept of emotion espoused by George Kelly (1955), we view emotion not as something intensely pathological but as functional in relation to the process of change, which is what readjustment is. Parents have to adapt to a new set of circumstances. They have to dismantle their projected model and then fill the void by re-constructing their values, plans, hopes and resources. Thus, it cannot be other than a relatively long process requiring time and well-thought-out support and planning. It is precisely with this rebuilding that counselling is intimately involved.

A number of stage models have been suggested for the process of adjustment to death, handicap or severe shock. In Table 15.1 we present such a model,

adapted from the work of Hall and Grunewald (1977) and other literature. The model is intended to guide professional considerations of counselling and not to be imposed on parents, since some will not display all the stages or reactions and many will oscillate between phases at different times and in different contexts. Parents can be organizing help and working with the infant and still have strong feelings of grief, anger and denial related to any of the many factors involved. Even after making an initial adjustment feelings return in different ways, levels and contexts. But if in the early counselling parents have learnt how to identify and analyse these, they are often more able to cope with new feelings.

This model is not applicable just to situations with new infants but also to any occasion when a diagnosis of severe handicap is made. The nature of the handicap and the preparedness of the parents for it are obviously influential.

In the case of the new infant, however, the situation is complicated by the development of attachment to the child: 'I found my own feelings and self-pity kept getting in the way of doing what I knew I had to, accept him as he is.' Emde and Brown (1978) noted three phases in the normal process of attachment. The first is the attachment to the dreamed-of child during pregnancy. The second follows the birth, with an upsurge of love and interest, manifested in daily care and interaction with the infant. It is this which may be crucial and

Table 15.1 Model of psychic crisis at disclosure of handicap.

		Manifestations		Needs
Parent is told → *Psychic crisis*				
	1 Shock phase ↕	Emotional disorganization, confusion, paralysis of actions, disbelief, and irrationality	Can last from two minutes to several days	Sympathy and emotional support
Frequent oscillation between phases	2 Reaction phase ↕	Expression of sorrow, grief, disappointment, anxiety, aggression, denial, guilt, failure, defence mechanisms	A process of reintegration through discussion	Listen to parent. Catharsis through talking out. Sympathy but honest. Facts on cause.
	3 Adaptation phase ↑	Realistic appraisal: parents ask, 'What can be done?' This is a *signal of readiness* to proceed with 'How can we help?'		Reliable and accurate information on medical and educational treatment and future
	4 Orientation phase	Parents begin to organize, seek help and information, and plan for future		Provide regular help and guidance in treatment
		→ Initial crisis over		→ Appropriate provision of services

may be damaged by separations at this time (Klaus and Kennell, 1976). The third comes after the neonatal period when the child's social signalling system, including eye contact and smiling, emerges. Both the latter stages are at risk in handicapped children. Before phase two can proceed the parents have to move sufficiently through the shock and reaction phases to turn energies into developing a knowledge and understanding of the new infant.

Having done this, they begin to orient and adjust. This can be seen as a 'functional acceptance' of the diagnosis, and the probability that the family will cope is increased. The concept of acceptance may be misused by professionals, particularly when parental hopes and expectations do not match those of professionals.

Since acceptance can never be defined in an absolute way, it is better to consider it functionally in terms of what purpose it serves. As such, it often coincides with the emergence of social signalling behaviour and the parent seeing the child as an individual rather than a handicap. However, if the behaviours are notably abnormal then this can affect phase three of the attachment process. Similarly, if at a later time the reality of the handicap is suddenly apparent, a new wave of feelings can be experienced and new reconstructing and orientation are required.

A dilemma faced by many paediatricians is whether to inform parents within the first days that the child is handicapped and so risk upsetting the attachment process or whether to delay it, against the wishes of the majority of parents, who want to be informed as soon as possible. Our own experience is that parents do not find possible interference with the process of attachment a good reason for withholding the information. Further, if one accepts the earlier notion of three phases in attachment, then it is clear that it is a long-term process and other factors than the diagnosis may be more influential. Recent research on the nature of mother–infant interaction is suggesting that guidance for some parents on the differences in development of the handicapped child and how this influences the interactions can be worth while. By altering the natural phasing and reciprocal patterns to compensate for the infant's difficulties, a more satisfying interaction can be facilitated (Berger and Cunningham, 1981).

Although we have discussed a stage model which is convenient to aid our understanding, we nevertheless also need to consider the processes by which parents traverse the stages. To do this, it is useful to see parents as constructing models of their world so that they can anticipate and therefore adjust to events (Davis, 1983). The first stage is therefore a period in which an existing model (of the anticipated child) is shattered by the disclosure of the diagnosis and the parents have no focus for their understanding. They have no framework to help them anticipate either the immediate or the long-term future. By nature, we assume that all people engage in the process of making the world meaningful, and therefore the process of reconstructing a new model of the world begins immediately. The reaction stage is the start: the parents engage in an exploration of their situation, they seek information, they explore consequences of various actions and their implications, and all the while they are in an aroused emotional state, which we see as functional in terms of the awareness of the need for change and the motivation to do so. Anger, aggression, denial, dependency and many other reactions can be seen as strategies which enable rapid exploration of possibilities and as such are prerequisites of change.

By the stage of adaptation, effective change has begun to be seen. There is the framework of an understanding that allows the parents to anticipate the future to an extent, if only to enable anticipation of what lines to pursue and what questions to ask. With the stage of orientation there is a working model that can guide parental behaviour; they know what to do. Of course, this is never static, but it is an understanding that will evolve with changing circumstances of the family.

The progress through the adjustment process is influenced by many factors and characterized by marked individual differences:

1 The nature of the child: physical, temperamental and rate of developmental progress.
2 Parents' past experience of mental handicap or any severe childhood disorders, previous difficulties with childbirth and other offspring, whether they have other children, have waited for many years to have a child, and so on.
3 Philosophy (in other words, their general model of life), parents' hopes, strivings and values. Often parents who particularly value intellectual skills have greater difficulty in accepting mental handicap than a physical handicap and vice versa. Some parents fear a child who will be disfigured or look peculiar.
4 Lifestyle: the difficulties that the child may cause in the present lifestyle of the family.
5 Relationship between partners: their relative strengths and weaknesses, support for each other and so on.

6 Emotion and adjustment; this is particularly complex, but any instability in the parent can become disproportionately crucial at this time.

7 How the parents and the infant are treated. The service provision and, last but not least, the social network resources.

However, one should not be daunted by the complexity. As noted in the introduction to this chapter, an appreciation of the feelings and needs of families and the use of model procedures for disclosure of diagnosis with skilled counselling can be highly successful. Most parents move through this adjustment period and become caring and attached to the child. Good counselling can help this process and reduce likely stress and pain.

COUNSELLING

Counselling can be carried out at many levels of sophistication. Most professionals can easily acquire the basic skills necessary to help parents to help themselves by providing appropriate support and information (see Cunningham and Davis, 1985). Several guidelines can be given on how to talk to parents:

1 Avoid all unnecessary jargon.

2 Do not give a lecture: let the parents ask questions. It is essential to allow the family to talk; the emphasis is on professional listening.

3 Allow pauses in the conversation and give the parents time to think; remember that silence often precedes embarrassment or difficult statements.

4 Try to get the parents to talk about and discover their own feelings, values, hopes, disappointments, and so on. Often it is best to present parables about other families which offer alternative views and allow the parents to draw their own conclusions and decide on relevance. When dealing with particularly sensitive areas of feelings this can be more acceptable. Some parents may prefer to read about such feelings and come to terms with them privately, rather than being forced through painful discussions with professionals or other parents.

5 Choose words carefully: an odd expression such as 'Had you not noticed something strange about the child?' can be misinterpreted out of all proportion.

6 Be as objective as possible in giving information about the child: be neither over-positive nor particularly negative.

7 Do not avoid honest responses saying that a particular question cannot be answered and why, or that you do not know the answer but will try to find out.

8 Try to give an accepting attitude to parents and child. Avoid any indications that the parents may be inadequate, for instance by talking in so complicated a manner that they do not understand or by suggesting that the child needs extra expertise which they do not have. If the child does need extra expertise explain why or how they can get this expertise.

9 Avoid giving the impression that you do not have time to talk to them. If you are scheduled to leave at a specific time, tell parents at the beginning, and some minutes before the time, remind them of it (preferably indirectly). Often the difficult questions for the parents to ask will be kept back and will come at this point, so always have some minutes in hand. If you go over the allotted time, parents appreciate this and realize that you do have time for them. This is a recognition of the value you place on them, the child and your own dealings with them. They are sensitive to people 'not caring because the child is handicapped and not worth the effort'.

All these are facets of more general characteristics of good counselling:

1 *Communication*: an ability to communicate both factual information and the personal qualities of the counsellor.

2 *Competence*: in knowledge and skills involved in working with handicapped children.

3 *Understanding*: an explicit framework for understanding the parent–professional relationship in terms of a consumer-partnership mode. This assumes that the parent and professional work cooperatively on a basis of variable equality, each aware of the other's expertise and responsibilities. It further assumes parental self-responsibility and that the essence of the relationship is negotiation not imposition.

4 *Respect*: respect for the family, valuing them and trusting in their strength and abilities rather than assuming that they are in any way inferior to the professional.

5 *Attending skills*: an ability to attend to what the parents and family say verbally and non-verbally.

6 *Empathy*: to attempt to see how the parents view their world, and what model they are using to make sense of their situation.

7 *Challenging*: once the parents' view of their situation is clear, the counsellor needs to be able, and to know when it is appropriate, to offer alternatives. This helps them to build more accurate and effective models. It can only be done within a relationship of mutual respect and with tact. It has to build on family strengths and be positive. Essentially, counsellors must *reflect* possibilities for the family and then have the skills to negotiate a mutually acceptable outcome.

8 *Ingenuity and flexibility*: no two counselling situations are identical. Each family has different needs and resources and so each plan and approach must be individual. This requires counsellors to use their ingenuity to blend skills and information.

9 *Evaluation*: good counselling must always have on-going evaluation of its goals in order to meet changing circumstances.

10 *Least intrusion*: the counselling should endeavour to produce the minimal disruption and alteration to the natural support system (unless it is pathological), at the same time enhancing the supportive capacity of the system.

11 *Success*: counselling should avoid making recommendations which are beyond the resources of the family. The plan should be built from small achievable steps. Throughout this process it is important to appreciate that parents have to adapt and adjust to each new piece of information given, each new set of events recognized. They have to consider new information in relation to past knowledge; they have to examine it from different perspectives before it is assimilated and understood; they have to reformulate it in respect of projected actions and consequences. This all takes time, so the organization of counselling and regular support is important.

These principles can be exemplified in the case of disclosure of diagnosis:

1 Parents should have the opportunity to have a second appointment with the professional or another informed person as soon as possible after the initial disclosure. At the first meeting the trauma is so great that little information is taken in. However, once this shock phase is over, the parent will probably need frequent opportunities to meet for support and information, though this must be negotiated with the individual parent and family. If the person who did the initial telling is

not able to maintain this contact, they should introduce someone else who can.

It is best if as few people as possible are concerned with providing the support and advice. Once the initial diagnosis and interviews are over, the paediatrician may play a less active role, with a community-based professional acting as the major resource.

2 Some parents find great comfort in meeting with another parent who has a similarly handicapped child. But not all parents are prepared to do this, so one must reach agreement with them first before making arrangements. It is also worthwhile carefully considering who the other parent should be. Merely having a handicapped child is not a sufficient criterion for being able to help a fellow parent at this time.

3 As far as possible, maintain the 'normality' of how parents and infants are treated in the hospital or baby clinic. Particular emphasis on special treatment appears to upset a number of parents.

4 Ensure that everyone dealing with the parents takes a similar approach and is aware of the treatment being given. Team meetings to review the position are essential.

5 If parents are going to develop a positive relationship to the infant they must feel they know him – that they understand him. It is a common psychological phenomenon to feel apprehensive or alienated from things we do not understand; how much more this must happen if it is your own child. They need information to help them make sense of the child, to interpret the child's behaviour, and to deduce the communicative intentionality of these behaviours. This is the foundation of their relationship.

In the first instance parents demand information centred around three common questions:

1 What is the handicap? How was it caused?
2 What are the consequences for the future? What will their child do or not do?
3 What can we do to help?

The last two questions are persistent and require on-going support services. Parents constantly have to interpret the meaning of the child's behaviour in order to develop new experiences to facilitate development (Chapter 18) and in order to anticipate implications for the future. Life-events, such as the birth of other children, changes in family structure and going to school, can produce recurrent crises, with a return of self-doubt and all the other feelings noted previously. Over time, families develop and change. Many values also change to allow adaptation to the changing life situations. Values used in caring for the baby based on feelings of protectiveness and responsibility may be challenged by increased pressures on the family as the child grows or as parents get exhausted by the demands of coping. Thus, the process of adjustment is recurrent, and continuing counselling may be required. If it is easily accessible, it may prevent, or at least prepare, the family for likely crises.

One pit-fall of such on-going counselling may be to produce dependency on the counselling services. Another is that new crises may lead to the professional re-opening the old case events and reviving old conflicts. On these occasions parents are often told, 'Well, we've been through this before. . . .' Too often, professionals use the presence of the handicapped child as a generalized explanation of all stress, again perceiving this in terms of unresolved previous difficulties. The focus has to be maintained on factors crucial to the solution of the current problems. This is central to counselling – that is, the evaluation of the situation and the development of coping strategies.

A further danger in long-term support is the feeling that new events are familiar. Professionals may become mechanistic in applying solutions instead of developing new and individual solutions to the issue. This can be generalized across families. Professionals can begin to anticipate events so well that they leave out the stage of joint evaluation and negotiation with parents and instead provide well-tried 'recipes'. Since these can be successful, they often hide the increasing dependency that can be engendered.

Despite such dangers, one point which cannot be overstated is the tremendous strength and support parents gain from knowing that there is someone who they can trust and who is always available. A phone number and the knowledge that someone will contact them periodically, even just to see if everything is all right and how the child is getting on, is always appreciated. It demonstrates that the child is valued by society.

CONCLUDING COMMENTS

The main aim of this chapter has been to review some current ideas on parent counselling and wherever possible to give clear statements of established methods that can be put into practice to improve services. A second aim has been to indicate the complexity of the area and point out how much

we still need to learn. It is our hope that as more professionals recognize and *evaluate* such issues in their everyday practice a more knowledgeable foundation for services will be attained. For the present, we can conclude that:

1 Well-organized parent counselling from the moment the diagnosis of handicap is suspected is essential.
2 It must understand the parents' and families' changing patterns of needs.
3 It must be regular, practical and available.
4 Given this, it will enable the parents to predict and prevent problems rather than hastily meet them when crises occur. Certainly counselling should never be withdrawn in the face of frustration and aggression. Hostility should not be met with hostility, no matter how disguised. Parents have the right to expect professional competence and understanding, and always to be fully involved in consultation and negotiation.

REFERENCES

Berger J & Cunningham CC (1981) Early development of social interactions in Down's syndrome and non-handicapped infants. In Teirikko A, Vihavainen R & Nenonnen T (eds) *Finland Speaks: Report of the EASE 80 Conference.* Helsinki: Finnish Association for Special Education with European Association for Special Education.
Cunningham CC (1982) *Down's Syndrome: An Introduction for Parents.* London: Souvenir Press.
Cunningham CC & Davis H (1985) *Working with Parents.* Milton Keynes: Open University Educational Enterprises Ltd.
Cunningham CC & Sloper P (1977a) Parents of Down's syndrome babies: their early needs. *Child: Care, Health and Development 3:* 325–347.
Cunningham CC & Sloper P (1977b) A positive approach to parent and professional collaboration. *Health Visitor 50:* 32–37.
Cunningham CC, Morgan P & McGucken RB (1984) Down's syndrome: is dissatisfaction with disclosure of diagnosis inevitable? *Developmental Medicine and Child Neurology 26:* 33–39.
Davis H (1983) Constructs of handicap: working with parents and children. *Changes 1:* 37–39.
Emde RN & Brown C (1978) Adaptation to the birth of a Down's syndrome infant. *Journal of American Academy of Child Psychiatry 17:* 299–323.
Folkman S & Lazarus RS (1980) An analysis of coping in a middle-aged community sample. *Journal of Health and Social Behaviour 21:* 219–239.
Gayton WF & Walker L (1974) Down's syndrome: informing the parents. *American Journal of Disabled Children 127:* 510–512.
Hall EC & Grunewald K (1977) Unpublished report. The National Board of Health and Welfare, S-10630, Stockholm, Sweden.
Kelly G (1955) *The Psychology of Personal Constructs.* New York: Norton.

Klaus MA & Kennell JH (1976) *Maternal–Infant Bonding.* St Louis: Mosby.

MacKeith R (1973) The feelings and behaviour of parents of handicapped children. *Developmental Medicine and Child Neurology 15:* 24–27.

Newson E & Hipgrave J (1982) *Getting Through to Your Handicapped Child.* Cambridge: Cambridge University Press.

Pueschel S & Murphy A (1976) Assessment of counselling practices at the birth of a child with Down's syndrome. *American Journal of Mental Deficiency 81:* 325–330.

Ray C, Lindsop J & Gibson S (1982) The concept of coping. *Psychological Medicine 12:* 385–395.

Springer A & Steele MW (1980) Effects of physicians' early parental counselling on rearing of Down's syndrome children. *American Journal of Mental Deficiency 85:* 1–5.

Chapter 16
Sexuality and Personal Relationships

ANN CRAFT & MICHAEL CRAFT

In 1971 the United Nations adopted a declaration of the rights of retarded persons which states that:

'The mentally retarded person has the same basic rights as other citizens of the same country and same age.'

It continues by saying that each mentally handicapped person has a right to 'such education, training and habilitation and guidance as will enable him (her) to develop his (her) ability and maximum potential.'

This chapter explores the issues which arise from the declaration of rights in the context of sexual expression. Any discussion has of necessity to be in general terms, but each person with a mental handicap is intellectually, socially, psychologically and medically unique (Saunders, 1981). It is these individual circumstances, individual capabilities and individually expressed needs which should shape education, counselling and intervention.

ATTITUDES OF SOCIETY

Because of the association of sexual activity with reproduction the traditional response of society towards the sexuality of those labelled 'mentally handicapped' was unequivocal: it was to be controlled to the point of extinction. The means of control were found in segregated and isolated colonies with preferential admission of women of childbearing age, harsh punishment of sexual behaviour, prohibition of marriage and laws permitting sterilization to prevent those who were (in the much quoted judgement of Justice Oliver Wendell Holmes) 'manifestly unfit from continuing their kind'.

Elements of this sexual oppression still persist, albeit often in more subtle forms. For example, many people believe the myths that (a) children are not sexual beings and (b) mentally handicapped individuals remain children for ever. Thus it follows that any expression of sexuality is seen as inappropriate, a 'problem' to be eliminated, because their 'childlike innocence' must be protected.

However, it is evident that attitudes are changing as the whole issue of sexuality is being more openly discussed. The literature on the subject now falls mainly into what might be called the enablement category – ways and means of helping individuals with mental handicaps develop their capacity for loving relationships in ways which are normal and acceptable to the society in which they live.

ATTITUDES AND CONCERNS OF PARENTS

We know from many sources (the media, novels, autobiographies and so on) that parents frequently have difficulty in coming to terms with their children's sexuality or in making a positive contribution to their formal sex education. Farrell (1978) found that while a majority of parents interviewed felt they ought to be involved in telling their children about reproduction and sex, only a minority actually claimed to have done so.

The presence of a mental handicap can compound the difficulty. Hammar et al. (1967) tell us, 'Puberty and the process of sexual maturation of the retardate created a stressful situation which most families were ill-prepared to handle.' Indeed, the adolescent's increasing physical maturity may precipitate a crisis for parents as fundamental as the one which occurred when their child was pronounced handicapped. As well as posing issues of management, parents are faced sharply with the fact that, whereas their friends and relations can look forward to the growing independence of their children, the adolescent with a mental handicap has

177

special needs for continuing care and protection (Fairbrother, 1983). It is not uncommon for parents to deny that their child has any sexual feelings at all, or to become over-protective and strictly control social contacts.

Parental concerns focus around real or anticipated inappropriate behaviour (Hammar et al., 1967; Kempton and Forman, 1976) and sexual ignorance which could facilitate exploitation. Many parents welcome school sex education programmes (Kempton, 1978; Watson and Rogers, 1980). Counselling can be of help to parents (Kempton and Caparulo, 1983) and groups where first-hand experience and support are offered to parents by parents are immensely valuable (Slater et al., 1981; Fairbrother, 1983).

ATTITUDES AND TRAINING OF STAFF

Sexuality can present management problems in any residential system, be it boarding school or old people's home, but it is undoubtedly a particularly sensitive area where the clients of the caring service have mental handicaps. Staff often feel that they have responsibilities for all areas of residents' lives and a duty to shield them from harm. This attitude is reinforced by the expectations of parents and management committees and can easily result in over-protection and over-control. This has implications not only for sexual expression, but also for the wider issues of maximal independence and personal growth, for we find it hard as caring professionals to allow people with mental handicaps 'the dignity of risk' (Perske, 1972).

Several surveys have looked at the attitudes and response of residential staff to the sexual behaviour of mentally handicapped people. Mulhern (1975) found that while 67 % of respondents felt that sexual frustration contributed significantly to most mentally handicapped residents' adjustment problems, the only forms of sexual release that received a major endorsement were private masturbation, brief kissing and private petting. As he says, 'A commitment to principles of normalization encounters severe strains in the area of sexual behavior.' Mitchell et al. (1978) found that 31.2 % of staff in three residential units considered that *no* sexual behaviour, not even simple physical contact, was acceptable. Again in America, Coleman and Murphy (1980) received responses to their questionnaire from 131 residential institutions for the retarded. Replies concerning the sexual activities of residents showed that 88 % of responding staff

approved of masturbation, but the disapproval rate rose sharply when sexual activity involved others. Even so, 56 % approved of private sexual intercourse between residents, with 25 % disapproving. Adams et al. (1982) found that staff in community-based facilities were not necessarily more liberal in their sexual attitudes than those in institutions. In Britain the Jay Committee (1979) reported that of staff questioned one-quarter of nurses in institutions and one-fifth of hostel staff thought that adult residents should be discouraged from developing sexual relationships.

All these studies prompt discussion of two very important issues: (a) official operational policies in day and residential services concerning the sexual needs and rights of the mentally handicapped clients, and (b) staff training about sexuality and mental handicap.

Operational policies and guidelines

These bring advantages to both the receivers of care and to the care givers. As we have seen from the surveys of staff attitudes, each unit is most unlikely to have staff who agree about what and where sexual behaviour is right and proper.

In the absence of set guidelines staff are frequently faced with situations to which they respond either as their personal feelings and attitudes demand or as they judge those above them in the hierarchy would wish them to react. For the mentally handicapped person this gives rise not only to an unjust position where he or she is ruled by other people's idiosyncrasies but also to confusion and inconsistency of management as one staff member forbids or punishes a behaviour another has allowed or even encouraged.

Policy guidelines usually serve to remind people of the law and show up overly restrictive written or unwritten rules.

Staff gain too when a unit has such an operational policy because it sets out clear guidelines which have been discussed and agreed throughout the hierarchy. People know where they stand, what is permissible, and who to approach for specific advice. Indeed, the discussion and debate at all levels which should precede the adoption of policies can be of great value.

A policy on sexual behaviour should not be a mere listing of rules or, worse, of proscriptions, but should contain positive statements of rights and possibilities in the context of the existing law and mores. For a comprehensive and thoughtful example see the document produced by Hounslow

Social Services Department (1983) entitled *Sexuality of Mentally Handicapped People – Guidelines for Care Staff*.

Policies should be regularly reviewed so that new staff and new clients are familiarized with them and any new circumstances can be taken into account.

Staff training

Training in the area of sexuality and mental handicap is an essential and challenging task (Kempton, 1983). In Britain over recent years there has been an increasing number of conferences and workshops run especially for staff by such bodies as the British Institute of Mental Handicap, the Family Planning Association and Castle Priory College. In the USA Hall and Sawyer (1978) report on a workshop format designed to develop guidelines for the sexual behaviour of clients, and Hall (1978) gives details of a training workshop intended to increase staff acceptance of sexual expression by mentally handicapped people.

Brantlinger (1983) found that an in-service training day for staff in a large residential institution resulted in a 'considerable redefinition of attitude concerning the sexual needs and rights of the retarded'.

In our view training courses should include features such as:

1 Factual information on the range of human sexual behaviour and response.
2 An exploration of attitudes towards sexuality.
3 An examination of the myths and fears surrounding sexuality and mental handicap in the light of modern knowledge.
4 A consideration of how environments (physical settings, living and working arrangements and interactions with staff) shape sexual behaviour.
5 Methods of improving the level of comfort and confidence that people have to discuss sexual matters openly and explicitly with mentally handicapped clients.
6 Consideration of the special needs and characteristics of people with mental handicaps which make socio-sexual education and consistent management of particular importance to them.
7 A discussion of basic counselling skills, emphasizing *listening* to what clients are saying.
8 Ways of working with parents, understanding their anxieties and helping them set realistic goals for their child's sexual behaviour and sexual fulfilment.

9 Techniques for teaching mentally handicapped people, bearing in mind the enormous range of handicap and ability.
10 Setting goals – What do we want this particular 'student' to *understand*? What do we want him or her to *do*? How best can we achieve these aims?
11 Reviewing suitable curricula and audiovisual resources.
12 Consideration of strategies which could be adopted to circumvent objections to the implementation of policies and programmes.

ATTITUDE OF MENTALLY HANDICAPPED PEOPLE TOWARDS SEXUALITY

In considering this essential piece of the complex jigsaw of sexuality and mental handicap we find that comparatively little is known. As Koegel and Whittemore (1983) point out, survey-orientated research methods have told us something about what mentally handicapped individuals know and/or have experienced as far as sex is concerned (though measurements are often dependent on caretaker or parent reports), but 'They have told us little, however, of the less identified but more important aspects of sexuality and the mentally handicapped – *their* feelings on a number of these issues and their continuing struggles to understand and experience sexuality within the context of their relationships with others.' These researchers' reports of an on-going study of community adaptation lift a corner of the veil and in doing so reveal the enormous diversity in attitude, experience and behaviour displayed by individuals who share the social label 'mentally handicapped' (Whittemore and Koegel, 1978; Koegel and Whittemore, 1983).

Watson and Rogers (1980) in their survey of ESN(M) children, also note that there has been a lack of regard to the attitudes of the mentally handicapped themselves. In each of four scales the ESN group were significantly more traditional in their attitudes than the normal control subjects. They comment that these conservative attitudes may be encouraged by parents and staff as a form of protection, but that there is a danger of confusion when the teaching model tends to be 'do as I say, not as I do'.

Edgerton and Dingman (1964) found that residents in a large mental handicap hospital evolved strict, puritanical rules of conduct to govern sexual behaviour and that transgressors felt guilty and were treated as such by other residents.

Hall et al. (1973) also noted a tendency for the mildly retarded adolescents surveyed to be conservative in sexual attitudes. All this should not be surprising when we consider the generally conservative views of significant adults in the lives of people with mental handicaps.

SEXUAL DEVELOPMENT

Physical development

The majority of persons with mental handicaps are in the mild and moderate range, and most of them will develop normal secondary sexual characteristics and reproductive capacities (Salerno et al., 1975). Studies of sexual maturation show a delay in physical sexual development as IQ decreases, although the various syndromes of mental handicap (except for Down's syndrome) do not seem to account for dissimilar patterns of growth between individuals (Mosier et al., 1962; Salerno et al., 1975).

Profoundly and severely handicapped people are more likely to be delayed in achieving sexual maturity (Alcorn, 1974; Hall, 1975) and have less pronounced sexual interest and impulses (Wolfensberger, 1972). Individuals with Down's syndrome make up about one-third of the severely handicapped population. While it is known that most of the females are fertile, with a 50% risk of producing a baby with the same chromosomal abnormality (Tricomi et al., 1964; Salerno et al., 1975), there is no reported instance of a true trisomy 21 male fathering a child. This may be due to hypogenitalism, impotence or incomplete sperm formation (Bovicelli et al., 1982). For a detailed discussion of reproduction and reproductive decisions in Down's syndrome see Jagiello (1981), Bovicelli et al. (1982) and Williams (1983). Among other syndromes contributing to mental handicap it has been suggested that brain-damaged females have a significantly earlier menarche than normal (Dalton and Dalton, 1978).

Psycho-sexual development

'Each family unit has its own sexual climate, formed by the attitudes the adults have brought with them from their families of rearing and, where there are two or more people *in loco parentis*, by the relationships the adults have with each other.' (Calderone, 1982)

We know that psychosexual development can be a process fraught with difficulties, with family interaction, cultural setting and educational approaches all having a bearing (Calderone, 1982; Goldman and Goldman, 1982; Craft, 1983b). Children with mental handicaps are even more vulnerable to distorting experiences. For example, it may be that parents are so overwhelmed by the birth of a handicapped baby that they tend not to prolong body contact much beyond that needed to feed and clean the infant. Rocking, stroking and fondling – in short, pleasurable and warm body contact – are important to future feelings about sexuality (Krajicek 1982).

Many mentally handicapped people are embarrassed about their bodies and say that sex is 'dirty'. As children they are often over-corrected as they show a natural curiosity about themselves, and ever afterwards have guilt feelings (Craft and Craft, 1978). Those who live in institutions are likely to be subject to even more distorting psychosexual experiences, as we shall consider in the following section.

SEXUAL BEHAVIOUR

We have already looked at some of the strands which go towards determining the sexual behaviour of people with mental handicaps – their own personal attitudes, those of the general public, and those of care-givers, whether parents or staff.

Living environments also play a significant part in shaping behaviour. We only have to think of the segregated institutions where homosexual activity became the tacitly accepted norm, not for the most part from personal choice, but rather because there was no choice. As Rosen (1975) states: 'Sexual behaviors in the handicapped can best be understood . . . as purposive behaviors learned according to unique experiences of the retarded person and the specific environmental influences to which he has been subjected. These include the extremely unnatural stimuli available to him in institutional settings, as well as the motivational and emotional consequences of inadequate learning and family experiences in the community.' Rosen goes on to make the important point that in institutions sex-related behaviour such as indiscriminate or inappropriate displays of affection, stripping or open masturbation may be tolerated, whereas in the community it may not be just embarrassing, but dangerous or illegal.

Lack of privacy and close supervision mean that sexual behaviour is inevitably visible, public and devalued. As Heshusius (1982) comments: '. . . one wonders how it still can carry the meaning of true affection and sensuality. Rather, it has turned into a caricature: intimate behavior watched by all, a position we ourselves would not want to be in.' Indeed, the whole question of privacy is one that it is essential to discuss when considering the policy guidelines.

Appropriate behaviour can usually be substituted for 'problem' behaviour.

The excellent manual devised by Mitchell et al. offers several strategies for correcting behaviour which causes concern because the time, place or partner is wrong. Ann Craft (1983) describes training techniques and discusses the ethical implications of deciding what behaviour is 'desirable' and what is 'undesirable'. Social and sex education programmes also have an important part to play, as ignorance is likely to be a significant factor.

Sexual exploitation of people who have scant knowledge of the sexual rules of the society in which they live is a very real danger (Kempton, 1977). Passiveness, acquiescence, dependency and respect for authority are all traits which tend to be tacitly or openly encouraged by the structure of our care systems. They make a mentally handicapped individual particularly vulnerable to sexual exploitation. Education programmes which encourage self-assertiveness, positive self-concept and personal worth and dignity, are increasingly needed as more and more people with mental handicaps move freely in the community.

Sexual offences. No study to date has satisfactorily explored the subject of sexual offences committed by mentally handicapped persons. Difficulties arise from the lack of standardization of measures used to determine IQ.

While ignorance of the law is no defence it is highly probable that a large number of the sexual offences committed by mentally handicapped individuals come about because of lack of knowledge and inadequate social education. For example, a man may be charged with indecent exposure when urinating in the street even though his real 'crime' was not knowing how to find the public toilets. A 16-year-old youth may find himself in court on a charge of indecent assault, having been caught playing a mutually enjoyable exploratory game with his mental peers aged five or six. A mentally handicapped adolescent may chance upon a be-

haviour, such as flamboyant masturbation, which happens to have sexual connotations but is very successful in gaining people's attention. All may give cause for concern, but require a course of action different from that needed for the 'true' sexual offender. The subject of criminality and mental handicap is discussed in Chapter 7.

SEXUAL KNOWLEDGE

Mentally handicapped people are highly likely to have large gaps in their understanding of sexual behaviour as a result of upbringing and individual cognitive deficits. They are often treated as perpetual children, who should have no curiosity about sexual matters. They may never ask questions because by the time they are ready to do so they have learned from those who care for them that anything to do with sexual parts of the body is embarrassing, dirty and not to be mentioned.

Their peers (an information source for normal youngsters) are probably just as ignorant, and they often find reading difficult. The sources of information that are available – advertising, newspaper pictures, cinema and television – distort sexuality rather than elucidating it. Andron (1983) found that the couples she worked with had gained a great deal of information from television: 'This has led to their extensive knowledge about babies born in six months or eleven months, ectopic pregnancy, twins with two different fathers, but not the more common ways these things occur.' Other researchers have also noted the widespread ignorance of those with mental handicaps, particularly in the areas of birth control, menstruation and venereal disease (Edmondson et al., 1979; Watson and Rogers, 1980; Gillies and McEwan, 1981).

Kempton (1976) reports that it is not unusual to find retarded couples who do not know that sexual intercourse exists or mentally handicapped women who believe sexual intercourse is meant to hurt the female and have therefore endured all kinds of unpleasant sexual experiences.

Indeed, the concept of sexual pleasure warrants a fuller debate than is possible here. The irony for mentally handicapped people is that education usually ignores the pleasurable dimension and successfully gets across the one aspect of sexuality (reproduction) which teachers and carers then strongly discourage their charges from exploring (Koegel and Whittemore, 1983).

Sexual ignorance is not bliss: it opens people to damaging and exploitative situations.

SEX EDUCATION

The reasons for sex education for people with mental handicaps have been well discussed (Gordon, 1975; Kempton and Forman, 1976; Craft and Craft, 1978). They can be summarized thus:

1 The vast majority of those with a mental handicap will develop normal secondary sexual characteristics. They need more help, not less, in making sense of these changes and the accompanying strong emotional feelings.
2 They need knowledge which will protect them from exploitation and from unwittingly offending others.

Formal and informal sex education

Most sex education occurs informally. It starts at birth and continues throughout life. The message comes across in many and various ways – the cuddling and warmth parents give to their children, the amount and quality of physical affection parents show for each other, elder siblings' behaviour with girlfriends or boyfriends, parental reaction as the child touches his or her genitals, advertising, television soap operas, with their stereotypes and crises, the response of teachers or care staff to an 'embarrassing' question. All these experiences are on-going sex education. The question we should ask, therefore, is not *whether* mentally handicapped people should receive sex education but *which form* will be the most helpful for a particular individual or group.

One important role of formal – that is, structured – programmes of sex education is to provide a filter for the informal learning experiences which are part of every human's life.

Context

It is our personal belief that 'formal' sex education is best placed in the setting of an overall health or social education programme. Either context provides for a holistic approach, emphasizing responsibility and relationships.

Teaching programmes and resources

There now exist many models for teaching all age groups of those with mental handicaps (see, for example, Special Education Curriculum Development Center, 1972; Brown, 1983; Craft et al., 1983; Livock, 1985; McNaughton, 1983a, b). There is also an increasing variety of audiovisual resources designed for use with such students, reviewed by Craft (1982). Adaptations can be made to suit students and circumstances. Local health education officers usually have a resources library.

Sex education for severely handicapped students

Those people with severe mental handicaps may pose special difficulties for parents, teachers and care staff, particularly in their sexual expression. It is important to remember in this context that sexual feelings and needs are present in *all* humans whatever their degree of handicap. Sexuality is *not* an optional extra that we in our so-called wisdom can choose to bestow or to withhold if an individual fails to score highly enough on some intelligence test.

In reality our choice is different. Here is a child with severe mental handicaps who, although his or her sexual maturation may be delayed, is going to reach puberty and adulthood with all the normal attendant physical and emotional changes. What is our response going to be? How best can we address ourselves to his or her sexual needs?

Setting goals is a valuable exercise because it requires decisions about the nature and complexity of teaching input. Two questions need to be posed:

1 What specifically do we want the student to *understand*?
2 What specifically do we want the student to *do*?

For example, in thinking about menstruation, we might decide that all that a particular girl can be expected to *understand* about the complex process is that it is a normal and natural occurrence – in short, that it is OK. This has to be put across by the matter-of-fact and comforting attitude and behaviour of mother or care staff. The 'do' components might be:

1 Tells or indicates to mother or care staff that her period has started so that she has help in the hygiene aspect.
2 Maintains modest behaviour: that is, does not tell or show everyone what is happening.

It might also be possible to train the girl to become more or less responsible for her own menstrual hygiene (Pattullo and Barnard, 1968), or to help her understand why she has periods and what is happening inside her body.

Answering the understand/do question can prevent would-be teachers from being overwhelmed by the task. While we would want to help severely mentally handicapped people understand as much as possible about their bodies and feelings, the 'do' component is always likely to be more important, for it is in behaviour, the acting out of feelings, that difficulties manifest themselves. The more unacceptable behaviour is, the more restricted and curtailed are opportunities for entertainment, outings or social interaction.

What topics should be covered in a teaching programme aimed at severely mentally handicapped individuals? One such programme for students with an IQ range of 35–54 chose five areas:

1 Bodily distinction;
2 Self care skills;
3 Family members and relationships;
4 Social interactions;
5 Social manners.

As skills were acquired parents and teachers decided to extend the complexity of information given. With very few exceptions the students mastered the objectives in the component areas and were also able to generalize these skills (Hamre-Nietupski and Williams, 1977; Hamre-Nietupski and Ford, 1981).

Verbal teaching can be enhanced by simple visual material such as pictures, body puzzles and felt cloth figures. Social situations and good manners can be acted out to demonstrate appropriate behaviour. Behaviour modification programmes might be used to teach specific self-care skills and to substitute appropriate public behaviour for acts which are unacceptable, such as open masturbation; or potentially dangerous, such as indiscriminate hugging and kissing (see also Champagne and Walker-Hirsch, 1982).

Because people with severe mental (and often physical) handicaps are likely to be more restricted we need to ask questions about the environment in which they find themselves. Given that it is normal for all humans to have sexual feelings and to gain pleasure from warmth and touch, where and with whom in a specific setting can a particular individual express what he or she feels sexually? If such behaviour is always seen as inappropriate some reassessment is needed. Could there be more private places? Could there be a more sympathetic response to severely mentally handicapped people holding hands, cuddling and hugging? (Assuming of course that the person being touched likes it too!)

Multiply handicapped people may be at a particular disadvantage because the touch they experience from others is an essentially impersonal attention to intimate and personal needs. An enjoyable way of encouraging touch and body contact is by games and exercises, which, besides toning muscles and relaxing tenseness, allow the opportunity for increasing awareness of 'self' and 'other'. Remedial gymnasts and physiotherapists have an important contribution to make here.

Inappropriate masturbation can cause much distress to parents and carers. A number of considerations need to be borne in mind. First, masturbation is a normal and natural human activity for both males and females. It is not realistic or appropriate to attempt to stop an individual any and every time he or she behaves in this way. Second, open masturbation may have a variety of 'causes' quite apart from the physical release and pleasure an orgasm brings; for example, lack of privacy in the living environment, confusing management styles, boredom, comforting oneself after failing in a task or when excluded from an activity, upsetting changes around him or her.

Before embarking upon any re-shaping of behaviour parents and care staff should think about physical environment (where is a private place?) and about the number and quality of rewarding and enjoyable experiences open to a particular individual during the course of the day. They should keep a written record of what was happening before the individual began to masturbate, and what happened afterwards. In this way a clear picture emerges of an individual and his or her needs in a particular setting (see Mitchell et al. for a manual of helpful procedures).

Masturbation is a learned behaviour. Most people learn for themselves the rate, friction and time span which bring orgasm. But some do not learn the 'trick' of it, often rubbing and touching but never continuing long enough to obtain release. Many parents report an overall improvement in behaviour when they have taught their son or daughter to masturbate successfully. For a severely mentally handicapped individual in residential care that approach cannot be made with the same informality or privacy. Any decision to teach a client to masturbate must be made collectively at a case conference. Reasons for the decision should be recorded and the responsibility for the teaching given to an individual professional who agrees to do this in accordance with the collective professional consensus.

Summary

In sociosexual teaching for children and adults with severe mental handicaps, begin with basics, evaluate and re-assess, and extend target objectives where possible. Ask what this individual needs to understand and do to avoid social embarrassment and for his or her own protection? Set clear and realistic targets. What teaching techniques or combination of methods can be used to reach these goals? Be simple and direct.

Effects of teaching

Many parents and teachers are concerned that giving sex education to mentally handicapped youngsters will somehow arouse appetites and stimulate sexual behaviour – behaviour which would not have occurred had Pandora's box been kept tightly closed. The underlying assumption is false because it implies that 'not telling' means 'no one does anything', and also that we can control all sources of information. On the contrary, informal sex education begins at birth and continues through life, and there is plenty of evidence that the withholding of structured information does not deter sexual activity in normal or handicapped members of the population (Kempton and Forman, 1976). Rather it causes confusion, needless fears, inappropriate behaviour and unwanted consequences.

In an evaluation of 31 courses which taught 430 retarded students by means of specially devised teaching slides, Kempton (1978) found that 'There were no reports that the staff was aware of serious inappropriate behavior that could be attributed to the programs.' Instead teachers commented on improved social behaviour, increased self-respect, more openness, and fewer feelings of guilt. Johnson (1981) also found that ' . . . group sexuality counselling produces positive changes in the sexual self-images of this population', providing them with practical coping strategies. Demetral (1981) compared the behaviour of 14 residents in a mental handicap hospital with their behaviour following a series of sex education lessons. He examined records for six months prior to the programme and for the six months following its completion. It was found that the amount of time spent by staff in counselling residents on such matters as masturbation and inappropriate menstrual behaviour decreased by nearly one-third.

Knowledge can enable people to make sense of themselves and their relationships. Brown (1983), in describing an education programme for 16–19-year-olds with multiple handicaps, reports, 'A knowledge of basic facts brings a sense of relief which allows many of them to move on to deal sensibly and maturely with personal issues and decisions. . . . '

Conclusion

Ultimately the education of individuals with mental handicaps about sexual matters is part of a much larger debate about mental handicap and adult status, and about the quality of life enjoyed (or permitted). In its more immediate focus the purpose of sex education is to avoid needless sexual casualties brought about by ignorance and fear.

SEXUAL COUNSELLING

There are many overlaps between sex education and sexual counselling for the giving of biological facts should always be in the context of people, their feelings and their relationships.

At present much of our sexual counselling for those with mental handicaps, their parents and care staff is crisis counselling. There is evidence, however, of a perceived need for counselling services which are readily available, not only in time of crisis, but before there are problems. This planned counselling should be wide-ranging. For example, a special school might ask a counsellor to come to an evening for parents of 10–12-year-olds to discuss aspects of puberty and handicap. While this would include a consideration of the preparatory information girls and boys need, it would also touch upon the attitudes and response of parents. What are their fears and anxieties? What changes do they expect? What difference is adolescence going to make to their management of the growing youngster?

The Warnock Committee (1978) on special educational needs commented that: 'At present, sex education and counselling on sexual relationships tend to be badly handled generally. This is unfortunate for all young people, but it is particularly serious in the case of young people with severe disabilities, whose opportunities for personal development through self-education are so limited compared with those of other young people, and for whom the problems of adolescence are likely to be increased by their disability.'

The report goes on to recommend that sexual and genetic counselling and advice on contraception should be readily available to youngsters with special needs and their parents. It also suggests that reference to sexual counselling should be made in all training courses for professionals who will be working with such adolescents.

In 1980 the National Development Group for the Mentally Handicapped produced a checklist of standards entitled *Improving the Quality of Services for Mentally Handicapped People*. Standards 92–94 are concerned with the provision of sexual counselling for staff, mentally handicapped clients and clients' families.

The counselling that parents and care staff need usually centres around management questions, but these cannot be resolved without reference to the attitudes and feelings of those doing the managing. A counsellor must be very sensitive to the issues involved (Kempton and Caparulo, 1983).

Counselling involves both a response to specific situations which have arisen, and preparation for future events and behaviour. It is a process which is an integral part of helping handicapped people to help themselves. Anyone can find themselves cast in the role of counsellor, whether parent, teacher, care staff or trainer. Not everyone is at ease with the task. Adults in close contact with mentally handicapped people should either be prepared to answer questions themselves about personal and sexual matters, or to refer the questioner immediately to another adult who can handle the subject. Fobbing off only raises anxiety levels. If the actual moment is inconvenient, set aside a time in the near future there and then, and make sure the date is kept. Counselling should never be merely the giving of advice or directions, for it needs to be an exploration of the situation as the mentally handicapped person sees it, and a working-through of the alternatives available.

Personal relationships

Care staff find themselves in the same position as parents when it comes to counselling in the area of friendships and personal relationships. In adolescence there is usually an upsurge of interest in the opposite sex and friendships become more intense. At best, friendships stimulate, aiding mental development and promoting an enthusiastic response to life and its rich possibilities. Some relationships, however, can hurt rather than help, and just as normal parents promote friendships with some of their children's circle and not others, so care staff would be expected to give frank encouragement or discouragement to those in their charge.

People with mental handicaps may need extra help in maintaining relationships because they are likely to lack the social skills which minimize frictions. They may not be good at recognizing mood signals, or at considering another's feelings. At a more practical level they may find it difficult to make telephone calls, write letters or keep dates. It is

well known that having a girlfriend or boyfriend can produce great improvements in social abilities! (Edgerton and Dingman, 1964.)

Particularly at the adolescent stage (which may well stretch into the twenties) friendships may be intense but short-lived, making the erstwhile friends miserable for a time. Normal adolescents learn by these experiences and mentally handicapped youngsters should be allowed the same opportunity. It is all part of growing up. Professionals may be called upon to advise parents with children at this stage; those with an only child are especially vulnerable and are likely to feel that it is the handicap, not adolescence, that is causing difficulties. It can be very comforting for parents to discover through informal discussions with other parents that their child is not the only one presenting 'problems', and that others have found ways of coping. Social workers and voluntary organizations can arrange these informal meetings.

Pre-marital counselling

There will be couples who become serious about each other, remain together for months rather than weeks, and begin to talk of marriage. Usually one or both will have a place in a system of care and the possibility exists of providing structured counselling.

For example, at one mental handicap hospital an operational policy on interpersonal relationships sets out guidelines for residents and staff. A couple talking of marriage are expected to 'go steady' for three months, and the implications of this are explained to them: that is, each should look after the other, not make dates with anyone else, and demonstrate by their mutual concern that their partnership is a constructive one. If all goes well during the three months and the pair wish to become engaged, a meeting is held with the couple, their next of kin and care staff. An arbitrary engagement period of six months is set, although it may be longer before the marriage takes place. The giving of a ring and a party announce the couple's formal intentions to everyone.

During the engagement period staff will take the initiative in counselling the pair, both separately and together, on what sex means in and out of marriage, the birth control methods usually needed, meeting each other's emotional needs, and the art of living together. Domestic training, cooking, budgeting and saving should also be covered, and the couple aided to think realistically of future plans. Obviously no two couples are exactly alike and counselling must be individually tailored. Are both mentally handicapped? If so, how competent are they expected, or proving, to be in looking after themselves? Were one or both brought up at home or in an institution? No studies have yet compared the marriages or child-rearing of those originally raised in institutions with those living all of their lives in the community, and it may well be that the former lack the models on which to base their own marital behaviour.

Counselling sessions should also explore the question of children. The couple will doubtless have views on the subject. Do they want children? How old is the wife? Do they understand that any woman over 35 runs a higher risk of having a handicapped child? Is the cause of their retardation known? If so, is there a genetic component? Are the couple likely to be mature enough to cope with the complete dependence of a child over many years? What do they feel are the advantages and disadvantages of parenthood? How financially independent are they likely to be? What sort of accommodation do they have? Many normal couples wait until they have settled down in marriage together before starting their family, and this has much to commend it. A mentally handicapped couple who wish for children can be advised to do the same. Others will not want the additional responsibility of children and will need counselling on appropriate methods of birth control. Here sterilization is probably the simplest and most effective method, for after completion no more attention is needed. It does raise the vexed question of informed consent, as mentally handicapped people are often easily influenced by authority figures (see section on sterilization below).

Post-marital counselling

We know that marital maladjustments, especially in the early stages of the partnership, are extremely common among normal partners. It might thus be expected that this would also be so where the couple are mentally handicapped, and here post-marital counselling can be of great benefit. It may only be a small problem, but it may be magnified because the couple do not have the interpersonal skill to handle it.

The maladjustment may be a sexual one and then detailed and experience-linked counselling will be needed. One couple in our Welsh survey illustrate this point (Craft and Craft, 1979). During their engagement Gareth and Helen explored with a counsellor the subject of marriage, and the responsibilities it would entail, in depth and detail.

Once they were married staff assumed all was well, until in fact the partnership reached crisis point. The *words* and even the *pictures* used beforehand did not match with their *experience*. Gareth was sexually unskilled and his first attempts at intercourse were clumsy. Not surprisingly Helen 'froze', making penetration impossible. This situation continued for almost a year until they were counselled about their specific difficulties. It was found that Helen was rather small; a minor operation made intercourse physically more comfortable for her. Gareth was prompted to be more gentle, Helen relaxed more and both gained enormously in satisfaction.

Counselling is a vital part of the support service professionals can offer the mentally retarded. The cardinal points to remember are that the counsellor must spend time listening and must talk *with* the persons concerned, not *at* them.

Sexual dysfunction

Ordinary members of society seek, or are directed to, sexual counselling because of sexual dysfunction. A wealth of literature now describes, categorizes, analyses and offers techniques to overcome the many and various things that can go wrong. However, the vast majority of this literature appertains to the so-called normal person, with an important small section concerned with physical handicap. There is very little which is specifically related to sexual dysfunction among those with mental handicaps. This is not surprising, as traditionally the weight of opinion has been against sexual function itself.

It is probable that the range and extent of sexual problems are similar for both 'normal' and 'mentally handicapped' people, but identification and treatment have been rarely reported. See, however, Craft (1981), Andron (1983) and Craft (1983b).

MARRIAGE

In recent years there has been much talk about the right of people with mental handicap to as normal a life as possible. It is normal in nearly every society for the majority of adult males and females to be married at least once in the course of their lives. In Western societies this is not true for those citizens labelled 'mentally handicapped'. Their legal and social status has been such that relatively few have ever married. Normally it is the married couple which forms the stable unit to produce and raise the next generation. It is this association of marriage with parenthood which led the guardians of society to make sure that as few mentally handicapped people as possible married or produced children. Indeed, in many parts of the United States sterilization was the condition of discharge to the community. The fear that people with mental handicap will produce retarded children in great numbers is still with us. However, nowadays methods of birth control are available to all and no one need produce children they do not want or more children than they can cope with. Marriage does not necessarily involve parenthood, and parenthood does not necessarily involve an unlimited number of children.

The literature – a caveat

Reviews of the literature concerning marriages where one or both partners are mentally retarded have appeared elsewhere (Hall, 1974; Craft and Craft, 1979). We would like to add a caveat. In our opinion there has been a tendency to confuse two separate populations; first, those in the community and institutions with IQs below 70 who have reached or are near their potential, and, second, those labelled 'mentally handicapped' and admitted to hospital (often via the courts) whose original IQ scores of 70+ were depressed by deprivative upbringing and personality disorder. Obviously the life chances for these two populations are rather different. Those in the second group may offend again, but it is highly likely that their IQs and abilities will rise over a period of time, so that eventually they will need little or no official care and guidance, and will merge with the general population (Craft, 1959). This has implications for the studies following up marriages among those labelled mentally handicapped. In Britain we know that the interpretation of the 1913 Mental Deficiency Act encompassed many people of dull normal intelligence who presented social problems as well as those with intellectual deficit, and thus included, for example, unmarried pregnant young women of average intelligence in receipt of 'poor relief'. The 1959 Mental Health Act facilitated the discharge of such people and on follow-up (Shaw and Wright, 1960; Mattinson, 1975) many were found to have married and settled down. The situation in the United States was not dissimilar. Floor et al. (1975) surveyed 214 discharges from a residential institution, 80 of whom had married. The mean IQ on discharge from the total sample was 76 (male 78.1, female 71.3). Among the reported characteristics of

the subjects, mention is made that 'All are orphans, or have families who are inadequate, disinterested or unwilling to accept the individual after discharge. The majority were institutionalized as adolescents, were referred from public agencies, and received State support'.

We need to remind ourselves that mental handicap is a dynamic, not a static, concept. It should be used to reflect *current* functioning, not past disabilities, especially among those once underfunctioning in intelligence because of personality disorders.

The subjects of the marital studies present further difficulties. Some studies look at couples where both partners have been labelled 'mentally handicapped', others where there are partners of normal intelligence, and others made up of subjects from both groups. Some studies look only at those discharged from mental handicap hospitals, often after long periods in an institution; others include those who have always lived in the community.

A number of studies are biased because of the method of selecting subjects. Unless there is a register of all mentally handicapped people in a particular area, or one is doing a follow-up of a cohort discharged from an institution, difficulties arise in locating subjects. The obvious and frequently used procedure is to contact social agencies, but if a couple is known to welfare departments it is probably because they have needed help of some kind. There must be other couples who manage without official assistance and who are virtually untraceable. Results of such studies have to be viewed against this background.

The marital studies have to be approached with caution. Besides the difficulties relating to the two populations and the subjects discussed above, each has to be viewed against its own social background, both in time and space. For example, Shaw and Wright (1960) give a divorce or permanent separation rate of 20%. From the standpoint of 1978 this does not sound excessive, but in terms of a follow-up done in the 1950s it compares unfavourably with statistics for the general population. None of the studies we have looked at have a control group. Admittedly, this would be hard to do, but the danger of the inappropriate use of middle-class standards is well known.

Support services vary enormously from area to area, and can be vital in keeping problems to a minimum. In Britain the disappearance of the Mental Welfare Officer with the reorganization of social service departments meant that in many areas mentally handicapped people were no longer visited regularly, and thus the chance to prevent or deal with problems before they escalated was missed.

The marital studies

Is it possible using pointers from the literature to predict whether a marriage will be of benefit to a particular couple? Edgerton (1967) concluded ' . . . it would seem that the sexual and marital lives of these retarded persons are more "normal" and better regulated than we could possibly have predicted from a knowledge of their pre-hospital experiences and their manifest intellectual deficits'. Mattinson (1975) looked at four obvious factors which might be of predictive value: recorded IQ score, length of time spent in hospital, behaviour in hospital and early history and background of deprivation. None of these factors on her sample of 32 couples correlated significantly with the achievement scores attained. Hall (1974) lists 18 factors appearing in the literature, which if present in significant number and/or degree can affect the 'success' of a marriage involving a retarded individual: for example, emotional disturbance of one or both partners, faulty childhood background, both partners being retarded, poor socio-economic background; length of institutionalization, and absence of sex education. As might be expected many of these 18 factors have a bearing on the stability of any marriage. Yet the reactions of human beings to each other and to circumstances are often *not* predictable. For example, for one couple in our own survey where the wife is classified as mentally handicapped, and the husband has episodes of schizophrenia (Craft and Craft, 1979), nine of these factors might be said to be present. True, their day is not complete without a row and both acknowledge the partnership to be unsatisfactory, but for the 28 years the marriage has lasted they have been apart only when one or other has needed to be hospitalized. Even then, full use is always made of opportunities to visit the sick or disturbed partner. As Hall (1974) says, ' . . . certain needs may be met in a marital partnership that cannot be met elsewhere'. We will return to this point in the section on subjective assessment.

Social functioning

Bearing in mind the difficulties in the literature, what do the studies tell us about the daily functioning of couples where one or both partners are retarded?

Several studies stress the importance of the support the couple receive in day-to-day living. This may be support from an official agency, or a private individual, someone Edgerton (1967) terms a 'befriender'. This is often a relative, but may be a neighbour, landlord or employer, someone who in many ways mediates between the couple and the world, particularly officialdom. All but one of the 12 couples in Andron and Sturm's (1973) survey depended on others in varying degrees for everything from advice to money.

In our survey of 45 Welsh couples (41 intact marriages), where one or both partners were mentally handicapped, 13 received no support from social agencies (Craft and Craft, 1979). Two couples lived in hospital married quarters with all the support that such entails, and a further four were in lodgings under a hospital guardianship scheme; the remaining 20 lived in the community and received help from social agencies, relatives or friends. This varied from intensive (at least weekly visits) to very infrequent help. Support may also be generated by the partnership itself. Mattinson (1975) reported a high number of couples (19 out of 32) who organized marital activities on a complementary basis; that is, the activities of husband and wife are different and separate but fitted together form a whole, with the skill of one partner supplementing the inability of the other. She writes: 'In many instances the active fit or complement made the whole greater than the sum of the two parts. This is true of many marriages, but with this group of subnormal people it seemed to be a particularly striking characteristic.'

As might be expected the problems the couples encountered were many and various, but not substantially different from those met within the general population.

Those who are handicapped are particularly vulnerable to the fluctuations of the economic climate. At the time of Shaw and Wright's (1960) survey 29% of the mentally handicapped husbands were not in employment. In Mattinson's (1975) study 14 husbands were employed irregularly and 6 were unemployed regularly; 12 were in regular employment. In our Welsh survey just over half of the husbands and one-third of the wives were in regular employment, either in an ordinary job or in sheltered workshops.

Some spouses run foul of the law. In Shaw and Wright's (1960) study 42 of the 197 husbands and 11 of the wives had come before the courts for a variety of offences. Of the 64 spouses in Mattinson's (1975) survey, 14 had been charged with offences since marriage, mostly for larceny. Andron and Sturm (1973) report that 9 of the 24 retarded people being surveyed were known to have had some police involvement, but comment, 'Most of the offences described seemed to be the result of suggestibility and vulnerability of many of the members of this group and their ignorance of the complexities of the law'.

Parenthood can present problems to some families. Shaw and Wright (1960) report that almost a third of families with one or more children were known to the National Society for the Prevention of Cruelty to Children or the local authority because of neglect or cruelty. There was evidence that families with three or more children were less successful from the point of view of social adaptation than small families. Of the 40 children born to the couples on Mattinson's (1975) survey, 6 (from three families) had been committed to the care of the local authority and 34 were being looked after by their parents. Of the 13 families with children under school age, 10 needed regular or intensive support or advice from health visitors or social workers, but none of the children appeared to be in dire need.

Other studies mention that previous sterilization is seen by many spouses as an ineradicable stigma and wives may use their childlessness as an excuse for all the difficulties present in the marriage (Edgerton, 1967). Andron and Sturm (1973) and Koegel and Whittemore (1983) mention the disappointments some couples feel at not being able to have a family.

As for many normal couples, housing can be an area of major difficulty. Those in council and public housing are reasonably secure, but many are not so fortunate and find themselves in rented accommodation of the worst sort. Living on top of one another in a small, dank and dismal room can exacerbate marital difficulties. At present, available placements in hostels and sheltered housing complexes are the exception rather than the rule for such married couples. In the future there may be changes. In a care system it seems just as sensible to cater for those who need support in units of two as it does for individuals who require substitute homes and help in daily living.

Subjective satisfaction

In the last resort marriage is a contract between just two people and so it is the partners themselves who must be the final judges. What does the partnership mean to them? Do they feel themselves worse or better off? Is there a discrepancy between their expectations of the relationship and perceived reality (an important potential source of discontent in marriages)?

Edgerton (1967) reports that marriage for someone discharged from a mental handicap institution is a highly meaningful status to achieve. It emphasizes a newly won position as a free and full member of the outside world. It is seen as a proof of normality. Marriage can also give a sense of relief because the couple are past the danger of being arbitrarily parted by a care system which all too often ignored friendships and personal preferences. As one Welsh couple expressed it: 'We're completely together, no one can separate us. It's just great, you know.'

Do the couples feel themselves better or worse off in the married state? Most seem to prefer being married, and given their often appalling past histories, it is hardly surprising that they draw much satisfaction from having a home of their own, a place in the community and a sense of family, one special person who cares very much about them. Of the 32 intact marriages surveyed by Mattinson (1975) 25 were considered by the spouses to be preferable to being single. Andron and Sturm (1973) report: 'All but one man said that married life was better than single life. The overwhelming reason given was the companionship marriage provided in contrast to their previous social isolation.'

In our Welsh survey of 45 marriages (1 divorced, 1 broken by death, 2 broken by involuntary separation, 41 intact) 18 partnerships were judged to be mutually supportive. In three marriages one partner was heavily dependent on the other, but this was in no way resented, rather it was an integral part of the satisfaction. Fourteen partnerships were judged to be affectionate, although there were some symptoms of stress. In four marriages one partner resented the dependency of the other. Two couples said they regretted their marriages, but had made no attempt (for 28 and 19 years respectively) to actually part. One husband sums it up: 'Marriage? It do beat being single!' (Craft and Craft, 1979.)

A number of studies, both British and American, say that many of these partnerships are characterized by a certain social isolation; they are what Mattinson (1975) calls 'cocooned' – that is, with few relationships outside the marriage. Andron and Sturm (1973) report, 'For most of the couples each spouse seemed to be the other's best friend and companion.' Twenty-two of our Welsh couples either kept very much to themselves or had contact mainly with family.

We know from studies of marriages and marital

breakdown that shared expectations tend to cement the partnership, while divergent views of the relationship impose an often fatal strain upon it. Commonly, the experiences of those with mental handicaps lead them to expect very little. They are often unidealistic about the marital state, and take things very much as they come. This may serve to increase their chance of happiness. As Mattinson (1975) comments, '[the] reality was usually so much better than anything they had known before; and an awareness of their limitations and often considerable ignorance of what went on in other people's homes enabled them not to overreach themselves and search for the finer subtleties of living.'

Conclusion

We have seen that in personal terms many marriages between handicapped people are 'successful', even when they present problems to others. Improving the quality of life experienced by handicapped people is the ultimate aim of our services. Bearing in mind that more mentally handicapped people are likely to marry in the future, how can we better prepare them for marriage and aid them after marriage? Four areas are important:

1 Sex education and counselling programmes in special schools, institutions and hostels, designed to help those with mental handicaps understand their own emotional and sexual needs and those of others.
2 Family planning advice and genetic counselling services staffed by professionals skilled in working with mentally handicapped people.
3 Support services, readily available. The flexibility of systems of care needs to be greater so that hostels and small group homes can give places as readily to married couples as to single people.
4 Sheltered housing developments and the use of council houses and flatlets, offer normal living environments in line with current thinking. Here there can be much service input to help a couple settle in, which can be withdrawn as need diminishes. Thus both capital cost and service cost can be optimized.

PARENTHOOD

In nearly all societies the normative pressure on married couples to become parents is very strong. The advent of safe and effective contraception has made it theoretically possible for ordinary couples to choose not to have children and there are discernible trends in this direction. Yet, according to one study only 1 % of the population of the United States considers marital union without a child to be a desirable state (Silka and Kiesler, 1977). What relevance does this have for mentally handicapped people in the community, who do their utmost to assume 'the cloak of competence' (Edgerton, 1967) and pass as ordinary citizens? On the one hand they are subject to normative pressures; on the other, they are likely to encounter serious opposition if they attempt to fulfil their reproductive potential. The disapproval voiced by parents and professionals is remarkably strong given that the label 'mentally handicapped' is applied to a very heterogeneous group of people and that there are very few properly controlled studies of parental competence.

Any consideration of parenthood in this context of mental handicap has to explore a number of different areas: potential and actual fertility, the possibility that the offspring of mentally handicapped parents will themselves be handicapped, and the competency of mentally handicapped parents both to care for their children and to create family environments which stimulate, not dampen, development.

Fertility

Fertility has two aspects: the biological capacity to reproduce, and effective reproduction (that is, the numbers of children actually produced). With regard to the first aspect, most people with mental handicaps are fertile at a biological level, although there are obvious exceptions such as Klinefelter's and Turner's syndromes. However, it is their social position, particularly for the severely handicapped, which militates against the actual production of children. Kirman (1975) states, '. . . in the main the effective reproductive capacity of the feeble-minded below IQ 70 is very limited and below IQ 50 it is statistically negligible'. This of course may change in the future as more people with mental handicaps remain in the community or marry while in care.

To compare effective reproduction we need to look at longitudinal studies. In analysing some of the data collected by the Minnesota Institute of Human Genetics, Higgins et al. (1962) show clearly that there is no correlation between measured intelligence and family size. The lowest IQ group, because of the small numbers who reproduce, have no more children per person than do the higher IQ groups. Although most professionals know of couples they judge to be mentally handicapped who have large numbers of offspring, this may well result from ignorance of birth control methods; and as we have seen in the literature concerning married couples, 'problem families' who are dull and have members with unstable or inadequate personalities may be labelled 'mentally handicapped' even when their measured IQ is above 70.

The inheritance of handicap

In the not-so-distant past, when the laws of genetic inheritance were less well understood, it was thought that parents who were handicapped (mentally or physically) were highly likely to pass on their disability to any offspring they produced. Eugenicists vociferously deplored what they saw as the disproportionate 'reproduction of the unfit', which could have only disastrous effects on the national 'gene pool'. While the laws of genetics are still not perfectly understood, we know enough to realize that 'handicapped parent' does not necessarily mean 'handicapped offspring.' The vast majority of people with mental handicaps have IQs above 50, with no detectable genetic causation for their handicap. Most of the remaining small proportion of severely and moderately handicapped adults are genetically impaired, and risks to any children can be estimated by genetic experts. In this latter group are chromosome 21 trisomies (Down's syndrome), and while there is no known case of a fertile male, the few females who have conceived run a one in two risk of passing on their extra chromosome to their children.

In the literature, studies of parents with mental handicaps estimating the percentage of retarded children vary enormously in their results. Hall (1974) reviewed 31 such studies dating from 1913 to 1965. The percentage of handicapped children produced ranged from 2.5 to 93.2. As Hall points out, these estimations vary so much because of differences in the studies themselves. Some of the obvious variables are mental handicap in one as opposed to both parents, psychometric assessment of IQs, type of handicap of parents (for example, genetic or social), IQ level of parents, death rate of children, and prenatal factors relating to socioeconomic level (malnutrition of fetus, prematurity and so on).

One of the most comprehensive of the studies is an American one reported by Reed and Reed (1965). The Minnesota Institute of Human Genetics selected 289 inpatients with IQs below 70 who had been institutionalized between 1911 and 1918 and traced first the patients' grandparents and then the latter's descendants forward to 1961. They could thus compare a group of mentally handicapped subjects with a group of 'normal' people in the community with similar genetic (and environmental) background. The sample eventually covered up to seven generations and included more than 80 000 people. The records available for 7778 of the children descended from the grandparents of the hospital group show that in the 89 instances where both parents had IQs under 70 nearly 40% of the children were also mentally handicapped (although it is worthy of mention that the *average* IQ of these children was 74). Where only one parent had an IQ below 70, 15% of the children were mentally handicapped (54% had IQs above 90), and of the 7035 children with neither parent mentally handicapped, 1% were mentally handicapped. It is generally accepted that children's measured intelligence tends to show a reversion towards the norm compared with their parents.

Reed and Anderson (1973) constructed a model of 100 000 persons to describe the general population, and suggested that 17% of the mentally handicapped children in the model population would have at least one mentally handicapped parent. The model thus predicts that the remaining 83% of mentally handicapped children in any generation have both parents in the normal range of intelligence, mental handicap occurring as a result of abnormal mutations, recessive genes and other chance pre- and post-natal factors.

Assessment of parental competence

Trying to assess the adequacy of parents with mental handicaps is by no means a simple matter. By what criteria do we judge the adequacy of any parent? Individuals in different stratas of society would give different answers. We know from the British National Child Development Study (Davie et al., 1972) that by the age of seven there are major differences between the children of various social classes in health, skills and scholastic attainment.

The literature is very scanty on this point of parental competence, and there is a notable absence of controls matched for such vital factors as social class and family income. What does seem certain is that the intelligence of the parents is only one of the many factors which have a bearing on child care. Other factors to take into consideration are the degree of marital harmony and stability, the psychiatric health of the parents, financial income, the number of pregnancies and the number of live children, use of support services, use of family planning, and whether or not the parents have histories of being institutionalized.

Environmental factors

We do know that environment can play an important part in the development or retardation of intelligence. A study by Barbara Tizard and colleagues (Tizard and Rees, 1976; Tizard and Hodges, 1978) showed that their two-year-old institutionalized subjects with a mean IQ of around 94 (slightly backward) developed in markedly different ways as they underwent different fates, and a statistically significant difference in IQs arose between the groups when retested. Amongst their findings, those adopted before the age of four, when tested at eight, had a mean IQ of 115. Those adopted after $4\frac{1}{2}$ had a mean IQ of 101 when aged eight. Those who remained in institutions had a mean IQ of 99. Those restored to their parents after the age of $4\frac{1}{2}$ had a mean IQ of 93 when tested at eight. The study of environmental variables is, however, complex, and the original papers should be studied for the many related variables involved, including the vexed question of how far bonding between child and parent affected the degree of communication, and thus of language, established.

Conclusion

Although we know that the mentally handicapped do not produce a disproportionately large number of children, we also know that their risk of having a handicapped child is greater, mainly for environmental reasons, than the risk facing a normal couple. However, that risk is statistical, and as we have discussed in the section on counselling, each couple is unique and ideally should have individual advice. There are couples who know they could not cope with the burden of parenthood, and nowadays no one need have unwanted children. There are others who long for a family of their own. Often this is an idealized dream as they have little or no practical experience of real babies who scream, need nappies changed, and have teething troubles. A number of studies looking at handicapped couples have reported the use of child substitutes, usually a pet who has affection lavished upon it. Other authors suggest that mentally handicapped people help in play groups and nursery schools and act as 'godparents' for children in hospital who do not receive many visitors.

While there is no real agreement on the skills necessary for good parenting, we know from the various studies on marriages between mentally handicapped people that many such couples do give what is judged to be at least adequate care to their offspring. It may be that these children would fare even better away from their natural parents, but that leads into the problematical realms of social engineering. It would not only be those of below average intelligence who would be in danger of losing their children.

BIRTH CONTROL

The existence of safe and effective non-permanent methods of contraception and thus of personal control and choice has a very important consequence for individuals with mental handicaps and for those who counsel them. In the past it was fear of the reproductive capacity of those labelled 'mentally handicapped' that gave rise to strict segregation and pre-discharge sterilizations.

Suitable methods

As with the general population there is no one preferred method for mentally handicapped people. In each case medical history, age, ability, living circumstances and personal motivation need full consideration.

Oral contraceptives

Use of these requires motivation and/or regular supervision. Many mildly handicapped women use the method successfully (Kempton, 1979). Polypharmacy is best avoided, so where other drugs such as anti-convulsants or anti-depressants are being taken another method of birth control might be more suitable (MacLean, 1979).

Intrauterine device (IUD)

For a sexually active woman who lacks supervision and sustained motivation an IUD would be the method of choice. To guard against the removal of the device by the woman or her partner one clinic cut the threads very short (MacLean, 1979). One danger is that the IUD may get dislodged, so checkups at shorter time-intervals than usual would seem sensible.

Medroxyprogesterone acetate (Depo-Provera)

One injection of this drug every three months inhibits ovulation, but there are disadvantages such as breakthrough bleeding and an unpredictable return of fertility after discontinuation (Kempton, 1979). Its main usefulness is as a short-term measure, for example to protect a woman against pregnancy during an episode of disturbed and promiscuous behaviour or for the female partner of a man who has just had a vasectomy.

Other non-permanent techniques

Methods such as the sheath, foam and the cap are not generally considered suitable, as they require understanding and manual dexterity. However, many mentally handicapped men have mastered the technique of using a condom and this should be encouraged.

Sterilization

Because of the permanence of this procedure the question of valid consent becomes very important (see below). The request for sterilization often arises from parents' fear that as their child develops physically he or she will act irresponsibly or be exploited. They may erroneously believe that sterilization removes not only the danger of pregnancy but all sexual drives and impulses, and would thus be in the best interests of everyone concerned. The facts, however, are otherwise.

Alternatives should always be considered first, with sensitive counselling for the handicapped individual, parents, or guardians and/or care staff. Decisions based upon temporary adolescent behaviour may well prove ill-founded in the light of maturation, aided by training and teaching.

For some, of course, sterilization is wholly advisable. MacLean (1979) describes the case of a woman with a mild mental handicap who had twice killed her children. She was highly distressed at the thought of having another baby but after counselling and sterilization became far less tense and was able to enjoy a stable and supportive relationship with her partner. Several of the married couples surveyed by Craft and Craft (1979) had requested sterilization to relieve them of the worry of potential parenthood, which they felt would threaten their ability to cope.

Effective delivery of services

Effective contraceptive methods are of no benefit to the population at risk if unaccompanied by an effective delivery of service. David et al (1976) carried out a pilot scheme in one American city to provide a specialized family planning clinic for clients with mental handicaps. In spite of wide publicity and direct contact with 37 institutions service uptake was disappointingly low – only 47 clients in a seven-month period (41 of them from one institution). MacLean (1979, 1983) reports on the success of a family planning clinic set up in a mental handicap hospital, bringing the service to the clients. Local family planning clinics are increasing their expertise in counselling and treating those with mental handicaps who live in the community.

Valid and informed consent

The question of informed consent is a vexing one, for it raises issues about the nature of mental handicap itself, about who decides who is incapable of giving a valid consent, and who then has the right to make a decision on behalf of that person. Not surprisingly, the courts of many countries have been heavily involved.

In Britain there is no set procedure beyond the requirement that the surgeon carrying out the sterilization should satisfy him or herself that the patient understands what is involved and what the consequences are. However, the judgement given in the case of *In re D* (a minor) ([1976] 1 All E.R. 326) reminds practitioners of the matters at issue, particularly when, as here, the mentally handicapped individual is a minor. The judge ruled that the operation was not in the best interests of the 11-year-old girl with a mild mental handicap. She rejected the paediatrician's proposition that where there is parental consent such a decision lies solely within the doctor's clinical judgement even when the purpose is non-therapeutic (that is, not simply for the health of the patient). It is likely, however, in the absence of a formal procedure, that many non-therapeutic decisions are never challenged.

In many American States and in Canada the pendulum has swung so far away from the eugenic excesses that it is virtually impossible to obtain sterilization at all (Evans, 1980; Gostin, 1980; Wolf and Zarfas, 1982). Karp (1981) comments on the absurdity of this position, which means in effect that unlike ordinary people, an individual with a mental handicap does not have the right *not* to reproduce, because no doctor will risk litigation by carrying out a sterilization operation. However, there are moves towards establishing a 'right to sterilization'. In 1980 the Supreme Court of Washington State required that the incompetent person be represented by a guardian *ad litem* at sterilization hearings, that the court received independent assessments, and that the views of the incompetent person be elicited and taken into account. Within this framework the judge must find by clear, cogent and convincing evidence that the individual is incapable of making his or her own decision about sterilization and is unlikely to develop sufficiently to make an informed judgment in the foreseeable future. It also has to be as convincingly proved that contraception is needed – in other words, that the physical capacity exists, the individual is likely to engage in sexual activity and the extent of the individual's disability renders him or her permanently incapable of caring for a child, even with reasonable assistance. Lastly, it must be found that there are no alternatives to sterilization (*In re Hayes*, 93 Wash 228, 608 P 2d 635; Appelbaum, 1982). These standards are likely to be widely followed. New Jersey has emulated them, with the additional standard that enquiry should be made into the likely effect of pregnancy or the birth of a child on the mentally handicapped woman.

Law and practice should ensure that sterilization is 'available to all and imposed upon none' (Gonzales 1982), but regrettably we are still some way off that ideal.

SUMMARY

Modern research has shown that many of society's fears concerning the sexuality of those labelled 'mentally handicapped' were ill-founded. With education, counselling and support individuals with mental handicap can be helped towards a better understanding of themselves and others, towards personally satisfying and socially acceptable relationships, and thereby to an overall enrichment of life.

REFERENCES

Adams G, Tallon RJ & Alcorn DA (1982) Attitude towards the sexuality of mentally retarded and nonretarded persons. *Education and Training of the Mentally Retarded 17(4):* 307–312.
Alcorn DA (1974) Parental views on sexual development and education of the trainable mentally retarded. *Journal of Special Education 8(2):* 119–130.
Andron L (1983) Sexuality counselling with developmentally disabled couples. In Craft A & Craft M (eds) *Sex Education and Counselling for Mentally Handicapped People,* pp. 254–286. Tunbridge Wells: Costello Press.
Andron L & Sturm ML (1973) Is 'I do' in the repertoire of the retarded? *Mental Retardation 11:* 31–34.
Appelbaum PS (1982) The issue of sterilization and the mentally retarded. *Hospital Community Psychiatry 33(7):* 523–524.
Bovicelli L, Orsini LF, Rizzi N, Montacuti V & Bacchetta M (1982) Reproduction in Down syndrome. *Obstetrics and Gynecology 59 (6)* (Supplement): 135–175.
Brantlinger E (1983) Measuring variation and change in attitudes in residential care staff towards the sexuality of mentally retarded persons. *Mental Retardation 21(1):* 17–22.
Brown H (1983) Why is it such a big secret? Sex education for handicapped young adults. In Craft A & Craft M (eds) *Sex Education and Counselling for Mentally Handicapped People.* Tunbridge Wells: Costello Press.
Calderone MS (1982) Children and parents as sexual people. *Health Education 13(6):* 27–30.
Champagne MP & Walker-Hirsch LW (1982) Circles: a self-organization system for teaching appropriate social/sexual behavior to mentally retarded /developmentally disabled persons. *Sexuality and Disability 5(3):* 172–4.
Coleman EM & Murphy WD (1980) A survey of sexual attitudes and sex education programs among facilities for the mentally retarded. *Applied Research in Mental Retardation 1:* 269–276.
Craft M (1959) Personality disorder and dullness. *Lancet i:* 856–858.
Craft A (1981) *Sexual Counselling for the Mentally Handicapped People , Parents and Care Staff.* (Slide presentation.) Graves' Medical Audio-visual Library, 220 New London Road, Chelmsford CM2 9BJ.
Craft A (1982) *Health, Hygiene and Sex Education for Mentally Handicapped Children, Adolescents and Adults: A review of Audio-visual Resources.* London: Health Education Council.
Craft A (1983a) Teaching programmes and training techniques. In Craft A & Craft M (eds) *Sex Education and Counselling for Mentally Handicapped People.* pp. 186–212. Tunbridge Wells: Costello Press.
Craft M (1983b) Sexual behaviour and sexual difficulties. In Craft A & Craft M (eds) *Sex Education and Counselling for Mentally Handicapped People.* pp. 38–52. Tunbridge Wells: Costello Press.
Craft M & Craft A (1978) *Sex and the Mentally Handicapped.* London: Routledge & Kegan Paul.
Craft A & Craft M (1979) *Handicapped Married Couples.* London: Routledge and Kegan Paul.
Craft A & Craft M (eds) (1983) *Sex Education and Counselling for Mentally Handicapped People.* Tunbridge Wells: Costello Press.
Craft A, Davis J, Williams M & Williams M (1983) A health and sex education programme: curriculum and resources. In Craft A & Craft M (eds) *Sex Education and Counselling for Mentally Handicapped People,* pp. 148–185. Tunbridge Wells: Costello Press.
Dalton ME & Dalton K (1978) Menarchial age in the disabled. *British Medical Journal ii:* 475.
David HP, Smith JD & Friedman E (1976) Family planning services for persons handicapped by mental retardation. *American Journal of Public Health 66(11):* 1053–1057.
Davie R, Butler NR & Goldstein H (1972) *From Birth to Seven.* London: Longmans.
Demetral GD (1981) Does ignorance really produce irresponsible behavior? *Sexuality and Disability 4(3):* 151–160.

Edgerton RB (1967) *The Cloak of Competence.* London: Cambridge University Press.

Edgerton RB & Dingman HF (1964) Good reasons for bad supervision: 'dating' in hospital for the mentally retarded. *Psychiatric Quarterly Supplement 38:* 221–233.

Edmondson B, McCombs K & Wish J (1979) What retarded adults believe about sex. *American Journal of Mental Deficiency 84:* 11–18.

Evans KG (1980) Sterilization of the mentally retarded – a review. *Canadian Medical Association Journal 123:* 1066–1070.

Fairbrother P (1983) The parent's viewpoint. In Craft A & Craft M (eds) *Sex Education and Counselling for Mentally Handicapped People.* pp. 95–109. Tunbridge Wells: Costello Press.

Farrell C (1978) *My Mother Said. . .* London: Routledge and Kegan Paul.

Floor L, Baxter D, Rosen M & Zisfein L (1975) A survey of marriages among previously institutionalized retardates. *Mental Retardation 13:* 33–37.

Gillies P & McEwen J (1981) The sexual knowledge of the 'normal' and mildly subnormal adolescent. *Health Education Journal 40(4):* 120–124.

Goldman R & Goldman J (1982) *Children's Sexual Thinking.* London: Routledge and Kegan Paul.

Gonzales B (1982) The international medicolegal status of sterilization for mentally handicapped people. *Journal of Reproductive Medicine 27(5):* 257–258.

Gordon S (1975) Workshop. Sex education for the handicapped. In Bass MS & Gelof M (eds) *Sexual Rights and Responsibilities of the Mentally Retarded.* Proceedings of the Conference of American Association on Mental Deficiency. Region IX, 1972. (Revised edition.)

Gostin L (1980) Sterilization and the law. *Parents Voice 30(4):* 16–17.

Hall JE (1974) Sexual behavior. In Wortis J (ed) *Mental Retardation (and Developmental Disabilities): An Annual Review, Vol. VI.* New York: Brunner/Mazel.

Hall JE (1975) Sexuality and the mentally retarded. In Green R (ed) *Human Sexuality: A Health Practitioner's Text.* Baltimore: Williams & Wilkins.

Hall JE (1978) Acceptance of sexual expression in the mentally retarded. *Sexuality and Disability 1(1):* 44–51.

Hall JE and Sawyer HW (1978) Sexual policies for the mentally retarded. *Sexuality and Disability 1(1):* 34–43.

Hall JE, Morris HL & Barker HR (1973) Sexual knowledge and attitudes in mentally retarded adolescents. *American Journal of Mental Deficiency 77:* 706–709.

Hammar SL, Wright LS & Jensen DL (1967) Sex education for the retarded adolescent: a survey of parental attitudes and methods of management in 50 retarded adolescents. *Clinical Pediatrics 6:* 621–627.

Hamre-Nietupski S & Ford A (1981) Sex education and related skills: a series of programs implemented with severely handicapped students. *Sexuality and Disability 4(3):* 179–193.

Hamre-Nietupski S & Williams W (1977) Implementation of selected sex education and social skills to severely handicapped students. *Education and Training of the Mentally Retarded 12:* 364–372.

Heshusius L (1982) Sexuality, intimacy and persons we label mentally retarded: what they think – what we think. *Mental Retardation 20(4):* 164–168.

Higgins JV, Reed EW & Reed SC (1962) Intelligence and family size: a paradox resolved. *Eugenics Quarterly 9:* 84–90.

Hounslow Social Services Department (1983) *Sexuality of Mentally Handicapped People – Guidelines for Care Staff.* (Available from Ms S Walmsley, Hounslow Social Services Department, The Civic Centre, Lampton Road, Hounslow TW3 4DN.)

Jagiello G (1981) Reproduction in Down Syndrome. In de la Cruz FF & Park SG (eds) *Trisomy 21 (Down Syndrome),* pp. 151–162. Baltimore: University Park Press.

Jay Committee (1979) *Report of the Committee of Enquiry into Mental Handicap, Nursing and Care.* Cmnd. 7468. London: HMSO.

Johnson PR (1981) Sex and the developmentally handicapped adult: A comparison of teaching methods. *British Journal of Mental Subnormality 27 Part I(52):* 8–17.

Karp LE (1981) Sterilization of the retarded. *American Journal of Medical Genetics 9:* 1–3.

Kempton W (1976) *Sexual Rights and Responsibilities of the Retarded Person.* Official Proceedings of the 103rd Annual Social Welfare Forum. National Conference on Social Welfare, Washington DC, June 13–17 1976. New York: Columbia University Press.

Kempton W (1977) The mentally retarded person. In Gochros H & Gochros J (eds) *The Sexually Oppressed.* New York: Association Press.

Kempton W (1978) Sex education for the mentally handicapped. *Sexuality and Disability 1(2):* 137–146.

Kempton W (1979) A review of intrauterine devices. *British Journal of Sexual Medicine 6(51):* 16–17.

Kempton W (1983) Sexuality training for professionals who work with mentally handicapped persons. In Craft A & Craft M (eds) *Sex Education and Counselling for Mentally Handicapped People.* pp. 53–77. Tunbridge Wells: Costello Press.

Kempton W & Caparulo F (1983) Counselling parents and care staff on the sexual needs of mentally handicapped people. In Craft A & Craft M (eds) *Sex Education and Counselling for Mentally Handicapped People.* pp. 78–94. Tunbridge Wells: Costello Press.

Kempton W & Forman R (1976) *Guidelines for Training in Sexuality and the Mentally Handicapped.* Philadelphia: Planned Parenthood Association of South Eastern Pennsylvania.

Kirman B (1975) Some causal factors. In Kirman B & Bicknell J (eds) *Mental Handicap.* pp. 67–99. Edinburgh: Churchill Livingstone.

Koegel A & Whittemore R (1983) Sexuality in the ongoing lives of mildly retarded adults. In Craft A & Craft M (eds) *Sex Education and Counselling for Mentally Handicapped People.* pp. 213–253. Tunbridge Wells: Costello Press.

Krajicek J (1982) Developmental disability and human sexuality. *Nursing Clinics of North America 17(3):* 377–386.

Livock P (1985) *Sex Education for People with Mental Handicaps.* London: Croom Helm.

MacLean R (1979) Sexual problems and family planning needs of the mentally handicapped in residential care. *British Journal of Family Planning 4(4):* 13–15.

MacLean R (1983) Birth control techniques and counselling for a mentally handicapped population. In Craft A & Craft M (eds) *Sex Education and Counselling for Mentally Handicapped People,* pp. 241–253. Tunbridge Wells: Costello Press.

Mattinson J (1975) *Marriage and Mental Handicap,* 2nd edn. London: Institute of Marital Studies, The Tavistock Institute of Human Relations.

McNaughton J (for the Schools Council) (1983a) *Fit for Life.* Basingstoke: Macmillan Education.

McNaughton J (1983b) Health, sex and hygiene education in

special schools. In Craft A & Craft M (eds) *Sex Education and Counselling for Mentally Handicapped People*, pp. 110–130. Tunbridge Wells: Costello Press.

Mitchell LK, Doctor RM & Butler DC (undated) *A Manual for Behavioral Intervention on the Sexual Problems of Retarded Individuals in Residential or Home Settings*. Available from Dr L Mitchell, Department of Counselor Education, California State University, Los Angeles, CA 90032, USA.

Mitchell LK, Doctor RM & Butler DC (1978) Attitudes of caretakers towards the sexual behavior of mentally retarded persons. *American Journal of Mental Deficiency 83(3):* 289–296.

Mosier HD, Grossman HJ & Dingman HF (1962) Secondary sex development in mentally deficient individuals. *Child Development 33:* 273–286.

Mulhern TJ (1975) Survey of reported sexual behavior and policies characterising residential facilities for retarded citizens. *American Journal of Mental Deficiency 79(6):* 670–673.

National Development Group for the Mentally Handicapped (1980) *Improving the Quality of Services for Mentally Handicapped People: a Check List of Standards*. London: Department of Health and Social Security.

Pattullo AW & Barnard KE (1968) Teaching menstrual hygiene to the mentally retarded *American Journal of Nursing 68(12):* 2572–2575.

Perske R (1972) The dignity of risk and the mentally retarded. *Mental Retardation 10(1):* 25–27.

Reed SC & Anderson VE (1973) Effects of changing sexuality on the gene pool. In de la Cruz FF & La Veck GD (eds) *Human Sexuality and the Mentally Retarded*, pp. 111–125. London: Butterworth.

Reed EW & Reed SC (1965) *Mental Retardation: A Family Study*. Philadelphia: Saunders.

Rosen M (1975) Psychosexual adjustment of the mentally handicapped. In: Bass MS & Gelof M (eds) *Sexual Rights and Responsibilities of the Mentally Retarded*. Proceedings of the Conference of American Association on Mental Deficiency, Region IX, 1972. (Revised edn.) pp. 97–113.

Salerno LJ, Park JK & Giannini MJ (1975) Reproductive capacity of the mentally retarded. *Journal of Reproductive Medicine 14(3):* 123–129.

Saunders EJ (1981) The mental health professional, the mentally retarded and sex. *Hospital and Community Psychiatry 32(10):* 717–721.

Shaw CH & Wright CH (1960) The married mental defective: a follow-up study. *Lancet i:* 273–274.

Silka L & Kiesler S (1977) Couples who choose to remain childless. *Family Planning Perspectives 9(1):* 16–25.

Slater J Fitzpatrick S & Carrins D (1981) Helping to overcome fears for the future. *Social Work Today 12(30):* 11–12.

Special Education Curriculum Development Center (1972) *Social and Sexual Development: A Guide for Teachers of the Handicapped*. Revised edition. Iowa City: University of Iowa.

Tizard B & Hodges J (1978) The effect of early institutional rearing on the development of eight-year old children. *Journal of Child Psychology and Psychiatry 19:* 99–118.

Tizard B & Rees J (1976) A comparison of the effects of adoption, restoration to the natural mother, and continued institutionalisation in the cognitive development of four-year old children. In Clarke AM & Clarke ADB (eds) *Early Experience: Myth and Reality*. London: Open Books.

Tricomi V, Valenti C & Hall JE (1964) Ovulatory pattern in Down's syndrome. *American Journal of Obstetrics and Gynecology 89:* 651–656.

United Nations (1971) *Declaration of General and Special Rights of the Mentally Handicapped*. New York: UN Department of Social Affairs.

Warnock Committee (1978) *Special Educational Needs: Report of the Committee of Enquiry into the Education of Handicapped Children and Young People*. Cmnd. 7212. London: HMSO.

Watson G & Rogers RS (1980) Sexual instruction for the mildly retarded and normal adolescent: a comparison of educational approaches, parental expectations and pupil knowledge and attitude. *Health Education Journal 39(3):* 88–95.

Whittemore RD & Koegal P (1978) *Loving Alone is not Helpful: Sexuality and Social Context among the Mildly Retarded*. Working Paper 7, Socio-Behavioral Group, Mental Retardation Research Center, School of Medicine, University of California, Los Angeles, USA.

Williams JK (1983) Reproductive decisions: adolescents with Down syndrome. *Pediatric Nursing 9(1):* 43–44, 58.

Wolf L & Zarfas DE (1982) Parents' attitudes toward sterilization of their mentally retarded children. *American Journal of Mental Deficiency 87(2):* 122–129.

Wolfensberger W (1972) *The Principle of Normalization in Human Services*. Toronto: National Institute on Mental Retardation.

Chapter 17
Bereavement

MAUREEN OSWIN

Experiences of loss cannot be avoided in the life of any human being. In early babyhood, a separation from our mother is perhaps the most frightening thing to happen to us, but we gradually accustom ourselves to this experience because we learn that the loved one returns. Longer and more traumatic experiences of loss in childhood, perhaps caused by parental illness, marriage breakdown, war or going into hospital, may cause lasting emotional damage. Adulthood brings a variety and an increase of loss experiences: for example, leaving the parents' home, moving house, unemployment, retirement, loss of abilities through illness, loss of status and self-esteem through ageing.

The ways in which we cope with our losses vary according to our philosophy of life, former experiences, the type of loss, the people around us and the sort of help we get. For example, people who become disabled through an accident may have their self-confidence restored by skilled rehabilitation, and mentally handicapped people leaving institutions may cope successfully with their new lives in ordinary neighbourhoods because they have been carefully prepared for the change and have welcoming neighbours and good support from community mental handicap nurses and other professionals.

BEREAVEMENT AND GRIEF

No previous experience of loss can adequately prepare anybody for the terrible finality of a loss caused by death. This time there can be no comfort-

ing promise to return. There is only the pain of irreversible loss that somehow has to be coped with and understood and explained to ourselves and to others. In the despair of a bereavement we may feel that nothing we have ever learnt in life has prepared us for such a blow as this.

When we are bereaved we may have to face various tasks which are very distressing, but they serve a purpose in forcing us to realize what has happened. For example, we probably *have* to talk about our loss because we need to telephone relatives, tell neighbours, perhaps organize the funeral and take responsibility for the legal formalities which follow a death. We have to speak the special words which are used at times of death: funeral, undertaker, coffin, grave, Chapel of Rest. Painful as these words are, they do make us realize what has happened. And in the weeks following the death this realization is further reinforced by the letters of condolence which have to be read and answered.

Our realization of loss is also reinforced by our sight and hearing. We are very conscious of a visual emptiness: the absence of the person is patently obvious – they have really gone, the face will not be seen again or the voice heard – and we see the evidence of the empty bed, the empty place at the table at mealtimes and the clothes no longer needed but requiring to be sorted out. We see the funeral cars and the flowers. The words and the music of the funeral service are heard. Being a mourner, attending the funeral, publicly declaring our loss, is one of the formal social ways in which we are helped to realize what has happened.

Studies of bereavement have been helpful in pinpointing common human reactions to loss through death. These include feelings of fear, loss of appetite, loss of intellect, exhaustion, tears, disturbed sleep, anger, depression, feelings of remorse, panic, disbelief about what has happened, passiveness, over-activity, thinking that the person is still there, wanting to talk continuously about the dead

This chapter is based on the preliminary findings of the author's research into bereavement and mentally handicapped people, including a survey of hospitalization following bereavement. The work was funded by the Rowntree Memorial Trust and undertaken at the Thomas Coram Research Unit, London. A full report will be available in 1986.

197

person, inability to concentrate, bad temper, moodiness.

A bereaved person may have any or all of these reactions, perhaps lasting only a few hours or prolonged for weeks. Sometimes they think they are recovering from the loss but then one or other of the reactions returns without warning, provoked by a sound or smell or sudden visual memory. Some bereaved people show their reactions, but others keep their grief very private; they may behave differently according to the company they are in, perhaps putting on a 'brave face' when with friends, but being overcome by anguish when alone.

GRIEF AND MENTALLY HANDICAPPED PEOPLE

There is no reason to suppose that mentally handicapped people will not suffer any of the normal reactions to bereavement which were listed above. However, they may have additional special difficulties due to:

1 Poor intellect and multiple disabilities which may deny them the many social, verbal, auditory and visual opportunities of realising the death which are available to more able people.
2 The failure of professionals and other people to recognize their normal grief.
3 The inappropriate way in which their services are organized.

Because of the wide range of intellectual, sensory and physical abilities amongst mentally handicapped people it would seem impossible to postulate about their perception of death. And it would be very unjust to contribute agreement to the popular but unproven views held by some professionals that mentally handicapped people's perception of death is very childish or that they have no emotional feelings about their loss.

What is important to bear in mind is that having a mental handicap will not preclude anybody from the wide range of normal bereavement reactions which have been listed, but will put them at risk of suffering additional problems. For example, mentally handicapped people who have multiple disabilities affecting sight, language, hearing and mobility may be denied many of the aids which help more able people to realize a death: those who are blind are denied the visual perception of their loss; a language disability will prevent opportunities for verbalizing the loss; other people may not include them in the conversations about the death which can be so

helpful in admitting loss and grief; those who are deaf and have language problems may not be able to understand the funeral service.

Mentally handicapped people who have severe physical disabilities may be barred from attending the funeral and getting to the graveside. Their physical disabilities may, indeed, have prevented them from visiting the sick person in hospital and gaining any preliminary understanding that the person was seriously ill and likely to die. Sometimes, severely mentally handicapped people are not included in the funeral ceremony because other people think that they will not understand it or will make a disturbance or will be very upset or maybe upset others. But funerals are a time for getting upset, and mentally handicapped people should have the same opportunities as more able people to mourn publicly and affirm their loss.

Some of the difficulties facing bereaved mentally handicapped people may be overcome by thoughtful planning and help; for example, they should be able to visit the dying person in hospital and attend the funeral. And they should have very careful explanations about what has happened and be included in the conversations about the death.

When professionals fail to recognize grief

Not all professionals who work with mentally handicapped people are familiar with the normal effects of bereavement. This ignorance may cause them to interpret a mentally handicapped person's *normal* grief reactions (such as anger, a temper outburst and inability to concentrate) incorrectly, as the behaviour of a mentally handicapped person being extra-difficult instead of the normal behaviour of a grieving human being.

Anybody who is bereaved, whether they are handicapped or not, may temporarily lose some of their mental abilities and they may find it difficult to do quite simple tasks such as writing a shopping list, using a telephone or even making a pot of tea. For this reason, it would be very unwise for professionals to try and assess a mentally handicapped person in the weeks following a major bereavement. Ignorance of normal grief reactions may result in the bereaved person being put onto to some elaborate training programme which will put extra stress on them, or may mean their removal to another residential facility and cause even more changes in their already disrupted lives.

It would seem that all professionals who work with mentally handicapped people should acquaint themselves with the normal reactions that occur when anybody is bereaved; thus they may avoid making mistakes which are going to cause the mentally handicapped person more pain.

DAY CENTRE STAFF AND BEREAVED STUDENTS

The staff of day centres can be a major source of help to their bereaved mentally handicapped students. They can support them in the days immediately after the death, and aid in the longer term by helping them to adapt to the changes in lifestyle which may be caused by the death. Day centre staff may also be helpful in preparing mentally handicapped students for loss and change long before a death occurs, by teaching them independence and advising them about some of the life experiences which adults have to face. Such preparation will not, of course, prevent the pain of loss, but it may give them additional strength when a bereavement does occur.

If the death happens when the student is at the day centre, one of the staff may have to break the news. Although this is a very difficult task, the day centre staff may be the best people to give the sad news because they are likely to be the most familiar of all the professionals known to the student and his family. Also, the day centre staff may have known the deceased parent very well and this can be a comfort to the bereaved person, for, if the person giving bad news can at once express and demonstrate their own genuine sorrow about the loss there is an immediate comforting sense of grief being shared.

A member of one day centre said: 'We knew his mum so well, and it was a shock for all of us to know that she had suddenly died. It was terrible telling him. But looking back now, we know it was best that one of us did it, although we were so tearful ourselves.'

GOING INTO RESIDENTIAL CARE FOLLOWING A BEREAVEMENT

The death of a parent is likely to provoke a series of losses. A person admitted to a residential care facility some distance away from the family home may have to leave his or her day centre and lose the support of the staff there, friends and the known daily routine. Leaving the neighbourhood will also mean losing familiar contacts such as shops, trades-

people, neighbours and perhaps married siblings and in-laws who live nearby.

Sometimes mentally handicapped people with elderly parents may not be known to the statutory services. Then, when a bereavement occurs, unknown professionals are called in to organize emergency residential care, primary bereavement help and long-term support. This can mean that grieving mentally handicapped people are suddenly surrounded by strangers at a time when, like all bereaved people, they need to be with familiar people in a familiar environment. There have been worrying instances of people going into residential care immediately following a bereavement and *never going back to their family home again*, and never receiving adequate explanations about what had happened to it. Having perhaps participated in their parents' household routines for twenty years or more, they must be dreadfully worried about their belongings, the care of pets and plants, about who has the key and where the letters are going; and they will be having to endure these worries at the same time as grieving for the dead parent. Such an accumulation of worry and grief will create an intolerably sad situation for them.

Some professionals do not recognize these worries because they do not expect mentally handicapped people to feel the same responsibilities as more able people would feel for the homes they have lost. However, one of the basic rules for any professional working with bereaved mentally handicapped adults is to recognize that they are not children and even if they cannot speak and do not appear to be very much aware of adult responsibilities, they are obviously going to be very worried about a home which they have suddenly had to leave.

Whatever decisions are taken regarding the residential accommodation of the mentally handicapped person on the first night following the death of a parent, it would seem important for them to return to the family home as soon as possible, even if only for a few hours, as they need to see for themselves that their house and belongings are still there and safe. When they do this they should be accompanied by a familiar person. In addition to the mentally handicapped person's worries about the physical care of their home, it must also be remembered that the family home represented their identity and therefore it should never just disappear from their life without some explanation. Professionals should make every attempt to link the old family home and the new placement by a full explanation about the future of the house and by allowing the bereaved person to take personal belongings and mementos from home to the residential care placement.

When a mentally handicapped person's understanding of the death is confused because of their intellectual handicap, or because they have not been told the complete truth, they may think that their parent has rejected them and is still living at home but does not want them back again. It is difficult to know the best way to help a person in this situation. Some may be helped by a visit to the home with a familiar caring friend who can show them that their parent is not there, and also explain that the parent did love them and want them but got very ill and could not get better and then died. However, some bereaved mentally handicapped people might not find this at all helpful. Each situation has to be carefully considered according to the needs of the individual, the only rules being that help should be given by familiar people and that the professional concerned should not make a decision alone but should talk about it with other members of the team. If there is an active local MENCAP group it could be very helpful for the professionals to talk about it with them also, as they would probably know the parents and the handicapped person. And, as always, knowledge about normal bereavement reactions must be brought to the discussion and to any decisions taken by the professionals.

The early findings of my research suggest that mentally handicapped people are at risk of multiple residential placements in the twelve months following a major bereavement: first, a short-term care emergency admission on the same day that the death occurred if there is nobody left at home to look after them; second, a move to a temporary long-term placement for the purpose of being assessed; and third, a final long-term placement. Some of the people met during the research had had as many as five different residential placements within the first twelve months of losing a parent.

It is obvious that multiple residential placements will be extremely upsetting, because at the same time as having to cope with the death of a close relative the bereaved person has to keep making new relationships with unfamiliar people who probably did not know the dead parent or their original home and lifestyle. Bereaved people in the early stages of their grief, no matter what their mental abilities are, should be with familiar people, so it would seem that professionals who organize multiple residential care placements are breaking a basic rule for bereavement support. And constant moves can serve little purpose in assessment, be-

cause it is doubtful if the staff in the various establishments will ever see these upset bereaved people functioning at their usual level of ability.

Long-term admission to a mental handicap hospital

Although the staff in mental handicap hospitals may be aware of the bereaved person's need for individual care, they may be unable to meet those needs because of organizational difficulties. Ideally, the bereaved person should have a member of staff specially assigned to them when they are admitted to a hospital, so that they can immediately begin relating to somebody who will be taking a long-term interest in them. But this may not be possible, and very soon the grieving person may be swamped by the traditional problems of long-stay hospital care, such as shortages of staff, constant changes of staff, too many residents in one ward, mass organization of care, routines of moving from activity to activity during the week and having nothing to do at weekends, noise and lack of privacy.

When a brief comparison is made between family life and hospital ward life it reveals the many differences which are likely to make newly admitted bereaved mentally handicapped people feel very insecure and unhappy; for example, they may not be allowed in the ward kitchen, whereas in the family home the kitchen may have been the focus of all social life; they may not have their own room in the hospital, whereas at home they may have had their own rooms and spent much time there on their own playing records and looking at magazines; they may not get out to the shops from the hospital but at home they may have enjoyed a daily trip to the corner shop; they might not be able to potter in the hospital garden like they did at home; and at home they may have helped aged parents and taken responsibility for household tasks, whereas in the hospital there may be no opportunity at all to be useful to others and to feel wanted.

When mentally handicapped people who have additional multiple physical and sensory handicaps are admitted to hospital for the first time immediately following the death of a parent, they lose not only their loved parent but also the familiar details of daily life which made sense of their world. As very dependent multiply handicapped people they may have led very sheltered lives and not attended day centres, and may have rarely left their houses since they reached adulthood and their parents became elderly. They may have been fed and dressed and washed by their own mother for years, in exactly the same manner, and she may have always said the same things to them while she did it. Since reaching adulthood and getting too heavy to carry upstairs they may well have spent their entire time in one room, the centre of the family life. In leaving the family home they lose the familiar environment of that room – its fabrics, sounds and smells. In the bigger environment of the hospital the lights may be brighter, sounds louder, more people will be passing, and voices, footsteps and clothes will be strange.

Some hospital staff, sensitive to the problems which face very dependent people, have agreed with the research hypothesis that multiply handicapped people suddenly admitted to hospital after a bereavement may be at risk of serious illness and may even die within two years of the bereavement, weakened by pining and despair and susceptible to infections.

WIDOWS

As would be expected, my research has found evidence of families suffering severe isolation following a bereavement. The family may have already been isolated for a number of years before the death occurred: for instance, it may have comprised an elderly mother and father and a middle-aged mentally handicapped son or daughter, with no in-laws and few friends or outside activities, their family life centring on the garden, the house, the television and the need to budget on a small income since the father's retirement. It is painful to think of widows left caring on their own for a speechless multiply handicapped son or daughter. Those who have been met in the course of the research have spoken of their intense loneliness: 'Dad and I did everything together and always worked to a routine looking after our boy. We were real partners: we did everything together. At nights Dad would undress John in front of the fire and get him ready for bed, and I'd make our drinks and then we'd watch the ten o'clock news and Dad would carry him up at a quarter to eleven. I cannot carry him up on my own so he has a bed made up here since Dad died.'

After the initial help given at the actual time of the death and the funeral, the widow and the handicapped son or daughter may have few callers and no invitations to go out. New widows who do not have severely handicapped dependent people to look after are able to go out and may eventually begin to adapt themselves to their widowhood; for example, many go on the package tour holidays which are popular amongst elderly widows and help

them to meet other people and develop new interests. But a widow's social activities may be curtailed when there is a very severely handicapped person to care for. Neighbours may not ask her out because they know that the handicapped person will have to come as well and they feel that they do not understand anybody with a handicap or cannot cope with a wheelchair. And the widows may be reluctant about the idea of putting their son or daughter into short-term care while they go away on holiday.

It is possible that widows in their fifties and sixties may be even more isolated than those in their late seventies and eighties. The older widows are likely to receive some services for elderly people and have contact with home helps, meals-on-wheels staff, district nurses and perhaps voluntary workers from a local church or a society concerned for the elderly, but the physically fit widow in her fifties or sixties who is not apparently needing any outside help may be acutely lonely. They express feelings of being rejected by society and especially by the statutory services: 'Social workers never come.' 'Haven't seen a social worker for years; I don't know what they would do if they came, but it would be nice to have someone to talk to.' 'It would be nice to get out more, but there's no car now of course, since Dad died.'

There are no easy answers about how to help these very lonely widows and their handicapped adult sons and daughters. Their problems are exacerbated by lack of day-care services, and by professionals failing to recognize the multiplicity of problems caused by a major bereavement.

At a practical level it is vital that these widows should have help to get out of the house. The loss of the husband often means the loss of transport: 'We used to go to the shops once a week in the car, and used it on Sundays to go to the park. But after Dad died I got rid of the car as I couldn't drive.' Some widows use the mobility allowance to have regular bookings with a car-hire firm whose drivers often get to know them well and seem like friends, but others do not have this friendly contact. Social service departments might use a voluntary driver to provide transport once a week to take a widow and her mentally handicapped son or daughter to the shops and the park; unlike the friendly car-hire driver, the volunteer will have time to help in the supermarket with the wheelchair and go for a walk in the park. This might seem like a luxury use of local rates and taxes, but it could be essential to the physical and emotional health of the widow in helping her to recover from her bereavement.

Pressure groups can influence public and government attitudes towards recognizing the needs of housebound lonely widows caring for a handicapped relative. For example, in Britain the Royal Society for Mentally Handicapped Children and Adults (MENCAP) has for many years been the main national spokesman for older parents of handicapped children. Their local branches may be a source of immense support to their widowed members. One of the biggest worries that widows face is the thought of their own death and what will then happen to their handicapped son or daughter. With this in mind, parents in the Harrow Weald group of MENCAP have drawn up guidelines to help each other with problems caused by bereavement.

SOME EFFECTS OF THE BEREAVEMENT

Parents have referred to their multiply handicapped sons and daughters losing some of their abilities after a bereavement, for example not walking so well, losing some of their speech, becoming more dependent, wanting to be fed, washed and dressed, being afraid about their widowed parent going out without them (even if only on a short trip to the post-box), being very 'clinging' when out and waking in the night and coming into the widow's bedroom to find out if they are still there. These reactions are normal and to be expected, indicating that the death has, understandably, affected the confidence of the person. People who are not handicapped also suffer loss of confidence when somebody close to them dies, but they may not show it in exactly these ways because they are not so intellectually and physically vulnerable as multiply handicapped people.

Some of the more able mentally handicapped people met in this research have not shown a loss of confidence after a bereavement but have actually become far more independent and have supported their widowed parent and started to take more responsibility in the house. One mother with a 29-year-old son living at home said that he was a tremendous support after she was widowed. He made himself responsible for locking up the house at night and checking that the garden gate was shut, and he took over many of his father's household chores.

Sometimes the bereavement results in the development of a behaviour problem, for example a refusal to leave the house and go to the day centre. This is understandable behaviour: the mentally handicapped person may fear that while they are at the day centre their remaining parent will disappear. Prolonged behaviour disturbances may need the advice of a psychologist or community nurse or a consultant psychiatrist specializing in problems of mental handicap.

THE NEED FOR SPECIALIZED HELP

Professor Joan Bicknell sees a vital need for help from a multi-disciplinary community mental handicap team, especially the psychologist, the psychiatrist and the community nurse, when the grief reactions are (a) prolonged to the extent that the quality of life is permanently threatened or (b) so severe that the presenting symptom requires treatment immediately, or (c) if there is an unusual presentation which is likely to be misdiagnosed and lead to inappropriate responses on the part of the care-giver. She illustrates these points with the following two stories.

John

Aged ten, John was referred to the psychiatrist in the mental handicap service for consideration for long-term hospital care. His presenting symptom was self-induced vomiting, which had already excluded him from his ESN(S) school and a children's home where he often stayed in holiday time. His parents, unable to cope with him, could see no alternative to hospital.

The history was that John had found his beloved grandfather dead in his chair six months previously. Since he had a severe mental handicap it was assumed that he did not understand and could not go to the funeral. He spent two weeks in the children's home while the family grieved over their loss and buried their loved one. John's vomiting started soon afterwards and so did irritability and aggression towards his younger sister. All the symptoms cleared with explanation that this was John's way of grieving, a visit to his grandfather's grave and a course of antidepressants. John soon returned to school, to the children's home and became his old happy self.

The link between his grandfather's death and John's symptoms had not been made by his family and John was at risk of symptomatic treatment for his vomiting and admission to a long-stay hospital.

James

This story illustrates a situation of multiple loss and a prolonged and severe bereavement response. James was mentally handicapped and lived at home with his parents. His father died first and James and his mother then lived together. As she became older and disabled, James's skills complemented hers and they managed to meet each other's needs. Together with their dog, they formed a close-knit family.

James's mother had been dead on the floor for two days when the barking of their dog attracted attention. James was taken into a pleasant small group home the same day, but was not allowed to keep his dog. He helped prepare for the funeral but decided not to go, and no one persuaded him to do so. He never went back to the family home and refused to walk down that road. He was immediately subjected to a course of surgical treatment for a deformed arm, a new dental plate was made, spectacles were provided for him and his medication for epilepsy was changed. One year later his epilepsy became out of control despite many years with few fits. James managed his own medication but it transpired that he was mixing up his tablets on purpose and often not taking them. On referral to a psychiatrist it was clear that he was deeply depressed and that his mismanagement of his epilepsy was a 'cry for help' and, some might say, a suicide attempt.

In treatment he was taken back to the family home and reintroduced to photographs of his mother and his dog, and he visited his mother's grave with the psychiatrist and was encouraged to cry there. After two years of psychotherapy James was well again and had adjusted to his new way of life.

Bicknell says that it is perhaps surprising that so many mentally handicapped people manage to work through a bereavement and regain their former personality and composure; in many cases this seems to be a tribute to the resilience of the handicapped person rather than to the sensitivity of the services. She recommends that as some mentally handicapped people may need specialized help with their bereavement problems (as did John and James), professionals should be aware of the indications for such help and the skills that are required for the assistance to be effective.

FANTASIES IN GRIEF

It is normal for newly bereaved people to look for the dead person or think that they have seen or heard them. They look down the garden expecting to see them digging or think that they hear their footsteps on the stairs. They may even fantasize a little that the person is still there and has not really died. The habits of years dwindle away only slowly and it takes time for the senses to adapt to the absence of a person long lived with, whose movements have been part of one's existence. Perhaps, too, the fantasies have a purpose in easing the hurt of immediate and total realization.

Some widows with a mentally handicapped son or daughter at home prolong the normal fantasies of bereavement and elaborate on them, pretending that the father is still alive and is in hospital or has gone on a journey. These widows could talk quite openly about what they were doing and could give reasons for it. What probably begins as an inability to tell their handicapped son or daughter the truth – intended to be just a temporary delay in doing so – develops over the months into a continuing pretence going well beyond the realms of normal grief fantasies. It is easy for a widow to maintain such fantasies when living a very isolated life with a mentally handicapped person who lacks intellectual understanding and verbal ability. When this happens it would seem to be a matter of some concern to family friends and professional workers because the mentally handicapped person is being denied the truth and the widows are denying themselves full realization of the loss.

It is understandable if some widows cannot bring themselves to tell their sons and daughters about the loss of somebody dear to them. It is inexcusable if professionals maintain a story that a dead relative is still alive. For instance, the staff in one hostel were pretending that the dead father of one of the residents was still alive and ringing up once a week to ask how she was. Other residents who knew that this was not true said they were very worried about the staff 'telling lies' as it was 'not fair' and 'she should know that her dad has died'.

There are several possible reasons why staff may be reluctant to speak the truth:

1 They may be afraid of losing control of their own emotions in talking about a sad event.
2 They may be unsure how they will manage to comfort and control the emotions of the mentally handicapped person, who might break down in tears or anger about the death.
3 They may believe that the mentally handicapped person is like a small child and will not understand the death, so it is not worth trying to explain it.
4 They may think that mentally handicapped people do not have the same emotions as people without handicaps so it does not matter if they are not told the truth.

It would seem that staff may be differentiating between what is right for people who are not handicapped and what is right for those who are. They may also lack confidence in their own professional abilities in working with people and taking responsibility for coping with sad events when necessary. It is understandable if professionals are worried about losing their own self-control and crying when telling the mentally handicapped person the sad truth, but crying is normal and to cry together and to grow closer through comforting one another is better than an evasion of the truth which merely leads to a negative pretence.

Perhaps professionals underestimate mentally handicapped people's strengths in being able to cope with normal human experiences and support other people. Some of the bereaved mentally handicapped people met in this research had been a source of tremendous help within their families when the death occurred, and at day centres and in hospitals and hostels it has often been the mentally handicapped people who have been most helpful to their fellow students and residents and staff when a bereavement has occurred.

TELLING THE SAD NEWS

It is important that the correct words are used in breaking news of a death: dead, death, died. These words should not be avoided, for they are part of the basic language of mankind and describe human experiences which belong to our perception of existence. After the news has been broken it may be possible to offer comfort by using traditional religious phrases such as 'gone to Jesus' if the person has a religious faith. When a person is placed in a residential facility it is important that staff respect the mentally handicapped person's religious beliefs, especially as they relate to what happens to a person after death.

The bereaved person should never be given bad news and then left alone for a long period or handed over to somebody else. The person who broke the news should try to remain with them for several hours and let them talk about what has happened. There should never be an abrupt change of subject or an attempt to 'jolly along' the person, and they should never be rushed into social activities straightaway, but unfortunately this does occur, because some residential care staff believe that the best way to help bereaved mentally handicapped people is to thrust them into activities which will 'take them out of themselves'.

CONCLUSIONS AND RECOMMENDATIONS

What can be done to ease some of the problems that face mentally handicapped people after a bereavement? The sort of help and support that is given will depend very much on local developments and the preparations made in advance by professionals. An inappropriate residential placement is less likely in those districts where there is an efficiently working community mental handicap team and a well-staffed community mental handicap nursing service. In such districts the parents and the mentally handicapped client are likely to know the local professionals. There may also be appropriate local residential care, and mentally handicapped people may be helped to live independent lives in homes of their own within reach of their families *before* their parents become elderly and die.

My research findings suggest the following recommendations; they have been discussed with professionals and parents at a number of seminars and conferences between 1981 and 1984, and some have already been put into practice in some districts in Britain.

1 All professionals working with mentally handicapped people should inform themselves of normal grief reactions. They should make contact with local branches of CRUSE, the organization concerned for bereaved people (Head office (1985): CRUSE House, 126 Sheen Road, Richmond, Surrey TW9 1UR).
2 Everyone coming into contact with bereaved mentally handicapped people should respect their right to be told the truth and to grieve.
3 Parents should try to have a plan of action in the event of deaths (for example, as in the Harrow Weald document). It could also be helpful if local branches of MENCAP had links with local branches of CRUSE.
4 Day centre staff should have a plan of action for the event of a student becoming bereaved while at the centre.
5 Immediate removal to an unfamiliar residential facility should be avoided when a bereavement occurs. It would be kinder for the bereaved person to have a professional or volunteer or friend staying with them in their own home for the first two or three nights and then to move gradually into the residential facility.
6 Assessment should be avoided in the early months following a bereavement, because the mentally handicapped person may be functioning at a lower level of ability during this critical time.
7 Multiple residential care placements should be avoided.
8 Every attempt should be made to ensure continuity of staff in the residential facility, with an assigned member of the care staff wherever possible.
9 If the bereavement results in the person losing their home they should have a full explanation about what has happened to it and they must be permitted to take into residential care some belongings which are important to them.

RECOMMENDED READING

Feifal H (Ed.) (1965) *The Meaning of Death*. New York: McGraw-Hill.
Lewis CS (1961) *A Grief Observed*. London: Faber & Faber.
Marris P (1974) *Loss and Change*. Boston: Routledge & Kegan Paul.

MENCAP (1983) *Emotional Responses of Mentally Handicapped People*. Report of the 16th Spring Conference on Mental Retardation, Exeter 1983. Exeter: South West Region of MENCAP. (Available from Royal MENCAP Bookshop, 123 Golden Lane, London EC1Y 0RT.)

Oswin M (1981) *Bereavement and Mentally Handicapped People*. London: King's Fund Centre.

Parkes CM (1972) *Bereavement*. London: Tavistock.

Pincus L (1976) *Death in the Family*. London: Faber & Faber.

Richardson R (1980) *Losses: Talking about Bereavement*. Shepton Mallet, Somerset: Open Books.

Toynbee A, Mant AK, Smart N, Hinton J, Yudkin S, Rhode E, Heywood R & Price HH (1968) *Man's Concern with Death*. London: Hodder & Stoughton.

Wertheimer A (1982) *Living for the Present*. CMH Enquiry Paper 9. London: Campaign for Mentally Handicapped People.

PART 4
EDUCATION

Chapter 18
Early Intervention for the Child

CLIFF C. CUNNINGHAM & P. SLOPER

This chapter is primarily concerned with intervention procedures for the mentally handicapped child in the pre-school years. A number of general points will orient the reader to the chapter:

1 The infants considered here are those who have a recognized primary condition such as Down's syndrome, associated with delayed development or future intellectual retardation, or whose development in the first months of life is so impaired that future severe retardation is highly probable. However, the presence of such a condition does not necessarily predict the extent of future handicap. A number of infants with such conditions will not eventually fall into the handicap range (i.e., less than two standard deviations below the norm on IQ scales). Indeed, an early pessimistic prognosis can lead to such low expectations on the part of those providing for the care of the infant that a degree of *secondary* handicap ensues – an example of a self-fulfilling prophecy.

2 Most of the information available in this area has arisen from work with Down's syndrome infants, this being the commonest single condition in mental handicap and easily recognizable at birth. The prognosis for this condition is probably one of the more favourable of the recognized conditions associated with mental handicap. Thus, the findings from Down's syndrome infants can provide useful models, but generalizations to other conditions must be made with caution.

3 Whilst there has been a decrease in the incidence of some mentally handicapping conditions, particularly of Down's syndrome, there has also been a decreased rate of mortality. This has resulted in an increase in prevalence, particularly of more severely handicapped children. No longer can the birth of such children be considered as a short-term problem for parents or society; instead the provision of an education for a normal life-span is required.

4 Increasing emphasis is being given to family care for such children. This calls for services which will help the family care for the handicapped child in the home and for changes in attitudes and support from the community.

5 In the case of some conditions which result in mental handicap, particularly those related to errors of metabolism such as phenylketonuria, galactosaemia and hypothyroidism (e.g. Bickel and Grubel-Kaiser, 1982), medical treatments have been notably successful. However, in the majority of conditions results have been less successful. Medical treatments of Down's syndrome, for example using thyroid or pituitary extracts, vitamins, siccacell, 5-hydroxytryptophan and serotonin therapy have not produced sustained beneficial effects (Coleman, 1973; Share, 1976) and do not appear to be any more successful than providing increased support for parents and stimulation for the infant.

The most recent series of studies in this area followed Harrell et al.'s (1981) report that the treatment of Down's syndrome children with thyroid, vitamin and mineral supplements resulted in beneficial effects on intellectual development and physical appearance. However, replications using double-blind trials (e.g. Weathers, 1983) have failed to confirm the results, and find no differences between those given the vitamin supplements and those given placebos.

Medical treatment has been most successful in improving the health of handicapped infants and in the early identification and treatment of additional biochemical or sensory dysfunction.

6 The increased knowledge of early child development and the evidence from research of the importance of stimulation during infancy, have considerably altered the conception of the infant

from one of being a mere passive recipient of information to one of an organism actively participating in interactions and of being responsive to early stimulation. If this is important for the normal infant, it is all the more so for handicapped infants, who are less well equipped to profit from their experiences.

We begin with a brief consideration of the 'nature' of mental handicap, followed by an overview of the main principles and methods of diagnosis, assessment and treatment that have been used. After this, research studies relating to the efficacy of intervention are briefly reviewed, and the last section deals with current issues and implications for future developments.

PRIMARY AND SECONDARY HANDICAP

There are two kinds of restriction impinging on the development of handicapped children: those resulting from primary conditions such as chromosomal anomaly, sensory or central nervous system damage and those resulting from secondary conditions such as parental handling, environmental deprivations or inadequate treatment of the primary conditions. Figure 18.1 gives an example of the interrelationship between primary and secondary handicap. The figure presents the cumulative percentages for the attainment of sitting without support. It compares the results of a number of studies of Down's syndrome infants with one study of normal infants.

If we assume that the curve for the normal infants (curve 1) reflects the 'maturational' development of sitting without support (that is, whilst it may be possible to shift the curve more to the left using training procedures, it will maintain the same shape) curve 2, consisting of infants who received intervention, which closely approximates to the shape of curve 1, may reflect the 'maturational' curve for Down's syndrome infants. Thus, the distance between curve 1 and curve 2 might represent the delay in development directly resulting from the inherent handicapping condition. This is called the primary handicapping condition. The distance between curves 2, 3, 4, 5 and 6 might reflect the effect of varying experiences which influence the development of sitting in such infants. This is called the secondary handicapping condition. Curves 5 and 6, which are for predominantly institutionalized Down's syndrome infants indicate far more delay in attaining the behaviour than curves 2, 3 and 4, for home-reared infants.

These secondary conditions are complex and as yet not fully determined; however, a number of points can be made. These relate to (a) the level of stimulation provided by the parents, (b) deprivation of experiences as a result of the primary condition, and (c) variability within the mentally handicapped population.

The parents may or may not provide the same level of stimulation as given to the normal child. They may believe that the child is unable to gain from such stimulation. They may be fearful of doing 'something wrong' and as a result not even try to do things which intuitively they feel are necessary. They may prevent the child from mastering skills such as feeding, dressing, walking and so on because it is more convenient to do things for the child, or because they have such low expectations of the child's potential that they feel such skills will never be attained. Their work or family commitments or lack of family or service support and organizational ability may not allow them to find the time to provide the opportunities for the child to learn and develop. Through embarrassment or inconvenience they may not take the child out, particularly if the child looks different or is difficult to manage. Exclusion from such everyday experiences as shopping, meeting a variety of people and seeing different places may be particularly damaging for the handicapped child.

The child may also be deprived of many experiences as a result of the primary condition. Extremely slow development on the part of the infant, together with the parents' inability to note small changes or understand the significance of small responses, may lead the parents to give up their efforts to stimulate the child – to settle for less than is possible. In this case a detailed knowledge of child development and training in observation can be most useful.

There may be 'hidden deprivation' effects even in 'good-quality homes'. For example, Francis (1971) and Jeffree and Cashdan (1971) reported observable differences in the type of interactions which took place between the parent and normal siblings and the parent and the handicapped child.

It is now generally recognized that the naturally occurring patterns of interaction between parent and child are influential on early development. But such interactions may be adversely affected by the child's handicap. Several studies with Down's syndrome infants from the first months of life have reported delayed and qualitatively different social signalling behaviours, including eye-contact, smiling and vocalizing, and at an older age chuckling

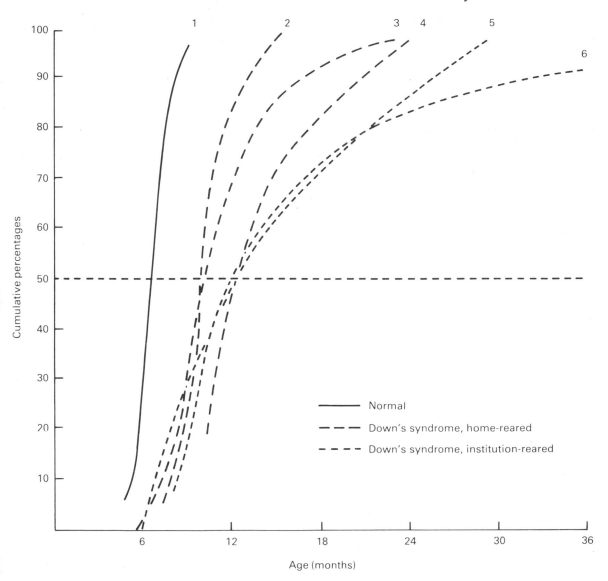

Fig. 18.1 Age for sitting without support.

1 Neligan & Prudham (1969). Normal infants n = 3831. Born 1960–62 City of Newcastle. Data collected by health visitors from parent reports and direct observation.

2 Cunningham (1976). Down's syndrome infants n = 67 home-reared. Born 1973–77 Manchester area. Data collected by researchers at six-weekly assessments in home.

3 Share & Veale (1974). Down's syndrome infants n = 123 home-reared. Born 1960–65 New Zealand. Data obtained from parent recollections.

4 Carr (1975). Down's syndrome infants n = 47 (40 home-reared, 7 institution-reared). Born 1963–64 London area. Data obtained by researchers at six-monthly assessments in home.

5 Taken from several studies noted in Penrose & Smith (1966), indicating range and means and including both institution-reared and home-reared infants.

6 Share & Veale (1974). Down's syndrome infants n = 26 institution-reared.

The data from the Carr (1975) and Cunningham (1976) studies is for the item 'sits alone steadily' from the Bayley Scales of Infant Development, which quote a range of 5 to 9 months and a mean of 6.6 months for this item. The remaining studies use the Gesell definition, 'sits unsupported and erect for one minute' (which includes no support by the arms). The range quoted from the Bayley standardization and that of the Neligan and Prudham (1969) survey are very similar. The Neligan and Prudham (1969) and the Share and Veale (1974) surveys are both based upon parent recollections of the age when the behaviour was attained, whilst the Cunningham and Carr studies are based upon assessments by qualified personnel. Thus, the former studies may have some error, erring toward a slightly earlier age than the latter. Despite the discrepancies, the studies are still quite consistent.

and laughter (e.g. Cicchetti and Sroufe, 1976; Berger and Cunningham, 1981, 1983). This appears to be linked to higher levels of maternal stimulation during interactions of mothers and their Down's syndrome children, as compared with non-handicapped pairs (Buckhalt et al., 1978; Buim et al., 1974), which becomes manifest in a more directive maternal style of interaction (Jones, 1977) with more vocal clashes and less reciprocal turn-taking (Berger and Cunningham, 1983). Richards (1974) noted for non-handicapped infants that if mothers did not allow the baby time to return a smile but instead continued to 'bombard' the infant, then the infant would often become tense and fretful. In attempting to cope with the anxieties generated for their infants, therefore, there appears to be a natural tendency for some mothers to 'bombard' the infant, which might produce a habit of intrusive interactions. Recently, Crawley and Spiker (1983) have reported that mothers of Down's syndrome two-year-olds, who combine directiveness and sensitivity in ways that provide stimulation value, appear to have more confident children. Also, they noted great individual differences and that almost half the mothers in their sample were rated as sensitive and not directive and intrusive. Affleck et al. (1982) argue that unless parents find their interactions with the infant pleasurable and satisfying they are unlikely to learn effective intervention and interactive skills.

In some recent work we have found that discussing interactions with parents, and advising them to imitate rather than initiate infant responses for short periods of time, to use more slowed-down and phased interactions and to elaborate child behaviour increased child responses and initiations and the interaction appeared more pleasurable. However, this has to be done with care as there are considerable individual differences between mothers and between infants and in some cases, when the infant fails to respond during such advisory sessions, mothers can become even more anxious. It is a case of patiently building upon mothers' own intuitive styles rather than intruding and imposing an incompatible alternative.

It is not only in the earliest behaviours that the behavioural difficulties of the child influence interaction with the environment. Considerable evidence exists to support the presence of learning difficulties in mentally handicapped children and adults, particularly in attentional mechanisms and in their ability to learn spontaneously from their experiences, for instance in the ability to direct their attention to relevant stimuli, to analyse and synthesize incoming information, to abstract and generalize and to do this without the aid of an adult (Clarke and Clarke, 1974). Unless the parent is aware of these difficulties and is guided in methods to compensate for them the infant will receive less than appropriate stimulation.

There is considerable variability within the mentally handicapped population. If one compares the range of age for sitting without support in the non-handicapped infants with the range in the Down's syndrome infants, it is immediately apparent that the latter has a wider distribution.

This conception of mental handicap has many implications for practice. Firstly, it strongly supports the need for early intervention. Secondly, and perhaps of importance to the physician faced with the parents of a recently diagnosed infant, it cautions against too-simplistic predictions of future attainments.

The greater variability found in the population reduces the possibility of predicting future individual progress. It is particularly noticeable in the quoted example that for the slower infants the delay in development due to the secondary handicap appears to be even greater than that due to the primary handicap, possibly because they have greater learning difficulties. If one accepts that development is hierarchical and that later abilities are built upon early ones, then the cumulative effects of the secondary handicap may be considerable. When we examine older handicapped children and adults, it is possible that a relatively large proportion of the handicap is secondary and could have been prevented. Thus, it is unwise to base future prognosis of the degree of handicap on observations of older individuals who have not received optimal stimulation from the early years.

Finally, all too often the primary condition and the degree of resulting handicap are confused as being the same. The loss of sight in one eye represents a 50% loss of the visual receptive mechanism, yet the resulting handicap is relatively small and is determined by the individual's lifestyle. The level of handicap will also be determined by the overall ability of the individual. A partial loss of hearing in a child of normal intelligence may have less handicapping consequences than the same level of impairment in a mentally retarded child who may not be as able to compensate for the loss. Indeed, the interaction between the two impairments may produce a greater handicap than the sum of the separate disabilities.

To summarize, in assessing any child one has to consider the primary handicap, the specific nature of the environmental experiences available to that child and the extent to which these are conducive to cognitive, emotional and physical growth.

Thus, a primary aim of early intervention is to ensure that the effects of secondary handicap are reduced to a minimum by the provision of the necessary environmental conditions to optimize the child's developmental potential.

DIAGNOSIS, ASSESSMENT AND TREATMENT PLANNING

Diagnosis and assessment are the necessary first steps to treatment. They have two functions: (a) to predict future problems and hence indicate preventive treatment and (b) to analyse existing problems and prescribe current treatment. For the parent of the mentally handicapped infant both functions are crucial. They are desperately in need of information which will tell them what the future may hold — what the child may achieve or may not achieve. Many also need to know what they can do now to help their infant. If treatment can prevent the occurrence of a secondary handicap and should commence as soon as possible, early diagnosis is essential.

Mental handicap is diagnosed in infants when a condition is recognized which is consistently associated with delayed development and future intellectual impairment or when assessments of the infant's rate of development indicate abnormally slow progress. Diagnosis of mental handicap in the infants should always lead to assessments of their actual and their potential development. A common first step is the assessment of the infant on standardized developmental tests. Standardized scales are made up of descriptions of typical infant behaviours arranged in hierarchical order. A number are closed tests only available to 'qualified' personnel (e.g. Bayley, 1969: Griffith, 1960); others (e.g. Illingworth, 1963; Sheridan, 1968) have been developed by paediatricians for the purpose of developmental screening. These scales indicate both the rate and the level of development. The level is expressed by the mental age (MA) and the rate by the developmental quotient (DQ). The mental age represents the mean score for the population at a given chronological age.* Generally the DQ is

calculated by dividing the MA by the chronological age and multiplying by 100.[†] The same method is used in intelligence tests to arrive at the IQ, and in both cases the mean quotient for the population is 100. Thus, the infant or child is considered to be mentally handicapped when the DQ or MA is significantly below average. By correlating the DQ with the later IQ it is possible to ask how much these early assessments foretell later ones. In the case of mentally handicapped populations the correlations are higher than with non-handicapped children, and developmental tests are considered to be more efficient predictors of later ability for such infants. Even so, they are not high enough to allow useful predictions of individual scores in the first year or two (Carr, 1975). However, as noted by Carr and confirmed in our research, a Down's syndrome infant who scored at a high level between 10 and 36 months is unlikely to score at the lowest level at four years or later, and vice versa, providing reasonable opportunities for development have been given. In cases where there is a likelihood of stimulatory deprivation (either hidden or manifest) then children with low scores can make rapid progress when remedial treatment is given. Thus, one has to take account of environmental factors. Of children with severe delay and multiple handicaps who show little evidence of development in the first year of life despite attempts to encourage development, most, if not all, remain in the profound range of handicap.

After the age of two years the correlations become increasingly high and more predictive for most handicapped children and 'offer a valuable source of intellectual estimate by the time the child is four years of age' (Fishler et al., 1965).

Thus, where infants are found to be functioning at a level significantly lower than average (more than two standard deviations below the norm) on developmental tests, there is a high probability that they will show some level of retardation in later years. Certainly, such findings suggest the need for treatment. However, neither the recognition of the condition nor developmental assessments before the age of two can be used with confidence to predict individual progress for the majority of children.

---

* If the mean score at eight months of age is 21, then any infant gaining a score of 21 can be designated as having an MA of eight months regardless of chronological age.

[†] There is some dissatisfaction with this method of deriving a quotient as it fails to take into account the variance of the population. The Bayley Scales of Infant Development, for example, use this variance and produce a developmental index (DI) not a DQ. This has implications for practice. For example, an infant aged 18 months may obtain a raw score of 103 on the mental scale. This would produce an MA of 12 months and a DI of 50. However, if the DQ is computed it would be $12/18 \times 100 = 66$.

Although standardized scales are extremely useful in pinpointing the child's developmental level in relation to established norms, their use alone does not give the comprehensive picture of the child's development which is needed for intervention and prediction. Thus, Illingworth's (1963) apparent success in predicting mental handicap in the first year of life is not just a result of using standardized tests of infant development, but is also a consequence of using these instruments in conjunction with a very full consideration of the child's previous history, rate of development and relevant physical and neurological findings. By taking into account clinical impressions, medical history and environmental factors in making an appraisal of the developmental abilities, one is more closely approximating the 'spirit' in which developmental testing was pioneered by Gesell (1939).

Within this appraisal, recent evidence, reviewed below, indicates the influence on development of such factors as parental education, family support networks, marital relationships, home organization, maternal involvement with the child and provision of appropriate play activities. This suggests that these should also be included more formally in early assessment. For example, the HOME Inventory (Bradley and Caldwell, 1979) contains 45 items in six categories, ranging from emotional and verbal responsivity to opportunities for variety in daily activities and is scored in the home through observation and interview.

Predictions also appear to improve when a clinical appraisal includes such factors as the quality of response, the child's general alertness, responsiveness, concentration and attention. This had led to the increasing exploration of temperament and infant behaviour scales (for example, the Infant Behaviour Record of the Bayley (1969) Scales of Infant Development), which may prove useful for predicting likely cognitive and emotional development and, more usefully, relationships between parent and child and factors that might produce stress in families of handicapped children (e.g. Beckman, 1983).

Concern has not just been directed at the limited perspective given by standardized tests but also at their appropriateness for mentally handicapped children when they have been developed on non-handicapped populations. Thus, the child's disabilities may distort the results and this raises doubts as to the validity of the assessment. One approach has been to modify current tests in relation to specific disabilities; an example is the Reynell–Zinkin scales for young visually handicapped children (Reynell, 1979). Zelazo (1979) and Kearsley (1981) have demonstrated the feasibility of perceptual–cognitive approaches to assessment which do not rely upon the motor responses typical of standard scales.

Another concern is the atypical developmental progress common to many handicapped children. Non-sequential development may be missed by keeping strictly to test protocols and normal developmental comparisons and so important information in constructing treatment could be missed. Most mentally handicapped children have plateaux – periods when little or no measurable change can be ascertained on standard developmental scales or their sub-scales.

An obvious problem is that if the child is assessed at the beginning of a plateau the DQ will be higher than if the assessment was at the end of the period. Similarly, whilst the mental age will remain the same the assessor may draw different implications as to the child's potential from these assessments. Thus, regular and frequent assessment is essential if a more reliable statement of potential is to be obtained.

These plateaux should not be considered as times of no development. Whilst often they are apparently related to specific difficulties, they frequently correspond to periods when the quality of response is being improved, and much consolidation of the behaviours is taking place. This is apparently a slower process in mentally handicapped children. They also reflect the difference in difficulty for such children between items of the developmental test. The size of the step between items is apparently neither too large nor too small for normally developing infants; however, for mentally handicapped infants far more information is needed of what behaviours are developing between these items. This is particularly important when one begins to use developmental scales to direct treatment.

Because of such concern, and because there is no purpose in assessing unless it leads to treatment, there has been an increasing movement away from normative testing alone to assessment in the context of treatment.

Treatment

A full assessment using developmental tests, detailed checklists, and observation of the child's behaviours in all spheres of development, motor, cognitive, social and emotional, provides a sound basis on which to plan treatment. Many intervention programmes have successfully used developmental scales as a basis for their curriculum. These scales provide:

1 A description of the hierarchical order of development of behaviours, each one leading to the next.
2 An indication, taken from the age norms, of when behaviours can be expected.
3 Measures of present performance, rather than future potential and hence some indication of particular strengths and weaknesses.
4 A profile of the range of behaviours which make up normal child development, which by implication are necessary for the normal development of the whole child.

The hierarchical order of behaviours (developmental milestones) is generally well established, but there are particular exceptions. In the area of gross motor development, normal children frequently do not crawl; instead, they bottom-hitch, and some apparently walk before they crawl. Such discrepancies are even more noticeable with mentally handicapped infants. Down's syndrome infants, for example, frequently clap hands and throw balls before they crawl or walk, even though such items appear later on developmental scales. Similarly, some behaviours seem more sensitive to treatment – for example scribbling with a pencil or looking at picture books – and so appear earlier in the repertoire of 'trained' infants than would be suggested by their order in the scales. Such observations reinforce the contention that it is necessary to look at the particular behaviours in terms of the prerequisite skills necessary to attain them rather than normative placement on a scale.

Such scales also, at present, emphasize gross motor and sensorimotor development and are less informed on socio-emotional behaviours and such areas as alertness, responsiveness and attentional skills. It is to be hoped that increasing knowledge of these areas will be used to enlarge these curricula and so maintain as complete a development of the whole child as possible (see, for example Seibert and Hogan, 1983).

Thus, whilst assessment on a developmental scale provides an initial statement of the child's strengths and weaknesses, it is necessary to follow this with more detailed observation and analysis of the skills that might develop next. This is important for mentally handicapped infants, as the step-size (the level of difficulty and the time it will take to develop the next behaviour) between behavioural items

noted in the scales may be too large or too complex for them. The more severe the mental handicap, the more likely this will be so, and the more essential is a detailed analysis of the required skill. Thus one moves from the normative basis of child development to an approach which emphasizes specification of the present level of skill or behaviour and the next smallest step required to achieve a new behaviour. The Behaviour Assessment Battery (Kiernan and Jones, 1982) is an example of criterion reference assessment. It attempts to define crucial early behaviours operationally, arrive at performance levels and sequence them in a series of small steps. The Battery has been devised specifically for profoundly handicapped individuals and can be used by psychologists, doctors, nurses and teachers.

The assessment constitutes the first stage in planning treatment. The next stage is to decide what it is we want the child to acquire. This is something which is relevant to the needs of the child and which he is ready to learn – that is, which we can expect him to acquire in the immediate, not the distant, future.

Developmental checklists and scales also provide a means for recording progress – an essential encouragement to the intervener, whether parent or professional. Parents also feel the need for some idea of what their child may achieve and when this can be reasonably expected. In the case of Down's syndrome, several studies have collected data which can provide some information (e.g. Carr, 1975; Share and Veale, 1974) and our own 'norms' are given in the appendix to this chapter. But it is crucial to understand that these are based on present samples who may not have been provided with optimal stimulation, so they may not indicate optimal progress.

As an example of a detailed programme, let us consider the behaviour of finding a hidden object under a cloth. This is part of object permanence. It appears at about 8–9 months in normal development. In most standard infant tests the previous item related to this is looking for a fallen object – one dropped off the edge of the table – at about 6–7 months. Thus, according to developmental scales, there is approximately two months between these items. If the handicapped infant is progressing at a slower rate then this difference could be much longer. Thus, having established that the child is beginning object permanence in looking for the dropped object, we must ask what are the next steps leading to finding an object hidden under a cloth and later under a cup. One sequence of behaviours could be the following:

1 When the infant is holding a noisy rattle and looking at it, cover it with a light cloth.

The criterial behaviour or objective is that the child will remove the cloth and look at or manipulate the rattle on say four or five successive attempts.

In practice, behaviours occur which themselves can be seen as sub-criterial behaviours or smaller steps. Typically, the infant:

  (i) drops the rattle and plays with the cloth, showing no further interest in the rattle;
  (ii) drops the rattle so as to play with the cloth, but then attends to the rattle when he or she realizes it has dropped or hears it land.
  (iii) shakes the rattle and cloth, often displacing the cloth;
  (iv) pulls the cloth off with the other hand and attends to it but still holds on to the rattle, sometimes 'banging' the two together;
  (v) removes the cloth, and attends to the rattle.

These sub-behaviours vary greatly according to the child and his or her ability level. Thus, observation of what the child does during the attempts to attain the behaviour are crucial. Frequently, difficulties are observed and new objectives must be worked out. Hence, the teaching is also part of the testing and vice versa. *If one has a sufficiently detailed curriculum the need for testing is redundant and one just teaches.*

The next steps, all of which could be further broken down depending upon the individual child's interaction with the teaching situation, might be:

2 Removes cloth from a silent object held in the hand.
3 Takes an object from the table, when the hand and object are covered by the cloth at the moment of grasping.
4 Removes cloth from a large noisy object, such as a squeezy doll or ball, which is placed on the table and gently moved.
5 Removes cloth from a half-hidden smaller object.
6 Removes cloth from a large silent object which is gently moved.
7 Removes cloth from still, silent objects of any size.

In all cases the infant would be expected to attend to the hidden object either with sustained visual inspection or reach and manipulation.

In teaching the behaviours a number of basic techniques are useful. Firstly, it is essential to ensure that the child is *attending* to the relevant parts of the behaviour. Thus, in placing the object on the table

one would make sure the infant was looking at it before hiding it. Indeed, one can frequently make the task easier by waiting until the infant starts to reach for the desired object before covering it.

Secondly, *prompts* are used. These may be physical prompts, such as guiding the child's hand to the cloth, forming a grip and removing the cloth. These can be particularly useful with mentally handicapped infants. There are visual prompts, such as shaking the object or pointing to it to attract attention. There are auditory prompts, such as tapping the object or using a noise-making object to attract attention, and also verbal prompts, such as 'look', 'find', 'give' and so on, which instruct the child to perform a particular behaviour. Prompts are useful to make the step-size smaller and to shape the new behaviour by a series of small steps which gradually become more and more like the final criterial behaviour. Most people intuitively use prompts but seldom plan how to reduce them. The art of teaching the child is knowing when to use the prompts and how to fade them out. Each completion of a successful behaviour or sub-behaviour should be reinforced by rewarding the child immediately after the behaviour has been demonstrated. A reward is anything which increases the likelihood of the behaviour being repeated. Simply, it is something which gives the child pleasure. Obviously, an interest in the task is the best means of rewarding the child and in the above example one would choose objects which the child appears to want and will try to attain. However, telling the child he is 'good', smiling, tickling, hugging and kissing can all be used and are used naturally by most parents. With very impaired children it is sometimes necessary to resort to more tangible rewards such as food or drink, but this is something of a special case. The important principle in using rewards is to be consistent and immediate.

In essence one is trying to *shape* up the child's behaviour by building on current behaviour (strengths), using prompts if necessary to ensure reasonable approximation and rewarding successive approximations until the new behaviour is achieved. One can view this task analysis – step-by-step, with immediate contingent rewards – as a form of rote training or conditioning. This would be particularly so if emphasis is placed on contingent rewards as the main factor in promoting behaviour change (learning). Alternatively, one can view the approach as an attempt to communicate with the child and overcome his inherent learning difficulties. For example, by breaking down a task in small steps, ensuring the child attends to the relevant aspect rather than complex input, by linking these steps together and shaping the new behaviour, one is compensating for the difficulties of directed relevant attention, abstraction and synthesis noted previously. In this sense the reward is important feedback, to tell the child he is doing it correctly. From this viewpoint, analysis and communication are emphasized and there is less stress on contingent rewarding.

Step-by-step shaping reduces the likelihood of failure for the child and so should reduce the possibility of loss of confidence, self-esteem and learning to avoid new or complex situations. Similarly, self-esteem will be more likely to develop if the interactions are not intrusive but sensitively directed. By allowing the child to control events and alter the programme one demonstrates to the child respect for the child's own right and ability to act on his or her environment. Thus, rigid enforcement of the programme may be undesirable and it is more appropriate to use the structure to direct how one elaborates on the child's own initiations.

In dealing with behaviour problems the emphasis is on establishing the relationship between the antecedent event which 'triggers off' the behaviour and the consequences which are reinforcing (rewarding) the behaviour and so maintaining it.

Whether building new behaviours or getting rid of unwanted behaviours parents will need the skills of observation, analysis, prompting, shaping and use of rewards. These constitute one basic component of early parent training and are common to the majority of approaches taken in parent involvement.

However, approaches vary considerably in how much emphasis is placed on the degree of systematic application and rigour. This can be illustrated using the object permanence example in relation to recording and assessing the child's progress. Since most handicapped children vary considerably, each stimulatory programme devised has to be treated as an experiment. One can never be sure that it will actually work or know how children will differ in their responses to it. Thus, a most useful approach is to record continuously during the teaching. Such recording methods use frequency, duration or time taken to respond. In the example of finding the hidden object one can record the number of times the child successfully uncovered and obtained the object. This would be the frequency.

In special cases of poor responsiveness or poor alertness, one might also note the time taken to respond and complete the behaviour. If one were training grasping of an object, sitting or standing, one might measure duration – how long an object was held or how long the child sat or stood. As well as this one may need to record whether a prompt was used to achieve the behaviour or not. Figure 18.2 shows a chart for finding an object hidden under a cloth.

Each day five trials were recorded at the end of the training sessions. As can be seen, the first day required constant prompting, but by the fourth day the infant had succeeded in five successful performances and thus it was decided to move on to the next step in the programme. This was achieved quite quickly and the child was ready for the third step. If no change was recorded over several days one would assume something was lacking in the training and re-analyse the task, the infant's abilities and the teaching techniques.

The detailed breakdown and recording techniques noted here are time-consuming and one must ask to what extent they are necessary and practical,

DATE	1.2.78					2.2.78					4.2.78					5.2.78				
TRIAL	1	2	3	4	5	1	2	3	4	5	1	2	3	4	5	1	2	3	4	5
1 Uncovers noisy rattle held in hand — with prompts	√	√	√	√	√	√	√	√			√									
1 Uncovers noisy rattle held in hand — without prompts									√	√		√	√	√	√	√	√	√	√	√

DATE	6.2.78					7.2.78														
2 Uncovers silent object held in hand — with prompts	√	√																		
2 Uncovers silent object held in hand — without prompts			√	√	√	√	√	√	√	√										

Fig. 18.2 Recording chart: finding the object hidden under a cloth.

particularly for the parent. Many parents can certainly understand and use these techniques but do not really have the time to develop them (this is discussed later). Thus, professional support in being able to provide objectives, task analysis and recording methods as well as analyse difficulties is important. The use of such techniques is relatively new and the extent to which they are necessary in relation to the individual child or area of development is unclear. The general answer is that the more handicapped the child – that is, the greater the child's difficulties and the slower the progress – the more one needs to get into very detailed analysis, teaching and recording.

However, the more detailed and vigorous the approach the more it has to be restricted to a small number of activities, and this may lead to other areas of development being neglected. Because of this, some intervention approaches have given parents a broader range of activities to be encouraged in a less vigorous way. They do not emphasize five training sessions per day per activity with recording; instead, they involve use in 'natural' play interactions.

The highly structured and systematic approach outlined above is typical of many current programmes, such as the Portage model (Shearer and Shearer, 1972), which is increasingly being used. It utilizes developmental checklists, curriculum cards specifying tasks and activity recording charts. Such approaches have been successfully used by a range of professionals including nurses, health visitors, speech therapists, physiotherapists, occupational therapists, social workers and teachers (e.g. Rayner, 1978; Revill and Blunden, 1979; Cunningham et al., 1982). It provides home visitors with a tangible package which is relatively easy to apply. It is recognized that it may not meet all parental needs and is increasingly being integrated into a more comprehensive approach which offers advice on behaviour difficulties, family and service problems.

The above discussion of treatment and assessment is necessarily brief and the reader is referred to such texts as Haring and Brown (1976) for details of analysis and teaching techniques for handicapped children, and to practical books directed at parents, for example Cunningham and Sloper (1978), Kiernan et al. (1978), Carr (1980) and Newson and Hipgrave (1982).

EARLY INTERVENTION RESEARCH

In this half of the chapter we will briefly review current research findings and implications. A number of positive guidelines can be derived from early intervention with disadvantaged (as distinct from mentally handicapped) pre-school children.

The disadvantaged child

Reviews generally concur that positive outcomes are found and no one programme is more effective than another, but several factors are essential.

1 The child must be enrolled in the programme from an early age. Around 18 months appears to be the crucial age, coinciding with the emergence of language.
2 The parent must be closely and actively associated with the programme and the home ecology of the child considered as a major variable in the intervention.
3 The programme needs specific and developmentally appropriate objectives and must be based on relatively systematic teaching approaches rather than general enrichment.
4 The programme has to be maintained over long periods of time.
5 Steps must be taken to provide for generalizations of the learning to new situations (Bronfenbrenner, 1975; Stedmann, 1977).

Lazer and Darlington (1978) carried out a study of twelve early intervention programmes considered to be well designed and evaluated. Findings showed that the children involved were less likely to be assigned to special education classes, to be retained within year grades or to drop out of school early. School achievements in both mathematics and reading were also improved. Effects on other, less obvious, areas were also found. The children showed more 'achievement orientation' and their mothers had higher vocational aspirations for them.

Caldwell (1983) concluded that in this area parent-mediated experiences have a more profound and persistent influence than similar experiences provided by some other person.

Since the handicaps of the children concerned in these studies are the result of social disadvantage and deprivation, one cannot directly extrapolate these findings to children with mental handicap; different variables may be influential.

Home v. institutions

Studies consistently report that infants and young children raised in the relatively unstimulating environments found in many institutions perform a lower developmental levels than those raised under favourable home conditions. These findings include both non-handicapped and mentally handicapped infants. In the case of Down's syndrome infants, it was found that the effects of institutionalization were relatively immediate and significant differences in developmental attainment between home and institutionally reared infants are reported by the second year of life (e.g. Carr, 1975; Francis, 1971). These findings are supported by studies which have changed the nature of stimulation provided in institutions and found improved functioning for mentally handicapped children (e.g. Lyle, 1959), premature infants (e.g. Solkhoff et al., 1969; Scarr-Salapatek and Williams, 1973) and non-handicapped infants (e.g. White, 1971).

It is not only the development assessed by standardized tests that is improved, but the whole 'style' that the child develops in interacting with his environment. Francis (1971) reports that home-reared Down's syndrome infants showed more initiative and exploration in play than those raised in the institution.

Institutions do not necessarily increase the handicap. It is the lack of stimulation, compared with that in the one-to-one caretaking situation usually found in the home, that appears to be critical, and not all institutions necessarily depress performance (Tizard and Tizard, 1974). Hunt et al. (1976) found that by increasing the number of caretakers in an orphanage for infants from poor backgrounds, faster rates of development of sitting and locomotion were attained. This extra 'untutored human enrichment', however, was only effective in these gross motor areas, presumably as a result of an increased handling of the infants which facilitated the pertinent motor mechanisms. When the staff were tutored to stimulate areas such as object permanence, the infants developed faster in these areas than controls, but not in other areas, such as verbal imitation, which were not tutored.

Thus, careful matching is needed between appropriate stimulation and the child's developmental status; the adults involved, parents or staff, need an understanding of both. Homes which fail to provide such stimulation may be just as depriving as institutions.

Intervention with parents of handicapped children living at home

There are now a number of studies reporting the effects of early intervention with severely handicapped children. In a recent review of 27 intervention studies, Simeonsson et al. (1982) found that 70 % were home- or home- and clinic-based, 81 % provided stimulation based on general concepts of development, 70 % specified roles for parents, 70 % used standardized instruments of infant and child development for evaluation, 45 % used control or contrast groups and 59 % used statistical treatment of data. Of those using statistical procedures, 81 % found significant results to support the effectiveness of the intervention.

Whilst, with few exceptions, such studies report high levels of parent satisfaction and changes in children's performance, they frequently lack contemporary controls and rely on retrospective comparisons with previous data; they often fail to use independent assessments or establish reliability of measures. They also frequently fail to report the characteristics of parents and homes and the representativeness of the samples, and fail to describe families who drop out. Details of the intervention programmes are often not given, whilst at the same time programmes vary considerably in length and frequency of child or parent attendances or home visits. Despite this, the evidence overall is for beneficial effects.

Several studies exemplify the diversity of approaches and results. For example, Wilkins et al. (1980) retrospectively examined the psychomotor development of 65 children with cri-du-chat syndrome raised at home. Using parental questionnaires and medical records, they found that achievement levels had been favourably influenced by the introduction of early special education.

One of the few controlled studies aimed at infants with cerebral palsy (CP) including a large proportion who were also mentally handicapped is that of Scherzer et al. (1976). Twenty-four children under the age of 18 months were observed for a period of at least six months in either experimental or control physical therapy programmes. The study used a double-blind design and found definite positive change in motor, social and management areas in favour of the experimental group. However, the authors noted that the younger the infant and the greater the global deficit the less evidence there was for change. They suggest that for very young CP infants stimulation in modalities other than motor should be given greater emphasis at this early developmental period. This observation is most significant and indicates the present lack of information on the interrelationships between content, techniques, aetiology and the developmental process in intervention studies.

In one of the few studies reporting no significant

effects of early intervention, Piper and Pless (1980) allocated 37 Down's syndrome infants (mean chronological age 9 months, range 2–23 months) to matched treatment and control groups. The treatment group received twice-weekly centre-based therapy for one-hour sessions and mothers were given written instructions for continuing activities at home. No information is given on parental education, social class variables, the representativeness of the sample, or access to other guidance and support services. This may be critical since the mean pre-therapy developmental quotients of *both* groups (79.4 and 78.9) were as high as those reported in other intervention programmes and much higher than scores for parents receiving little assistance (Cunningham, 1982). This suggests that these infants were functioning at a relatively optimal level, possibly as a result of parents having a more positive approach.

Both Connolly and Russell (1976) and Cunningham and Mittler (1981) report significant differences between Down's syndrome children in delayed treatment groups starting at six months and those starting treatment earlier. However, Cunningham (1982) found that this difference occurred for mental scale scores on the Bayley Test of Infant Development and not motor scores. The delayed group did not significantly differ on motor scores at six months, but were significantly in advance of previous similar samples (e.g. Carr, 1975), suggesting that changes in social attitudes and practices influence parental conceptions and attitudes toward Down's syndrome infants and consequently influence parental behaviour and the developmental outcome of the child.

The positive outcomes of intervention are reported to diminish after the programme ceases in many studies of socially disadvantaged children, particularly if parents are not involved (Bronfenbrenner, 1975). Studies of mentally handicapped children suggest a similar effect (e.g. Harris et al., 1981; Webster-Stratton, 1982).

For example, Harris et al. (1981) compared scores on a 21-step hierarchy of speech behaviours checklist for 11 pre-school autistic children before and after their parents were taught operant procedures by attending a series of ten weekly training groups. The children showed significant gains on the checklist, and these were maintained at a follow-up one year later. However, there was no evidence of improvement beyond that achieved at the end of the training and the authors conclude that there is a need for continued parent support and training for new skills.

To some extent this is related to the extent that parents can independently continue to develop and apply appropriate intervention activities. Baker (1977) carried out a 20-week training programme for 160 families from diverse backgrounds, all of whom had a handicapped child between 3 and 14 years of age. After training, groups given training were significantly better than a control group. A follow-up fourteen months later found that the trained parents had maintained their knowledge of teaching principles and the children had maintained the advances made during the programme. However, there were fewer planned, formal teaching sessions. Only 16 % had embarked on teaching new tasks and 22 % on tackling new behaviour problems. Instead, 86 % were found to be carrying out some teaching efforts, but this was mainly incorporated in daily routines and incidental teaching. The authors concluded that parent training programmes should begin by encouraging formal teaching and then move towards incidental teaching, as this is more likely to be maintained. Many parent training workshops aim to teach parents basic teaching and management skills which become 'internalized' and can be used in everyday interactions (Cunningham and Jeffree, 1971).

Whilst short intervention programmes and parent workshops have generally demonstrated effectiveness, few have examined more long-term effects.

Two longitudinal studies of early intervention with Down's syndrome children which used contemporary treatment and non-treatment groups are those of de Coriat et al. (1968) and Ludlow and Allen (1979). De Coriat et al. provided 'psychomotor' stimulation from birth and assessed the 189 children at six-monthly intervals until five years of age. The difference between the two groups was significant throughout and at five years of age the median IQ was 61 for the treatment group and 42 for the non-treatment group.

Notable is the study of Ludlow, who was working in a situation closely comparable to the community health physician and child health clinic. She compared three groups of Down's syndrome children from the first years of life. One group was reared in institutions ($n = 8$–23) and two were home-reared: the parents and children of one of these regularly attended a developmental clinic and were given advice and support ($n = 29$–63), while in the other group parents had no access to such facilities and received no regular counselling ($n = 23$–71). Consistent significant differences were found between the three groups from the first year of life:

these were of a similar magnitude to those in de Coriat et al.'s study, and persisted up to the ninth and tenth year of age.

We found similar levels of mean developmental scores and IQs in a longitudinal, home-based intervention study of a representative cohort of 181 Down's syndrome infants. The children were visited at least every six weeks until two years of age and parents were given support and guidance. From two to five years, six-monthly follow-up assessments were carried out, and by three years all children were also enrolled in various pre-school facilities. The range of developmental scores at age five was from IQs less than 20 to 95.

Hayden and Haring (1977) have also reported more advanced development for 94 Down's syndrome children enrolled in a structured pre-school programme from six months to six years old and mainly centre-based. They concluded that the longer the child had been in the study the greater the gains made, but unfortunately they do not give information on whether later enrollers catch up with early ones, and if not, whether there is a critical age or developmental level when permanent secondary handicap ensues as a result of non-treatment.

Whilst such studies report positive effects, at least in the pre-school period, the majority of children in the current programmes appear to remain in the handicapped range, suggesting major constitutional limits to what can be achieved.

Longitudinal studies on mixed aetiological samples report similar results. Sandow et al. (1981) conducted a three-year home-support programme for pre-school severely mentally handicapped children divided into two matched groups, visited at home at either two-week or eight-week intervals and provided with educative programmes for general development. Successive IQ scores indicated that both groups were more advanced than a control group living in another locality and receiving no intervention. However, whilst the most frequently visited group made faster progress initially, the less frequently visited group made greater progress by the end of two years, although this difference disappeared by three years. The authors suggest that the more frequently visited mothers may have become more reliant and dependent whilst those in the less-visited group maintained the role of 'protagonist' rather than observer and trainer, and this supported their self-esteem and confidence (Sandow and Clarke, 1978).

Thus, it would appear reasonable to conclude that early intervention does facilitate the child's development but that many issues have arisen from the literature. Before considering these we will discuss the methods of parent involvement that have been used.

Methods of parent involvement

Materials

One important finding from the research is that the socio-economic and educational level of the parent is not generally correlated with ability to learn and apply techniques for training and stimulating the child. However, parents experienced in obtaining information from lectures and written material obviously find these more helpful than those without such experience. The latter need far more individual assistance. Studies indicate that demonstrating the techniques (Nay, 1975) and using modelling and role-playing (Hudson, 1982) is probably the most effective approach for all parents and that validated instructional manuals can be particularly useful (Heifetz, 1977). The use of videotape courses has increased in recent years and has proved successful for such content areas as play and language (McConkey et al., 1982) and parent interactions (Webster-Stratton, 1982). They have also proved useful in assessment and evaluation of parent–child interactions and behaviour disturbances (e.g. Bidder et al., 1981).

Workshops

A major approach has utilized parent workshops (e.g. Cunningham and Jeffree, 1971) and parent groups. Typically, parents meet at regular intervals with a professional course organizer/tutor and discuss general topics of interest or receive a structured course designed to teach assessment and teaching skills and/or child management skills (Holland and Hattersley, 1980; Firth, 1982). Recent approaches have combined reflective group counselling focusing on parental emotional needs and behavioural training aimed at education and management techniques (e.g. Hornby and Murray, 1983). Tavormina et al. (1976) compared various approaches but concluded that a combination of reflective counselling and behavioural techniques was most successful. Such workshops are often related to specific areas, such as language or behaviour modification (see Yule and Carr, 1980, for a review of methods and materials). Generally, such groups should not exceed ten to twelve parents, should be planned and organized with clearly stated objectives in agreement with the parents, and if possible should be led by an experienced person who is neither too authoritative nor too laissez-faire.

Home/clinic-based programmes

The second major approach in early intervention is based on home visiting and/or regular attendance at some centre. In the first months after the diagnosis many parents do not wish to meet others and need time to adapt and decide when they are ready to do this. This is a formative period when they are developing attitudes and interactive patterns with the infant (see Chapter 15) and so home visiting is essential.

Each of these approaches has its advantages and disadvantages and there is little evidence to support any one in particular. However, most studies find that parents gain considerable benefit from meeting in groups with parents of similar children in age and condition and that these rate highly on lists of priorities.

The mechanisms which make such groups beneficial are not fully understood. However, three aspects appear important.

First, most parents question whether they are doing the right things for the child and whether the child is making satisfactory progress. Social support groups give parents a reference base from which to assess these questions and confirm or develop their own actions. They also indicate that their feelings and concerns are shared by others, and this can provide emotional support and influence their sense of confidence and self-esteem.

Secondly, parents can view their child from different perspectives and gain new ideas and information on ways to interact and cope.

Finally, the act of discourse with others offers a major learning method. Concepts are articulated, analysed, re-phrased and repeated, which helps assimilation and internalization. Thus, they become more readily available to influence everyday interactions.

Domiciliary visits provide much necessary information on home circumstances, extend the possibility of including other members of the family and provide concentrated effort on parent and child whilst clinic, school or workshops provide the opportunity to meet with other parents. A comprehensive approach providing both these aspects would seem most advisable, particularly in the early years.

The Honeylands Project (Rubissow, 1976) provided a comprehensive service of home visiting, centre-based groups, family support, child-teaching activities and respite care. Burden (1980) evaluated the effect on parents and found that those receiving the service showed fewer signs of stress and more positive and realistic attitudes to their situation than a control group.

As the child gets older and development becomes more complex many parents appear to prefer that the main responsibility for teaching the child is taken on by professionals. Thus, in some intervention programmes, the children attend a pre-school facility and receive specific structured teaching from trained personnel (Hayden and Haring, 1977) and parental involvement in daily teaching is reduced.

CURRENT ISSUES

Because parents are parents, not professionals, and have unique feelings about their children, they are often less able to be as detached and objective about 'teaching' their children. Thus in helping some to develop and internalize the observation and interaction skills it can be useful to use children other than their own in initial training and to use video-recording, role-playing and so on. Further, having convinced parents that their efforts can help the child, and conversely therefore, that lack of effort or inappropriate management can hinder the child, parents can become increasingly anxious that they are not doing enough. Thus, it is important to select and organize initial training activities that lead to successful outcomes. Having developed a reasonable level of skills and experienced success, parents can more easily cope with later attempts which are not successful.

There is an increased debate, however, about whether parents want to bear the responsibility of teaching their handicapped child and about the dangers that certain approaches to parental involvement may increase stress. By emphasizing the importance of the parental role and the need for systematic regular teaching, parents, usually the mothers, can find themselves placed under considerable pressure. They have to take on the role of teacher or therapist, transporter and manager, not only of the home, but of contacts with a wide range of professionals (Doernberg, 1978; Lacoste, 1978). Increasingly, society is opening up wider opportunities for family activities, emphasizing individual development and, particularly for mothers, activities beyond the family. Thus, if the mother considers time for herself she may suffer 'such guilt that it is not worth it' (Doernberg, 1978), which may then lead to resentments and damage the family interactions. The question of how worth while is the possible cost to the family of small changes in the handicapped child must be addressed. Parents are also beginning to question the nature of early intervention. Fulwood (1981) for example notes that 'no sooner is one skill mastered than another skill is presented' and there is little time to enjoy 'the simple sweetness of success'. Many parents who are removed from access to active services or whose child enters full-time education comment that their first reaction is of relief.

Such reactions appear to be voiced by a minority of parents in the first years of the child's life (Baker, 1977; Sloper et al., 1983). Most find that carrying out activities with the child is therapeutic and do not differentiate these from other forms of support.

Crucial to this debate is how necessary a high rate of home visiting and intense daily programming is for the child's development.

In a series of recent studies with Down's syndrome infants under two years of age, we have investigated the effects of different intensities and frequencies of home visiting on the rate of development (i.e. mental and motor ages). Little difference was found at the age of two years between the high-intensity groups (highly structured systematic programmes as described earlier) and the less-intensive groups (a lower frequency of training and recording, but still based on structured activities), and all groups had comparable levels of development to those previously reported (e.g. Ludlow and Allen, 1979). Visiting rate, whether weekly, two-weekly or six-weekly, was not correlated with developmental outcome, but parents did prefer two-weekly visits.

This confirms Sandow et al.'s (1981) finding of no overall differences between groups visited every two weeks and every eight weeks. It is possible that alternative approaches to intervention, focusing on different aspects (more on relationships and interactions) and using different outcome measures, will produce different results. However, for the present it would appear that providing parents with checklists of normal development derived from standardized scales, insights into the use of observation, analysis and shaping and prompting techniques, regular support, information on child development and help in interpreting the child's behaviour is as beneficial in the long term for the infant's development as more intensive intervention approaches, with set daily exercises and detailed records. Of course, more intensive methods may be needed for particular behaviours and with very slow children, although in the latter case one has to question

seriously the cost-effectiveness regarding family input and gains made.

Unlike Sandow et al. (1981) we found no evidence of dependency related to frequency of visits. However, we emphasized the importance of parents acting for themselves and tried to avoid merely providing recipes for activities, and we also attempted to 'wean' parents onto using other sources by gradually reducing visiting rate over time.

Thus, most approaches to parent involvement and early intervention appear to work and most parents receiving them report high rates of satisfaction. This suggests that the crucial variable is not so much the service but the way it is operated – how it meets parents' needs and the interpersonal skills and competence of the professionals involved. Clearly a flexible approach which is sensitive to the needs and reactions of the family as a whole is foremost. We require investigations of the implications of differences within and between families in relation to service provision and the child.

McConkey and McEnvoy (1984) compared mothers of handicapped children who enrolled for an evening workshop with those who did not, comparing them on family background variables, attitudes to play and interactions. Significant differences were found on maternal attitudes and on interactions. Course-refusers appeared more confident about their role as parents but paradoxically were less likely to play with the child. The authors conclude that these parents did not share the assumptions of the course – that the behaviour of the child was modifiable and their interactions could be effective – and this may be related to the social ethos of the culture.

Bee et al. (1982) carried out a longitudinal study of pre-school non-handicapped children and found that for mothers of low-educational backgrounds, measures of the social support network, home organization, life changes and expectations of child development predicted cognitive and language attainment at three years old. Connell and McConnel (1981) carried out a follow-up study of 45 primary-school-age children treated operatively for hydrocephalus in infancy and found significantly higher ratings of emotional disturbance in children whose parents were rated as having negative attitudes towards them and interpersonal difficulties. Piper and Ramsay (1980) found positive correlations between HOME inventory scores of Down's syndrome infants and developmental level similar to that reported for non-handicapped groups and concluded that either a highly stimulating and organized environment with increased maternal involvement may prevent a major decline in mental functioning or the handicapped children who initiate interactions and manifest development facilitate increased maternal involvement.

Such studies are beginning to indicate the range of variables involved. The most frequently recurring ones are maternal involvement, expectations, knowledge and/or perception of child development, parent–child interaction, positive adaptation, family support and social support networks. This suggests that much of the success of early intervention may arise from the support, information and attitudes it brings with it, which facilitate interaction and involvement with the child. It may be that these are equally if not more important in the early years than intensive highly structured teaching. If this is so, we may be able to avoid many of the potential dangers voiced about such intensive approaches and match interactions more closely to family and child's needs. The core of early intervention, however, is well established. It is regular contact with parents focused on practical guidance relating to the child's development and the nature of the learning difficulties, and the implications this has for the family.

Finally, in recent years the content of early intervention, concentrating mainly on activities derived from developmental tests, has been questioned. It is seen as limited and directed at products of development rather than processes. Seibert and Hogan (1983), for example, argue that the objectives of early intervention should be concerned with functions and concepts rather than specific behaviours and have produced an alternative curriculum. Similarly, it is argued that such approaches tend to focus on the child and may ignore the relationship between the parent and child, the suggestion being that it is this relationship acting through everyday interactions that mediates the learning and development of the child. Thus, both parent and child will profit more if the parent encourages and permits the infant to initiate interactions and regulate their pace; the parent is then following the infant's lead and promoting interactions appropriate to the baby's activities (Affleck et al., 1982).

Current emphasis on physical and cognitive development may inadvertently minimize attention to social development. During the pre-school years mentally handicapped children need to broaden their experience outside the home – to mix with other children, encounter a variety of experiences and increase their ability to communicate with different people. In the pre-school period there is a strong argument for placing the child with non-handicapped peers to aid social development and encourage contact within the neighbourhood for child and parent. In these early years the difference between many mentally handicapped children and their peers is less marked and there is little evidence of the children being bullied and teased and they are not generally isolated in pre-school settings (Guralnick, 1980; Field et al., 1981). However, staff inexperienced in special education do need support and guidance, often initially to give them confidence. If the integration is to be more than locational, interactions have to be planned and encouraged (e.g. Essa, 1978) for instance, by reinforcing appropriate interactions in both handicapped and non-handicapped children, and structuring imitation and peer modelling (Snyder et al., 1977).

CONCLUSIONS AND FUTURE NEEDS

There is sufficient evidence to demonstrate that the provision of early intervention has a positive effect on the development of many young handicapped children. Further, the provision of support and training for the parents is an essential part of this and provides a necessary therapy for the parents.

There is sufficient information concerning early child development, techniques of stimulation, techniques and approaches to parent training and a knowledge of parental needs from which to build early services.

The climate is favourable. The reports of both the Court Committee (1976) and the Warnock Committee (1978) have outlined in some detail a framework of how such services might be developed.

This is not to argue that more research and investigation is unnecessary. There is insufficient information on the interrelationships between programme content, techniques, aetiologies and the stages of development of the infant. How intensive does early stimulation need to be? How does it vary with developmental level or with areas of development or both? How does this vary with age or aetiology? What are the influential processes in infant–parent interaction and within families? With regard to individual differences of infants, parents and families and their interaction with various intervention approaches, the evidence points to the need for programmes to be flexible and adaptive rather than rigid and prescriptive. The importance of the child's social experience is an area which has received insufficient attention, and the question of how best to ensure the optimal development of the child's social skills and community contacts remains unanswered. However, many of these questions will only be answered as more and more services are set up and evaluated. Current reliance on developmental scale scores for assessment or evaluation is insufficient. Measures related to other aspects of the child's development, home environment factors, parental adjustment, reduced stress and so on are required.

Finally, early intervention in the formative period may be particularly important in providing a foundation for the family's and the child's future development and for the prevention of avoidable secondary handicaps to both. The relationship that services establish with families at this time may be particularly significant to this process. Thus, we must increase our endeavours to understand its complexities and develop flexible services which meet the individual needs of the consumers—the children and their families.

Appendix Mean and range of ages for achieving early developmental behaviours in infants with Down's syndrome.

Behavioural item	Mean age (months)	Range (months)	No. of babies
Gross motor			
Holds head up for 15 seconds	3	$1\frac{1}{2}$–$5\frac{1}{2}$	24
Balances head and holds it steady when swayed	5	3–$8\frac{1}{2}$	31
Rolls from back to front and front to back	8	4–11	37
Sits without support for one minute or more	10	7–$15\frac{1}{2}$	37
Sits steadily for ten minutes or more and is well balanced	11	$8\frac{1}{2}$–$15\frac{1}{2}$	35
When lying down pulls himself up to sit	$14\frac{1}{2}$	$8\frac{1}{2}$–24	35
Pulls to standing position on furniture	$16\frac{1}{2}$	10–24	33
Walks with hands held	$17\frac{1}{2}$	10–30	30
Stands alone	$21\frac{1}{2}$	$15\frac{1}{2}$–36	29
Walks three or more steps without support	24	$15\frac{1}{2}$–42	27
Fine motor			
Holds cube using fingers against palm	$4\frac{1}{2}$	$1\frac{1}{2}$–7	30
Grasps cube, using thumb and fingers to hold it	$6\frac{1}{2}$	4–10	34
Can pick up object the size of a currant	12	$8\frac{1}{2}$–$15\frac{1}{2}$	35
Picks up object the size of a currant using thumb and forefinger only	20	12–36	31
Adaptive			
Visually follows dangling ring in circular movement	3	$1\frac{1}{2}$–$5\frac{1}{2}$	18
Grasps dangling ring	7	4–11	36
Picks up cube	8	$5\frac{1}{2}$–10	36
Holds two cubes	8	4–11	35
Picks up neatly and directly	10	7–14	37
Pulls ring by string deliberately	$11\frac{1}{2}$	7–17	36
Removes cloth to find hidden toy	$13\frac{1}{2}$	10–21	35
Puts cube in cup	$16\frac{1}{2}$	10–24	24
Attempts to imitate scribble	$15\frac{1}{2}$	10–21	35
Puts three cubes in cup	19	14–30	29
Puts a peg in pegboard two or more times	23	17–36	24
Builds a tower of two cubes	22	$15\frac{1}{2}$–30	26
Social			
Smiles when touched and talked to	3	$1\frac{1}{2}$–$5\frac{1}{2}$	18
Approaches image in mirror	$6\frac{1}{2}$	4–10	37
Communication			
Vocalizes to smile and talk	4	$1\frac{1}{2}$–$8\frac{1}{2}$	28
Turns to sound	7	4–11	36
Says da-da, ba-ba etc.	11	7–18	37
Reacts to 'no'	14	11–24	35
Responds to familiar words by gestures etc.	$13\frac{1}{2}$	10–18	35
Jabbers expressively	18	$12\frac{1}{2}$–30	35
Says two words	22	$15\frac{1}{2}$–30	25

The data presented is the result of a study of early development in Down's syndrome. The infants were visited every six weeks and assessed on the Bayley Scales of Infant Development (Bayley, 1969), for the first two years of life.
From Cunningham and Sloper (1978) by courtesy of the publishers, Souvenir Press.

REFERENCES

Affleck G, McGrade BJ, McQueeney M & Allen D (1982) Promise of relationship-focused early intervention in developmental disabilities. *Journal of Special Education 16:* 413–430.

Baker B (1977) Support systems for the parent therapist. In Mittler PJ (ed) *Research to Practice in Mental Retardation, Vol. 1 Care and Intervention.* Baltimore: University Park Press.

Bayley N (1969) *Bayley Scales of Infant Development.* New York: Psychological Corporation.

Beckman PJ (1983) Influences of selected child characteristics on stress in families of handicapped infants. *American Journal of Mental Deficiency 88(2):* 150–156.

Bee HL, Barnard KE, Eyres SJ, Gray CA, Hammond MA, Spietz AL, Synder C & Clark B (1982) Prediction of IQ and language skills from perinatal status, child performance, family characteristics and mother–infant interaction. *Child Development 53:* 1134–1156.

Berger J & Cunningham CC (1981) The development of eye contact between mothers and normal and Down's syndrome infants. *Developmental Psychology 17(5):* 678–689.

Berger J & Cunningham CC (1983) Development of early vocal behaviours and interactions in Down's syndrome and nonhandicapped infant–mother pairs. *Developmental Psychology, 19(3):* 322–331.

Bickel H & Grubel-Kaiser S (1982) Inborn errors of metabolism – consequences of long-term treatment for the individual, as derived from observations in phenylketonuria. In Cockburn F & Gitzelmann R (eds) *Inborn Errors of Metabolism in Humans. Lancaster:* MTP Press.

Bidder RT, Gray OP & Bates RM (1981) Brief intervention therapy for behaviourally disturbed pre-school children. *Child: Care, Health and Development 7:* 21–30.

Bradley RH & Caldwell BM (1979) Home observation for measurement of the environment: a revision of the pre-school scale. *American Journal of Mental Deficiency 84:* 235–244.

Bronfenbrenner U (1975) Is early intervention effective? In Friedlander BZ, Sterritt GM & Kirk GE (eds) *Exceptional Children, Vol. 3, Assessment and Intervention.* New York: Bruner/Mazel.

Buckhalt JA, Rutherford JB & Goldberg KE (1978) Verbal and nonverbal interaction of mothers with their Down's syndrome and non-retarded infants. *American Journal of Mental Deficiency 82:* 337–343.

Buim N, Rynders J & Turnure J (1974) Early maternal linguistic environment of normal and Down's syndrome language-learning children. *American Journal of Mental Deficiency 79:* 52–58.

Burden RL (1980) Measuring the effects of stress on the mothers of handicapped infants: must depression always follow? *Child: Care, Health and Development 6:* 111–125.

Caldwell BM (1983) A landmark study. Commentary in Slaughter DT Early intervention and its effects on maternal and child development. *Monograph of the Society for Research in Child Development, no. 202, 48,* pp. 87–89.

Carr J (1975) *Young Children with Down's Syndrome.* IRMMH Monograph 4. London: Butterworths.

Carr J (1980) *Helping Your Handicapped Child.* Harmondsworth: Penguin.

Cicchetti D & Sroufe LA (1976) The relationship between affective and cognitive development in Down's syndrome infants. *Child Development 47:* 920–929.

Clarke ADB & Clarke AM (1974) Mental retardation and behavioural change. *British Medical Bulletin 30:* 179.

Coleman M (1973) *Serotonin in Down's Syndrome.* New York: Elsevier.

Connell HM & McConnel TS (1981) Psychiatric sequelae in children treated operatively for hydrocephalus in infancy. *Developmental Medicine and Child Neurology 23:* 505–517.

Connolly B & Russell F (1976) Interdisciplinary early intervention program. *Physical Therapy, 56(2):* 155–158.

Court Committee (1976) *Fit for the Future.* Report of the Committee on Child Health Services (Chairman: SDM Court). Cmnd. 6684, 1 and 2. London: HMSO.

Crawley SB & Spiker D (1983) Mother–child interactions involving two-year-olds with Down's syndrome: a look at individual differences. *Child Development 54:* 1312–1323.

Cunningham CC (1976) Parents as therapists and educators. In Kiernan CC & Woodford P (eds) *Behaviour Modification with the Severely Retarded.* IRMMH Study Group 8. Amsterdam: Elsevier.

Cunningham CC (1982) Psychological and educational aspects of handicap. In Cockburn F & Gitzelman R (eds) *Inborn Errors of Metabolism.* Lancaster: MTP Press.

Cunningham CC & Jeffree DM (eds) (1971) *Working with Parents: Developing a Workshop Course for Parents of Young Mentally Handicapped Children.* Manchester: National Society for Mentally Handicapped Children (North West Region).

Cunningham CC & Mittler PJ (1981) Maturation, development and mental handicap. In Connolly KJ & Prechtl HRF (eds) *Maturation and Development: Biological and Psychological Perspectives.* London: Spastics Society International Medical Publications and Heinemann Medical.

Cunningham CC & Sloper P (1978) *Helping Your Handicapped Baby.* Hyman Horizons Series. London: Souvenir Press.

Cunningham CC, Aumonier M & Sloper P (1982) Health visitor support for families with Down's syndrome infants. *Child: Care, Health and Development 8:* 1–19.

De Coriat LF, Theslenco L & Waksman J (1968) The effects of psychomotor stimulation on the IQ of young children with trisomy-21. In Richards BW (ed.) *Proceedings of the 1st Congress of the International Association for Scientific Study of Mental Deficiency.* Reigate, England: Jackson Publishing.

Doernberg NL (1978) Some negative effects on family integration of health and educational services for young handicapped children. *Rehabilitation Literature 39(4):* 107–110.

Essa F (1978) The preschool setting for applied behaviour analysis research. *Review of Educational Research 48(5):* 537–575.

Field T, Roseman S, De Stefano L & Koewler JH (1981) Play behaviours of handicapped preschool children in the presence and absence of non-handicapped peers. *Journal of Applied Developmental Psychology 2:* 49–58.

Firth H (1982) The effectiveness of parent workshops in a mental handicap service. *Child: Care, Health and Development 8:* 77–91.

Fishler K, Graliker BV & Koch R (1965) The predictability of intelligence with Gesell developmental scales in mentally retarded infants and young children. *American Journal of Mental Deficiency 69:* 15.

Francis SH (1971) The effects of own-home and institutional-rearing on the behavioural development of normal and mongol children. *Journal of Child Psychology and Psychiatry 12:* 173.

Fulwood D (1981) Mum or supermum? *Australian Citizen Limited* (August): 241–247.

Gesell A (1939) Reciprocal interweaving in neuromotor development. A principle of spiral organization shown in the patterning of infant behaviour. *Journal of Comparative Neurology 70:* 161.

Griffiths SR (1960) *The Abilities of Babies.* London: University of London Press.

Guralnick MJ (1980) Social interactions among pre-school children. *Exceptional Children 46(4):* 248–253.

Haring NG & Brown LJ (1976) *Teaching the Severely Handicapped Vol. 1.* New York & London: Grune & Stratton.

Harrell RF, Capp RH, Davies DR, Peerless J & Ravitz LR (1981) Can nutritional supplements help mentally retarded children? An exploratory study. *Proceedings of the National Academy of Sciences, of the USA 70(1):* 574–578.

Harris SL, Wolchik SA & Weitz S (1981) The acquisition of language skills by autistic children. Can parents do the job? *Journal of Autism and Developmental Disorders 11:* 373–384.

Hayden AH & Haring NG (1977) The acceleration and maintenance of developmental gains in Down's syndrome school-age children. In Mittler PJ (ed) *Research to Practice in Mental Retardation, vol. 1, Care and Intervention.* Baltimore: University Park Press.

Heifetz LJ (1977) Behavioural training for parents of retarded children: alternative formats based on instructional manuals. *American Journal of Mental Deficiency 82:* 194–203.

Holland JM & Hattersley J (1980) Parent support groups for the families of mentally handicapped children. *Child: Care, Health and Development 6:* 165–173.

Hornby G & Murray R (1983) Group programmes for parents of children with various handicaps. *Child: Care, Health and Development 9:* 185–198.

Hudson AM (1982) Training parents of developmentally handicapped children: a component analysis. *Behaviour Therapy 13:* 325–333.

Hunt JMcV, Mohandessi IK, Ghodssi M & Akiyama M (1976) The psychological development of orphanage-reared infants: interventions with outcomes (Tehran). *Genetic Psychology Monographs 94:* 177–226.

Illingworth RS (1963) *The Development of the Infant and Young Child: Normal and Abnormal.* Baltimore: Williams & Wilkins.

Jeffree DM & Cashdan A (1971) The home background of the severely subnormal child: a second study. *British Journal of Medical Psychology 44:* 27.

Jones OHM (1977) Mother–child communication with pre-linguistic Down's syndrome and normal infants. In Schaffer HR (ed) *Studies in Mother–Infant Interaction.* London: Academic Press.

Kearsley RB (1981) Cognitive assessment of the handicapped infant: the need for an alternative approach. *American Journal of Orthopsychiatry 51:* 43–55.

Kiernan C & Jones MC (1982) *Behaviour Assessment Battery,* 2nd edn. Walton-on-Thames: NFER-Nelson.

Kiernan CC, Jordan R & Saunders C (1978) *Starting Off.* London: Souvenir Press.

Lacoste RJ (1978) Early intervention: can it hurt? *Mental Retardation 16:* 266–268.

Lazar I & Darlington RB (1978) *The Lasting Effects After Pre-School.* (OHDS) 79–30178. Washington DC: US Dept of Health, Education and Welfare.

Ludlow JR & Allen LM (1979) The effect of early intervention and pre-school stimulus on the development of the Down's syndrome child. *Journal of Mental Deficiency Research 23:* 29–45.

Lyle JG (1959) The effect of an institution environment upon the verbal development of imbecile children. 1. Verbal intelligence. *Journal of Mental Deficiency Research 3:* 122.

McConkey R & McEnvoy J (1984) Parental involvement courses: contrasts between mothers who enrol and those who don't. In: Berg J (ed) *Proceedings of 6th International Congress of IASSMD.* Toronto: University Park Press.

McConkey R, McEnvoy J & Gallagher F (1982) Learning through play: the evaluation of a videocourse for parents of mentally handicapped children. *Child: Care, Health and Development 8:* 345–359.

Nay RW (1975) A systematic comparison of instructional techniques for parents. *Behaviour Therapy 6:* 14.

Neligan G & Prudham D (1969) Norms for four standard developmental milestones by sex, social class and place in family. *Developmental Medicine and Child Neurology 11:* 413.

Newson E & Hipgrave J (1982) *Getting Through to Your Handicapped Child.* Cambridge: Cambridge University Press.

Penrose LS & Smith GF (1966) *Down's Anomaly.* Edinburgh: Churchill Livingstone.

Piper MC & Pless IB (1980) Early intervention for infants with Down's syndrome: a controlled trial. *Pediatrics 65:* 463.

Piper MC & Ramsay MK (1980) Effects of early home environment on the mental development of Down's syndrome infants. *American Journal of Mental Deficiency 85(1):* 39–44.

Rayner H (1978) The Exeter home-visiting project: the psychologist as one of several therapists. *Child: Care, Health and Development 4:* 1–7.

Revill S & Blunden R (1979) A home training service for pre-school developmentally handicapped children. *Behavioural Research and Therapy, 17:* 207–214.

Reynell J (1979) *Reynell–Zinkin Scales for Young Visually Handicapped Children.* Windsor, Berkshire: NFER Publishing Co.

Richards M (1974) *The Integration of a Child into a Social World.* Cambridge: Cambridge University Press.

Rubissow J (1976) Honeylands – a family help unit in Exeter. In *Early Management of Handicapped Disorders* IRMMH Review of Research and Practice, no. 19, London: Institute for Research into Multiple and Mental Handicap.

Sandow SA & Clarke ADB (1978) Home intervention with parents of severely subnormal, pre-school children: an interim report. *Child: Care, Health and Development 4:* 29–39.

Sandow SA, Clarke ADB, Cox MV & Stewart FL (1981) Home intervention with parents of severely subnormal pre-school children: a final report. *Child: Care, Health and Development 7:* 135–144.

Scarr-Salapatek S & Williams ML (1973) The effects of early stimulation on low-birth-weight infants. *Child Development 44:* 94–101.

Scherzer AL, Mike V & Ilson J (1976) Physical therapy as a determinant of change in the cerebral palsied infant. *Paediatrics 58:* 47.

Seibert JM & Hogan AE (1983) A model for assessing social and object skills and planning intervention. In McClowry D & Richardson S (eds) *Infant Communication: Development, Assessment and Intervention.* New York: Grune & Stratton.

Share JB (1976) Review of drug treatment for Down's syndrome persons. *American Journal of Mental Deficiency 80:* 388.

Share JB & Veale AMO (1974) *Developmental Landmarks for Children with Down's Syndrome (Mongolism).* Dunedin: University of Otago Press.

Shearer MS & Shearer DE (1972) The Portage project: a model

for early childhood education. *Exceptional Children 39:* 210–217.

Sheridan M (1969) *The Developmental Profiles of Infants and Young Children.* London: HMSO.

Simeonsson RJ, Cooper DM & Scheiner AP (1982) A review and analysis of the effectiveness of early intervention programs. *Pediatrics 69:* 635–641.

Sloper P, Cunningham CC & Arnljotsdottir M (1983) Parental reactions to early intervention with their Down's syndrome infants. *Child: Care, Health and Development 9:* 357–376.

Snyder L, Apolloni T & Cooke TP (1977) Integrated settings at the early childhood level: the role of non-retarded peers. *Exceptional Children 43(5):* 262–266.

Solkhoff N, Yaffe S, Weintraub D & Blase B (1969) Effects of handling on the subsequent development of premature infants. *Developmental Psychology 1:* 765.

Stedmann DJ (1977) Important considerations in the review and evaluation of educational intervention programmes. In Mittler PJ (ed) *Research to Practice in Mental Retardation, Vol. 1 Care and Intervention.* Baltimore: University Park Press.

Tavormina JB, Hampson RB & Luscomb RL (1976) Participant evaluation of the effectiveness of their parent counselling groups. *Mental Retardation 14:* 8–9.

Tizard J & Tizard B (1974) The institution as an environment for development. In Richards MP (ed) *The Integration of a Child into a Social World.* Cambridge: Cambridge University Press.

Warnock Committee (1978) *Special Educational Needs.* Report of the Committee of Enquiry into the Education of Handicapped Children and Young People (Chairman: HM Warnock). London: HMSO.

Weathers C (1983) Effects of nutritional supplementation on IQ and certain other variables associated with Down's syndrome. *American Journal of Mental Deficiency 88:* 214–217.

Webster-Stratton C (1982) The long-term effects of a videotape modelling parent-training program: comparison of immediate and 1-year follow-up results. *Behaviour Therapy 13:* 702–704.

White BL (1971) *Human Infants Experience and Psychological Development.* New Jersey: Prentice-Hall.

Wilkins E, Brown JA & Wolf B (1980) Psychomotor development in 65 home-reared children with Cri-du-Chat syndrome. *Journal of Paediatrics 97:* 401–405.

Yule W & Carr J (1980) *Behaviour Modification for the Mentally Handicapped.* London: Croom Helm.

Zelazo P (1979) Reactivity to perceptual–cognitive events: application for infant assessment. In Kearsley RB & Sigel I (eds) *Infants at Risk: Assessment of Cognitive Functioning.* New Jersey: Lawrence Erlbaum.

Chapter 19
Education and School Leaving – Background and Philosophy

DAVID NORRIS

HISTORICAL ASPECTS OF SPECIAL EDUCATIONAL PROVISION IN THE UNITED KINGDOM

No government ever gets out of bed and declares, 'Today we are going to do something enlightened to help people with special needs', unless pressure has been brought to bear in such a manner as to *compel* that government to do something to enhance the lives of people with special needs. As with many aspects of statutory reform the story of the way in which we meet the needs of people with mental handicap is one of administrative inertia interspersed with sudden flurries of public concern.

When one considers England's behaviour towards people with mental handicap in the context of the power and riches of which she was once possessed it is difficult to escape the conclusion that, as a nation, England herself was a slow learner. It is interesting to note that it was only one hundred and fifty years ago that Parliament disbursed the very first state funds for the education of the nation's normal children.

In 1833 Parliament voted £20 000 for the education of our young. Even then the government refused to have anything to do with its spending. Four-fifths of the money went to the National Society for Promoting the Education of the Poor in the Principles of the Established Church throughout England and Wales and the remainder to the Nonconformists – the British and Foreign School Society.

To this day one can still see old schools bearing the legend 'National School' or 'British School' above the door. To have suggested that some of this money should have been given to educate children who displayed severe learning disorders would not really have been regarded as outrageous – just silly. The fact that a greater sum of money was devoted to

the restoration of the kennels and stables in the royal residences was not thought to be incongruous.

A detailed history of legislation and its impact on the provision of educational services for the severely retarded child is not provided here. The reason for not doing so is that, in large measure, there is very little to say. While the 1913 Mental Deficiency Act made provision for the care and education of the feeble-minded, the training of the imbecile and the occupation of the idiot, it cannot be said to have advanced significantly the emotional, social and intellectual stimulation of people with severe learning disorders, and it added nothing to their dignity.

When large conflicts are resolved people often seem to display feelings of confidence, optimism and resolution. The 1944 Education Act, at the end of the Second World War, was a major piece of social legislation. This offered education to all children according to age, ability and aptitude – unless they had a mental handicap, in which case they were excluded from the provisions of the Act.

At about this time England was in a state of some legislative ferment. The whole nation was striving towards a more just and humane society, in which the sick, the old, the jobless and the socially vulnerable were to be offered the protection of the community, underpinned by statute. At the same time, however, we managed to ensure that as far as education was concerned the severely retarded child was quite specifically and quite deliberately denied access to the nation's educational system. Such is the ugly history of real underprivilege.

Public disquiet over the conditions surrounding those with mental illness or mental handicap led to the 1959 Mental Health Act, which, for all its faults, managed to bring the mentally disordered into the twentieth century. In spite of the manifold improvements to which this Act gave rise the severely mentally retarded child was still denied access to our educational system.

Many people still clung to the view that the stimulation of children with severe learning disorders was a medical problem, and for that reason the education of such children was controlled by doctors and not teachers. Norris (1968) made the comment that if it really *were* a medical problem the medical profession was singularly reticent on the subject. In an analysis of three widely read medical journals over a five-year period (1962–1966) only five papers were found on topics related to the education or training of mentally handicapped people. One of these was by a doctor and dealt with the management of a sheltered workshop.

It was inevitable that such a state of affairs could not be sustained, and eventually the Education (Handicapped Children) Act was passed in 1970. As a result of this Act the nation opened its school doors to children with severe mental handicap on 1st April 1971. Shortly after this Act the Government established a Committee of Enquiry in 1974 under the chairmanship of Mary Warnock. Its function was to review the educational provision being made for children and young people handicapped by disabilities of body or mind. The report was published in 1978. Two of the main proposals were (a) that the child with special needs should receive more integrated and less segregated education and (b) that various categories of disabled schoolchildren would be subsumed under one heading, 'special needs'.

Arising out of the Warnock report, the Education Act of 1981 states that where possible children with special educational needs should be educated in normal schools. While it deals with other aspects of special education this one proposal to admit handicapped children to normal schools, if sensitively handled, could revolutionize the way in which future generations regard their handicapped fellows. It could enhance their daily lives and increase their subsequent social integration.

One must now wait and see if the spirit of the Act will be reflected in the will of the people. More enlightened commentators might suggest that there is no need to wait – only a need to do. Public protestations of private piety underpinned by administrative inertia have been too often in the past the main impediments to reform.

Barclay (1960) describes the responses of intellectually normal children going to school with mentally handicapped youngsters. In doing so she mentions a cockney girl who makes the comment to the mother of Jane, a child with severe mental handicap: 'Jane isn't as clever as me, I'm five. I know she's weak in the head but she's my best friend and I love her all the same'.

This child had probably not read Samuel Johnson, who comments (in *Rasselas*), 'example is always more efficacious than precept', but her behaviour certainly supported the truth of the statement. As long as we insist that in the rearing of the young of our species one group of children is isolated from another because of differences in their intelligence we sustain folklore and perpetuate bigotry.

AWAY FROM A PHILOSOPHY OF SPECIAL EDUCATION

Philosophy is concerned with principles, not practices, and while there is a clear need in very many cases to adopt different practices in response to individual needs, the principles which impel their adoption are no different from those which lie at the root of practices surrounding the education of the gifted child.

In discussing education Peel (1956) comments that 'the purpose of education is the promotion of a well-integrated personality capable of exercising such responsibility in society as his powers allow'. If one accepts the notion that it is moral and necessary to offer education to all children it is difficult to see, when one examines Peel's comments, why this view should not apply to slow learning toddlers and their normal siblings and to older children studying physics and biochemistry and their age peers learning to acquire the skills of literacy.

SCHOOL-LEAVING READINESS

In recent years there has been a great deal of discussion and activity to ensure that retarded children stay at school until they reach the age of nineteen. Whilst it is entirely reasonable to try and ensure that such children are offered the maximal educational input, there are many who would benefit by leaving school before the age of nineteen if there were somewhere for them to receive continuing education.

In many schools one sees older adolescent pupils who have been in the same school since their infancy. It was there that they received their potty training, it was there that they learned to sing 'Baa Baa Black Sheep' and it was there that the dinner lady cut up their meat at lunch time. It is difficult for young men and women who can talk, go to pubs with their parents and friends and form attachments with the opposite sex to regard themselves as developing young adults if the dinner lady who cut their meat up when they were toddlers is still doing the same thing at a different table in the same room. It is difficult for many to let loose the bonds of infancy and to become aware of their own maturity if they can still hear 'Baa Baa Black Sheep' still being sung in another classroom down the corridor. Continued proximity to the echoes of early childhood can often be an impediment to the growth of self-awareness and the pursuit of personal development.

THE EDUCATIONAL FUTURE OF THE RETARDED SCHOOL-LEAVER

The problem that presents itself to school-leavers with mental handicap is that, for many, the process of leaving school is too often accompanied by a marked diminution of educational opportunity. While at school their day was substantially devoted to classroom activities; in the day centre for adults with mental handicap the prospect of maintaining this measure of educational stimulus diminishes significantly.

At the time of leaving school many are at a stage of their cognitive and educational development which should allow for a marked growth in skills of literacy and numeracy, and it is at this very time that they are offered less educational support than they were offered at school. While so many of us protest to an awareness that retarded people learn more slowly than the rest of us, we send them to a day centre which offers a decreased measure of educational instruction and then ask them to maintain their learning progress. The need for continuing education persists and is not being met nationally.

An illustration of the extent to which we are not meeting this need can be found in numerous articles and accounts of schemes in which mentally handicapped people are attending colleges of further education. While such schemes are of undoubted value, the sad thing about such accounts is the excitement and pleasure with which they are described. Such ventures should be a matter of routine. The fact that a group of mentally retarded ladies and gentlemen go to college for one day a week should not acquire such significance as to warrant an article in the local paper.

The longer we regard the opening of public facilities to a particular group of citizens as some kind of adventure the longer we will take to adopt a more civilized view of affairs. After all, it would be surprising to pick up a newspaper carrying a headline which read, 'Clean water available in Rickmansworth'!

While there may be some who regard this view as extreme, such people should be reminded of the euphoria which surrounded the establishment of the National Health Service or the days when council house estates were built without off-street parking facilities because people who lived in such houses would not have cars. That which was wonderful yesterday will be routine by tomorrow. The sooner we press ahead to ensure the provision of further education facilities for those with mental handicap on a routine basis, the sooner they will be able to establish their own identity as members of the community.

Day centres for mentally handicapped people are facing an almost impossible task and one can only admire the way in which staff in such centres are responding to the situation confronting them. They are asked to deal with a wide range of people presenting a full range of problems and they are forced to work in premises which were designed as imitation factories.

This situation came about because the local authorities who built them – having little experience and less knowledge of industry – were deceived into the fatuous belief that because handicapped people could assemble plastic toys and pack things into boxes that was where their future lay.

The government spent many millions of pounds in buying land, building factories (called training centres), employing and training staff and then offering them free of charge to private industry complete with a captive labour force (called mentally handicapped people). The wages paid can only be described as inadequate. The huge capital investment which the nation had made in providing such establishments was ignored when private industry came to calculate the number of pennies it would pay the workers. In more recent years such token wages have often been euphemistically described as incentive payments or training allowances.

Fortunately, economic adversity has intervened and, as a result of massive unemployment, industry is less able to supply sub-contract work to day centres. In addition to this, staff in such units are re-evaluating their own function and reconsidering the social future of people with mental handicap.

As part of this process day centres are making increasing attempts to provide a greater measure of continuing education. There are not enough staff (Baranyay, 1981), but one must also examine the training opportunities available to such staff. It is anomalous that those teaching mentally handicapped children are offered three or four years' full-time training whilst those anxious to involve themselves in the further education of the same children when they leave school are only offered two years' part-time training.

Whilst Dixon (1979) mentions an encouraging instance of staff in day centres being offered further training, it is believed that enhancement of the educational future of mentally handicapped people can only be adequately achieved after a re-evaluation of the training facilities open to staff engaged in this field. If we were to undertake such an exercise it would also be appropriate to re-examine the kind of further education facilities we now provide, with a view to enhancing the range and style of provision available to the mentally handicapped school-leaver.

SOME PROPOSALS FOR RE-STRUCTURING THE SYSTEM AFTER SCHOOL

The need for re-structuring the post-school system is apparent: our present day-centres are faced with too wide a range of problems under one roof. They are asked to provide emotional, social and intellectual stimulation to teenagers just out of school and appropriate occupations for mature adults. They are called on to supply a range of activities which are emotionally satisfying and socially valuable for middle-aged people and, increasingly, to ensure that elderly people with mental handicap can maintain some measure of fulfilment and sustain a quality of life which is still enriching and satisfying. In addition to this they are asked to make special provision for people with behavioural disorders and for those suffering from profound mental handicap – often associated with severe physical disability.

The following model has been proposed (Norris, 1982) as offering a range of therapeutic climates which would be more flexible and more capable of offering appropriate education, support or training to those handicapped people in need of these facilities. It depends on the committed involvement of our education service on a routine basis.

If we want extended education for mentally handicapped people it seems nonsense that we seek to provide this facility without insisting that the educational system assumes a major role in its provision. It is suggested, therefore, that the following post-school facilities should be provided by the local education authorities: a further education establishment, an advanced training unit and self-catering flats. It must be noted that there are limits to how long a person can attend these facilities.

The further education establishment

Children leaving school would not go straight to a day centre. Instead they would be offered continuing education constructed on a prescriptive basis. Part of this process would be a thorough assessment of each student's strengths and an examination of his or her particular needs. As a result of this assessment an individual programme would be drawn up for the student to follow. This procedure is necessary as the wide range of learning disability presenting itself in a given group of retarded young people makes it inappropriate and less effective to offer all students the same educational diet.

Thus school-leavers would be offered access to an environment designed quite specifically to develop individual skills and, as far as possible, to remedy individual areas in which they under-function. They would be exposed to a fairly structured imaginative regime in which they could mature emotionally and socially in a climate which was itself mature, made sensible demands and provided an appropriate model.

While educational experiences would be designed to promote continued cognitive development, opportunities would be offered to develop interpersonal and social skills as an integral part of this process.

It is suggested that this facility could in very many areas form part of the local college of further education. Under such circumstances the retarded students could follow their own courses and, at the same time, have access to the facilities of the students' union and be able to mix in the wider world of the college.

The duration of the course offered to those attending would be determined by the needs of each student but it is not anticipated that it would be less than two years. It is also proposed that opportunity should be provided for people with mental handicap to apply for this facility later in life if their level of maturity suggests that they would benefit by attending a further course.

The advanced training unit

The function of this unit, which would be controlled by the further education sector of the local authority, would be to offer an intensive training course to those ex-students of the further education college if it were believed that they were able to live independently or with minimal support, or would be able to work in open employment, should jobs be available. As part of their training course the students would be subjected to increasing amounts of stress and made to work a full working day.

This training would examine and promote the students' capacity to organize their own affairs, tolerate fatigue and boredom and exercise judgement. It would place them in a situation in which the development of free choice formed a central part of the training programme. Part of the course would insist that the student spend time in a training hostel and graduate to a self-catering flat. These facilities would be an integral and essential part of the training course. There would be a resident tutor on the premises who would ensure that the student was given an understanding of diet, housekeeping, shopping and self-care and could put these skills into practice.

Self-catering flats

The self-catering flats would be geographically distant from the day training component of the advanced training unit. The training programme would insist that students ultimately travelled alone to the place in which they lived. If they *really* wanted to become independent they would have to learn to be independent. Clearly this process must be planned, and it must be aware of and sensitive to the needs and nature of the individual student. The residential element would not be introduced at the beginning of the course but would form a central component of the whole training process.

There are far too many people with mental handicap who are forced to live at home with their parents for years and years, not because they cannot be trained to live independently, but as a reflection of two factors, parental anxiety and lack of opportunity. If we really mean it when we plead for the enhancement of the lifestyle offered to mentally handicapped people we will provide the opportunity for them to enhance their *own* lifestyle. We will let them go hungry if they cannot cook and get lost if they cannot travel. We will let them do what we have done – make their own mistakes. This does not of course apply to all, but to those who have

some prospect of success and yet are denied their right to fail. It must be stressed that if this sort of development is to succeed there must be a considerable amount of rethinking on the part of many parents. Too frequently one sees parents allowing their own solicitude to become the greatest impediment to the enhancement of their own handicapped offspring, and without active parental encouragement this sort of venture will be diminished in its effectiveness.

Other services

Other services for mentally handicapped people should stay within the ambit of the social services departments. Thus the hostels, group homes, facilities for the profoundly handicapped, sheltered workshops and day centres would continue to offer a service to the majority of clients. The question of the nature and conduct of our day centres lies outside the scope of this chapter (see Chapter 22). However there will be many who mature at a later stage in their lives and this increased level of maturation would make it appropriate for them to be offered a course at the advanced training unit.

EDUCATION AND TRAINING – SOME CONSIDERATIONS

Training cannot go on for life even though it can occur throughout life. As the term is commonly employed, training implies the acquisition or development of skills which will be called into use or put into practice at a later time. During the course of one's life, however, one may require periods of training or re-training in order to allow one to acquire additional skills, to adapt to changes in life events or to prepare to meet new demands which may present themselves.

From this it follows that the mentally handicapped school leaver has a future whose training needs are probably not much different *in principle* from those of his normal fellow. For many years now mentally handicapped children have left school and been offered a future in day centres in which their time has been devoted in large measure to boring and repetitive tasks, like assembling bits of plastic or stamping doctors' prescription pads, and this process has been called 'training'. It is not training: it is occupation.

Fortunately, a shortage of work and an increasing professionalism on the part of the staff in such units is bringing this state of affairs to a close. If we intend to provide training we should do so in the context of a *training course*. These courses must have specific objectives and they must be capable of evaluation. The student must be able to *fail*. Such failure may be a reflection of the student's performance or it may be a function of the course design. A process of continuous monitoring of such courses will give us the evidence which will allow us to make the necessary adjustments to improve their effectiveness. It seems bizarre that we can construct and conduct training courses for remedial teachers and psychologists anxious to involve themselves in the training of handicapped people, while ignoring the anomaly that we do not construct courses for those whom they allege to serve.

Although the view has been put forward that training cannot go on for life it is stressed that education *must* go on for life. While all training is learning and not all learning is training, the need for learning is continuous. No matter what form education takes, without its influence people will subside and under-function. Education should both arouse hunger and remain a nourishing process which sustains the mind and enriches the person. Its function is not merely to inform but to disturb and, in the process, it compels those involved to examine themselves and invites them to re-examine others.

Those who are intellectually handicapped and socially vulnerable are particularly at risk. Without the sustenance of continuing stimulus we help them to earn the diminishing pejoratives with which they are too often surrounded. Day centres for people with mental handicap must be seen as facilities in which those for whom they were established are offered a social, emotional and intellectual climate in which they can learn with other people and thereby discover themselves.

REFERENCES

Baranyay E (1981) *Towards a Full Life*. London: National Society for Mentally Handicapped Children and Adults.

Barclay JE (1960) The child permanently at home. In *Community Care of the Mentally Handicapped*. Proceedings of the Conference of the National Society for Mentally Handicapped Children.

Dixon K (1979) Staffing resources. In Dixon K & Hutchinson D (eds) *Further Education for Handicapped Students*. Bolton: Bolton College of Education (Technical).

Meeting Special Educational Needs: A Brief Guide to the Warnock Report. London: HMSO.

Norris D (1968) Some observations on the school life of severely retarded children. *Journal of Mental Subnormality* (Monograph supplement).

Norris D (1982) *Profound Mental Handicap*. Tunbridge Wells: Costello.

Peel EA (1956) *The Psychological Basis of Education*. London, Oliver & Boyd.

STATUTES

Mental Deficiency Act 1913. London: HMSO.

Mental Health Act 1959. London: HMSO.

Education Act 1981. London: HMSO.

Education (Handicapped Children) Act 1970. London: HMSO.

Education Act 1944. London: HMSO.

Chapter 20
Education and School Leaving – Practice

MARK ROBERTS

Nine o'clock in the morning at a special school for retarded children. In the driveway the minibuses and ambulances, having collected the children from their homes, are arriving and disgorging their passengers. School staff are at hand to give help to those who need it, and to keep a sharp eye open for one or two potential 'runners', who might decide to make a dash for the front gate and the excitements of the main road. The children stream in through the front door: Joanne, Paul, Kitty, Jon-jon, Sally, Stewart. . . . About a quarter of them have Down's syndrome, though the signs are less obvious than they used to be – mercifully there are very few 'pudding-basin' haircuts these days. Stewart, a profoundly retarded Down's syndrome boy, decides to sit down on the floor in the middle of the entrance-hall: 'Come on, Stewart, we don't want any sit-down strikes today!' But Stewart will not budge.

Some children walk in briskly and confidently. Elizabeth dances in – she dances everywhere, all day. Apollodorus potters in slowly, humming a tune to himself – he seems quite unaware of his surroundings. John waves a bag of books and proudly announces: 'I've done all my homework!' Wendy, a girl with severe cerebral palsy, is pushed along in her wheelchair: 'Good morning, Wendy.' Alex is today's birthday boy: 'Look what I got for my birthday!' – a transistor radio whose small size belies its devastating volume. His teacher congratulates him with a brave smile.

In this particular school the pupils are aged from seven to eighteen, but most schools of this kind take children from the age of two or three. Like all other pupils, they can leave school at the age of sixteen; most, however, now stay until they are nineteen. A few of the children have syndromes with unfamiliar names – 'cri-du-chat', 'Pierre Robin' – but medical aetiologies are not a major concern for teachers when they are planning children's work-programmes: it is of more importance to know what each child can *do*.

Stewart is still sitting on the hall floor. Outside it is starting to rain; the process of unloading the buses is speeded up. Andrew gets carried into school, although this is against the rules: 'You needn't expect this every day, Andrew!' A commotion in the hall, – Apollodorus has tripped over Stewart; he falls down; his nose hits the floor first; he stops humming and starts yelling; anxious staff bustle around him. . . . Amid the confusion, Stewart gets to his feet and walks slowly off to his class; an evil grin irradiates his ginger-freckled countenance. There are those who say that the life of a severely handicapped child is not worth living; Stewart knows different.

If we could go back to 1970, we would see children like these arriving each morning not at a school, run by the local education authority, but at a 'junior training centre', run by the local health authority; these children were officially classified as 'unsuitable for education' and were excluded from the education system. In most cases this decision was taken if a child was found to have an intelligence quotient of less than 50 (approximately). In April 1971, as noted elsewhere in this book, all children, no matter how severely handicapped, became entitled to 'education'. Looking forward to this change, a leading authority on mental handicap (Mittler, 1969) said: 'Educational and training facilities are likely to improve substantially in the coming decade, and more teaching and other staff are being trained. In general, it seems probable that the training and teaching of the mentally handicapped will involve a more professional approach. . . . ' It is difficult to say how far this moderately optimistic view has been justified by events: as in most fields of education, standards of work vary greatly from one place to another. It has to be said that some schools for the mentally retarded are still not greatly different from the 'junior training centres' which existed before 1971. In the course of this chapter I will mention some of the factors which at present militate against educational progress, but first I will try to give a picture of what one might reasonably *hope* to see being offered to mentally retarded children in our schools. What might a discriminating parent of a retarded child expect from a special school in the 1980s in terms of the 'more professional approach' envisaged by Mittler?

PROFESSIONALISM AND THE SCHOOL

First I must express a personal view that professionalism has little to do with membership of a so-called 'profession'; it has to do with the achievement of the highest possible standard of work. The discriminating parent will be impressed not so much by the number of letters after the names of the staff as by evidence of what they can actually *do* for a retarded child. Such a parent will want to know as much as possible about the school's curriculum and how it meets each child's individual needs. This parent will also want to know whether the school consults parents, and keeps them clearly informed, about their children's education; professionals may often use technical jargon among themselves, but they must also be able to explain their work to their customers in plain English. This matter of professional accountability to parents will be dealt with later in this chapter.

But first there is the matter of the curriculum, which has been defined as 'a school's plan for facilitating a child's growth and for developing selected skills, ideas, attitudes and values' (Department of Education and Science, 1975). This is not the only possible definition of a curriculum but it is a serviceable one, and the key word in it is 'plan'; without such a plan, a school cannot operate professionally at all, because it has no clear idea of what it is trying to achieve or of how it is trying to achieve it. A special school's curriculum must never be rigid – it must be able to adapt to changing needs – but it should provide a clearly structured framework, enabling head teacher and staff to make a preliminary assessment of how a prospective pupil's needs can best be met within that framework, or of how the framework would need to change to accommodate that pupil's needs.

Let us take the case of a seven-year-old retarded child who is presented for admission to a special school. The staff will want to know about his physical abilities, his language development, his self-help skills (dressing, undressing, washing, eating, etc.), his behaviour and relationships with other people, and any aptitude which he may have shown for reading, number, art, music and so on. The staff should be able to relate this information to their already existing programmes of work, which will cover these and other areas of development and which will form the main substance of the curriculum. They should then be able to tell the child's parents, at least in outline, how the school would aim to advance his development in each of these areas; obviously, it will take some weeks or months for the staff to know the child well and to plan his work programmes in detail.

What degree of professionalism will the special school bring to the planning of this child's educa-

tion and training? The answer will depend on the degree of professionalism which it has brought to the planning of its curriculum in general for the school as a whole. And the answer will therefore vary greatly from one school to another: in some schools the task of planning a curriculum has hardly begun.

ORGANIZATION AND THE CURRICULUM

Curriculum construction in a school for mentally retarded pupils is no simple task, for at least two reasons. Firstly, the range of ability in a school for the mentally retarded is wider than in any other type of school: there may be only fifty or sixty children in a school, but they may range from a relatively bright eight-year-old, who is perhaps beginning to read, down to a 17-year-old who has virtually no communication or even eye-contact with those around him, and who may additionally be immobile and incontinent. The curriculum must be sufficiently adaptable to meet the full range of needs presented by this wide variety of pupils. Secondly, there is very little published guidance available on the subject: although there are certainly useful books and material dealing with individual areas of the curriculum, there are very few which give guidance on the development of the curriculum as a whole. In this respect schools must, to a great extent, rely on their own efforts.

Figure 20.1 is an attempt by one school to summarize what appear to be the main areas of the curriculum appropriate for retarded children; it also suggests how some of those areas may relate to each other. This book is not the place to explain this model in detail (see Rectory Paddock School, 1983), but I will briefly refer to the main division within it – that between the 'developmental core curriculum' and the 'applied curriculum'. This division arises from ideas suggested by Clarke (1965) and Gulliford (1971). The aim is to identify certain essential areas of learning, what Gulliford calls 'key activities', and to develop them by means of highly-structured work-programmes, adapted as precisely as possible to each child's individual needs. These areas are grouped together in the 'developmental core curriculum', so called because it comprises what may be regarded as the central or 'core' areas of the child's development. The skills and knowledge gained through the developmental core curriculum should be generalized and given practical application in those activities listed in the 'applied curriculum'.

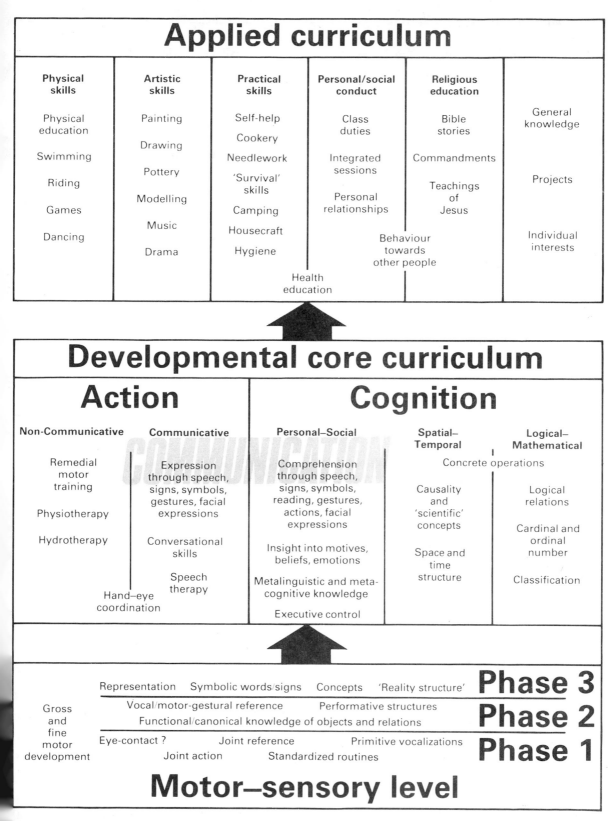

Applied curriculum

Physical skills	Artistic skills	Practical skills	Personal/social conduct	Religious education	
Physical education	Painting	Self-help	Class duties	Bible stories	General knowledge
Swimming	Drawing	Cookery	Integrated sessions	Commandments	
Riding	Pottery	Needlework		Teachings of Jesus	Projects
Games	Modelling	'Survival' skills	Personal relationships		
Dancing	Music	Camping			Individual interests
	Drama	Housecraft	Behaviour towards other people		
		Hygiene			
		Health education			

Developmental core curriculum

Action

Cognition

Non-Communicative	Communicative	Personal–Social	Spatial–Temporal	Logical–Mathematical
Remedial motor training	Expression through speech, signs, symbols, gestures, facial expressions	Comprehension through speech, signs, symbols, reading, gestures, actions, facial expressions	Concrete operations	
Physiotherapy			Causality and 'scientific' concepts	Logical relations
Hydrotherapy	Conversational skills	Insight into motives, beliefs, emotions	Space and time structure	Cardinal and ordinal number
	Speech therapy	Metalinguistic and meta-cognitive knowledge		Classification
Hand–eye coordination		Executive control		

Representation   Symbolic words/signs   Concepts   'Reality structure'   **Phase 3**

Vocal/motor-gestural reference   Performative structures   **Phase 2**
Functional/canonical knowledge of objects and relations

Gross and fine motor development

Eye-contact ?   Joint reference   Primitive vocalizations   **Phase 1**
Joint action   Standardized routines

Motor–sensory level

Fig. 20.1 A framework for curriculum development.

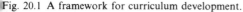

This type of curriculum structure may have implications for the organization of the school and of its daily timetable. A basic principle for the organization of any school is that *the curriculum should dictate the organization, and not vice versa.* The curriculum, and the aims and objectives it includes, are the very purpose of the school's existence; methods of organization are merely instrumental to the achievement of those aims and objectives. The implementation of a core curriculum, adapted closely to individual children's needs, may necessitate some departure from the usual organization, under which each child is placed in a certain class and does all his or her work with that class. For certain highly structured programmes it may be more effective to place the children in groups according to the stages which they have reached in those programmes. For example, a certain time may be fixed for work each day on a communication skills programme which is divided into four levels. Each child is placed at one of those levels according to the stage of language development he has reached; at the appointed time each day, he leaves his class base and goes to join the other children who are working at the same level as himself. When staff are teaching to very precise, programmed objectives, this kind of organization may give them a better chance of achieving results than if they are working with 'mixed-ability' groups, which may, however, be appropriate for other activities.

The curriculum in practice

The foregoing paragraphs (together with Figure 20.1) have outlined, in general terms, a possible approach to curricular development and organization in a school for retarded children. We will now briefly consider what such an approach may mean in practice for individual children. For example, let us take that reprobate, Stewart. Having made an enjoyable start to his school day, he proceeds from the entrance-hall into his classroom: 'Hullo, Stewart!' One of the staff undoes the buttons on his coat and pulls both sides of it up to his shoulders, but no further: a progress chart on the wall indicates that he must try to complete the task of removing his coat without any further help. Once he has learnt to do this, he will be taught the next step in the 'backward-chaining' sequence: he will have to pull the sides of the coat up to his shoulders unaided. The next step will be to undo the buttons himself, and so on. The teacher has devised this programme by analysing the whole task of coat-removing into a chain of small steps, which are then taught 'backwards', so that the last step is taught first; in this way, the child can achieve success – the completion of the task – as early as possible in the training process. This strategy is used frequently in teaching severely retarded children, especially in teaching self-help skills; it is, of course, vital that parents should be kept fully informed of these procedures, so that they can apply them when the child is at home.

Stewart's next port of call is the toilet area: although he is twelve years old, he is still going through the process of toilet-training. Then comes the day's first timetabled session, lasting 35 minutes and allocated to work on cognitive development. Clearly this is an extremely wide field: for pupils at the highest level of ability in the school it covers number work, awareness of spatial and temporal relations (including spatial measurement and learning to tell the time), and the beginnings of very simple 'scientific' concepts involving explanation of cause and effect in the world around them. But at Stewart's level the cognitive programme means learning 'object-permanence' – the fact that physical objects continue to exist when he cannot see them, learning to imitate a series of actions, and learning to relate two objects in space or two events in temporal sequence – things that a normal child learns in the first year or two of his life.

In the second session of the morning Stewart works on a programme of motor development tasks devised by the teacher in consultation with the school's physiotherapist. At this time, the more able children in the school are mostly working on their reading, using a variety of approaches designed to make the most of their individual abilities. Some children, for example, are able to use letter-sounds to help them recognize words; others may find this quite impossible, but may have a relatively good memory for the shapes of whole words. However, few retarded pupils are likely to achieve a standard of reading above that reached by a normal child at the age of eight. Whatever method may be used for teaching retarded children to read, there is one essential requirement, and that is that they must be helped to see the purpose of reading, namely to get the meaning from the text (Figure 20.2).

The third session of the morning is devoted mainly to improving the children's language and communication skills. Obviously, these skills do not exist in isolation from cognitive development, but there are specific language skills which need to be taught to many of the children: it may take them a long time to learn to construct sentences of two or

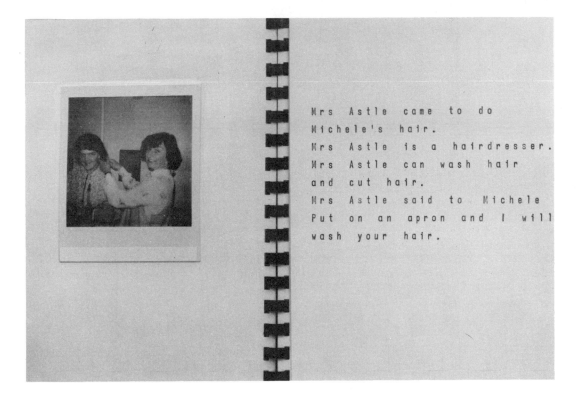

Mrs Astle came to do
Michele's hair.
Mrs Astle is a hairdresser.
Mrs Astle can wash hair
and cut hair.
Mrs Astle said to Michele
Put on an apron and I will
wash your hair.

Fig. 20.2 Books about the children themselves help to emphasize the meaningfulness of written language.

three words. Stewart's limited abilities will not allow him to achieve even that. His utterances mainly take the form of squeaks, chuckles and an occasional bellow of indignation. To these, staff are working to add a small repertoire of manual signs taken from the Makaton sign system – for example, signs for 'drink', 'biscuit' or 'toilet' (see Chapter 29).

After this it is time for lunch. This is an important training session for Stewart, who is being taught to feed himself with a spoon. It requires constant attention from a member of staff: Stewart takes the view that spoons are a wonderful invention but hands are quicker, especially for purloining one's neighbour's chips. The more able children in the school can, of course, feed themselves and perhaps serve themselves at the table. On some days senior pupils will have cooked their own lunch, having first visited local shops to buy the ingredients (Figure 20.3). The resulting lunch will probably consist largely of convenience foods, which the pupils will realistically be able to manage with minimum supervision by staff: there is little value in pupils producing a *cordon bleu* meal under constant direction by the teacher, because they will certainly not

be able to produce such a meal unaided when they have left school. Staff must always be realistic in setting objectives for their pupils.

This is not to say that staff should ever set an arbitrary ceiling upon what their pupils may achieve, nor cease to urge better provision for pupils after they have left school. The progressive types of development envisaged by Norris (Chapter 19) will stand a better chance of realization if schools provide increasingly strong evidence of pupils' potential for independent living and for benefiting from advanced training (Figure 20.4).

There is, of course, no hope of independent living for Stewart and other profoundly handicapped pupils, but there is always hope of teaching them basic skills that will make them less of a burden to others and so widen their possibilities for a fuller life; there is hope, too, of increasing their awareness of the world around them, their physical competence in coping with its demands and their possibilities for communicating with other people. These were the main aims of Stewart's morning timetable, which centred upon the 'developmental core curriculum'. Staff will continue to pursue these

Fig. 20.3 Practical skills: shopping and telephoning.

Fig. 20.4 Using a tandem to learn the Highway Code.

aims during the rest of Stewart's day within the wider context of the 'applied curriculum', covering those activities shown in the top part of Figure 20.1.

PROFESSIONALS GALORE

The above paragraphs have given a brief sketch of some of the work which takes place in a school for mentally retarded children. In tackling this work, teachers are (or should be) able to call upon a wide variety of other professionals to bring their own specialized skills to bear. Some of these are discussed in the last part of this book. The job of the physiotherapist, whether full-time or part-time, is bound to be important because of the large proportion (perhaps 50%) of retarded pupils who have either mild or severe degrees of physical handicap; for the most severe cases of multiple handicap most schools of this kind have a 'special care' class, which is equipped with many aids and special facilities for coping with these pupils' often appalling disabilities (Figure 20.5); in practice, the physiotherapist will probably spend much of his or her time working with these children and advising teachers and other staff as to how to handle them (Figure 20.6). The help of an occupational therapist, if one is available, will also be valuable to staff, particularly in this special class; the occupational therapist should be able to advise on each child's needs as regards specialized physical aids and equipment and assist in obtaining them.

Although teachers in a school for retarded children should be as expert as possible in the development of pupils' communication skills, they will often be able to benefit from consulting a speech therapist about certain children with special communication difficulties. Speech therapists are in short supply, especially those with much knowledge of, or willingness to work with, retarded pupils, and a school may therefore be allocated as little as one day a week of speech therapy time; into this limited time the therapist must try to fit assessments, discussions with staff, interviews with parents, writing of reports, and periods of therapy with individual children. An additional part of the job is

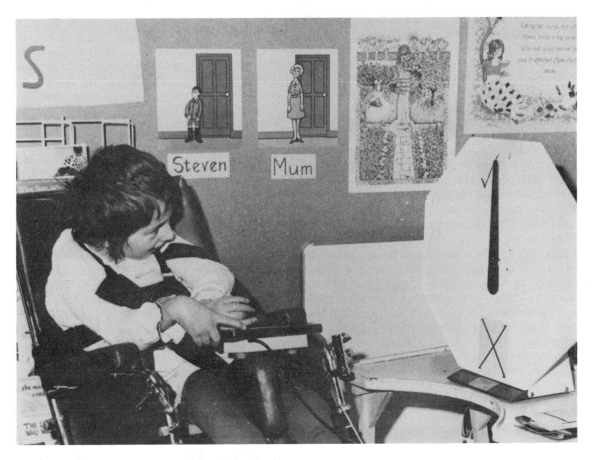

Fig. 20.5 Electronic communication board for children in the special care class.

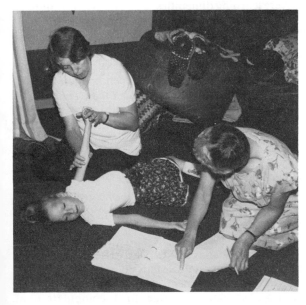

Fig. 20.6 Assessment by physiotherapist and teacher.

investigating and advising upon children's difficulties in feeding: the therapist's specialized knowledge of the mouth and throat relates directly to the problems some children have in biting, chewing and swallowing.

Another, probably even less frequent, visitor to the school is the educational psychologist. The job is often difficult to define, and it varies greatly from one psychologist to another. Some find themselves with an excessive case-load, which prevents them from visiting schools regularly to talk to school staff and to offer them advice. But the psychologist who has time can be a valuable help to the teacher in dealing with certain children, perhaps by investigating and assessing specific learning difficulties, by suggesting ways of managing behaviour problems, by helping to explain difficulties to parents, or by contributing to the staff's work in curriculum development. Looking to the future, an additional job for the psychologist may be in helping the school to carry out research projects (about which more below).

A school for retarded children will inevitably contain pupils with defects of sight or hearing and the school should be able to call upon specialist teachers or advisers to assist in these cases; they will be able to arrange, or to carry out themselves, assessment procedures which may give the teacher valuable information about pupils' visual or auditory possibilities; they will also be able to advise on the provision of appropriate aids.

The list of professionals who may visit special schools for various purposes is lengthy. To those already mentioned we must add school doctors, school nurses, dental officers, 'oral hygienists', and social workers, who may come from the local department of social services or from voluntary bodies such as the Invalid Children's Aid Association. Teachers must learn how to make the most of any help that these people can give, whilst avoiding the temptation to spend more time in talking to other professionals than in actually teaching children. They must avoid spending too much time in large meetings and massive case conferences. The First Law of Meetings is that, as a general rule, the usefulness of any meeting is in inverse proportion to its size.

ACCOUNTABILITY TO PARENTS

'The relationship between parents and the school which their child is attending has a crucial bearing upon the child's educational progress. On the one hand, if parents are to support the efforts of teachers they need information and advice from the school about its objectives and the provision being made for their child: on the other, a child's special needs cannot be adequately assessed and met in school without the insights that his parents, from their more intimate experience of him, are able to provide. Close links between schools and parents must therefore be established and maintained, as we have stressed throughout this report.'

(Warnock Committee, 1978)

Whilst agreeing with every word of the above paragraph, one cannot help noting that consultation with parents is recommended only because it is thought expedient for the child's progress, and not because parents are thought to have any natural right to such consultation: accountability to parents as clients or customers does not, perhaps, come naturally to many professionals in the state education system. But certainly, as the Warnock Report recommends, special schools must strive continuously to build a close working relationship with parents.

What does this mean in practice? It means that parents must be welcome in the school at any time, must be fully consulted about their wishes for their child's education, and must be given proper, written reports on their child's work at regular intervals. 'Home–school notebooks', recommended by the Warnock Committee, are an essential means of daily communication between teacher and parent, and staff should try to write in them every day, saying something about what the child has been doing in school. The school's parent–teacher association is another important point of contact between home and school – provided that it is used not only to raise money for the school but also to facilitate the exchange of views and information between parents and staff.

If a school makes itself genuinely accountable to parents, then the views and wishes of those parents are bound to affect the curriculum. Figure 20.7 shows how decisions on the curriculum can reflect both parental and professional points of view. This model may appear over-simplified in that any views emanating from government sources, whether national or local, are excluded from it; this is done on the grounds that education is essentially a matter between teachers, parents and children. The model can thus be applied to independent as well as to state schools.

RESEARCH AND THE CURRICULUM

'Knowledge of teaching children who . . . have severe learning difficulties. . . . is still in its infancy,' said the Warnock Committee. This seems a critically important point to those who believe that the right kind of education can radically improve the mental and general functioning of retarded children; for that improvement depends upon *increasing our knowledge of how to teach these children*. So long as that knowledge is allowed to remain 'in its infancy', we cannot expect much progress. Therefore, our most urgent priority must be to increase that knowledge, and, if we want to see knowledge increased, we naturally look for help to the researcher.

But that familiar cliché 'the yawning chasm between research and practice' applies to special education as much as to so many other things. As long ago as 1975, Clarke and Clarke wrote, 'the results of research need to be disseminated more rapidly so that practical steps do not lag, as so often occurs at the moment, many years behind the findings . . . doubtless due to a combination of

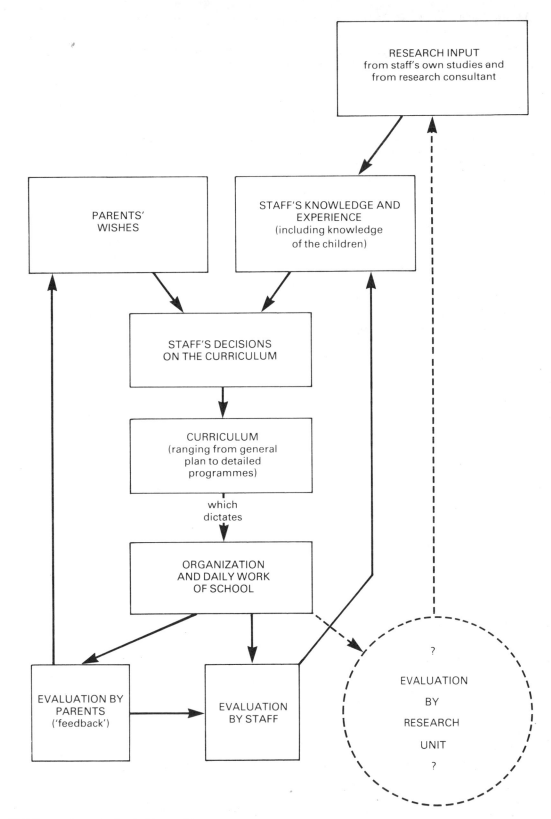

Fig. 20.7 Factors in curricular decision-making.

inertia, conservatism, poor communication, vested interests. . . . ' But it is still the case that research journals, often containing reports directly relevant to the education of retarded children, are read by only a few teachers; the translation of research findings into teaching strategies is attempted by even fewer.

Is this just the fault of teachers? Mittler (1969) urged greater efforts *by the researcher* to 'justify his existence' by relating his research more closely to 'practical problems of disordered learning as seen in the classroom and in the home'. But, even now, any teachers who wish to interest researchers in practical, school-based projects or raise the necessary finance from research-funding bodies may rest assured that they will find it an uphill struggle.

Our aim, I suggest, should be for special schools themselves to become so far as possible, research establishments, with teachers and researchers working together. It may be possible, in some cases, to build a research unit at the school or to make rooms available to be adapted for this purpose; something of this kind was foreshadowed in the Warnock Report (para. 8.13), and the benefits of such an arrangement would be considerable for all concerned. Another useful innovation is the appointment of a part-time 'research consultant' – preferably someone who is experienced in using research methods and reviewing research findings and who also has experience of special education. Such a person can assist the staff of the school in assimilating published research findings and in setting up research projects in the school. As teachers, we all need the help of researchers in evaluating with ruthless objectivity the effectiveness of our curricula and teaching methods; where it is clearly established that a curriculum is not effective we must be prepared to face that unwelcome fact and go 'back to the drawing-board', remembering that schools exist not to enable teachers to feel complacent but to enable children to be educated.

In Figure 20.7, 'evaluation by research unit' is included as a tentative possibility, but the ultimate aim must be for the whole school to become, in a sense, a research unit – an information-processing system, assimilating knowledge, deciding what parts of it may be useful, framing hypotheses, testing them out and seeing whether they work *in a school*, incorporating the results into work-programmes, evaluating and fine-tuning those programmes over a period of years, exchanging information with other schools operating in a similar way, and so continuing the process until the 'special educational needs' of mentally retarded children become objects of real knowledge and intelligent planning.

THE QUESTION OF INTEGRATION

The last few paragraphs have emphasized that if a better education is to be provided for retarded children the most essential requirement is more knowledge and more effective application of that knowledge. Some readers may feel that this point is so obvious that no one is likely to dispute it, but such readers will be mistaken. Tension is becoming apparent between two contrasting approaches: some take the view (advanced above) that the most urgent need is for more knowledge and, so far as possible, a scientific and experimental approach to educating the retarded, even if this means some degree of separation of the retarded from other children for this purpose; others take a quite different view, maintaining that such separation is unacceptable on moral or political grounds: 'Whether or not children with a wide range of handicaps should be involved in ordinary schools primarily involves a moral choice in the same way that advocacy of comprehensive or grammar schools involves choosing between different kinds of society' (Booth, 1983). Separation may also be regarded as unnecessary: ' . . . children can be educated within ordinary schools irrespective of the severity of their handicap' (Booth, 1983). This raises the obvious question: But will they be educated to the highest possible standard? This is the heart of the 'integration' debate. There is no space to pursue it here, but in Chapter 19 Norris discusses the subject and, in this connection, the possible effects of the Warnock Report and the 1981 Education Act.

Those who are wary of extreme points of view may tend to agree with Mittler (1979): 'The question of whether mentally handicapped pupils should be taught in special or ordinary schools should be seen as one of reconciling the child's educational and learning needs with the need to maintain contact with ordinary children in the community'. Staff of special schools can help to effect that reconciliation by establishing close links with local primary and secondary schools, with regular visits of children between them (Figure 20.8). For a description of such a scheme in practice see Taylor and Hagedorn (1978). Staff should also ensure that integration takes place within their own schools, with regular contact between their more able pupils and those who are very severely handicapped.

Fig. 20.8 Integrated sessions with pupils from primary and secondary schools.

Nevertheless, there is little doubt that the tension referred to above, between two contrasting educational approaches, will still be unresolved when the next edition of this book comes to be written.

Tension, however, is far from the mind of Stewart at 3.30 in the afternoon: he cannot tell the time, but the sight of the minibuses outside the front door evokes pleasant associations of home and Mum and Mars bars. He toddles through the open door with the rest of the children. Anxious staff are once again watching out for the runners, and (just in case) a 'long-stop' is on duty by the gate. Suddenly there is a hullaballoo outside the front door: someone has pulled Wendy's hair, but nobody saw who did it. Stewart, a picture of innocence, toddles slowly on towards his bus. . . .

REFERENCES

Booth T (1983) Integrating special education. In Booth T & Potts P (eds) *Integrating Special Education.* pp. 1–27. Oxford: Basil Blackwell.

Clarke ADB (1965) The role of learning transfer in development. In Loring J (ed) *Teaching the Cerebral Palsied Child.* pp. 171–179. London: Spastics Society/William Heinemann.

Clarke ADB & Clarke AM (1975) *Recent Advances in the Study of Subnormality,* 2nd edn. London: MIND (National Association for Mental Health).

Department of Education and Science (1975) *Educating Mentally Handicapped Children.* Education Pamphlet No. 60. London: HMSO.

Gulliford R (1971) *Special Educational Needs.* London: Routledge & Kegan Paul.

Mittler P (1969) *New Directions in the Study of Learning Deficits.* Lecture given to the Institute for Research into Mental Retardation. Subsequently printed in Clarke, ADB & Lewis MM (eds) (1972) *Learning, Speech and Thought in the Mentally Retarded.* pp. 1–13. London: Butterworth.

Mittler P (1979) *People Not Patients.* London: Methuen.

Rectory Paddock School (1983) *In Search of a Curriculum: Notes on the Education of Mentally Handicapped Children,* 2nd edn. Sidcup. Kent: Robin Wren Publications.

Taylor K & Hagedorn J (1978) A happy mixture. *Junior Education 2 (4: April):* 8.

Warnock Committee (1978) *Special Educational Needs: Report of the Committee of Enquiry into the Education of Handicapped Children and Young People* (Chairman: HM Warnock). London: HMSO.

Chapter 21
Special Education in the United States

AARON H. ARMFIELD

In the United States the movement towards providing special education was started by parents of handicapped learners. They were joined by the new professional group of special educators, and the combined groups carried the message to the general public that disabled people deserved the rights and opportunities enjoyed by all citizens. That manifesto was embodied in the Education for all Handicapped Children Act of 1975 (PL94-142). The rules and regulations for implementing that legislation reflected the social concerns of the nation and gave direction to the developing art of special education. On the subject of evaluation, they requested that discrimination based on race, cultural background or the presence of handicapping conditions be eliminated and that evaluation be used to document educational need and progress. They called for nationwide systematic location of children needing special services at the earliest age possible – a reflection of the need to reduce or eliminate the effect of disability through educational intervention. Suggested parental involvement at every stage of the educational process was described in highly detailed language. The 'zero reject' principle, a rule against excluding any type of disabling condition, meant that approaches that had been totally foreign to the schools would need to be considered. Expensive equipment would need to be purchased and alternative or augmentative communication would be necessary to provide education to multi-handicapped students. Changing public attitude was a beginning. New assessment instruments, teaching methods and materials, therapeutic devices, and communication programmes with parents were needed. The effort to provide a free, appropriate education for all children was begun.

PARENTAL PARTICIPATION

Parent activism

The nature of family participation in the special child's education has changed radically from twenty years ago. At that time, volunteer groups composed mostly of parents of handicapped children had organized and were financially supporting education, recreation and vocational training programs for children who were not regarded as the responsibility of government schools and programmes. The United Cerebral Palsy Association and the National Association for Retarded Children were two well-known groups who helped to pioneer educational services for the handicapped.

As the programmes supported by parent groups grew into community volunteer agencies who employed specialized professionals, it became obvious to many that special education could be an important resource to the community at large by greatly improving the productive life of some of its most handicapped citizens and reducing the need for institutional care. Families and specialized professionals, many of whom were newly trained to provide services for the handicapped, joined forces to find a way to shift some of the overwhelming financial burden of educating handicapped learners to the general population. A series of court cases and legislative bills culminated in the passage of the Education of All Handicapped Children Act of 1975.

Parent rights

PL 94-142 was remarkable in the extent to which it advanced the concept that parents could be involved in making decisions about their child's

247

education. The fundamental procedure of due process was defined in a set of rights:

1 Parents must have an opportunity to have a hearing about any matter of concern to the student's identification, evaluation, placement or free appropriate education.
2 A surrogate parent who has precisely the same rights in the educational process as a natural parent must be appointed by the state educational agency if a student is a ward of the state or if the student's parents are unknown or unavailable.
3 Parents may obtain an independent evaluation, by a certified examiner independent of the local educational agency, of their handicapped child.
4 Parents are entitled to written notice from the school regarding changes in identification, evaluation, placement or the provision of a free appropriate education with accompanying reasons for the action in the parents' native language or dominant mode of communication.
5 Parental consent must be obtained by the school following full information about the case in the parents' dominant language before the first evaluation of the child.

Parental participation in planning

In addition to this delineation of rights, parents were further encouraged to be involved by PL 94-142. Requirements for the development of an individualized educational programme (IEP) were given extensive description. Parents were to be included in the process along with the teacher, programme supervisor and the evaluator. The purpose of the IEP was to give the parents an opportunity to suggest goals, inquire about teaching methods, learn about assessment procedures, hear systematic reports on progress and voice approval or disapproval. Parental access to their child's educational records and interpretation of the contents of those records were also provided in PL 94-142.

It appears that most IEP planning sessions are quite amicable and that parents are quite accepting of the school's efforts on behalf of their child. A number of schools apparently desire active participation of parents. There is a growing trend for schools to increase the role of parents aggressively. The trend includes parent training and family support projects.

Parent training

A programme of training parents for the IEP process is generally co-sponsored by an advocacy group and the school. Invited speakers may include legal experts, advocates, parents and curriculum advisors. Topics may be parental rights, IEP procedures, home and school instructional planning, parent and school responsibility, local school practices and specific handicapping conditions. The purpose of the training is to encourage parents to feel confident about participating in planning and to increase the frequency of positive contributions from parents.

Several projects have concentrated on training parents to help provide educational intervention in the home. This is especially true of projects for early education of the handicapped where teachers go to the home on a regular basis to help parents prepare appropriate developmental activities for their child. Some schools ask parents to come to the classroom to act as volunteers for short periods of time to help the parents better understand the programme in which the child is enrolled and then to support certain educational goals in the home. It is fairly common for teachers to involve willing parents in a school–home training programme on a specific skill or behaviour to be acquired by a student.

Family support

Much has been written about the stages of parental adjustment to a handicapped child. However, the needs of the handicapped at successive stages of development present an ever-changing challenge to siblings, parents, relatives and neighbours. The impact of a growing handicapped child on his or her environment is complex. Single-parent families, second marriages, adoptive parents, foster parents, extended family members, ethnic heritage, and economic hardship are a few of the complicating factors which can dramatically influence the presence of a handicapping condition. Several schools have cooperated with other social agencies and volunteer agencies to provide parent study groups and counselling on family needs such as sex education. Such projects address a great need and appear to be expanding.

ASSESSMENT

Functional assessment

The first step in the individualized educational planning process is to identify the present level of educational functioning. That identification requires that each student's skill and abilities be assessed. In a culturally pluralistic society that is attempting to assess the learning potential of students who have previously been considered uneducable, appropriate and fair assessment is a major challenge.

Functional assessment approaches are being developed to meet the practical needs of schools who wish to identify, plan for and provide appropriate instruction to special students systematically. Assuming that present behaviour is the cumulative result of unique inter-relationships of hereditary and environmental factors, functional assessment is the attempt to describe as accurately as possible those behaviours that are present or absent. That approach provides a basis for planning an IEP at a child's current level of functioning. Analysis and planning may include functioning in language, perceptual, adaptive, self help, emotional, social, gross and fine motor skills and achievement in academic areas.

Assessment for planning

The type of assessment that is called for in PL 94-142 is continuous and involves a general-to-specific evaluation process. Major assessment steps are:

1 Screen and identify exceptional students.
2 Conduct a comprehensive, functional assessment of the student's ability to perform.
3 Determine appropriate educational placement.
4 Design IEPs.
5 Monitor individual student progress.
6 Evaluate programme effectiveness.

Non-discriminatory assessment

An accurate assessment of a handicapped learner's capabilities and limitations is difficult at best. Assessments were once completed using instruments designed for average students. PL 94-142 suggested certain underlying assumptions regarding assessment:

1 Assessments must be appropriate to the handicap.
2 Assessments must be free of cultural and linguistic bias.
3 Assessment data must come from multiple sources and be directed toward programming.
4 Assessment results must provide comprehensive descriptions of current levels of functioning.

Adapting and creating assessment tests which are handicap-appropriate and free of cultural and linguistic bias is a continuing activity. New tests are

being developed with non-verbal sections, with scores standardized with handicapped learners included, and with separate standardized scores for specific social and racial groups. Some schools have developed local sets of norms for true peer evaluation, but previously published non-verbal scales appear to be more frequently used.

Comprehensive assessment ingredients

The first step in the process of identifying students who can profit from special education is screening. Early identification efforts often involve the use of developmental checklists, behaviour problem rating scales, readiness measures and sensory tests. The device used the most is one which is intended for children younger than six years and surveys functioning on landmark developmental tasks such as gross motor skills, fine motor skills, adaptive skills, language behaviours and psychosocial capability. Passes or fails on such activities provide an estimate of development or developmental delay. Collection of estimates then provides a basis for highlighting or selecting a particular function for comprehensive analysis.

Comprehensive assessment procedures require a great deal of qualitative and quantitative information from a range of sources, such as the direct observation of behaviours, classroom climate scales, behaviour ratings, actual child performance, interviews with the family, anecdotal records and school achievement. Direct observation allows behaviour to be sampled in a natural setting and can yield information on which stimulus affects which behaviours in what way.

Time sampling, recording data on behaviour for a specific length of time, can accurately describe the frequency and duration of a certain behaviour pattern. Event sampling, on the other hand, narratively describes the chain or sequence of preceding and succeeding behaviours throughout an activity. Combining the techniques of time and event sampling can provide a teacher with an objective analysis that lends itself to planning appropriate interventions. Checklists and rating scales can provide structure to a teacher's or parent's subjective impression of a child's behaviour. Rating scales can also focus the attention of the observer on an important behaviour which could otherwise be overlooked.

Norm-referenced assessment scales are employed to compare an individual child's knowledge, performance and skills with those of a representative group of peers. Familiar examples are intelligence and achievement tests. For them to be of value in a multi-cultural society requires that great care be taken to ensure that the peer group against which a score is compared is truly representative. Norm-referenced tests are important to the process of determining placement and type of classroom instruction. Historically, such scales have had little relationship to behaviours tested and behaviours taught in the classroom.

Criterion-reference assessment scales can provide a record of progress on the mastery of specific educational skills. While norm reference provides a comparison of a student with a representative group of peers, criterion reference provides a comparison of a student's current performance with that student's past performance of a skill which has instructional relevance. To measure the progress of skills over time in this way, a teacher must analyse skills that a student has not yet acquired along a given instructional sequence; this is task analysis. Once the task has been analysed, the teacher focuses on the unacquired skills. Criterion-reference assessment and task analysis are important tools in carrying out an individualized educational programme.

By using a comprehensive set of assessment tools, from screening to norm-referenced measures, reasonably fair and effective evaluation can be made of a student and an educational programme. This requires the involvement of several specialised professionals and, hopefully, the child's family.

EARLY EDUCATION OF THE HANDICAPPED

Public support

Acceptance of the belief that the environment played an important part in the development of the child was a major impetus for creating early education programmes in the USA. The logic of providing cognitive stimulation to all normal children was applied to handicapped children who lacked the ability of most children to interact with the environment. Such logic also suggested that early intense stimulation could reduce, if not eliminate, the impact of handicapping conditions upon future development. Thus, early educational intervention for handicapped children might be said to have been based upon the philosophical application of the homely admonition that a stitch in time saves nine.

In 1965 Project Head Start was initiated, to provide compensatory programmes for economi-

cally disadvantaged preschool children. Services to be provided included: (a) educational intervention, which could be home-based instruction, centre-based instruction or a combination, (b) medical intervention, which emphasized nutritional education as well as the identification of physical and mental health problems and some intervention programmes, and (c) family services, which helped families with information on social services available for families and provided training in parenting skills.

At least 10% of the children enrolled in a Head Start programme must qualify as being handicapped. This has contributed to the development of mainstreaming as a concept because of the reported acceptance of disabled by non-disabled children in these programmes. The field of assessment of the abilities of young children has also been stimulated by this requirement, as each programme must provide evidence concerning the proportion and type of handicapped children enrolled.

In 1968 the Handicapped Children's Early Education Assistance Act was enacted to fund projects for research on the specific needs of young handicapped children, curricula to meet the specific needs, demonstration of curricular techniques in practice, training of personnel, and the implementation of the research, curriculum and personnel-training programmes throughout the country. The funded projects have produced field-tested programmes in early-childhood screening and assessment, educational intervention curricula and parent and para-professional training.

The Education for All Handicapped Children Act (PL 94-142) made at least two important contributions. First, children as young as three were included. Second, it required that each state and local school conduct a search designed to identify all handicapped children and youths in each agency's jurisdiction. This effort helped to find at least the most handicapped at an early age and, in many cases, to provide an educational intervention programme.

Identification and screening

The identification of children who may need early intervention generally occurs through referral or screening. Obvious medical conditions such as cerebral palsy or spina bifida are likely to be noticed and referred by a physician or a child's parents. Less serious conditions will occasionally be referred by parents or professionals, but a large number of learning handicaps would remain unattended without an organized screening programme.

Screening tests have been organized for quick examination of large numbers of children to locate children who might need special services. The tests are conducted at child day-care centres or at community fairs where families are provided with information on child development and a free developmental check-up.

A referral or screening programme must be followed by assessment. This may include evaluation of sensory functions such as hearing and vision, development of gross and fine motor skills and speech and language development. Self-help skills, such as eating, dressing and toileting and unusual behaviour patterns, such as severe tantrums or withdrawal, are also checked.

Intervention models

When it is determined that a child is in need of special services and the child's strengths and weaknesses have been assessed, an IEP is designed. The intervention programme will generally fall into one of three programme models: home-based, centre-based, or a combination of home-and school-based. Centre-based programmes will typically be for children requiring the services of several specialized professionals such as physical therapists and physicians and/or specialized equipment. Home-based programmes employ teachers who visit the home to train and support parents in an intervention programme. The teacher will provide assessment or help the parents assess a child's abilities and then help them evaluate progress. The teacher may provide some instructional materials or aid the parents in locating or developing the material. Planning the use of the instructional materials designed to stimulate development is led by the teacher, but includes the active participation of the parents. A home- and school-based programme combines the advantages of the other two models by offering the specialized attention available in a centre and home follow-up support for the family.

Assessment and intervention programmes have been very much influenced by theories of development which suggest that development follows sequential stages. Developmental checklists that are used to assess abilities and upon which progress is charted are based on a combination of theory and organized record-keeping. Instruction or therapy is then based upon the premise that certain skills or abilities will probably follow successful completion of the child's present stage of development. The use of developmental theories has contributed greatly to the logical organization of early educational intervention programmes. There is an obligation, however, for the programme to evaluate the efficacy of its developmental theory base as it is applied to assessment, planning and intervention. Comparison between programmes regarding their experience could provide the world at large with added perspective on the field of early childhood development.

MAINSTREAMING

The process of mainstreaming, or placing special students in educational settings with regular students, has been an objective in schools for more than a decade. The process was actively supported by special educators who observed or reasoned that handicapped students who associated only with handicapped students were likely to develop the characteristics of a handicapped subculture. The movement was welcomed by school administrators, who feared, for philosophical or economic reasons, the proliferation of special classes for students with mild learning handicaps. The funding formula for PL 94-142 was designed to encourage schools to adopt actively the principle of the least restrictive environment for special learners. A theoretical model which suggested that a graduated choice of environments, ranging from regular classes to hospital schools, would serve a gradually decreasing population from mildly handicapped to profoundly handicapped was considered to be ideal.

Implementation

In practice, an overwhelming majority of identified mildly handicapped learners are placed in regular or resource classes in which they physically see both regular and special students every day. A large proportion of moderately handicapped are placed in self-contained classes in regular schools and participate in some non-academic activities with regular students several times per week. Severely handicapped students are often mainstreamed in the same way or are transported for part of each day, from a special school to a regular school, for specific activities. Classrooms for profoundly handicapped students may be found as self-contained units in regular schools, but such students are seldom integrated with regular students.

The process of mainstreaming generally consists of at least four different areas: physical presence, participation in such non-academic areas as art, music, vocational and recreational activities, participation in academic activities and social interaction. Physical presence and participation in school activities could lead to spontaneous social interaction between regular and special students. Social interaction seems to occur in groups of younger children, but as children mature and begin to discriminate against people they perceive to be different, careful planning is required of teachers for social interaction to occur.

Nearly every disabled learner attending a publicly supported school is physically present, at least part of the day, in a regular school building. Separate schools for children who are severely (profoundly) handicapped or medically fragile still exist, but are rare. Privately financed schools are also rare, but are available to families who have enough money. Physical presence in a regular school describes a very wide range of situations. Some special classes are housed in small, temporary additions beside the main building, some classes are grouped in a separate wing, some classes are randomly located next to regular classes attended by children of the same age, and many mildly handicapped students are placed in a regular class with their age peers. No statistical analysis exists which could provide an authoritative national description of the current proportion of physical settings for special learners. A general rule appears to be that a high number of special classes in regular school buildings are placed away from the high traffic areas. However, the opportunity for handicapped learners to come in contact with regular learners at some time during every school day appears to exist in most American schools.

Participation in non-academic programmes with regular students appears to be common amongst mildly handicapped and some moderately handicapped students. The effect of the participation is difficult to measure or describe, but the participation usually serves as a starting point for other participatory activities.

Academic integration of mildly handicapped students is often supported by a resource or consultant teacher. Special students will generally go from the regular class to a resource room for specific subjects, such as reading or mathematics, or to receive remedial instruction in the specific academic areas, in addition to attending regular classes with regular students. The types of children with learning handicaps served by a resource room are generally those with average intelligence who have reading or mathematics problems, with mild cognitive deficits,

with mild or moderate behaviour disorders, with temporary emotional adjustment problems, with mild to severe sensory disabilities (vision and hearing), or with moderate to severe orthopaedic disabilities.

The status of social integration of special students with regular students is mercurial, at best. Casual observation in some schools in which there is the physical presence of special students suggests that social integration does not exist in any form. Hostility of regular faculty toward the presence of special students appears to still exist in those schools. In contrast, there appears to be an easy integration and acceptance of handicapping conditions on the part of faculty and students in other schools. The difference appears to be dependent upon the leadership of the school administration. A frequently used programme in the latter situation is one in which students who demonstrate a high level of responsibility in the regular class are rewarded with the privilege of tutoring or aiding special students. When these programmes are encouraged by teachers, a sense of pride is instilled in both sets of students.

Overall, the majority of special students are physically placed in some type of regular school facility. Many of the students with sensory or orthopaedic handicaps have been integrated into regular academic programmes with resource teacher support. Social integration between special and regular students has been accomplished in schools where administrators have carefully orchestrated positive personal exchange.

TECHNOLOGY IN SPECIAL EDUCATION

The physical appearance of special classrooms has changed since the day when the teaching materials in a class for slow learners consisted of cast-off texts from the regular classes. Many classrooms now are filled with attractive books, instructional games and technologically advanced electronic equipment. Materials and equipment have been specially prepared for learners with specific limitations. Much of it has been made possible through the application of space-age technology.

Computer and programmed instruction

Computer and teaching machine programmed instruction has almost all been prepared for individualized use. Further, programming instruction requires task analysis – analysis of skills, abilities or knowledge that must be learned in a given instructional sequence to reach a specific goal. Continuous assessment and self-pacing is also part of the programme. Many students find programmed instruction attractive enough to consider the time spent on the machine as a reward for completing other work. It appears to be a very welcome and extremely valuable tool for providing individualized instruction.

Teachers have begun to use the computer as an aid for planning. First, a comprehensive list of educational goals that are appropriate for the selected population of students is prepared. Parents are offered the comprehensive list as a start for selecting, in discussion with the teacher, educational goals for their child. The selections are entered into the computer and then a complete description of goals and associated activities is printed for distribution to all concerned. Many of the programmes are designed to include descriptions of assessment procedures, suggested teaching activities and evaluation techniques that can be associated with each of the educational goals.

Using the computer as a tool in the diagnostic/prescriptive teaching process is accomplished with programmes that are designed to retrieve (a) suggestions for remedial teaching activities (b) available resources that may be applicable to the given situation (c) further or additional assessment procedures and (d) evaluation techniques that are keyed to diagnostic data yielded by certain diagnostic instruments. While the intention of the planning programmes and the diagnostic/prescriptive teaching programmes is to aid the individual student, accumulation of programme records can provide a school system with information on trends and future needs.

Recorders

Audio and videotape recorders have high educational value. An obvious problem for a student with a reading problem is dealing with the printed word. Particularly for a student with limited visual comprehension but good audio comprehension, an audio tape recorder offers an opportunity to hear the reading material that is required in the class. Many students without limitations find listening to recorded stories and other material to be a rewarding experience. Self-recording can become an adventure in performance for a student for whom oral reading is a dreaded exercise. It allows for rehearsal, self-appraisal and a record of a student's best effort.

A major resource provided by videotape is professionally prepared instruction which brings in the outside world to the classroom. In addition, some interesting experiments with videotape have been explored. One involves recording for a certain length of time a student who has behaviour problems. Later, the teacher and the student discuss the behaviour exhibited by the student and the impact of that behaviour on the rest of the class. It can be a revelation to a student to see himself or herself as others do and to observe the environmental consequences of that behaviour. Often, the student will have had no previous awareness of the relationship between a specific behaviour and undesired consequences. A sequential series of recording sessions and discussions can help a student develop self-monitoring and modification skills. Another experiment has been used to help students form realistic, positive self-concepts by producing a self-commercial – a self-description of valuable personal assets on video tape. Preparation for the production requires considerable introspection and self-evaluation. Describing oneself before a camera requires elements of realism and fortitude. These experiments suggest that videotaping has potential as a tool for improving behaviour and social performance in the classroom. There are experiments in the development stage which will combine computer programming with video instruction. The potential seems unlimited.

Technology for deaf and blind students

The dramatic improvement in acoustic, optical and sensory technology has had great impact on the availability of alternative devices for students with sensory handicaps. The miniaturization and advanced performance of acoustic equipment has made it possible to improve or augment the auditory reception of nearly every person with a hearing limitation. Language development and hearing augmentation teaching programmes are being used with hearing-impaired infants and young children to capitalize on the available combination of technology and language-stimulation techniques. With the exception of electronic equipment, nursery and pre-school programmes for deaf children appear to be nearly the same as programmes for normal children.

Technology that allows a visually impaired or blind student to appreciate visual images is now available. One of the first of such devices was the Optacon, which delivered an image of individual letters to the fingers by means of vibrating pins. The

Kurzweil Reading Machine is a small computer that converts print into speech. Electronic devices that provide audible information have been developed to teach mathematics, spelling and other academic subjects. Some of the inventions have been transformed into toys for sighted children.

Variable-speed tape recorders are used to compress speech. This allows a visually handicapped student, with practice, to listen to recorded speech at a speed approaching that of slow-normal reading. Braille now has very limited use in the USA classroom.

Technology for multi-handicapped learners

Technological advances have provided multi-handicapped students with access to the world at large. Any one or a combination of the electronic devices for the deaf or visually impaired may be applied to an individual student's specific need. Voice-activated equipment is offering mobility and voice-simulators are giving speech to a growing number of people who were previously non-ambulatory or non-communicative. Modern technology offers many wonderful opportunities to those handicapped people who are fortunate enough to be part of a family or school programme with the financial resources to provide them.

ALTERNATIVE AND AUGMENTATIVE COMMUNICATION

Alternative communication

An interesting phenomenon has been occurring in the form of experimental approaches in establishing communication with persons who find it impossible to use speech or who have limited ability to express themselves with speech. Although the deaf community has long used manual communication, the use of manual communication for those who can hear, even those without speech, has been considered to be primitive and regressive. A common opinion has been that speech is the only way for hearing people to learn to communicate, if they were to learn at all. A similar attitude has prevailed to the use of pictographic symbol systems other than printed English for written communication.

Experiments with manual and symbolic communication with severely retarded people had been conducted, but the major impetus for widespread practice was manual communication experiments with chimpanzees. When it appeared that chimpanzees could acquire a small expressive vocabulary

the field of communication for non-verbal hearing people changed. Teachers, speech therapists, researchers and other professionals began to try programmes designed to teach manual or pictographic symbol systems to severely retarded and multi-handicapped people.

Choosing vocabulary

Questions immediately arose. Which signs or symbols should be taught first? What is the typical composition of an effective small vocabulary? Are signs or symbols more useful? The lack of experience with dealing with very small vocabularies was compounded by the lack of experience in communicating at all with non-verbal people.

A variety of guidelines were suggested for choosing initial vocabulary. Those guidelines relied heavily upon identification of objects, activities, or persons with great attachment to the handicapped person. Survival ('eat', 'drink' and 'toilet') and socially obligatory ('hello' and 'goodbye') words were identified as a possible starting vocabulary. Further study of the handicapped persons's environment, language development and common practice among other non-verbal populations were also suggested as parts of a logical system for choosing an initial vocabulary. Perhaps the most common practice for initiating a sign vocabulary has been for a therapist or teacher to go through a book of illustrated signs and choose signs for reasons known only to that therapist or teacher. That person has then begun to teach his or her best approximation of the chosen sign.

A number of studies, formal and informal, are under way which may help practitioners to determine the alternative communication vehicle (types of signs, types of symbols, or a combination of the two) which may be the most effective for a certain student. It would seem unfair and impractical to consider all signing and all symbol approaches to have the same value for every non-verbal person.

Psycholinguistics

Attention is being given to the nature of language development as it is applied to a limited vocabulary. Language development has usually been studied amongst children with normal cognitive development. Comparing a normal beginning vocabulary to that appropriate for a severely delayed child has pitfalls. The study of the normal acquisition of language with identified semantic values and the study of potential for early semantic combination may have value for use with severely delayed children. For example, a very small expressive vocabulary of nouns and verbs has more potential for making two-word expressions than does a large vocabulary of only nouns.

Augmentative communication

As systematic study of alternative communication for non-verbal persons has begun, interest has arisen concerning the use of signs or symbols to augment speech as a means of accelerating verbal language acquisition among students with delayed or unintelligible speech. Because signs or symbols are generally only used with key words being taught or to accentuate meaning, principles of language development became critical. The signs or symbols are meant to be an augmentation tool to enhance language development. The field of psycholinguistic development is too new and uncertain to provide obvious answers to questions concerning how and in what way can augmentation stimulate language acquisition.

Practice appears to suggest that teaching the receptive and expressive use of signs or symbols to children with delayed or unintelligible speech helps some students express themselves more effectively and accelerates language development. It may be that those students have responded to the stimulation of augmented speech or to the more consistently presented communication that is required of a teacher using augmentation.

Individualized communication

The question of which alternative approach is best seems to be a very individual matter for those who cannot speak but have good cognitive skills. Voice simulation and computer- stored retrieval information systems have great value for those with motor handicaps. The appropriate system generally depends upon the cognitive level of the person who will use it. Determing the cognitive level of a severely motor-handicapped, non-verbal child is a challenge!

Professionals working with non-communicative or language-delayed students have much to look forward to. There is considerable on-going experimentation with both augmentative and alternative communication approaches which promise to provide many helpful suggestions for implementing individualized language development programmes.

SPECIAL VOCATIONAL EDUCATION

Employment as a goal

Vocational training for special students is organized to prepare students for employment. Most programmes incorporate career education and experiences through which a student learns about work as a part of living into the curriculum. Vocational education often emphasizes skills and abilities directly relevant to occupational opportunities in the local area or to a student's unique abilities. Vocational and career education become integrated as the student reaches adulthood. Many schools offer a work/study programme, where the school arranges for either sheltered or competitive employment on a part-time basis while the student remains in school. The work/study programme offers teachers an opportunity to reinforce general work skills such as in communication or human relations.

Preparing special education students for employment is a challenge for several reasons. A primary aim of special programmes for younger children is to integrate them into regular education. When a special student who has participated a great deal in regular education programmes reaches adulthood, a special vocational programme may seem regressive. Many schools operate vocational programmes which effectively integrate special and regular students. Full-time special students at that age are generally people with persistent disabilities. Unemployment and competition for employment are high.

Legislation

There has been considerable national attention to the problem of employment of the handicapped. The US Congress has required that 10 % of federal funds for vocational education be devoted to providing vocational education for handicapped students. The Education for All Handicapped Children Act (PL 94-142) includes students up to 21 years old. The Comprehensive Employment and Training Act of 1978 (PL 95-524) was designed to help communities provide on-the-job training for the unemployed or under-employed. The Rehabilitation Act of 1973 (PL 93-112) requires agencies with government contracts to have an active programme for hiring handicapped workers and forbids discrimination against the handicapped.

Low-status employment

All of the attention to the matter of unemployed or underemployed handicapped adults has brought positive results, but it is far from being resolved. In addition to simple unemployment, many of the jobs held by handicapped people are jobs considered to have very low status. The association between low-status employment and handicapped people may be unavoidable, but it is a concern to counsellors who wish to avoid exploitation of handicapped people and to parents who hope for the best possible for their child. In general, prospects of employment for handicapped people remain poor.

A number of factors contribute to the challenges which remain in the area of vocational education of handicapped people: general unemployment, a shortage of professional training programmes for special vocational teachers, a shortage of employer training, and a need for improved vocational curricula. There is much to learn and much to do about the employment of the handicapped person.

CULTURAL DIVERSITY

Many diverse cultural groups have immigrated to the USA for a wide variety of reasons. Each culture has attempted to retain certain characteristics such as language, skills and rituals that were unique to its culture. Some groups have been more eager than others to assimilate into the mainstream of society. The mainstream has primarily been a reflection of the mores, attitudes and normative values of the earliest settlers from Europe. English has been recognized as the standard language.

Minority children in special education

When a large number of publicly supported schools began to offer special classes to handicapped learners, a disproportionate ratio of minority children began to appear in those classes. It became clear that there was a tendency for children from groups whose non-assimilation included language and social value differences to be identified by schools as students who needed special education. Simultaneously, civil rights were being claimed by minority groups in dramatic social and legal confrontations. Many conflicting explanations and solutions were offered. Obvious to everyone, however, was the fact that some groups of minority children were being asked to respond to at least two different cultures and that the school was being asked to be the agency to help them become successful in the two worlds.

Because members of minorities were often poor, there was a tendency to consider minority children deprived. In fact, culturally deprived as a term somehow suggested that a minority child might be suffering from the handicap of being reared in a culturally different home and from being exposed to two different languages. Recognition of the separateness of cultural difference and poverty led to the support of bilingual education as a reflection of the large element of biculturalism in the nation. Several federal programmes were meagrely funded to provide bilingual education.

Fair assessment

PL 94-142 was neutral on the subject of bilingual education, but it made it incumbent upon the schools to communicate with parents in their native language and to provide non-discriminatory evaluation for students. Communicating in a parent's native language required translators. Providing non-discriminatory evaluation required the development of new culture-fair testing devices and restandardization of common testing devices according to local, social/economic or racial norms to be able to compare a student's performance with a representative group of peers.

The use of culturally fair assessment approaches has reduced, but not eliminated, the concern that a disproportionate ratio of minority students are identified as having special needs. Equal opportunity and rights in the educational system is only a part of balanced cultural pluralism. It is possible that the majority of citizens will accept cultural pluralism as a positive force and that acceptance will be reflected in the schools in the form of non-discriminatory testing, more individualized education, and clearer communication between the school and the family.

SUMMARY

Many schools are now aggressively seeking parental involvement in the education process by sharing decision-making and by providing training designed to help parents provide some educational treatment at home. New perceptions of child development are being formed as schools and parents explore early intervention approaches. The concern for providing assessment and evaluation which does not discriminate on the basis of race, cultural background or handicap is shifting the assessment base from rather verbal to non-verbal. Evaluation is becoming continuous and comprehensive, drawing data from a wide range of sources. Technology is revolutionizing the structure of classroom management and is making individualized education a reality. Inclusion of multi-handicapped students is stimulating the imaginative use of alternative communication techniques. The complexity of the impact of the growing handicapped child on his or her environment is beginning to be realized. There is much to learn.

RECOMMENDED READING

Hallahan DP & Kauffman JM (1982) *Exceptional Children: Introduction to Special Education*, 2nd edn. Englewood Cliffs, New Jersey: Prentice-Hall.
Haring NG (ed) (1982) *Exceptional Children and Youth*, 3rd edn. Columbus, Ohio: Merrill
Kirk SA & Gallagher JJ (1983) *Educating Exceptional Children*, 4th edn. Boston: Houghton Mifflin.
Smith RM, Neisworth JT & Hunt FM (1983) *The Exceptional Child: A Functional Approach*, 2nd edn. New York: McGraw-Hill.

Chapter 22
Social Education Centres and Employment

BARRY GRAY

'You are doing a very good job keeping them off the streets'

This comment was made to me by a county council Official Visitor who had just spent several hours at the adult training centre (ATC) that I used to manage. The comment was very hurtful (unintentionally so), because that particular ATC, like many others at that time (1977) was proud of the programmes it provided for the adults who attended. The programmes were based on many of the recommendations of the National Development Group for the Mentally Handicapped (1977) and the goal for virtually all these programmes, as perceived by the staff, was to increase independence and community participation. On reflection, the comment can be seen as an accurate one. There we were, in line with most other ATCs, congregating up to 100 adults with intellectual impairment and expecting that their individual needs could be met in ways which were similar to the rest of society.

What are adult training centres (ATCs) and social education centres (SECs) for? This seems to be a crucial question. Unfortunately, there does not appear to be a uniformly agreed answer. An examination of current service delivery will also raise the question: who are the clients? Are they the people who attend daily or the parents and families of those people? I would promote the notions that the clients are the people who attend daily and that the needs of these people can be met using generic community resources. However, whilst ATCs and SECs are with us, there are many practices that can be introduced in order to meet the needs of the people in a more valued way.

The National Development Group for Mentally Handicapped People (an independent advisory body set up by the Secretary of State for Social Services in 1975 and disbanded in 1981) recommended that ATCs should be renamed social educa-

tion centres (SECs) and this was intended to reflect the role of the ATC as being educational in its broadest sense. This suggestion was not readily accepted, but before we examine some possible reasons let us consider what ATCs and SECs are.

What are ATCs and SECs?

ATCs and SECs are establishments provided, on the whole, by local authority social services departments. They offer day services for people with intellectual impairment from the age of 16 years. People 65 or older do attend some centres; this indicates an unclear policy with regard to elderly people with intellectual impairment.

HISTORICAL DEVELOPMENT OF ATCs AND SECs

The Lunacy and Mental Treatment Acts 1890–1930 placed responsibilities on local authorities to provide institutional and community services to people with intellectual impairment. The services provided were custodial in nature and separate from the bulk of the population. Provision for training, occupation and supervision was made in the 1913 Mental Deficiency Act and by 1938 there were some 60 local authority and 95 voluntary centres, providing a total of about 4000 places. A decline in provision was brought about by the 1939–1945 war and in 1948 the responsibility for providing institutions for people with intellectual impairment not living at home was transferred from the local authorities to the new hospital authorities.

The 1959 Mental Health Act and Section 12 of the Health Services and Public Health Act (1968) put beyond doubt local authorities' duty to provide training centres for people with intellectual impairment. In 1964 an independent national training body was set up to promote the provision of training for the staff of centres and to approve courses of training. This body was known as the Training Council for Teachers of the Mentally Handicapped and in 1974 the work of this body was absorbed into the Central Council for Education and Training in Social Work (CCETSW), who now have responsibility for the training of many groups of staff working in local authority social services.

Up until 1971 the centres were making provision for children as well as adults, but the Education (Handicapped Children) Act 1970 transferred the responsibility for provision to the education service, so what had been known as junior training centres became special schools. (It should be noted that not all children with intellectual impairment were being provided for in centres before 1971.)

The White Paper *Better Services for the Mentally Handicapped* (DHSS, 1971) emphasized the need to shift away from hospital-based care to care in the community and suggested how health and local authorities could best provide the full range of services needed. This paper also indicated the number of places that local authorities should provide; generally speaking, authorities are progressing well in meeting these targets.

Providing places is one thing; what actually happens to the people who fill these places is quite another. To guide the management of centres there have only been three publications which have received national distribution. They are by the Ministry of Health (1968), Whelan and Speake

(1977) and the National Development Group for the Mentally Handicapped (1977). These publications have certainly helped to create the current philosophy of ATCs and SECs and careful study of them will highlight the problem faced by many centres today: namely, what are their aims and how are they achieved?

Before we attempt to answer that question, it will be useful to have information about the people who attend centres. Whelan and Speake's (1977) survey of 305 ATCs in England and Wales gives the figures shown in Tables 22.1–22.5.

Although many local authorities are increasing the number of places for people with profound intellectual impairment there may still be too many such adults remaining in their place of residence during the day.

THE CURRENT PHILOSOPHY: AIMS OF SECs AND ATCs

Once you have overcome the plethora of ambiguous statements like 'develop each individual to his/her full potential', then it would be true to say that most local authorities claim that the aim of their centres is something like this: 'to provide programmes in the areas of daily living skills, social skills, work and leisure skills and educational skills to meet the individual needs of the people attending'. In addition to this there would probably be a claim to be providing this service in line with the (much misunderstood) principle of normalization. (For detailed accounts of the principle of normalization see O'Brien (1981), Wolfensberger (1972) and Wolfensberger (1980)).

The first problem to be encountered when examining these aims is that, for most non-handicapped adults, daily living skills, social skills, work and leisure skills and educational skills are catered for in different settings and with different people. We go to our own ordinary houses, ordinary work and adult institutions of education (adult education classes, colleges of further education, colleges of higher education, polytechnics, universities etc). If some of our work skills are catered for by these establishments we may still go to other places for further training (on-the-job training schemes, agricultural colleges, technical colleges, salesmanship colleges etc.). To try and meet all these needs in one establishment for people with intellectual impairment is hardly adhering to the principle of normalization.

Table 22.1 Basic information for 305 adult training centres in England and Wales.

Total number of places officially provided.		24 983	
Total number of trainees on the register		24 252	
Total number of individuals on the waiting list		1 127	
Number of trainees with multiple handicaps (medically diagnosed)	male	503	2.1%
	female	395	1.6%
	total	898	3.7%
Number of trainees considered to be special care cases	male	726	3.0%
	female	660	2.7%
	total	1 386	5.7%
Number of trainees receiving medication at the centre	male	1 551	6.4%
	female	1 507	6.2%
	total	3 058	12.6%

From Whelan and Speake (1977), with kind permission of the authors and the publishers.

Table 22.2 Age of trainees and types of handicap.

Age range	Mental handicap only		Physical handicap only		Mental illness only		Both mental handicap & physical		Both mental handicap & mental illness		Unknown or other		Total			
	M	F	M	F	M	F	M	F	M	F	M	F	Male	%	Female	%
16–19	2060	1599	8	8	15	20	290	225	59	26	26	25	2458	*10.1*	1903	*7.9*
20–24	2661	2356	27	10	36	55	382	358	150	71	34	27	3290	*13.6*	2877	*11.9*
25–29	2038	1775	14	7	44	27	302	232	80	55	23	26	2501	*10.3*	2122	*8.8*
30–34	1191	1109	8	7	70	33	128	148	57	61	9	5	1463	*6.0*	1363	*5.6*
35–39	731	648	11	4	45	29	80	96	36	30	9	10	912	*3.8*	817	*3.4*
40–44	448	477	14	2	69	35	61	60	30	27	3	3	625	*2.6*	604	*2.5*
45–49	360	347	16	4	72	40	45	44	21	25	13	19	527	*2.2*	479	*2.0*
50–54	354	281	23	4	76	41	39	44	22	24	7	2	521	*2.2*	396	*1.6*
55–59	178	149	33	9	54	56	18	35	13	16	6	6	302	*1.3*	271	*1.1*
60–64	108	77	20	5	27	28	9	11	4	2	3	1	171	*0.7*	124	*0.5*
65 +	50	40	18	1	21	18	5	3	2	1	2	1	98	*0.4*	64	*0.2*
Total	10179	8858	192	61	529	382	1359	1256	474	338	135	125	12868		11020	
%	42.6	36.5	0.8	0.3	2.2	1.6	5.6	5.2	2.0	1.4	0.6	0.5	53.1		45.4	

(Missing data 1.5%)

From Whelan and Speake (1977), with kind permission of the authors and the publishers.

Table 22.3 Incidence of specific clinical conditions.

Sex	Down's syndrome	Cerebral palsy	Epilepsy	Other	Total
Male	2799	531	1251	518	5099
Female	2558	428	985	407	4378
Total	5357(*22.1%*)	959(*4.0%*)	2236(*9.2%*)	925(*3.8%*)	9477(*39.1%*)

From Whelan and Speake (1977), with kind permission of the authors and the publishers.

Table 22.4 Special care units and special care cases.

Number of centres with no special care units and no special care clients	82
Number of centres with no special care units but with special care clients	193
Number of centres with special care units	43
Number of centres not stating	14
Total number of centres involved in this analysis	332

From Whelan and Speake (1977), with kind permission of the authors and the publishers.

Table 22.5 Sex distribution of special care cases.

	Male	Female	Total
In 43 special care units	300	266	566
In 193 centres with no special care units	510	456	966
Total	810	722	1532

From Whelan and Speake (1977), with kind permission of the authors and the publishers.

The second problem is that the aims may be so wide in their scope that it is very difficult to produce clear objectives. Is the objective to find people employment, increase integration into the community or increase literacy? What are the centres? Places of work? Places of occupation? Educational establishments? Leisure centres? Whilst the centres try to be all of these things the adherence to the principle of normalization will be problematic.

However, the current situation is that centres are all these things, and some centres would be seen as being other things as well – community resource centres and family support centres. ATCs and SECs are a good example of where a genuinely caring section of society tries to meet the needs of a group of people with handicaps. In fact, the resultant service possibly goes only a little of the way because of many of the unconscious influences on our attitudes and behaviours. Why do we continue to congregate handicapped people? Why do we have almost 100 % unemployment for people with intellectual impairment and some 12 % for other people? Why do we continue to miss out on the opportunities of providing people with handicaps the models of non-handicapped people that the rest of us enjoy? Why are people with handicaps often denied the access to enjoy the rights and responsibilities the rest of society have? The answers may lie in the views that society and some professionals hold of people with intellectual impairment.

Wolfensberger (1969) has categorized the ways society views people with intellectual impairment into nine social roles:

1 As a subhuman organism.
2 As a menace.
3 As an object of dread.
4 As an object of pity.
5 As a burden of charity.
6 As an eternal child.
7 As a holy innocent.
8 As an object of ridicule.
9 As a diseased organism.

If a person or group of people are placed into one or more of these roles, it is not difficult to imagine the labels, forms of address, types and sitings of buildings, professional workers and social expectations that will be used in services for such groups. For example, subhuman beings may be called 'low-grade' or 'cabbages', spoken to like animals, kept in zoos, looked after by trainers and expected to learn tricks. When staff of ATCs and SECs are introduced to this concept, they can readily see how the service has been influenced by these underlying, somewhat unconscious attitudes. When asked to describe a role that they, the ATC or SEC staff, would like to see promoted for the people who attend their centres, they readily arrive at this sort of conclusion: 'to view people with intellectual impairment as individual developing people with the same rights and responsibilities as any other citizen'. The real challenge is – to provide a service that promotes that image of the people who attend our centres. That is why we have the centres – to promote that image, not to keep people off the streets, not to provide a break for parents and residential staff and not to fulfil the low expectations that are often held about people with

intellectual impairment. This challenge is met in our existing centres by:

1 Emphasizing the individual and providing a system or systems to support that emphasis.
2 Providing good models.
3 Thinking about what we ask people to do.
4 Becoming aware and educating others.
5 Valuing the individual's background and age.
6 Using the best and lots of it.
7 Being part of the local scene.
8 Making it all look good.

These are now discussed in more detail.

Emphasizing the individual and providing a system/s to support that emphasis

One of the more positive developments for people with intellectual impairment over the last decade has been the increasing use of language and systems that stress the individual rather than that person's apparent membership to some heterogeneous group (the mentally handicapped or some diagnostic category). In the USA there are some states where federal funds are withheld from programmes unless it can be shown that they employ a system of Individual Programme Planning (for detailed accounts of Individual Programme Planning see Blunden (1980), California Instructional Television Consortium (1978), Perske (undated).) Individual Programme Planning (IPP) is not new and most centres will be employing a system that incorporates part of this idea. Some centres have developed a system that closely resembles IPP without ever being aware of that particular framework (e.g. Gray, 1978) and, in a way, this demonstrates the soundness and common sense of this particular procedure. There are perhaps two particularly important aspects of IPP: first, the system allows for individuals to be fully involved in decision-making (a very powerful feature of creating positive images) and, second, the system has a built-in procedure of accountability.

Briefly IPP is a process and a written plan. The process involves five steps.

Step 1: forming a team

The function of the team is to make decisions about future training programmes and opportunities for the person with intellectual impairment. With this in mind, it is important that members of the team have real interest in, a considerable knowledge of, and regular contact with the person. Far too often in the past people with intellectual impairment have been subjected to placements, routines and rhythms that have been decided by people who have not known the person whose life they are so affecting. So the team should consist of the person with intellectual impairment, his or her family member or advocate where necessary and about six other people who have regular contact with that person. The manager or principal officer should not automatically be included; in fact, their inclusion might be the exception rather than the rule. People can be co-opted onto the team as is felt appropriate.

Step 2: collecting information

The central questions here are what sort of information is wanted and in what form and manner it should be gathered and recorded. It is important for the team to create an atmosphere of equal status and one way of assisting towards this goal is for the written and verbal reports to be readily understood by all the members. That means avoiding (for IPP meetings) jargon and specialized assessment techniques that only those with appropriate training can interpret. The team should be aware of the possibility of teaching these skills to all members but initially any system that categorizes members of the team should be avoided. A well written list of strengths and needs without vague, 'fuzzy' statements is a good starting point. Information concerned with the person's quality of life should be included.

Step 3: meeting as a team

The team can decide who will chair the meeting, but where possible it should be the member of the team who takes on the role of coordinator/key worker. Some teams may not need anyone to chair the meeting: again, whatever works without creating barriers is the goal. It is sensible to set a time limit for the meeting: $1\frac{1}{2}$ hours should be sufficient. Where the team meets is an important consideration, as is the physical layout of the venue. Again all those aspects that will help to create a supportive, relaxed atmosphere should be aimed for.

Step 4: writing and implementing the plan

All members of the team should be encouraged to contribute and if possible all should record the decisions. The particular format is perhaps not too important, but it should include the following sections:

1 Name of person.
2 Address.
3 Date of birth.
4 Date of meeting; date of next meeting.
5 Those present.
6 Strengths/needs.
7 Ideal situations: residential; educational; work; leisure.
8 Priority needs.
9 Goals; person/people responsible; outcome.
10 Target dates.
11 Resource deficiencies.

Part of the role of the coordinator or key worker is to ensure that the plan is implemented, and this person should be skilled at reinforcing the positive behaviours of other team members.

Step 5: regular reviews

The IPP meetings should take place at least every 12 months. Wherever possible a six-monthly cycle should be instigated. Individual members of the team are likely to feel more valued if they are informally contacted between meetings on a regular basis. This again can be part of the role of the coordinator.

The IPP system allows for joint decision-making and should provide people with clear responsibilities.

Providing good models

One of the most powerful ways we learn appropriate behaviours is by imitating people we perceive as having something to offer us. We are much more likely to imitate behaviours that are exhibited by people we can readily associate ourselves with (people of similar background, profession etc.) or by people who are exhibiting behaviours in what is obviously a high-status situation. For example, teachers develop a style that is very influenced by the teachers they saw as pupils or students and by observing the responses that their colleagues receive for their teaching behaviours. Also, many amateur sportsmen can be seen adopting the behaviour of some of their sports idols, whom they can never hope to equal.

We know this to be true and yet we seem to forget it when designing services for people with intellectual impairment. We seem to surround handicapped people with other handicapped people. There are some centres with over 200 people attending daily, and some local authorities appear to be compounding the problem by making centres 'multi-purpose'. When one man with intellectual impairment was asked what he thought about other types of handicapped people attending his centre he replied, 'Actually, me and most of my friends at the centre would like to be surrounded by normal people'.

There are important things to remember about imitation and the staff at centres should be aware of at least the following steps.

1 Identifying what to model and who are likely to imitate.
2 Arranging for the desired behaviour to be present, exhibited and repeated.
3 Providing positive feedback for the imitator.
4 Promoting a learner's identification with a model.
5 Surrounding others, especially vulnerable people, with good models.
6 Being a good model.
7 Having positive models in place in situations that are new or equivocal to the learner.

Thinking about what we ask people to do

If someone is observed putting matchsticks into a wooden jig with 50 small holes in it, no great feeling of competence or value is attached to the task. If, on the other hand, someone is observed placing electronic components into a printed circuit board, then the value and apparent competence increases. In fact, the fine motor skills for both tasks are very similar and both are activities/jobs undertaken by ATCs and SECs. Both jobs may be valuable to society, but the way they are carried out is also important.

Similarly, if we see an adult entering a college building and partaking in educational classes with other adults, we again have the impression of someone learning valued and, one hopes, appropriate skills and gaining knowledge for their development. If an adult is seen in a room with other adults finger-painting or using childish educational material, the message is quite different.

With leisure activities the same principle applies. Handicapped adults using the local swimming pool with non-handicapped adults on a Saturday morning give quite different messages about themselves than if they were using the pool at a special time during the day when only other handicapped people were present.

The problem faced by the ATCs and SECs is whether they should be places of work, education or leisure. Whilst they remain part of the personal social services this problem will remain. It might be overcome if the social service departments would stop seeing the day service in terms of separate buildings and developed a planning system that was based on the future of individuals and their individual needs.

Becoming aware and educating others

In order that the day services for adults promote the image of the people being served as individual developing human beings with the same rights as any other citizen, then they need to become aware of devaluing practices. Many of these practices are based in the unconscious. For human services to be responsive to the needs of their consumers it is necessary for actions to be based in the conscious. An example that should make the point is with regard to language. Even today it is possible to visit ATCs or SECs where the staff continually refer to the adults who attend as either 'low-grade' or 'high grade', and this is often done in their presence and in the presence of members of the public. The staff probably have no intention of devaluing the people, but if they stopped and thought about those particular labels they would realize that they are better suited to vegetables or eggs. This is important to understand, because other people hearing these labels will associate the adults talked of with sub-human organisms, and this will lead to low expectations. Whilst it is hoped that this example makes the point, it should be recognized that language is only one way of conveying messages to other people. The buildings, the people you are next to, the things you are doing and the staff employed to work with you, will also convey these messages.

Becoming aware of the importance of this and the mass of negative messages that pervade our current services is important. It is equally important to try and change the situation, for that will help in changing the perceptions and expectations the general public have of adults with intellectual impairment.

Responsive and committed service workers should also be aware of the power of the media in transmitting messages about people with handicaps. Wherever positive images and high expectations are noted, the authors, presenters etc. should be informed of their good work and told why it is good.

Valuing the individual's background and age

This is all about treating people in ways that any other person of their age would feel comfortable with and providing a service that any other adult would expect.

Perhaps this 'age-appropriateness' is the most difficult aspect for service workers. The concept of mental age does not help: a person of 35 years of age may have some of their abilities developed to a similar extent as an average four-year-old child, but that does not mean that that person should be treated as a four-year-old for most of the time. If you continually treat an adult as a child then the adult will learn to behave as a child. This 'treatment' is not only with regard to the activities, routines and official programmes an individual partakes in, but also with regard to what Shackleton-Bailey (1981) has called the 'Hidden Curriculum'. This hidden curriculum refers to the language, labels, tone of voice and, in a general sense, the respect and expectations that are shown to the individual.

This is one of the challenges that face the day services – how to provide surroundings, materials and activities that are consistent with the person's chronological age but that will also be responsive to the person's developmental needs.

One useful way of testing how the day centre is responding to the ages of the people attending is to imagine that you are a visitor from outer space.

Forgetting why things are the way they are, just concentrate on what you see and write down some ideas about the age of the people attending. Many centres look like and have an atmosphere like nursery or junior schools; the special care/needs units often look and feel like playgroups (Figures 22.1 and 22.2).

There has to be a commitment and a belief that it is right and proper to treat adults as adults regardless of any handicap (this is important in raising expectations), as many people who are receiving the service will appear 'happier' when treated like children. They may well believe that they are children and will have embarked upon what Nirje (1980) calls the handicap career.

Using the best and lots of it

As well as giving messages about people's ages and backgrounds, the way the day services are delivered will also indicate how worthy and important the people are who receive the service. For people with intellectual impairment, who may well have already been relegated to one or more of nine low-status roles mentioned earlier (p. 261), it is important that the things that surround them are equated with high

Fig. 22.1 Who does this belong to?

Fig. 22.2 Who does this belong to? (Taken at the same Adult Training Centre as Figure 22.1.)

who has been unable to develop eating skills for 30 years may need a lot of intensive effort before they can learn those skills.

Being part of the local scene

If we are to deliver a service that allows the people who use it to interact with and join the rest of the community, then we have to avoid measures that make that difficult and encourage ones that make it more likely to happen. Grouping people together in large numbers (30 is a large group of people) allows the people to have most of their needs for personal relationships met within the group. This does not encourage people with handicaps to form relationships with non-handicapped people. We need to find ways of dispersing our service throughout the community so that individual needs can be met in the facilities that other members of the community use (colleges, factories, offices, leisure centres, pubs, houses etc.). This, of course, raises the question of why we need ATCs or SECs.

The ATC or SEC should allow physical integration by being accessible and within easy reach of all the generic services other adults use (shops, banks, pubs, cafes, cinemas etc.). It will also help if the building itself looks like other buildings in the neighbourhood and there are no signs that mark it as being different. Social integration will be helped if the activities and routines are carried out in the presence of non-handicapped adults (other than staff). This means using generic resources at times when other people use them, not, as so often is the case currently, using them at special times when only people with handicaps are being served.

Making it all look good

The way the service is delivered transmits powerful messages about the consumers or users of the service. Again, for people who for one reason or another have a lot of catching up to do, it is important that attention is paid to how these services look. They need to be not only what we ourselves would perhaps accept, but they need to be what we would actually desire. This means beautification of the physical environment and having activities that look worthy and desirable. For the staff it means paying attention to their own appearance and behaviour.

Space does not permit a detailed account of how to do this and I would certainly not claim to know all the answers; however, it is hoped that the preceding section has identified some general

status and high expectations. This means using the best that is available and not making do with secondhand products and other people's cast-offs. This clearly involves a political decision. If we can get people to the moon and spend vast amounts on sophisticated defence systems, then we need to ask questions about the amount of the economic wealth we allow for those people with handicaps. Consider people who are unable to get themselves about independently and so need support. The style and appearance of the wheelchairs, for example, that are provided are such that most people resist the idea of having to use one for as long as possible. Surely we could design and manufacture supports that look desirable and worthy. The same principle applies to all areas. People who have problems learning should have ready access to our most developed technologies.

In addition to using the best we need to recognize that people with intellectual impairments will also require lots of these new technologies. Our interventions and treatments need to be intense. Someone themes. Whilst one of the conclusions that could be drawn from these themes is that we should not have ATCs or SECs as separate buildings providing separate services, we do have them, and it is possible to introduce some of these themes into our existing services. The Avro Centre in Southend is an example of where staff have thought about and attempted to introduce many of the elements mentioned. If the enhancement of people's positive images is related to the voice they have then the Avro Student Committee (Williams and Shoultz, 1982) stands as a fine example of what can be done within the existing system.

STAFF TRAINING

What sort of training is going to provide an individual with the right sort of knowledge and skills to be part of an ATC or SEC that is in the business of promoting the positive image of adults with intellectual impairment? It seems to me that there needs to be an emphasis on two main aspects in any training scheme; they are (a) encouraging the right sort of attitudes and (b) providing appropriate levels of knowledge and skill.

Traditional courses in mental handicap covering such topics as aetiology, prevalence, clinical syndromes and prevention may do much to enhance the differentness and, in subtle ways, emphasize the negative qualities of people with mental handicap. That is not to say that these topics are not important, but there needs to be a real commitment to emphasizing the human qualities of the people and intense attempts at raising expectations.

Current training for staff working in ATCs and SECs is provided by the Certificate of Social Service (CSS), validated by the Central Council for Education and Training in Social Work, and by some two-year full-time courses, validated by various bodies (such as the University of Hull and the Council for National Academic Awards). The CSS model has great potential as it can be a real partnership between colleges and service delivery agencies. Certainly training that has a commitment towards people working together should produce people who are able to create a more responsive service. The Jay Committee (1979) recommended that nurses should be trained with social services staff.

Further joint reports by the General Nursing Council and the Central Council for Education and Training in Social Work (GNC/CCETSW 1982) using the CSS model have added support to the idea of joint training. It is perhaps a comment on the existing problems of working together that as far as I am aware no such joint training exists (in 1985).

EMPLOYMENT

The concept of work in our culture

When adults (in employment) are asked which five aspects of their lives they would least like to lose, then their job/work is usually in the list of factors that they, presumably, regard as very important. Figure 22.3 shows the ways in which work may be so important to the adult members of our society. Time, energy and submission to a certain amount of control can be viewed as costs to the individual, and the following can be seen as benefits to the individual.

Status. This will vary according to the type of work undertaken, but having a paid job is valued by our society and a certain amount of status goes along with this.

Money. For most adults their paid job is their sole source of income and, again for most people, this allows them to make choices about many things, including the activities they do, the sort of holiday they have, the kind of accommodation they live in and how they spend their leisure time.

Self-image. Earning an economic wage usually means paying taxes and contributing to society's wealth in a tangible way. This is just one aspect of having a paid job that helps to increase the self-image of the worker.

Security. Most jobs also carry with them some possibilities of providing for economic security for the future. This may be in the form of a pension scheme or individuals may be able to plan and make their own savings schemes. Being a paid employee also allows people to partake in many schemes that our society permits to help people at particular points in their lives (such as mortgages and hire purchase arrangements).

Friends. For many adults work provides an opportunity to make positive relationships with other adults. It should be noted that for most of us that means positive relationships with non-handicapped people!

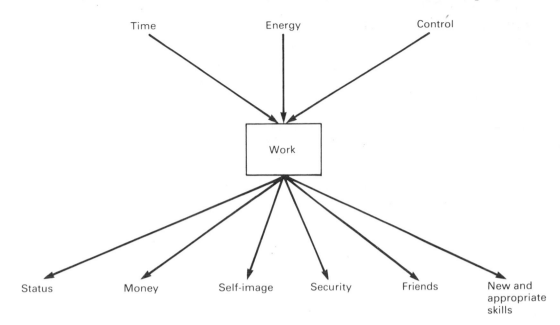

Fig. 22.3 Ways in which work may be important to adults.

New and appropriate skills. The behaviours that are allowed and encouraged at work are usually those behaviours which also allow us to join in many other activities in the community. The way we dress, eat and talk to one another in the adult setting of work gives us models of how we behave in other circumstances.

The current level of unemployment (over three million in the UK) and the rapid growth of technology may mean that as a society we have to review our concept of work. It may well be that we will all have to share the work that is available and we will all have more leisure time to fill. Money helps in allowing access to different forms of leisure and it may be that we need to consider leisure as a service that society as a whole provides for its members. At the moment, the situation is that most of the valued leisure pursuits have to be paid for, and this in itself provides a whole industry. It may be argued that with unemployment rates so high and with the already massively disproportionate rate amongst adults with mental handicap (certainly over 90 %) it is a waste of time and energy to try and train people and find them employment. When asked what to do instead it might be suggested that the centres concentrate on social education and leisure pursuits. This does not accord adults with mental handicap the same status as other citizens. As Len Murray (1981) put it, 'but all

are people and our fellow citizens, and all are exposed to the same risks by the blight of the unemployment: risks to their dignity and self-respect, to their health, to their normal participation in the community, to their income, while the country as a whole becomes poorer'.

Perhaps the argument that will be most persuasive is the economic one. Whelan and Speake (1981) estimate that if a third of the people attending ATCs and SECs were placed in *sheltered* employment the overall annual benefit (money that used to be spent in providing the service) would be between £63 million and £77 million. Obviously the benefit increases if people are placed in open employment.

In order to find people employment careful consideration has to be given to:

1 skills required;
2 assessing the skills;
3 training for work;
4 choosing a job;
5 providing support;
6 overcoming possible obstacles.

These topics are sensibly covered in Whelan and Speake's (1981) *Getting to Work* which is recommended for some good practical suggestions to meet people's employment needs.

One dilemma that continually faces staff working with people with mental handicap is nicely highlighted when considering employment. That is the whole question of whether to train people in the appropriate skills so that they can increase their opportunities to partake in more normal activities (such as paid employment) or, on the other hand, to place people in these situations (provide the opportunities), even though they may not have the appropriate skills, and provide them with support that can be gradually removed. Most adults take jobs at which they are not competent to begin with. Many jobs have 'probationary' periods during which the employer endeavours to provide support and training for the employee in that particular work task. There is usually an expectation on behalf of the employer that the person will eventually become competent. For people with mental handicap we need to raise our expectations. This is one of the values of the Pathway Scheme (for a full account of this scheme contact The Pathway Employment Service, 169 City Road, Cardiff or MENCAP National Centre, 123 Golden Lane, London).

The Pathway Scheme is sponsored by the Royal Society for Mentally Handicapped Children and Adults (MENCAP). Basically it is a scheme designed to provide employment opportunities for adults with mental handicap. The Pathway Officer searches out potential employers in the neighbourhood and that employer identifies someone within the work setting who will act as a support to the employee with mental handicap. The wage is the going rate for the job. Half the wage is paid for by MENCAP and the support worker is paid a bonus (also funded by MENCAP). The scheme lasts for a fixed period (usually six months), at the end of which there is no obligation on the employer to take the person on as a bona fide full-time employee.

The results of the Pathway Scheme are most encouraging. The rate of people being given full-time employment after a placement on the scheme is high, and many employers request further people to place after they have experienced the scheme.

In Britain, the Manpower Services Commission (MSC) also funds employment schemes that do not exclude people with mental handicap. The local Jobcentre and the local disablement resettlement officer are the best sources for current information on these schemes.

The King's Fund Centre's (1984) *An Ordinary Working Life* is an excellent source for a more detailed discussion of the concept of employment for people with intellectual impairment.

Alternatives to work

Whilst the potential of many people with mental handicap for employment is grossly underestimated and underutilized, the fact remains that large numbers of people with handicaps cannot obtain work. It is worth considering some alternatives to work which might provide some of the benefits employment brings. The late Jack Tizard (1979) produced a most stimulating monograph on this question and his suggestions may be summarized under the following headings.

Leisure

The concept of 'leisure' and its uses has been neglected by social scientists and leisure time has too often been viewed in a negative way – as an escape from obligations or as freedom from work. There needs to be a change of view regarding leisure. It should be seen as giving a person the freedom to enter into a choice of activities, and these activities must be linked with the psychological needs which work generally fulfils (p. 266).

Participation in voluntary work

This is seen as a particular way of providing the person with a sense of personal worth and involvement in society at large. The person with mental handicap can be viewed as a giver rather than a receiver of services. Tizard mentions some of the volunteering that is currently being carried out by people who attend ATCs and SECs and also refers to schemes of volunteering for house-bound adults.

Adult education

The Russell Committee (1973) envisaged a 'society in which the whole lifelong learning needs of all citizens would be taken as the field with which the national educational system is concerned in its basic planning structures and expenditure'. This adult education is not to be seen simply as a course of basic education in literacy and numeracy with a course of social education, but also as providing a whole range of opportunities for recreational pursuits for those living without work. It is important that this service be provided in existing adult education centres and is not seen as a separate segregated 'special' service.

Life at home

Homemaking has become much more of a real possibility for people with mental handicap. Plans exist for the closure of all hospitals for the mentally handicapped. Places which are similar to the dwellings of most other citizens in our society are beginning to be recognized as the alternative to large-institutional care. Projects like those taking place in the Wessex Region (Mansell et al., 1983) demonstrate that adults with severe and profound mental handicap can live in ordinary houses.

An adult life of homemaking is an alternative to one of employment. Care needs to be taken to allow opportunities for people living at home to supplement their incomes if required and to keep links with other people in the neighbourhood.

A community work approach

Here Tizard describes the Stone House project. This project was established in a small centre of heavy industry (population 50 000) in the English Midlands. In essence, the service was delivered in a non-institutional way and operated an 'open-door' policy.

The above examples show how, with a little thought, real and valuable alternatives to work can be found. None of these alternatives included the ATC/SEC as it currently exists. This should be noted by those who are planning services. ATCs and SECs tend to be segregative in their effects, whatever their intention. (Note that the opposite of segregation is *not* creating 'multipurpose' centres where people with mental handicap mix with people with different handicaps; it is delivery of services so that people with handicaps spend most of their time with non-handicapped people).

THE EXCITING CHALLENGES

Evolving change in the existing ATCs and SECs

The points discussed on pp. 259–266 can be viewed as outlining a principle that stresses both means and ends for the SECs and ATCs. The challenge within that principle is for the service providers to develop good working relationships with existing generic facility agencies. This is one of the main aims of the Association of Professionals for Mentally Handicapped People and many of their publications and activities are to be recommended. Similarly, Campaign for Mentally Handicapped People have published several useful reports and papers that stress service delivery adhering to this principle.

Local authority social services departments should recognize that the service they provide is for adults with intellectual impairment. Whilst the parents and families of these people may have more apparent political clout it is the needs of the individuals themselves that should be catered for by the day service.

Perhaps the most exciting challenges within the centres come with the recognition that the people have a right to speak for themselves. Not only is there the challenge of equipping people with the skills required to represent themselves, but also, far more difficult, there is the challenge of listening to what they say!

The planning process

Services for people with intellectual impairment should be planned on an individual basis. When the planners are encouraged to produce projections of what opportunities and possible experiences are most appropriate for individual people, then we may see flexibility and innovation in the service delivery that, it could be suggested, is currently missing. Plans that are based on an individual's needs are also more likely to influence the elected members of local government who make resources available.

The nature of local social service departments may be such that they are unable to respond to these challenges and it is possible that many of the needs of the adults currently attending ATCs or SECs could be more appropriately met by existing agencies offering services to other adults (education departments, the Manpower Services Commission etc.). However, there are examples of where, even within the constraints of large bureaucratic social service departments, ATCs and SECs can develop exciting and flexible programmes for the individuals who attend (For example, Sturminster Newton ATC, Dorset; Avro Training Centre, Southend, Essex; the mobile bus centre in North Yorkshire; Bishopsgate ATC, Hampshire; Camperdown ATC, Newcastle upon Tyne.)

REFERENCES

Blunden R (1980) *Individual Plans for Mentally Handicapped People: A Draft Procedural Guide.* Cardiff: Mental Handicap in Wales – Applied Research Unit.
California Instructional Television Consortium (1978) *Way to Go* Baltimore: University Park Press.
DHSS (Department of Health and Social Security) (1971) *Better Services for Mentally Handicapped People.* Cmnd. 4683. London: HMSO.
GNC/CCETSW (General Nursing Council/Central Council for Education and Training in Social Work Joint Working Group on Training for Staff Working with Mentally Handicapped People) (1982) *Co-operation in Training*, parts I & II. London: GNC & CCETSW.

Gray B (1978) Programme planning in an adult training centre. *Apex 6(3):* 3–5.

Jay Committee (1979) *Report of the Committee of Enquiry into Mental Handicap Nursing and Care.* Cmnd. 7468-I and 7468-II. London: HMSO.

King's Fund Centre (1984) *An Ordinary Working Life.* Project Paper 50. London: King's Fund Publishing.

Mansell J, Felce D, Jenkins J, Dekock U & Toogood S (1983) A Wessex Home from Home. *Nursing Times* (3rd August): 51–56.

Ministry of Health (1968) *Local Authority Training Centres for Mentally Handicapped Adults: Model of Good Practice.* London: HMSO.

Murray L (1981) Foreword. In Whelan E & Speake B. *Getting to Work.* London: Souvenir Press.

National Development Group for the Mentally Handicapped (1977) *Day Services for Mentally Handicapped Adults.* Pamphlet No. 5. London: Department of Health and Social Security.

Nirje (1980) The normalisation principle. In Flynn RJ & Nitsch KE (eds) *Normalisation, Social Integration and Community Services.* Baltimore: University Park Press.

O'Brien J (1981) *The Principle of Normalisation, A Foundation for Effective Services.* London: Campaign for Mental Handicap.

Perske R (undated) *Individual Programme Planning . . . Getting all Helping Persons to Root Together.* Joint Commission for Accreditation of Hospitals, California State College, Sonoma.

Russell Committee (1973) *Adult Education: A Plan for Development.* Report of a Committee of Enquiry into Adult Education. London: HMSO.

Shackleton-Bailey M (1981) *The Hidden Curriculum: Winchester.* Videotape. Winchester: Hampshire Social Services Department.

Tizard J (1979) The Education of the Handicapped Adolescent. Alternatives to Work for Severely Handicapped People. In Clarke ADB & Tizard B (eds) (1983) *Child Development and Social Policy – The Life and Work of Jack Tizard.* pp. 185–228. Leicester: British Psychological Society.

Whelan E & Speake B (1977) *Adult Training Centres in England and Wales,* Manchester: National Association of Teachers of the Mentally Handicapped and University of Manchester Hester Adrian Research Centre.

Whelan E & Speake B (1981) *Getting to Work.* London: Souvenir Press.

Williams P & Shoultz B (1982) *We Can Speak for Ourselves.* London: Souvenir Press.

Wolfensberger W (1969) The origin and nature of our institutional models. In Kugel MR & Wolfensberger W (eds) *Changing Patterns in Residential Services for the Mentally Retarded.* Washington DC: President's Committee on Mental Retardation.

Wolfensberger W (1972) *The Principle of Normalisation in Human Services.* Toronto: National Institute on Mental Retardation.

Wolfensberger W (1980) A brief overview of the principle of normalisation. In Flynn RJ & Nitsch KE (eds) *Normalisation, Social Integration and Community Services.* Baltimore: University Park Press.

Chapter 23
Further Education, Adult Education and Self-advocacy

MATTHEW GRIFFITHS, JANET WYATT & JOHN HERSOV

FURTHER EDUCATION

In 1983, approximately 50% of all young people who left Inner London Education Authority day schools for children with severe learning difficulties became full-time students at mainstream non-specialist colleges of further education, which cater for students with a wide range of needs and abilities (Griffiths, 1984). Figures for the rest of the country vary, but the principle of the right of young people with mental handicap to have provision made for them in their local college of further education is being increasingly recognized.

This chapter will not attempt to describe the multiplicity of courses and programmes which are offered by individual colleges. Each college which offers this provision has developed it along its own lines, to suit the facilities which it has to offer and the demands made on it by schools and parents. Thus any overall picture would be hugely complex and possibly of little value. What will be attempted instead is the outline of one concept of a coherent philosophy and rational structure which underlines the extremely diverse provision for young people with mental handicap that exists in colleges of further education. The philosophy which should underpin the provision, however it is actually presented, should, I* believe, have as its centre *development* and *transition*. For any young person a course at college or university provides both a particular expertise and a period of transition from their dependent role in the school-based world of childhood to an autonomous and independent role in the adult world. This transition takes place on two levels – firstly, as the result of changing perceptions of self within the student as he or she develops and matures in a new and more demanding environ-

ment and, secondly, as a result of the changing perceptions of society towards the young person as that person moves into a more independent role, which is seen as bringing him or her on to equal terms with full adults.

Traditionally most young people with mental handicap have not made this transition, either by a college course or by starting work, and so as mature adults they retain all the components of a childhood role – dependence, passivity, submissiveness, naivity and childlike behaviour. Such adults perceive themselves to be children, and society as a whole reinforces and is reinforced in this belief. The major role of further education is to stimulate such young people into adolescence and to enable them to begin the period of transition which will, optimistically, end with as many of this group as is possible having a clearly defined image of themselves as fully adult, and with society having a similar concept of this group of people as being adults with specific difficulties, rather than post-pubescent children.

Contents of courses

Colleges of further education can provide courses which clearly signal by style or content the fact that schooldays and childhood are over. To that end the content of most courses includes teaching aimed at developing the following:

(a) an awareness of self;
(b) an awareness of others;
(c) appropriate adolescent or young-adult behaviour and relationships;
(d) choice- and decision-making;
(e) new skills, especially leisure skills;
(f) the beginning of self-advocacy
(g) an awareness of the community and its facilities;
(h) risk-taking
(i) self-care

---

* Matthew Griffiths.

(j) a concept of the student's changing role within the family.

A vital element of every college course is the fact that it is offered in a non-segregated, mainstream institution. The students will be, possibly for the only time in their lives, in day-long contact with their non-handicapped peers and have similar rules and expectations applied to their behaviour. This aids their own and society's perception of their increasing autonomy.

The process of transition begins in the final year at school, when the first contact that young people make with the college of further education local to their school is usually as members of a 'link course', (Table 23.1). The link course should be explicitly about moving away from school and its functions. Ideally this course consists of a full day at college each week; a programme planned jointly by the school and the college is offered. The day may include two or three specialist subjects such as pottery, woodwork, home crafts, sport or drama, at least one of which should be totally new to the students or offered in a way which is totally different from that in which it is offered at school. The day should also include a tutorial period which enables the course tutor to help the students make sense of their day at college and reinforce experiences and notions of transition as well as deal with problems as they arise.

As well as initiating transition the link course also aims to be (a) preparatory to a full-time course or (b) a selection process for the full-time course as well as a preparation for those who move on to it.

The link course as preparation for the full-time course

If the link course is seen as purely preparatory to the full-time course the selection of which young people should attend is left entirely to the school and the school's perception of what abilities are necessary to 'cope' with college. The college staff will probably never meet the young people who have not been selected and they will move into an adult training centre (ATC) or social education centre (SEC) on completion of their school career.

This kind of link course will concentrate on the familiarization of students with the buildings, routines, subject areas and personnel of the college and on the smooth movement of young people onto the full-time course, so that they can reap the maximum benefit from their two years of full-time provision. This kind of link course is particularly common when a college has several schools for children with severe learning difficulties within its catchment area and can therefore offer each school a limited number of link and full-time places. These constraints can produce a tight well-structured link course with very clear aims and objectives and strong continuity with the full-time course, but because of the high value of places in this situation many young people who could benefit from college provision are excluded before they even leave school. Inappropriate selection is sometimes practiced in schools, even when there is no particular pressure for places, because of misunderstandings about the level of competence required by the college.

The link course as a selection process for the full-time course

When the link course is seen as part of the selection process for the full-time course, the school and college staff should ideally agree to meet regularly to discuss the performance of the students and

Table 23.1 Further education provision and the transition from school to adulthood

Course	Approximate age of students	Emphasis
Link course: one day at college, four days at school	18–19 years	Moving on from school. Familiarization with college building(s), students, staff. Introduction to college facilities (canteen, common room, library, workshops etc.).
First year of full-time further education	19–20 years	Developing an adolescent self-image. Developing an awareness of others. Developing appropriate behaviour. Learning and developing skill areas.
Second year of full-time further education	20–21 years	Taking responsibility for self. Beginning of self-advocacy. Awareness of the community and its facilities. Moving on from college – choices available.

ultimately to make joint decisions about those young people who could benefit from the full-time course, and those whose needs could be more appropriately met elsewhere. This places the onus on the link course to take a group of young people with a wide range of abilities and to ensure that the course provides valuable and stimulating experiences for those young people who will not move on to the full-time course as well as a preparation and introduction for those who do. This type of course therefore has more general aims than the purely preparatory link and may not be as neat in its structure, but it does enable a wider range of students to have access to the college environment and it enables more informed decisions to be made about those young people for whom there was some doubt either about their ability to benefit from a full-time college course or about the college's ability to cope with them.

The selection process has been dealt with at length because arguments about which young people are able to benefit from further education are unresolved. There are those who believe that access should be given to all young people, however profound their handicap (Beresford et al., 1984), while others maintain that a college of further education cannot meet the needs of every potential student. I would suggest that if the model of the further education course as transition is used, the college experience will benefit those who are able to begin that transition at college-entry age. For young people who are not yet able to begin the transition an alternative placement is more appropriate, with different opportunities for moving into a more adult role being provided when they are more able to take advantage of them.

The minimum level of maturity

At present the level of maturity which is considered to be necessary varies widely from college to college, but I would suggest that most colleges would agree on a list of abilities which allow a student to begin the movement towards adult life and to function in a large, non-adapted building with the level of supervision and support considered desirable. Such a list would include the following:

1 Basic ability to make known and cope with bodily needs – clothing, food, lavatory, hygiene and so on.
2 Ability to cope with a large building and unfamiliar people without undue apprehension or distress.
3 Ability to function in a group situation and to function without constant supervision,
4 Ability to respond to verbal instruction and to communicate, whether by speech or a speech alternative.
5 Ability to refrain from extremes of anti-social or dangerous behaviour.

School leavers who are judged to be able to benefit from the full-time course either prior to the link course or from their performance during that course rarely drop out of the course during their two full-time years.

As young people progress through further education their gains in maturity, independence and awareness can be spectacular, considering their disabilities, particularly when they have had high-quality provision at a school which was committed to transition during the link period and the student's parents are also aware of, and committed to, their son or daughter's movement into adulthood. It is a disheartening fact, however, that progress is often not maintained. Young people who have moved out of segregated education into unsegregated further education are moved back into a segregated ATC or SEC at the end of the course. They may remain in a segregated centre for the whole of their adult life. The effect of this can be stultifying unless the centre is of a particularly high calibre or there is a strong link with a good adult education institute where people are able to continue the transition, or having completed it, to continue to receive education which allows them to retain the independent, decision-making, risk-taking aspects of adult life. Further education at its best thus provides young people who have severe learning difficulties with a bridge to the adult world and the dignity of an adult self-image. It may also provide the only two years of such people's lives in which they are not daily segregated from the rest of the world.

ADULT EDUCATION*

To understand the levels and types of adult education offered to adults who are called mentally

---

* The author's (Janet Wyatt) experience of adult education lies within the inner London area, and she has written from that basis. In discussion with adult educators from other areas she finds that experiences are similar wherever adult education is involved with people who are called mentally handicapped. What literature there is implies the same pattern of development. Further information can be obtained from the author.

handicapped in the mid 1980s we need to look at the way adult education has developed over the last 15 years.

Some managers of adult training centres, under government pressure (DHSS, 1971) to provide training for their clients, requested assistance from adult education institutes (AEIs). At the same time adult education was looking for new growth and closer links with the community at large, and several institutes made a positive response.

At this point there was little experience of, or educational guidelines for, developing the learning skills and abilities of adults who had been classified as mentally handicapped. Traditional tertiary educational values were therefore used as a starting point, with literacy and numeracy as the important subjects, together with some 'general education', based on literacy and numeracy, or the acquisition of language as a preliminary to literacy and numeracy. There was also some 'leisure activity' provision – physical education, sports, art and craft, and conventional forms of simple dance and music.

For many students, who because of their label of 'ineducable' or their minimal schooling had never been exposed to these types of experience, this proved valuable. Tutors from adult education visited ATCs on a regular, weekly basis, taking small groups of students, and using methods based on tertiary education practice. Emphasis was placed not only on educational skills learnt, but also on social training. In the best examples of provision the ATC staff and the AEI staff worked in close consultation.

Inevitably this type of provision was best suited to the more able adult whose main problem had been lack of opportunity and sufficient concentrated attention. Expertise did not extend to meeting the needs of more severely handicapped adults, or those whose ability could not be given room to develop within conventional types of educational provision. In an attempt to meet these needs a 'therapy' role was adopted, for which in most instances the tutors concerned had neither the ability nor the expertise. Adults who were called mentally handicapped became the recipients of good intentions instead of becoming adult learners; their role was passive. The criterion of a good class was that 'they enjoyed themselves'.

There were some tutors, working with both students who were called mentally handicapped and mainstream students, who noted marked similarities in subject ability between the two seemingly disparate groups, and began to question some of the assumptions underlying this provision. Students emerged who had real subject ability. Their commitment to their area of study and the quality of work produced were of a high standard. For some of these students access to adult education classes with tutors who were sympathetic to the concept of integrating adults who are called mentally handicapped with mainstream adult students has proved successful without any additional assistance. For some it has been helpful to have a volunteer within the class to give added support, particularly at a social level. The danger here is that the volunteer helper may adopt a tutor role for which he lacks the ability, and the student then loses the opportunity to learn from the subject expert. The volunteer receives knowledge on behalf of the student, and becomes a learning filter – or block!

For many other students, the learning patterns were significantly different. The subject ability was real, and the subject could be presented in an adult manner, but learning needed to be broken down into discrete stages, and built up at a pace and in a manner which the students could accept and retain. In some subjects special learning materials had to be developed which were both adult in concept and comprehensible to the students. Tutors with subject expertise had to re-evaluate not only their teaching methods, but also the very nature of their subject. For the thoughtful and enquiring tutor this could only add to their own comprehension of their subject, and many tutors welcomed this opportunity to re-examine their work in a wider context. Groups of tutors met together to discuss these implications and to gain mutual support.

Location of education sessions was seen to be important. There was pressure by tutors to bring students into an adult education environment, with its facilities for the different subject areas and atmosphere of adult learning.

The areas of ability where most significant developments took place were initially in arts subjects (music, art, dance, drama and so on). The classes were of normal duration – two or three hours, and in some cases the students had two classes a day for one day a week. Many significant discoveries were made:

1 The individual subject ability of students did not correlate with the assessment of general ability. For instance, some so-called low-ability students were found to have very high bodily–kinesthetic ability. Musical intelligence of a high order was not necessarily matched by verbal or social skills.
2 Students were able to concentrate for long

periods, though the effort which some, unused to working at this level, made spontaneously was exhausting, and they needed time to adjust to the demands made by the subject.

3 The hidden curriculum was significant for all students involved. Personal growth, a developing sense of self-worth and the necessity for working with a group of people with similar interests combined to enhance social skills and competence, often dramatically.

4 There was evidence of overspill into other subject areas. One ability, and its recognition by the student and by other people, acted as a stimulus to other areas of potential growth.

5 Some students with real ability developed slowly, and patience and faith was needed on all sides to accept that their growth was both real and valid.

6 Opportunity for choice was a new experience for many of the students, even at the rudimentary level of choosing between coffee and tea in the canteen. It was a basic skill to be learnt before students could approach the wider decision-making skills essential to real learning, as opposed to rote learning, or training.

Does this evidence indicate that educational assumptions are made on too narrow a basis? Are the instruments of measurement used to identify mental handicap valid? What real abilities are buried within people because of a narrow view of 'intelligence'? Are there other intelligences which are relevant to adult society which have had no opportunity for growth within the narrow curriculum laid down for people with a mental handicap?

What is mental handicap? Is it a condition with no amelioration? Is it something that can be modified with training? Or is it the result of societal attitudes? Are our assumptions of what is normal, and our desire that people should conform to that normality, overwhelming the potential for growth and development through innate abilities?

During the early 1980s significant developments have taken place within adult education for several reasons:

1 The continuation and development of the work of the previous decade.

2 The changing pattern within ATCs, most of whom now run training and/or educational programmes as a normal part of their work.

3 Widening opportunities in the community, as people who are called mentally handicapped leave hospitals and live in hostels or group homes.

4 The new self-advocacy developments, where people who are called mentally handicapped have opportunity to enter into dialogue with those who work with them, and with a wider audience.

Within the current adult education provision there is a much broader curriculum. This includes practical subjects like self-help skills, budgeting and cookery, both basic and more advanced. Students with minimal literacy skills are enabled to put their thoughts on paper to disseminate them to a wide audience using tape recorders and secretarial assistance. This does not negate the need for literacy skills; it stimulates the desire for those skills, with the realization that what they write is relevant and powerful, unlike 'The cat sat on the mat'.

Self-advocacy, which is discussed below, is a real and vital aspect of this development. Political issues are being pursued, and people who are called mentally handicapped are demanding to be taken seriously. There are other developments, too numerous to mention in this brief overview.

There is still too little opportunity for students to choose their own areas of study. In an area of education where adult students are free to select not only the subjects but also the institute and tutor of their preference, students who are called mentally handicapped do not have adequate opportunity to make real choices, which should be based on experience. All too often referral agencies dictate the subject area. There are still institutes where the 'therapy' model is present and real educational opportunities are lacking; indeed, some have yet to call these people 'students', even though they enrol them as such!

Let us hope that the emerging student power in our midst will overcome paternalistic and custodial attitudes, so that tutors and students together can pursue real educational goals, and make a positive contribution to human knowledge, skills and attitudes.

SELF-ADVOCACY

Self-advocacy is the term used to describe both the principle and process of mentally handicapped people speaking for themselves. The principle encompasses the desire to be taken seriously, treated as adults and equals and viewed by others in terms not of their handicaps but rather of their ability. It need not only be with words or through committees. It may consist of composing or playing a piece of music, creating a dance or movement sequence or drawing a picture. Creative subjects have proved to be a rich source of communication for mentally handicapped people, not just as an opportunity to 'enjoy themselves', but more importantly to demonstrate their ability to concentrate and master techniques which enable them to communicate with others more effectively.

Although it is much harder for people with little or no language to communicate their needs and wishes, the principle remains the same; there is simply more pressure on professionals or parents to interpret those people's means of self-expression. When talking here of mentally handicapped people and self-advocacy I* am particularly thinking of people with language, especially in the context of meetings and conferences, but would stress that from my experience the range of people capable of acquiring the appropriate skills is much wider than might be assumed. It is not just the 'high-grade' ones (whatever that means) who can achieve this.

Although many of its recipients quite reasonably object to the label 'mentally handicapped', it is used here for the purpose of literary convenience. The debate about alternative 'labels' is not without value, but sometimes proves a distraction to other important issues. This section will refer to the developments familiar to me at the time of writing (May 1984) in the field of self-advocacy in Britain, and will then go on to consider the implications of these developments for future service provision for mentally handicapped people in this country.

Williams and Schoultz (1982) give a readable and detailed account of developments in the USA and in Britain over the previous decade. In 1984 nine mentally handicapped people and nine professionals travelled to the USA to attend the International Self-Advocacy Leadership Conference organized by the Washington group People First; this provided an opportunity to experience at first hand the ways in which self-advocacy has developed in the USA and a chance to share ideas about how it can develop further on both sides of the Atlantic.

An increasing number of centres and hostels have committees of users which exercise varying amounts of influence and power. Members of any discussion group have to learn a variety of skills. Listening to one another, speaking clearly and to the point, sharing and developing their ideas, and gaining confidence which may lead to speaking in public are skills which take time to master. There is no set time

limit, as each person is different, but what is done with this expertise will depend on the aims of the group.

The MENCAP Metropolitan Region Participation Forum group have organized two seminars at which mentally handicapped people spoke on topics they had chosen themselves like 'What do we mean by handicap?', 'Who makes the rules?' and 'Where we live'. Videos of the seminars were made as training aids for other interested parties. Members of this group as well as students from the City Lit Adult Education Institute in London have been invited to speak to groups of professionals and parents at conferences and on training courses (including medical students and staff on an SEC induction course). In certain cases, clients at centres and residents at hostels have contributed to the process of interviewing new staff. The skills learnt are thus transferred. For individuals, acquiring these skills may help them to live more independently in the community by moving into group homes and flats. It may also help them to negotiate with the professionals in their work and leisure programmes.

Clearly, these developments in self-advocacy have profound implications for the world of mental handicap. Professionals and parents need to accept that there should be far more meaningful consultation with mentally handicapped people over decisions affecting their lives. For some people this will necessitate a considerable change of attitude, and they will also need training. If there is to be real participation by mentally handicapped people, then discussions may well proceed at a slower pace and in less complex language than usual; the way that decisions are arrived at may have to change too, for real participation should not mean that service providers just listen politely and then go ahead and do what they were planning to anyway! Some people may feel that mentally handicapped people speaking up and questioning things is an implicit threat to the status quo. However, it is too easy to dismiss what they say as merely echoing other people or as unrealistic; you have to be prepared to explain the matter clearly, examine the available options and offer them the choice, remembering that choice-making is also a skill to be learnt.

Ultimately, self-advocacy must pose the question, 'How much do "they" need us?'. Currently, professionals help people to speak for themselves. But what if a self-advocacy group decide that they do not want help from professionals and moreover are diametrically opposed to what is being provided? Will professionals negotiate with them while

---

* John Hersov.

accepting the possibility that they might have to back down? Obviously, we hope it that would not happen because we hope that are all working in everyone's best interests. But what if the recipients say 'No'?

Self-advocacy is a dynamic process which covers casual conversations and interpersonal relationships as well as committees, public meetings and conferences. The current rate of progress suggests that the future will be very exciting.

REFERENCES AND RECOMMENDED READING

Further education

Gathercole C (Ed.) (1984) *An Ordinary Working Life*. London: King's Fund Centre.

Griffiths M (1984) *First Destinations of Special School Leavers*. Unpublished.

Adult education

DHSS (Department of Health and Social Security) (1971) *Better Services for the Mentally Handicapped*. Cmnd. 4683. London: HMSO.

Edwards B (1979) *Drawing on the Right Side of the Brain*. London: Fontana//Collins.

Gardner H (1983) *Frames of Mind: The Theory of Multiple Intelligences*. London: Heinemann.

Rogers C (1983) *Freedom to Learn for the 80s*. Columbus. Ohio: Charles E. Merrill.

Self-advocacy

City Literary Institute (1982) *Speaking for Ourselves* (videotape). London: City Literary Institute.

City Literary Institute (1983) *Have we a Future* (videotape and information pack). London: City Literary Institute.

Williams P & Schoultz B (1982) *We can Speak for Ourselves*. London: Souvenir Press.

PART 5
INTERVENTION

Chapter 24
The Dynamics of Teamwork

SHEILA HOLLINS

This part of the book is devoted to intervention, with contributions from a number of authors with different professional backgrounds, including nursing, social work, psychology, psychiatry and the remedial therapies.

Educational interventions were covered in Part 4, and the demanding roles of parents in assessment and intervention were discussed in Chapter 13. Study of the information provided in this final part about the range of skills acquired by the various professionals during training and the appropriate application of these skills in different settings should enable a fuller use of each discipline to the advantage of the patient or client.

Inter-disciplinary teams

Such sharing of knowledge permits the development of multi-disciplinary and, ultimately, inter-disciplinary teamwork. An accurate understanding of the true extent of another therapist's expertise, and an acknowledgement of areas of overlapping interest and skill should lead to more appropriate referrals and expectations. However, the mere existence of a number of different professionals all appointed to work with people with mental handicaps in the same setting does not guarantee teamwork. Stories about so-called team-members who do not talk to each other are legion. 'Inter-disciplinary' working implies an interchange between different disciplines. Traditional professional boundaries may be threatened and such interchange will only take place in an atmosphere of mutual trust and respect. These considerations are not restricted to clinical teams: clear parallels can be seen in sport. The cricket team with members who are reluctant to pull their weight will not achieve its objectives. Although different team members owe their position in the team to their skill as a batsman, bowler or fielder, at times the batsman must also bowl as well as he is able.

Figure 24.1 shows a number of different models for client/professional interaction when more than one specialist is involved. As can be seen, multiple individual consultations may lead to confusion about who is responsible for what, to the possibility of repetition and overlap, and to wasted time for specialists and client alike. Multiple simultaneous consultations can be overwhelming for the client, with an enormous pool of expertise remaining largely untapped. Extensive team liaison may leave the client out in the cold, unless one team member is clearly identified to communicate with the client and to help him represent his own interests.

Inter-disciplinary staff training at both initial and in-service training levels might provide a model for cooperation and understanding which would reap benefits in professional teamwork. Inter-disciplinary jealousy based on more traditional styles of working in which different disciplines are perceived as having higher or lower status can be both a destructive and an inhibiting force.

Key workers

Within the multi-disciplinary team the person identified to communicate with the family is known as the 'named person', the 'key worker' or the 'lead member'. In choosing a key worker the person on the team with the most appropriate skills is identified. That person will be the family's contact point with the team. The key worker may invite other professionals to contribute their skills at different times, but no professional would get involved with a client without speaking to the key worker. The key worker thus coordinates the service delivery but does not necessarily deliver it himself.

In the United States another system of health care delivery has been described called cross modality (or cross-discipline) (Modrow and Darnell, 1979).

The idea here is to identify one therapist as the primary therapist who will deliver a range of treatments himself, his colleagues on the team acting

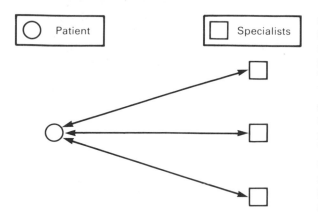

a Multiple individual consultations – Confusion

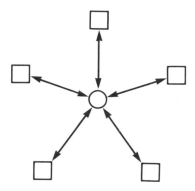

b Multiple simultaneous consultations – Overwhelmed

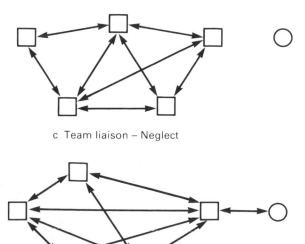

c Team liaison – Neglect

d Team liaison <u>and</u> communication with patient

Fig. 24.1 Types of team organization (Holt, 1977); in each diagram the circle represents the patients and the squares the specialists.

as teachers and consultants. This can be taken one step further so that the parent or carer is the primary therapist, and is taught to assess needs and implement all treatment programmes under supervision. This approach is being used to some extent in the UK by psychologists in their work with residential care staff. For some years parents have been participating in home intervention programmes where they become the therapist or teacher for their child. This could be a way of spreading resources and enhancing the skills of those who have 24-hour responsibility for people with mental handicaps. Such an approach sounds encouraging, but there are risks of diluting skills and of applying treatment inappropriately.

Link person

Inter-agency liaison is as important as interdisciplinary teamwork. One way of achieving this is for the team to appoint a link person to each local referral agency or facility. This person's role is to maintain a dialogue between the team and the facility, and to bring specific requests for help back to the team.

SUCCESSFUL TEAMWORK

One purpose of teamwork is to pool the skills of individuals and so produce a better result than that which could be achieved by each individual working on their own. The total effect should be greater. Another purpose is to attend to the development of individual ability among team members.

In their book *Organisation Development Through Teambuilding* Woodcock and Francis (1981) outline their nine 'building blocks' of team effectiveness:

1 Clear objectives and agreed goals.
2 Openness and confrontation.
3 Support and trust.
4 Cooperation and conflict.
5 Sound procedures.
6 Appropriate leadership.
7 Regular review.
8 Individual development.
9 Sound intergroup relations.

Of these I would link the need for clear objectives and sound procedures with the need to continually evaluate effectiveness in achieving goals. Cooperation should be enhanced where there is a shared office base providing efficient management and secretarial services as well as central recording of information.

Clear objectives

The fundamental question to ask about any team is whether clients benefit. Unless one member of the team is identified appropriately as the person with the necessary skills and experience to work directly with the client, referral to a professional team may well have been a waste of time. In such a circumstance referral to an individual specialist might have met the client's needs more effectively. However, problems are almost always complex and changing; no one person is likely to have all the answers all the time.

Individual development

In the business world computer analysis has been used to produce profiles of individual team members. The idea is to identify the strengths and weaknesses of each member so that appropriate demands will be made, utilizing skills to the full and offering support and help to avoid failure. I would hope that our clinical teams will never reach the stage when a computer will be needed to make decisions about delegation of responsibility!

In a fully competent professional team one would expect to see adequate recognition of skills without unnecessary competition, and enough support to enable professional growth for each individual member. There is no scope for prima donna performances – the team gets all the glory! Sometimes one team member may find himself overworked to a degree which is detrimental both to his efficiency and his sanity. This most commonly occurs with newly appointed enthusiastic workers taking on too many clients without realizing the full extent of the job, or with committed longer established staff who try to maintain the same level of service provision when job vacancies occur and remain unfilled. Such overwork may be a symptom of an individual's inability to set realistic limits. Some teams may feel the need for a staff support group to engender the development of trust, loyalty and support and to increase cooperation between its members. Such meetings help to clarify objectives and to dispel feelings of isolation and to explore the extent of individual responsibility. Confrontation may be used constructively in a supportive group setting to resolve differences. A regular time and place may need to be set aside with an independent group leader.

Leadership

Leaderless teams result in chaos, but leadership styles must vary to suit particular circumstances (Figure 24.2). For example, inexperienced newly appointed team members will respond to firm leadership offering support and encouragement. On the other hand, a new team comprised of experienced staff accustomed to working independently will require a more flexible leadership.

For some time now there has been movement away from medical coordination of services for people with mental handicaps. It is not necessarily the prerogative of the doctor in the team to be the chairperson. Many teams sensibly elect a chairperson for a limited period, or regularly rotate this responsibility round the whole team. Such measures avoid the leader being made a scapegoat when something goes wrong, and increase the likelihood of appropriate delegation. Commitment to the efficient functioning of the team is shared in this way.

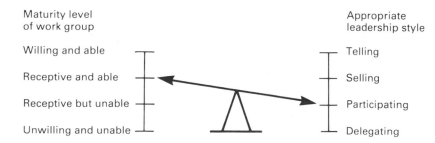

Fig. 24.2 The leadership style balance (Woodcock and Francis, 1981).

The chairperson's task is primarily to facilitate the business of the meeting. Thus he will come well prepared to the meeting with minutes and agenda.

During the meeting he will aim to begin and end on time and he will invite comment and foreshorten unnecessary diversion. He will represent the team to other agencies or delegate this function.

Leadership skills are not inherent, but can often be learnt, and management and leadership courses are becoming standard and essential components of continuing training for all professional groups. Issues about leadership and responsibility occupy the committees of all health and social service professional staff.

The team coordinator or chairman does not necessarily carry responsibility for the clinical work of the team. The model recommended by the Inner London Education Authority (1979) to its Child Guidance Units is described as follows: 'responsibility for professional judgement and action lies with the professions concerned in their respective spheres, for in this they are autonomous. . . . If the 'lead' member in a particular case is concerned about the part being played by a colleague he/she should bring the matter to the attention of the team coordinator, who may be able to resolve the difficulty in discussion with the senior team member in the profession concerned. . . . '

In 1977 the Royal College of Psychiatrists adopted a report on the question of the consultant psychiatrists' responsibilities. I quote: 'Administrative or management issues can be decided on a corporate basis because the standing between the disciplines is on a basis of equality in arriving at a management decision. This method generally cannot be applied to professional opinions relating to individual patients,' and again: 'Each doctor must formulate his own opinion, whether assisted in this process by others or not. Multidisciplinary in this context, from the medical point of view, is a process of consultation, the final decision resting with the Consultant on matters where the Consultant has the final responsibility. Similar conditions may apply to other professions when the central responsibilities germane to these disciplines are involved.'

Rohde (1984) recommends that the Royal College (a) issues a revised statement continuing to reaffirm the consultant's role as leader of the clinical team in the hospital, but taking into account the continued movement into multi-disciplinary teams and community psychiatry, and considering that in some settings (in planning and outside the National Health Service) the consultant may not be the automatic leader, and (b) takes the initiative in contacting other professional bodies for an interdisciplinary statement on ethics in community psychiatry.

DIFFERENT TEAMS

For any professional working in mental handicap membership of one kind of team or another is a certainty. Whether it is a community nursing or residential care team or a multi-disciplinary specialist team based in the hospital or the community, many of the factors in effective teamwork described in this chapter will still be relevant. However, vertical professional hierarchies or membership of more than one team may interfere with loyalty to the multi-disciplinary team. For example, community nurses are responsible for their clinical work to a senior nurse manager in a vertical hierarchy. The possibility arises that the senior nurse could put aside the decision of the community mental handicap team without being a member of that team. Similarly the clinical psychologist is responsible to the district psychologist, and the social worker to the director of social services.

A good team will develop to meet local needs, so it is not possible to describe the composition of a typical mental handicap team. However, in the United Kingdom one model which is being adopted widely by district health authorities is that of the community mental handicap team (CMHT). The idea is to have a team based in the community which will accept referrals from any source and will meet the specialist health-care needs of people with mental handicaps (Figure 24.3). For the reader who plans to use this part of the book to understand more fully the scope of the community mental handicap team, chapters are included first of all from the four disciplines that are generally considered to make up the essential nucleus of such a team: the community nurse, the social worker, the clinical psychologist and the psychiatrist in mental handicap. These chapters are followed by contributions from some of the other members of a community mental handicap team: namely the speech therapist, physiotherapist, occupational therapist and dietitian. The range of interventions described is not fully comprehensive; there are many other skills which are regularly contributed through CMHTs, for example those of the community physician.

Team members

David Sines (Chapter 25) explores the position of the community nurse as a full-time member of the

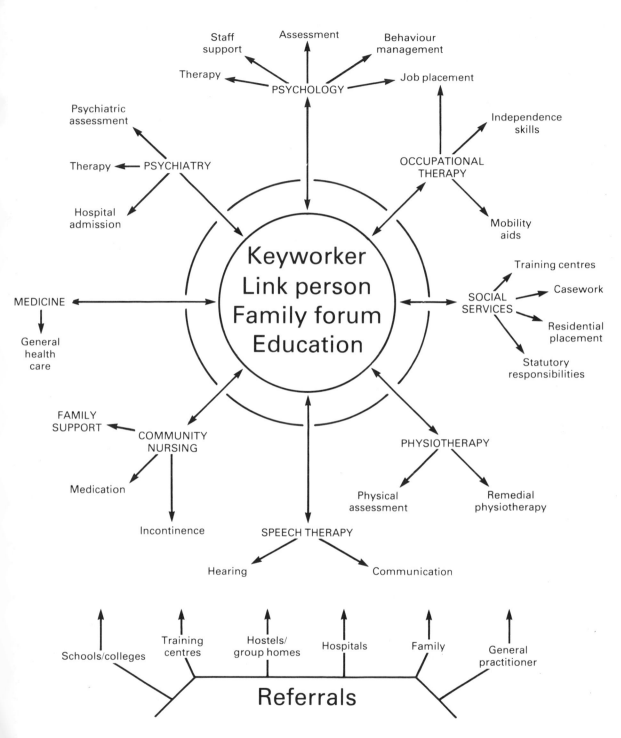

Fig. 24.3 The community mental handicap team.

CMHT. The training of community nurses is described, with a resume of the wide range of activities for which they have to be prepared. Special health care needs such as epilepsy are discussed from the point of view of community management. The emphasis is on preview and anticipation of crises rather than crisis intervention.

Peter Gilbert (Chapter 26) describes the central role of the practising social worker within the multi-disciplinary health care team. The consultative aspects of the social worker's role, particularly in enabling generic social workers to do case work with people with mental handicap and their families is discussed. He explains that the social worker has a broad knowledge of specialized resources and will participate in assessment of need, in providing support, counselling and arranging practical help as necessary.

Peter Wilcock (Chapter 27) outlines the idea that the work of the psychologist is as consultant to other practitioners and parents, with the emphasis on assessment as an entree to individual programmes. He illustrates some theoretical descriptions of the psychologist's skills, with examples of current good practice.

Andrew Reid (Chapter 28) offers case histories and clinical cues to illustrate the presentation of mental illness in a person with mental handicap. He discusses psychiatric diagnosis and the range of different treatment modes available.

Margaret Walker (Chapter 29) explains the speech therapist's role as concerned with every aspect of developing communication skills in human relationships. Assessment of language development and advice to, and work alongside, teachers and parents and others living or working with mentally handicapped people is discussed. A description of non-verbal communication systems is included and their relationship to total communication is explored.

Brenda Blythe (Chapter 30) outlines the variety of assessments and treatments for which the physio-therapist has, or may have, been trained and the different settings in which a physiotherapist might work with people with mental handicaps.

Berendean Anstice and Rosemary Bowden (Chapter 31) consider the occupational therapist first in a variety of practice settings and then as a manager.

Using generic services

Where possible the community mental handicap team will assist people with mental handicaps in using the ordinary health services provided for the rest of the community. There are a number of medical specialists who will have a particular interest in medical problems associated with mental handicap. John Patten (Chapter 34) has simplified neurological assessment to aid the early recognition of significant symptoms and signs. John Corbett and Desmond Pond (Chapter 33) have written an account of epilepsy and its management and have included consideration of the psychosocial aspects of epilepsy.

Phillipa Russell (Chapter 32) has written about the role played by voluntary organizations in promoting discussion and contributing to the provision of adequate services for people with mental handicaps. She emphasizes the increasing importance of such organizations and the growing cooperation between statutory and voluntary bodies.

Michael Craft and Ian Berry (Chapter 36) emphasize the role of the professional in managing and anticipating aggression. They also consider the particular difficulties which may occur when aggression is encountered in community settings, and the implications for staff training.

CONCLUSION

Team work is seldom easy; perhaps surprisingly, it can be satisfying despite some personal loss of professional autonomy.

In mental handicap there are particular pressures associated with the inescapable fact that disabilities do not go away. The isolated professional is at risk of 'burn-out'. Within a multi-disciplinary team there are opportunities for supporting periods of stress within a framework of realistic expectations for the outcome of any intervention for a client or family.

REFERENCES

Gordon NS (1981) Personal view: the team approach in helping children with learning difficulties with particular reference to the doctor's role. *Child: Care, Health and Development* 7: 195–199.

Holt KS (1977) The handicapped child. In Mattingly S (ed) *Rehabilitation Today* Ch. 14. London: Update Books.

Inner London Education Authority (1979) *Relationships and Leadership in Child Guidance Units*. London: ILEA Medical Department.

Modrow CL & Darnell RE (1979) Dietetic services in a cross-modality system. *Journal of the American Dietetic Association* 74(3): 341–344.

Rohde PD (1984) The future of the consultant in psychiatry: a continuing debate. *Bulletin of the Royal College of Psychiatrists* (April): 65–66.

Royal College of Psychiatrists (1977) The responsibilities of consultants in psychiatry within the NHS. *Bulletin of the Royal College of Psychiatrists* (September): 4–7.

Woodcock M & Francis D (1981) The nine building blocks of team effectiveness. In Woodcock M & Francis D *Organisation Development Through Teambuilding*. pp. 118–157. Aldershot, Hampshire: Gower.

Chapter 25
The Role of the Community Nurse

DAVID T. SINES

Community nurses are able to provide a unique contribution to the care of people with mental handicaps by bringing the skills which they have acquired during their previous training in mental handicap hospitals and carefully adapting these to the needs of people living in the community. A new philosophy of care has emerged in liaison with other colleagues working in the community mental handicap team (see Chapter 2).

It is important to note that wherever the needs of people with mental handicaps present themselves there will be a requirement for flexibility of approach in providing the care that they and their families require. The community nurse and the social worker often work together to share their skills and resources, providing a joint approach to care without losing their own professional identity. It is necessary to ensure that each member of the team has a clearly defined role when planning the delivery of care to each individual, although there may be some areas of overlap.

In the United Kingdom community nurses often form the full-time members of community mental handicap teams, with social work colleagues. Emphasis on team work is important and, during induction training programmes, community nurses usually spend a considerable time working with other professionals in the care team, understanding and appreciating how their own roles will develop and merge during the course of their everyday work.

This chapter considers the role of the community nurse (mental handicap) in the United Kingdom and draws upon examples of the work performed by community nurses in different teams throughout the country. It is not expected that each community nursing team should aim to provide all the services outlined since regional variations may reduce or inhibit the performance of certain tasks. Before considering the role of the community nurse in detail it may be helpful to consider the training and preparation which community nurses undertake before working with mentally handicapped people and their families.

TRAINING OPPORTUNITIES FOR COMMUNITY NURSES

Nearly all nurses in the United Kingdom specializing in this field have spent some time working in mental handicap hospitals gaining a variety of experience with different client groups. The majority hold a statutory qualification, the Registered Nurse for the Mentally Handicapped certificate (RNMH), which is gained on completing a three-year course. There is also a two-year course and qualification which enables learner nurses to proceed to enrolment as qualified nurses. With the two-year course more emphasis is based on practical aspects of care and promotional opportunities are limited.

In 1982 the General Nursing Council, the body then responsible for the statutory training of nursing in the United Kingdom, published a revised RNMH syllabus for nurses training to work with people with mental handicaps. The syllabus covers a wide range of opportunities and experiences which nurses are likely to encounter during their professional career in both hospital and in the community. In the revised syllabus the following definition, of nursing people with mental handicaps (adapted from Henderson, 1961) is offered: 'The function of the nurse is directly and skilfully to assist the individual and his family whatever the handicap in the acquisition, development and maintenance of skills, giving the necessary ability [for them] to be performed unaided; and to do it in such a way as to enable independence to be gained rapidly and as fully as possible and in an environment that maintains the quality of life that will be acceptable for those citizens of this day and age.'

The new syllabus provides experience for learner nurses in both hospital and community settings. It includes practical placements at schools, hostels, adult training centres and visits with community nurses and other domiciliary staff such as health visitors and social workers. The syllabus is wide in its concept and emphasizes the education and training of the person with a mental handicap and the support required by the family. An understanding of social policy, the processes involved in planning individual client care and the skills of counselling and communication are included. Naturally the nursing element is of greatest importance and consideration is given to the care required by the following groups of people with special needs:

1 Multiply handicapped people.
2 People with sensory handicaps.
3 People with associated behaviour problems.
4 Elderly people with mental handicaps.
5 People with profound mental handicaps.

Post-basic courses for community nurses are available in the United Kingdom; these vary from courses of one month's duration to a more intensive course following a full academic year at a local college of higher education. In all post-basic courses emphasis is placed on practical community experience with established teams. The development of additional skills such as the following is usually included:

1 The principles and practices of community nursing.
2 The role of the nurse in the community.
3 Family relationships.
4 The use of the nurse/patient relationship.
5 Behaviour modification.
6 Relevant sociological trends.
7 Health and social service policy.
8 Management appreciation.
9 Health education and teaching techniques.
10 Interviewing and counselling skills.
11 Research methodology.

THE PROFESSIONAL ROLES OF THE COMMUNITY NURSE

As a basic principle the community nurse aims to offer nursing care, support and understanding for each person with a mental handicap and his or her family in response to identified needs. The nurse's primary aim is a preventive approach to care

by reducing the consequences of any mental handicap to a minimum whilst encouraging the person and the family to have as near normal a lifestyle as possible. The nurse also aims to encourage the individual to develop to his or her full potential although it should be acknowledged that from time to time frustrations and over-stimulation may be counter-productive in the process. The community nurse should also plan for potential crises which may be identified during the course of an individual's life and generate strategies which may be available to relieve and reduce problems to a minimum.

The nurse assessor

The nurse's role in assessing the needs of individuals and their families is a prerequisite to planning the delivery of care in the community. Assessment entails the gathering and collection of information regarding identified needs as perceived and experienced by the person with a handicap, the family and the nurse. In order to carry out a comprehensive assessment the nurse may use one of several formalized assessment schedules based on a system of individual care planning. 'The nursing process' is a term that is used to classify a system of systematic data collection which is based on four main principles:

1 Assessment of individual needs.
2 Planning the care required.
3 Implementing an individual care plan.
4 Evaluating the success or failure of the intervention.

Assessments should take into account the person's strengths and weaknesses and should lead to the implementation of a carefully planned programme, tailored to the needs of the individual. A full functional assessment should take into account the following:

1 The physical requirements and factors which may result from the handicap and require intervention.
2 Social factors involved in the individual's life at home.
3 Psychological factors.
4 Emotional influences.

Assessment should be on-going and continuous, leading the nurse to identify individual abilities and patterns of behaviour in the areas of (a) self-help skills, (b) communication skills, (c) medical/clinical factors, (d) behaviour and (e) the family and home.

Self-help skills
1 Feeding
2 Washing and personal hygiene
3 Oral hygiene
4 Care during menstruation
5 Toilet habits and continence

Communication skills
1 Identifiable standards of verbal communication
2 Degree of comprehensibility of individual speech patterns
3 Non-verbal communication and systems of communication

Medical factors/clinical
1 The presence of additional physical handicaps, for example cerebral palsy
2 The degree of any sensory handicap, such as partial sight
3 The degree of any associated organic disease, for instance Parkinsonism or diabetes
4 Impairment of mobility
5 The presence of epilepsy, its presentation and method of control
6 The administration of any medication and occurrence of side-effects

Behaviour. The nurse will be careful to consider both positive and negative aspects of an individual's behaviour and will assess the appropriateness of such behaviour to the individual's lifestyle and environment at the time. Problems such as self-mutilation, temper tantrums or disturbed sleep patterns will be noted and may be referred to a psychologist following the initial assessment.

The family and home. Through observation of verbal and non-verbal communication the community nurse should be able to obtain a reasonable impression of the family's circumstances during preliminary visits to the home. Factors noted will include adequate warmth, ventilation and security within the home (adequate locks on doors etc.). The family's coping mechanisms should also be identified, along with other members of the extended family or the neighbourhood involved in the care of the person with mental handicap. Specific fears, anxieties, wishes and expectations presented by the person and by the family should also be noted.

Following such assessment of the individual's handicap and the family's care for him or her the community nurse should be able to suggest to the community mental handicap team the kind of services that the individual may require. A care plan may then be formed for each individual and his or her family following full discussion by the team.

The nurse clinician

Traditionally, nurses have administered treatment prescribed by medical staff. In the last decade in the United Kingdom the nurse's role has widened in certain situations to one of innovator and primary professional, both advising and implementing care programmes independently. This development has encouraged a new professional status within the field of nursing for people with mental handicaps.

The nurse can be involved in any aspect of the physical or total nursing care required by each person; this may involve sharing bathing and direct physical treatments in the home with district nursing colleagues. Assessment and monitoring of any physical ailment, whether it be a common cold, influenza or an open wound, will be part of the community nurse's duty during regular visits to clients at home. The degree to which the community nurse may be directly involved in treating these may depend upon the nurse's liaison with local general practitioners, consultants and the district nurse. In some areas community nurses are involved in helping to dress and feed people with mental handicaps as part of training programmes.

Community nurses may be involved in teaching parents and people with mental handicaps appropriate methods to obtain desired standards of oral hygiene, often in liaison with dentists and oral hygienists.

The presentation of physical handicap such as seen in cerebral palsy has presented a challenge to community nurses in the community, and they may work closely with physiotherapists and remedial gymnasts to provide passive movements and therapy in the home. The supervision of bathing, exercises to improve eye–hand coordination and postural drainage may be part of the community nurses' clinical role with families. Supervising walking exercises and the introduction of appliances such as walking frames, tripods and wheelchairs may also be part of their role.

Community nurses can play an important role in the management of epilepsy by monitoring the frequency and type of seizures. The nurse's role is to teach the family to record in detail the frequency and presentation of fits as they take place. The importance of this procedure is that it assists the doctor to make a firm diagnosis, which will then lead to the recommendation of appropriate treatment.

Many people with epilepsy will be taking anti-convulsant drugs and community nurses may be involved in the monitoring of these drugs and their side-effects. Some community nurses have taken training as venesectionists and take blood regularly for serum anticonvulsant level monitoring.

Some community nursing teams have formed crisis-intervention services (Figure 25.1) to help with the following types of emergency:

1 Status epilepticus.
2 Behavioural disturbance.
3 Problems arising from stress exhibited in families with members with mental handicap.

Very often these problems occur outside normal working hours and immediate and practical sup-port is often called for. The coordination of services usually involves the organization of a nursing duty rota alongside the medical duty rota. In one service used in two London Boroughs seven community nurses share a duty rota to provide continuous cover (Sines and Bicknell, 1985). Calls to the service are monitored by the local hospital switchboard, who will then page the designated community nurse on duty by radio. The community nurse may then contact the family, assess the situation and decide upon an appropriate course of action. For example, this may involve:

1 Discussion of the problem over the telephone, with the offer of a follow-up visit the next day.
2 Discussion with the duty doctor or other agencies.
3 Home visit and the possible administration of emergency medication.
4 The arrangement of short-term care.

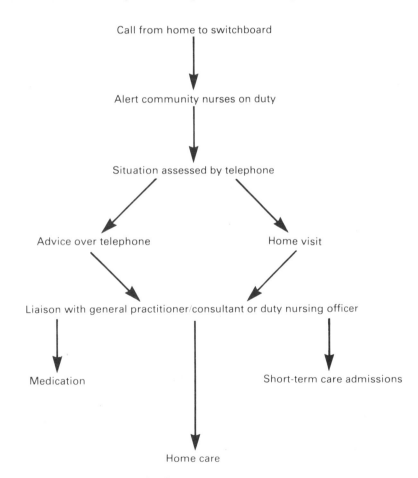

Fig. 25.1 A crisis-intervention service: one example of an 'on-call' service.

This particular service is useful in the management of epilepsy, particularly when drugs are being reviewed or changed and the possibility of additional seizures may be anticipated. Community nurses may administer emergency medication and offer a telephone contact at all times; this may avoid unnecessary admission to hospital. Other examples of the community nurse's clinical tasks are:

1 Escort of families to district general hospitals for medical appointments.
2 Management of menstruation.
3 Regulation of bowels.
4 Support and advice about physical problems involving cardiac and respiratory diseases and diabetes.
5 Knowledge of services such as dentistry, ophthalmology and chiropody.

The nurse therapist

Referrals to the community mental handicap team may sometimes be to modify undesirable or unsuitable behaviour or, in other cases, to develop certain areas of self-help skill, such as the promotion of continence. Behaviour modification programmes may be formulated for the community nurse to supervise at home, school or training centre. The community nurse will be an important link in the therapeutic process by keeping the community mental handicap team informed of the progress of each programme and of any problems or changes which have occurred since the programme was originally implemented. The community nurse may also act as the point of liaison between all the agencies involved in the individual's care whilst a programme is being produced. For example, a toileting programme being introduced to someone at home will also need to be followed up at school and in any short-term care unit the child may be attending.

For the under-fives a more systematic approach may be used, such as that found in the Portage system of home education (Shearer and Shearer, 1972). The Portage system illustrates the use of behaviour modification and allows a carefully planned model of intervention. Community nurses may act as 'home advisers' for the Portage system and visit families on a regular basis to introduce new ideas and methods, to provide stimulation and to teach techniques to develop self-help skills in the young pre-school child. The nurses usually meet psychologists, speech therapists and other members of the pre-school team to discuss progress and to plan the forthcoming week's activities. Baseline data are collected and a checklist completed following a comprehensive assessment schedule provided by the Portage team. Weekly activity charts are left with parents with instructions regarding the next week's tasks. The community nurse, through the process of modelling and role-play, ensures that the family understands the instructions for the week's activities.

In hospitals, hostels and group homes the community nurse may be involved in the development and implementation of self-help skill training programmes which lead to independence.

Social skill training will be particularly important for this group of people, who are training to live independently in the community. Close liaison with adult training centres, social services staff and the multi-disciplinary team will be necessary to provide a consistent and successful programme. The monitoring and implementation of programmes for after-care for people who have lived in hospitals also provides an important role for the community nurse.

Working with social workers, psychiatrists and psychologists, the community nurse may have an important role as co-therapist in psychotherapy and family therapy. The concept of psychotherapy for people with mental handicaps through the group process is becoming more important and the community nurse, following close supervision from other professionals, may be involved in the exploration of group feelings. The process of family therapy is one other area in which the community nurse may be involved on a contractual basis with social workers and doctors.

The nurse adviser

From time to time the community nurse may be asked for advice on specific problems or issues relating to mental handicap and, in order to answer or provide satisfactory advice, it is necessary for the community nurse to have at his or her disposal a wide variety of resources. These resources may be other professionals in the team or simply a 'library' of resource information which may act as a guide when information is requested.

Many people working in the community regard the community mental handicap team as a resource centre to offer such advice. Staff working in residential establishments, day-care centres and schools are examples of people who may call upon the community nursing services on matters relating to the care of mentally handicapped people. In some areas community nurses have established 'drop-in' clinics open to anyone to call in to seek information or simply for a 'chat'. Advice on residential school placements, residential facilities, clubs, clothing for people with disabilities, aids and appliances for incontinence and mobility, financial benefits and legal rights are some examples of the information which may be requested. On a more individual basis parents may request help to deal with a problem which may then require further investigation and referral to the community mental handicap team.

The nurse manager

As with any professional group a certain amount of management is required to run effective services. The community nurse is responsible for a case load of individual people who require planned and systematic care. The development of a satisfactory communication system between team members, the public and other establishments involved in the care of people with mental handicaps is important and may involve much of the team's time.

The community nurse should also maintain an individual care plan for each person that he or she is involved with which should be available to any member of the community mental handicap team.

The nurse counsellor

Parents may form a firm relationship with a community nurse who visits regularly and the community nurse should respond in such a way that he or she will be accepted as someone who can enable the family to discuss their feelings and problems without fear of prejudice or judgement. Drawing upon their own experience and sharing feelings and frustrations with parents, community nurses may share many of the problems which parents have found difficult to express during their everyday care for their handicapped son or daughter. The value of any counselling which the community nurse may offer will be enhanced by practical help and advice.

The community nurse may use many of the basic tools of counselling such as careful listening, the observation of verbal and non-verbal communication and the parents' general method of expression. Counselling on a basic level such as this is an essential part of the community nurse's role. In some areas community nurses have taken advanced courses in individual counselling and have entered into 'in-depth' work with families.

Community nurses should plan for the long-term goals in relation to life events which will occur during the ordinary pattern of a person's life. It is well known that certain 'critical stages' such as puberty, school-leaving and the emergence of a secondary handicap may all require specific help and advice as they occur and the community nurse may assist families to adjust to such problems through careful preparation and counselling. This is particularly true during adolescence, when sexual awareness and puberty may present families with additional problems.

The nurse coordinator

During the course of the care of a mentally handicapped person many problems may emerge which will require the support and intervention of several professionals. The community nurse may offer a point of contact for families and may coordinate the services which the family require.

Arranging attendance at dental, chiropody and ophthalmology clinics may form an important part of the community nurse's role; this requires liaison with clinical medical officers, general practitioners and the primary care team. Liaison with volunteers and the coordination of volunteer schemes and rotas may also form part of the community nurse's work. Examples of other services which may be coordinated by community nurses are:

1 A home sitting service (family relief schemes).
2 Special-care holidays.
3 The coordination of short-term care and long-term care admissions.

The nurse teacher

Community nurses may be involved in informal and formal teaching of professionals and volunteers in the community. Parent workshops may be offered to families to help them to gain more skills in the care and training of their son or daughter in order to reduce the symptoms of handicap to a minimum. Here the emphasis is usually placed on problems presented by families, and behavioural strategies may be introduced to help them cope more adequately. The role of the nurse in health education is also important and community nurses are increasingly appreciating their role as educators to individuals through the promotion of positive attitudes to health and handicap and to the general public to encourage and promote the acceptance of people with mental handicap in the community.

The nurse mediator and befriender

It has often proved necessary for the community nurse to form a befriending relationship with people with mental handicap by establishing a firm rapport in a non-judgemental fashion. Community nurses have enabled some individuals to develop their own social skills and self-confidence by helping them to attend clubs in the community and to work generally towards greater integration in their neighbourhood. Others have attended self-awareness groups and sex counselling courses run by community nurses where the contribution of both the nurse and the mentally handicapped person is encouraged.

Community nurses may often mediate between the family and other professionals working with them, for example with the Department of Health and Social Security in respect of benefits, the local social services department with respect to day-care placement and the health authority for adequate but unusual incontinence wear. Such representation may involve an interpretation of parents' feelings regarding certain situations or bureaucratic decisions.

SUMMARY

In the United Kingdom, over the past ten years, the role of the community nurse for people with mental handicap has evolved. The pace at which this evolution has progressed has been regulated by the release of financial resources by health and social services departments and by a growing awareness of the need for a nursing component in the new caring philosophy to help people with mental handicap live in the community.

It may be argued that many of the functions performed by community nurses may be performed by other professionals, such as social workers and health visitors, but the community nurse aims to have a close rapport with the person with a handicap by using the experiences which he or she has gained during a 24-hour caring situation. It is this empathy that has formed the basis of the partnership between the nurse and parents of people with mental handicap in the community.

Emphasis on a local model of care avoiding stereotypes of 'model services' is important if families are to receive the care and support which they require. Services should be flexible and adapted to local needs, with parents and people with mental handicap helping to plan for their own futures.

REFERENCES

Community Psychiatric Nurses Association (1978) *The Role of the Community Psychiatric Nurse*. A submission to the Royal College of Psychiatrists.

Cornforth A, Johnson K & Walker M (1974) Makaton vocabulary – teaching sign language to the deaf mentally handicapped. *Apex 2(1):* 23–25.

English National Board for Nursing, Midwifery and Health Visiting (1980) *Syllabus for a Post-basic Approved Clinical Studies Course in Community Nursing for Mentally Handicapped People*. London: English National Board for Nursing, Midwifery and Health Visiting.

General Nursing Council (1982) *A New Syllabus for Nurses for the Mentally Handicapped*. London: General Nursing Council for England and Wales.

Hall V (1980) *The Community Mental Handicap Nurse: A New Professional Role. Mental Handicap Studies Report No. 11.* Bristol: Bristol University Department of Mental Health.

Henderson V (1966) *The Nature of Nursing: A Definition and its Implications for Practice, Research and Education*. New York: Macmillan.

Jay Committee (1979) *Report of the Committee of Enquiry into Nursing Care of the Mentally Handicapped*. Cmnd. 7468/I. London: HMSO.

Kratz C (1976) The clinical nurse consultant. *Nursing Times 72(46)* (November 18): 1792–1793.

Mittler P et al. (1980) *The National Development Group – A Plan for Action*. London: HMSO.

Owens G & Burchenall P (1979) *Mental Handicap: The Social Dimensions*. London: Pitman Medical.

Shearer SM & Shearer DE (1972) 'The Portage Project' – a model for early childhood education. *Journal of Exceptional Children* 36: 217.

Sines DT (1981) *Community nursing in two boroughs* (unpublished paper).

Sines D (1983) Incontinence–helping people with mental handicap. *Nursing Times 79(33)* (August 17): 53–55.

Sines DT & Bicknell J (1985) *Caring for Mentally Handicapped People in the Community*. pp. 329–333. London: Harper and Row.

Chapter 26
The Role of the Social Worker

PETER GILBERT

DEFINING SOCIAL WORK

Social work in the mental handicap service is something of a paradox. Knowledgeable and caring social workers are much in demand from parents, voluntary organizations and other professions – Simon (1981) puts the specialist social worker and the nurse at the heart of the community mental handicap team – and yet the role that the social worker is meant to fulfil often appears ill-defined.

One reason for this confusion is the fact that, like doctors in the eighteenth century and nurses in the nineteenth, social workers are not seen as requiring any particular expertise or training. A further reason is that the legislation relating to the mental handicap services in the United Kingdom, in contrast to the layered mass of law relating to child care, gives an inadequate and threadbare framework on which to base a social work service.

Defining what a profession does is never easy and is dependent on historical perspectives, professional attitudes and current pressures. The Younghusband Working Party, reporting in 1959, saw casework as 'a personal service provided by qualified workers for individuals who require skilled assistance in resolving some material, emotional or character problem'.

This emphasis on a personal service to people in trouble has widened to embrace a changing emphasis on groupwork and community work in the British Association of Social Workers' 1977 description of the social work task as 'enhancing the personal and social functioning of an individual, family, group or neighbourhood'.

The tensions between casework and community work and between a legislatively-defined and a needs-centred task focus are still with social work, as highlighted in the Barclay Report (NISW, 1982). Perhaps it is healthy that some of the 'helping professions' are in a state of flux, while others have a more defined role, because needs will not always be met by legislative prescription, and flexibility is a necessary part of caring.

THE NEED FOR SOCIAL WORK

Anderson (1982) writes: 'Social workers deal with people who are in conflict with some norm of the society in which they live . . . sometimes they are not aware that they are in conflict; sometimes they have set out to create the conflict. The essence of the social work task is the resolution of that conflict'. While this definition of social work has relevance in many other areas, such as work with families experiencing multiple difficulties and juveniles in conflict with the law, it has a special application in terms of people with a mental handicap, who may well transgress social norms without realizing it and will need additional help in negotiating their way through the increasingly complex maze that is the route towards essential needs in our society.

Social work is of course firmly based on a legislative framework that expresses, in a confused and confusing way, the often contradictory governmental concerns of societal care and social control. Government has recognized that in an industrial society which requires mobility of labour while wishing to preserve the extended family, where world wars have fractured relationships, denuded families and spread the traumas of separation, and where changes in production have had widespread effects on status, employment and roles, a body of people is required to resolve, by means of counselling and material help, the crises of hardship, change, separation and loss.

MODELS OF SOCIAL WORK

Just as a psychiatrist may be a proponent of chemotherapy or psychotherapy, so a social worker may subscribe to one of a number of models of working. Inevitably, the different theories have their own particular strengths and weaknesses, so many counsellors opt for an eclectic approach, which often means a bit of everything!

Any method must be carefully evaluated against basic human values, because, as with any vulnerable group, working with mentally handicapped people can tempt the worker to disregard the human rights of the individual in pursuit of perceived professional goals. Such values should focus on (a) *the reality of human existence*, which means that professional intervention is needed not only to mobilize the dormant capacities in the individual, but also to effect change in the environment, (b) *the dignity of the individual* and his or her right to life, acceptance, the rights and responsibilities of citizenship and the inalienable citizenship of humanity, and (c) *the right to self-determination*, which entails an acceptance that in a true partnership between workers and the individuals and families they serve, people have a right to resist or modify the advice they are receiving to meet their own unique needs and circumstances (see Mittler and McConachie, 1983).

Bearing in mind the value systems of both worker and consumer the main models of social work practice are social casework, family therapy, group work and community work.

Social casework with individuals and families has tended in recent years to move away from the psycho-social model, developed by Hollis and founded on Freudian personality theory, to more of a problem-solving model, where the relationship between worker and client is used to mobilize the latter's innate strengths to overcome actual deficits such as loss of a limb or a loved one, intellectual handicap or financial impoverishment, role inadequacy and emotional disturbance. The caseworker attends to what the client is saying, then responds in a way that helps the individual first explore his or her behaviour and then develop new coping mechanisms (Egan, 1975).

As more schools of thought have developed there has been a tendency for workers to draw on many strands, in an eclectic approach to coping with the range of problems and lack of time experienced in a public welfare agency.

Schools of social work in the United Kingdom are likely to teach a variety of casework models (for a fuller discussion see Butrym, 1976):

1 problem-solving;
2 functional;
3 behaviour modification;
4 task-centred;
5 unitary.

Family therapy. While the caseworker may use the family as an aid in work with an individual member, the family therapist aims at 'the transformation of the family into a more perfectly functioning group' (quoted in Walrond-Skinner, 1976). Because of the evidence concerning the effect of the birth of a handicapped child on the family as a unit and the method's development as a multi-disciplinary approach, family therapy is being used more frequently in this field.

Groupwork. As the White Paper *Better Services for the Mentally Handicapped* (DHSS, 1971) stated, 'Many parents obtain relief and reassurance from contact with other parents of mentally handicapped children.' Experience shows that most parents feel very isolated, and groups for sharing experiences, hopes, fears and strategies for coping are a useful support not only in the early years but at other points of crisis such as entering and leaving school.

Community work. Despite the growth in community resources since 1959, the very low base and essentially segregationist model of care in Britain has meant that mentally handicapped people and their parents are often put in the difficult position of having to accept facilities that divorce the individual from family and neighbourhood. Work with individuals and groups should lead into a wider community and into political action to restore the opportunities that are denied to so many handicapped people and their families.

HISTORICAL BACKGROUND

Because the phrase 'social work' has such a very 1960s ring to it, it is easy to see the activity itself as a recent phenomenon. In fact it properly relates back to the 1913 Mental Deficiency Act, which, despite its overriding concern with social control, gave the impetus to a casework, placement and resource service by its obligation on local authorities to ascertain the numbers of mentally 'defective' people in their area, supervise them and provide residential care or care under guardianship if necessary.

The Report of the Royal Commission in Lunacy and Mental Disorder in 1926 pinpointed the need for contact between institutions and families; lack of contact had been one of the prime reasons for the failure of the Philanthropic movement of the previous century (Ryan and Thomas, 1980). As the report stated, 'The transition from asylum life to the everyday world is a stage of peculiar difficulty. . . .'

Despite a growing awareness of the needs of families, advances in the psychiatric field which produced a move towards rehabilitation, and developments in other services such as child care, social work with mentally handicapped people and their families remained fundamentally static up to 1959. Lack of training and professionalism (Timms, 1964, quoted in Browne, 1982) and the isolation of the residential services for mentally handicapped children and adults after the National Health Service took control of them in 1948, meant that there was a confused approach to families. As Bayley (1973) points out in his Sheffield Study, 'There appeared to be a general uncertainty among the mental welfare officers about the sort of service they should be trying to offer to the subnormal and their families, let alone how to offer it.'

The 1959 Mental Health Act abolished the requirement to visit that had been bitterly resented by many families, but meant that many then had no support at all. Bayley reports that of the severely mentally handicapped adults in his study, living at home, 44% were not visited by a mental welfare officer. Bayley's families did not express great satisfaction with the mental welfare officers in Sheffield, but it is fairly clear from the literature and from experience that other professionals, agencies and institutes appreciated having contact with a welfare agency which had a designated interest in mental handicap. This relationship between social workers and other interested professionals was effectively ruptured by the creation in 1971 of the unified social services departments.

The essence of the report of the Seebohm committee (1968), which heralded the change, was that there should be a family service where all client groups would be served by professionals with a common training. This should free them from the tunnel vision of focusing only on damaged or deviant individuals. As the report declares, 'The families of mentally disordered people tend to suffer from inter-related social disabilities. . . . The social worker should be concerned with the whole family . . . to make a family diagnosis . . . take wide responsibility and mobilise a wide range of resources.'

With better training and counselling skills and a relative increase in community resources, social workers should have been able to operate more effectively in their work with families. In fact the research by Goldberg et al. in the late 1970s demonstrates the low priority given to work with mentally handicapped people and their families and the tendency for them to be allocated unqualified workers and to be on an agency review rather than designated to a particular worker, who could monitor needs and act appropriately over a longer period (Goldberg et al., 1978). This finding, which is acknowledged to be general, conflicts sharply with the 1971 White Paper's view of the social worker as a long-term coordinator (DHSS, 1971).

Recently specialization has started to reappear in social service departments. Whether this will be the 'more precise social service strategy' that Goldberg et al. demanded, only time will tell.

WHAT DO FAMILIES WANT FROM SOCIAL WORKERS?

Bayley's detailed study in the early 1970s showed not only how many very severely handicapped people were being cared for by their families, and how much sheer hard work was involved, but also the ineffectiveness of the professionals assigned to assist them. Day care was one of the most sought-after provisions and as the Mental Welfare Officers often could not provide this it made 'the social work help . . . offered irrelevant' since 'casework help only makes sense when a family's basic needs are met' (Bayley, 1973).

Glendinning's more recent research highlights similar problems of the lack of appropriate help and the fact that families are put in the position of supplicants rather than their needs being anticipated. Research pinpoints several needs that social workers should be able to meet.

People may need *someone to talk to* outside the immediate family about developmental or other crises or about problems relating to the daily grind of caring: 'You know, you just feel as if you are on your own with them and you have no one to talk to. . . . I would like to have someone to talk to' (quoted in Glendinning, 1983).

Social workers should be able to provide *practical help* with day care, respite and residential care, family holidays and aids and adaptations, and *sensitive responses to the ambivalent feelings* such help arouses: 'We went on holiday a fortnight ago and it was marvellous. Not that I wanted to be rid of Frances but parents of ordinary children don't realize just how lucky they are to be able to get out and about. . . . I hate taking her into hospital, but I do enjoy my holiday and she seems to settle down' (quoted in Glendinning, 1983).

Under section 1 of the 1970 *Chronically Sick and Disabled Persons Act*, social services departments have a duty to provide *clear and concise information*: 'I do feel it would be a lot easier if there were a comprehensive booklet covering *all* help and advice for the handicapped child' (parent in West Sussex survey).

Families need social workers to ensure *liaison between agencies*; also, the British system of provision is complex and families often need help to find their way round the maze of resources or brokerage skills to negotiate financial or other provision. In countries such as the USA and Australia, where public and private agencies jostle together, services are complicated by federal and state interests. Rees and Emerson (1983) identified 150 agencies providing direct and indirect services for families with handicapped children in New South Wales and saw services as based on 'the traditions of agencies and the interests of professional groups rather than on the priorities . . . of the mothers'.

THE ROLE OF THE PAEDIATRIC SOCIAL WORKER

For all parents the birth of a handicapped child is a shock, which throws them into confusion. The event strikes at all the hopes, dreams and aspirations for their creation and unleashes fears and fantasies which had remained submerged: " 'He has Hurler's syndrome. . . . In English you call it . . . er, gargoylism.' Through the thickening fog in my head I heard him, and into my punch-drunk consciousness swam hideous figures, straight off the pages of *Notre Dame de Paris* – gargoyles. Monstrous creatures carved in stone . . . Oh God, not that. . . . Not my son" (Craig, 1979).

Cunningham and Sloper have outlined a model of the 'psychic crisis' that is likely to overtake parents at such a time (Chapter 18). The manifestations of the four phases – shock, reaction, adaptation and orientation – require empathy, emotional support, accurate information sensitively delivered, realistic hope for the future and services which maintain continuity of approach between hospital and community services (see also Lonsdale et al., 1979).

While the paediatrician has the responsibility to inform the parents of their child's handicap and is in the best position to discuss causation and prognosis, the paediatric social worker should be able to give parents the emotional support and time to absorb the information they have received, and to

listen for questions hinted at or half stated that can be answered there or then or referred to the paediatrician. For, as McCormack recalls, 'It is not a case of not knowing the answers, but of not even knowing the questions' (McCormack, 1978).

Other duties are:

1 Protecting the interests of the child under the requirements of the 1969 Children and Young Persons Act. For example, in the 'Alexandra case' of 1981, Hammersmith social services sought and obtained a care order for a baby with Down's syndrome after her parents had refused her a routine life-saving operation. 'Alexandra' was fostered for a time and eventually returned to her parents (for a fuller discussion, see British Association of Social Workers, 1982).
2 Ensuring that adequate information is given about the provisions which supplement or replace parental care.
3 Counselling for other members of the family if needed and advising on the support that should be forthcoming from statutory and voluntary agencies in the community.
4 Liaising with staff in the hospital and community to ensure continuity of care.
5 Ensuring that parents find hospital reviews purposeful and useful.
6 Keeping hospital staff informed of the changes in social care in the community so that realistic advice can be given and decisions taken.
7 Being aware of the feelings of medical and nursing staff in relation to handicap and the trauma of informing parents.
8 Ensuring that casework responsibility is taken over by the community social worker when appropriate.

THE ROLE OF THE SOCIAL WORKER IN THE MULTI-DISCIPLINARY TEAM

Many parents feel that between the ages of 2 and 19 years they relate primarily to the local education authority but that from the time when their child leaves school they are unsure whether to turn to the National Health Service or social services. The multi-disciplinary team is seen as one way of unifying service provision and it is right that staff from the two major departments serving adults should be brought together. As Simon (1981) states, 'Each community mental handicap team (CMHT) should have two full-time members – the community nurse in mental handicap and the social worker.' As probably the only local authority representative in a health service team the social worker has a vital liaising role: 'He represents the link between families in their homes, the wider community and the services which should be available within that community through social service and voluntary agencies' (Simon, 1981).

Intervention in delicate family situations, complicated by a growing cultural complexity and factors such as an increasing divorce rate, requires that an accurate social assessment report is made by the social worker to place the individual within the family unit, and the family into a wider kinship and community context. Although the social assessment (Figure 26.1) is an onerous task for parents to complete with the social worker, most people welcome it as a vehicle for discussing past difficulties, looking at current challenges and facing the future.

Although the increase in multi-disciplinary work will mean an inevitable, and largely beneficial, interchange of roles, it is likely that both colleagues and families would expect the social worker to have a good working knowledge of financial benefits, domiciliary provision under the 1970 Chronically Sick and Disabled Persons Act, and other sources such as the Family Fund and other charitable trusts.

The social worker will have a direct counselling role with individuals, parents, siblings and groups (see Anderson, 1982). As has been stressed by the research literature this intervention can only be successful if *both* emotional and practical concerns are attended to:

'Henry' had been in a mental handicap hospital under a court order and on release was very torn between a desire for independence and a hankering after the structured life of the hospital. The social worker empathized with 'Henry's' ambivalence and helped him apply for a council flat and to approach the disablement resettlement officer (DRO). When 'Henry' gained and then lost employment, the social worker gently resisted the idea of 'Henry' going to a hostel and adult training centre (ATC) even for an assessment period. 'Henry' has been found another job, and, with additional help from other members of the CMHT, is well settled into the local community.

Many referrals to the multi-disciplinary team will come from area social workers (see Gilbert and Spooner, 1982) and the team's specialist social worker should be the coordinator of such referrals rather than replacing the area social worker, who may have known the family for some time. One ethical problem that the area social worker frequently faces is the question of whether, for example, the parent or the mentally handicapped person is the client when the question of the latter's

living situation arises. In such cases the specialist should be able to help the team come to a realistic appraisal of the individual's abilities and to assess realistic priorities.

The social worker will clearly be the link person for the team with the growing number of local authority facilities: fostering and boarding-out schemes, schools, ATCs and social education centres (SECs), hostels, community projects and so on. The arrangements for assessment in social service facilities will probably be done through the social worker. It may also be seen as useful for the team, and for social services as a whole, for the specialist social worker to have responsibility for making links with voluntary societies, of which there are a growing number, and gaining and disseminating knowledge on voluntary placements such as L'Arche, Home Farm Trust and CARE. Information on these and other matters could usefully be collated into a handbook and distributed to parents and agencies (e.g. Gilbert and Hollingdale, 1985).

All members of the team will have an educative role within the NHS and local authority. The social worker within the CMHT is in an ideal position to organize exchange placements between agencies to promote better understanding of each others roles, approaches and challenges.

The social worker in the team may be warranted by the local social services department to act under the child-care legislation or be an 'approved social worker' under the 1983 Mental Health Act or both. It is unlikely that the specialist would use these powers, as it would normally be more proper and sensible for the area social workers to do so. The specialist will, however, be able to advise NHS colleagues on, for example, the powers of and limitations on the local authority in the child-care field, and the increased responsibility for all concerned under the 1983 Mental Health Act to seek an alternative treatment method to hospital admission.

As in all disciplines, the social worker's role as a planner should start with the consumer. For instance, an isolated parent may express a desire to meet other parents with a handicapped child. The social worker would ascertain whether there was a similar desire in other families, and if the group was formed other needs would be likely to get highlighted. Such needs, for example respite care or an information booklet, could then be forwarded on to social services, NHS or joint care planning teams at district or supra-district level.

Many imaginative schemes that provide support for families have started off as ground-level projects

SOCIAL REPORT

Sub-heading	Prepared by	Date	Information Source

Name	
Address	
Reason for referral	
Diagnosis	

FAMILY	Relationship	Name	Age	Occupation	Address
			Underline subject's name		

Home	*Rent* *Area* *Description (physical): number of beds and amenities etc.*
Family history	
Client history	
Family relationships	
Social contacts and relationships	*Neighbours, friends, involvement with church, clubs etc.*
Agency contacts	*General practitioner* *Health visitor* *Probation* *Mencap/voluntary society*
Benefits	*Attendance allowance, mobility etc.*
Client's current occupation	*Schooling, work, housewife?* *Salary/wage etc.* *Attitudes to occupation*
Leisure	
Health	
Current concerns	
SUMMARY	*Brief synopsis: problem-orientated evaluation in* *own words and action thought necessary*

Fig. 26.1 A social report form.

and then developed with official backing (see Pugh, 1981), a good example being the Contact-a-Family groups in London.

Sometimes a large gap in services is identified which only a political initiative can rectify, and the social worker should work with families during this time.

SOCIAL WORK IN THE MENTAL HANDICAP HOSPITAL

With so much publicity concerning the multi-disciplinary team it is sometimes forgotten that a large population of mentally handicapped people still live in mental handicap hospitals. Though improvements have taken place in recent years the hospitals still bear the imprint of segregationist policies, and as Morris stated in her 1960 study *Put Away*, 'subnormality hospitals are isolated not only geographically and socially, but also from the mainstream of both medical and educational advances' (quoted in Smith, 1970).

The presence of a social worker within the hospital with a 'chance of getting to know at least some of the residents and their needs' was seen by the National Development Group for the Mentally Handicapped (1978) as vital to the effective functioning of the establishment. Unfortunately, social service departments have never given this a high priority and Jones's 1975 report of one English region found that 'There were only three whole-time (one qualified) and four part-time social workers for all the mental subnormality hospitals in the region, too preoccupied with work related to admissions and discharge to undertake other work with patients, their families and the community' (quoted in Younghusband, 1978).

Since 1974 hospital social workers in England and Wales have been the responsibility of social services departments not the NHS, and their presence has sometimes been seen as 'a threat to the social equilibrium of the regime' (Smith, 1970).

In places where a realistic level of social work input has been reached the social worker can make a vital contribution to the staff team through:

1 The compiling of social histories to help other staff understand the resident's background and the circumstances of his or her family – To give the resident 'a past life', which so many of the older adults lack through inadequate reports on admission.

2 Attendance at case conferences to help them come to fully multi-disciplinary decisions, by looking at the individual in the context of his or her family.

3 The maintenance of links between residents and relatives, voluntary visitors or community associations.

4 The investigation of suitable placements for residents following multi-disciplinary assessment.

5 Liaison with other staff within the hospital regarding training before community placement, liaison with placement staff and liaison with the residents during the trial period.

6 Liaison with specialist social work staff who may have expertise on sensory handicaps, communication skills and aids not possessed by the hospital staff.

7 Advice concerning residents' welfare rights, and also the rights of relatives who may not be visiting because of financial hardship.

8 Undertaking statutory functions in regard to hospital children in the care of the local authority.

9 Liaison with area social work staff in respect of statutory duties under the 1983 Mental Health Act.

10 Taking part in education for other staff on the social aspects of care for mentally handicapped people, community resources, the needs of families, counselling and so on.

11 Providing a counselling service for staff on matters which do not fall under the jurisdiction of line management or occupational health.

THE FUTURE

As specialism begins to reappear in social work, speeded by the new mental health legislation's statutory insistence on additional training for the social workers operating under its auspices from October 1984, social workers in the mental handicap field are appearing in CMHTs, special schools and area offices.

It is essential, however, that this is not a haphazard growth and that specialists do not become isolated from their colleagues in a geographical and developmental Gulag Archipelago. My own preference would be for a specialist team with many links so that the members are sensitive to consumer needs, agency demands, professional developments and legislative changes, and are accessible to those who need them when that need arises.

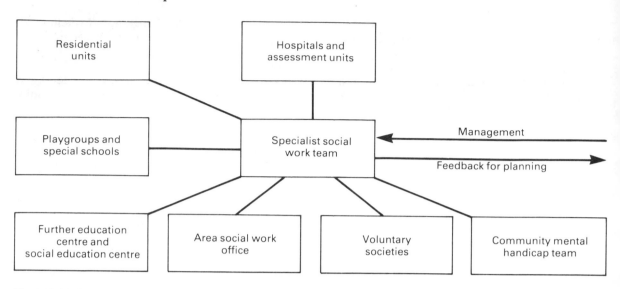

Fig. 26.2 Model for a specialist team.

Basically the post-Seebohm service should have added more resources, expertise and a wider perspective to work with mentally handicapped people (DHSS, 1971: para. 76). Instead, the service has become more remote to families and agencies and a rapid return is needed to the role of the social worker as envisaged by the White Paper: 'Many people . . . have a contribution to make in advising parents. . . . The person best placed to act as a co-ordinator is likely to be the social worker, who should take her part in the multi-disciplinary team as soon as handicap is suspected and thereafter maintain a continuing relationship with the handicapped child and his family.'

A specialist team of social workers should have a *liaison* role with the agencies that families will have contact with, so that accessibility and trust can go hand in hand (Figure 26.2). Allied to this should be a *monitoring* service (see Gilbert, 1983) where visits should be offered to those families without a social worker, at crucial development times, because, as Glendinning points out, 'Many parents felt that a routine, regular visit from a social worker would help enormously. It would lend a sense of security. . . . Their current needs could be readily identified and future ones anticipated and planned for' (see Glendinning, 1983: Chapter 7).

If the need for social work in this field is evident now, the movement from formal residential care, and increased social mobility, high unemployment, and cultural fractures are all likely to increase it. No profession, however, can simply maintain like Shakespeare's Wolsey that their 'profession is to

cure such sorrows'; social work must develop to meet consumer demand and legislative change.

BIBLIOGRAPHY

Anderson D (1982) *Social Work and Mental Handicap*. London: Macmillan.

Bayley M (1973) *Mental Handicap and Community Care*. London: Routledge & Kegan Paul.

British Association of Social Workers (BASW) (1977) *The Social Work Task*. BASW, 16 Kent Street, Birmingham B5 6RD.

British Association of Social Workers (BASW) (1982) *Guidelines on Social Work with Severely Handicapped Infants*.

British Association of Social Workers (BASW) (1983) *Towards Extraordinary Services for People with a Mental Handicap*.

Browne EE (1982) *Mental Handicap: The Role for Social Workers*, University of Sheffield & *Community Care*.

Butrym ZT (1976) *The Nature of Social Work*. London: Macmillan.

Central Council for Education and Training in Social Work (CCETSW) (1974) *Social Work: People with Handicaps Need Better Trained Workers*. London: CCETSW.

Craig M (1979) *Blessings*. Sevenoaks, Kent: Hodder & Stoughton.

Davies M (1981) *The Essential Social Worker: A Guide to Positive Practice*. London: Heinemann.

DHSS (Department of Health and Social Security) (1971) *Better Services for the Mentally Handicapped*. Cmnd. 4683. London: HMSO.

Egan G (1975) *The Skilled Helper*. Monterey, California: Brooks Cole.

England H (1986) *Social Work as Art: Making Sense for Good Practice*. London: Allen & Unwin.

Gilbert P (1983) New services, new strategies. *Community Care* (March 31): 20–21.

Gilbert P & Hollingdale J (1985) *Coping with Mental Handicap in Horsham, Crawley and Mid-Sussex*. Chichester: West Sussex County Council.

Gilbert P & Spooner B (1982) Strength in unity. *Community Care* (October 28): 17–19.

Glendinning C (1983) *Unshared Care: Parents and Their Disabled Children*. London: Routledge & Kegan Paul.

Goldberg E, Warburton RW, Lyons LJ & Willmott RR (1978) Towards accountability in social work: long-term social work in an area office. *British Journal of Social Work 8(3):* 253–287.

Hanvey C (1981) *Social Work with Mentally Handicapped People*. London: Heinemann.

Kupfer F (1982) *Before and After Zachariah*. London: Victor Gollancz.

Lonsdale G, Elfer P & Ballard R (1979) *Children, Grief and Social Work*. Oxford: Blackwell.

McCormack M (1978) *A Mentally Handicapped Child in the Family*. London: Constable.

Mittler P & McConachie H (eds) (1983) *Parents, Professionals and Mentally Handicapped People*. Beckenham, Kent: Croom Helm.

National Development Group for the Mentally Handicapped (1977) *Mentally Handicapped Children: A Plan for Action*. Pamphlet No. 2. London: HMSO.

National Development Group for the Mentally Handicapped (1978) *Helping Mentally Handicapped People in Hospital*. London: Department of Health and Social Security.

NISW (National Institute of Social Work) (1982) *Social Workers: Their Role and Tasks. (Barclay Report)*. London: Bedford Square Press.

Payne M (1982) *Working in Teams*. London: Macmillan.

Philip M & Duckworth D (1982) *Children with Disabilities and Their Families: A Review of Research*. Windsor, Berkshire: NFER-Nelson.

Pugh G (1981) *Parents as Partners*. London: National Children's Bureau.

Rees S & Emerson A (1983) Confused and confusing: services for mentally handicapped children. *Australian Journal of Social Issues 18(1)*.

Ryan J & Thomas F (1980) *The Politics of Mental Handicap*. Harmondsworth, Middlesex: Penguin.

Schreiber M (ed) (1970) *Social Work and Mental Retardation*. New York: John Day.

Seebohm Committee (1968) *Report of the Committee on Local Authority and Allied Personal Social Services*. Cmnd. 3703. London: HMSO.

Simon GB (ed) (1981) *Local Services for Mentally Handicapped People*. London: British Institute for Mental Handicap.

Smith G (1970) *Social Work and the Sociology of Organisations*. London: Routledge & Kegan Paul.

Todd JF (1967) *Social Work with the Mentally Subnormal*. London: Routledge & Kegan Paul.

Walrond-Skinner S (1976) *Family Therapy*. London: Routledge & Kegan Paul.

Younghusband E (1978) *Social Work in Britain 1950–1975, Vol. 1*. London: Allen & Unwin.

Younghusband Working Party (1959) *Report of the Working Party on Social Workers in the Local Authority, Health and Welfare Services*. London: HMSO.

Chapter 27
The Role of the Psychologist

PETER WILCOCK

The tasks undertaken by psychologists working with mentally handicapped people have expanded and diversified to such an extent that it is now necessary to consider their contribution in a number of different roles.

The contents of this chapter have been chosen to cover a broad range of areas and types of skills the reader may expect to find in a practising psychologist. An attempt has been made to keep it client-centred, and it is not intended to be a manual for psychologists. The method chosen has been to describe processes necessary to meet a variety of different needs of people with mental handicap, within which the role of the psychologist is considered implicit rather than being made explicit.

The organization and structure of the chapter has been influenced by Bender's suggestion that the roles of the psychologist working with people in the community can be described at three different levels (Bender, 1976). This model has been adapted slightly to consider the psychologist's work with people with mental handicap.

Level 1. Work that has a direct impact upon the lives of people with mental handicap, such as assessment and design of teaching programmes.

Level 2. Working indirectly through other staff to help larger numbers of people with mental handicap. This level includes staff training and counselling and systems to help maintain direct teaching work.

Level 3. Working with managers to influence policy and planning within broader service systems, for example developing strategies for creating change within systems, influencing policy at wider levels and evaluating services.

LEVEL 1: WORK THAT HAS A DIRECT IMPACT UPON THE LIVES OF PEOPLE WITH MENTAL HANDICAP

Assessment and goal planning

Mittler has described the move away from routine standardized assessment to the application of assessment procedures to aid the development and planning of learning objectives (Mittler, 1979). This necessarily includes an analysis of the environments in which learning is to take place and in which the skills being taught are to be used.

He emphasizes the essentially inter-disciplinary nature of the psychologist's role if he is to be effective. In this context the contribution to assessment, for example, may be to help members of other disciplines frame their own questions and obtain the information to answer them. This contribution may then be expected to extend to providing advice about the selection of goals for intervention and devising strategies to achieve them usually based on behavioural principles.

Concern with assessing a person's needs in the context of his real life has considerable implications which will be discussed later. Before doing so, however, it is appropriate to make some general points about the nature of assessment which has itself been the subject of much controversy.

Kiernan and Jones (1982) differentiate between 'administratively-oriented assessment' and assessment designed to 'identify more precise strengths and weaknesses in the abilities of the individual'. The former is required to help make decisions about the placement of an individual and depends on the use of rapid screening procedures, which are usually norm-referenced. It is in this area that Kiernan and Jones consider traditional intelligence testing to have some value despite the strong criticism to which it has been subjected over the years. It is unfortunate that, for mainly historical reasons, the use of intelligence tests assumed such a dominant role in classifying a person as mentally handicapped, because, although the importance of social competence in defining mental handicap was recognized, the standardized intelligence test for many years provided the only simple objective measure available to workers in the field. Tragically for the person with mental handicap, once a label was assigned following an IQ test, it was taken as representing not only his degree of impairment in intellectual functioning but also his other behavioural characteristics. Gould (1981) summed it up well when he stated that 'few tragedies can be more extensive than the stunting of life, few injustices deeper than the denial of an opportunity to strive or even to hope, by a limit imposed from without, but falsely identified as lying within'.

Although assessment tools are becoming increasingly relevant and sophisticated, the people for whom they must be useful (i.e. mentally handicapped people) usually have to be considered administratively at a number of points in their lives. There is a danger that in the need for quick and apparently objective tools, administrators will perpetuate the use of the neat and deceptively attractive IQ. For example, there is a residential establishment for people with mental handicap where the authorities have produced a sliding scale of charges according to IQ (Campaign for Mentally Handicapped People, 1983). The administrators are making predictions about a person's needs and behaviour based on his measured IQ: the lower this is the higher is their charge.

As far as possible, placement decisions should result from attempts to match a person's identified needs with the establishment that will be best able to meet them. By their very nature, the norm-referenced tests that may be used to make placement decisions have to measure areas of functioning that are not influenced by external variables. They are carefully designed to avoid areas where, for example, earlier training may influence the results and hence will produce very little information of much value to those trying to establish a person's real needs for teaching.

One major step forward should result from the 1981 Education Act. This has shifted the emphasis to looking at a child's needs rather than his handicaps, so that decisions can be made about the best way to help him learn. This will have considerable implications for educational psychologists, who will have to consider not only how best to obtain this information but also how to ensure that it results in positive learning programmes within school settings.

The major purpose of assessment must be to define the entry point to a teaching curriculum (Mittler, 1979). Taking this concept one step further raises two related questions. First, who is the 'client'? Second, given that a person will have a number of different educational needs at any point in time, how can relative priorities be judged?

There are now a considerable number of multi-dimensional and developmentally based checklists which are designed to identify individual needs and help answer such questions (e.g. Adaptive Behaviour Rating Scales – Nihira, 1974; Progress Assessment Charts – Gunzburg, 1976; Behaviour Assessment Battery – Kiernan and Jones, 1982; Hampshire Assessment for Living with Others – Shackleton-Bailey, 1980; Portage Checklist – Bluma et al., 1976; Bereweeke Skill Teaching System – Jenkins et al., 1982). The reliable completion of such checklists demands that information must be obtained about a person's behaviour in the most significant settings of his day-to-day life. It is well known that people develop different sets of behaviours in different environments and hence assessment will need to be carried out in several settings, for example at home, and at school or adult training centre. Thus when asking who the client is, assessment must acknowledge that it is not simply a person but someone who exists in the context of different environments.

One of the initial tasks will be to draw up a list describing the person's strengths and needs. The identification of strengths is important for at least two reasons. First, it will provide valuable information about where to begin teaching so that it may reasonably be expected to result in success. Most people with mental handicap have had much experience of failure in their lives and achieving early success is important if they are to realize that learning can be an enjoyable experience. Second, concentrating on a person's strengths will alter the perceptions about him held by other people with whom he comes into contact. Problem-oriented approaches can easily result in a person only ever being perceived as the receiver of services while continually concentrating on his weaknesses devalues him as a person and will have a destructive influence on his self-perception.

Identifying a person's needs is fundamental to beginning the teaching process as is the recognition that these needs may assume different priorities in different settings. For example, teaching a child colour and shape discrimination might be considered an early priority at school but at home his parents would probably consider this to be less important than for him to be able to dress and feed himself. On the other hand his ability to sit down and occupy himself constructively for reasonable periods of time would be considered important in both settings. The significance here is that goal planning as well as assessment needs to occur across rather than within settings. A balance must be achieved where, although the needs of the individual are considered paramount, it is also recognized that these have to be tempered by the needs of the other people who are significant in his life. It is only in this way that working compromises with realistic chances of success can be agreed. There is also little point finding out how a person behaves in different environments if the subsequent attempts to change his behaviour are limited to only one environment.

Focusing on a person's positive characteristics may also be applied to a consideration of outcomes of intervention. Part of the teaching may necessarily involve working with behavioural problems, but goals can be stated in terms of achieving positive alternatives rather than just eliminating the problems. This 'constructional' approach has been fully described by Goldiamond (1975) and provides an alternative to the problem-oriented approaches that developed out of the early behaviour-modification work. Goldiamond initially presented his model in terms of working with non-handicapped people with social problems but it can be readily applied to work with mentally handicapped people.

The constructional approach emphasizes the functional analysis of behaviour – that is not just what a person does but what he gets for what he does in a particular situation. The person's behaviour is viewed as a logical and understandable response to his environment and the assessment involves analysing what this relationship may be. A high frequency of disruptive or self-mutilating behaviour, for example, may be maintained because he has learned that it is the only way he can gain attention quickly. Instead of purely working to eliminate such behaviour the constructional approach suggests identifying (or constructing) alternative and appropriate ways that the person can gain this attention. The task for staff then becomes the positive one of teaching these alternative behaviours. Thus the approach demands that part of the assessment of the behaviour must be the assessment of constraints imposed by the environment and how these may themselves be modified.

Behavioural teaching techniques where the individual is used as his own control have added a further dimension to the concept of assessment. The whole process is perceived as a continuous feedback cycle where assessment continues throughout the process of intervention and attempts to discover what factors will increase desired or decrease undesired behaviour. Valuable information about a person's learning style will also be obtained and will influence future teaching strategies.

Teaching

It is important to realize that the mentally handicapped person is in a learning situation all the time. His experiences must not be dichotomized into teaching and non-teaching, or the significance of those which occur outside formal teaching sessions may be ignored or misunderstood.

Approaches to providing learning opportunities for mentally handicapped people may be roughly categorized into three sorts, although there is bound to be some overlap.

Informal approaches

There are at least two dimensions to making sure that the settings in which mentally handicapped people find themselves provide naturally occurring learning opportunities. First, adequate and appropriate materials must be available and easily accessible rather than being locked away until a member of staff brings them out. One of the striking results of moving mentally handicapped people into normal housing is the way in which they begin to undertake some simple domestic tasks without needing intensive teaching first. This is the result of such opportunities being naturally available rather than either not being available at all or available only when a timetable allows.

Second, staff must remain actively aware that their clients have a 'past, present and future, all of which are directly relevant to programming' (Ziarnik, 1980). This 'proactive' approach involves anticipation and action prior to an event rather than waiting to react until after an event occurs.

Structured informal approaches

The development of informal learning environments, although crucial to the on-going success of any teaching, will not in itself necessarily produce change. The process can be taken a stage further by exposing a person to an environment that is engineered to provide appropriate experiences. Careful observation will be necessary to observe his reaction to specific materials available within his setting and to note the interactions between himself and other people in the setting. Although goals need not be set at the outset, knowing what they are will guide decisions about what materials should be made available and what types of staff interaction are necessary. Structuring the environment in this way helps ensure that progress in some identified direction is maintained.

This type of approach has resulted in the 'room-management' model, as described by Porterfield et al. (1978), Porterfield (1979) and McBrien and Weightman (1980). In this work activity periods of a specific duration are introduced and staff are given detailed instructions about how they should behave during this time. They are designated as either 'room manager' or 'individual helper' according to a schedule agreed beforehand.

The room manager's tasks include giving each trainee a choice of materials and prompting him to begin using them. He is also expected to place other materials within each trainee's reach, talk to those who are busy, and praise and offer alternative materials to trainees who have completed a task.

The second member of staff can then work relatively undisturbed with individual students for short periods on goals tailored to meet those people's needs. In this way it is possible to provide time for individual work with all students during the activity period. This approach is particularly demanding on staff and it is essential that active support by managers is planned into the system in order to maintain it.

Structured intensive approaches

Although the provision of informal learning opportunities must underlie any attempt to teach mentally handicapped people, there will also always be a need for structured intensive teaching back-up. The actual balance will be determined by the needs of the individual. Systematic teaching approaches have been well described in the literature (e.g. Kazdin, 1980; Yule and Carr, 1980; Schopler et al., 1980) and basically involve the following steps.

1 Initial assessment and its need to be interdisciplinary has been discussed in some detail. This assessment will have resulted in the selection of long-term goals, which are necessary to give the teaching an overall direction. These goals must be carefully defined and will usually be related to helping the person towards greater independence.
2 Task analysis will help identify the steps necessary to achieve the long-term goals. It may also identify the need for sideways steps in a programme to teach skills without which it will not be possible to move forward. For example, a person may have to learn how to grasp before being able to learn to feed himself independently.
3 Specific teaching objectives must be set so that at any point in time it is clear what the teaching programme is trying to achieve. These must be written in explicit behavioural terms and describe what a person will be able to do after teaching that he could not do before.
4 The actual teaching strategy must be chosen. The teacher must remain flexible so that the strategy can change as more experience about working with an individual is gained. Which specific techniques are to be used and strategies to cope with possible behavioural problems must be decided.
5 The appropriate setting for the teaching, together with the need for generalization into other settings must be considered (see Colvin and Horner, 1983).
6 Appropriate reinforcers will have to be chosen. These must be defined in relation to the student rather than the teacher and it may be necessary to experiment in order to find what is rewarding for a particular person. Planning strategies for initially delivering and then fading out reinforcers or moving from arbitrary to naturally occurring reinforcers is an essential part of the teaching process.
7 It is important to ensure that the teaching programme is written down in a way which will ensure that it can be implemented as consistently as possible by the different staff who may be involved. Written records will also help determine its success.

Evaluation and record keeping

Recent trends in teaching have placed the responsibility to achieve success firmly on the teacher rather than making it the mentally handicapped person's responsibility to learn. Some form of monitoring is necessary not only to demonstrate that learning is taking place but also to help identify appropriate changes if success is not being achieved. It is worth remembering that the pace of teaching can be too slow as well as too fast, and a bored student will soon lose interest and may become disruptive.

Maintaining good records is thus very important, although care must be taken to ensure that record systems do not become so overwhelming and punitive to staff that the intervention fails on these grounds. It is not always easy to predict what the right balance will be at the outset for any person or any programme, but with sensitive monitoring it will become more obvious as the teaching progresses. This may involve keeping very simple records or perhaps testing at regular intervals to ensure that behaviours are being learned. The more relevant the teaching the greater are the chances that the new skills will be used in a day-to-day context, thus providing the opportunity both to practise them and to monitor that they are being maintained.

Administrative aspects

It would be naive to assume that once all the necessary preparation has been completed it then becomes merely a matter of implementing the teaching. In order to be successful there are a number of other key issues which the psychologist must be aware of in addition to those relating to assessment and teaching.

Perhaps most important is the provision of on-going support to those doing the teaching since it will not very often be the psychologist himself. Teachers, like their students, need to achieve success and there is a danger that failure will undermine their own feelings of competence. The psychologist must therefore be prepared to plan time to work alongside the staff he is supporting. In this way he will gain an understanding of their difficulties and will also demonstrate that he has the basic skills necessary.

Teaching will be doomed to failure if staff are not adequately trained and motivated, if there is competition due to internal politics, if there is lack of support from senior management or if the implementation of teaching is given low priority when compared to the day-to-day administrative tasks which are necessary to maintain the setting in which it should be occurring. These types of issues often need dealing with at higher levels; the psychologist's role in tackling them is considered in Chapter 4 by Berry.

The increasingly inter-disciplinary nature of the work brings its own set of problems. The most crucial of these is the process by which the actual decisions concerning a mentally handicapped person's life and needs are taken. There will be a number of different disciplines, possibly from a variety of different agencies, involved at any one time. Frequently they will be unaware of what each other is doing and decisions taken in isolation may result in contradictory strategies being employed in parallel, leading to confusion for the staff and the mentally handicapped person concerned.

The emerging concept of the Individual Programme Plan (IPP) is designed to reduce and if possible eliminate such confusions (see Blunden, 1980; Felce et al., 1981). This approach is both inter-disciplinary and inter-agency and broadly speaking brings people together regularly to make joint decisions, although the practical and political implications of doing this must be clearly understood. Wherever possible, mentally handicapped people themselves or their relatives or advocates should attend the meetings which will make major decisions concerning their lives. The psychologist is likely to already have working relationships with many of the people involved and has an important role in supporting the establishment of such systems and their continued working.

The purpose of the IPP meeting is to consider all aspects of a mentally handicapped person's life and agree objectives for that person. These are usually related to increasing competence and independence and will cover areas such as living and working situations, financial issues, increasing social and leisure opportunities and identifying skill needs and blocks to learning. Goals are set with a six-month time scale or less attached to them and this dictates the frequency of the meetings.

The system depends on the appointment of a 'key worker' who knows the client well and may see him frequently. The key worker's job is to contact all the different people concerned with a client and to obtain an overview of his strengths and needs; these are listed and form the agenda for the meeting (Figure 27.1). The key worker acts as convener and ensures that all the relevant people know its date and time.

As the list is worked through at the meeting a record is drawn up which summarizes the discussion and identifies the objectives together with the name of the person responsible for achieving them. This may involve them in direct action or it may require beginning the assessment and teaching process as already described. The follow-up meeting reviews progress and sets new objectives which will in turn be reviewed at agreed future dates.

Application of research findings

In the enthusiasm to develop systems helping mentally handicapped people to take more active social roles, it is important to remember that there is also an expanding body of experimental research findings which may be of value when tailoring individual teaching programmes.

For example, Hogg and Mittler (1983) have stressed the importance of looking at psychological

Individual programme planning (IPP) – needs list

Client's name **Philip Smith**   Key worker **Mrs Ansell.**

Form completed **September 1982 .**   (month, year)

Meeting to be held on **14th September 1982**   (day, month, year)

---

1. *Predicted requirements and need for admission*

    Long-term accommodation

    Short-term care   **Planned stays at Wood Lane Hostal.**

    Day care/training   **Regular attendance at adult training centre (ATC)**

    Education

    Work

    Finance

---

2. *Training priorities: skills client needs to acquire in the next six months*

    Self care   **Shave and wash himself. Comb hair fasten buttons**

    Domestic   **Turn off taps, clear table, wash up.**

    Daily living
    Community living   }

    Communication   **Speak more to other people.**

    Personality and social
    adjustment   }   **Runs rather than walks. Has**
    Behaviour problems   }   **run off down road. Rocks**

    Close personal relations

    Use of leisure

    Physical development   **Use hands more.**

Needed in the next six months in the areas of:

3. Health/hygiene

4. Physical appearance and coordination

5. Social relationships/companionship

    Needs someone to befriend him and encourage him to talk.

6. Opportunities for increased or different occupation:

    Household

    Day care/work   **Spend some time in main ATC workshop
as well as special needs unit.**

    Leisure   **More outdoor activities. Swimming. Likes animals.**

7. Opportunities for participation in community events

Programme planning team (Please tick people contacted before IPP meeting and write in their names)

Key worker	**Mrs Ansell**	Psychologist	
Relatives/advocate	**Mr/Mrs Smith**	Social Worker	**Mrs Blackman**
Residential care/person in charge	**Mr Johnson**	Psychiatrist	
ATC manager		Speech Therapist	
Special care unit manager	**Mrs Carter**	Physiotherapist	
Teacher		Other	

Fig. 27.1 A model for an Individual Programme Planning
meeting agenda and record (Felce et al., 1981).

processes underlying competent behaviour in areas demanding skilled performance. They have brought together a collection of papers which consider aspects such as non-oral communication skills, perceptual–motor skills, and the relationships between motor skills performance and factors such as job design and information processing. The psychologist is probably the key professional in maintaining a current awareness of such research and advising local workers about its implications for individual mentally handicapped people.

LEVEL 2: WORKING TO HELP LARGER NUMBERS OF MENTALLY HANDICAPPED PEOPLE

It is becoming increasingly clear that psychologists can no longer afford the luxury of restricting their work to clients, either individually or in groups. To use their skills to the greatest effect they must look for ways of helping produce change for greater numbers of mentally handicapped people, even though they may have little or no direct contact with most of them. This may range from the transference of skills in staff-training programmes to the provision of on-going support to those who have the responsibility to care for and teach mentally handicapped people in whatever setting.

Staff training

The psychologist's specialist and in-depth knowledge of human learning can equally well be applied to the preparation of staff-training programmes as to the teaching of mentally handicapped people. The advent of behaviour modification in particular emphasized the need for a new set of skills at direct-care level and presented psychologists with a new set of challenges.

In basic staff education programmes they can be expected to introduce direct-care staff to the broader psychological and developmental implications of being a person with mental handicap. In England the developing courses for the Certificate in Social Services (CSS) and the new training syllabus for registered nurses in mental handicap (RNMH) will continue to make demands for psychologists to be involved at this level. Perhaps pointing the way to the future, a joint working party of the General Nursing Councils and the Central Council for Education and Training in Social Work has published two reports (GNCs/CCETSW, 1982, 1983) indicating lines of collaboration in the training of staff working in National Health Service and local authority residental services.

It is essential that staff training is a multi-disciplinary team exercise. Being a member of such teams provides psychologists with one of their key roles, namely advising members of other disciplines about effective teaching models and overall strategies for training programmes. The essence of true teamwork is the sharing of skills, knowledge and experience and nowhere is this more vital and fundamental than in the preparation of staff-training programmes. The proper inter-disciplinary presentation of staff training will in itself provide a model of interaction for participating students to take away with them.

Staff-training workshops will provide the psychologist with formal opportunities to pass on skills to others and will have a considerable spin-off in supporting the team's work on a day-to-day basis. The emphasis of such training, which clearly must be on the acquisition of skills by students, must also introduce a knowledge of underlying theories as an essential component of teaching if the skills are to be used in an insightful way and not merely discarded when difficulties are experienced in practice (Berger, 1979).

The form of the teaching is as important as its content and the trend towards experiential methods is significant. As Mittler (1983) has pointed out, research has revealed the difficulties experienced even by highly skilled staff in integrating behavioural methods of teaching with their day-to-day work. A major implication for the shift to skills teaching is the responsibility to provide follow-up support in vivo. Staff need on-going help and support as they practise and improve their skills back in their working situation with their own real clients.

Casey et al. (1983) describe a workshop series that attempted to come to grips with this problem. Attendance was restricted to pairs, one of whom had to be a psychologist, the other a member of staff with whom they were working. Before attending the first workshop they were asked to make an initial assessment of a child. The workshop provided a mixture of theoretical and practical teaching and participants returned to their home setting with agreed goals and suggested strategies of intervention. Follow-up workshops one term and then one year later provided opportunities to discuss progress and practical dfficulties that had been experienced.

Another staff training model that attempts to come to terms with these difficulties is the EDY (education of the developmentally young) model developed by McBrien and Foxen (Foxen and McBrien, 1981; McBrien and Foxen, 1981). This model was primarily designed for teachers working with severely handicapped children in ESN(S) schools but is being increasingly used by other professionals.

The EDY model provides an in-service course for staff whose responsibility it is to implement teaching, together with a workshop to help staff learn the skills of teaching other staff. The workshop is aimed at people such as psychologists and advisers who may be expected to influence teaching practice in schools and who, once they have attended an EDY course, are expected to set up and run similar courses in their own areas.

The in-service part of the training takes place in four phases. Phase 1 consists of ten one-hour practical sessions covering aspects of the behavioural teaching approach. Trainees are expected to read written units before attending each session and then watch a video demonstration of a teacher using the techniques to be learned for that session. The main emphasis is on role play and simulated practice with a child and this takes place at three levels. First, the instructor teaches the trainee who plays the role of a child; second, these roles are reversed; third, the trainee works with the real child while being observed by the instructor. Feedback to the trainee about his performance is built in at all stages.

The status of the trainee now changed to that of trainer he enters phase 2 of the programme, which is designed to consolidate his learning. This entails running a programme for an individual child over the course of a term while receiving support from the instructor. Detailed records are kept and feedback is provided on a weekly basis. Phase 3 is the generalization phase, during which instructor support is gradually 'faded out' and the trainer is encouraged to tackle more difficult children and tasks.

The final phase is concerned with principles of classroom management, which enables the skills learned with individual teaching to be used in group settings. The materials are available as self-instructional texts designed for use by small groups under the guidance of a tutor rather than for individual study. (Foxen and McBrien, 1981; McBrien and Foxen, 1981).

Some implications of community-based services

The continuing trend towards dispersed community-based services presents psychologists with the challenge of applying their skills and expertise in new and unfamiliar settings. As well as working alongside community nurses, they will have increasing involvement with primary care workers such as health visitors, social workers and teachers. Part of this work will be to encourage the formation of local community networks to improve communications and coordination of services and to provide support to each other.

Another vital aspect of this role is to work alongside individual primary care workers where the task is not purely to take over referrals but to work with the referers themselves. In this way they can be helped to develop insight into ways of gathering reliable information about their clients, how to analyse it in functional terms and how to develop strategies of intervention within their clients' own home settings. This may involve changing setting conditions and manipulating consequences to eliminate problem behaviours or it may involve positive teaching programmes to help the client and family increase independence. It is hoped that over time the primary care workers will become more skilled, confident and independent themselves.

As the number of smaller residential homes for mentally handicapped people increases it is becoming necessary for psychologists to rethink how best to provide support to their residents and staff. This new set of demands on their time means that current models of working closely alongside staff in residential settings, as mentioned previously, may be becoming unworkable before they have really been established.

Some of the overall goals of such work have been listed as follows (Parks, 1978):

1 To ensure the implementation of individualized client service plans.
2 To ensure that staff are adequately trained to perform their jobs.
3 To establish procedures to attempt to avoid crisis situations.
4 To ensure that adequate support is provided by other community agencies or professionals.
5 To help prevent re-institutionalization of the client.
6 To assist staff in finding personal and professional satisfaction in their work.

The precise nature of the input will vary from home to home, depending upon the needs of the residents and the skills of the staff in post. As Parks points out, the role may be that of trainer where staff skills are few, or facilitator in settings where staff have adequate experience. The onus is clearly on the psychologist to be sensitive to such issues and plan his involvement accordingly.

Curriculum development

The curriculum that exists within a setting will provide one of the major constraints as to what teaching may occur within that setting. Psychologists have a useful contribution to make within a service system or setting (such as school, adult training centre or hospital) in guiding the design of curricula with educational relevance for its students.

One concept is that of the 'core curriculum' for, say, a school, which includes skills considered to be fundamental to all the children in the school and which has the flexibility to take sideways branches to meet the needs of any individual child. Thus the curriculum is not allowed to inhibit the learning that is available and allows teachers to respond quickly and appropriately to changes in the child or his needs. It also has to be recognized that core-aspects for any individual child may have to be taught through the use of non-core aspects of the curriculum. Bearing in mind the comments about assessment made earlier, this approach also makes clear the need to consider both the mentally handicapped person and his context and has to be interdisciplinary. Above all it emphasizes that curriculum development should be considered as a dynamic process, not a one-off event.

The whole concept of curriculum development is considered in greater depth in Chapter 20.

Staff and family counselling

So much emphasis is often placed on the need for intensive individual work with mentally handicapped people that the psychological needs of the other people who play a significant part in their lives may be overlooked. The psychologist can indirectly, but none the less valuably, help maintain effective services for mentally handicapped people by being available to provide such support or helping others provide it. Maintaining staff enthusiasm when a large amount of effort does not seem to be producing much in the way of results is as essential as the teaching process itself.

Direct-care staff are under increasing pressure to reconsider their own personal value systems and become aware of how their own attitudes and beliefs will be influencing their work. It is possible that at some time an individual member of staff will need the opportunity to discuss in depth his own feelings about his work. This will often be most usefully done outside line management structures and the confidentiality of such discussions must be respected.

The members of families of mentally handicapped people also need recognition that they have a set of psychological needs quite apart from, although obviously influenced by, having a mentally handicapped member. One danger of working intensively with mentally handicapped people who still live at home is that placing the emphasis heavily on intervention may cause feelings of inadequacy and demoralization in their parents. By focusing only on intervention, psychologists may imply that they expect parents to have come to terms with having a handicapped child and that they are expected to get on with the teaching and coping with the job in hand. It is important that family members are allowed to discuss how having a handicapped relative affects their own feelings and emotions and how it may have shattered their aspirations. They must be encouraged to realize that experiencing what they may consider are negative feelings is quite legitimate. Pressure must be taken off them to 'adjust' when they feel they cannot, and support must be available on those occasions when their intense grieving feelings are re-awakened and experienced.

The current trend in using teaching packages within the home (e.g. Portage) or other settings (e.g. Bereweeke Skill Teaching System) has highlighted the lack of training in counselling skills received by most professionals. Such packages may channel thinking in narrow and rigid ways because they sometimes meet staff needs rather more effectively than they meet client needs. Psychologists must consider the responsibility to provide access to counselling skills for staff to be as important as the transfer of intensive teaching skills.

Another group who may need access to counselling support are mentally handicapped people themselves. As well as having their own psychological needs as people, the emphasis attached to learning new skills and participating more fully in public life also exposes them to a range of feelings and emotions that they may need the opportunity to talk through. Failure to recognize and meet this set of needs is likely to reduce the value of all the other inputs to their development.

Administrative aspects

It will be clear by now that however skilful staff may be in assessing individual needs, drawing up teaching programmes and being able to teach, this will all come to nothing if the settings within which all this has to occur are not supportive or sympathetic. Bearing in mind the wide range of settings into which psychologists' roles take them, a consideration of the administrative aspects of their work is particularly important if they are to be really effective.

The preparation of the culture within which the skills of the psychologist must be transferred to other staff and used in practice by those staff is an essential part of the process. The most fundamental issue to consider is how decisions are made which have a direct influence upon the behaviours and learning opportunities provided to a person with mental handicap.

There is a need within any setting for staff to be able to come together to discuss whether the opportunities exist to implement specific management programmes and to work towards the achievement of teaching objectives. The implications for resources and time, and possible constraints, need to be identified. This must be done by those staff responsible for the day-to-day operation of the setting, and decisions about the form of implementation or relative priorities when there are competing needs must include these staff if they are to stand any chance of success. Regular staff meetings must be held and, as new and different needs are identified, a process of negotiation will begin; at the end of the negotiation agreement about practical ways forward must be reached. Different members will have to accept that their ideals may well not be achieved and must agree to an acceptable and achievable compromise. These meetings will also allow an overall perspective of current work being undertaken to be maintained. It is very easy in practice to overlook the cumulative effects of setting up a number of individual programmes for a number of different people.

If these meetings occur on a regular basis they will provide important opportunities for staff to support each other and will allow peer-group monitoring of the work. A member of staff is less likely to be destructive or obstructive if he is not only involved in the decision-making but also likely to be challenged by his own colleagues.

Opportunities to discuss on-going problems will provide staff with a greater understanding of the difficulties being experienced by other colleagues and may induce greater tolerance. Such sharing of difficulties between team members will also play a key role in helping develop real teamwork.

When things go wrong, as they invariably will

from time to time, such meetings allow public and constructive discussion about why and what steps can be taken to avoid future failure. Finally and perhaps above all, they allow the lowest status staff, who are usually the bulk of the workforce, to make a valuable contribution to the running of their own work environment and doing this will greatly increase their motivation and result in better outcomes for their clients.

LEVEL 3: WORKING WITH MANAGERS TO INFLUENCE POLICY AND PLANNING

From time to time, fundamental issues will arise which may need the involvement of a line manager at more senior level or may have implications that will affect a range of other service providers. At this level the psychologist is beginning to enter the arena of creating systems change within an organization or service. It may be necessary to negotiate with a school head teacher, a director of nursing services or a manager of an adult training centre to gain their support for change. Such change may include examining curricula and restructuring timetables, re-deploying staff, experimenting with different decision-making models or providing cover to allow staff training. The increasing move into the community and need for inter-agency collaboration makes a consideration of work at these sorts of level even more important and psychologists must acquaint themselves with a knowledge of some of the fundamental strategies for creating change within systems, whether the system be an organization or a service agency (see, for example, Emery, 1969, 1981).

When the need for change is identified the initial response is likely to be resistance and unwillingness to disturb the equilibrium within the system. For example, under-manned and under-resourced organizations engage in more self-maintenance behaviour, so making demands for change without providing the necessary resources will disturb the equilibrium and will be resisted. Psychologists attempting to create change must also recognize that such proposals are often perceived as an implied criticism of current practice and hence a threat to the self-esteem of staff members.

Positive ways to unfreeze systems must be discovered. Power will be held formally within legitimately constituted bodies and will also be held informally by key individuals. Identifying these people and gaining their support will be crucial to understanding these formal and informal sub-systems. It will be important to move towards establishing jointly agreed goals and to begin to plan their achievement. This will include identification of necessary resources, planning realistic steps forward and developing structures to monitor and evaluate. The possibility for future change must be built into the new system if it is not to become as rigid and inflexible as the first.

Perhaps most important of all is the need to develop trust by working with other people in an atmosphere of mutual respect. Personal style is an inherent part of the change process and this must be recognized by psychologists if they are going to fulfil a role as change agents. One of their tasks must be to help people working at direct-care level by creating supportive networks at senior management level.

The increasing role of psychologists in influencing policy decision-making provides opportunities to guide service developments in line with underlying philosophies. In England it is being accepted that the principles of normalization should guide the development of services at both the broad level and when considering goals for mentally handicapped individuals. Normalization has been well described by Wolfensberger (1972) and PASS, a system designed to evaluate services in relation to this philosophy, has been designed by Wolfensberger and Glenn (1975). It is essential that the practising psychologist is familiar with such tools and the psychologist's role in the evaluation of services is considered in more detail in Chapter 4.

The 1982 reorganization of the National Health Service into autonomous district health authorities has created a new set of opportunities for clinical psychologists to influence policy-making. Many district health authorities have set up unit management teams to manage and plan for mentally handicapped people and these teams may have clinical psychologists as core or co-opted members. These psychologists are then in a position to guide strategic planning of services to mentally handicapped people in their district as well as create day-to-day changes.

Educational psychologists are in an especially significant position to influence decision-making following the 1981 Education Act, which has increased both their importance and their numbers. Some local authority social services departments now also employ psychologists to advise about their developments as well as to provide direct services to mentally handicapped people. Thus psychologists are in significantly influential positions within each of the three main service agencies in the UK. It is a situation that they must use to the benefit of mentally handicapped people in general if they are to maintain their credibility with service managers.

Psychologists have also made a significant contribution at a national level through membership of bodies such as the National Development Group for the Mentally Handicapped and the National Development Team. The former produced a range of important publications which provide examples of psychological principles and practice enshrined in official government reports (National Development Group for the Mentally Handicapped, 1978, 1980). As members of the National Development Team psychologists have been able to apply principles of developmental programming to local services where the team has been called in to advise.

The volume of government reports and discussion documents in recent years (e.g. Jay Committee 1979; Warnock Committee, 1978) has created a demand for formal responses from psychologists and the Department of Health and Social Security now routinely includes the British Psychological Society on its list of bodies for consultation. The implications are that individual psychologist should keep themselves informed about the broader perspectives of their work and actively involve themselves in creating change at this 'macro' level.

Research

The speed of recent developments in services for mentally handicapped people owes much to research undertaken by psychologists, who are one of the few professional groups for whom research design and methodology are included as part of basic training.

The need for psychologists to maintain an awareness of current experimental research and its possible use for their work with individual mentally handicapped people has already been referred to. Other areas that merit further investigation include approaches to establishing the needs of mentally handicapped people, how they can be assessed, how they vary and the evaluation of services to meet these needs. Current trends need to be accompanied by research into the effectiveness of alternative models of care, for example the use of normal housing for even the most handicapped people, processes to facilitate the working of interdisciplinary teams and the implications of dispersing services throughout the community to make them more local. A high priority must be for more intensive study to help profoundly and multiply handicapped people, including those with severe behavioural difficulties.

Finally, it is worth mentioning the contribution that could be made by the many applied psychologists working in the field who do not feel they have the time to commit to formal research projects. Much of the work they undertake, such as developing intervention techniques, applying research findings or experimenting with different service models, may be considered as empirical research. The individual psychologist's training gives him the knowledge to build systems of monitoring into his work and the information gained from this should be disseminated as widely as possible to stimulate other workers into new directions and help them avoid traps and pitfalls. Monitoring does not have to be very sophisticated to be useful and many service psychologists could make a considerable contribution by disseminating their ideas and ensuring that they are not lost to the service. Kiernan has pointed out that research tends to be very slow and there is a danger that fashions may change before specific techniques have been optimized (Kiernan, 1983). Although he was referring to non-ral communication his point is equally valid in a general sense.

BIBLIOGRAPHY

ender M (1976) *Community Psychology*. London: Methuen

erger M (1979) Behaviour modification in education and professional practice: the dangers of a mindless technology. *Bulletin. British Psychological Society 32:* 418–419.

uma S, Shearer M, Froman A & Hilliard J (1976) *Portage Guide to Early Education*. Portage, Wisconsin: Co-operative Educational Service Agency.

unden R (1980) *Individual Plans for Mentally Handicapped People. A Draft Procedural Guide*. Cardiff: Mental Handicap in Wales – Applied Research Unit.

ampaign for Mentally Handicapped People (1983) Newsletter 34 (Autumn). Campaign for Mentally Handicapped People, 12a Maddox Street, London W1R 9PL.

asey G, Hunt H, Paddon A & Wilcock P (1983) Paired associates: a workshop model for effecting change. *Child: Care, Health and Development 9:* 137–144.

olvin G & Horner R (1983) Experimental analysis of generalisation: an evaluation of a general case programme for teaching motor skills to severely handicapped learners. In Hogg J & Mittler P (eds) *Advances in Mental Handicap Research*, Vol. 2. Chichester: Wiley.

nery FE (ed) (1969) *Systems Thinking*, Vol. 1. Penguin Education Modern Management Readings. Harmondsworth, Middlesex: Penguin.

nery FE (ed) (1981) *Systems Thinking*, Vol. 2. Penguin Education Modern Management Readings. Harmondsworth, Middlesex: Penguin.

lce D, Jenkins J, Toogood A, Mansell J & de Kock U (1981)

Individual Programme Planning: Handbook for Keyworkers. Winchester, Hampshire: Health Care Evaluation and Research Team.

Foxen T & McBrien J (1981) *Training Staff in Behavioural Methods: Trainee Workbook*. Manchester: Manchester University Press.

GNCs/CCETSW (General Nursing Councils and Central Council for Education and Training in Social Work Joint Working Group on Training for Staff Working with Mentally Handicapped People) (1982) *Co-operation in Training. Part I: Qualifying Training*.

GNCs/CCETSW (General Nursing Councils and Central Council for Education and Training in Social Work Joint Working Group on Training for Staff Working with Mentally Handicapped People) (1983) *Co-operation in Training. Part II: In-Service Training*.

Goldiamond I (1975) A constructional approach to self control. In Schwartz A & Goldiamond I (eds) *Social Casework – A Behavioural Approach*. New York: Columbia University Press.

Gould SJ (1981) *The Mismeasure of Man*. New York: Norton.

Gunzburg HC (1976) *Progress Assessment Charts*. Birmingham: SEFA/Stratford Social Education Publications.

Hogg J & Mittler P (eds) (1983) *Advances in Mental Handicap Research* 2. Chichester: Wiley.

Jay Committee (1979) *Report of the Committee of Enquiry into Mental Handicap Nursing and Care*. Cmnd. 7468. London: HMSO.

Jenkins J, Felce D & Mansell J (1982) *The Bereweeke Skill Teaching System*. Windsor, Berkshire: NFER-Nelson.

Kazdin AE (1980) *Behaviour Modification in Applied Settings*. Homewood, Illinois: Dorsey Press.

Kiernan C (1983) The exploration of sign and symbol effects. In Hogg J & Mittler P (eds) *Advances in Mental Handicap Research 2*. Chichester: Wiley.

Kiernan C & Jones M (1982) *Behaviour Assessment Battery*. Windsor, Berkshire: NFER-Nelson.

McBrien J & Foxen T (1981) *Training Staff in Behavioural Methods: The EDY In-Service Course for Mental Handicap Practitioners. Instructors' Handbook*. Manchester: Manchester University Press.

McBrien J & Weightman J (1980) The effect of room management procedures on the engagement of profoundly retarded children. *British Journal of Mental Subnormality 26:* 38–46.

Mittler P (1979) Training, education and rehabilitation. In Craft M (ed) *Tredgold's Mental Retardation*, 12th edn. London: Baillière Tindall.

Mittler P (1983) How effective is staff training? Talk to *Tenth Annual Conference, Association of Professions for the Mentally Handicapped, Digby Stewart College, London*.

National Development Group for the Mentally Handicapped (1978) *Helping Mentally Handicapped People in Hospital. Report to the Secretary of State for Social Services*. London: Department of Health and Social Security.

National Development Group for the Mentally Handicapped (1980) *Improving the Quality of Services for Mentally Handicapped People: A Checklist of Standards*. London: Department of Health and Social Security.

Nihira K (1974) *The Adaptive Behaviour Rating Scales*. Washington DC: American Association for Mental Deficiency.

Parks AW (1978) A model for psychological consultation to community residences – pressures, problems and program types. *Mental Retardation 16(2):* 149–152.

Porterfield J & Blunden R (1979) *Establishing Activity Periods in Special Needs Rooms Within Adult Training Centres: A*

Replication Study. Research Report 7. Cardiff: Mental Handicap in Wales – Applied Research Unit.

Porterfield J, Blunden R, Blewett E & Beynon M (1978) Profoundly handicapped adults can do much more. *Teaching and Training 16(1):* 3–11.

Shackleton-Bailey M (1980) *Hampshire Assessment for Living with Others.* Winchester: Hampshire Social Services Department.

Schopler E, Reichler R & Lansing M (1980) *Individualised Assessment and Treatment for Autistic and Developmentally Disabled Children,* Vol. II. Baltimore: University Park Press.

Warnock Committee (1978) *Special Educational Needs: Report of the Committee of Enquiry into the Education of Mentally Handicapped Children and Young People.* Cmnd. 7212. London: HMSO.

Wolfensberger W (1972) *The Principle of Normalisation in Human Services.* Toronto: National Institute on Mental Retardation.

Wolfensberger W & Glenn L (1975) *PASS 3. A Method for the Quantitative Evaluation of Human Services.* Toronto: National Institute on Mental Retardation.

Yule W & Carr J (eds) (1980) *Behaviour Modification for the Mentally Handicapped.* London: Croom Helm.

Ziarnik JP (1980) Developing proactive direct care staff. *Mental Retardation 18(6):* 289–292.

Chapter 28
Psychiatry and Mental Handicap

ANDREW H. REID

Over the last 20 years there has been a change in concepts of care for mentally handicapped people. It is widely held that it is preferable for them to remain in the community, with either their natural or foster families, and if this is not possible then care within a small group or community home or hostel environment is considered preferable to care in hospital. Some advocates of community care policies maintain that all retarded people can be cared for in this way. The reality is that whereas most retarded people can be managed in the community, there are a substantial number who by reason of physical dependency or psychiatric or behaviour disorder, require the resources and facilities of medical and nursing care in hospital. The diagnosis of psychiatric and behaviour disorders has, therefore, assumed a much greater significance since they are a potential source of distress both to the patient and to his or her family, since they may determine residential placement and since they often give rise to major problems of management. Moreover, these psychiatric and behaviour disorders are frequently treatable and occasionally preventable. Their identification is therefore of considerable clinical importance.

For various reasons, mentally retarded people have an increased vulnerability to psychiatric illness.

Firstly, there is the factor of structural brain abnormality or brain damage. Nearly all severely and profoundly mentally retarded people have major structural brain abnormality, and substantial numbers of mildly retarded people will be similarly affected. The abnormality may be determined by a wide variety of agencies including genetic causes as in tuberous sclerosis, infective causes as in the rubella syndrome, toxic causes as in the fetal alcohol syndrome, or trauma as in child abuse. Brain damage has effects on behaviour, personality, affect, memory, language and intellectual function, as well as on motor and sensory function, depending on the site, the developmental period at which

damage was sustained and the nature of the process concerned. It may predispose to disturbances in levels of activity, irritability and noisiness, and to defects in social and emotional control. Given the present state of knowledge some of the very pressing and intractable behaviour problems one encounters, particularly among more severely mentally retarded patients, can only be categorized as brain damage syndromes. Brain damage also predisposes to epilepsy and it has been shown very clearly that the prevalence rate of epilepsy is increased among mentally retarded people, particularly among the more severely retarded and multiply handicapped groups, where rates in excess of 50% can be found. The relationship between neurological abnormality, intellectual retardation, epilepsy and psychiatric disorder has been demonstrated very clearly by Rutter and his colleagues in their Isle of Wight survey. They showed that in the total child population in the Isle of Wight the overall prevalence rate of psychiatric morbidity was 6.6%; where there were physical disorders not affecting the brain the rate rose to 11.6%, but where brain disorders were present the rate rose to 34.3%. The effect of epilepsy was shown by a further study of two groups both with lesions above the brain stem. In the group without seizures the prevalence rate of psychiatric disorder was 37.5%, whereas in the group with seizures it was 58.3%.

Secondly, there are the problems associated with the fact of handicap and the effect of handicap on lifestyle and interpersonal relationships. Retarded children and adults are vulnerable to the adverse social consequences of educational failure and social rejection. In childhood they may not be acceptable as playmates by other children, and as they grow up they tend to be denied status and satisfaction. In adult life their employment prospects are poor and they are less likely to marry than their more gifted contemporaries.

These social factors summate with organic brain dysfunction and family stresses to bring about a

317

high prevalence rate of psychiatric disorder in mentally retarded people of all ages.

PSYCHIATRIC SYMPTOMATOLOGY

There are, however, problems in formulating concepts of psychiatric disorder in mentally retarded people.

These may arise in the first instance from incomplete or rudimentary development of spoken language. Language development and vocabulary is usually limited in mentally retarded people, and more severely retarded patients frequently have no spoken language at all. Much psychiatric symptomatology is, however, integrally related to language. For example, thought disorder, hallucinations, delusions and ideas of influence and of significance rely for their identification on a certain level of verbal fluency and it is not possible to establish the presence of these symptoms in people with an IQ much below around 40. Furthermore, where there is a certain level of language development but it is of limited extent, it may not be sufficient to convey the nuances of meaning necessary to establish the presence of such symptoms as obsessional phenomena, for example. On the other hand, symptoms such as change of mood in the direction of elation or depression can usually be picked up by a sensitive observer, even if the patient is unable to tell one about it.

It may also be difficult to decide what significance to attach to a phenomenon which in a normally intelligent person would be construed as suggestive of psychiatric disorder. For example, echolalia in normally intelligent patients is often regarded as suggestive of a schizophrenic illness, and disorientation for time and place or incontinence of urine as suggestive of a dementing process. In mentally retarded people these phenomena will usually be explicable on a developmental basis and be of no specific psychiatric significance.

Some psychiatric symptoms may have different significance in a mentally retarded person and a normally intelligent person. For example, restlessness in a normally intelligent adult may be a symptom of a manic state, an agitated depression or a confusional or dementing disorder, whereas in severely mentally retarded patients it may be a persistent and long-standing phenomenon, perhaps related to brain damage. Likewise, self-injury in the general population may signify a depressive illness, a cry for help from a patient with difficulties in his or her social life and adjustment, or it may be a manifestation of an underlying personality problem. In mentally retarded patients it may in addition be a self-stimulatory phenomenon and related to boredom or social isolation. It may be secondary to perceptual difficulties in deaf, multiply handicapped children, attention-seeking in the setting of a large, over-crowded and under-staffed ward, physiologically determined as in the Lesch–Nyhan syndrome, a symptom of early childhood autism, or possibly even a response to abnormalities in pain sensation secondary to malfunctioning of the endorphin system.

Certain items of behaviour are particularly associated with mental retardation but within that context are of very variable significance. For example, intense ritualistic, stereotypic and manneristic behavioural patterns are particularly, although not exclusively, associated with more severe degrees of mental retardation. In this population they may be a symptom of early childhood autism but they may also be pleasurable, or related to excitement or anticipation. They may be developmentally determined and akin to hand and finger regard in small babies. They may have a symbolic significance. They may be imitative, related to boredom, and susceptible to modification through the provision of alternative activities and stimulation, although there are some patients in whom certain types of sensory stimulation serve paradoxically to increase the phenomenon. Finally, stereotypy may be of no psychiatric significance at all.

There may also be difficulties in interviewing mentally retarded people arising from limitations of language and defects in attention and concentration. It will usually be necessary to get to know the patient first and to rely on frequent short sessions rather than the long interviews used in general psychiatry. It may be necessary to use media such as play, or to carry out the assessment with someone present who knows the patient well and can interpret. It is always important to make a longitudinal appraisal, to note changes in such observable parameters as facial appearance and social responsiveness and to enquire after changes in functions such as levels of activity, sleep and feeding patterns. It is helpful also to obtain an account from an outside person who knows the patient well, for example, parents, siblings, teachers or care or nursing staff.

PREVALENCE

One of the main problems in establishing prevalence rates for psychiatric disorder in mentally retarded people arises from the difficulty in defining what constitutes a case. In the field of mental retardation the psychiatrically disordered population overlaps with the physically handicapped and dependent population on the one hand, and on the other with a large number of retarded patients whose behaviour or personality is unusual in some respects, but whose strange ways would not be regarded as indicative of psychiatric disorder were it not for the fact that their intellectual retardation makes them dependent on others. The situation is analogous to geriatric psychiatry where unusual personality traits or eccentricities only present management problems when the old person is no longer able by reason of mental or physical impairment to look after himself or herself.

It is, however, important to attempt to establish prevalence rates since these determine the range, type and extent of services required. Accordingly various investigators have tried, some of them using standard definitions of psychiatric disorder. Studies have been carried out on populations of retarded people of various age ranges and degrees of retardation, both in hospital and in the community. There seems to be emerging a consensus that prevalence rates of psychiatric disorder are higher among more severely mentally retarded people, and among patients in hospital as opposed to non-hospital accommodation: prevalence rates of around 50% are reported for significant psychiatric disorder in patients in hospital. These high rates are the result of admission policies which have tended, quite appropriately, to selectively admit to hospital mentally retarded patients who are physically dependent, psychiatrically disturbed or both. Amongst this 50% are to be found some patients with functional illnesses such as manic-depressive and schizophrenic psychoses, grown-up cases of childhood psychiatric disorders, acute and/or chronic brain syndromes (delirium and dementia), and many more with neurotic, personality or behavioural problems, sometimes associated with epilepsy.

RELATIONSHIP BETWEEN BEHAVIOURAL PATTERNS AND MENTAL RETARDATION SYNDROMES

There has also been considerable interest in the extent to which particular types of behavioural patterns are associated with specific mental retardation syndromes. The most obvious example of

this approach is the commonly held public stereotype of the patient with Down's syndrome as being friendly, sociable and fond of music. Unfortunately, when the proven data are reviewed, the established associations turn out to be meagre.

Down's syndrome patients are certainly in the main friendly, responsive and socially acceptable. They are, however, quite likely to show conduct disorders in childhood, sometimes as a result of family and handling problems consequent on the presence of a mentally handicapped member. For some curious reason they seem less vulnerable than ordinary children to early childhood autism. In adult life they may develop affective or paranoid disorders but these often turn out to be prodromal features of a dementing process. This is the most specific association there is in the whole field of mental retardation between psychiatric syndrome and diagnostic category. All, or nearly all, Down's syndrome patients over the age of 35 show EEG, neuropathological and neurochemical changes characteristic of Alzheimer's disease. The increased liability extends to the various types of chromosomal abnormality underlying Down's syndrome, but the presence of a normal cell line in mosaicism may protect the patient against the development of the dementing process. Not all Down's syndrome patients with neuropathological evidence of Alzheimer's disease at autopsy will have shown a dementing syndrome in life, but this may partly reflect the difficulty in identifying the presence of intellectual deterioration in patients who are originally severely mentally retarded. The presence of these Alzheimer-type neuropathological changes in the brain is reflected in the rising prevalence rate of epilepsy in Down's syndrome patients as they get older. The reason for this increased vulnerability to Alzheimer's disease is not known. Were it better understood it would almost certainly add fundamentally to our knowledge of senile dementia in patients of normal intelligence.

Paul was a moderately mentally retarded man with Down's syndrome who died at the age of 52. He came from a caring family with a professional background. He was admitted to hospital when his parents were elderly themselves and could no longer cope. Over the last five years of his life he showed progressive memory deterioration, manifest in failure to recognize his brother when he visited. The deterioration was less apparent in the residential setting where he remained pleasant and cooperative although staff noted that there were times when he appeared lost as to his precise whereabouts. At the age of 52 he developed grand mal epilepsy for the first time in his life and thereafter his deterioration accelerated. At autopsy he showed characteristic neuropathological changes of Alzheimer's disease with brain atrophy and widespread senile plaques and neurofibrillary tangles.

The search for other associations has been less rewarding. Tuberose sclerosis was once considered to be associated with a particular behavioural syndrome suggestive of catatonic schizophrenia, but the behavioural patterns in question are widespread amongst severely and profoundly mentally retarded adults, and bear no relationship clinically to schizophrenia. Phenylketonuria has been linked with a tendency towards persistent hyperkinesis but again this behavioural pattern is non-specific and widespread in severely and profoundly mentally retarded adults. Phenylketonuria is, moreover, now a largely preventable condition.

The other area in which there has been considerable interest is that of the chromosomal abnormalities. Following the discovery in the 1960s of a high prevalence rate of the XYY genotype amongst males at some top-security hospitals, the idea of a genetically-determined form of criminality was put forward. It has now been shown that the XYY genotype is quite widely distributed in the normal population and its identification at birth does not by any means indicate that the individual concerned is predestined to a life of crime. The consensus of present opinion is that the presence of the XXY chromosome constitution carries an increased likelihood of mild mental retardation, and the XYY constitution similarly but to a lesser extent. The greater the degree of genetic abnormality the greater the severity of mental retardation. The verdict on the view that the XYY anomaly predisposes to criminality is 'not proven', and the association may merely be with slightly increased impulsivity. The XO (Turner's) syndrome, so long linked with mental retardation and anorexia nervosa, has now been shown to be of little psychiatric significance.

EARLY CHILDHOOD AUTISM

This syndrome is dealt with extensively in Chapter 14 but it is reviewed briefly here for the purpose of completeness.

Early childhood autism was originally identified by Kanner in 1943, although there had been descriptions of children who were almost certainly autistic in the literature before. Originally it was considered to be caused by abnormalities in the parent–child interaction, and it was believed that autistic children were potentially of normal intelligence. This laid a terrible burden of guilt and responsibility on parents and it is now widely accepted that the vast majority of these children are indeed mentally retarded, often severely so, and the observed abnormalities in the parent–child interaction are the result of the immense difficulties inherent in attempting to relate to an autistic child.

Early childhood autism can be defined as a condition which starts before 30 months of age, characterized by an autistic-type failure to develop interpersonal relationships, delay in the development of speech and language, and ritualistic and 'compulsive' phenomena. Using strict diagnostic criteria the prevalence rate amongst the childhood population overall is around 4.5 per 10 000 children, with boys being affected around three times as frequently as girls. However, it is now becoming increasingly apparent that early childhood autism represents a spectrum of conditions, with relatively few children showing the complete, nuclear syndrome and many more showing features of early childhood autism such as social impairments, repetitive behaviour and abnormalities of language and symbolic activities, either alone or in combination.

Early childhood autism is often associated with organic brain damage, for example infantile spasms, rubella embryopathy and severe perinatal complications. These organic factors are reflected in the development of epilepsy in approximately 30% of autistic children at around the age of adolescence. Recently it has become clear that there is also a strong genetic component.

In making the diagnosis in infancy, the failure to develop pre-verbal and social communication can be very evident to an experienced observer or parent. During babyhood the lack of eye contact and failure to cuddle or come for comfort are apparent. In childhood there are abnormalities in the comprehension and expression of speech. Many autistic children are, and remain, mute, while others show pronominal reversal, echolalia and abnormalities in the intonation and timing of speech. This central language impairment extends to understanding and thinking, and lies behind the abnormal patterns of social interaction and the marked deficits in creative and imaginative play so evident in these children. The autistic child may show strange fears, for example of open stairs, or fascinations, for example with the smell or texture of hair, or mirror gazing. Insomnia, restlessness and screaming may occur. There may be abnormalities in visual perception which lead the autistic child to focus on the periphery of a picture or environment rather than on the whole. Autistic children also show complex, manneristic and stereotypic movements which are of absorbing interest to them and which are performed in preference to normal imaginative play. These stereotypies include finger posturing, hand-flapping, rocking and twirling, rituals involving spinning and stereotyped play with such objects as a piece of wool or strip of paper. Autistic children show a resistance to change and a drive towards the preservation of sameness. Pain sensation may be dulled and self-injury such as hand-biting, head-banging or eye-poking may occur. Adolescence may bring problems with inappropriate sexual behaviour. In adult life some of the most pressing problems, including hyperkinesis, screaming, insomnia and self-injury, tend to fade, but the language impairment, resistance to change, abnormal preoccupations, stereotyped phenomena and social isolation all tend to persist. A few patients develop depressive illness.

Sheila is aged 25, severely mentally retarded and suffers from early childhood autism. She is very set in her ways, communicates very little and prefers to spend her time on her own in stereotyped play with a stick or comb. She has the curious habit of 'using' parts of other people's bodies such as their hands to get them to do something she wants, for example opening a fridge door or acquiring a glass of milk, notwithstanding the fact that she can perform these functions herself perfectly adequately. From time to time she becomes clearly depressed, disinterested in her usual stereotypic play, emotional and anorexic and has disturbed sleep. These episodes last a few weeks and may sometimes, but not always, be traced back to changes in her routine. They respond well to treatment with amitriptyline.

Follow-up studies show that, overall, around two-thirds of patients with early childhood autism will remain severely handicapped and unable to lead an independent life. Many will eventually be cared for in a long-stay residential setting. Only a very small percentage will ever be able to cope with regular paid employment, but there have been moving accounts of occasional patients with such a happy outcome.

Unfortunately, there is no reliably effective medical or psychological treatment for early childhood autism. Hyperkinesis, screaming or self-injury may respond partially to phenothiazines or butyrophenones, and a few patients seem to benefit from lithium. Insomnia may require night sedation. Good control of fits is essential and there is some evidence to suggest that the newer anticonvulsants such as carbamazepine can exert a beneficial effect on aggressiveness and overactivity. Appropriate education is very important and there has been progress over the last few years through the application of behavioural techniques in the educational setting. Speech therapy may help in the acquisition of speech, or may encourage non-verbal means of communication, but gains made in the treatment setting tend to be hard to maintain outside. In adult life the provision of structured and stimulating activity is important, and parents, relatives and care staff need to be involved in the treatment programme so that a concerted approach is possible.

HYPERKINETIC SYNDROMES

Over the last 40 years the concept of a hyperkinetic syndrome characterized by a chronic, sustained, excessive level of motor activity relative to the age of the child has gained popularity. It is said to be more common in boys and to be accompanied in many cases by distractability, short attention span, disturbed sleep, excitability, temper tantrums and low frustration tolerance. Aggressive and antisocial behaviour, specific learning problems and emotional lability are often considered to be part of the syndrome. Premature birth, perinatal abnormalities, temporal lobe epilepsy and diencephalic abnormalities have all been implicated as possible causes. The hyperkinetic syndrome has come to be identified with the rather elusive concept of minimal brain dysfunction.

This concept of the hyperkinetic syndrome has been challenged, however. Attention has focused on the problem of defining hyperkinesis and on the wide disparity in reported prevalence rates between the USA and the UK. It now seems likely that overactivity in children of normal intelligence is related more to conduct disorders than to a hyperkinetic syndrome as such. Amongst more severely retarded, brain-damaged and epileptic children, however, hyperkinetic syndromes undoubtedly occur.

It is not clear what happens to these severely retarded hyperkinetic children in adult life. In some patients the hyperkinesis persists for many years although it may fluctuate in intensity. It may be accompanied by some elevation of mood, and may present with a clinical picture resembling chronic hypomania.

Paul is aged 43, epileptic and severely mentally retarded. He is playful, mischievous, always on the go and very thin. He shows very marked echolalia, in which there is a quality of mimicry. He is buoyant and cheerful in his mood but there is an aggressive streak in him and at times of peak restlessness he can be aggressive towards other patients. Clinically he presents with a behavioural pattern suggestive of chronic hypomania but he has shown very little response to phenothiazines, butyrophenones or lithium. He showed a little improvement with a behavioural approach aimed at increasing his attention and concentration span but this failed to generalize from the structured treatment setting to the daily living environment. He showed slightly more response to carbamazepine, to the point where he can now be engaged in some simple day-to-day constructive activities.

In some patients the hyperkinesis wanes during adolescence, to be replaced by inactivity in adult life, whereas in others the restlessness gives way to aggression and antisocial behaviour.

Jean is aged 22, epileptic and severely mentally retarded. She was an extraordinarily powerful, restless child and an immense problem at home and school. Eventually she was admitted to hospital when her very caring mother had a depressive illness and attempted suicide. She could never be contained within the school setting but over the last few years hyperkinesis has waned to be replaced by a more normal level of activity. She is still, however, very significantly aggressive although there is often a component of boisterousness or exuberance rather than intent to injure. Behavioural treatments and drugs, including tranquillizers and stimulants, have proved relatively ineffective and the most fruitful approach by far has been to keep her involved in as many energetic, out-of-doors, activities as possible.

As can be seen from the case histories a variety of treatment approaches may be tried. Stimulants may be helpful in severely hyperkinetic children but there is concern about their possible retarding effects on growth and they may increase stereotypy. Additive-free diets have been advocated but their efficacy is uncertain since double-blind trials are difficult to construct and placebo effects hard to eliminate. In due course they may find a place. Phenothiazines and butyrophenones may alleviate the restlessness and lithium or carbamazepine may prove helpful in adults with overactivity accompanied by mood elevation. More recently behavioural approaches which attempt to prolong the attention and concentration span have claimed some success. Environmental change and manipulation with the provision of space and suitable activities may also help.

AFFECTIVE DISORDERS

Affective disorders occur in mentally handicapped patients and there may be an increased vulnerability, and an earlier age of onset, in this population as compared with the general population. Prevalence rates of around 1.5 % for patients actually suffering from an episode of affective psychosis at a particular point in time have been reported from several hospital surveys.

George is aged 23 and severely mentally retarded with primary autosomal microcephaly. He is of pleasant and gentle disposition and lovingly cared for by his parents. His first affective illness occurred at the age of ten when for some weeks he appeared profoundly depressed with delusions of imminent blindness and of his teeth falling out. His sleep was disturbed with early morning wakening, his appetite was impaired and he showed little interest in his usual activities. He recovered on treatment with amitriptyline and has since had two further shorter and less serious depressive episodes.

Episodes of affective disorder may be related to such apparent precipitating events as childbirth, bereavement, viral infections including influenza, glandular fever, viral hepatitis, brain pathology and cerebral arteriosclerosis. In some patients there seems to be a psychogenic precipitant but in many the illness seems endogenously determined. An affective disorder may occur once only or the illness may run a relapsing course with recurrent episodes of depression, mania or both. Depression is more common than mania although this tendency may not be as marked as in patients of normal intelligence. In severely retarded patients the disorder may run a regularly cyclical course.

Karen is aged 30, profoundly mentally retarded and blind with a variant of Schilder's disease. The disease ran a rapidly progressive course between the ages of 7 and 13 but has now been static for many years. At the age of 13 she developed a regularly cyclical affective psychosis with periods of excitement, restlessness and elevation of mood, alternating with periods of near stupor, on an almost exact ten-week cycle. When elated her sleep is greatly reduced and there is tachycardia; her face is suffused and there are accompanying changes in haematocrit (packed cell volume). This cyclical psychosis has not responded at all to phenothiazines, lithium or bromocriptine. On the basis that it might be a form of periodic catatonia thyroxine in large doses has also been tried but to no avail.

Diagnosis is based on the usual clinical grounds of change in mood accompanied by appropriate alterations in psychomotor activity and thought processes. In mentally retarded patients who are verbally fluent the diagnosis should present few problems; in more severely mentally retarded patients who may have little or no language the diagnosis is more difficult and relies on careful observation by relatives or care staff who know the patient well and who can sense abnormalities of affect. These observations must be backed up by information about changes in such parameters as sleep, appetite, level of activity and social responsiveness.

Mentally retarded patients who are depressed may find it difficult to verbalize their mood state: they may complain more of being fed up than depressed, or they may present with aggressive or irritable behaviour, with regression or with prominent somatic and hysterical symptoms. In mildly mentally retarded patients who are depressed there may be florid, affectively-loaded, delusions and hallucinations, ideas of guilt or failure leading to suicide or attempted suicide, diurnal variation of mood and sleep disturbance, usually in the direction of decrease but occasionally of increase.

Jean is aged 40, moderately mentally retarded and a child of an incestuous mother–grandfather union. There is a family history of suicide. She also suffers from psoriasis and torsion dystonia. She manifests an unstable affective disorder in which at times she becomes seriously depressed and inclined to self-injury, on one occasion even setting fire to her nightdress. She also shows manic swings in which she is excitable, impulsive, talkative and her sleep is seriously disturbed with combined initial insomnia and early morning wakening. When manic her mood state is particularly unstable and labile and she can be dangerously and impulsively assaultive to staff or other patients. Her illness has responded partially to treatment with lithium but this unfortunately exacerbates her psoriasis. Nursing staff always know when she is becoming depressed because her hair is limp, her skin texture pasty and her eyes dull and listless.

Mentally handicapped patients suffering from mania may present with an unusual clinical picture. As a result of the limitation in verbal ability, wit and humour may be conspicuously lacking, and flight of ideas, clang associations (association of words with similar sounds) and rhyming may be rudimentary. Mood elation may be poorly sustained and replaced by excitement, irritability and restlessness. Some patients may behave in an assaultive manner. Delusions and hallucinations may be grandiose and wish-fulfilling and there may be increased or inappropriate sexual activity.

Sometimes patients show a combination of manic and depressive symptomatology and in the resulting mixed affective state there may be an abundance of delusions and hallucinations, together with some perplexity, suggestive of a confusional state.

Affective disorders may occur in patients with a wide variety of physical and neurological disorders, including epilepsy, but there does not seem to be any specific liability. The frequency with which affective disorders occur in mentally retarded patients with these conditions merely reflects the multiple physical pathology so often encountered in this population.

Peter is aged 52 and severely mentally retarded with athetotic cerebral palsy. He also has a spastic dysarthria which renders phonation difficult and language intelligibility is poor. Over the course of a few weeks nursing staff noted that he was becoming emotional, with frequent temper tantrums and aggressive outbursts. He became concerned about his health, complained of sore feet and abdominal pain, and expressed the delusional idea that he had a hole in his stomach which was causing him to waste away. He seemed clinically depressed. He was started on amitriptyline and within a period of around two months was back to his usual self.

Affective disorders usually respond reasonably satisfactorily to appropriate psychiatric treatment, although the outcome depends to some extent on previous personality strengths and weaknesses. Depression usually responds to treatment with an antidepressant drug of the tricyclic group such as imipramine or amitriptyline. Side-effects such as dry mouth, glaucoma, urinary retention in men, or drowsiness with amitriptyline, may pose problems and the dose needs to be titrated against response and side-effects. Occasionally a manic swing can be precipitated by antidepressant medication. Other drugs which may be prescribed for depression include the newer tricyclics (which have no clear advantages over the older preparations), tetracyclic drugs such as mianserin, and monoamine oxidase inhibitors such as phenelzine. In selected cases of severe depression, particularly where there is much anguish and suffering, or danger to life from food refusal or suicide ideation, electro-convulsive therapy may be the most effective and speedy way of bringing relief. Mania is treated in the usual way by drugs of the phenothiazine group such as chlorpromazine, or the butyrophenone group such as haloperidol. These drugs have a rapid onset of action and are particularly useful in allowing quick control of manic overactivity. They are usually well tolerated in mentally handicapped patients, but they can precipitate such neurological side-effects as dystonic reactions, akathisia, rigidity, tardive dyskinesia and other parkinsonian symptoms. Mania can also be treated with lithium but this drug takes time to be effective and it is customary to combine it with chlorpromazine or haloperidol in the early stages. There has been anxiety in the past over the combination of lithium with haloperidol and there have been sporadic reports of irreversible brain damage precipitated by the combination. Although the association is by no means proven it is probably prudent not to prescribe lithium to patients receiving more than 20 mg haloperidol per day, and to ensure that blood lithium levels are not allowed to rise above 1.0 nmol/l in patients on combined therapy.

Along with specific drug treatment for mania and depression it may also be necessary to promote sleep through the judicious use of such sedatives as chloral hydrate, or a benzodiazepine such as oxazepam. Attention will also need to be given to the maintenance of an adequate nutritional state. In depressed patients, constipation may be a problem.

In the longer term lithium is a useful prophylactic against recurrent attacks of bipolar manic-depressive psychosis, and possibly also of unipolar recurrent depressive psychosis, in mentally handicapped patients. Unfortunately, the response to lithium is frequently only partial and patients with rapidly cyclical affective disorders in whom episodes occur with great frequency rarely seem to gain satisfactory relief. Drug levels of lithium need to be carefully monitored and some brain-damaged mentally handicapped patients may not be able to tolerate a full therapeutic dose. The normally quoted therapeutic range is around 0.8–1.2 nmol/l but it seems increasingly likely that reasonably satisfactory control can be obtained at levels below this – around 0.4–0.6 nmol/l – and these lower levels are often tolerated much better in older and brain-damaged mentally handicapped patients. Acute intoxication with lithium can give rise to alarming and dangerous side-effects including nausea, vomiting, tremulousness, polyuria and polydipsia, weight gain, oedema, disturbance of consciousness, coma and even death. Possible longer term side-effects of prolonged treatment with lithium include hypothyroidism and renal damage. Notwithstanding these limitations lithium can be a valuable drug in the management of recurrent affective disorders in mentally handicapped patients if it is carefully monitored.

SCHIZOPHRENIC AND PARANOID DISORDERS

The inter-relationship of schizophrenia or dementia praecox to mental retardation has been of interest to clinicians and research workers for many years. Originally it was considered that the onset of schizophrenia in the first few years of life could of itself bring about severe mental retardation and the term 'pfropfschizophrenia' was coined. The term was later used to denote a particular form of schizophrenia occurring in mentally handicapped patients and running its own distinctive course. The term eventually came to mean different things to different investigators and it has now been finally dropped. There has also been controversy about the feasibility of diagnosing the various sub-types of schizophrenia – simple, hebephrenic, catatonic and paranoid – in mentally retarded patients. Some research workers have maintained that simple schizophrenia is particularly common; others have stated that it is quite impossible to identify such a featureless and ill-defined illness in a mentally retarded population. The consensus view now inclines to the latter.

There is some evidence from Swedish whole-population surveys that there is a modestly increased liability to schizophrenia in people of mildly subnormal intelligence. Surveys of in-patient populations of mental handicap hospitals in the UK have come up with prevalence rates of around 3.5% and it is clear that schizophrenia is a significant problem in the field of mental handicap.

Schizophrenic disorders may have an acute onset, perhaps with some clouding of consciousness as in the so-called oneiroid state, but more usually the psychosis seems to develop insidiously out of a previously unusual personality. It is sometimes possible to identify what seems to be a clear precipitating event but more often this is not the case. It is certainly true, however, that schizophrenia is to some extent responsive to environmental change and manipulation and relapses are frequently related to emotional stress and tension, often within the family circle. The age at onset of schizophrenia in mentally handicapped patients is similar to that in patients of normal intelligence and is usually during the second and third decade of life. There is nothing distinctive about the natural history and it may run a chronic and persisting course or there may be prolonged remissions. With the passage of time patients may show a varying combination of hebephrenic and catatonic symptoms, or a residual defect state with impairment of volition and emotional blunting.

The diagnosis of schizophrenia is clinical and based on various symptoms which tend to be language-based. The significance of these symptoms has to be evaluated against the background of previous personality, the mode of onset of the disability and the course of the illness. The main symptoms include ideas of influence, 'made' experiences, auditory hallucinations, thought disorder, primary delusions and abnormalities of affect and of motility. A degree of verbal fluency is required for patients to describe these diagnostic features and it is impossible to identify the condition in mentally retarded patients with an IQ below around 40. Schizophrenia may occur in more profoundly retarded patients who have no language but in the absence of a convincing biological test the diagnosis cannot be sustained.

Jessie is aged 43 and mildly mentally retarded. She suffers from a persistent schizophrenic psychosis and entertains some strange and fantastic somatic delusions, for example that she has a new and an old hand, that the configuration of her neck and shoulders changes from day to day, and that her face is back to front. She hears voices at night emanating from people outside the hospital, telling her that she is being 'infected' by the other residents and that she should be off on her former itinerant way of life. She is pleasant and friendly but very feckless, deteriorated in her social behaviour and she needs considerable prompting and supervision in matters of personal hygiene. Her more florid symptoms are contained through the prescription of flupenthixol by intramuscular injection at fortnightly intervals but her psychosis is still running an active course after many years.

Mentally retarded patients with schizophrenia may show abnormalities of affect including incongruity or inappropriate cheerfulness. Some patients are socially withdrawn but others are surprisingly warm and accessible. Thought disorder is expressed in abnormalities of speech but the significance of these abnormalities has to be assessed in the light of the patient's innate level of speech development. Ideas of influence and of self-reference may be dramatic and delusions naive and wish-fulfilling. Hallucinations tend to be of auditory type but may extend to the visual, tactile and olfactory modalities. Some patients may be noisy, restless and impulsively aggressive.

Paranoid syndromes may be of various types. They may be of acute onset and associated with such precipitating factors as operation, infections or intoxication with alcohol or drugs. Under these circumstances the paranoid state is more appropriately seen as originating in a toxic confusional state. An acute paranoid state may also be precipitated by intense stress in a vulnerable personality.

Joanne was mildly mentally retarded and a dependent girl who wanted very much to be looked after. She was aged 16 when she contracted a marriage to an intelligent man 14 years older than she and of Pakistani origin. He took her to his own country where she was horrified by the way of life, customs and food, and she developed delusional beliefs of being poisoned by curry. She had been rejected by her mother in early years and when she was admitted to hospital she misidentified older members of female staff as her mother in a clear wish-fulfilling manner. Her difficulties were exacerbated by her inability and reluctance to look after her young baby. The whole fabric of delusions and hallucinations cleared almost immediately when she and her husband separated, the child was taken into care and she achieved a supportive hostel placement.

Persistent paranoid schizophrenic syndromes, however, more usually develop slowly and progressively out of a previously abnormal personality and affect an older age group. In the early stages they may be characterized by anger, irritability and a sense of grievance and there may be marked depressive symptoms. Delusions may involve relatives, friends, neighbours or caring staff and be forcibly held. Voices may criticize, accuse, taunt or discuss and there may be assaultive behaviour.

James was aged 69 and mildly mentally retarded. He had worked satisfactorily for many years in a sheltered employment situation as a farm labourer. He was always a solitary, rather dour individual who did not take kindly to company. When he grew older he went to live with his sister and developed the persistent and delusional belief that she was systematically robbing him. He eventually attacked her with a poker, injuring her. He was admitted to hospital where his paranoid delusional beliefs persisted and extended to include persecution at the hands of external agencies. With time, however, the heat and anger went out of his delusional ideas and his behaviour gave rise to little concern.

There are no proven associations between physical pathology and schizophrenia in people with mental handicap. Schizophrenic disorders occur in patients with a wide range of neurological disabilities including epilepsy, and it is not clear whether the association between epilepsy and schizophrenia in people with mental handicap is causal or coincidental.

Donald is aged 50 and mildly mentally retarded. He suffered from tuberculosis in childhood with cerebral involvement and now has a right hemiparesis with choreoathetotic movements of the right arm superimposed on a coarse static intention tremor. He also suffers from grand mal epilepsy. He became unwell during his twenties, hearing voices threatening him, commenting on his actions and seeing people staring malevolently through the window at him. He took to fighting off his imaginary persecutors and there were problems with aggressive behaviour. At the time of admission to hospital he described how he could read people's minds by the use of hearing aids and he expressed the view that others could read his thoughts and cause his thinking patterns to become mixed up. He was preoccupied with sexual and erotic themes and even now, many years later, he is still actively hallucinating, hearing voices accusing him and occasioning damage to his body.

The differential diagnosis of schizophrenia in mentally retarded patients can be difficult. Isolated symptoms such as catalepsy may occur in the absence of other schizophrenic phenomena and should not be taken as indicative of schizophrenia. Some retarded patients seem to have a sustained and vivid fantasy life and these fantasies are recounted to the interviewer with a conviction suggestive of delusions. They may be derived from remnants of childhood thinking patterns or relationships, or they may have a clearly wish-fulfilling component: they should not be interpreted as psychotic phenomena.

Schizophrenia usually responds in some degree to treatment with the phenothiazine group of drugs. Those most commonly in use are probably chlorpromazine and thioridazine, the longer-acting oral preparations such as pimozide, and the longer-acting injectable preparations such as fluphenazine decanoate and flupenthixol. Chlorpromazine is usually effective in allowing rapid control of acute schizophrenic excitement. Butyrophenones have also been used in the treatment of schizophrenia with varying success. The management of the acutely disturbed schizophrenic will also involve the use of a night sedative such as oxazepam, perhaps prescribed along with one of the phenothiazines to control nocturnal restlessness and induce sleep. The use of phenothiazines and butyrophenone drugs involves the risk of side-effects including skin photosensitivity, blood dyscrasias, liver disorders and such neurological sequelae as acute dystonic reactions, parkinsonism, rigidity, akathisia and oculogyric crises. Tardive dyskinesias consisting of bucco-linguo-masticatory movements, and occasionally tardive dystonias, are emerging as troublesome and persistent side-effects of longer-term treatment with phenothiazines. Anticholinergic drugs which may be helpful in the parkinsonian syndromes may actually be implicated in the genesis of tardive dyskinesias and dystonias. A further possible risk of phenothiazines, and particularly of the injectable preparations, is the development through time of depressive symptoms; the clinician should be alert to this.

The treatment of schizophrenia also involves sustained and intensive efforts at rehabilitation once drug control of acute symptomatology has been gained. Patients are often subsequently left with defects in volition and social skills; behaviour modification programmes may help.

The outlook for schizophrenia has improved substantially over recent years, and many schizophrenic patients can now be maintained in the community, either in a family setting or, when the emotional involvement in such a setting is too high, in a small group home or hostel environment. Some patients will eventually be able to resume a completely independent life and cope with the demands of society including a job under conditions of open employment. Others will require sheltered employment or day-care services. The successful maintenance of schizophrenics in the community demands support and sustained follow-up. This can best be achieved by outpatient clinics specializing in the after-care and maintenance of schizophrenics in the community. Community psychiatric nurses are usually attached to these clinics and play a key role in them, monitoring progress, encouraging compliance, supporting families and other caring agencies, identifying early signs of relapse and maintaining contact with defaulters.

ACUTE AND CHRONIC ORGANIC BRAIN SYNDROMES: DELIRIUM AND DEMENTIA

Delirium

Delirium is usually the result of a temporary, toxic, biochemical process affecting the function of the brain as in the delirium of fever or alcoholism. It is particularly common at the extremes of life. Clinically it is characterized by clouding of consciousness, which is usually worse at night, disorientation, impairment of memory, illusions, hallucinations (especially in the visual modality) and an affective change, usually of fear, although occasionally of euphoria. Attention and concentration are impaired. Paranoid misinterpretations and transient fleeting delusions are common. Behaviour may be severely disturbed and the patient is usually restless. There are often accompanying physical symptoms such as tremulousness, tachycardia, profuse sweating, dehydration and chest and renal complications. Fits are not uncommon and the condition can endanger life.

There is nothing distinctive about delirious reactions in mentally retarded patients, the content of the delirium reflecting the patient's innate intellectual endowment. Delirium can be precipitated in retarded patients by the usual agents including drugs, dehydration, uraemia, hypothyroidism, cardiac failure and chest infection. With the increasing tendency towards integrating retarded patients into the community, it is to be expected that a few mildly retarded people will manifest such alcohol-related problems as delirium tremens.

Rena is now aged 64 and moderately mentally retarded. She lived at home with her parents until they died and then on her own with a great deal of help from neighbours and health and social services. Over the years she became enormously fat, unable to leave her flat and eventually bed-fast. Her physical health and personal hygiene deteriorated, she became doubly incontinent and her condition eventually came to constitute a public health hazard. She refused admission to inpatient care, but eventually this became necessary. When she did come in she weighed 25 stone (350 lb; 160 kg) and could not weight-bear and it was necessary to construct a small crane to move her. On physical examination she was found to have a massive fibro-adenomatous tumour weighing nearly 30 lb (13 kg) arising from a thick pedicle in the left thigh. There was also gross lymphoedema of the legs. Her hair and features were coarse and her skin was thickened and dry. Her voice was gruff. She was found to be grossly hypothyroid with a serum thyroxine (T_4) level of 26 nmol/l and a thyroid-stimulating hormone level of 27.4 mu/l. She had thyroid antibodies present in high titre. Within a few days her mental state deteriorated, she appeared confused, out of contact with her surroundings and had visual hallucinations, claiming to see ambulance men in the ward and her home help pulling off her bed clothes. She was considered to be suffering from an acute confusional paranoid hallucinatory state associated with hypothyroidism (myxoedema madness) and was started on thyroxine in small doses. Her physical and mental state gradually improved although there were problems with her cardiac state. She lost weight and regained mobility and it was eventually possible to resect the tumour. She is now euthyroid but there are still chronic behaviour problems with her stubborn cussedness and dirty habits.

Treatment of delirium begins with treatment of the underlying cause such as chest infection and cardiac failure. In the delirium of alcoholism, vitamin B_1 by injection as Parentrovite (vitamin B and C injection) is widely believed to promote recovery. Treatment is otherwise symptomatic. Sleep should be encouraged by a sedative such as chloral hydrate or a benzodiazepine such as oxazepam. Daytime restlessness and excitement may need to be controlled by a tranquillizing agent such as chlormethiazole or chlordiazepoxide. The presence of fits may necessitate the prescription of an anticonvuls-ant, and nutritional and fluid balance need to be carefully monitored.

Dementia

Dementia is characterized by a deterioration and disintegration in the intellectual, affective and be-havioural spheres. It is nearly always progressive and occurs in the setting of clear consciousness. It is usually thought of in connection with the elderly but it can occur at any age, including childhood, when it is sometimes known as childhood dis-integrative psychosis.

Among the progressive brain disorders which may be associated with the childhood disintegrative psychoses are the lipidoses, the leukoencephalo-pathies, the leukodystrophies and subacute sclero-sing panencephalitis. Huntington's chorea, which is a progressive heredofamilial neurodegenerative disorder combining a progressive dementia with choreiform movements, usually has its onset in adult life but it may rarely develop in childhood. Severe and uncontrolled epilepsy with frequent grand mal seizures and anoxic brain damage can be associated with a childhood disintegrative psy-chosis, although uncontrolled epilepsy may itself be a symptom of progressive brain disease. Some conditions such as severe dehydration with gross electrolyte imbalance, lead poisoning, brain trauma or tumour and measles, herpes, vaccinial and rubella encephalitis can also produce catastrophic deterioration in intellectual function, behaviour, personality and loss of developmental skills. The condition is not usually progressive once the under-lying pathology is corrected or subsides and in essence these non-progressive disorders leave behind a condition of static childhood mental retardation.

Dementia is more usually considered in relation to the psychoses of senescence, in particular ar-teriosclerotic dementia and Alzheimer's senile and presenile dementia. The subject of dementia in retarded patients is important and becoming more so as the life expectation of mentally handicapped people increases. Community and hospital-based surveys so far tend to suggest that, with the exception of Down's syndrome, mentally retarded patients are no more and no less likely than the rest of the population to develop a dementing process.

Diagnosis is made on the usual clinical grounds, including failure of grasp and comprehension, progressive deterioration in orientation, and failure to elaborate new impressions or think in conceptual terms. Deterioration in thinking is reflected in loss of vocabulary, nominal dysphasia and persever-ation. Eventually speech becomes grossly disorga-nized with both expressive and receptive dysphasia. Memory failure is initially most marked for recent events but progresses to involve more remote ones. Attention and concentration are impaired and the patient may fatigue readily. In the early stages there may be affective changes including anxiety, depres-sion, agitation and hypochondriacal preoccup-ations. Organic lability tends to occur in dementias of vascular origin. There are changes in behaviour, with the emergence of new and alien behaviour patterns such as disinhibited sexual activity, ag-gressiveness and attention-seeking hypochon-driasis. Hygiene and personal appearance are neg-lected, feeding habits deteriorate and incontinence of urine and faeces may supervene. There is a progressive loss of self-care skills in such fields as washing, bathing and shaving. Sleep patterns may be severely disrupted with some patients turning night into day. Awareness is impaired and judge-ment and insight are progressively lost.

The diagnosis of dementia in mentally retarded patients depends on eliciting a history of decline. For the diagnosis to be established, therefore, it is necessary to know the patient's premorbid level of intellectual functioning, social competence and self-care skills. There may be difficulties in this, particu-larly in more severely mentally retarded patients whose previous level of ability may have been very modest.

The differential diagnosis and investigation of dementia in mentally retarded patients involves a good clinical history with particular attention to the evolution of the disorder, backed up by careful physical examination to identify any neurological signs and such physical symptoms as high blood pressure, uraemia and hepatic insufficiency. Chest and skull X-ray, full blood examination with folic acid and vitamin B_{12} assays, urea, electrolytes and liver function tests, precipitation tests and thyroid function tests should all be carried out. EEG examination, particularly if repeated over a period of time, may help establish the diagnosis: increasing and generalized slow-wave activity including delta frequency components is highly suggestive of a dementing process. Cerebral angiography may identify unilateral lesions such as a subdural haematoma or clarify the vasculature of a tumour. Many of these neuroradiological investigations have been superseded by computed tomographic scanning, which is non-invasive and which can identify with considerable accuracy the presence of brain atrophy.

Where a treatable cause of dementia can be established, treatment is directed in the first instance to the underlying condition, for example hypothyroidism or conditions such as cerebral tumour or subdural haematoma. More usually no treatable pathology can be identified and treatment then is symptomatic and aimed at controlling insomnia through the use of sedatives such as chloral hydrate, oxazepam or chlormethiazole, and daytime restlessness through tranquillizing agents such as thioridazine. The maintenance of good physical health, and the treatment of anaemia and urinary or chest infections, may be helpful and may sometimes serve to minimize the level of confusion. There is little point in attempting to reduce blood pressure in a patient with hypertension and establish multi-infarct dementia.

Where a senile or multi-infarct dementia develops in a mentally retarded patient who is already in hospital, then continuing nursing care should be delivered in that hospital. Where a dementia develops in a person with a mental handicap who is living in the community with his or her family then it may well be appropriate to organize care through the mainstream psychogeriatric services. This may include the day hospital, holiday relief admission and eventually longer term residential care in either the hospital psychogeriatric service or local authority home for the elderly, according to nursing and dependency needs.

John was aged 67 and severely mentally retarded. He had been looked after at home by his mother until she died and he was admitted to mental handicap hospital. He remained an inpatient for around ten years and then his sister took him to live with her when her husband died. They got on well for some years and then he began to deteriorate. His limited verbal ability diminished further and he had several small strokes. There were problems with nocturnal restlessness and getting lost within the house, and he became physically very frail. There were occasional episodes of incontinence of urine. He was referred for psychogeriatric assessment, started in attendance at the geriatric psychiatry day hospital and arrangements were made for intermittent short-stay admission to the psychogeriatric inpatient unit. This proved helpful to his sister and enabled her to continue with his care for some time, although eventually he required admission to longer-term inpatient hospital care.

NEUROTIC, CONDUCT AND PERSONALITY DISORDERS

It is uncommon to find conventional anxiety, obsessional and hysterical neuroses in mentally handicapped patients. Disturbances of conduct based on psychodynamic and interpersonal conflicts in the family, school or residential setting abound, however, and require elucidation and understanding. Classical psychoneurosis as observed in general adult psychiatry occurs rarely if at all.

In the matter of obsessional neurosis it requires a degree of intellectual sophistication to experience and describe the various components of true obsessional symptomatology, including the feeling of subjective compulsion, the struggle against compulsion and the retention of insight. This sophistication is beyond all but very marginally mentally handicapped people and it must be very uncommon to come across obsessional neurosis as such in a patient with any significant degree of intellectual retardation. On the other hand rituals, resistance to change and stereotyped patterns of behaviour do certainly occur, and frequently, in mentally retarded people. These rituals should not be confused with obsessions. They are often deeply engrained, pleasurable, actively sought after and there is no component of distress or struggle.

Hysterical symptoms are common and sometimes gross in retarded patients. This is probably a function of increased suggestibility. In day-to-day clinical practice the meaning and gains of hysterical symptomatology are usually readily apparent. Often hysterical symptoms, including trivial hypochondriasis, are simply attention-seeking. This can be a difficult problem in the setting of a living environment which may be overcrowded, understaffed, unstimulating and lacking in the opportunity for privacy. Sometimes florid hysterical symptoms, including regression to an infantile level of development, occur in the setting of stress and threat to feelings of inner security.

Beatrice was aged 35 and mildly mentally retarded. Although physically robust she had been cosseted and over-protected by her mother and brought up to regard herself as utterly incapable of holding her own in the community. She wanted nothing more than to be looked after. Whenever her inner dependency needs were threatened by the suggestion of rehabilitation, she regressed. At such times she would revert to an infantile pattern of behaviour, taking to her bed, curling up in the fetal position, wetting, soiling and wailing loudly. This proved a major problem for many years until it was eventually possible to inch her into a hostel-type setting where her dependency needs were satisfied and her lifestyle was more commensurate with her abilities.

Hysterical symptoms may also arise on the basis of an underlying affective disorder.

Treatment of hysterical symptoms should be directed in the first instance towards eliciting their meaning and significance to the patient, and modifying and relieving any precipitating and perpetuating factors when that is possible. Where hysterical symptomatology is arising on the basis of an underlying affective disorder, treatment should be directed towards relieving that disorder through appropriate antidepressant medication.

Neurotic disorders characterized by states of disproportionate anxiety, fearfulness, depression and phobias are also common in mentally retarded people. Phobias may be situation-specific as, for example, in school phobias. There is nothing distinctive about school phobia in a retarded as compared with a non-retarded child. The symptomatology is usually secondary to separation anxiety and may include a whole range of somatic symptoms including stomach pains and morning headaches which miraculously disappear later in the day when school has been avoided. Sometimes a phobia may be a very circumscribed phenomenon as, for example, in the little Down's syndrome boy who functioned socially at a good level considering the extent of his disability, but who was reluctant to leave the house because of a specific fear of dogs. This phobia responded rapidly to a behaviour therapy approach using desensitization. Adults with anxiety-based neurotic disorders may present with depression of mood, with self-injury or with various types of acting-out behaviour related to an inability to verbalize their difficulties. Anxiolytic drugs of the benzodiazepine group may be helpful in cases where anxiety is a prominent feature, although the benzodiazepines can generate dependency problems and it is prudent to use them in small doses and for limited periods of time.

Retarded patients of all ages frequently present with, for want of a better term, a conduct or behaviour disorder. These disorders are often related to conflicts or problems in the family, school or residential setting. The psychogenesis may be quite apparent to the observer, but they can prove very hard to modify. They are often the outcome of attitudes and ways of relating and handling of many years' duration, and they may be very deeply engrained.

Shona is aged 17 and severely mentally retarded. She comes from a middle-class family whose social life and ambitions are frustrated by her continuing dependency and obvious differentness. Her father copes by opting out, giving in to her and leaving the responsibility to her mother, who feels enormous resentment towards her daughter but overcompensates by being excessively conscientious and solicitous. Shona senses the underlying resentments and conflicts and reacts by exploiting and manipulating her parents. Behaviourally based intervention, carefully planned, monitored and sustained over a long period, has made little difference to the handling problem and Shona's chronic behaviour disorder persists. Likewise, a psychotherapeutic approach focusing on the family psychodynamics serves principally to support the mother but has not enabled change to take place.

Sometimes it is possible to intervene effectively, however.

Joyce, aged 25, is mildly retarded and comes from a large, caring, but not very intelligent family, who tend to over-protect and supervise her, thereby denying her the opportunity for growth and independent living. The emotional links in the family are strong and the parents are very concerned not to seem to be putting her away. In this setting Joyce misbehaved repeatedly, stripping off her clothes in public places, shouting and swearing loudly and running away, particularly at night. It was possible to explore the problems through interviews in the family group setting and thereby enable separation to take place without guilt or resentment. Joyce is now at the point of moving into a hostel placement with a view to eventual group home living in the community and her behaviour disorder has settled down meanwhile.

There are times when admission to residential care is the outcome of a severe behaviour disorder.

George, aged 35, is severely retarded with Down's syndrome. His parents are in their seventies and frail. As their circle of interests and activities contracted, so did his, to his immense irritation. He became very frustrated, negativistic and aggressive in his behaviour, soiling and refusing to dress or wash and he took to striking his elderly mother. His parents could not cope and eventually, much to their distress, there was no alternative but to admit him to hospital care, where he enjoyed the company and activities and his behaviour problem resolved completely. His parents still visit and he will go out with them for the day, but he is adamant that he will not return home on a longer-term basis.

Personality and temperament are important aspects of mental handicap about which little is known and there are major problems in defining what is meant by personality disorder in mentally retarded people. One form of personality disorder which is fairly widely recognized, however, is that of psychopathic or antisocial personality disorder. Psychopathy is defined in terms of a total disregard for social obligations, lack of feeling for others, impetuous violence or callous unconcern. The behaviour pattern should be such as to be regarded as abnormal within the peer or cultural group, and is not susceptible to modification through experience or punishment. Psychopathy is regarded as predominantly, but not exclusively, a male problem and this is certainly so in the field of mental retardation. By definition the term cannot be applied to patients with more than a mild degree of mental retardation since a certain level of intelligence is inherent in the diagnostic criteria. Some mildly mentally retarded psychopathic men may present major problems through sustained and seriously aggressive antisocial behaviour, sometimes including deviant sexual activities. They can give rise to serious management problems in whatever residential setting they are accommodated, be it home, hostel, mental handicap hospital, prison, secure unit or state hospital.

Personality disorders in retarded patients are not susceptible to curative treatment. Time may exert a beneficial effect, however, and many personality problems become less intrusive as the patient gets older. Management of personality disorders is difficult and demanding, and calls for qualities of insight into personal relationships, consistency, firmness or flexibility as appropriate, and imagination. Some nursing or residential care staff have an almost intuitive ability to handle patients with personality problems. Drugs have a relatively modest role although phenothiazines may take the edge off irritability and aggressiveness. Good anticonvulsant drug control in patients who are epileptic is obviously important. Appropriate social and recreational outlets are required, and structured, interesting and worthwhile activity can go a long way to minimize management problems. Conversely, boredom can result in the exacerbation of tensions and difficulties. For some patients a limit-setting approach may be necessary, with rewards and privileges tied to acceptable behaviour. There are times when containment is the only realistic goal, although more positive aims should be substituted as soon as possible.

FORENSIC PSYCHIATRY AND MENTAL HANDICAP

It is difficult to be precise about the nature of any relationship between mental retardation and criminality. Mentally retarded people tend to be suggestible and may as a result be led into petty criminality. They may be exploited by their partners in crime and led into taking the most risky roles. They are probably less successful in concealing their actions, less effective in getting away and more likely to be caught than their fellow criminals. These factors would tend to lead to overstatement of the connection between mental retardation and criminality. On the other hand, the police may well choose not to charge a person who is obviously mentally abnormal and frequently take such a person home or even direct to hospital. Likewise, courts tend preferentially to seek a hospital disposal. Against this background it is hard to assess the significance of reported prevalence rates for criminality among retarded people. The situation is further complicated by ambiguities and uncertainties about the diagnosis of retardation at the borderline level of intelligence, and by lack of

precision and consistency in many of the intelligence tests presently in use. Ostensibly it would seem that there is little direct link between defectiveness of intelligence and crime beyond sexual offences and arson, in which it does seem clear from wide-ranging criminological surveys that mentally retarded persons are more frequently implicated.

The explanation of the association between sex offences, arson and mental retardation is perhaps relatively simple. Sexual offences by retarded males are probably related to difficulty in finding suitable sexual partners, coupled with a reduced awareness and appreciation by the retarded person of the significance of his behaviour. A mildly retarded male is, for example, likely to have a normal sexual drive but to be an unattractive sexual partner for a normally intelligent female. He may find a retarded female partner and such relationships may be stable and supportive. Failing this, however, children may seem a more attainable and less daunting object of his sexual drive. Retarded women may be suggestible and gullible. They may be manipulated and exploited sexually and be vulnerable to casual sexual encounters and prostitution. Fire-raising may be related to the combination of thrill and child-like fascination with fire, allied to a similar lack of awareness and insight into the potentially appalling consequences of arson. Sex offences and fire-raising in mentally retarded patients may prove persistent and repetitive and require careful monitoring. Most such offences are fortunately trivial but some cause significant distress or damage and a few are attended by disastrous consequences.

The other forensic aspect of mental handicap which has recently aroused interest is that of the retarded person's ability to cope with normal police interrogation and custody procedures. It is well known that many retarded people are compliant, anxious to please and will say 'yes' to almost any suggestion if they think this is the reply the questioner wants. This suggestibility can be a major problem in the legal/judicial setting, where it is not uncommon for retarded people to confess to offences they have not committed to terminate stressful interview situations, or in naive endeavours to please. It is imperative that there should be recognized safeguards for retarded people in the matter of court procedures involving them and that these safeguards should be honoured.

TREATMENT APPROACHES

There are certain fairly well established psycho pharmacological treatment approaches to the mai functional and organic psychoses. These have been indicated at the appropriate point in the text of this chapter. Psychotropic drugs may also be helpful in the management of certain problem behaviours, for example abnormal aggressiveness, in the absence of a recognized psychiatric illness. The phenothiazine group of drugs, including chlorpromazine, and the butyrophenones such as haloperidol can prove significantly useful in this respect. Lithium may also exert a non-specific effect on aggressiveness and irritability, and there is some evidence to suggest that the newer anticonvulsant drugs, including carbamazepine, may have a place. The danger lies in the temptation to use drugs of these groups to control behaviour problems which are related to unsatisfactory living conditions and an unstimulating environment. In such circumstances the main thrust of treatment should be towards the improvement of these living conditions, but clinicians are often left in the unenviable position of being obliged to do the best they can within the constraints of limited resources. In general terms, it is good practice in the field of mental retardation to use psychotropic drugs sparingly, at minimal dose levels and to keep their continuing prescription under regular review.

There is also scope for far more input than has previously been considered possible in the field of psychotherapy. Individual in-depth analytical psychotherapy is probably inappropriate in view of the limitation in intellectual capacity, but simple group therapy and the harnessing of peer-group pressures can go a long way to minimizing socially unacceptable behaviour. It is also possible in the group setting to explore a wide range of topics related to independent living, such as financial management, housing, sexuality and the use of leisure time. Psychodynamic insights in the family setting may complement behaviour therapy, whereas each in isolation may be ineffective.

Behavioural treatments are also making a significant contribution to the management of disturbed behaviour in mentally retarded patients. Amongst the behaviour problems which can be approached through behaviourally based techniques are aggression, hyperactivity, stereotypy, self-injury and pica. The techniques used include identifying behaviour for acceleration and deceleration, enhancing attention span, rewarding an alternative activity, withdrawing socially rewarding responses to inappropriate behaviour, over-correction, obliging a patient to perform an incompatible response, isolation and the use of time-out and aversion. Helpful though these techniques are, none has proved reliable in all cases. The problem behaviour is rarely eliminated completely in the training situation and the improvement may fail to generalize satisfactorily to the less structured living environment. There are also ethical problems in the use of aversion techniques. Even so behavioural insights have made a valuable contribution to the understanding and management of behaviour problems in mentally handicapped people.

Any treatment approach has to be set against the context of the residential environment and the degree to which the mentally retarded person's rights as a human being are respected. All too often the residential environment falls short of acceptability and, far from enabling and promoting normal behaviour patterns, some living situations are positively anti-therapeutic. It is against this background that the philosophies of normalization and personalization and the advocacy movement have taken root. These have been admirable developments and have contributed much to progress over the last ten years. At times, however, these philosophies have tended to become items of faith and unconstructively adversarial, but they have served to draw attention to the imperative need for a civilized living environment which is conducive to personal development and socially acceptable behaviour. In the absence of such an environment the impact of clinical psychiatric and behavioural treatment approaches will be substantially diminished.

The specialist therapist professions also have an important contribution to make to the management of psychiatric and behaviour problems in retarded people. Frequently retardation is accompanied by defective development of speech and language. Speech defects may serve to identify a retarded person as abnormal and can lead to ridicule and ostracism, with much resulting unhappiness. Communication problems can generate frustration and tension which can be acted-out in socially unacceptable behaviour. Speech therapy can sometimes help with these problems by enhancing communicative abilities, either directly or through the use of such non-verbal means of communication as Makaton and Blissymbolics, and through fostering a residential milieu which is communication-based. Likewise physiotherapy and the provision of suitable aids to motility may enable a retarded person to partake of a wider circle of activities and social outlets, thereby relieving frustration and enhancing the quality of life. The specialist therapist professions have a direct and valuable contribution to make to the prevention and treatment of psychiatric and behaviour problems in mentally retarded people.

ORGANIZATION OF A PSYCHIATRIC SERVICE TO PEOPLE WITH MENTAL HANDICAP

The 1948 National Health Service Act brought the care of mentally handicapped people very much within the sphere of responsibility of the National Health Service. This was, to some extent, an accident of history, although the motives for the decision were humane. Mental handicap, however, crosses into the separate professional disciplines of education and social work, and over the last 30 years these disciplines have developed their own distinctive and more substantial contribution and expertise. Other disciplines including clinical and educational psychology, the specialist therapist and remedial professions, and the voluntary agencies, also have a valuable and increasing contribution to make. Along with these developments there has been a shift of emphasis away from the residential setting and towards the provision of facilities and services in the community. Mental handicap is therefore viewed in a very different perspective now than it was 30 years ago. The medical contribution is seen as much more focused and related to unique medical skills in such areas as diagnosis, developmental assessment and the delivery of specialist treatment and remedial procedures in infancy and early childhood, to the general medical care of vulnerable and physically disabled people of all ages, and to the diagnosis, assessment and treatment of psychiatric disorders in mentally handicapped children and adults. There are various possible organizational frameworks within which to deliver the psychiatric contribution. It can be delivered by a full-time specialist in the psychiatry of mental handicap, working with both children and adults and having a whole-time commitment in the field. An alternative framework is to integrate the psychiatric care of mentally retarded children into a comprehensive child psychiatric service and

the psychiatric care of mentally retarded adults into a comprehensive adult psychiatric service. There are arguments for and against each model and neither are mutually exclusive. In the end the deciding factor will be the quality of recruitment. Whatever the organizational pattern that emerges, the psychiatric input is likely to move increasingly in the direction of a consultative rather than a residential care responsibility, and this latter role will be reserved for a much more selected group of mentally handicapped people.

ACKNOWLEDGEMENT

I am grateful to the editor of *MEDICINE International* for permission to base parts of this chapter on my article 'Diagnostic problems in the mentally handicapped', which was published in *MEDICINE International* (1983) Vol. 1, pp. 1554–1557.

SUGGESTED FURTHER READING

Aman MG (1982) Stimulant drug effects in developmental disorders and hyperactivity: towards a resolution of disparate findings. *Journal of Autism and Developmental Disorders 12*: 385–398.

Day K (1983) A hospital-based psychiatric unit for mentally handicapped adults. *Mental Handicap 11*: 137–140.

Evans DP (1983) *The Lives of Mentally Retarded People*, Boulder, Colorado: Westview Press.

Gibbens TCN & Robertson G (1983) A survey of the criminal careers of hospital order patients. *British Journal of Psychiatry 143*: 362–369.

Reid AH (1982) *The Psychiatry of Mental Handicap*. London: Blackwell Scientific.

Reid AH (1983) Psychiatry of mental handicap: a review. *Journal of the Royal Society of Medicine 76*: 587–592.

Rutter M, Tizard J & Whitmore K (eds) (1970) *Education, Health and Behaviour*. London: Longman.

Sovner R & Hurley AD (1983) Do the mentally retarded suffer from affective illness? *Archives of General Psychiatry 40*: 61–67.

Tait D (1983) Mortality and dementia among ageing defectives. *Journal of Mental Deficiency Research 27*: 133–142.

Wing L (ed) (1976) *Early Childhood Autism*, 2nd edn. London: Pergamon.

Wing L & Gould J (1979) Severe impairments of social interaction and associated abnormalities in children: epidemiology and classification. *Journal of Autism and Developmental Disorders 9*: 11–29.

Chapter 29
The Role of the Speech Therapist

MARGARET WALKER

If we cannot communicate our needs, thoughts, feelings and desires to others then all our experiences, our opportunities for learning and indeed our overall quality of life are severely reduced. The development and maintenance of all human relationships depends on a shared means of communication. It is through this medium that parents, care-givers and teachers shape, expand, educate and support the child through all the experiences of life to adulthood. The success and manner in which daily living activities and work patterns are established, friendships and lasting relationships are made, and personality and individuality are expressed, depend largely on whether we can communicate adequately and whether the form of our communication is accepted and understood.

Frequently, people with a mental handicap have limited, inadequate or poorly developed communication. This causes great frustration for everyone but particularly for the individual. Often it will lead him or her to express this in antisocial and inappropriate behaviour, thus increasing the problem. The identification of the communication needs of a handicapped person and the planning of suitable remediation and management programmes must be given the highest priority and wherever possible should involve the expertise of a speech therapist.

The speech therapist

The title of speech therapist is rather confusing. It suggests that the therapist deals only with problems affecting speech and speech articulation. In reality, the speech therapist's work includes all aspects of human communication, across the entire age range. It covers simple communication, expressed by gesture, facial expression, grunts and sounds, eye contact and gaze, and complex language, expressed in speech, sign language, symbols, reading and writing.

Speech therapy training differs from one country to another. In the United Kingdom and the Irish Republic it is a specialized training course at degree level. It involves the theoretical study of the development of the various forms of human communication, the factors which influence them and the problems which will interfere with development or are acquired. Training in treatment methods and procedures is given and practical experience is gained in clinical and educational environments. Related subjects such as psychology, neurology, anatomy, physiology, linguistics and phonetics are also studied in considerable depth.

When qualified, speech therapists work alongside parents, teachers, psychologists, nurses, occupational and physiotherapists, nurses and doctors in schools, hospitals, special units and centres with a variety of children and adults with communication problems. These may include developmental language delay, voice production problems, cleft palate, stammering, hearing losses, speech defects, mental handicap, autism, cerebral palsy and acquired problems resulting from a 'stroke', laryngectomy, and other neurological diseases or traumas.

Some speech therapists work as members of a team of professional workers specializing in a particular area of handicap, such as mental handicap, child development or adult rehabilitation.

The speech therapist in the field of mental handicap

The speech therapist brings to mental handicap a unique knowledge of human communication and its related problems which spans the entire age range, together with an understanding and appreciation of the important relationship between cognitive, physical, linguistic and psychological processes involved in gaining effective communication and language skills.

Mental handicap, in turn, will make special

demands on this knowledge and experience, as it does for any professional worker in the field. Because all the learning processes in mental handicap will be at a slower rate, the small stages through which the non-handicapped person passes smoothly and almost unnoticed will have greater significance. Information on the learning sequences of particular skills, the sub-skills or components which go into making up the skill and the relationship between one skill area and another will be of the greatest importance.

It will not be surprising, therefore, to find the speech therapist concentrating her attention at times on work areas that one would not expect. For example, she will, when working with mentally handicapped people of all ages, refer, if necessary, to the very early pre-speech communication that occurs between the mother and infant and which is in fact the foundation of all later communication. This may seem unusual, but it is during this early period of life that the reciprocal patterns of communication – turn-taking routines, use of eye contact and gaze to communicate and direct communication, use of pointing and gesture, sound-making and sound play – are established and upon which the later development of language depends (Grove and Walker, 1984). People with a mental handicap often miss out on some of the vital components at this early stage; this will hinder their communication development and the loss needs to be identified.

Another example of the breadth of a speech therapist's work in mental handicap and the need to look at related skills and sub-skills would be the programmes carried out on feeding and diet by speech therapists in close association with physiotherapists, dietitians, parents and other workers. Correcting such feeding patterns as sucking, swallowing and chewing has a direct connection with speech sound production. The precise movements of speech sounds and the rapid synchronization of sounds into words needs mature muscle function and tone, which is usually achieved from satisfactory feeding patterns.

There are five main areas to which the speech therapist contributes in mental handicap:

1 Assessment of a handicapped person's communication skills and needs.
2 Evaluation of assessment results and recommendations for remediation.
3 Sharing the information gained from the assessment and discussing recommendations with parents and other professionals.
4 Planning suitable remedial programmes where required and implementing programmes or advising and supporting others who may carry out the programmes instead of the speech therapist.
5 Contributing to an overall care plan for a person with a mental handicap, as a member of a team, for example a community mental handicap team, behaviour modification team, curriculum planning team for schools or social education centres or a computer-based learning programming team.

Let us look at each area in more detail.

ASSESSMENT

It is necessary first to define communication and language: communication is the process whereby messages are transmitted; language is the highest form of communication, where words/signs are used in a symbolic form and according to rules of grammar which enable an infinite number of meanings and propositions to be generated.

For purposes of assessment it is necessary to consider all forms of communication, including eye contact, gesture, single words, spoken language, sign language and so on, and to regard communication as a two-way process involving the person sending the message and the person receiving it (Walker, 1980).

There are many formal assessments and tests which the speech therapist may use in her assessment. Before starting, it will be necessary to consider what the assessment should tell us and, having established this, to choose appropriate assessment measures from those that are available, and where they are not, to use careful observation techniques.

The assessment should scrutinize the two aspects of the communication process, that is the input and output of both the handicapped person and those people in daily or frequent contact with him. Only by making the two aspects of the process compatible can effective communication be achieved. The kind of information required from the assessment will be:

1 How much does the handicapped person understand of our speech? If he does not seem to understand speech then what form of non-verbal communication used by us does he understand?
2 How much and in what manner does the handicapped person express himself? Are there additional handicaps, e.g. hearing loss, speech or

movement problems that interfere with production of speech or gestures?

3 How much of his speech or non-verbal communication can we understand and in what form? Is it always intelligible or only occasionally, or after many guesses, or only when the subject is known?

4 How do we communicate to him and what type of communication do we use? Is it at the level he will understand? Do we communicate appropriately as often as we could?

5 Can the handicapped person's communication skills be developed further? Can communication opportunities be increased? If so, how?

In an attempt to provide some of the answers to these questions the following areas are investigated: communication skills, associated cognitive learning processes, additional handicaps, communicative behaviour, and the communication used with the handicapped person.

Communication skills

Firstly, the speech therapist assesses the current level of the handicapped person's communication skills, on the following dimensions: (a) comprehension ability (understanding) and (b) expressive ability.

Formal assessments will be used (see references at the end of this chapter), but often a combination of formal assessments with clinical observation is the best way to gain a complete picture, because the range that the tests cover does not always adequately assess the full range of mental handicap, particularly for the profoundly handicapped person. Reference is also made to checklists and to developmental programmes which cover the development of early communication skills (see references).

The objective at this stage is to gain details of the form of communication that the person understands and uses. The range will be very wide and runs along a continuum of increasing complexity. It can include, for example, the handicapped person for whom speech and signing is too difficult, who relies only on rituals and cues from routine patterns of care, tone of voice, touch and so forth in order to be able to comply and who makes his feelings and needs known by very basic means – laughing, grunting, screaming, pushing, pulling and resisting. Even at such a basic level of communication, details will be needed of the precise cues the person follows, and the variations in, for example, vocal tone and touch to which he will respond, as well as some idea

of the intentions he has behind the laughing, screaming, pushing and so on. By contrast, someone who has developed an understanding of spoken language, and has good expressive speech, will need a completely different kind of assessment. It will be necessary to analyse sentence length, linguistic structure, vocabulary range and speech or sign quality to assess if these are as effective as they could be.

Associated cognitive learning processes

Many cognitive processes are intricately woven into the acquisition of communication skills, so an assessment of communication skills should include information about these processes because of the relevance they have in programme planning. The processes to be assessed are:

1 Length of attention and concentration span.
2 Length of auditory and visual short-term memory.
3 Visual and auditory perception (recognition).
4 The ability to retrieve and recall information that has been learnt.
5 The ability to form associations, to generalize and to categorize concepts.

From observation of the handicapped person and experience gained during the assessment the speech therapist will form an impression of the person's abilities in these areas, but more specific information needs, if possible, to be obtained. There are formal assessments (see references) which give some of this information, provided the range of the test suits the handicapped person's range of ability. If these are not suitable the speech therapist uses her clinical judgement based on observation and special assessments she devises herself.

Additional handicaps

If present or suspected any additional handicaps should be assessed, as these may be severely hindering the development and functional use of comprehension and expressive abilities. Some of the major associated handicaps are considered here.

Hearing loss. This can vary in degree from a mild to a profound loss, and the causes may be temporary or permanent. All hearing losses should be carefully investigated as early as possible because the effect on communication development is very serious. Even a mild to moderate loss will reduce concentration and understanding, slow down responses to sounds and speech and make speech-sound imitation very difficult. A severe-to-profound loss will seriously interfere with the acquisition of language development, both comprehension and expression. Other forms of language and communication methods, such as sign language and gesture, need to be introduced as early as possible, so that the handicapped person can develop effective communication through another medium.

Visual impairment. This will also vary in degree and will affect communication development according to its severity. Apart from the obvious handicap of not being able to see objects and people referred to clearly, the handicap, if severe, will seriously restrict opportunities to experience and explore the environment with the same freedom as a sighted person, so it may also restrict understanding of language.

Physical handicap. Physical problems which affect expressive communication may be part of a general problem of physical handicap or specific to the speech muscles or limbs. Speech production requires normal breath production and laryngeal movement and normal movement of tongue, lips and soft palate. Signing requires normal movement of one or both (preferably both) upper limbs, but, although fine movement is preferred, signing as used in a scheme such as the Makaton vocabulary can tolerate clumsy hand and finger movement and still be understood.

Immature speech sound production. This is quite common in mental handicap. It is unfortunate if this is allowed to persist as it reduces the quality of the handicapped person's expressive speech and sometimes causes unnecessary frustration and confusion. Care must be taken though to discriminate between what seems to be immature speech resulting from a lack of experience and opportunities to copy good speech models and receive correction and, on the other hand, an earlier stage in the acquisition of speech sounds, which is in keeping with the person's general level of development.

Specific articulatory disorders. Dysarthria results from neurological damage affecting the speech muscles and causes drooling, swallowing difficulties and clumsy tongue and lip movement. *Articulatory dyspraxia* results from neurological damage affecting the learning of speech patterns needed to produce speech sounds. Both dysarthria and articulatory dyspraxia will affect speech production

and may indirectly restrict language development. The extent of the restriction will depend on the severity of the disorder, and they require very careful assessment.

Cleft lip and/or palate. Cleft lip and/or palate can occur in association with mental handicap or in isolation. The cleft is usually repaired surgically, and results are generally successful, but sometimes lip and palatal movement can remain restricted and voice quality can remain hypernasal. Exercises may help or further plastic surgery may have to be carefully considered.

Specific language disorders. Dysphasia is a specific neurological disorder. The person with dysphasia has difficulty in appreciating the meaning of spoken language and in expressing his thoughts in language. It is a problem right at the centre of the language process and it varies in severity and may affect both comprehension and expressive language abilities or only one aspect. Dysphasia may be a congenital condition or acquired in later life as a result of brain damage, for example a stroke.

Language and communication difficulties are usually very prominent in a person who has *autism*. The severity of the difficulties will vary with the degree of autism that the person has. Since the person will have difficulty interpreting and coding in-coming stimuli and in personal inter-relationships, communication and language development is usually seriously affected. Stereotyped learning of communication skills often occurs and communicative behaviour is poorly developed.

Mental illness. A person with a mental handicap, like someone who is non-handicapped, may also experience a mental illness. This possibility has to be considered by the speech therapist, because some forms of mental illness can present as a speech and language disorder or as inappropriate communicative behaviour, as for example in schizophrenia, paranoia, personality disorders and depression. Pre-senile dementia is known to occur in middle-aged people with Down's Syndrome, and with the increase in life expectancy for people with this syndrome, the speech therapist may come into contact with it more than before.

The speech therapist's training equips her to assess most of the additional handicaps discussed above, but in practice she will refer some to other specialists with particular expertise amongst the team of professionals working in this field for their assessment, if this has not already been done. For example, she will refer a person with a suspected hearing loss to an audiologist for a full audiological report and refer a person with suspected visual impairment to an ophthalmologist. She will also discuss her results with other members of the team to compare the effect of an additional handicap on communication with the effect it has on function in other areas.

Communicative behaviour

It has already been mentioned that communication is a two-way process involving an interaction with someone else. For this to occur satisfactorily, not only must both partners in the interaction communicate at the same level, but they must transmit and receive the information within a subtle framework of behaviour patterns which are specific to human communication and to their respective cultures. Sometimes these skills are under-developed in a mentally handicapped person and he will need to be shown how to use the communication skills he has in a socially acceptable manner and to his advantage. Examples of this range from very basic needs, such as knowing how to respond and take turns in conversation, to the more sophisticated, such as knowing how to modulate his voice to suit the occasion and setting, knowing how to distance himself with people to whom he is speaking or signing, for example not coming too close and embarrassing someone, using appropriate vocabulary which is in keeping with his age (sometimes childish features are retained unnecessarily), knowing how to express his right to refuse things in an acceptable form, and knowing how to assert himself.

It is also necessary to assess the level of play in the young child and the level of imaginative ability in both the young child and the adult. The development of these abilities is closely related to communication development and provides opportunities to develop, practise and rehearse communicative behaviour essential for real-life experiences.

An assessment of communicative behaviour would not be complete without a measure of the handicapped person's motivation to communicate. In fact motivation underlies the incentive to learn. Many mentally handicapped people have a reduced motivation to communicate and it is very difficult but necessary to devise ways of making it a worthwhile and rewarding experience for them. A measure of how eager or disinclined a person is to communicate is essential for the future planning of

remediation programmes and it is also important to have information about the person's level of frustration at not being able to communicate and the negative ways in which they express their frustration.

Communication used with handicapped people

Finally, it is essential to assess the type of communication used by those in daily contact with the handicapped person – parents, care-givers, teachers, therapists and so on. There are no formal assessments to gather this information, so the handicapped person's needs, as revealed by the four areas of assessments discussed so far, and the communication experience provided for the handicapped person by his environment are compared. It will be necessary to obtain answers to the following questions.

1 What length of sentence, complexity and range of vocabulary is used in speaking to the handicapped person?
2 Is any augmentative communication used to support speech, such as gestures or signs? If so, details of the form and complexity are needed.
3 Is any type of alternative communication, for example a symbols board or picture board, used and at what level?
4 Are the topics of shared communication compatible with the handicapped person's experience and interests? Does education and training take this into account?
5 Is everyone aware of the communication needs of the person with additional handicaps? For example, in the case of a hearing loss, does everyone when conversing with him ensure that they are facing him, to provide the best opportunity for him to lip-read, to see facial expressions and read signs or gestures clearly?
6 What opportunities are there for communication and are these fully utilized? Assessment of the whole environment should be made, so other demands on parent and staff time and the ratio of staff to handicapped people need also to be realistically considered in relation to communication opportunities for the handicapped person.
7 Do parents, staff and any others involved have any background knowledge of communication development and any experience in skills-training procedure.

EVALUATION

It will be realized by now that there is enormous variation in the communication skills and needs of people who are described under the blanket term of mental handicap. This is why it is so vital to have a speech therapist assess in depth as described above, so that the handicapped person's skills and needs are individually identified. Having assessed the level and type of communication skills, the level of associated cognitive processes, the identification of any additional handicaps, the appropriateness and level of communicative behaviour, and the type and level of communication used in the environment of the handicapped person, the speech therapist will have a clear picture of the person's communicative ability and needs and the possible presence of any difficulties that may be interfering with the development. It is then necessary for her to evaluate the results.

First, a comparison will be made between the level of the handicapped person's communication skills and his general level of ability, for example, his self-help skills, occupation or work and his psychological assessment, if available. Ideally the communication skills and general ability should match fairly well, which would indicate that communication skills are developing or have developed in phase with other skill areas and that everything is satisfactory. More often than not the two do not compare evenly. Frequently the level of communication skills is below that of other areas, and the reason for this needs to be confirmed. Factors already revealed from the speech therapist's assessments, such as an additional handicap or poor environmental opportunities, may well account for this. Occasionally the reverse occurs: communication ability exceeds other areas of skills development, and in this case it serves as a target towards which other skills are aimed.

Second, the speech therapist will compare the handicapped person's levels of achievement for the various components that contribute to communicative ability, to ensure that they are all developing effectively. Comprehension ability will be compared with expressive ability and should ideally be the same, but allowance can be made if expressive ability is about three to six months behind comprehension ability. Attention span, memory retention for speech and the production of speech sound or signs should also be the same as the individual's overall level of ability.

After making these two comparisons the speech therapist will be able to summarize her findings and make recommendations where necessary for the introduction of a remediation programme, for corrective therapy, for the provision of a speech aid, or for specialized training and advice to be given to

parents or others. She will also look at the long-term plans being made for the handicapped person to see whether the handicapped person's opportunities to achieve these could be enhanced if his communication skills could be realistically extended.

SHARING ASSESSMENT RESULTS AND MAKING RECOMMENDATIONS FOR REMEDIATION

The results of the speech therapist's assessment and the recommendations she makes for remediation have great significance to the parents of a handicapped person and to professional workers and others. Generally, the speech therapist circulates a report providing this information and she is always prepared to allocate time to discuss the results and the implications for the handicapped person and those in close contact.

There are two applications of the information gained from the speech therapist's assessment. First, there is the broad application to communication in general use. Some examples of this would be:

1 The teacher working in a school with the handicapped person needs to take the speech therapist's results carefully into consideration as the teacher's level of communication used through all curriculum areas should be compatible with the child's level of communicative ability.
2 The nurse trainer or psychologist writing the instructions for a behaviour modification programme for dressing, toileting, feeding and so on needs to consider the speech therapist's results so that the instructions are appropriate to the person's level of communicative ability.
3 The parent or play-therapist needs to bear the speech therapist's information in mind when demonstrating a new toy or simply looking at a book with the handicapped person.

Secondly, there is the specific application within programmes devised by the speech therapist in close collaboration with parents and others to provide specific remediation, to correct, or encourage the development of certain communication skills.

PLANNING REMEDIAL PROGRAMMES AND IMPLEMENTATION

As a result of the comprehensive assessment, the speech therapist is able to select or devise programmes to cover the total needs of a handicapped person. This may comprise a series of approaches. For example, it could involve a specific programme to correct some elements of speech production, a language stimulation programme and advice on providing more extensive opportunities for communication experience. What she does have difficulty in achieving in some cases is finding sufficient time to implement all aspects of the programme.

Unfortunately, speech therapists working in mental handicap are often in short supply in the UK. As a result, those working in the field try to work as closely as possible with parents and other professionals to share their expertise so that the handicapped child or adult may receive sufficient and consistent training and stimulation. This can work very effectively for the training of basic skills and free the speech therapist to undertake specialized areas of treatment and remediation which need her unique expertise. It also has certain advantages in that it results in a wider group of people becoming more adept at using appropriate communication techniques and they in turn share their opinions and suggestions about the programmes with the therapist, which broadens her perspective of the work. A good example of this is the Makaton Vocabulary, which is a language programme devised by the author (see references) and which illustrates the widespread multi-disciplinary use of a speech therapy programme.

Speech therapists in mental handicap tend quite often to design their communication programmes with the active participation of other workers and parents in mind. Their programmes must therefore not only provide the essential stimulation for the handicapped person, but must be planned clearly for others to implement. Often preliminary training or demonstration of how to use the programmes is given first to the parents and professionals who will use them because experience and confidence has to be built up. Continued monitoring and support throughout the programme is essential in case modification is required.

One very large and dramatic change that has occurred in remediation programmes over the past ten years has been the introduction and now the widespread use of non-verbal communication systems, such as sign language and symbols, to support speech. Speech therapists in the UK have pioneered this work with colleagues from other professions. They recognized two needs:

1 The need to provide some handicapped people with an augmentative form of communication which would provide them with a method of communicating and which could be linked with speech and act as a facilitator.
2 A need to provide the multiply handicapped person with a symbol system of communication, because the nature of the handicap would make it impossible to speak or sign adequately.

The Makaton Vocabulary (see references) is a language programme which is generally used with speech and signing but can also be used with symbols. The signs used with the Makaton Vocabulary are from British Sign Language. The Makaton Vocabulary is the most widely used system throughout the UK and is attracting interest abroad. Makaton symbols have recently been developed to use with the vocabulary to provide communication for physically and intellectually handicapped people and as a link to reading.

Blissymbolics (see references) are used across the entire range of physically handicapped people as a very effective symbol communication system, and are used throughout the UK and abroad. The Blissymbolics organization have a wide range of practical and technical aids to assist in the use of Blissymbolics with extremely physically handicapped people.

Rebus symbols, either those from the Peabody Rebus Reading Scheme or new British rebuses (see references), are being found extremely useful to develop language and reading skills in children with a mental handicap, and rebus use is steadily growing throughout the UK.

THE SPEECH THERAPIST MEMBER OF THE TEAM

Mention has already been made of the speech therapist's role in sharing her skills, so it is not difficult to see how she will fit into any team of workers in mental handicap.

Many speech therapists contribute as members of a community mental handicap team, and a speech therapist can if necessary take on the role of key worker if she is considered to be the appropriate member; she will then enlist the services of other members where she considers it necessary.

A great deal of time and effort can be saved if it is possible to have a speech therapist involved in, for example, a behaviour modification planning team or curriculum planning team, as she can, by virtue of her training, anchor the programme plans to the level of the communication needs of the handicapped person, which is difficult to do when other, varied skills training is being planned.

Finally, because the speech therapist has established links with community speech therapy services, she is able to make a contribution to community-based programmes for mentally handicapped people. She can work with the very young handicapped child in the home with parents, establishing early communication programmes in association with other early areas of skills development, and she can support handicapped people newly integrated into society.

CONCLUSION

There have been speech therapists working in mental handicap for many years and, despite the numbers being few, they have made a major contribution to the quality of life of mentally handicapped people. The need to improve communication between the non-handicapped and handicapped person continues to be a challenge and is particularly relevant with the emphasis on the integration of more people with a mental handicap into society.

REFERENCES

Grove N & Walker M (1984) Communication before language. In Walker M (ed) *The Makaton Vocabulary Development Project Research Information Service II(2,3,4)*.

Walker M (1980) Communication. In Simon GB (ed) *The Modern Management of Mental Handicap.* pp. 151–173. Lancaster: MTP.

Language assessments, checklists and programmes

Reynell Developmental Language Scales (revised edn) Windsor, Berkshire: NFER–Nelson.

Bloom and Lahey Language Assessment and Programme. In Bloom L & Lahey M (1978) *Language Development and Language Disorders* Chichester, West Susses: Wiley.

LARSP. In Crystal D, Fletcher P & Garman M (1976) *The Grammatical Analysis of Language Disability: A Procedure for Assessment and Remediation* London: Edward Arnold.

The Carrow Test of Auditory Comprehension of Language. Windsor, Berkshire: NFER–Nelson.

Illinois Test of Psycholinguistic Abilities (revised edn) Windsor, Berkshire: NFER–Nelson.

The English Picture Vocabulary Test (EPVT) (Brimar & Dunn) Educational Evaluation Enterprises, Owre, Newham, Gloucestershire.

The British Picture Vocabulary Scales Windsor, Berkshire: NFER–Nelson.

PIP Developmental Charts (Jeffree & McConkey) Sevenoaks, Kent: Hodder & Stoughton.

The REEL Test – Receptive and Expressive Emergent Language Test (Bzoch & League) Henry Kimpton, Great Portland Street, London W1.

Sentence Comprehension Test (Wheldall, Mittler & Hobsbaum) Windsor, Berkshire: NFER–Nelson.

The Aston Index (2nd edition) (Newton & Thomson) Learning Development Aids, Wisbech, Cambridge.

First Words Language Programme (1979) (Gillham B) London: Allen & Unwin.

Two Words Together (1983) (Gillham B) London: Allen & Unwin.

Pre-Verbal Communication Schedule Thomas Coram Research Unit, 41 Brunswick Square, London WC1N 1AZ.

Sequenced Inventory of Communication Development (SICD) Windsor, Berkshire: NFER–Nelson.

Portage Project Windsor, Berkshire: NFER–Nelson.

Wessex Revised Portage Language Checklist Windsor, Berkshire: NFER–Nelson.

Derbyshire Language Scheme Mark Masidlover, Educational Psychology Service, Amber Valley & Erewash Area Education Office, Grosvenor Road, Ripley, Derby DE5 3JE.

Makaton Vocabulary (see below for address, etc.).

Bereweeke Skill Teaching System Windsor, Berkshire: NFER–Nelson.

Early Language Training Programme for the mentally handicapped child Drake Educational Associates, 212 Whitchurch Road, Cardiff CF4 3NB.

Feeding

Helping the handicapped child with early feeding (Warner J) Winslow Press, 23 Horn Street, Winslow, Bucks MK18 3AP.

Behaviour checklists

Behaviour Assessment Battery (BAB) (Kiernan & Jones) Windsor, Berkshire: NFER–Nelson.

Communication Behaviour Rating Curriculum In Leeming, Swann, Coupe & Mittler *Teaching Language and Communication to the Mentally Handicapped* Schools Council Curriculum Bulletin 8. London: Evans/Methuen Educational.

Play

Symbolic Play Test: Experimental Edition (Lowe & Costello) Windsor, Berkshire: NFER–Nelson.

Assessments for dyspraxia, dysarthria and dysphasia

Nuffield Dyspraxia Programme Nuffield Centre, Royal National Throat, Ear and Nose Hospital, Grays Inn Road, London WC1.

Frenchay Dysarthria Assessment (Enderby P) Windsor, Berkshire: NFER–Nelson.

Minnesota Test for Differential Diagnosis of Aphasia (Schuell) Windsor, Berkshire: NFER–Nelson.

Alternative and augmentative communication systems

Blissymbolics Information from Mrs E Davies, National Advisor, Blissymbolics Communication Centre (UK), South Glamorgan Institute of Higher Education, Western Avenue, Llandaff, Cardiff CF5 2YB.

Makaton Vocabulary Information from Mrs M Walker, Director, Makaton Vocabulary Development Project, 31 Firwood Drive, Camberley, Surrey.

Learning with Rebuses – Glossary of Rebus and Teaching Packs (developed in the UK by Judy van Oosteram and Kath Devereaux) EARO, The Resource Centre, Back Hill, Ely, Cambridgeshire CB7 4DA.

Peabody Rebus Reading Program (1967) (Woodcock RW) American Guidance Service. Available from NFER–Nelson, Windsor, Berkshire.

Information on UK speech therapy services

Local level. District Speech Therapist, Local Health District Offices.

National level. College of Speech Therapists, Harold Poster House, 6 Lechmere Road, London NW2 5BU.

Chapter 30
The Role of the Physiotherapist

BRENDA BLYTHE

The physiotherapist working in the field of mental handicap has a broad and challenging role. She has at her disposal a range of specialist treatments with which she can considerably improve her patient's quality of life. She must assess not only his current problem, but his present and future expectations in order to help him to achieve the satisfaction of as independent a lifestyle as possible. She must observe his physical abilities, allowing for psychological, psychiatric and environmental constraints. Her treatment plan can range from intensive physical therapy and the selection of aids for a cerebral-palsied child in hospital to the discussion of a change in diet and exercise habits for a mildly handicapped overweight community client.

ASSESSMENT

The aim of physiotherapy assessment is to establish the extent of function, control of movement and range of physical abilities and to define the limitations imposed by the handicap and its underlying cause. The assessment is divisible into three stages:

1 *Symptom analysis* – how the therapist describes the disability and its effects.
2 *Physical examination* – physical examination of the patient and observation of his signs.
3 *Interpretation* – the evaluation of all available information, including the reports of other professionals, consideration of possible drug side-effects and the formulation of a treatment plan.

Symptom analysis

This can be the most difficult stage, as the person with mental handicap often does not complain of pain and may be unable to define its site. He may feel apprehensive about being assessed, or inhibited by the presence of family or care-workers. The therapist must make the occasion informal and

allow the patient to talk to her alone, where appropriate.

There are advantages if the initial assessment of a community client takes place in his own home. Here the therapist can evaluate environmental factors which may affect treatment. The therapist will usually have to rely on a case history given by the family or care-workers, and must take into account the emotional relationship between the informant and client. The family may not have come to terms with the realities of the handicap, or they may have unreasonable expectations of future development and an overoptimistic view of treatment benefits. They may be overprotective and consequently deny him the opportunity to develop self-help skills. It is therefore essential to discuss every aspect of the proposed treatment plan with all the carers to ensure a similar standard of expectation.

Physical examination

Observation

The ambulant mildly handicapped adult. Watch him carefully as he comes into the room and sits down. Study his face for unusual pallor or cyanosis, grimacing, orofacial dyskinesia, wincing or festinant gait. Is there abnormal posture to protect a painful area? Is there unequal weight distribution as he walks? What footwear does he have? How does he cope with a step or the edge of the carpet? Is he breathless if he has come upstairs? Watch if he chooses a high or low chair. How good is his muscle control and spatial awareness as he sits down. Can he coordinate the requisite fine movements if he is given a cup of tea?

The non-ambulant severely handicapped child. The therapist should watch the child unobtrusively in his own surroundings. She should talk at length to his parents, encouraging them both to be involved and discover what they consider to be the biggest problem looking after their child. If the therapist relates her treatment to their needs and the child's, they will be more willing to incorporate her suggestions into home routine. They may like to know of other parents with similar problems.

Is the child's resting position normal? Does he consistently return to an abnormal position (Levitt, 1977)? Are his active movements within the normal range for his chronological age? At what level is he functioning? There is considerable variation within the developmental norm, and some children miss out stages completely. Observe the child's reaction to his environment. Does he watch other children, moving himself if necessary to do this?

There are many different methods of recording assessment findings (Holt, 1965; Holt and Reynell, 1967; Sheridan, 1973; Finnie, 1976; Parry, 1980; Cheyne Centre for Spastic Children, 1985; Portage, 1985) and an accurate record will take time to compile and should be regularly up-dated, but it is an essential part of management. During the assessment of daily living skills the therapist should observe and note the degree of help required and use of aids, so that she may later decide whether these should be retained or phased out during treatment progression.

Physical testing

This should always be done with the minimum discomfort to the patient, and an appropriate explanation, particularly when clothing is being removed. The room should be warm and quiet, and the therapist unhurried. Key areas to be investigated will be obvious from the medical history, X-ray reports and so forth.

The skeletal system. When joint involvement is suspected, look for oedema, bruising, muscle wasting and deformity. Palpate for signs of soft tissue injury and crepitation and measure joint range. Loss of function is often the only relevant factor to the patient, who measures recovery by freedom from pain and return of skills.

When deformity is present the therapist must decide if it is due to recent change in posture to relieve pain, which the patient can correct himself, or whether it is of longer standing with adaptive soft tissue changes and bony damage. It may be possible to modify some soft tissue changes, for example by regular icing of spastic muscles, but orthopaedic intervention is necessary to modify bony damage. Hip replacements have been found to be very

successful, but the postoperative positioning and exercise required after soft-tissue correction such as adductor tenotomy is more difficult to achieve.

The respiratory system. People with mental handicap, both at home and in residential care, often do not have the opportunity, motivation or encouragement to take adequate exercise. Consequently they are prone to an above-average incidence of chest infections and respiratory problems. This is particularly relevant in Down's patients, whose predisposition to chest infections (Kirman and Bicknell, 1975) is often combined with hypotonia (Cowie, 1970), which makes movement slow and more difficult, especially if there is an additional congenital heart abnormality (Kirman, 1976). They also have difficulty blowing their nose, and so often have catarrhal congestion.

If there is chest deformity there will be diminished capacity and decreased exercise tolerance. Count the respiration rate (it should be 16–20 per minute). Listen to the breathing sounds and watch for dyspnoea or signs of pain. Feel chest movement whilst the patient is in long sitting (with the back supported and a small pillow under the knees), encourage regular slow breathing by manual pressure, with intermittent rests to prevent hyperventilation. Note if he has a dry cough due to irritation. If sputum is present encourage expectoration. If blood is coughed up it should be reported as it may indicate a serious underlying condition (Cash, 1959). If the patient has difficulties understanding instructions it is easier to assess exercise tolerance during functional activities.

The nervous system. There is often a scattered distribution of physical abilities and deficits, and certain signs, symptoms and tests can tell the therapist if the lesion is of the central or peripheral nervous system. An assessment should be made of sensory abilities and deficits, proprioceptive senses and stereognosis (Bannister, 1969). Passive limb extension will demonstrate muscle resistance, and reflexes should be tested to further assess muscle tone and the state of nerve conductivity. Test for Babinski's sign by stroking the outer border of the sole of the foot. Normally after about a year the first toe will plantarflex and the foot will dorsiflex (Cash, 1977). If spasticity is present the whole foot will dorsiflex, with flexion at the hip and knee (Draper, 1965).

If there is loss of sensation it is important to alert the patient and carers and pad and cover high-risk areas to prevent injury.

Coordinated voluntary movements should be tested, and the ability to maintain posture and balance assessed. Variations in gait are significant; for instance, a broad-based gait may indicate loco-motor ataxia (Gardiner, 1959). Muscle power should be tested according to the Medical Research Council gradings 0–5.

Interpretation

The therapist must now collate all the evidence of her own investigations and those of her colleagues in other disciplines, and plan the treatment that will promote maximum improvement in her patient's quality of life. This may include environmental changes like structural alterations to his accom-modation, or persuading over-protective parents to let their epileptic child swim or ride a bicycle. The patient's potential can be achieved through habili-tation (promoting body control and abilities to cope with the environment or adapting the immediate environment to accommodate body control) or rehabilitation (redeveloping control and abilities which may have been lost through injury or loss of opportunity for use). To be effective the treatment should become part of the patient's way of life, and only if it is consistently encouraged and reinforced can there be any realistic hope of sustained improvement.

TREATMENT

Treatment can be divided into broad categories, each designed to promote fuller participation in life skills and the development of personal independence:

1 Mobility – (a) body control and movement; (b) walking, (c) footwear, and (d) wheelchairs.
2 Eating.
3 Toilet training.

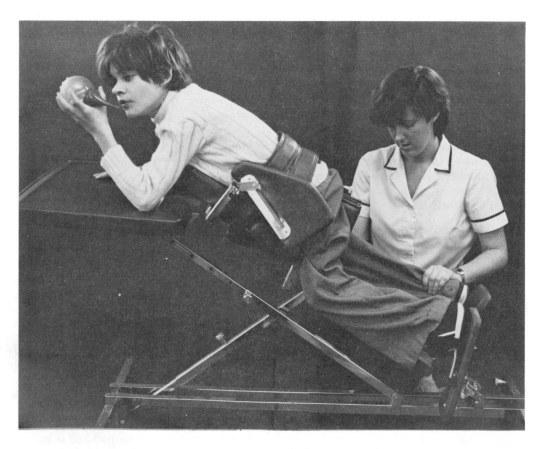

Fig. 30.1 Extension in orthokinetic inclined stander.

4 Dressing.
5 Bathing.
6 Recreation.
7 Common medical conditions.

Mobility

Body control and movement

To be able to move a specific part of our body, we need to be able to stabilize the rest of it. It is the physiotherapist's role to assess and develop her patient's degree of control and the development of normal patterns when abnormal ones are present, eliminating these by positioning and aids*, to enable purposeful movements to be achieved. During the early stages mats, wedges, rolls, side-lying and inclined padded boards and crawlers may be used (Figure 30.1),[1, 2, 3, 4, 5] together with manual support and stimulation.

The most functional position for acquiring and using self-help skills is sitting, which provides a broad-based position with variable degrees of support. Failure of her child to sit up by six to nine months often causes a mother to bring the child to the attention of her doctor. The provision of the correct chair is crucial to the development of independent abilities and prevention of deformities due to prolonged poor posture and muscle imbalance. It should provide just sufficient support to complement the patient's muscular control, so that maximum function can be achieved. This can range from almost complete support in the highly adaptable Action chair[6] through the range of supportive Kirton chairs (Figure 30.2)[7] and Camp Tumbleform chairs[8] to rising-seat chairs[9] to assist the arthritic geriatric.

In addition to firm support in a mid-line position, each chair must be comfortable and stable and of correct size, depth and height, so that hips, knees and ankles are symmetrical and supported at 90° for functional activity sitting, except for children with extensor spasm thrust whose hips should be held at less than 90°. The chair arms and seat heights should be at the correct levels for the occupant and the working surfaces being used.

Arrange for the patient to try a selection of chairs[10, 11] and modifications; with the help of mobility allowance the multiply handicapped now

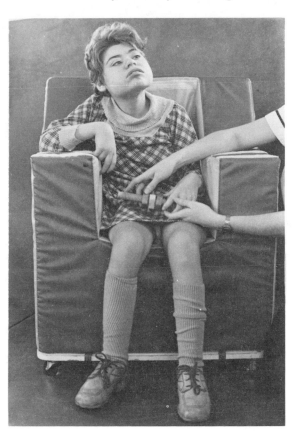

Fig 30.2 Kirton chair.

have an attractive range from which to choose. But, however well-fitting his chair, every patient should be encouraged to make frequent position changes; a change of visual or auditory stimulation can motivate the more handicapped. No chair should be so firmly fitting that it eliminates the 'fidget' factor.

The enjoyment of movement can be encouraged by hydrotherapy and water play. To promote maximum relaxation and consequent improvement in pain-free movement the water should be at 36°C (97°F), with a surrounding air temperature of 24°C (75°F). For severely physically handicapped patients the use of a shower trolley (Figure 30.3)[12] or chair and ramp avoids an awkward lift. For small groups or individual therapy a jacuzzi pool has the additional benefits of massage and circulatory stimulation.

Walking

'Will he walk?' is the question asked by every parent with a backward baby. It is the most demonstrable

---

* Sources of the equipment and aids mentioned are listed at the end of this chapter and indicated in the text by superscript numbers.

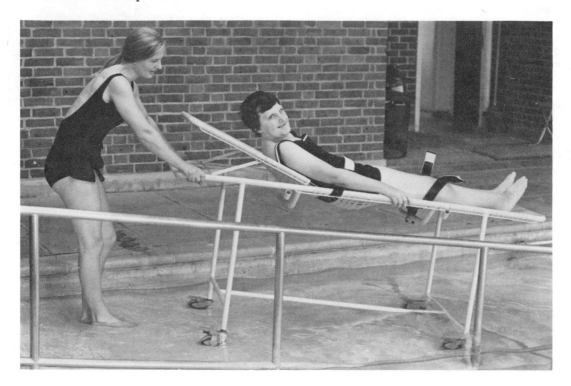

Fig. 30.3 Pool access by shower trolley.

sign of independence. Individual advice on how to encourage the child will be dependent on the handicap and can range from kicking and bicycling games for leg strengthening, to the use of standing frames[13] and boxes,[14] supportive footwear, 'cheyne' gaiters[15] for knee support, below-knee irons or full-length calipers, and exercises to promote interaction and coordination of the muscle groups within the postural reflex (Wittleman, 1965).

Sit-through baby-walkers[16,17] are useful to give the sensation of weight-bearing without transmitting the full body-weight through the legs, but should not be used long enough for the child to become 'lazy'. Baby-bouncers are not recommended for spastic or athetoid children as they aggravate the existing abnormal movements. Push-along toys are helpful; they need two hands to propel and so promote symmetry and stability, but add weights so they do not tip. Give the child encouragement and opportunity, but only minimal physical help. Make achievements fun, but do not tire him out.

It has been said that people with mental handicap can be recognized by their 'institutional' gait. There

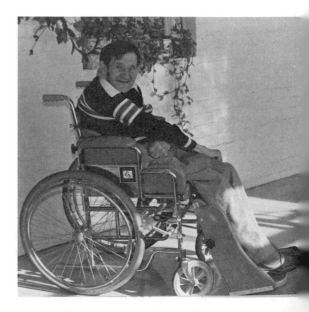

Fig. 30.4 Everest & Jennings Postura wheelchair.

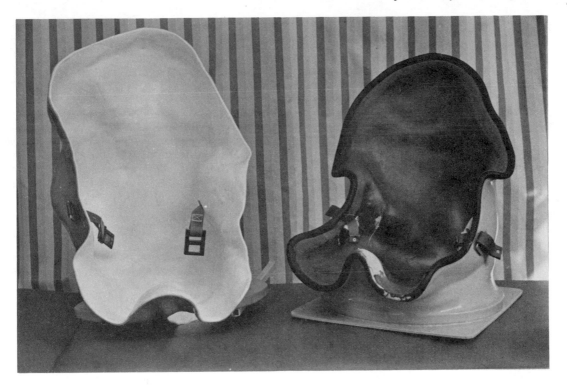

Fig. 30.5 Chailey Heritage moulded seats, the left hand seat shown before padding.

are many possible causes for abnormal gait patterns: orthopaedic conditions, muscle imbalance, lack of co-ordination, involuntary movements, psychiatric disability, chiropody problems and ill-fitting footwear, not to mention drug side-effects, for instance in the treatment of parkinsonism. Any pain, stiffness or tension will lead to immobility, slumping, stooping or awkwardness (Grieve, 1980, Figure 30.6).

Recent gait assessment research (Grieve, 1980; Little, 1981) has highlighted the use of checklists and designed manuals, ambulation profiles, foil walkways, gait mats and foot switches in addition to video film and the 'eyeball' analysis instinctively practised by all trained therapists. Treatment may include referral to an orthopaedic consultant, physical medicine specialist, chiropodist or psychiatrist. Within physiotherapy it may include the use of walking frames, such as the Atlas frame[18] for the hemiparetic who does not do well with tripod sticks, the Rollator,[19] to give maximum stability to the elderly confused, or a light-weight two-wheeled walker,[20] which is easier to turn and less likely to catch in the aptly-named and lethal slip mats or carpets.

The provision of the correct walking stick – equal in length to the distance from the distal crease of the patient's wrist to the ground (Sainsbury and Mulley, 1982) – can often give enough confidence to overcome mild unsteadiness and maintain independent mobility. Check that the handle is comfortable and the ferrule intact. Special retractable-spiked sticks are available for use in slippery conditions.[21]

Footwear

The provision of comfortable well-fitting footwear is one of the most fundamental but often overlooked ways of encouraging mobility, particularly in the elderly. Various problems must be accommodated, from basic orthopaedics to fitting the typical short, wide, deep flat feet of the Down's syndrome patient. People with mental handicap do not often complain of foot problems, so careworkers must be particularly vigilant. The intervention of an orthopaedic surgeon and regular chiropody can minimize the need for special footwear.

The therapist should have knowledge of a wide selection of footwear. Each patient must be carefully measured, noting the depth, length and width

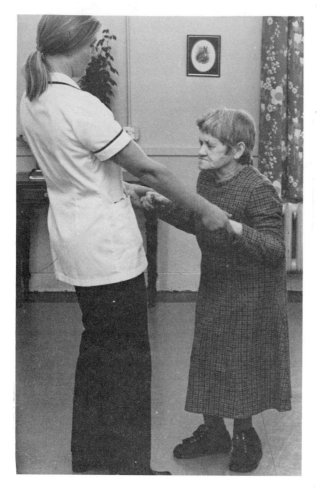

Fig. 30.6 Physical support.

of the foot, shape of heel and size of ankle. Some suppliers provide an 'odd' size service[11] and one will convert a right or left shoe to the opposite.[22] To protect against excessive damage, footwear can be fitted with toe or welt guards, or sprayed with Shoeguard.[23] Piedro boots give ankle support, but Biffa boots or John Locke[24] shoes may be sufficient, with heel floats or sole wedges to ensure correctly balanced weight-bearing. Patients are more likely to wear attractive footwear that they have helped to choose for themselves. Drushoes[24] provide foot protection for non-ambulant patients, and for cold weather lined lambswool bootees give extra warmth.[25, 26]

Wheelchairs

Choose a wheelchair that gives maximum safe independence – robust for outdoor use, lightweight and narrow for home. Let the patient feel the difference between chairs with propelling wheels at the front or the back. Which is more comfortable and stable? Which can he control? Check that his back, thighs and feet are well-supported. Does he need a pommel, footbox, thoracic cushions, head support or shoulder harness in addition to a lap strap? Always have a shoulder harness with two attachment points front and back, to prevent chafing at the neck, and to allow for adjustment for winter clothes. Will he need folding or removable footrests, desk arms or a tray? Would he benefit from protective hand mittens?[27]

For the more severely handicapped, choose a well padded supportive chair to promote a corrective and functional position (Figure 30.4)[28]. For those needing additional support within their wheelchair, a moulded (Figure 30.5)[29,30,31] or matrix[32] seat should be considered.

Eating

Eating provides a popular focus of social interaction which people with mental handicap share. The appropriate training and utensils can help to ensure social acceptability in community life. Valuable modelling can be encouraged in residential units by arranging for staff to eat with residents free of charge.

The physiotherapist helps formulate eating programmes by advising on a firm well-supported midline sitting position (see 'Body control and movement', above) for the physically handicapped and assessing and encouraging the patient's ability to achieve independent hand, arm, head and jaw and eye–hand coordination. During the training period it may be appropriate for the patient to use wide or loophandled cutlery, deep-shaped Manoy plates, Dycem non-slip mats and adapted cups[5] to maximize weak movements, or give direction and function to inaccurate ones, but aim to progress to conventional utensils. Over-protective families should be firmly discouraged from helping unnecessarily.

Toilet training

Two fundamental questions need to be answered before embarking on toilet training. Does the patient have primary incontinence due to a neurological developmental lag or secondary incontinence, usually of emotional or drug-induced origin? Is it realistic to expect continence, or should the therapist offer practical advice on incontinence aids to minimize the patient's discomfort and the relative's embarrassment?

Why has continence not been achieved? The normal child does not indicate his need to go to the toilet until he is a year old, and may not have full bladder control until eight years old. Can the patient get himself to the toilet? Can he indicate his need in time for someone to take him? He may need a walking aid, which should be kept within reach at all times. Are the toilet doors wide enough for a wheelchair, and can he transfer safely, or are handrails needed? Is the seat height right? Can he balance and cope with clothing or would elasticated trousers or Velcro fastenings help him to become independent?

Having dealt with the practical aspects, start a routine of regular potting or toileting, giving appropriate verbal praise, or if communication is a problem, use the same word or sign for toilet each time. Discard the protective pads during this stage to make him more aware of accidents. Full continence takes longer to achieve in the handicapped, particularly for boys, and there will inevitably be setbacks and accidents.

With secondary incontinence it is important to obtain a detailed history of loss of continence. It often relates to changes in routine or to domestic upheaval. Medical investigation should be done to rule out infective or metabolic aetiologies, after which a programme of behaviour modification and regular toileting with reinforcements and rewards can be tried, in conjunction with the use of appliances.[11]

Dressing

Everyone has preferences for particular clothes, but people with mental handicap may need advice on selecting styles that make independent dressing easier and synthetic materials like Courtelle and Terylene that will withstand regular laundry care, particularly for those with incontinence problems.

Choose light, warm, loose-fitting clothes, with wide neck and armholes to encourage those who find dressing slow and difficult. Incorporate front-fastenings, Velcro and zips in seams or with large ring pulls for those with coordination problems.[11] Long-handled dressing hooks, shoehorns and stocking aids may help. Choose non-flammable materials where available.

For wheelchair users use short front-opening jackets and sweaters, with extra width across the back, and well-fitting sleeves for those who self-propel. Poncho tops and warm leg muffs are good for winter use, and those with poor circulation, and are not as hazardous as trailing blankets.[25, 26]

See how far the patient can dress himself, identify the problem areas and plan a daily routine. A secure position is essential. For the severely cerebral-palsied child a side-lying position may be best, minimizing extensor thrust and allowing head and shoulders to be brought forward more easily and the limbs to bend. If a sitting position is possible, see that the back is well-supported and the hips well flexed. A stool may be sufficient for the less handicapped, against the wall or near a safety rail, if necessary. Let the patient have the satisfaction of achieving the final stage of putting on each garment, and progress to leaving more of the task to finish. Always dress the less mobile arm or leg first in patients with hemiplegia, or similar disability, and undress that limb last.

Bathing

A warm bath is one of the most pleasurable activities of self-care. How intensified this satisfaction must be for the sensorily deprived multiply handicapped person, who cannot complain that he is hot and sticky or cold and stiff and is unable to alter his position. To gain maximum relaxation and benefit the wheelchair user's transfer in and out of his bath must be smooth and secure. The Aquajac[33] bath seat offers this. It consists of a seat on a vacuum cushion, which can be raised to bath side height for transfer, and then lowered into the water. It is a compact and portable aid for home use, as an alternative to the many designs of hoist (Chartered Society of Physiotherapy, 1975), and avoids the need for gantries and frames. As another alternative, the side-opening Parker bath[34] allows sitting transfer from a wheelchair, and then pivots backwards to allow immersion. For the mildly handicapped, bath steps, bath seating and a non-slip mat or non-slip flower shapes[35] may be sufficient.

These aids and the provision of showers and seats[36] will allow the patient the dignity of maximum independence in bathing, but care should be taken to check water temperature, particularly for those with sensory deprivations. Check non-slip floor surrounds and the accessibility of an alarm and someone within earshot for the epileptic patient. The provision of medicated bath lotion will be of benefit to Down's syndrome patients and others with similar dry skin problems.

Recreation

The Year of the Disabled awoke an awareness of the sporting and recreational needs of people with mental handicap. Several specialist organizations were already providing some of these facilities. The Riding for the Disabled Association (Chartered Society of Physiotherapy, 1975; Walker, 1978) provides both the physical benefits and challenges of coordination and balance required to master a new dimension of movement and the opportunity to establish a rapport with the pony, that can fulfil a communication need that some handicapped people find difficult to express.[37]

Many people find personal fulfilment through swimming (Cadogan, 1978). In addition to the physical benefits (see 'Body control and movement', above) an integrated swimming club offers the opportunity to compete on equal terms with non-handicapped members, and this shared enjoyment will promote personal confidence and further community integration. Initially the therapist can encourage the handicapped person to enjoy the water by giving physical support. This must be done with care and empathy, as some people with mental handicap find touch intrusive. Once confidence grows, buoyancy aids can be used as required. Epileptic swimmers should always retain their aids and be accompanied in the water.

Music and movement is another field in which the natural abilities find rewarding expression. This can range from the shared pleasure of listening to classical music together to the familiar action songs of a one-to-one assisted movement class (Davies, 1981).

Play therapy cannot start too soon. Every child, from about six weeks, learns through simple repetitive games, and vocalizing when given attention. How much more essential is the stimulation for the backward child. An interesting way of providing this has been their integration into playgroups with non-handicapped children (Lovell, 1973). Initially the therapist will usually need to teach the skill or guide the handicapped to use toys (Upton, 1979), but there is a strong incentive to copy other children's activities which promotes participation and interaction within their peer groups.

Yoga is of benefit to patient and therapist alike. Every physiotherapist can bring many of its advantages to her patients by incorporating yoga principles in her work, but she should submit herself to careful instruction before attempting to teach advanced postures. The calm, deliberate 'slow-motion' approach of yoga in 'which the restless mind is calmed and the energy directed into constructive channels' (Iyengar, 1970) is particularly appropriate for the tense and anxious. They will benefit from improved circulation and muscle tone, better breathing control and restful sleep, in addition to a feeling of improved well-being and decrease in tension. Instruction should be to a small group in a quiet, pleasant room, warm but airy and free from interruptions and distractions.

Horticultural success and pleasure can range from the individual with a collection of cacti to the commercial level of the Kehelland Horticultural Centre on a 16-acre site near Camborne in Cornwall (Hills, 1983). The sale of produce covers the running costs of the centre, which trains twenty-four workers with mental handicap. The projects of the Home Farm Trust and Camphill Villages offer similar creative opportunities for natural gardening talents and country crafts. On a smaller scale, but growing in popularity, is wheelchair gardening. The therapist can share her patients' challenge to find the most appropriate wheelchair and special tools – desk arms and the narrow Streamliner chair giving easier access to raised garden beds or greenhouse, and long-handled tools to extend reach (Chaplin, 1973; Disabled Living Foundation, 1972; Growth Point).[11]

Common medical conditions

People with mental handicap have a higher incidence of medical problems, and will require a simplified explanation of proposed treatment, and particular care if electrical treatment is contemplated. It must be established that the patient understands that he must not touch the equipment, will be able to comprehend and report any feeling of discomfort, and will not endanger himself if he has an epileptic fit during treatment.

Chest complications

These can often be successfully treated by postural drainage and percussion (Cash, 1959) in conjunction with antibiotics. Expectoration can be encouraged in children by a variety of play activities, and increased chest expansion can be encouraged by blowing games. For older patients, a programme of bending and stretching activities can be devised, remembering that exercise tolerance may be limited in Down's syndrome patients with heart defects.

Varicose ulcers

Varicose leg ulcers are an additional hazard to the sedentary patient who is not encouraged to keep mobile and active. Encouraging the elderly to walk to the toilet independently is an excellent prophylactic. It is vital to instigate early treatment at the first sign of ulcer formation. The use of protective sheepskin and water beds and a regimen of ultraviolet light treatment, surrounding tissue massage and elevation have been found to be of benefit, together with the application of carbon dressings and zinc-oxide bandage to prevent the confused patient from irritating the wound.

Post-operative care

There is often intense apprehension post-operatively, magnified by the inevitable pain and possible restriction of movement through surgery, dressings or splinting. Reassurance is the first essential, ideally by a therapist who has been known to the patient prior to surgery and who would have prepared him for his ordeal. The appropriate chest therapy, passive and active exercise and rehabilitation often needs to be taken at a slower pace than usual, using appropriate rewards and encouragement. Shorter and more frequent therapy sessions than usual will be required, as the patient cannot be relied upon to continue his treatment independently.

Epilepsy

Physiotherapy has not yet evolved a treatment to diminish the number or severity of epileptic fits, except in a few anecdotal reports of diversional activities being able to prevent a fit from occurring. However, the therapist can provide a range of protective helmets which will minimize injury during a fall. The majority of these are made from circumferential strips of polythene, foam and leather secured by chin straps. For patients who habitually fall in a particular way, additional 'buffers' can be incorporated, or part-solid skull caps can be made. To minimize the social ostracism still sadly experienced by some epileptics wearing helmets, protective crowns have been designed to fit inside hats. An excellent form of camouflaged helmet has been developed by the David Lewis Centre, who mould an individual reinforced plaster-zote skull cap, which is then covered by a wig chosen to blend with the patient's natural colouring.[38]

Spasticity

In addition to the programme of supportive positioning and exercise outlined for spasticity in cerebral palsy, the application of ice is of considerable benefit. An ice pack is held over the appropriate muscle group by a towel for 10–15 minutes, followed by passive and active assisted movements. We have noted, as did Hartviksen (Lee and Warren, 1978), a reduction in muscle spasticity by this local application of cold. In one particular patient it resulted in the knee joint becoming sufficiently extensible to permit assisted weight-bearing and sessions in a standing frame, associated with all the benefits of an upright posture. Children tolerate these applications surprisingly well. They should take place in a warm room, with the patient comfortably dressed, except for the area to be treated. We use visually and auditorily stimulating toys to divert attention.

Arthritis

Warm wax baths have proved a safe and enjoyable form of pain-relieving therapy prior to the more active treatment of arthritic hands. Several of our patients with mental handicap have had successful total hip replacement for osteo-arthritis and knee arthrodesis, and have been able to re-learn a pain-free walking pattern.

Recent injuries

Patients with mental handicap often cannot understand the need for a particular post-trauma regime. It is therefore important that they receive early treatment reassurance and early return to pre-injury function, before deeply ingrained apprehension overcomes them and they lose the ability or forget the relevance of the temporarily lost skill. The use of ice is safer than ultrasound, as heat concentration may not be reported, and infrared treatment is similarly preferable to shortwave diathermy. For soft tissue injuries it has been found that silicone oil is an enjoyable treatment to promote early healing, as it is safe, soothing and non-invasive, in addition to its high-oxygen, fast healing properties.

Obesity

Once medical investigation has been done to establish the cause of obesity and the appropriate drug change or slimming agent has been prescribed, the physiotherapist should monitor a regimen of exercise and appropriate diet in conjunction with the dietitian. The cooperation of family and care-workers is essential as people with mental handicap often cannot understand the need for a selective diet, cannot discriminate between high- and low-calorie foods and have difficulty refusing foods they like if they are available.

DIFFERENT SETTINGS IN WHICH THE PHYSIOTHERAPIST MIGHT WORK WITH PEOPLE WITH MENTAL HANDICAP

The continuing trend over the past decade for people with mental handicap to retain or return to their rightful place in the community has brought a dramatic change in the physiotherapist's role. She will always have an essential contribution to make for long- and short-term residents in the special resource centres, not only promoting their independence and improved quality of life, but also as part of the multi-disciplinary team preparing them for appropriate community accommodation. This will include assessment and training, and evaluating the proposed placement and support services.

As more people with mental handicap remain within their families the therapist must expand her domiciliary role within the community mental handicap team, and increase her involvement in residential and day schools, hostels, day centres and group homes. She must have a working knowledge of the community social services, recreational facilities, district general hospital provisions and specialist centres' resources, and ensure that her client has access to each as required.

She must take a broad and flexible view to meet the new challenge of a changing role (Blythe, 1985).

ACKNOWLEDGEMENTS

I would like to thank Mrs L. M. Angel, Mr G. Blythe MBE, Mrs H. Gillam-Smith, Dr H. G. Kinnell, Mrs E. A. Oliver, Mr J. B. Oliver, Miss. L. Oliver, Mr H. L. Troughton and Miss J. E. Weller.

REFERENCES

Bannister R (1969) *Brian's Clinical Neurology.* Oxford: Oxford University Press.
Bluma S, Shearer M, Frohman A & Hilliard J *Portage Guide to Early Education.* Portage Project CESA 12, Box 564, Portage, WI 53901, USA.
Blythe BLG (1985) Physiotherapy and mental handicap. *Physiotherapy 71(3):* 115.

Cadogan DR (1978) Swimming: a physiotherapist's view. *Physiotherapy 64(11):* 325.
Cash JE (1959) *Textbook of Medical Conditions for Physiotherapists.* London: Faber & Faber.
Cash JE (1977) *Neurology for Physiotherapists.* London: Faber & Faber.
Chaplin M (1973) Gardening in rehabilitation. *Physiotherapy 59(3):* 80.
Chartered Society of Physiotherapy (1975) *Handling the Handicapped.* London: Chartered Society of Physiotherapy.
Cheyne Centre for Spastic Children (1985) *Physical Ability Chart.* Centre for Spastic Children, 61 Cheyne Walk, London.
Cowie V (1970) *A Study of the Early Development of Mongols.* Oxford: Pergamon.
Davies EM (1981) *Let's Get Moving.* Age Concern, Bernard Sunley House, 60 Pitcairn Road, Mitcham, Surrey.
Disabled Living Foundation (1972) *The Easy Path to Gardening* Disabled Living Foundation, 346 Kensington High St, London.
Draper IT (1965) *Lecture Notes on Neurology.* Oxford: Blackwell Scientific.
Finnie N (1976) *Handling the Young Cerebral Palsied Child at Home.* London: Heinemann Medical
Gardiner MD (1959) *The Principles of Exercise Therapy.* London: G Bell & Sons.
Grieve DW (1980) Monitoring gait. *British Journal of Hospital Medicine* (September): 198–203.
Growth Point Magazine Horticultural Therapy, Goulds Ground, Vallis Way, Frome, Somerset BA11 3DW.
Hills A (1983) Handicapped trainees down on the farm. *The Remedial Therapist.*
Hittleman RL (1965) *Be Young with Yoga.* A Thomas & Co.
Holt K (1965) *Assessment of Cerebral Palsy.* London: Lloyd-Luke.
Holt K & Reynell J (1967) *Assessment of Cerebral Palsy II.* London: Lloyd-Luke.
Iyengar BKS (1970) *Light on Yoga.* London: Allen and Unwin.
Kirman B (1976) General aspects of Down's syndrome. *Physiotherapy 62(1):* 6.
Kirman B & Bicknell J (1975) *Mental Handicap.* Edinburgh: Churchill Livingstone.
Lee JM & Warren MP (1978) *Cold Therapy in Rehabilitation.* London: Bell & Hyman.
Levitt S (1977) *Treatment of Cerebral Palsy and Motor Delay.* Oxford: Blackwell Scientific.
Little H (1981) Gait analysis for physiotherapy departments. *Physiotherapy 67(11):* 334.
Lovell LM (1973) The Yeovil Opportunity Group: a playgroup for multiply handicapped children. *Physiotherapy 59(8):* 251.
Parry A (1980) *Physiotherapy Assessment.* Beckenham, Kent: Croom Helm.
Sainsbury R & Mulley GP (1982) Walking sticks used by the elderly. *British Medical Journal 284:* 1751.
Sheridan M (1973) *Children's Developmental Progress.* Windsor, Berkshire: NFER Publishing
Upton G (1979) *Physical and Creative Activities for the Mentally Handicapped.* Cambridge: Cambridge University Press.
Walker GM (1978) Riding for the disabled. *Physiotherapy 64(10):* 297.

EQUIPMENT REFERENCES

1 Kirton Designs, Bungay Road, Hempnell, Norwich, Norfolk NR15 2NG.

2 Camp Therapy, Nothgate House, Staple Gardens, Winchester, Hampshire.

3 Rifton, Robertsbridge, East Sussex.

4 Ortho-Kinetics, 24 South Hampshire Industrial Park, Totton, Southampton.

5 Nomeq, Melton Road, West Bridgford, Nottingham NG2 6HD.

6 See Dawson R & Huddleston S (1983) The Action Chair. *Physiotherapy 69(2):* 38.

7 Kirton Designs, Bungay Road, Hempnell, Norwich, Norfolk NR15 2NG.

8 Camp Therapy, Nothgate House, Staple Gardens, Winchester, Hampshire.

9 The Powell Seat Company, 70 Lodge lane, Derby DE1 3HB.

10 Easy Chairs for the Arthritic: Royal National Hospital for Rheumatic Diseases, Upper Borough Walls, Bath.

11 Disabled Living Foundation, 380–384 Harrow Road, London W9 2HH.

12 Linido: Amilake Ltd, Haslemere Industrial Estate, 20 Ravensbury Terrace, London.

13 Remploy Medical Products, 415 Edgware Rd, London NW2 6LR.

14 Rifton, Robertsbridge, East Sussex.

15 Cheyne Centre for Spastic Children, 61 Cheyne Walk, Chelsea, London.

16 White Lodge Walker: Nomeq, Melton Road, West Bridgford, Nottingham NG2 6HD.

17 Cell Barnes: Modern Tubular Productions, 188 High Street, Egham, Surrey.

18 Atlas Walker: Carters J & A, Alfred Street, Westbury, Wiltshire.

19 Rollator Walker: Carters J & A, Alfred Street, Westbury, Wiltshire.

20 Adult Scandinavian Walker: Day's Medical Aids, Litchard Industrial Estate, Bridgend, Mid-Glamorgan.

21 Therapy Weekly, 4 Little Essex Street, London WC2R 3LF.

22 JE Brown, Kings Road, New Oscott, Sutton Coldfield, West Midlands.

23 North Hill Plastics, 49 Grayling Road, London N16 OPB.

24 John Drew, 433 Uxbridge Road, Ealing, London.

25 Dermalex, 146–154 Kilburn High Road, London NW6 4JD.

26 Donald Macdonald (Antartex) Ltd, Lomond Industrial Estate, Alexandria, Dunbartonshire.

27 Wheelies: Stadium Shop, Stoke Mandeville. Buckinghanshire *or* Beakbane, PO Box 10, Stourport Rd Kidderminster, Worcestershire.

28 Everest & Jennings, Princewood Rd, Corby, Northamptonshire.

29 Medical Engineering Unit, Queen Mary's Hospital, Carshalton, Surrey.

30 R Taylor & Son (Orthopaedic) Ltd, Compton Works, Woodwards Rd, Pleck, Walsall, West Midlands.

31 Chailey Heritage Hospital, Newick, East Sussex.

32 Hugh Steeper Ltd, 237 Roehampton Lane, London SW15 4LB.

33 Aquajac, Mountway Ltd, Brecon Rd, Abergavenny, Gwent.

34 Parker Baths, Rondar, Queensway, Stem Lane, New Milton Hampshire.

35 Bristol Products Company, West Chazey, Upper Warren Avenue, Caversham, Reading, Berkshire.

36 Dansk Pressalit UK Ltd, Pressalit House, 25 Grove Promenade, Ilkley, West Yorshire.

37 Riding for the Disabled Association, Avenue R, National Agricultural Centre, Kenilworth, Warwickshire.

38 David Lewis Centre for Epilepsy, Therapeutic Workshop, Warford, Nr Alderley Edge, Cheshire.

Chapter 31
The Role of the Occupational Therapist

BERENDEAN ANSTICE & ROSEMARY BOWDEN

The profession of occupational therapy has grown steadily over the last 50 years, and continues to grow at the rate of about 6% a year. Occupational therapy is the treatment of physical and psychiatric conditions through specific activities in order to help people reach their maximum level of function and independence in all aspects of daily life. Its approach is a holistic one, and aims to rehabilitate where possible, to maintain where total rehabilitation is not possible, to assist in readjustment where conditions are deteriorating, and at all times to consider the quality of life.

With these approaches in mind, it is not difficult to see that occupational therapy has a major contribution to make in the habilitation and care of people with mental handicap. However, before looking in detail at the role of the occupational therapist, it is necessary to understand some of the background training, in order to set in context the service that the therapist provides.

TRAINING

The training is a three-year full-time period of study which can broadly be divided into four main categories. The first is the academic study of basic sciences, such as anatomy, physiology and psychology, leading on to medicine, psychiatry and associated subjects. It includes training and practical experience in all types of physical, vocational and social assessment; it involves learning communication and counselling skills, as well as programme planning, recording and evaluating. The second area of learning is gaining knowledge of a variety of practical skills to treat physical, psychiatric and social conditions. Skills such as self-care techniques, work processes, craft and trade activities with exercise or vocational potential, creative educational and leisure pursuits and social skills.

The third element of training consists of 1200 hours of clinical experience in a hospital or community setting. Of this experience half will have a physical orientation, while the other half will have a psychiatric orientation. The final element of training involves the acquisition of management skills and the analysis and application of occupational therapy techniques. Occupational therapy is applicable to many different illnesses and activities, and the skill of the therapist is the accurate use of the therapeutic link between the activity and the illness.

After successful completion of the training period, the therapist is able to work in a variety of different settings and across a wide range of handicaps. Of these handicaps, mental handicap is now a major area in which occupational therapists are involved, in a variety of settings, as this chapter will explain.

SERVICE OBJECTIVES

Before looking at the detail of the work content, some broad objectives of the occupational therapy service for people with mental handicap can perhaps be summarized as follows:

1 to contribute to the development in each individual of the skills necessary to lead as full and as independent a life as possible;
2 to identify, prescribe and supply such specialist equipment as is necessary to promote independence;
3 to contribute to the mobilization of resources to provide input where the skills of the individual cannot be matched to the demands of living;
4 to assist in the long-term settlement and maintenance of individuals in an environment consistent with their needs and abilities;

5 to assist handicapped people to adjust to changing circumstances in their own lives or their environment;

6 to assist in the care and support of families and carers;

7 to consider at all times the quality of life both of the handicapped people and of their families, and assist each individual to derive maximum satisfaction from living.

ASSESSMENT

The key to the development of therapeutic programmes is the accurate assessment and definition of individual objectives. The assessment will need to show abilities as well as disabilities, so that the programme can build on the former and develop the latter. The assessment will cover all the activities of daily living (ADL), from getting up in the morning to going to bed at night. This includes self-care, domestic, employment and social skills, all of which make up the ability of an individual to meet the demands of integrated living. In addition, an assessment of the person's ability to communicate effectively, to make appropriate use of leisure time, to manage money, to use community resources, and to modify behaviour according to circumstances, must all be established if a picture is to be created of the individual, and an understanding reached of his or her particular needs.

No man is an island, and the assessment procedure must also encompass his emotional and sexual needs and the needs of the people who play or will play a significant role in his life.

MEETING OBJECTIVES

Having defined needs and abilities, the occupational therapist will then develop programmes aimed at maximizing ability and minimizing disability. It is only when individuals are functioning at their own optimum level that they can be helped to make realistic decisions about their future, and the environment in which they feel most at home. Very often many of the life experiences taken for granted by able-bodied children, will have been denied to the child with a mental handicap. Some of the processes of maximizing ability that the therapist will introduce may include providing for the first time opportunities to experience 'mainstream life', with the risks that this involves. The particular contribution of the occupational therapist is the ability to understand disability and its effects on 'normal' functioning, and then to plan, carry out and modify programmes which are focused at both a practical and an emotional level so as to meet the objectives, and yet provide realistic and varied stimulation.

One-to-one work

How these programmes are implemented will be varied and encompass a number of settings. Some of the work will be with an individual in a one-to-one setting, while other work will take place as part of a group activity. For the more profoundly handicapped, the need for individual attention will be apparent, for these individuals have particular needs that do not always derive maximum benefit from the group situation.

Similarly, those with behaviour problems require some one-to-one attention if their particular needs are to be met and their behaviour modified in a manner which is both therapeutic for them and for a group as a whole. For some of the activities, for instance domestic skills, cooking, shopping and self-care, a mixture of one-to-one or group settings can provide a therapeutic variety which meets individuals' needs. Education and social skills may benefit from this variable approach (Figure 31.1).

Group work

There are two main types of group work, both of which meet rather different objectives. In 'non-specific' group work, the membership of the group and the objectives of the activity are less clearly defined than in a 'specific' group activity. This does not mean that un-directed and aimless activity takes place in non-specific group work, but it caters for a range of different abilities and needs in a less structured environment. Activities such as art, pottery or woodwork or music and movement, can provide an excellent medium in which handicapped people can learn such things as teamwork skills and communication and group tolerance, but the less specific nature of the activity makes it less defined in function.

Specific group work will have more clearly defined objectives, and the group membership will have been carefully selected and matched to ensure compatibility of need. Activities such as social skills, literacy and numeracy skills, communication skills and so on can all be undertaken in a group whose membership remains largely the same, who are at broadly similar levels of development, and

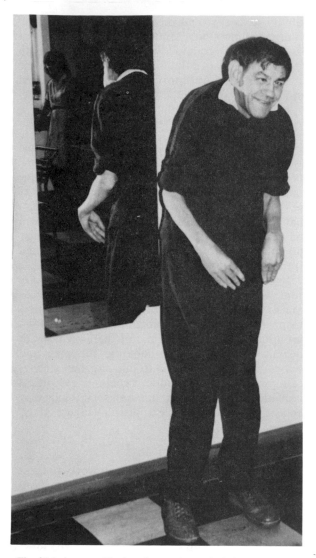

Fig. 31.1 A man with chronic spastic paralysis in a one-to-one session. There is lively awareness and coordination.

who develop a group identity in an atmosphere of mutual respect (Figure 31.2).

The majority of activities will take place within these two frameworks. The types of activity that will be covered can be roughly split into the following categories.

Activities of daily living

With the focus on the development of the skills of independence, it is obviously of great importance to develop in the individual the ability to deal with the practical necessities of living (Figure 31.3). The level at which this independence training is pitched and the type of activity undertaken will obviously be dictated by the need and abilities of each individual person.

For the person with a more severe handicap the first objective may be quite basic things such as toilet training, independent feeding or dressing, while for the more able the objective may be the whole range of domestic skills, including such things as simple budgeting, planning, purchasing and cooking of meals, as well as care of hair and personal presentation, use of make-up and the need for personal hygiene. The full range of activities that go to make up a normal day will need to be assessed and developed. Where possible the development of these skills will take place in as normal an environment as is possible (Figure 31.4). Thus shopping may be done in the local shops, cooking in a kitchen with normal domestic equipment, and social skills in a local restaurant. One of the main things that a therapist will be helping the individual to learn is the ability to transfer skills and techniques to different situations.

Knowledge of learning theory enables the occupational therapist to recognize a plateau in skill learning early. A plateau can denote a range of skills that have been attained, and it is then important for the programme to be switched to select another activity, which being new to the handicapped person, provides new interest and a different learning opportunity. At an appropriate time a programme that moves on from the plateau can be introduced to increase the skill level. Thus, concentration spans can be extended by work in the kitchen or in physical activity or some educational task. Similarly, social skills can be learned through outings or in discussions or recreational activities.

Communication

In addition to the activities of daily living, it is of the utmost importance that individuals are able to communicate with those around them at a variety of levels. Wherever possible the development of normal speech is encouraged, and occupational therapists and speech therapists work closely together to ensure a uniform approach. Where normal speech is not possible, then the development of specialist communication systems such as Makaton (see Chapter 29), can overcome some of the difficulties. In these instances the techniques are taught by the speech therapist, but the occupational therapist uses the same processes during the course

Fig. 31.2 Group music session, including the three people in the individual photographs. Differing specific needs are included in a happy general activity.

Fig. 31.3 Positioning used in music learned to enable independent drinking to take place.

Fig. 31.4 Washing-up is an essential part of cooking and eating for everyone.

of activities and in any contact with the individual. In this way, the learning is not only reinforced but developed.

Education

While many of the formal educational classes may be undertaken by teachers, the occupational therapists, in the course of daily-living training, can introduce an educational element into the activity process. Education in the occupational therapy department is carried out in essentially two forms: *applied education*, which is taking education and relating it to daily events, such as shopping, budgeting and general day-to-day management, and *pure education*, a follow-up from stages attained in formal education. This is particularly helpful during holiday periods when teachers are absent. So activities will include such things as the knowledge, understanding and handling of money, quizzes and games aimed at general knowledge, and discussions at various levels and on different topics; these can both develop communication skills (Figure 31.5) and broaden general knowledge.

Work-related skills

The development of independence and the acquisition of new skills must focus on the individual leading as normal and as integrated a life as possible. Even though the percentage of unemployment amongst people with mental handicap is greater than in the able-bodied population, the assessment of work potential and the acquisition of the necessary skills for employment must feature as part of the programme. The nature and the extent to which this features will obviously be determined by the needs of the individual but it is an important element. Many of the activities undertaken will have implications for the work environment. The ability to work alongside and communicate with fellow workers, to have reasonable spans of concentration, and to have developed some work tolerance is important if people with mental handicap are both to find employment and then to keep it. Modern technology is opening many horizons in the fields of employment, and occupational therapists are now using it quite extensively in their departments and in their treatment programmes. Microcomputers are used both as tools to improve communication and to improve understanding and learning. Therapists are involved in the development of work-experience programmes, where individuals can have a taste of employment, and can prove to employers their skills and abilities.

Fig. 31.5 Writing practice for an older man as a part of group discussion.

Leisure

All work and no play makes Jack a dull boy, and in the same way as is necessary in the able-bodied world, the development of a satisfying use of leisure time features quite highly in any occupational therapy programme. Apart from adding another appropriate dimension to the individual's life, activity can improve physical and psychological well-being and mobility and help to burn off undirected and unused energies. Likes and dislikes in recreational pursuits are very personal affairs, and the occupational therapist will attempt to establish with individuals, by helping them to try a number of different activities, those which fulfil their needs and interests and which contribute to the satisfying use of their time (Figure 31.6).

Counselling

While much of the work of the occupational therapist with handicapped people can encompass

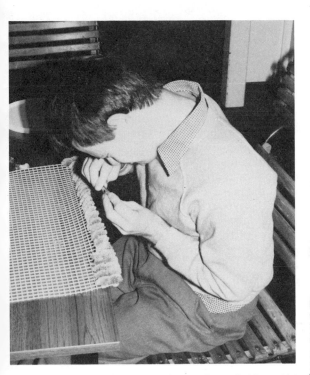

Fig. 31.6 Complete concentration on a chosen hobby, which can be carried out unsupervised when it has been learnt.

the role of counsellor, there are perhaps one or two areas where very specific counselling takes place. The first is with individuals in terms of helping them adjust to changes in their environment or their own situation. Bereavement, loss of friends and relatives, or major life changes will have as profound an effect on people with mental handicap as on anybody else, and the care and counselling that is needed at these times must not be overlooked. Equally the whole area of emotional and sexual needs is one in which mentally handicapped people can experience considerable difficulties. Sexual education and counselling about emotional and physical relationships all comes within the brief of a holistic approach to the normalization process.

In addition to counselling the individuals with handicaps, occupational therapists are frequently involved in the support and counselling role for relatives of handicapped people. Dealing with handicap may be a life-long commitment, and the stress that this creates in families should never be under-estimated. There is a considerable counselling task in helping both the clients and the carers. The development of independence for a child or adult with a handicap can be a painful and frightening process for the relatives. Helping the relatives to

understand the process of development and to 'let go' and encourage independence despite the risks takes time and considerable skill to achieve. Similarly, for those more profoundly handicapped people who may never experience totally independent living, the experience of a different environment and being cared for by different people can be very traumatic. The families of these people need considerable support in helping them to undergo and accept this new experience, before it is forced on them at a time of crisis. Occupational therapists are quite often involved in the development of self-help and mutual support groups for relatives of handicapped people, as well as being involved in voluntary groups such as toy libraries and adventure playgrounds.

Behaviour modification and social skills

One of the key factors in integration of handicapped people is their ability to behave in a manner which society finds acceptable. Occupational therapists are sometimes involved in formal behaviour modification methods such as token systems, but are invariably involved in the modification of an individual's behaviour and the development of social skills through the practice of realistic activities. Going shopping will teach people how to use their communication skills and what behaviour is required of them in the environment of a supermarket. Eating in a restaurant will show them what is demanded of them when eating in a public place as opposed to a hospital dining room. Going to a disco will teach them how to behave in social settings, and a work environment will show what is expected of them by other employees. Sometimes, if working from a hospital base, the use of these real facilities may not be possible, but occupational therapists will attempt to create situations which represent reality as near as possible, as part of the process of moving on to the real thing.

SPECIAL CARE

There is perhaps one group that deserves specific mention. These are the people for whom it is sometimes determined that 'special care' is required. While these people may well be involved in some or all of the mainstream of activities, there may equally be occasions where their care is undertaken separately. Nearly always they are the more severely handicapped, and frequently they are people with multiple handicaps. It is important with these profoundly handicapped people to develop the bond which is built up over months or even years of daily contact, encouraging the individuals to play, explore and respond to their environment. The need for warmth and human contact is high and through this a special relationship forms. An additional contribution of occupational therapy with this group of people can be quite clearly defined. As a member of a multi-disciplinary team, the occupational therapist would be responsible for certain aspects of an individual's needs and for devising the relevant programmes. These aspects will include:

1 advising on the suitability and use of equipment (educational, rehabilitative and communication);
2 modifying equipment to tailor-made specifications;
3 planning and teaching various activities in order to promote useful movement – both fine motor control (such as finger and hand dexterity) and gross motor control (such as trunk flexion);
4 assessing and teaching daily-living skills related to the potential of the individual, for example feeding techniques and the use of specialized feeding equipment, toilet training, independent mobility;
5 advising activities that develop concentration spans and stimulate communication, both verbal and non-verbal.

Some of these tasks may be undertaken in conjunction with the physiotherapist, in which cases the physiotherapist is likely to concentrate on mobility and gross motor control, while the occupational therapist concentrates on the development of independence in daily-living activities and on fine motor control, particularly in upper limb function. If there is a speech therapist involved then it will be essential to absorb that work into the programme as a whole. However, as with any multi-disciplinary work the coordination of effort and uniformity of approach are essential elements and should involve all those caring for the individual: habilitation needs to be a 24-hour concept if it is to have the greatest effect. In all areas of working, the occupational therapist will be substantially involved in the development of programmes which enhance this uniformity of approach and which therefore create the maximum habilitative environment for the individual.

SETTINGS IN WHICH OCCUPATIONAL THERAPISTS WORK

The tasks that occupational therapists undertake,

modified according to circumstances and individuals, can be seen to be happening in various settings around the country. The most obvious are discussed below.

Hospital departments

With the trend towards community care and the subsequent policy not to admit to hospital anyone who could enjoy a fuller life in the community, the residents of hospitals and the patients that come to occupational therapy departments are now very often the more severely and multiply handicapped. Thus the type of activities identified in the section above, on special care, can predominate in certain sections of these departments. However, for many patients there is now a trend to move them into more community-oriented settings. This is being done in a number of ways. The first is the locally based hospital unit which is considered in the next section.

Locally based hospital units

While still within the aegis of National Health Service provision, the small locally based hospital units (LBHUs) are attempting to remove the most destructive elements of institutionalization. They are being planned and built to provide a more home-like environment, in a community which has significance to the residents it caters for. Staff working in the units have less clearly defined roles, and although a shift system is in operation, the work staff undertake is quite varied. Occupational therapists are involved in these environments, and in addition to undertaking the specific types of activity already mentioned are quite substantially involved in the training of other staff and in the development of therapeutic programmes. Some of these LBHUs have day-care placements, or day-care units attached, where handicapped people from the community come for all or part of their day. Sadly the shortage of occupational therapists seldom allows for a therapist to be identified for each individual unit, but services are stretched as far as possible to ensure that these units and the day-care establishments that go with them do have some occupational therapist's time for some part of each week, or on a consultancy basis.

Community mental handicap teams

In order to meet the needs of handicapped people now remaining in the community, many areas are developing community mental handicap teams

(CMHTs), in which occupational therapists play a significant role. Some of these teams are staffed by health service personnel only, and some on a joint basis with local authority social services departments. The aims of the teams are to identify mentally handicapped individuals in the community, to make an initial assessment to determine the needs of the individuals and to provide or organize such services as are necessary. This may be either in the form of direct input to the individuals in their own homes from the team or via a supporting agency. On occasions attendance at some of the community or hospital facilities must be arranged if the individual is to develop independence skills and achieve the objectives already mentioned. For those handicapped individuals who are settled in a community environment, the team will visit to monitor the situation and be alive to need before it presents as a crisis. Extensive work is also done in liaising with other agencies and bodies such as housing authorities, voluntary organizations and community support groups.

Another substantial role of a community mental handicap team is that of community development. While the aim is to match the abilities of the handicapped individuals to those demanded by society, it may not be possible to do so to the extent that means that society does not have to make any compromises. Heightening public awareness, levels of tolerance and involvement, and assisting compromises to accommodate handicapped members of society, is essential if handicapped people living in the community are not to be as isolated from the mainstream of life as they were when living in large, remote institutions.

Local authority teams

Some local authority social services departments do now identify teams to work with people with mental handicaps or have employed individual specialists, including occupational therapists, to undertake some of the work. Where there are community mental handicap teams or where there are community developments from the National Health Service there is an obvious need for close cooperation and good communication. Occupational therapists, as the one profession employed in any numbers by both local authorities and the National Health Service, do quite often form the bridge, alongside the hospital-based social workers.

In addition, the main occupational therapy service within local authorities (which focuses on aids and adaptations to assist handicapped people to remain at home) will also encompass the needs of mentally handicapped people, usually when there is associated physical handicap. The assessment will relate to the needs of individuals within their physical environment, which can then be adapted to minimize its handicapping effects. Thus alterations to access, kitchens and bathrooms or the provision of alternative sleeping accommodation can be organized where need is established by the occupational therapist. These facilities are usually financed jointly between a housing improvement grant and a local authority social services department grant, with contributions from individuals which vary according to their circumstances.

Group homes

One form of independent community living that has developed quite rapidly over the last few years is the group home. These are usually standard district council houses and offer accommodation for three or four individuals who have varying needs of community support. Community mental handicap teams or staff from local authority teams are often involved in the maintenance and care of individuals living in group homes. The training and preparation for people to live within a group home is of paramount importance, and will often be the responsibility of the occupational therapy department back at the hospital base. Group homes are developing with differing levels of formal support and it is important that people are prepared at the appropriate level and that the assessment process defines the appropriate provision for them. However, there are now more people coming into group homes who have never lived in an institutional environment, and whose need for group home living is as a result of the death, illness or frailty of caring relatives. In these instances, helping the group to form a cohesive identity, share tasks, and develop mutual respect is a task which cannot be overlooked and is one in which occupational therapists, along with community nurses and social workers, should be involved. Again the shortage of occupational therapists often mitigates against this being performed at an optimum level.

Adult training centres (ATCs)

Adult training centres (ATCs), provided as part of the service resources of local authorities, offer a variety of programmes on a Monday-to-Friday basis for mentally handicapped people. There are some occupational therapists working within these units, but they are the exception rather than the rule. However, occupational therapists developing close links with adult training centres and with sheltered workshops do forge good and effective links with the staff of these units. Being involved in the development of ATC programmes for individuals and in individual reviews can also give the occupational therapist the opportunity of working through these with the family concerned if that person is living in the community. This is yet another way of ensuring consistency of approach and reinforcement of skills. Similarly, helping adult training centre staff to develop new techniques, new activities and new ideas can assist in the provision of varied and stimulating programmes.

For the occupational therapist working in a community team the knowledge and expertise of adult training centre staff and sheltered workshop staff about the abilities and behaviour of individual mentally handicapped people can greatly enhance the ability of the therapist to offer appropriate services and mobilize appropriate resources within the community and domestic environment.

Hostels

Many local authorities provide hostels as their main source of residential care for mentally handicapped people. The size of these hostels varies considerably, but virtually all have a policy of training with a view to independent or minimal support living. Here again, working with the staff of the hostel, the occupational therapist can assist in the development of appropriate training programmes to develop independence skills. The hostel staff are also able to give accurate and detailed assessments about the needs, abilities and deficiencies of each individual, so that when community living is considered it is done in an appropriate and planned fashion.

Child assessment units

Where child assessment units are established there is frequently an occupational therapist involved, often working with both health and social services. The aim is to assess the abilities and disabilities of the child so that a comprehensive understanding of the particular needs can be established and appropriate treatment plans made. This is obviously a matter of teamwork, and occupational therapists work closely with physiotherapy, speech therapy, nursing and social work colleagues as well as, of course, the medical staff.

Many of the children seen in these assessment units are multiply handicapped and will be referred for assessment as soon after the diagnosis as possible. The occupational therapist will be looking at general physical functioning such as muscle tone, balance, mobility and hand function, and with older children will also assess social skills and independence. The assessment will aim to show the developmental delays and identify the areas towards which treatment could effectively be concentrated.

The treatment will most often focus on the development of personal independence as well as developing concentration spans, hand–eye coordination and so on. Occupational therapists work with parents and children in small groups and will involve them in such things as Portage schemes, which are structured patterns of learning in which parents and therapists modify and select specific tasks to meet objectives. Parents play the predominant therapeutic role with therapist support and constant review and reappraisal of the child's performance. Much of the group work is also aimed at supporting parents and helping them to help each other.

Nursery schools and special schools

Some children with mental handicap are placed in mainstream nursery schools, others in special schools. Much of the occupational therapist's time in the school environment will be spent working with teachers, helping them to devise programmes and activities with developmental potential. This will involve such things as handling techniques, correct posture and seating, appropriate positioning to maximize ability, ideas for games with exercise potential and play with developmental potential. For children with a mental handicap who are in mainstream schooling, integration with able-bodied classmates will be very important. The occupational therapist can help the teacher to ease the integration process by offering ideas and working together in group sessions to develop the necessary social and physical skills.

Working with teachers on programmes to increase body awareness, balance and coordination, as well as to improve hand–eye coordination and general hand function, can provide the special element necessary to allow the less handicapped children to keep up with their more able peers. The occupational therapist can demonstrate ideas and methods which the teachers can then pursue.

Some children may need specialist equipment and it will be the occupational therapist's responsibility to prescribe this and arrange its purchase. Some may need adapting to tailor-made specifications and may be used both at school and at home. As a result, the therapist liaises extensively with both the education department and the local social services for equipment provision.

THE ADVISORY ROLE

Apart from direct patient–client contact, occupational therapists are now more and more seen and used in an advisory capacity for a wide range of personnel. Advice may concern the care or management of a mentally handicapped person, for instance for care staff of hostels, instructors in ATCs, social workers, nurses, volunteers or relatives. Alternatively, advice may be sought on such things as design features of new buildings or voluntary developments or service initiatives. On these latter issues, the role of the occupational therapist manager will be of considerable importance and will be discussed next.

THE OCCUPATIONAL THERAPIST AS A MANAGER

Having looked in detail at the contribution of the occupational therapist in direct contact with patients, and having demonstrated the breadth and range of work in which occupational therapists are involved, it is essential also to consider the role of the occupational therapist as a manager. An experienced occupational therapist can make a substantial contribution to the management tasks of both district health authorities and social services departments. This management can be at two levels – firstly, in an individual unit, such as a hospital occupational therapy department or social services team, and secondly, in the rather more embracing role of a service manager.

With the establishment of the district occupational therapists' posts, head occupational therapists' positions in hospitals and principal occupational therapists' posts in social services departments, the role of the occupational therapist as a service organizer, as a trainer and as a contributor to service development is now better recognized. An occupational therapy manager is able to respond to service needs and developments by the appropriate deployment of resources. With changing patterns of care and with new initiatives in the provision of services, it is important to have at the helm an individual who is aware of the strengths and weaknesses and resource availability of occupational therapy staff. An individual in a position to mobilize resources which accommodate new initiatives, as well as maintaining priority areas during periods of leave or sickness, can greatly enhance the continuity of care. With occupational therapy being numerically a small profession, this type of effective organization becomes more essential if priority areas are to receive the service they deserve.

Forward planning policy and service development

The effectiveness of a service will depend very substantially on the strategy framework in which it is provided. Developments which are piecemeal and unplanned seldom produce the continuity of provision which mentally handicapped people of all abilities require. An occupational therapy manager as a member of the team developing services and policies can add a further dimension to the deliberations. Policy strategies will depend on the availability and suitability of staff, new developments will depend on the suitability and appropriateness of building design, and a multi-disciplinary team approach will need to be formulated on accurate and realistic knowledge of skills and resources of each member. In these types of issues, the occupational therapy manager can make a major contribution, but the structure should allow the individual to be an integral part of the planning machinery and not merely a specialist brought in as the occasion arises.

Supervision and organization of service delivery

As with any type of service, differing tasks require differing levels of experience and expertise. It is important to develop a pattern of services and career structure that uses staff skills appropriately to ensure that scarce skills are directed to where they can have most benefit. Some of the more routine and repetitive tasks can be undertaken most successfully by occupational therapy helpers, provided they have the support and supervision of qualified and experienced occupational therapists. The more detailed work, programme planning, review and evaluation, and the complex one-to-one or specific group activities need to be provided by qualified occupational therapists. Most hospital occupational therapy departments have a career structure which provides for a head occupational therapist and appropriately graded staff answerable to that individual. This is not necessarily the case in social services, where many occupational therapists work single-handed, answerable to the senior social worker or leader of the team in which they are located. The question of supervision is one of crucial importance if standards of professional performance are to match the goals and objectives of the service. These standards of performance, along with the needs for further training and areas of potential development, can only be properly identified by a senior and experienced member of the same profession. Thus for services to develop in excellence, it is of very significant importance to have a career structure which allows a therapist to develop those skills and work up through differing levels of competence, with the opportunity to share and learn from more experienced members of staff.

Training

Apart from identifying and making arrangements for appropriate on-going training for staff, an occupational therapy manager should have a major input into the training programme for both district health authorities and social services departments. In a department which has the staffing structure to allow good clinical experience, the provision of clinical placements for occupational therapy students is very important if the therapists of the future are to have the range of experience and learning that will equip them well in their work. However, input into the training programmes of other staff dealing with mentally handicapped people should be seen as another integral part of an occupational therapy manager's role. This should also include initiating and developing training courses, seminars and discussions aimed at the improving of services as well as the important area of induction courses for new staff of all disciplines.

Research and evaluation

Any service, if it is to be forward-looking, needs to be the subject of review and evaluation so as to be responsive to changing demands. A specific commitment to a research and evaluation programme can not only provide a lively appraisal of current standards and levels of service delivery, but can also give opportunities for staff to develop the techniques of critical analysis and subsequent redefining of goals, objectives and initiatives. This not only improves standards of performances, but provides stimulation and job satisfaction for a continual effort to improve service provision. In this way it is also possible to determine the cost-effectiveness of the service delivery and develop strategies based on real data rather than supposition.

CONCLUSION

It is almost impossible to list a set of techniques that can be called the practice of occupational therapy. The skill of the therapist is in the assessment of need and the devising of appropriate therapeutic programmes that are designed to meet that need and to achieve the objectives set out at the beginning of this chapter. An appropriately managed and allocated occupational therapy service can make a major contribution in the multi-disciplinary approach to the integration and well-being of mentally handicapped people, be it in the community or in a residential environment.

Chapter 32
The Role of the Voluntary Organizations

PHILIPPA RUSSELL

WHAT IS THE VOLUNTARY SECTOR?

'[The voluntary sector] should cooperate closely with the State services, perhaps even carrying out specialised work under agency arrangements . . . but whatever the decision made, it must be taken in full knowledge of the needs to be met and bearing always in mind that it is the historic role of charity to pioneer and take risks. . . . [It has] greater flexibility, ability to set new standards or to undertake new work without seeking fresh statutory powers . . . to make additional or more special provision for people suffering from certain types of disadvantages or disabilities . . . to work outwards from the individual in need to help the services he needs rather than the reverse process of discovering the individual and providing a service. . . . '

Although written thirty-five years ago, the Nathan Report highlighted the changing role of the voluntary sector as it moved from Victorian philanthropism (usually aimed at 'salvage' operations for unwanted or orphaned children funded through individual charitable contributions) to the specialist services for professional agencies often provided today (Nathan Committee, 1950; Wolfenden Committee, 1978).

Whilst the emphasis on innovative good practice and flexibility still remains, the payment of fees on a contract basis and growing professionalism must imply some accountability to other agencies, and the growth of jointly financed voluntary/statutory initiatives and planning strategies clearly indicates the major shift in our thinking not only about *how* to work together but about what the voluntary sector can offer.

The Oxford English Dictionary describes a voluntary organization as 'maintained or supported solely or largely by freewill offerings and free from state interference or control'. However, this is not wholly accurate in the handicap field, since many voluntary agencies have major injections of funding from local and central government. Indeed, as the joint report from the National Council of Social Service and Personal Social Services Council (Unell, 1979) clearly showed, Victorian philanthropism has been in continuing decline as a source of finance for voluntary activity, and fees for professional services rendered now form the major part of annual income. Such fees imply a degree of accountability to the sponsoring agency; they also impose greater coordination with existing health, education and personal social services in a given area.

In general families with handicapped children encounter four principal systems of care:

1 Informal *'social caring'* – the 'gift relationship' described by Titmuss, in which friends, family and the wider community provide informal networks of support.
2 The *'commercial system'*, more common in the USA, in which the client purchases direct services.
3 The *statutory system*, which theoretically offers universal coverage and agreed standards, but has all the associated problems of size, inflexibility and removal from direct public involvement in service delivery.
4 The *voluntary sector*, which in fact complements, supplements and influences the other systems listed above. Historically, all our statutory services have emerged from voluntary initiatives and pressure groups. Although the role of pressure group and independent critic is an important part of the voluntary sector's work, it should be emphasized that many voluntary organizations are innovators and risk-takers and persuade through good practice rather than political campaigns.

The diversity of the voluntary sector makes it difficult to extrapolate common objectives and philosophies. However, most organizations would recognize five common aims:

1 to recognize special needs and to organize constructive responses;
2 to pioneer and establish services by a process of exploration, examination, research and demonstration projects;
3 to present to central and local government evidence of needs and recommendations for meeting them;
4 to act as a lobby for public and government recognition and acceptance of the need for such services (and, since the allocation of resources requires a much wider recognition of need by the general public, to present such evidence in both a popular and a professional format);
5 to encourage self-help and active participation in decision-making and service provision by the *clients* themselves.

COMPETITION WITH THE STATUTORY SECTOR?

The specialism of some voluntary agencies and their ability to provide a monitoring service from an independent stance have sometimes led to accusations that they are seeking to 'take over' professional tasks from statutory agencies. However, the work of the voluntary sector has traditionally complemented rather than supplanted universally available statutory services. As Shearer wrote in the *Guardian* in 1980, the voluntary sector would not be half as effective if it also had to achieve some kind of *minimal national standard* and endeavour to provide *universal* coverage.

The majority of voluntary organizations are cost-effective compared with similar statutory services. However, despite their origins in Victorian philanthropism, they are not necessarily cheaper. Specialist services such as those provided by the Spastics Society's schools at Meldreth Manor or Beech Tree House or the Queen Elizabeth Foundation's assessment centre at Banstead Place cannot be cheap. But they are good value for money. They can be very specific in their client group. In the age of 'small is beautiful', they do not have the enforced administrative constraints and costs of many larger bureaucratic agencies.

A constant misapprehension even in professional circles about the nature of voluntary provision is that it inevitably relies heavily on 'volunteering'. Many voluntary agencies are more professional than the professionals. The specialist social work services of the Invalid Children's Aid Association or

the Spastics Society can, therefore, complement generic local authority services on an equal footing. Smaller case-loads often permit more constructive work – but such work is unlikely to be effective without liaison with other professional agencies already working with the families.

Some voluntary organizations do indeed use volunteers in ways which make them adjuncts to local services (such as the specially trained welfare visitors of the Royal Society for Mentally Handicapped Children and Adults or the Kith and Kids parent workshops) (Pugh, 1982). But in general the voluntary sector seeks to provide direct services, which – because of the enforced good housekeeping caused by constant accountability to statutory agencies who may partially fund them, to the consumers and to the fund raisers – are often excellent value for money.

THE PROBLEMS OF FUNDING

Although the majority of voluntary organizations are cost-effective, a major problem for many local branches of national bodies and grass-roots organizations is that we are at a stage of developing expectations and declining resources. Many local authorities have felt it necessary to cut back drastically on grants to voluntary agencies and few small organizations (and indeed very few larger ones) have reserves on which to draw in hard times. Although some voluntary organizations are successful in fund-raising (some, like the Church of England Children's Society are seeing a significant increase in funds received despite the recession), such fund-raising in any event forms only a small part of the overall budget. For many voluntary organizations, the 'core' secretariat depends on funding from local or central government, with the project work often being separately funded from a variety of resources. Hopefully, continued take-up of joint finance arrangements will ensure more collaborative efforts and secure revenue in the future. But again, many voluntary organizations cannot plan ahead on the same timescale as local authorities or health authorities. Their services are, therefore, vulnerable in hard times, precisely when they may most be needed.

FAMILY NEEDS – OPPORTUNITIES FOR COLLABORATION?

There can be few more distressing situations for a family than the discovery that a child is mentally handicapped. Traditionally, parents of handicapped children have themselves been regarded as emotionally aberrant. As Hewett (1970) noted, 'The general tendency to characterize parents of handicapped children as guilt-ridden, anxiety-laden, over-protective and rejecting beings is unfortunate.' She went on to comment that the common characteristics of parents appeared to be much more the need for money, services and information. Without these, counselling would be of little value. Indeed, the underlying tenet of successive Government reports, such as those of the Court Committee (1976), the Warnock Committee (1978) and the Jay Committee (1979), has been the concept of partnership with parents, with parents being offered the tools with which to work effectively with their child. In effect, parental skills need adequate support if they are not to become deficits in the context of the day-to-day difficulties of caring for a handicapped child (Russell, 1983).

The exact patterns of relationships between support services, therapeutic facilities and educational facilities (and the mechanisms by which a proper mix is achieved for individual families in order to minimize family burden and maximize positive expectations) are often unclear. As the Warnock Committee noted: 'although we tend to dwell upon the dependence of many parents on professional support, we are well aware that professional help cannot be wholly effective – if at all so – unless it builds upon the *parents'* capacity to be involved. Thus we see the relationship as a dialogue between parents and helpers working in partnership'. It is in parental *involvement* that the voluntary sector has been so uniquely successful both as enabler and as facilitator for services the parents may need.

It is generally accepted that most parents go through a sequence of reactions in adapting to the idea that their child is handicapped. Initial shock leads to denial and hostility, with orientation and adaptation following. However, the sequence may vary in individual families, and some research (Cunningham and Sloper, 1977; Gath, 1978; Cunningham, 1979; Chapter 15) has found that families may be more unhappy a year after the birth than at the time of the actual diagnosis. In effect, parents may have treasured unrealistic expectations about their child during the first few months of life, but have to accept the diagnosis if services fall off at around one year old and also when the child begins to differ conspicuously from his or her peer group in the community. Such parents, without support, may well be labelled as 'negative' and 'hostile' by successive professional agencies. They will also have low expectations of their child.

The American paediatrician Brazleton (1976) suggested that the success of any intervention programme, whether health or educational, should be measured not only by the child's developmental gains, but also 'by increased family comfort, decrease in the divorce rate, lower incidence of behaviour problems in siblings. . . . ' He accepted that such criteria might be seen as 'soft signs', but recognized that a child's enhanced performance in terms of motor development or cognitive gains would certainly be influenced by the suitability of the treatment programme to the family's needs. He also noted that *voluntary* agencies were often more effective in adopting a 'whole-family' approach than their professional counterparts.

THE CONCEPT OF 'SELF-HELP'

The 1970s and '80s have seen the emergence of a strong professional commitment to working in families. The development of Portage and other home-based learning schemes has identified not only the capacity of parents to become educators as well as carers, but also, importantly for all services, the corresponding and critical necessity to meet parents' emotional needs before they can help their child in any structured way. The 'self-help' movement began with the development and expansion of MENCAP's local groups in the 1950s and has since proliferated in diverse settings, with small groups frequently attached to child development centres, schools and adult training centres. The concept of 'self-help' is a seductive one for service providers and planners. Enabling parents to become more competent as well as confident may be seen as reducing the needs for alternative services. Prevention may avoid family crisis. However, there is growing evidence that 'self-help' cannot exist in a vacuum but should be seen as part of a network of provision. Spontaneity is important, but so is the enabler. MENCAP groups have always had a tradition of working with support from their regional and national offices. Another example of the new breed of voluntary self-help groups is Contact a Family, where national direction and support enable local groups to meet parents' needs.

THE ROYAL SOCIETY FOR MENTALLY HANDICAPPED CHILDREN AND ADULTS (MENCAP)

MENCAP is the largest of the voluntary organizations concerned with mental handicap in the UK.

With 40 000 members in some 500 local societies, served by 12 regional offices, it provides a major network of parent support. Local groups are largely autonomous, but use the national organization for information, collaboration on policy issues and as a resource for service development.

In 1974 MENCAP established their Voluntary Welfare Visitors Scheme, with the object of providing accurate information, advice and counselling to parents on their local services. In order to provide acceptable standards on a national basis, and to ensure that the 1500 welfare visitors were well equipped to foster a good working relationship both with parents and with local statutory agencies, a training scheme was developed. The training offered is divided into two main components. One covers the basic legal framework and statutory rights, the second the social security system, allowances and benefits and a good working understanding of the different professionals who might help mentally handicapped people and their families. All welfare visitors are encouraged to attend regular seminars and meetings, both at national and regional level, in order to keep up to date with the development of services and changes in legislation. The national office issues a regular Welfare and Rights Communications Pack. Welfare visitors must agree to follow a 'code of practice', which has been compiled by MENCAP partly in order to help them in their work but also to ensure that complex issues like confidentiality are carefully considered and understood.

Historically, MENCAP developed primarily to meet *parents'* needs. In the 1980s it has also developed innovative work with mentally handicapped people themselves, whose needs complement but may not be the same as those of their families. The rise of self-advocacy in the USA has had its parallel in the United Kingdom, and much of MENCAP's work is now directed to helping mentally handicapped people acquire skills in order to help themselves. For those whose lack of communication skills is compounded by multiple handicap and isolation in a hospital setting, the Advocacy Alliance (initiated by a consortium of organizations including MENCAP) is pioneering the use of independent citizen advocates and exploring strategies for recruitment, training and support which will make them more effective. For many major voluntary bodies like MENCAP, the question 'Whose rights?' will become an area of major concern in the 1980s. The civil-rights perspective emerging in educational, health and social services has already shown that parents and their children can have different but complementary rights which needs exploration and sometimes intervention. In this context, MENCAP, like many other voluntary organizations, has an expanding and challenging role to play in the next decade.

CONTACT A FAMILY

Contact a Family arose from a pilot project in two London boroughs. The project aimed to bring together families with children with any disability on a neighbourhood basis. The groups offered mutual support, guidance and encouraged autonomy. They also aimed at maximum integration with local statutory services and voluntary agencies such as MENCAP. Other groups developed in different parts of the country, guided by community workers accountable to the central office, but essentially developing according to local needs. However, groups as disparate as these sited in inner-city areas and in rural Gloucestershire found they had certain common aims. Firstly, the groups worked with the whole family, moving away from the largely mother-centred services usually available. Siblings, grandparents and friends could all be involved. Secondly, each group endeavoured to help parents meet each other as near as possible to their own homes. The parents were gently encouraged to provide mutual support (such as shared transport, baby-sitting and play schemes) but also to define their own needs and influence local service development collectively. Thirdly, and most importantly, each group was served by the community worker, who could take an objective view of national and local issues. Many individual families lack sufficient courage or conviction about their own right to services to tell the service-providers what they actually want. Many more need the 'honest brokers' found in a good voluntary organization in order to understand or use services (such as respite care schemes) which do exist.

The links between local groups and the national office ensure that local groups, whilst flexible and individual, are aware of national trends and can look for advice on particular practical issues such as running play schemes, organizing parents' groups or producing information material. The use of local volunteers can be more effective because a community worker can recruit, train and deploy volunteers. Practical initiatives by Contact a Family include Saturday Clubs (for the whole family), regular coffee mornings, 'Share a Family' schemes – matching families with others needing befriending or help and 'Share a Weekend' – an annual weekend for establishing networks of local groups and forging links with other voluntary organizations working in the field. Voluntary organizations, like statutory service providers, need to be inter-disciplinary, and collaboration is a primary aim.

AN ORDINARY LIFE

A major shift in the philosophy of care for mentally handicapped people (and their families) has been towards the concept of an 'ordinary life' in the local community. Although statutory services will be key providers in terms of acute and specialist health care, education, housing and day care, the voluntary sector has always played a prominent role in developing pilot projects to provide good-quality care on a local basis (King's Fund Centre, 1982).

A major cause of admission to long-term and institutional care has always been a family crisis which prevented the existing family from continuing its caring role. In recent years, respite or relief care has also been recognized as having a positive role for the mentally handicapped person. It can offer new friends, contacts, a chance to sample another lifestyle and an invaluable first step to the inevitable move away from the family home when parents age and can no longer cope. Voluntary organizations, with their direct consumer involvement, have played a significant role in encouraging local authorities to develop appropriate patterns of care. The well-documented Leeds Respite Care Scheme (using local families recruited by the local authority social services department) arose from discussions with a local branch of MENCAP. The Crossroads Care Attendance Scheme (a network of local groups providing practical help at critical periods of the day to families with a handicapped member) has recently been extended to include mentally handicapped people. A number of organizations, like the Leonard Cheshire Foundation, have pioneered the concept of care *within* the home through peripatetic care-workers, rather than removing the mentally handicapped person in order to deal with family difficulties. A number of voluntary organizations at local and national level have themselves set up short-term care projects; for example, the Tuberous Sclerosis Association acquired and now runs, with local authority financial support, a staffed group home in Oxfordshire for local families.

The proliferation of successful short-term care schemes, usually based within a local community and using paid and supervised caring families, is leading to another development – namely that of finding long-term placements for mentally handicapped children and young people and developing family-placement and boarding-out schemes for young adults.

National Children's Homes and Barnardos have both established pilot projects to place and support mentally and multiply handicapped children in long-stay foster family placements. Barnardos' implementation of the 'core and cluster approach' clearly highlighted the need to establish such schemes within an existing infrastructure of good-quality care and to link caring families with services which exist for all similar families in the local community. Barnardos are similarly initiating a project to place some of the children remaining in mental handicap hospitals in more appropriate placements in the community. They and a number of other voluntary organizations have been better able to utilize the Government's £3 million initiative to develop pilot schemes for multiply handicapped children in the community than many statutory agencies. Their involvement also highlights the immense spectrum of provision in the voluntary sector, ranging from small local projects run on a self-help basis (with local authority financial support) to national initiatives where the voluntary organization utilizes joint funding and any special monies available from central and local government and will look to local or health authorities for running costs when placements are established.

The belief that children should live in families rather than in institutions (and concern that child-care principles are often not adequately implemented in large health service settings) has also led to interest in the development of adoption placements for mentally handicapped children. Parents for Children, an independent adoption agency, has pioneered family placements and has developed recruitment and placement strategies which take account of special needs, the particular problems of matching atypical children to what are often atypical adopting families and the additional need to ensure that on-going support is available. A DHSS-sponsored evaluation of Parents for Children (together with a separate evaluation of the adoption allowances introduced under the Children Act 1975) is in turn being carried out by another voluntary organization, the National Children's Bureau. In an age of increasingly generic approaches to service delivery (whether in health, education or social services), it is interesting to reflect that the national voluntary organization is becoming in effect the *specialist* agency and may not only seek to demonstrate its own philosophy of care, but may also accept commissions from local and central government in order to test out hypotheses and explore and evaluate new service concepts in action.

Although many of the voluntary organizations concerned with mental handicap in the United Kingdom developed as child-oriented bodies, the past decade has seen a shift in emphasis, perceiving mentally handicapped people as a whole and moving away from arbitrary and irrelevant cut-offs in services at critical points such as the transition between school and adult life. Although provision in adult and further education has greatly improved, much pioneering work was done by organizations like MENCAP (which runs its own residential units for people over 16), by CARE and Home Farm Trusts (whose philosophy is shifting away from large residential communities to smaller residential units with links with the local community) and by the Spastics Society (whose residential colleges meet the needs of multiply handicapped young people). Many residential courses run by voluntary organizations now serve as bridges to more integrated provision in the community. MENCAP has also pioneered a project which demonstrates the feasibility of supported integration of mentally handicapped people into adult education courses – an important initiative not only in terms of enhanced educational opportunities but also because of the conspicuous lack of good-quality leisure opportunities for many adult mentally handicapped people.

Employment opportunities for mentally handicapped people have also given the voluntary organizations the chance to develop and demonstrate skills. MENCAP's Lufton Manor Rural Training Unit has successfully trained a large number of mentally handicapped people to work in horticulture or farming. Pengwern Hall runs a successful village shop. MENCAP's Pathway Scheme, using local employment officers who find placements and then support both employer and employee as 'foster workers' in the first vulnerable weeks, has also demonstrated that people with mental handicaps may not only work with 'ordinary people' but may also be highly regarded by their employers.

Housing initiatives have received considerable impetus from the relaxation of Housing Corporation rules (with regard to support for housing which also includes a degree of care) and

from the belief that a residential service (as opposed to housing provision) is needed in order to provide flexible and individual approaches to people with special needs. The King's Fund Centre's (1982) Ordinary Life project has also had considerable impact not only in promoting the developing of positive and imaginative thinking about residential services but also in encouraging collaboration amongst those with an interest in service provision. Voluntary organizations have historically provided most of the residential provision in the United Kingdom, the shift first to health service and then to local authority care coming comparatively late. In the 1980s collaboration between statutory and voluntary agencies (particularly through the joint funding initiatives which may now include housing under the Health and Social Services and Social Security Adjudications Act 1983) seems likely to encourage the trend towards small, local and integrated residential units and a more creative approach to the support services which they will require.

However, pilot projects and new initiatives must be seen as part of a wider network of provision. Organizations like Campaign for People with Mental Handicap and the Independent Development Council for Mentally Handicapped People have a policy-making and review role (with no direct services) and they, like MENCAP and the Spastics Society, take a critical and objective overview not only of individual developments but also of national trends.

EDUCATION

As the Warnock Committee (1978) noted, 'the history of special education in the United Kingdom is largely a matter of voluntary effort'. The United Kingdom has traditionally had a 'mixed economy' in both mainstream and special education, with independent and non-maintained schools coexisting with the maintained sector. However, there is a distinction in that independent or non-maintained schools offering *special* education provision are indirectly supported by local education authorities, who pay for almost all of the pupils registered at those schools. Indeed, the voluntary sector could not survive without, in effect, meeting the requirements for specialist services made by the local authorities.

Many of the educational initiatives by the voluntary sector were, and are, highly specialist. They cater for children with complex learning difficulties, multiple handicaps, speech and language disorders and, increasingly, severe behaviour problems. Such schools are usually residential and pioneer new approaches for a small but complex group of children such as those who are deaf, blind and mentally handicapped.

But although voluntary organizations have been traditional providers of educational provision, they also have a major (and ultimately more significant) role to play in working within the statutory educational system. The Education Act 1981 is the first piece of education legislation to formally recognize the contribution of the voluntary sector as provider, counsellor and advocate. The Act requires, in Section 10, that health authorities draw parents' attention to relevant voluntary organizations if they consider that their child may have special educational needs and are of the opinion that a voluntary body might be able to help. A central concept of the report of the Warnock Committee (1978) was that of the 'named person', who would direct parents to sources of information and help and act as a liaison person with other agencies in ensuring that family and child got as much as possible from the educational system. Section 7 of the Act requires local education authorities, when making the statement of special educational needs, to give parents the name of such a person. Although the specific functions outlined in the Warnock report are not written into the Act or indeed into the accompanying circulars and regulations, it is clear that many voluntary organizations and local education authorities will collaborate in utilizing their mutual resources in performing this role.

The new civil-rights perspective in the Education Act 1981, which confers rights and responsibilities on parents in the assessment of their child's special educational needs (and which offers recourse to an appeals procedure if they are dissatisfied with the provision offered) must have major consequences for voluntary organizations. In the USA the development of parent coalitions (established nationally with federal funding in order to provide an enabling and supportive service for parents under Public Law 94-142) has shown how effective voluntary organizations can be not only in providing befriending and information services but also in developing advocacy and other services to operate for and on behalf of parents. The expertise of the voluntary sector in the United Kingdom is already adapting to the new demands. It seems probable, therefore, that the voluntary sector's traditional provision of largely residential educational facilities for children of school age with complex special

needs or of services for pre-school children through Pre-school Playgroups Association, opportunity groups, home teaching schemes and other support networks will be complemented by an advisory role. In addition, there is already evidence that many voluntary organizations are working directly with education authorities, as well as with parents, in order to maximize the 'partnership' advocated by many recent government departments as a cornerstone of working with parents.

IN CONCLUSION

In the 1980s the role of the voluntary organizations as providers, initiators, policy-makers and innovators seems secure. Indeed, the inclusion of voluntary organizations as partners in joint-funded initiatives or as pilot service providers for specialist groups (such as mentally handicapped children leaving hospital residential care: DHSS, 1983) indicates that their scale of operation is growing in some areas similar to those of statutory service providers. However, the strength of the voluntary sector has been that it is capable of flexibility and change. It can respond to need at both the micro and the macro level. It must also face the consequences of a developing role in service provision in terms of competition with statutory bodies for available funds and also in terms of the philosophical basis of a voluntary service. As Hess (1982) noted, 'There is something about volunteerism that is very subversive – in this country at least. It flies directly in the face of the two conventional wisdoms of our time – professionalism and corporatism.'

In the case of voluntary organizations in the United Kingdom, conflicts may exist where 'self-help' could be seen as reducing the apparent need for a proper professional service from a statutory agency. Conversely, it can be strongly argued that 'self-help' and the development of personal and community autonomy and confidence should complement but never compete with a good minimum statutory service provision. The debate will go on. It must and does transcend the availability (or otherwise) of resources, and there is good evidence that the voluntary sector will continue to respond, to provide, to monitor and evaluate and increasingly to influence profoundly the policies which ultimately dictate provision in our own 'mixed economy' of service provision for mentally handicapped people and their families.

The voluntary and statutory sectors have some aims, responsibilities and structures in common and others that diverge. Social services departments, for example, must be multipurpose and endeavour to provide universal coverage. The voluntary sector can be specific, either in terms of specialist services or as an enabler and convenor of small local self-help projects. However, both sectors are becoming increasingly linked in planning and also in terms of the financial dependence of the voluntary sector upon local and central government for funding. If the general decline of voluntary contributions as a factor in voluntary sector income continues (Unell, 1979), it seems probable that many voluntary organizations will depend not only upon grants but also upon fees for services rendered. Many voluntary organizations in the mental handicap field provide residential care. Such care often enhances client choice. It frequently reflects what parents want. But those voluntary bodies which were pioneers may also have to please social services or health authorities who will actually place and finance the residents. The time has come to take up Dr David Owen's challenge and accept that 'the danger is that we merely repeat the old and familiar slogans about the value of voluntary effort and stop short of a serious analysis of what the voluntary movement really is' (Owen, 1976). In effect, it is a process, innovative, flexible and increasingly complementing statutory service provision and directly accountable to local or central government.

REFERENCES

Brazleton T (1976) Case findings, screening, diagnosis and tracking: discussant's comments. In Tjossem T (ed) *Intervention Strategies for High Risk Infants and Young Children*. Baltimore: University Park Press.

Court Committee (1976) *Fit for the Future. Report of the Committee of Enquiry into Child Health Services*. Cmnd. 6684. London: HMSO.

Cunningham C (1979) Parent counselling. In Craft M (ed) *Tredgold's Mental Retardation*, 12th edn. London: Baillière Tindall.

Cunningham C & Sloper P (1977) Down's syndrome infants: a positive approach to parent and professional collaboration. *Health Visitor 50(2)*: 32–37.

DHSS (Department of Health and Social Security) (1983) *Health Service Development: Helping to Get Mentally Handicapped Children out of Hospital*. Health Circular HC(83)21; Local Authority Circular LAC(83)15. London: DHSS.

Gath A (1978) *Down's Syndrome and the Family*, London: Academic Press.

Hess C (1982) *Surviving the '80s': an Alternative Approach. Voluntary Action Leadership*. New York: Fall.

Hewett S (1970) *The Family and the Handicapped Child*. London: Allen & Unwin.

Jay Committee (1979) *Report of the Committee of Enquiry into Mental Handicap Nursing and Care*. Cmnd. 7468. London: HMSO.

King's Fund Centre (1982) *An Ordinary Life* KFC Project Paper 24. London: King's Fund Centre.

Marrs L (1984) Should a special educator entertain volunteers? Interdependence in rural America. In *Exceptional Children* (January): 361–366.

Nathan Committee (1950) *Report of the Committee on the Law and Practice Relating to Charitable Trusts* (Chairman: the Rt Hon. Lord Nathan). Cmnd. 8710. London: HMSO.

Owen D (1976) *In Sickness and In Health – The Politics of Medicine*. London: Quartet Books.

Pugh G (1982) *Parents as Partners*. London: National Children's Bureau.

Russell P (1983) The parents' perspective of family needs and how to meet them. In Mittler P & McConachie H (eds) *Parents, Professionals and Mentally Handicapped People: Approaches to Partnership*. London & Canberra: Croom Helm.

Unell J (1979) *Voluntary Social Services: Financial Resources*. (Joint report of the National Council of Social Service and Personal Social Services Council) London: Bedford Square Press.

Warnock Committee (1978) *Special Educational Needs: Report of the Committee of Enquiry into the Education of Handicapped Children and Young People*. Cmnd. 7212. London: HMSO.

Wolfenden Committee (1978) *The Future of Voluntary Organisations*. London: Croom Helm.

Chapter 33
The Management of Epilepsy

JOHN CORBETT & SIR DESMOND POND

Epilepsy is one of the most frequently occurring additional major handicaps in people with mental retardation, and as such has important implications for the pattern of care which the person with mental handicap needs and receives.

Epilepsy is not a disease in itself; seizures are an important outward manifestation of the neurological dysfunction underlying particularly severe mental retardation, and the prevention or early effective treatment of epilepsy may in certain instances be an important measure in alleviating the burden of handicap. The handicap of epilepsy places additional stress on families and others caring for people with mental handicap, and with the increasing emphasis on community care it is essential to plan services to allow ready access to the additional facilities which are required for the treatment of epilepsy.

Finally, seizures themselves and the long-term anticonvulsant treatment which is required may further impair learning in the person with mental handicap and have important links with behaviour disturbance; a knowledge of these problems is required of all those responsible for the delivery of services. No longer can epilepsy be considered as a narrow medical problem: available knowledge must be shared by the whole team responsible for care.

In this chapter the prevalence and outcome of epilepsy and its relationship to the main causes of mental retardation will be considered, together with the prevention and treatment of epilepsy.

PREVALENCE OF EPILEPSY IN PEOPLE WITH MENTAL RETARDATION

In the general population of schoolchildren the prevalence of epilepsy is 0.5–0.7%, and seizures are more frequent during the first years of life. Before the age of five years, 3–8% of all children experience one or more epileptic seizures (Aicardi, 1980).

Epidemiological studies suggest that 3–6% of children with IQs between 50 and 70 suffer from continuing epilepsy (Rutter et al., 1970; Peckham, 1974). The figure is higher in those children whose seizures are complicated by other handicaps. Until recently, most studies have been of institutional populations, and this accounts for the higher figure of 19.5% given by Margerison (1962) for 'high-grade' institutional populations.

Very few total population studies have been carried out and even fewer follow-up studies reported. Richardson and his co-workers (1981) studied the distribution of seizures in a population classified as mentally retarded in childhood, in the city of Aberdeen; they were followed up to the age of 22 years. Of this sample 24% had some history of persistent seizures at the age of 22, while seizures had occurred in 19% in the pre-school years and 13% in each period of early-, late- and post-school years.

This study was of all those children born in the years 1951 to 1955 who were resident in the city in 1962. A child was defined as mentally retarded if at any time up to the age of 15 years they had been placed in a special school, training centre or hospital for retarded children. This is an administrative definition of mental retardation and generally included people with IQs of less than 75.

Of the young people with *severe* mental retardation, that is with IQs of less than 50, 44% had experienced one or more seizures by the age of 22 years, compared with 19% of those with IQs of 50 or greater. For those with some history of seizures, there was no significant association between IQ and degree of seizure impairment (Richardson et al., 1981). For the total population, 40% had experienced seizures for more than ten years, whereas 21% had seizures over a period of less than one year.

Males with mental retardation were almost four times as likely as females to have seizures, and the chance of young people with mental retardation having some history of seizures was more than forty times that of their non-retarded peers. In an epidemiological study of severely retarded children under the age of 14 years from the Camberwell district of South East London, it was found that 32% had had a seizure at some time during life, but although many of these continued to be labelled as 'epileptic' and received anticonvulsant drugs for long periods of their childhood, only 19% had suffered a seizure in the year prior to the study (Corbett et al., 1975). This increase in seizures in the severely retarded and those in contact with services for the mentally handicapped persisted into adult life and, with increasing age, more of those with epilepsy tended to be in institutions (Corbett, 1974).

In this study, as in others, there was a very marked increase in the frequency of seizures in the more severely retarded, so that nearly 50% of those who were profoundly handicapped had had fits, usually occurring for the first time in early infancy.

This very marked increase in seizures in the severely retarded is understandable as most children with IQs of under 50 have overt signs of brain damage. As in the Aberdeen study epilepsy was more frequent in boys; in the Camberwell study 39% of boys had suffered from seizures, compared with only 26% of the girls. It is possible to distinguish four situations during early infancy when brain damage associated with epilepsy is particularly likely to occur: perinatal brain damage, infantile spasms and Lennox–Gastaut syndrome and febrile convulsions.

Seizures and brain damage in the peri-natal period

The causes of neonatal seizures are very varied, and it is convenient to classify them according to the times at which the cause first operated – pre-natal, peri-natal or post-natal.

Most frequently, they are related to intrapartum hypoxia or trauma with consequences such as brain haemorrhage and oedema. Less frequently, they are due to post-natal infection, metabolic disorder or developmental defect. Different factors come into play according to the time of the first seizure. The seizures are usually related to pre- or peri-natal brain trauma or early hypoglycaemia (within three days of birth), hypocalcaemia and/or hypomagnesaemia (within four to eight days after birth).

Most studies suggest that the outcome for neonatal seizures is poor, in terms of both intellectual development and persistence of seizures, although it is dependent on the underlying cause, and the outcome of those with, for example, late-onset hypocalcaemia is better.

Follow-up studies of children with seizures occurring between 28 days and one year after birth suggest that persistent seizures are more common in those with mental retardation (73%) than in those without (18%) (Chevrie and Aicardi, 1979). Neonatal seizures tend to be multifocal in origin, although status epilepticus is not common. It is usual to try to stop seizures in neonates pharmacologically; however, some authors express the opinion that there is no difference in outcome or subsequent development between the treated and non-treated groups.

Infantile spasms

The onset of infantile spasms, or West's syndrome, is commonly between the ages of three and eight months. In about half the cases, they are of unknown origin, whilst the rest are associated with brain damage of various kinds, ranging from tuberose sclerosis to inborn errors of metabolism (Jeavons and Bower, 1964); 80–90% of both cryptogenic and symptomatic cases are associated with mental retardation (Lacy and Penry, 1976).

A distinctive EEG pattern of hypsarrhythmia is seen most frequently during the second year of life (in 75%), the frequency dropping to 7% between the 5th and 9th year, and to 1% between the ages of 10 and 19 years. Of the 75% who survive, 10% will be mildly retarded, 16% normal and the remainder severely retarded, although in the cryptogenic cases the outlook is somewhat better, with 37% showing normal development (Jeavons et al., 1973).

Like many other forms of epilepsy associated with severe encephalopathy in early childhood, infantile spasms are often followed by severe regression in behaviour and cognitive development. In some cases, language development and social relationships are particularly affected in a way similar to that seen in early infantile autism (Taft and Cohen, 1971). In cryptogenic cases, there has usually been a period of apparently normal development, and the condition is probably more appropriately entitled non-progressive disintegrative psychosis of childhood (Corbett et al., 1977).

Early treatment with steroids is usually beneficial in respect of both clinical and EEG improvement, and as there is evidence that the outlook for mental development may be better in the group treated early, it seems possible that in this instance the seizures themselves may be responsible, at least in part, for the intellectual deterioration which is seen.

Lennox–Gastaut syndrome

Around the age of 3–5 years, sometimes following infantile spasms or arising de novo, progressive seizures sometimes develop which are also associated with intellectual deterioration. Although this has been given the name Lennox–Gastaut syndrome or petit mal variant, it is not dissimilar to West's syndrome, and may in fact simply be a version of that disorder beginning somewhat later in life, but still in the pre-school period. A variety of seizure types occur, with tonic, atonic (drop or astatic attacks), myoclonic seizures and absences. The EEG shows high-voltage spike or sharp and slow wave complex activity at 1.5–2 Hz which is more regular than in hypsarrhythmia. Sometimes the frequency of seizures is so high that 'minor status epilepticus' can be recognized on the EEG, and clinically there is a fluctuating confusional state which may persist for weeks or even years. It is particularly important to recognize this in children with severe mental retardation as it may be treatable. In 20 % of cases of the Lennox–Gastaut syndrome the seizures start after the sixth year of life; in this case, there is often preceding intellectual impairment and evidence of brain damage (Barriera et al., 1980).

Febrile convulsions

Febrile convulsions occur in 2.5 % of children under the age of five years. In the majority of cases they are isolated and benign, but complications occur in about 9 % (Millichap, 1968). Complications are particularly likely if status epilepticus occurs; it may give rise to infantile hemiplegia with subsequent hemiatrophy of the brain. There may also be severe mental retardation (if there has been severe cerebral oedema) and subsequent temporal lobe epilepsy, which, like infantile hemiplegia, may be associated with subsequent hyperkinetic behaviour disorders (the so-called HHE syndrome). In one study of 100 patients with temporal lobe epilepsy, a third had a history of prolonged febrile convulsions lasting more than 30 minutes (Ounsted et al., 1966; Falconer, 1971). The most common pathology in temporal lobe epilepsy is mesial temporal sclerosis, due to metabolic factors operating during status epilepticus. Prolonged febrile convulsions as a cause of mental retardation are often difficult to distinguish from other conditions associated with acute brain damage in early infancy such as 'acute infantile hemiplegia' or 'acute toxic encephalopathy'. Prevention of status epilepticus may be possible if the seizures can be terminated rapidly by the use of rectal diazepam and by antipyretic therapy (Wilson, 1981).

Prophylaxis of febrile convulsions in selected cases, using phenobarbitone or sodium valproate, has to be weighed against possible side-effects of the drugs and is best restricted to those with a high risk of subsequent convulsions, particularly those with a history of seizures in the first year of life, those with seizures between the ages of one and three years who have a family history of epilepsy and those with two or more febrile convulsions (Majkowski, 1977). The risk of subsequent seizures is higher in infants with pre-existing cerebral palsy or mental retardation, so that the risk for developing epilepsy by the age of 20 years is 2.5 % for children with febrile convulsions, without prior neurological disorders, without prolonged seizures and without focal seizures, while seizures develop in 17 % of those with such complications (Annegers et al., 1979).

EPILEPSY IN PARTICULAR MENTAL RETARDATION SYNDROMES

There have been very many accounts of the association of mental retardation with epilepsy in isolated case reports of particular conditions. Some of the main syndromes associated with epilepsy are listed in Table 33.1. While epilepsy is reportedly rare in Down's syndrome, kernicterus and cretinism (Crome, 1965), it is much commoner in conditions associated with evidence of more extensive or localized brain damage, such as spastic cerebral palsy, and almost universal in those where extensive cortical involvement is associated with severe mental retardation. For example, in the Sturge–Weber syndrome or tuberose sclerosis, if the subject is severely mentally retarded (that is with an IQ of less than 50), then seizures seem almost inevitable. Similarly, in biochemical disorders such as phenylketonuria or homocystinuria, if the metabolic condition is untreated, epilepsy is common, and again there is an association in treated cases between the intellectual level and frequency of the seizures. It is likely that both are related to the severity of the biochemical disorder, although in some cases the seizures themselves may lead to further intellectual impairment.

In some conditions associated with mental retardation, epilepsy, often taking the form of West's or Lennox–Gastaut syndrome, may be a presenting or predominant symptom, while in others, such as meningitis, seizures presenting at the onset have

Table 33.1 Epilepsy associated with specific mental retardation syndromes.

	Epilepsy	West's syndrome	Lennox–Gastaut syndrome
Metabolic abnormalities			
Phenylketonuria	+	+	+
Maple syrup urine disease	+	+	
Hyperornithaemia	+	+	
Isovaleric acidaemia	+	+	
Non-ketotic hyperglycaemia	+	+	
Pyridoxine dependency	+	+	
Leucine-sensitive hypoglycaemia	+	+	+
Tay–Sachs disease	+	+	
Lipoidosis G_{M1} and G_{M3}	+		+
Metachromatic leukodystrophy	+		+
Homocystinurea			+
Dysplastic conditions			
Tuberose sclerosis	+	+	+
Sturge–Weber syndrome	+	+	+
Megalencephaly	+		+
Other cerebral malformations	+	+	+
Aicardi syndrome	+	+	
Pre-natal infections			
Cytomegalovirus	+	+	
Syphilis	+	+	
Toxoplasmosis	+	+	
Post-natal infections			
Purulent meningitis	+		+
Acute encephalitis	+		+
Subacute sclerosing panencephalitis	+		+
Post-immunization encephalopathy	+	+	
Post-traumatic	+		
Chromosomal abnormalities			
Down's syndrome		+	

serious implications for future intellectual development. The nature of the epilepsy and prognosis are largely related to the severity of the cerebral insult and the age of onset.

Epilepsy in Down's syndrome

In the past, it was generally believed that epilepsy was rare in Down's syndrome (Kirman, 1951; Illingworth, 1958), but with the increased longevity of people with this condition over the past few years epilepsy has been reported increasingly frequently and seems to occur in 8–20 % depending on the age of the sample (Levinson et al., 1955; Seppalainen and Kivalo, 1967). Recent studies suggest that the incidence of epilepsy in Down's syndrome is age-dependent. In subjects under the age of 20 years it was found in 1.9 % and by the age of 55 had reached 16 % (Veall, 1974). Other studies (Tangye, 1979) have shown an even higher frequency, so that after the age of 55 years it reached 71.4 %. It seems

possible that this may be related to the Alzheimer-like changes seen in the brain of older subjects with Down's syndrome and the onset of dementia, but clear evidence for such an association is thus far lacking.

In younger subjects with Down's syndrome, infantile spasms are occasionally seen, and both this condition and the myoclonic seizures which sometimes develop seem to respond to pyridoxine (McCoy et al., 1964). Further evidence for an underlying biochemical abnormality in some cases of epilepsy associated with Down's syndrome is found in the precipitation of seizures by 5-hydroxytryptophan given to improve muscle tone in young Down's syndrome infants (Coleman, 1971).

Epilepsy and cerebral palsy

Children with cerebral palsy, usually resulting from pre- or peri-natal brain injury, frequently suffer from epilepsy, 36 % having a life-long history.

Where both the degree of mental retardation and cerebral palsy are severe the frequency is even higher, and in the Camberwell study seizures were reported in 60%, compared with only 20% of severely retarded children without cerebral palsy. Now that these children have been followed up for ten years, it is apparent that epilepsy is the commonest cause of death in this population. The rate is highest in spastic children and lowest in those with athetoid cerebral palsy. Infantile hemiplegia, which is more frequently post-natal in origin, has a particularly high incidence of seizures (see above), and occasionally where the seizure disorder proves resistant to anticonvulsant treatment, neurosurgical intervention is indicated if the degree of retardation is not too severe.

Epilepsy and behaviour disorder

It is generally recognized that there is a strong positive association between inter-ictal behaviour disorders and epilepsy. In schoolchildren with epilepsy in the general population, approximately 25% have been found to suffer from significant psychiatric disorder (Rutter et al., 1970; Mellor, 1977), while in children with complicated epilepsy who are in institutions this rises to nearly 70% (Corbett and Trimble, 1983). In children with severe mental retardation, the association is less marked, possibly because of the strong association with severe cerebral palsy, and there are few systematic studies of adults with mental retardation, although there is a well-recognized association between hyperkinetic behaviour disorders in children and schizophrenic-like illness in adults with temporal lobe epilepsy. Generally speaking, however, there is little that is distinctive about the type of psychiatric disorder which is seen and there is little evidence to support the concept of a typical epileptic personality (Tizard, 1962; Verduyn, 1980).

Acute disturbances can also occur in the pre-ictal phase (a well-recognized, but poorly understood condition). Some people, for example, become irritable and moody before an attack and are said to be 'working up to a fit'. Acute disturbances can also occur during the aura of the seizure itself, though this only lasts for a few seconds, or in the confusional state that often accompanies the complex partial seizure. Temporal lobe attacks have been said to be uncommon in people with mental retardation, but this is by no means the case and may arise from the patients' difficulty in describing their subjective experiences during the attack.

Particular caution is needed in the use of the term 'epileptic equivalent', which suggests that children may suffer from paroxysmal disturbances of behaviour which have an epileptic basis although they are not accompanied by any of the typical signs of an attack. Sudden outbursts of temper and violence were particularly liable to be regarded as having an epileptic basis, especially in the older literature. Failure to distinguish temper outbursts without any epileptic basis from true seizures, may lead to anticonvulsants being unavailingly increased and to a failure to recognize emotional and environmental causes for behaviour disturbances.

Post-ictal behavioural disorder usually take the form of short-lived confusional states, which may be maintained by brief minor epileptic attacks passing almost unnoticed, but serving to continue the general disruption of cerebral activity. Episodic behaviour disorders that are related to true ictal or post-ictal states are likely to respond to treatment with anticonvulsants, and this may be an important diagnostic point as non-ictal disorders do not usually respond in this way.

A number of factors may be implicated in the relationship between inter-ictal behaviour disorder and epilepsy. As these often interact, it may be difficult to identify the relative contribution of each in an individual case. They include the seizure frequency and chronicity, seizure type, the site and extent of underlying neurophysiological disturbance as shown on the EEG, the age of onset of the seizures, underlying brain damage, psychosocial influences and drug therapy. In the clinical situation, it is necessary to consider each of these factors individually, and their relative contribution to the clinical picture which is seen.

Intellectual deterioration

It has long been recognized that a minority of patients with long-standing epilepsy show progressive intellectual deterioration. Pond (1974) has argued that the proportion of deteriorated patients does not appear to increase with age and that deteriorated adult patients had shown early evidence of this phenomenon in childhood.

Some causes of intellectual deterioration, such as West's syndrome and the Lennox–Gastaut syndrome, status epilepticus and underlying neurodegenerative disorders, have already been considered, but in other cases there is no evidence of these disorders and in such instances the same list of factors as has been incriminated with behaviour disorders needs to be considered.

Early studies suggested that a high seizure frequency was more common in those with intellectual deterioration (Chaudhry and Pond, 1961), although more recently increasing attention has been paid to the effects of long-term anticonvulsant therapy as a significant and possibly preventable cause of intellectual deterioration (Corbett and Trimble, 1983).

Epilepsy and childhood psychosis

Apart from those cases where infantile spasms or epilepsy associated with an acute encephalopathy in early childhood may be incriminated in the aetiology of childhood autism or psychoses, the prevalence of epilepsy is not greatly increased in most children with this condition. Seizures do, however, occur in approximately one-third, usually in later adolescence. There is a risk of these being precipitated by epileptogenic psychotropic medication given to control behaviour disturbance. In many cases, the seizures are isolated and do not require long-term anticonvulsant medication. In some cases there appears to be progressive behavioural disturbance associated with psychomotor seizures which may be difficult to treat (Corbett, 1983).

TREATMENT

The additional handicap of epilepsy causes particular problems for families and others caring for the mentally retarded child. Anxiety and fear for the life of the child, engendered by the seizures themselves, frequently compound the sense of partial bereavement caused by the presence of the handicapped child in the family.

It follows that there is a particular need to facilitate access of people with epilepsy and mental retardation to outpatient services for epilepsy. Special investigations such as EEGs and neuroradiology will need to be carried out at hospital.

However, on-going supervision and monitoring of serum anticonvulsant levels may be best carried out by the same team of specialists visiting special schools, adult training centres or residential facilities in which the handicapped person works or lives. This also provides the opportunity for staff counselling and support.

ANTICONVULSANT THERAPY

The general principles of treatment of epilepsy in people with mental retardation are similar to those for non-retarded subjects. The situation is complicated by the fact that little is known about the long-term effects of anticonvulsant drugs on the behaviour or intellectual performance of people with mental retardation. Clinical side-effects of anticonvulsant medication are more difficult to distinguish from the underlying neurological disorder, and seizures are often more complex and severe.

Modern anti-epileptic therapy is based on clinical knowledge of both the differential diagnosis of epilepsy and the pharmacokinetics of anticonvulsant drugs. The International Classification of Seizures provides some insight into the differential diagnosis in older children and adults. However, in the newborn and in early infancy seizures are less well systematized except in the case of a few well-defined syndromes.

Measurement of plasma anticonvulsant drug levels has clearly shown that there is a significant correlation between the plasma level and the clinical effects; however, the relationship between drug dose and blood levels varies greatly among different subjects.

In combination many anticonvulsant and other drugs interact, resulting in inhibition or stimulation of the drug metabolism through enzyme induction.

It is important to know not only the effectiveness and side-effects of an individual drug, but also the absorption and elimination rate (that is, the metabolic half-life) and the time taken to achieve a steady-state therapeutic level.

The indications for the use of different anticonvulsants are similar in retarded patients to those in people of normal intelligence and are summarized in Table 33.2. Where possible, a minimum number of drugs, and if possible a single one of proven low toxicity, should be used, bearing in mind the additional burdens placed on those caring for the retarded.

Among the other chronic disturbances in metabolism which are likely to remain undetected in people with mental retardation are those involving folic acid and calcium. Both require monitoring, and although there have been no specific studies of folate metabolism in mentally retarded populations, it is clear that children on long-term anticonvulsant (particularly phenytoin) therapy who show intellectual deterioration tend to suffer from folate depletion (Trimble et al., 1980). There have also been a number of reports of calcium deficiency in patients receiving long-term anticonvulsants, and this has been confirmed in mentally retarded patients with epilepsy (Viukara et al., 1972).

Table 33.2 Drugs of choice in various types of epilepsy.

Type of epilepsy	EEG	Drugs of choice	Therapeutic blood level (mg/l)	Range of maintenance dose (mg/day)
Generalized seizures				
Tonic–clonic (grand mal)	Spike and wave	Carbamazepine	4–10	600–1400
		Sodium valproate	60–100	600–2000
Absence seizures				
typical (petit mal)	3 Hz spike and wave	Ethosuximide	4–10	750–1500
atypical	Poly-spike and wave	Sodium valproate	60–100	600–2000
Myoclonic seizures	2 Hz spike and wave	Sodium valproate	60–100	600–2000
		Clonazepam	0.02–0.07	0.1–6
Partial seizures				
Simple/complex (psychomotor)	Temporal spike and wave	Carbamazepine	4–10	600–1400
Partial, becoming generalized	Spikes and sharp waves	Carbamazepine	4–10	600–1400

Unwanted side-effects

Phenobarbitone

Unfavourable behavioural changes have been estimated to occur in 20–75% of children receiving phenobarbitone as prophylaxis for febrile convulsions in infancy (Thorn, 1975; Heckmatt et al., 1976; Wolf and Forsythe, 1978). Although Camfield et al. (1979) found no significant differences in IQ between toddlers treated with phenobarbitone and those treated with placebo after 8–12 months, there were effects on memory that were related to serum levels and effects on comprehension which were related to duration of treatment. In a recent comparative trial of monotherapy with four major anticonvulsants in previously untreated children with epilepsy, five of the first ten (50%) children randomized to phenobarbitone developed hyperactivity or aggressive behaviour or difficulty in coping with school work necessitating withdrawal of the drug (McGowan et al., 1983).

There have been few systematic studies of the use of phenobarbitone in older people with mental retardation, and although it remains one of the most effective anticonvulsants in the prevention of febrile convulsions in infancy, its use is limited in patients with brain damage by its tendency to exacerbate behaviour disorders.

Phenytoin

Acute intoxication with phenytoin leads to a confusional state sometimes referred to as 'encephalopathy', which is associated with neurological signs of toxicity, especially nystagmus and ataxia. It has become apparent that a chronic picture of progressive degenerative disorder may also occur without classical cerebellar signs, and this may also occur with relatively low dosages (Logan and Freeman, 1969; Vallarta et al., 1974). This can occur in adults, but has been noted especially in children, particularly those with pre-existing mental retardation or brain damage. In such instances, further deterioration in intellectual function, in the absence of more classical signs of toxicity, may be overlooked or mistakenly regarded as part of an underlying progressive neurological disease.

Valproate

A few examples of an encephalopathy associated with sodium valproate have been reviewed by Davidson (1983). He regarded them as examples of acute toxicity with stupor and drowsiness as a prominent feature. It is not clear whether these are associated with drug interactions, especially with barbiturates, exacerbation of epilepsy or an effect on arousal mechanisms (Reynolds, 1983a).

Benzodiazepines

The behavioural effects of these drugs have been reviewed by Trimble (1983). In the same manner as barbiturates, there are reports of varying degrees of irritability, aggression, hyperactivity and antisocial behaviour in up to 50% of patients, especially children. While clonazepam and nitrazepam may be effective in the Lennox–Gastaut syndrome, one of the major disadvantages of the diazepam derivatives is the tendency for tolerance to develop; diazepam is probably best reserved for the treatment of status epilepticus, where it may be most effective when given rectally.

Ethosuximide

A number of reports have appeared of 'psychosis' or 'encephalopathy' precipitated by this drug, and Roger et al. (1968) described 15 cases and reviewed the earlier literature. It is relevant that a number of these patients have been mentally retarded young adults with a history of psychiatric disorder, and Wolf (1980) has emphasized the role of this drug in precipitating 'alternating' psychosis with 'forced' normalization of the EEG.

Carbamazepine

There are few reports of serious behaviour disturbance with this drug (Reynolds, 1983b) but Dalby (1975), reviewing its psychotropic effects, mentions examples of irritability aggression, confusion, or psychiatric breakdown, mainly in brain-damaged patients also on other drugs.

It is clear from this brief review of the adverse effects of anticonvulsant therapy that particular care needs to be taken in mentally retarded populations in minimizing these effects. This can be best achieved if a single anticonvulsant is prescribed or the number kept to a minimum, if careful monitoring is undertaken not only of anticonvulsant blood levels, but also by clinical and psychological assessment to detect early signs of behavioural or cognitive deterioration.

CONCLUSION

When epilepsy occurs in association with mental retardation it presents particular problems in management because of its association with other handicaps. It is an important challenge to all those working in the multidisciplinary team caring for retarded people.

REFERENCES

Aicardi J (1980) Seizures and epilepsy in children under two years of age. In Tyner JH (ed) *The Treatment of Epilepsy.* pp. 203–250. Philadelphia: Lippincott.

Annegers JF, Hauser WA, Elverback LR & Kurland LT (1979) The risk of epilepsy following febrile convulsions. *Neurology 29:* 297–303.

Barriera AA, Lison MP & Fernandez AL (1980) Incidence of cases of Lennox Gastaut Syndrome with onset before and after 6 years of age, aetiological factors and intellectual level. *Arqivos Neuro-psiquiatria 38:* 341–351.

Camfield CS, Chaplin S, Doyle AB, Shapiro SH, Cumming SC & Camfield PS (1979) Side effects of phenobarbitone in toddlers. Behavioural and cognitive effects. *Journal of Paediatrics 95:* 361–365.

Chaudhry MR & Pond DA (1961) Mental deterioration in epileptic children. *Journal of Neurology, Neurosurgery & Psychiatry 24:* 213–219.

Chevrie JJ & Aicardi J (1979) Convulsive disorders in the first year of life: persistence of epileptic seizures. *Epilepsia 20:* 643–649.

Coleman M (1971) Infantile spasms associated with 5-hydroxytryptophan administration in patients with Down's Syndrome. *Neurology 21:* 911–919.

Corbett JA (1974) Epilepsy and mental retardation. In Parsonage MJ (ed) *Total Care in Severe Epilepsy.* Proceedings of VIth International Symposium on Epilepsy. London: International Bureau for Epilepsy. pp. 85–87.

Corbett JA (1983) Epilepsy and childhood psychosis In Wing JK & Wing L (eds) *Handbook of Psychiatry, Vol. III, Psychoses of Unknown Aetiology.* pp. 198–202. London: Cambridge University Press.

Corbett JA & Trimble MR (1983) Epilepsy and anticonvulsant medication. In Rutter M (ed) *Developmental Neuropsychiatry.* pp. 112–129. New York: Guildford Press.

Corbett JA, Harris R & Robinson R (1975) Epilepsy. In Wortis J (ed) *Mental Retardation and Developmental Disabilities, Vol. VII.* pp. 79–111. Bruner Mazel: New York.

Corbett JA, Harris R, Taylor E & Trimble M (1977) Progressive disintegrative psychosis of childhood. *Journal of Child Psychology & Psychiatry, 18:* 211–219.

Crome L (1965) In Hilliard LT & Kirman BH (eds) *Mental Deficiency.* pp. 225–273. London: Churchill.

Dalby MA (1975) Behavioural effects of carbamazepine. In Penry JK & Daly DD (eds) *Complex Partial Seizures and their Treatment.* Advances in Neurology 2. pp. 331–344. New York: Raven Press.

Davidson DLW (1983) A review of the side effects of sodium valproate. *British Journal of Clinical Practice 27 (Suppl.):* 79–85.

Falconer MA (1971) Genetic and related aetiological factors in temporal lobe epilepsy: a review. *Epilepsia 12:* 13–31.

Heckmatt J, Houston A & Dodds K (1976) Failure of phenobarbitone to prevent febrile convulsions. *British Medical Journal i:* 559–561.

Illingworth RS (1958) *Recent Advances in Cerebral Palsy.* London: Churchill.

Jeavons PM & Bower BD (1964) *Infantile Spasms* Clinics in Developmental Medicine 15. London: Spastics Society International Medical Publications/Heinemann.

Jeavons PM, Bower BD & Dimitrakoudi M (1973) Long term prognosis of 150 cases of 'West syndrome' *Epilepsia 14:* 153–164.

Kirman BH (1951) Epilepsy in mongolism. *Archives of Diseases of Childhood 26:* 501–503.

Lacy JR & Penry JK (1976) *Infantile Spasms.* New York: Raven Press.

Levinson A, Friedman A & Stamps F (1955) Variability of mongolism. *Paediatrics 16:* 43–54.

Logan WJ & Freeman JM (1969) Pseudodegenerative diseases due to diphenylhydantoin intoxication. *Archives of Neurology 21:* 631–637.

Majkowski J (1977) Ethical, legal and medical aspects of pharmacological prophylaxis of epilepsy. In Majkowski J (ed) *Post-traumatic Epilepsy and Pharmacological Prophylaxis.* pp. 129–138. Warsaw: Polfa.

Margerison JH (1962) *Proceedings of the London Conference on the Scientific Study of Mental Retardation.* London: International Association for the Scientific Study of Mental Deficiency.

McCoy EE, Anast CS & Naylor JJ (1964) The excretion of oxalic acid following deoxypyridoxine and tryptophan administration in mongoloid and non-mongoloid subjects. *Journal of Paediatrics 65:* 208–214.

McGowan MEL, Neville BGR & Reynolds EH (1983) Comparative monotherapy trial in children with epilepsy. *British Journal of Clinical Practice 27(Suppl.):* 115–118.

Mellor D (1977) *A Study of Epilepsy with Particular Reference to Behaviour Disorder.* MD Thesis, University of Leeds.

Millichap JG (1968) Clinical evaluations and manifestations. In Millichap J G (ed) *Febrile Convulsions.* pp. 17–36. New York: Macmillan.

Ounsted C, Lindsay J & Norman R (1966) *Biological Factors in Temporal Lobe Epilepsy.* Clinics in Developmental Medicine 22. London: Spastics Society MEIU/Heinemann.

Peckham C (1974) National Child Development Study (1958) Cohort. Personal Communication.

Pond DA (1974) Epilepsy and personality disorders. In Vinken PJ & Bruyn GW (eds) *Handbook of Clinical Neurology, Vol. 15.* pp. 576–592. New York: Elsevier.

Reynolds EH (1983a) Iatrogenic disorders in epilepsy. In Williams D (ed) *Modern Trends in Neurology 5.* pp. 271–286. London: Butterworths.

Reynolds EH (1983b) Mental effects of anticonvulsant medication: a review. *Epilepsia 24 (Suppl. 2):* 85–95.

Richardson SA, Koller H, Katz M & McLaren J (1981) A functional classification of seizures and its distribution in a mentally retarded population. *American Journal of Mental Deficiency 85:* 457–466.

Roger J, Grangeon H, Guey J & Lob H (1968) Incidences psychiatriques et physiologiques du traitement par l'ethosuccimide chez les Epileptiques. *Encephale 5:* 407–438.

Rutter M, Graham P & Yule W (1970) *A Neuropsychiatric Study in Childhood.* London: Spastics International Medical Publications/Heinemann.

Seppalainen AM & Kivalo E (1967) EEG findings and epilepsy in Down's syndrome. *Journal of Mental Deficiency Research 11:* 116–125.

Taft LT & Cohen MJ (1971) Hypsarrhythmia and infantile autism: a clinical report. *Journal of Autism & Childhood Schizophrenia 1:* 26–27.

Tangye SR (1979) The EEG and incidence of epilepsy in Down's syndrome. *Journal of Mental Deficiency Research 23:* 17–24.

Thorn I (1975) A controlled study of prophylactic long-term treatment of febrile convulsions with phenobarbital. *Acta Neurologica Scandinavica 60 (Suppl.):* 67–70.

Tizard B (1962) The personality of epileptics: a discussion of the evidence. *Psychological Bulletin 59;* 196–210.

Trimble MR (1983) Benzodiazepines in epilepsy. In Trimble MR (ed) *Benzodiazepines Divided.* pp. 65–91. Chichester, West Sussex: Wiley.

Trimble MR, Corbett JA & Donaldson D (1980) Folic acid and mental symptoms in children with epilepsy. *Journal of Neurology, Neurosurgery & Psychiatry 128:* 27–34.

Vallarta JM, Bell DB & Reichert A (1974) A progressive encephalopathy due to chronic hydantoin intoxication. *American Journal of Diseases of Children 128:* 27–34.

Veall RM (1974) The prevalence of epilepsy among mongols related to age. *Journal of Mental Deficiency Research 18:* 43–48.

Verduyn C (1980) Social factors contributing to poor emotional adjustment in children with epilepsy. In Kulig BM, Meinhardi H & Stores G (eds) *Epilepsy and Behaviour.* pp. 177–184. Lisse, The Netherlands: Swets & Zeitlinger.

Viukara NMA, Tannisto P & Kaumo K (1972) Low serum calcium levels in forty mentally retarded subnormal epileptics. *Journal of Mental Deficiency Research 16:* 192–195.

Wilson JT (1981) Antipyretic management of febrile seizures. In Nelson KB & Ellenberg JH (eds) *Febrile Seizures.* pp. 231–239. New York: Raven Press.

Wolf P (1980) Psychic disorders in epilepsy. In Canger R, Angeleri F & Penry JK (eds) *Advances in Epileptology: the XIth Epilepsy International Symposium.* pp. 159–160. New York: Raven Press.

Wolf SM & Forsythe A (1978) Behaviour disturbance, phenobarbital and febrile seizures. *Paediatrics 61:* 728–730.

Chapter 34
The Role of the Neurologist

JOHN PATTEN

The neurologist's role in mental handicap is a wide-ranging one. It includes documenting the neurological correlates of classical disorders, occasionally identifying the disorder causing mental handicap by virtue of the neurological findings; estimating the type, extent and treatment possibilities in some of the acquired disorders, such as head injury, leading to mental handicap; and the detection of new neurological disorders in the already compromised central nervous system. The neurologist also assumes a very important role in the recognition and treatment of epileptic disorders, the latter complicating the whole field of mental handicap, and including the particularly difficult associated behavioural disorders, some of which may be related to anticonvulsant medication.

It should never be forgotten that mental handicap is a symptom and not a diagnosis, and continuing efforts to establish the medical basis of the child's disability should be made. Accurate diagnosis may also enable a clearer prognosis for future expectations to be made.

GENERAL CONSIDERATIONS

Until the age of two, only physical findings and motor development can be used to assess the child's progress. Tests of long-term value assessing intellectual development only assume significance between the ages of four and six, and the recognition of previously unsuspected specific learning disabilities may cast doubt on the presence of global defects necessary to allow an accurate diagnosis of mental handicap to be made. In the first three years of life, in addition to neurological assessment, it is vital that audiological, ophthalmological and speech therapy assessments are made as a prerequisite to formal intelligence testing. Quite wide variations in the speed of acquiring motor skills and the loss of primitive reflex responses are found in normal

children, so that, although suspicions of abnormality may occur, it may be impossible to give an accurate answer as to whether or not motor deficit exists in the first year to 18 months of life. Some of the classical neurological findings of brain damage also require maturation in other brain pathways to become apparent, so that apparently new abnormal physical signs, especially in the field of movement disorders, only really become manifest after 18 months of age. They may then be incorrectly ascribed by the parents and other interested parties to falls or insignificant injuries occurring within the first 18 months of life, rather than being accepted as late developing evidence of pre-existent brain damage. Having established such findings, a yearly review, watching for the development of further new signs, is important. If early assessment and the ages when developmental milestones were reached did not give any strong indication of disability, such findings may then be evidence of new or progressive metabolic or structural brain disease. It must be stressed, however, that the vast majority of children with mental handicap will not have physical signs of nervous system damage, and, in most instances, those with such signs will clearly be suffering from cerebral palsy due to relatively obvious peri-natal factors.

Examination of the nervous system in children is always difficult and, in the very young, extremely unstructured, any opportunity to observe any particular function being taken as and when it presents itself, giving the observer the impression that it is all rather haphazard; indeed, it is, unless there is continuous vigilance, watching everything the child does or attempts to do carefully and critically. In normal children up to the age of two, a simple play approach to the examination is used. Between two and four a more structured approach can be introduced, and some cooperative four-year-olds will allow as complete and accurate a neurological assessment as one could ever hope to achieve. From four, an adult-type assessment of the nervous system can be attempted, only the worst attention-seeking type of child proving taxing to the point of impossibility. In those with mental handicap the two-year-old approach is required at virtually all ages; formal instructions are usually not understood, or specifically resisted. For example, attempting to look at the fundi may well provide the best opportunity to assess forced eye closure during the whole examination! Even in the most uncooperative person patience, smiling, talking quietly, praise for cooperation and, particularly, the close attendance of a parent or much-loved ward nurse or helper will eventually make the effort both possible and worth while. It is important to recall that mental handicap is about intellectual function. Motor skills and sphincter disturbances in themselves are often only slightly delayed, and are often in no way proportional to the severity of the intellectual deficit. Therefore, even in the most severely intellectually handicapped child, little or nothing in the way of physical findings may actually be elicited by the most diligent examination. Nevertheless, such examination must be attempted, and the following section provides some indication as to how this can best be achieved in this difficult situation.

NEUROLOGICAL ASSESSMENT

The behaviour of the child, his posture, alertness, inquisitiveness, balance, gait and reaction to the surroundings can all be noted whilst obtaining a history of the pre-natal, peri-natal and post-natal period of the child's life from the parents. Information on developmental milestones, performance comparison with siblings, and the observations of skilled paramedical staff all form an important part of this assessment. If a lengthy history is necessary, it may be best to be brief initially, and examine the child as soon as he seems to have relaxed and settled into the situation. Throughout the interview, the posture when sitting, facial expression and habits with hands, fingers or face should be noted; visual movements and interest in objects should be observed and encouraged. Simple toys or inexpensive and preferably unbreakable clinical equipment can be pressed into use. Unfortunately, ophthalmoscopes are very popular, and are best kept hidden both before and after their use! Startled responses to noise, in or outside the room, often provide an unintended hearing test, and telephone calls, although unwelcome, serve a similar purpose, but may provoke an overwhelmingly lasting interest in the hand-set throughout the

rest of the consultation. Within five minutes, a fairly good idea of the degree of difficulty likely to be experienced during the examination and the best approach to performing it can be gained by the experienced examiner.

Talking to the child, asking to see his toy, or allowing him to hold a flashlight, are all good starting ploys. The size and shape of the head can be noted by direct observation, noting in particular any asymmetry or peculiar shape, the position of the ears and the location of the orbits; if appropriate, the fontanelle can be palpated. A formal measurement of the skull size around the largest occipitofrontal circumference should be made to assess whether macro- or microcephaly exists, with various diagnostic possibilities. External characteristic features, such as the naevi of Sturge–Weber syndrome, the rash of adenoma sebaceum, the mutilated lips of Lesch–Nyhan syndrome and the facial abnormalities of hypertelorism and craniostenosis, and the shape of the jaw and dentition are all noted.

The size, shape and reactivity of the pupils can be assessed with a flashlight, but fast observation is required before the flashlight is grabbed by the patient, providing simultaneous evidence of the normality of the pupil, of intact vision in that eye, assuming that the other has been occluded by the examiner, and of the strength and dexterity of the patient's upper limbs. Using the flashlight again, the movements of both eyes can usually be seen in all directions with the head held still by the examiner as the flashlight is taken in all directions. The accommodation reaction can also be seen by bringing the flashlight towards the child, making final observation on the pupils with the flashlight turned off to avoid a constriction due to the direct light reflex. The flashlight can again be used to make an assessment of the visual fields, bringing the lighted flashlight in from outside the normal range of vision and seeing if the child immediately responds and looks in that direction. Using this technique, a blind eye, or even a hemianopic field defect, can often be detected.

Direct inspection of the retina and optic nerve head assumes special significance when there is a mental handicap, as many of the common conditions produce characteristic abnormalities of the retina and optic nerve. It is beyond the scope of the present text to discuss all the characteristic appearances, but these should be well known to those experienced in this field. Ophthalmoscopy, even with a cooperative patient, is not easy, and in this situation it can be difficult, if not impossible. Dim lighting will help to dilate the pupil, and if an intriguing object can be held by an assistant at the end of the examination couch to attract the attention of the child then a quick glimpse of the retina and disc may be possible. The loss of interest in the item is heralded by the macula lutea flashing into view as the patient looks straight at the ophthalmoscope instead of at the object. If the examiner is patient, eventually all the important features of the optic disc can be seen, but considerable expertise is necessary to draw definite conclusions from the fleeting glimpses often afforded. Checking the size of the eyes themselves and whether or not ptosis of either lid is present completes examination of the eyes. It is important to remember that telangiectasia of the conjunctivae (Louis-Bar syndrome) is almost invariably misdiagnosed as conjunctivitis when first detected.

The movements of the facial muscles are next observed. This should include an assessment as to whether there are any spontaneous tics, grimaces or habit spasms, and whether the face moves symmetrically on smiling or eyebrow raising. The latter may easily be studied by holding a flashlight about 45 cm ahead of, and above, the patient's head. Pouting, teeth showing and tongue protrusion, biting, teeth clenching and wide mouth opening can all be achieved by imitation of the examiner in most instances, allowing the seventh cranial nerve, the motor part of the fifth nerve and the twelfth nerve to be tested in quick sequence. Most patients will attempt to say 'Ah' on invitation, but gag reflex testing is not necessary and, if attempted, is likely to terminate the whole proceedings very abruptly. Abnormalities of the teeth, the shape of the palate and the size of the tongue can all be assessed during these manoeuvres.

The jaw jerk, pout reflex and palmar–mental reflexes can all be attempted at this stage, but very gently. The tendon hammer is tapped onto the examiner's finger resting on the mental process of the patient's chin in the midline: the jaw snaps shut in a positive test. The pout reflex is elicited by gently tapping the upper lip just below the nose with the tendon hammer: the lips pout involuntarily in a positive test. The palmar–mental reflex is elicited by gently scratching the palm of the hand while observing the lower lip: the skin over the mental process puckers on the side that is stimulated in a positive test. These reflexes all provide evidence of preservation of primitive reflexes, and are indicative of bilateral upper motor neurone lesions.

While performing the above tests, general observations as to whether the patient sits or lies nor-mally, has any preferred posture, whether a preferred upper limb always reaches for the object, or if both upper limbs always seem to move in unison (mirror movements) will have been made. The accuracy of such movements, the presence of tremor or the intrusion of random involuntary movements should have been noted. Examination of the limbs and trunk should begin with general observations on limb symmetry, posture and, in passing, the state of the nails and the skin, looking for subungual exostoses, ichthyosis, rashes, cafe-au-lait patches, amelanotic naevi, or strawberry naevi. The trunk, both the front and the back, should be similarly inspected, special attention being paid to the shape and length of the neck, the presence of kyphosis or scoliosis, midline defects in the nape of the neck or over the sacral area, naevi in the same areas, a dermal sinus or abnormal tufts of hair over the nape of the neck or sacrum, and shagreen patches (areas of thickened skin with a slight sheen, usually found over the loin or lower back).

Tone should be tested in all limbs by gently flexing and extending the limbs at all joints, feeling for muscle stiffness, rigidity, spasticity, or contractures preventing joint movements and causing joint deformity. The patient should be asked to hold his hands straight out in front of him to command or imitation, if necessary, and to attempt to hold the position. Further observations on symmetry can be made at this time and attempts made to get the patient to maintain this posture with the eyes closed. Involuntary writhing posturing of one or other upper limb may indicate athetosis, sudden jerky movements indicate chorea, downward drift implies pyramidal deficit and up-and-down swaying indicates a defect in postural sensation. Upward drift with external rotation of the forearm normally indicates cerebellar deficit. This relatively simple test, which can be performed by most patients, can give useful clues to defects in pyramidal, extrapyramidal, posterior column sense and cerebellar function, and is an extremely useful screening test which is quickly and simply done and relatively reproducible in different testing sessions.

The reflexes in the upper limbs should then be elicited, with both limbs in a comparable position, ideally with the hands on top of one another and held by the examiner in this position. If different positions of each arm are allowed, reflex asymmetry may appear which has no real significance. It is important to remember that the supinator jerk, in particular, is quite painful for the patient, and, if possible, a single elicitation is desirable to maintain patient cooperation. Remember that an absent reflex is much more significant than a brisk reflex: it always requires explanation. Power in individual muscle groups can be tested, but this is usually difficult. Hand grips, which are, unfortunately, the least helpful test, are usually performed with great enthusiasm, particularly if the examiner pretends that he is being hurt. Minor, more complex tests, such as finger abduction and elbow extension, which have much more diagnostic significance, are uncertainly or indifferently performed. The assessment of power and dexterity of a limb based on general activities throughout the examination may be more reliable.

Coordination testing again presents problems. One of the best tests involves the subject touching his own nose and then the examiner's index finger, which is moved to a new position between each movement. This tests speed, accuracy and dorsal column sense, and allows further assessment of visual function and power to be made. Unfortunately, most patients prefer to keep one finger on their nose, and then attempt to touch the examiner's nose with a finger on the other hand. On occasions, allowing this may enable some information to be obtained, but the to-and-fro test of a moving target provides an excellent test of power, coordination and sensory feedback, and, if the examiner's finger is moved into a suspected hemianopic field, a further test of visual function. Formal testing of two-point discrimination, posture sense and light touch is usually impossible. Sometimes, however, posture sense testing can be performed by making a game of it, asking the child to move the other hand in the direction of movement of the finger on the tested limb. Pinprick testing of sensation is rarely going to provide useful information in the examination of the person with mental handicap, and may well produce permanent non-cooperation if attempted.

Lightning speed on the part of the examiner with an orange stick is required to elucidate the four abdominal reflexes, in view of the tickling sensation that is involved leading to much giggling and resistance to further efforts. Interestingly, in congenital and neonatal acquired conditions, the abdominal reflexes often escape unscathed, even in the presence of an extensor plantar response. However, absence of one abdominal reflex on occasions may provide the only clinical evidence of the presence of a neurofibroma on the appropriate nerve root, and the test is certainly worth performing.

Examination of the legs is much less helpful in general. The symmetry of the limbs is important, because congenital or infantile hemisphere lesions often cause more marked under-development of the leg and foot on the affected side than is apparent in the arm. The younger the child, the more useful this finding may be. The position of the feet is also helpful; increased passive tone and inwardly turned and plantar-flexed feet with extension of the big toe is typical of a spastic paralysis of a lower limb. Fidgety leg movements with random movements of the ankle and toes are typical of chorea. Trophic changes in the feet, ulcerated toes and marked vasomotor changes may indicate sensory or autonomic denervation, and are a common consequence of spina bifida. Calluses in unusual positions on the feet may also indicate abnormal foot posture during movement that may not be immediately apparent on simple examination. The passive tone in the legs can be tested by gently rolling the leg with the hands around the knee, and then suddenly attempting to lift the knee with both hands. A spastic leg will fly straight up in the air; the normal, or hypotonic leg, just flops and folds at the knee over the examiner's hand. Gentle attempts to elicit ankle clonus can be made, recalling that the upward pressure on the foot must be maintained to elicit clonus: it is not sufficient merely to dorsiflex the foot briskly. The knee and ankle jerks should be examined, again bearing in mind that the ankle jerk is quite painful, and careful attempts should be made to elicit the response on the first test. The knee jerk can usually be elicited, unless the patient insists on holding his legs firmly extended when lifted behind the knee, in which case the response may be incorrectly thought to be absent. It is important that the quadriceps muscles are relaxed when attempting this test.

Plantar responses present similar problems, and are fortunately left to the end of the examination by tradition. The stimulus must be a noxious one, and again, only one valid attempt may be permitted by the patient. It is vital to elicit this response correctly. The stimulus (a Yale or car key is ideal) should be pulled firmly up the lateral aspect of the foot, and then across the pad of the foot to the ball of the big toe, and off. Great care should be taken not to scratch the palm of the foot, or the base of any of the toes. Extension of the big toe is the positive response, and the big toe should be watched carefully. It is often impossible to see what the other toes are doing and, with only one attempt likely, the big toe response is the most important.

Sensory testing in the legs is subject to the same strictures as in the arms. Rarely is it going to provide helpful information, and even more rarely is it going to be possible to perform; in the interests of patient cooperation, both for this and for subsequent examination, it is probably best avoided.

Finally, formally watching the patient walk in underpants may be as informative as all the preceding examination. Indeed, in many cases, the reason for referral to the neurologist has been the development of a 'funny walk', and the question as to whether or not this indicates progressive or new pathology. A very important additional consideration in gait disturbance is the possibility that the gait is an imitation of another disabled patient, or attention-seeking in its own right. A truly bizarre gait usually presents no problems, but occasionally a well-imitated gait in an institution patient who has made a study of fellow residents can be an immense diagnostic challenge. A hemiplegic gait in childhood will always produce a combination of a fully flexed arm and hand (it rarely dangles by the side – a mistake made by less skilled imitation), and a stiff circumducting leg, with a scuffing foot. Attempts to walk faster emphasize the deficit, as the knee will not bend. Under these circumstances the simulator will start to bend at the knee. A paraparetic gait will usually produce a fixed slight flexion deformity at both knees, the feet both scuffing the ground, rather like someone trying to walk with his knees roped together, the hands in this instance usually flailing limply at the sides to improve balance. A gait modified by choreiform movement disorder may become very bizarre. In its mildest form, odd jerking of the head or sudden unusual posturing of the hands may produce a somewhat contrived appearance. In its most severe forms, sudden jolts may extend the trunk or throw the patient off balance, producing a lurching, reeling gait. Choreoathetoid movements produce the most extreme gait and movement disorder of all. The patient walks bent at the hips and knees, with the arms flailing and the hands and fingers hyperextending and posturing, the head often thrown back. Attempts to speak whilst talking may jolt the head and eyes into bizarre positions, almost throwing the patient over. This picture is particularly characteristic of kernicterus brain damage. If the patient's basic gait is fairly normal, attempts to watch him hop, skip or jump can all be made, increasing the degree of difficulty, depending on the patient's abilities, but usually the observed gait provides the best guide to diagnosis.

Having established the nature of the neurological deficit, it is then important to decide whether these findings are consistent with the clinical history as presented by the relatives or hospital staff, and consistent with the likely cause of the patient's other disability, or whether these findings represent a new feature, suggesting additional or progressive disease. As the most identifiable neurological substrate to mental handicap is cerebral palsy, this decision is usually fairly easy, but in conditions such as tuberose sclerosis and neurofibromatosis the high incidence of other central nervous system (CNS) lesions raises very real new diagnostic possibilities; in the patient with pre-existent CNS findings, considerable skill and a high index of suspicion must be brought to bear on each problem. In this respect, it is important to evaluate as clearly as possible the new symptoms which the patient may have mentioned, or, more importantly, the new observations of his family or nurses.

NEW SYMPTOMS OR DISABILITIES REQUIRING NEUROLOGICAL EVALUATION

Behavioural changes

In view of the essentially intellectual problems of the vast majority of patients with mental handicap, changes in these parameters may well provide the most sensitive index of change. In the alert adult even marked changes in intellect may be diagnostically taxing and in the adult with a mental handicap, starting from such a low baseline, almost impossible to sort out. In general, if close observers note a change, then the observations are ignored at peril. The general features of progressive change in behaviour or intellect may be divided into rough categories.

Abnormalities of consciousness and attention are very sinister and require urgent evaluation. Intermittent change may indicate an epileptic process, even if clear-cut convulsive features are not apparent. Progressive drowsiness or lack of attention in usual interests may indicate a metabolic problem, diabetes, renal failure, drug toxicity or rising intracranial pressure, and any combination of drowsiness with vomiting requires urgent exclusion of this group of disorders. Abnormalities of interest and progressive apathy and inertia may suggest a frontal lobe lesion, and this may be accompanied by disinterest in eating, speaking or pursuing normal hobbies. Such lesions are very likely to produce epileptic events and, as these may be purely nocturnal, special observation may be necessary to establish this feature. Disorders of the posterior hemispheres depend on cerebral dominance. Disorders of the right parietal lobes would tend to produce loss of acquired skills, manifest as increasing clumsiness, falls, difficulty with dressing and difficulty with orientation in the ward, hospital or home. All these symptoms may be accompanied by evidence of a mild left hemiparesis. An element of left-sided neglect may be apparent if the patient tends to walk into the door frames or other patients on his left-hand side. Left parietal lobe lesions tend to produce dramatic changes in speech skills; the incorrect use of words or failure to communicate at all should raise this suspicion, and as signs of a mild right-sided motor or sensory deficit may be in evidence.

Examination of such patients requires special attention to be paid to altering head size and shape in the young child, evidence of hemianopic field defect, asymmetrical motor skills or responses and sensory deficit. Formal psychometric assessment, which is so helpful in the normal patient, may be precluded by the pre-existing level of skills. In the adult patient, usually in the late teens and early twenties, sudden behavioural change may indicate a growing awareness of social limitations and the low likelihood of ever leading a normal family life like his contemporaries and siblings. Antisocial behaviour may occur for the first time in years, often directed at siblings or parents, and may incorrectly raise the suspicion of new pathology.

Balance and brainstem disorders

As discussed previously, the possibility of simulated or imitative gait disorder is extremely high in this group of patients, and is a common cause of neurological referral. A change in gait involving imbalance or falls, particularly if injury is sustained, requires prompt and careful assessment. There are three main diagnostic categories: drug toxicity, raised intracranial pressure and tumours.

Patients on sedatives, mood-enhancing drugs or anticonvulsants may have accidental or deliberate overdoses, or may, for reasons that are not clear, develop toxicity to agents previously taken for years without trouble. Drowsiness, imbalance and ataxia, very frequently accompanied by slurred speech and nystagmus, is the typical picture produced by drug toxicity, and this possibility should always be suspected when the patient has access to medication.

Patients with arrested hydrocephalus, previous subarachnoid haemorrhage, meningitis or congenital anomalies of the posterior fossa and upper cervical spine causing mental handicap may all develop progressive or intermittent hydrocephalus, due to outflow obstruction at aqueduct, fourth ventricle or basal cistern level, and this is usually manifest as ataxia, and frequently accompanied by headache and vomiting – the cardinal features of raised intracranial pressure. In extreme situations, intellectual impairment may be paralleled by increasing headache, and it is important to realize that papilloedema may take several weeks to develop in such a situation, and that the absence of papilloedema, together with normal findings on CNS examination, does not exclude the possibility of rising intracranial pressure. Patients with tuberose sclerosis and patients with neurofibromatosis are also particularly likely to develop tumours, blocking the circulation of CSF, and in all these instances computed tomographic scanning is indicated to exclude developing hydrocephalus.

Posterior tumours of all types can occur in association with mental handicap, and in neurofibromatosis the high frequency of pontine gliomas and acoustic nerve tumours may lead to a picture of progressive incoordination. The picture may evolve extremely slowly, and the patient may become extremely ataxic without any suggestion of papilloedema on fundal examination. The advent of vomiting is, again, an extremely important feature, and as an important general rule any patient with headache, unsteadiness and vomiting should be regarded as suffering from raised intracranial pressure or a posterior fossa tumour until proved otherwise by appropriate investigations.

Visual disturbances

In the intact adult, surprisingly complete loss of vision in one eye, or a hemianopic field defect may occur without the patient recognizing the problem. Loss of vision in one eye will only interfere with distance and stereoscopic vision, and may produce an apparent increase in clumsiness, such as knocking over glasses and cups, or difficulty in getting food onto a spoon. A hemianopic field defect may lead to apparent clumsiness until it is realized that the patient always bumps into things on one side alone, and seems startled when approached from that direction. Clinical assessment should relatively easily identify such defects, but the need to do such an evaluation may only arise from a skilled observer rather than from the patient's own observations.

Headache

The assessment of headache is one of the most finely-honed clinical skills in the neurologist's repertoire. In 99% of cases the history is the only information that will provide the diagnostic clue, physical examination and further studies rarely providing any additional useful information. It is important to realize that, even in this situation, there can be no substitute for a careful history, which may be time-consuming and unrewarding. Once again, one is faced with lack of sophistication in descriptive language, and the usual assessment may be quite impossible. There are several visual clues, however, that may be helpful. Most patients will involuntarily locate accurately the main area of pain with their hands while attempting to describe it, and this is often more reliable than the claimed descriptive localization. It is therefore important, even if the patient's sole history consists of 'head hurts', to watch exactly what he does as he says this, the facial expression often indicating the degree of anguish experienced, and the involuntary movement of the hand being a remarkably accurate localization of the main headache. The following may be very helpful pointers.

1 The palm of the hand or a finger pointed at one or other eye will usually indicate a migraine-type headache, and, if associated by others' descriptions of drowsiness, prostration or vomiting in attacks, makes migraine a certain diagnosis.
2 If both hands are raised to the temples, pressing in on the head, a migrainous headache is again possible, but if the patient indicates that the whole head is encircled by pain, then a tension headache becomes more likely, particularly if the observer's account includes the observation that the headache seems to come on more in the evenings, or when the patient is under obvious stress.
3 One hand placed on the vertex, pressing down, usually indicates a psychogenic headache, often due to depression, and this type of headache tends to be present 24 hours a day.
4 The headache of raised intracranial pressure is surprisingly non-descript in type. Like migraine, it tends to be worse in the morning or on bending, and may also be associated with vomiting, drowsiness or unsteadiness, so that, in some instances, the confident exclusion of pressure headache may be impossible.

It should again be stressed that papilloedema develops very slowly. The cooperation required for the careful fundal examination may not be forthcoming, and further investigation may be required to exclude raised intracranial pressure completely. This is never a decision to be taken lightly, as computed tomographic scanning in this situation will require general anaesthesia, with all the risk attendant to such a procedure.

Collapses, altered consciousness and 'turns'

Fortunately, in this particular aspect of neurological diagnosis, the patient's own history is often the least important aspect, information given by the bystander or paramedical observer being far and away the most important part of the history. In general, too much emphasis has been placed upon whether the patient cries out, is incontinent of urine, or injures himself. All may happen in a syncopal attack, and observers should be closely questioned, not for what they diagnosed, but as to what they actually observed.

Simple faints

Faints, or syncopal attacks, are, unfortunately, rarely simple. The location and circumstances of the patient at the time of collapse may present great diagnostic dilemmas. There is usually some form of prodrome, and the patient may say that he feels hot, dizzy, sweaty, sick, shivery or strange. If he gets the opportunity, he may then describe visual fragmentation or 'blacking out' of vision, or state that he has gone blind, followed by a rushing noise in the ears or deafness. By this stage, attempts to get to fresh air or the toilet may lead to the actual collapse occurring in a dangerous setting, with consequent head injury. The description of the fall is usually that the patient fell 'like a sack of potatoes', a 'crumpling-up' type of collapse, but the eyes often roll up and a fine shivering movement with extension of the limbs almost always occurs, and is invariably incorrectly identified by bystanders as a 'convulsion'. The most important observations are the patient's colour: 'white as a sheet', 'waxen' or 'as if dead' are the typical descriptions, and of major diagnostic importance. Unconsciousness may last several minutes, and a mild degree of confusion on recovery is common. Drenching sweat, nausea and, very frequently, vomiting, characterize recovery, and – perhaps the ultimate diagnostic clue – attempts to get the patient to walk to a chair or bed, or out into the fresh air, promptly result in another collapse. Such episodes are faints, and with the exception of careful exclusion of autonomic neuropathy (check lying and standing blood pressure) and cardiac anomalies (valve lesions, septal defects or arrhythmia) no further investigation or specific treatment is necessary.

Breath-holding attacks

Breath-holding attacks usually occur in early childhood and tend to happen when the child is frustrated and angry, or, like syncope, may occasionally follow trauma. In the latter instance, the child usually looks as if he will cry, but then goes progressively red, then blue in the face, and may then collapse, showing brief eye-rolling and, perhaps, slight twitching. Such episodes can look remarkably like seizures, and it is often only the recurrence during similar characteristic situations which enables the diagnosis to be made. Whenever collapses seem to be an alternative to an explosive temper tantrum, frustration or crying with pain, then the diagnosis can be strongly suspected. Most children grow out of this type of episode by five or six years of age.

Minor epileptic attacks

This deliberately vague title has been used to emphasize the concept of minor epilepsy. True petit mal epilepsy is very rare (less than 2.5% of all childhood epilepsy), and almost never occurs in pure form as a result of brain damage or inherited metabolic cerebral disease. It is, therefore, extremely rare in mental handicap. However, it has a nice, cosy diminutive sound to it, and is much liked by the parents of children with epilepsy. However, such licence should not be allowed in case someone acts upon the inaccurate diagnostic label and prescribes anti-petit-mal medication, which will usually provoke major convulsions, and can even lead to status epilepticus.

Most minor epileptic attacks in brain-damaged children are temporal lobe attacks (psychomotor seizures or complex partial seizures). They may range from brief episodes (lasting 15 to 90 seconds) of altered behaviour, with apparent fear, confusion or loss of awareness, accompanied by lip-smacking, chewing, repetitive movements, head-turning, to more complex automatic acts, such as tearing up a book or paper, taking off clothing, turning a TV set on and off. Such prolonged or dramatic manifestations may culminate in a collapse or generalized convulsion. Any form of aggressive or unpleasant behaviour in the attack is extremely unusual, but on recovery a period of confusion and irritability is quite common, and attempts to help the patient may be rebuffed physically, although unprovoked assault is extremely rare.

Most classifications include myoclonic and akinetic falls in the category of minor epilepsy. Unfortunately, such forms of epilepsy are very common in brain-damaged children, and the akinetic fall is almost specific to mental handicap. Both present considerable hazards to the patient, being characterized by sudden falls. Myoclonic epilepsy typically occurs in the morning around breakfast time; a series of jolts may lead to food being dropped or thrown across the table, culminating in a fall with a major convulsion. Akinetic falls are much more serious and happen completely without warning; all postural tone is lost and, if sitting, the patient may crash face-down onto the table or, if standing, fall flat on his face, often sustaining severe facial lacerations. Such patients typically have flattened broken noses and multiple scars on the forehead, and most front teeth are missing behind swollen, scarred lips. Not only are such attacks dangerous, but they are also extremely refractory to treatment.

Major epilepsy

Major epileptic fits usually occur in the night, or soon after awakening. In brain-damaged patients, a more random pattern is seen, with frequent daytime attacks showing a tendency to become serial or culminate in attacks of status. This introduces the risk of further brain damage in the already impaired patient. Major attacks are characterized by the sudden loss of consciousness, with tonic spasm, which may produce a forced expiration, causing a gasp or a cry. During the tonic phase, the patient will become deeply cyanosed and will appear to be straining. It is extremely unusual for the head and back to be arched during this phase (see below). After 30 to 90 seconds the patient usually goes limp, resumes breathing and will start to convulse clonically. This typically consists of synchronous flexing movements of the arms, and extension movements of the head and legs, the patient often banging his head and heels against the ground. This stage usually lasts a few minutes, and is followed by a very deep sleep, during which the patient may be hardly rousable. Because of this, the duration of an attack is often grossly overestimated, and, occasionally, status epilepticus is mistakenly diagnosed because the deep sleep is mistaken for unconsciousness due to the previous fit. Incontinence of urine is common, but not inevitable, and injury depends upon whether or not a fall was involved. Tongue-biting is infrequent, and is a strong diagnostic pointer.

Children and young adults with mental handicap are prone to imitative behaviour, and those with genuine epilepsy soon discover that an attack will bring a difficult confrontation to an end. Simulated or hysteroid epilepsy is a difficult and common problem in an institutionalized patient. The important clues are a tendency to arch the back in an attack, and for the movements to be semi-purposeful and desynchronized, so that the impression of a patient 'lashing out' rather than convulsing is common. Classical attempts to prove non-organicity by testing the corneal reflexes and plantar responses are helpful more in the fact that the simulating patient will hold the eyes tightly closed, preventing testing, and the plantar responses may provoke withdrawal or lashing out at the examiner with the leg – as good a diagnostic test as the response itself!

Status epilepticus can occur in both minor and major epilepsy. Whenever a mentally handicapped patient shows marked alteration in attention and motor skills, the possibility of minor status epilepticus should be considered. Drooling, jerky movements, falls, zombie-like states would all be suggestive. Although intravenous diazepam may temporarily arrest this condition, permanent control may be very difficult and take days or weeks to achieve. Major epileptic status is life-threatening and a potentially brain-damaging emergency. Injury during the fall, aspiration and suffocation are the immediately obvious fatal consequences, but repeated anoxic episodes, combined with electrolyte and hydration problems, may further damage the patient's brain. Prompt aggressive treatment is essential. The management of epilepsy is separately considered in Chapter 33.

SPECIFIC DISEASE ENTITIES OF NEUROLOGICAL SIGNIFICANCE IN MENTAL HANDICAP

It is obvious that patients with limited cerebral function and physical disability have little reserve when they become ill for any reason. Minor febrile illnesses may provoke behaviour change, drowsiness, confusion and epileptic fits, a feature easily suggesting meningitis. Squints, spasticity and ataxia will all worsen with pyrexia or general ill health, and may be mistaken as indicating new progressive neurological deficit. Therefore, the neurologist, when assessing an acutely ill patient with neurological deficit, should take particular care with the general medical component of the examination. Certain diseases, however, include a distinct possibility of further neurological developments as a direct complication of the disorder, and these are worth listing separately.

Tuberose sclerosis

70 % of children with tuberose sclerosis have a mental handicap. The characteristic tubers in the brain which give this condition its name may become large enough to act as space-occupying lesions in their own right, but, more frequently, due to their tendency to occur in an intraventricular position, may obstruct the foramen of Munro, producing hydrocephalus. This may result in drowsiness, ataxia, nausea, vomiting and, ultimately, papilloedema and unconsciousness.

Neurofibromatosis

10 % of patients with neurofibromatosis have a mental handicap. The characteristic peripheral nerve tumours (subcutaneous neurofibromas) seem to provide some protection against the development of a formidable array of central nervous system tumours. Intracranial and spinal tumours appear more likely to occur in patients whose main peripheral manifestation is café-au-lait patches. Proximal neurofibromas, particularly in the posterior mediastinum and retroperitoneal tissues, have a tendency to become sarcomatous, so sudden enlargement of such a mass or progressive disability in the arm or leg may suggest malignant plexus infiltration. Some will invade the spinal canal and produce spinal cord compression. Optic nerve gliomas occur frequently in patients with neurofibromatosis, with an estimated incidence of 20 %. Progressive visual failure in one or both eyes will be the presenting symptom, and the high incidence would suggest that regular screening of vision should be an important part of the continuing assessment of such children. Acoustic neuromas are less frequent and the typical very slowly progressive unilateral hearing loss may pass unnoticed by the patient. When the size is sufficient to distort the brainstem, vomiting and ataxia will occur. All other types of intracranial tumours, particularly meningiomas, are more likely to occur in patients with neurofibromatosis. Half of the patients with neurofibromatosis who develop seizures have an intracranial tumour. Malignant hypertension or subarachnoid haemorrhage may be produced by phaeochromocytomas, which occur in 5 % of neurofibromatosis patients, so that paroxysmal headache, cerebrovascular accident or subarachnoid haemorrhage may occur and prompt a search for an underlying phaeochromocytoma.

Sturge–Weber syndrome

50 % of patients with Sturge–Weber syndrome have mental retardation. This condition, which is characterized by a large strawberry naevus, is almost invariably complicated by epilepsy, and such attacks are notoriously resistant to treatment. Cerebrovascular accidents are common in these patients, owing to a tendency to develop a thrombotic occlusion of both arterial or venous channels, which are usually abnormally developed.

Hydrocephalus

Children with hydrocephalus are particularly likely to develop problems with progressive ataxia. This in turn will lead to frequent falls, and relatively trivial cerebral trauma may produce a subdural haematoma. This may produce further enlargement of the head, or change in pre-existing symptoms, and exclusion of this possibility by CT scanning may be necessary on numerous occasions.

CONCLUSION

In this chapter I have tried to give some idea as to the role of the neurologist in discovering evidence of mild development disorder or localized damage to the nervous system in patients with mental handicap. Rarely would the neurologist be the primary physician involved; more frequently, the need for evaluation of new, different or progressive additional disability leads to neurological referral for the first time, and evaluation of such a patient requires a knowledge of what normally does happen, and what possibly could happen. Some of the more frequent entities have been discussed in detail. As the main reason for referral is because of the observations of lay people, parents, childminders, social workers, nurses and other hospital staff, and not because of the patient's own complaint, extensive coverage of common presenting symptoms has not been given. Instead, the importance of taking such eye-witness accounts into very serious consideration, and performing a neurological assessment with all the possibilities in mind have been stressed. The continuing role of the neurologist in such patients is often in the management of epilepsy, and this is the subject of Chapter 33.

Within the last few weeks of preparation of this manuscript, the application of the principles outlined has enabled the recognition of the following cases:

1 A boy of 11 with mental handicap due to neurofibromatosis, with progressive clumsiness, who had developed bilateral optic nerve gliomas.
2 A 23-year-old girl with Down's syndrome who had a faint incorrectly identified by bystanders with nursing qualifications as epilepsy.
3 A girl of 26 with tuberose sclerosis who complained of head pain, who had hydrocephalus of the left lateral ventricle due to blockage of the left foramen of Munro by a tumour.

All these have, hopefully, benefited from the neurologist's efforts on their behalf.

Chapter 35
The Role of the Dietitian

SALLY DAY & SHEILA HOLLINS

How can dietitians fit into the changing pattern of services? Dietitians have begun to play a part in the mental handicap field in both institutional and community settings. The range of skills the dietitian needs in this work will be shown by tracing her involvement from before conception through to adulthood. How her skills relate to the skills of other disciplines will be explored, and an account given of the changing role of the dietitian as the special health care of people with mental handicap moves into the community.

THE DIETITIAN IN GREAT BRITAIN

The British Dietetic Association was formed in 1936 and there are now 2000 dietitians, most of whom work in the National Health Service. Entry to the profession is usually through a four-year degree course which leads to state registration.

The emphasis in a dietitian's work is on promoting health and preventing disease. She (except for 20 men all are women) works in close liaison with a wide range of other professionals. Much of her work, whether with professionals or individual clients, comes into the category of health or nutrition education.

In 1974 the first community dietitian to be employed by a health authority was appointed, although community dietitians had worked in social services and health boards previously. Many more dietitians working in the hospital service are developing a part-time interest in work in the community, and there are now forty whole-time community dietitians. The British Dietetic Association defines the aim of this new community work as follows: 'to promote health and prevent disease amongst the local population, by improving nutrition, *and* increasing public awareness of the link between nutrition and health'. An increasing number of dietitians are being appointed to new posts in mental handicap and mental illness.

The role of the dietitian in mental handicap – another 'way forward'

The literature on this subject is sparse. However, interest in mental handicap was stimulated when the DHSS (1977) published a paper called *The Way Forward*, which directed dietetic resources into the care of people with mental handicap. The role of the dietitian in fields other than the acute service is slowly being accepted.

THE DIETITIAN WORKING IN AN INSTITUTION

From reports of work within institutions we can learn something about the role some dietitians have developed. An excellent account of what is possible was written by Bandini in 1982. For one hospital population of nearly nine hundred in the United States there was an increase in the number of dietitians employed from one to seven. A note of caution here: this is an unusually high level of provision! The primary role of each dietitian was to formulate an individual nutritional care plan for each resident. An inter-disciplinary approach was used, so that the different factors affecting each person's nutritional needs could be taken into account. Dietary interventions were considered necessary for half of the residents, and some of the diet changes recommended are described by Bandini.

The dietitian prepared menus for special diets. She also tried to meet individual food preferences and to include modifications to the texture of the food offered. In the management of under- or overweight she recommended portion-controlled diets. Nutritional supplements between meals were sometimes necessary to provide an adequate daily food intake. Snack programmes were prepared for use by ward staff as behavioural reinforcers. Other interventions included nutritional counselling and consultation with other professional staff.

The experience of dietitians in less well-staffed institutions suggests that individual diet planning is a goal to work towards. Initially, the lone dietitian struggles to gain acceptance on the team, and ignorance about her expertise and her potential role means her initial emphasis is on educating other staff (Schafer, 1976; Modrow et al., 1979).

The relationship between nutritional status and an institutional lifestyle

There are some constraints on lifestyle imposed by the institution which can be related to nutrient deficiency and not to the quality of the diet delivered to the ward. For example the long-stay elderly person who never sees the sun may be low in vitamin D (Thomas, 1980). The old practice of doing a 'dental clearance' will restrict food intake to a soft diet. Shortage of staff may cause feeding to be a chore – to be got through very fast. Foods with soft texture can be force-fed by so-called 'bird feeding'; perhaps with oatmeal added as a filler, resulting in dilution of the meal (Modrow, 1979). This dangerous practice, in which the head is extended and food scraped off the spoon on to the palate and upper teeth, is more likely to result in choking than offering a more solid diet. Moreover, in some institutions staff have been in the habit of mixing all the components of the soft or puréed diet together – the meat, vegetable, fruit and custard. In addition, there is the difficulty of providing an adequate diet for the person who eats quantities of rubbish, for example cigarette ends, used tea bags or even black plastic bags. The person who regurgitates his food is also at risk of weight-loss and nutritional deficiency (Hardingham, 1983).

THE DIETITIAN IN THE COMMUNITY

Prevention

Pre-conception clinics offer not only genetic advice to prospective parents, but also nutrition and health education. Some experts believe that nutritional factors, possibly in interaction with many others, play a larger part in prompting or preventing fetal damage than anyone has ever imagined in the past. One centre advocates that nutritional health should be a prime concern for two years before and after each pregnancy (Barker, 1983). The dietitian needs to be aware of current research into selective supplementation of maternal diets with micronutrients. Before conception parents may be advised to have their body levels of toxic minerals, such as cadmium or lead, assessed so that benign

antagonists can be offered. This area of work is highly controversial. More conventional advice to mothers during and after pregnancy concerns the use of tobacco and alcohol and the preparation of infant diets.

The dietitian's role here will be largely a preventive one, although we cannot always separate prevention from treatment or cure, and as the child grows up prevention gives way to treatment.

Developing eating habits and skills

With a small child, some food may be invested with magical qualities as 'good for the child'. Food preparation and eating occupy such a significant part of the pre-school child's day that the dietitian's relationship with the mother could be a crucial one. For example, the dietitian will be concerned to achieve a sufficient nutrient intake in the infant with cerebral palsy and to prevent obesity in the child with Down's syndrome. In addition, we all know that food is a potent reward and reinforcer, and there is a danger that the child's love of food will be exploited to elicit good behaviour.

Problems in feeding are seen with many infants and pre-school children who have handicaps (Mills and Hedges, 1983; Aumonier and Cunningham, 1984). A handicap may affect one or more aspects of the total feeding process, such as sucking, biting, chewing or swallowing. If a special diet is required food may be unappetizing, and mealtimes may become a battle ground. With a lack of help and nutritional advice during the crucial stages of weaning, behaviour problems may develop. These range from regurgitation to throwing food or only eating one or two food items. Developmental motor problems may result in continued spoon feeding by the parent. Experimentation with different food combinations as well as the expression of choice is thus limited.

'They miss out on so much that other people can enjoy.' 'Let her eat what she wants.' Such attitudes quickly lead to dietary imbalance, perhaps to vitamin deficiency, obesity, dental caries or constipation (Caliendo et al., 1982). At the same time parents may be bombarded with fringe advice on the need for dietary supplements of unproven value (Wickens, 1983).

Trahms (1984) has spoken of her work in the diet self-management of phenylketonuria, stressing that nutrition education must match cognitive and motor development. In group work with children of different ages, she recycles the same basic concepts according to their developmental age.

Working with other professionals

In childhood the paediatric dietitian must be part of the child development team, working closely with the speech therapist, physiotherapist and occupational therapist. These other professionals not only overlap in their interests, but may also know more about some aspects of eating. For example, the physiotherapist will be concerned with positioning at mealtimes. She will be aware of skeletal problems, and will endeavour to establish a symmetrical sitting position with vertical head control. If someone's hands are needed to maintain balance, they cannot be used for eating.

Part of the speech therapists' role is to develop the muscles used in speech – the same muscles as are used in chewing and swallowing. Controlled chewing and swallowing patterns are needed before intelligible speech will develop. Liquidized food is quicker to feed someone with, but bulky food is easier to get hold of and gives more practice at swallowing. If mealtimes are seen as normal opportunities for social interaction, both language and dietary objectives may benefit. Many people with mental handicap can be caused extreme frustration by their lack of choice when it comes to food, although choice can be offered by the use of photographs or alternative communication systems.

The occupational therapist will be involved in the mechanics of feeding. She can recommend appropriate aids, such as sticky-backed sheeting which grips utensils, and she will be trying to stimulate increasing independence in eating and other self-help skills.

The psychologist will have advice to offer on the management of behaviour problems (Pope and Buck, 1982).

However, none of these other professionals has the same broad background in nutrition and food as the dietitian. For example, a doctor may not know that children with Prader–Willi syndrome have reduced energy requirements and need a very low-carbohydrate diet (Coplin et al., 1976). The physiotherapist may not be aware of the increased energy requirements of the child with athetoid cerebral palsy. An occupational therapist may not consider the client's nutritional status during a cookery session: someone who is overweight may be taught to bake a cake.

Changing needs in adolescence and adulthood

As a child grows up, some maladaptive eating patterns may persist. Socially acceptable eating habits assume more importance in adulthood. In addition an individual adult is more likely to achieve a balanced diet if the childhood diet has been varied. The dietitian has a clear role in educating parents and teachers – the people who decide what a child will eat. Without the ability to apply these basic principles an individual can never be independent. Thomas (1980) included ignorance in her list of eight risk factors in the aetiology of malnutrition (Table 35.1). Dietary goals for the general population of increasing unrefined carbohydrate and fibre and decreasing fat, sugar and salt intake should be reflected in nutrition education for people with mental handicap.

In a group home a resident will need skills in menu planning, budgeting and shopping. All of these will require him to make choices. He will have to learn to follow a recipe and learn simple cooking techniques. He will have to use household equipment. This will apply equally to the person with a disability who has grown up at home and to the individual who is being habilitated into the community following years of institutional care. For the latter the dietitian must remember that the person will have none of the skills required to live outside, coupled with a severe loss of confidence (Table 35.2).

Concessions will have to be made in dietary planning. For example, convenience foods may be very important, because of their ease of preparation when practical skills are limited (Thomas, 1983).

Table 35.1 Risk factors in the aetiology of malnutrition in the elderly (Thomas, 1980).

Ignorance
Loneliness
Disability
Poverty
Poor dentition
Drugs
Decreased taste and smell
Impaired appetite

Table 35.2 Habilitation of institutionalized people.

Problems that the person has
Lack of the skills required to live 'outside'
Severe loss of confidence

Skills to be taught will include:
Managing money and a budget
Using household equipment
Shopping and cooking
Communication and transport

Table 35.3 Aims of cookery course

Sensible eating pattern – not favourites every day
Enable food choice
Measure ingredients – use spoon or cup
Time – use a clockface
Temperature – use shades of red and blue

For the person with a physical disability, a microwave may prove to be the safest oven. Food can be cooked and reheated safely without the container getting hot.

Some special pictorial cookery books have been designed for the adult market (Spear, 1980; Nutrition Information Pack, 1981; Canada Resource Pack, 1984). One procedure or practical skill is shown at a time. Cups and spoons can be used as the simplest form of measure, a clockface can be used to indicate times, and the colours red and blue to indicate temperature (Table 35.3). Another method of teaching choice of food and menu planning has been developed in Bath by Clark with stick-on pictures of different food items.

Spear described some problems commonly experienced in this kind of work:

'The first group of four residents in the halfway house were typical, in that between them they had accumulated 120 'institution years'. They had not prepared anything in a kitchen during this time. Meals had arrived cooked, served and ready to eat. They had no conception of 'raw' or 'cooked', of how to recognize basic ingredients. Eggs, for example, had always arrived boiled and peeled, so that the idea of eggs in shells was new to them. Until recently even tea poured from the pot had had milk and sugar added already. No practical culinary skills could be assumed.'

For the person with a more severe mental handicap developing such skills may not be possible. However, with higher staffing levels in the community than is customary in an institution, perhaps more attention will be given to individual needs. The goals should be a varied diet with attention to food preferences and constant awareness that taste is a sense which can give a great deal of pleasure, even to someone who, at first sight, shows little awareness of his surroundings or lacks the most simple skills.

SUMMARY

The dietitian's role has changed considerably since the establishment of community dietitian posts ten years ago, with increasing stress on health education and prevention. Because of the small number of dietitians compared with the other professions allied to medicine the dietitian has had to adopt a catalytic role, spreading nutritional advice and education more widely by working through others.

The profession has set up a number of special interest groups: the Community Nutrition Group is well established and the newer Geriatric and Mental Health Groups are developing. This will in turn lead to a wider acceptance of these newly created posts.

The role of the dietitian in current practice

1 The provision of an advisory service on all aspects of nutrition in mental handicap both in health and disease.
2 Setting up nutrition education programmes for health and social service professionals and others working within mental handicap. Also to participate in in-service training of dietitians.
3 Carrying out nutritional assessments of those with mental handicap who may be at risk of nutritional deficiencies and being involved in individual dietetic management and the process of feeding.
4 Initiating and actively participating in any nutrition research being undertaken by the members of the mental handicap team.
5 The dietitian should be a member of the mental handicap team in order to establish her role with the medical, nursing and paramedical staff involved with mental handicap, and also to liaise with social services and the voluntary organizations.

CONCLUSION

The dietitians' role is an exciting and a challenging one. Dietitians could make a major impact in this field if they first acknowledged their own role, and then informed senior planners, both medical and paramedical. Labelle, in the 1984 Ryley–Jeffs Memorial Lecture, said that it is the responsibility of those with specialized knowledge about nutrition to ensure that their expertise is disseminated more widely. Twenty years ago Umbarger (1965) delivered a paper on the same theme in Texas. She was talking to nurses and nutritionists, imploring them to recognize the importance of eating to people with disabilities. We would add another plea: to remember that we are talking about 'the meal' – about the sharing of food with the community in which we live. That community may be our own family, a group of friends, or the residents and staff of a ward in an institution. The meal we share retains the same central importance in all our lives.

REFERENCES

Aumonier M & Cunningham C (1984) Health and medical problems in infants with Down's syndrome. *Health Visitor 57* (May): 137–140.

Bandini L (1982) Providing individualized nutritional care in a state institution for the mentally retarded. *Journal of the American Dietetic Association 81(4):* 448–450.

Barker W (1983) Mental Handicap Week Conference *Nutritional Possibilities in Reducing Mental Handicap*. Reported in *Beacon* Spring 1984, MENCAP, London.

British Dietetic Association, Daimler House, Paradise Street, Birmingham BBl 2BJ.

Caliendo MA, Booth G & Moser P (1982) Iron intakes and serum ferritin levels in developmentally delayed children. *Journal of the American Dietetic Association 81:* 401–406.

Canada Resource Pack (1984) *Homemaking and Feeding Problems*.

Clark M (1984) Personal communication.

Coplin SS, Hine J & Gormican A (1976) Out-patient dietary management in the Prader–Willi syndrome. *Journal of the American Dietetic Association 68(4):* 330–334.

DHSS (Department of Health & Social Security) (1977) *Future Developments 1–14. Priorities in the Health and Social Services 'The Way Forward'*. London: HMSO.

Drug and Therapeutics Bulletin (1984) Rational use of vitamins. *Drug and Therapeutics Bulletin* (May).

Hardingham A (1983) *Report on the Dietetic Work at Springfield Hospital, London*. Unpublished paper.

Kings Fund Centre (1980) *An Ordinary Life* Project Paper 24. London: King's Fund Centre.

Labelle H (1984) *Placing Nutrition on the National Agenda*, 34th Memorial Lecture of the Violet Ryley – Kathleen Jeffs Foundation, Toronto, July 1984.

Mills YL & Hedges CA (1983) The feeding process and the nutritional needs of handicapped infants and preschoolers. *TECSE 3(2):* 33–42.

Modrow CL & Darnell RE (1979) Dietetic services in a cross-modality system. *Journal of the American Dietetic Association 74(3):* 341–344.

Nutrition Info Service (1981) *A Manual on Food and Nutrition for the Disabled* (1981) Nutrition Info Service, Ryerson Polytechnical Institute Library, 50 Gould St, Toronto.

Pope C & Buck R (1982) Spoonful of success. *Nursing Mirror* (14 July): 14–18.

Schafer DS (1976) Physical therapy management of patients through cross modality. *Physical Therapy 56(6):* 676–680.

Spear S (1980) A cookery book for self-catering mentally handicapped. *Journal of Human Nutrition 34:* 54–57.

Thomas S (1980) *A Study of the Nutritional Status of 14 Long-stay Patients, Springfield Hospital, London*. Unpublished paper.

Thomas LD (1983) *Teaching Nutrition to the Mentally Handicapped*. Unpublished paper.

Trahms C (1984) Child Development and Mental Retardation Center, University of Washington, Seattle. Teaching diet self-management using developmental concepts. Paper presented at *Workshop on Recent Advances in the Dietary Treatment of Inborn Errors of Metabolism*, The Sick Children's Hospital, Toronto, July 1984.

Umbarger B (1965) Role of the nutritionist or dietitian in clinic services for the mentally retarded. *Mental Retardation 3(5):* 25–26.

Webb Y (1980) Feeding and nutrition problems of physically and mentally handicapped children in Britain: a report. *Journal of Nutrition 54:* 201–285.

Wickens C (1983) Can vitamin supplements improve the IQ of children with Down's syndrome? *BDA Adviser* (Summer): 22–24.

Chapter 36
The Role of the Professional in Aggression and Strategies of Coping

MICHAEL CRAFT & IAN BERRY

Aggression is a common enough phenomenon in the general population, all too common in fact. Wife- and husband-beating, violence on the football terraces and vandalism in public buildings all feature in our daily newspapers. Crimes involving physical aggression to person or property are increasing.

Aggression can be defined as unprovoked attacks on other humans, material things, or even on oneself. Many people would differentiate between verbal aggression and actual physical harm.

Naturally, the public has a right to be protected against those who have proved themselves capable of physical aggression. Prison sentences deal with some, and for those whose behaviour becomes so extreme their families or local communities are unable to tolerate it, admission to a mental handicap or psychiatric hospital may be sought. The unfortunate paradox is that aggression is frightening and a mental handicap hospital may refuse admission on the grounds that it may not have the necessary treatment facilities available. In addition, it is arguable that, particularly for those people with mental handicap, management of most problems is best achieved in the natural environment where what has been learned is most likely to be used. Hospitals, even those with specialized treatment facilities, should be a last resort.

What follows here is a discussion about strategies of coping with aggression, outlining both theory and practice.

THEORIES OF AGGRESSION

There are four major explanatory theories of aggression: psychoanalytical, ethological, learning and neurophysiological.

Psychoanalytical theory

This explains aggression as one of the instinctual forces driving people towards the twin poles of love and destruction. Freud outlined what he called 'the death wish'. According to this theory, the release of aggressive energy in actual violence allows the individual to reduce aggressive feelings for a while. It has a 'cathartic effect', allowing the internal reservoir of aggressive feelings to spill over from time to time in aggression towards people or property. Thus agricultural workers who have a physically more violent occupation than office workers are felt to be less subject to frustration, which can be one result of pent-up aggressive feelings. The damming-up of aggression can cause other deleterious results by working through the subconscious of the individual. The outcome can be destructive, with reactions such as guilt, over-strict morality, over-eating, excessive smoking, alcoholism, anxiety and tension states, or constructive, when aggression is diverted to physical outlets such as gardening, sawing wood, mountain climbing and walking. The theory suggests that treatment might be needed both for too much and for too little deployment of actual aggression if the norm of society does not allow adequate expression.

In his later writings Freud considered the role of aggression in the relationship between groups. For him, it was inevitable that a group would manifest aggression to people who were not members of that group. Out-group hostility served the function of holding the group together. Such a theory can be seen to apply directly to the relationships between ward staff and inpatients in a mental handicap hospital or the trainees at an adult training centre and the surrounding community for example.

Ethological theory

Writers such as Lorenz (1967) suggest that aggression, or the 'aggressive instinct' is intimately connected with the survival of the species. It is a drive operating in the interests of the species and in its present variety of forms is derived from our evolutionary past. There is little need to dwell on such theory here, partly because of the necessary absence of empirical proof and partly because of the sparseness of research on *human* aggression (Tajfel, 1978).

Learning theory

Learning theorists do not accept the Freudian and ethological views. They believe that aggression is strongly influenced by learning and situational factors and that biological factors tend to play a smaller part (Bandura, 1973). Aggressive behaviour is strengthened (reinforced) by its consequences. For example, if a child who throws a temper tantrum is given sweets or immediate attention of any other pleasurable sort, then it is probable, but not inevitable, that he will produce tantrums more frequently in future. The relationship between a behaviour and its consequences is not as entirely straightforward as this. The child may not have tantrums more often: instead they may last longer or become more extreme. Any reinforced behaviour may increase in frequency, duration, intensity or any combination of the three. Also, it may be observed that although a child has been 'rewarded' with immediate attention, sweets and so on there is no subsequent strengthening of the tantrum behaviour. Amongst the possible explanations are that some other behaviour is being so consistently and powerfully reinforced that the child is preoccupied in indulging in that behaviour; alternatively, it may be that the attention or sweets are not reinforcers for that particular child. An error practitioners often make is to speculate about the nature of reinforcing consequences, when the only valid and reliable method of determining these is through systematic observation and analysis of behaviours, their antecedents and consequences. This explanation may to some extent account for the maintenance and modification of aggressive behaviours, but it does not account for their occurrence in the first place.

The frustration–aggression hypothesis was until fairly recently one of the most influential explanations of aggressive behaviour. This hypothesis was uncompromising; aggression is *always* a consequence of frustration. For a time, this view was considered axiomatic and research ignored the possible influence of other variables on aggression, together with the issue of how such behaviours were learned. Certainly the use of physical force to remove obstructions which get in the way of a desired outcome can be viewed as the use of aggression to reduce frustration, but it is not a sufficient explanation for all instances of aggression. Also it does not account for the different patterns of aggressive behaviour.

A modified version of this hypothesis was later produced which stated that frustration leads to an *instigation* to aggression. Overt aggression will occur only if there are no more powerful competing responses which may inhibit the aggression. For example, if someone in authority frustrates an individual, the latter may respond with compliance, a response which may be strong enough to inhibit aggression. However, he may displace that aggression onto some other target.

Social learning theorists such as Bandura (1969) believe that the target of aggression, the environments in which it is manifested, and the form which the aggression takes is particularly influenced by social experience. A distinction has to be made to begin with between the learning of physically destructive and painful behaviours and their subsequent usage. If such behaviours could only be elicited by frustration then there would be a high mortality rate amongst karate and army weapons instructors.

The use of learned aggressive skills is considerably influenced by exposure to aggressive models. Parke et al. (1977), for example, noted that children who watched violent films were more willing to engage in aggressive behaviours. Not only did the children learn new techniques for aggression through observation, but any inhibitions they had about the use of aggression were weakened, and they also became more desensitized to violence, in that they were no longer upset or aroused by such behaviour. It would be unfair to conclude from studies such as this that one way to reduce aggression in people with mental handicap would be to deprive them of the opportunity to watch films on television. The evidence seems to suggest that prolonged exposure to a steady diet of televised violence over a period of years may sometimes contribute to the occurrence of overt aggression.

Direct provocation from other people has also been found to be a powerful elicitor of aggressive behaviour. Provocation usually results in retaliation in kind. Modelling may be in evidence here again. People with mental handicap are perhaps more likely to model provocative behaviours directed at them as they may have few alternative responses within their limited repertoire of behaviours. Moreover, aggression elicited in this manner has an unsettling way of escalating (Goldstein et al., 1975). People who have been subjected to frequent provocation and who have learned to reciprocate can act in this manner even when not subject to attack; they have merely learned that 'others' intend to do them harm.

Learning theorists have also come to realize the importance of other social factors in modifying and determining aggressive behaviour. For example, the perceived legitimacy of aggression in certain circumstances will determine its usage. The best known study is that of Milgram (1974). Milgram found that adult subjects were prepared to inflict astonishingly heavy 'punishments' (electric shocks) on people for no other reason than the insistence of the experimenter. The experimenter's authoritative status as a scientist and his supposed specialized knowledge legitimized this behaviour. Such a finding may be relevant to aggression in mentally handicapped people in a number of ways. The use of certain aversive techniques by psychologists and psychiatrists, even though strictly controlled, may cause direct carers to see the use of such techniques in general as having legitimacy. From a rather different point of view, aggression may be perceived as legitimate by a mentally handicapped person if society tolerates such behaviour by attributing it to the person's 'handicap'.

Some behaviourists have developed the work of Bandura and others in an attempt to show that such phenomena as anger and aggression are as much subject to covert cognitive factors as to identifiable environmental and social evocation. Cognitive behaviour modifiers view anger as an emotional response to provocation; the anger is exacerbated by tension and agitation and may manifest itself as physical aggression. Whether aggression is manifested at all is partially dependent upon how well the potential aggressor has learned to use covert language and images in the control of his own behaviour (Meichenbaum, 1977). There is a possible implication of this view for the treatment of aggression in mildly mentally handicapped people which will be discussed later.

Neurophysiological theory

The fourth explanation of aggression is the neurophysiological theory. Certain types of brain damage are known from both animal experiments and

accidental damage in man to cause the recipient to be more aggressive. This is probably by interference with centres of inhibition. Such results have been interpreted as supporting both psychoanalytic and learning theories, and are well observed in people with extensive brain damage from birth, who have frequent epilepsy thereafter. The term 'epileptic personality' is here a misnomer, for although there are some hundreds who are indeed selectively admitted to hospital on account of their aggressive behaviour disorder, they are likely to be just the most severely affected of the half a million epileptics in the United Kingdom.

In animal experiments damage to parts of a cat's thalamus causes it to show 'thalamic rage': the unfortunate animal, apparently contentedly purring and drinking milk, responds to a pin-prick with a three-second burst of extreme, spitting rage before resuming its purring and drinking. Twenty years ago tracts leading to the thalamus from the frontal lobe used to be severed in humans in the operation known as prefrontal leukotomy. These earlier operations gained a bad reputation because they often left an apathetic, listless individual without reactions. Now, as a result of the advance of knowledge in recent years, smaller tractotomies are effected, using stereotactic surgical techniques, often in the temporal lobe. In drug-resistant temporal lobe epilepsy with psychotic episodes, or violent aggressive outbursts, it may be possible to excise the discharging focus. Sometimes the focus is in the amygdaloid nucleus, a large collection of brain nuclei on the antero-medial wall of the temporal lobe. By means of high-frequency electrical stimulation, the suspect nucleus or focus can be located, and stereotactic division of small tracts between the medial and lateral nuclei bodies is possible. In successful cases the result is decreased emotional hyperactivity, fewer fits, less EEG activity from the discharging focus, and fewer anti-epileptic drugs required thereafter. There should be no deadening of personality as a result.

THE PREVENTION OF AGGRESSION

Aggressive behaviour in people with mental handicap often causes further distress to an already distressed family or makes the work of caring staff even less tolerable. Clearly, identification of the circumstances which can lead to an aggressive incident is the most effective prevention.

Aggression can be unpredictable, but most incidents do develop out of a situation that builds up over time. One can divide the factors behind a potentially dangerous situation into the historical situation, the susceptible group, the potential protagonist and the provocative incident.

The historical situation

The background is often the same in these situations. A group of people with violent records are kept together on a ward or in a unit, not necessarily with keys, but by nursing policy. There may well be lack of work opportunities or limited leisure activities, leading to boredom and a build-up of energy and tense atmosphere. This is the general background against which violent incidents occur and are remembered. Each watches to ensure that no one is more favoured than he and each may come to feel he has a legitimate grievance and that he is not able to secure redress within the limitations that obtain. He feels that the people who are with him are either cold or unfeeling or antagonistic. In a residential home or mental handicap hospital it is usually possible to identify the potentially violent situation.

The susceptible group

Property can be damaged by one violent person on his own, but much more damage is done by a group in violent action. In a residential situation such action takes time to build up, and needs a susceptible group. By this is meant a group of people, some of whom may have a history of violence, who may be placed together against their own wishes and dislike each other in consequence, and who may have a hatred of authority figures resulting from their handling by parents, teachers or police. The nurse or care assistant faced with the responsibility of managing this group may not be in a position to separate or scatter such an ill-matched assembly, but it may be worth trying. The allocation of different jobs in different areas may be possible. The attempt to get people to talk, even to laugh together, may help. Stories from the day's newspaper, the radio or even gossip – preferably constructive – about people known to the group may gain their attention.

The potential protagonist

The potential protagonist is the one likely to break into violence given the right historical situation, the presence of a susceptible group and appropriate provocation. Indeed, there may be several such

people in the group and the flashpoint of one may be different from that of another. It is rare for the potential protagonist not to show signs of the coming explosion. There are those trained to violence and skilled at concealing their feelings, such as soldiers, mafiosi or professional criminals, who may give no sign of the violence to come. It is debateable whether these people should be called more 'normal' than those about to be described, but it is true that by training – the result of learning theory – the more 'normal' the average soldier, the better he can school himself to swift and efficient violence.

This is not so for mentally handicapped people in a residential situation. Because of their historical background and upbringing, usually full of conflict between the feelings they feel and the good behaviour they are taught, the clash between emotions is almost always expressed in facial and bodily signs. Such signs have to be looked for, and weighed against knowledge of that person's past behaviour. For instance, the quiet reserved introvert may need much greater provocation to reach his flashpoint for violence than the habitually noisy extrovert. Each human is genetically differently endowed in the way he may respond to stimulus, so there is considerable variety in the signs different humans can present in the face of stress or provocation.

Negative signs foretelling the protagonist's outburst may be his sudden silence, his retirement to a corner, or the absence of facial colour in one who reacts to stress by an overactive sympathetic nervous system.

Positive signs foretelling an outburst are a flushed face for one with an overactive parasympathetic system or as the result of high blood pressure, tense, twitching face, eyes that fail to look at one directly, jerking hands, a body that is agitated and hops from one foot to another and fists that clasp and unclasp.

Psychiatry is full of signs to see – if one knows what to look for and has been taught to understand what one sees. It is very rare for a person under psychiatric care to cause violence that is completely unsignalled.

The provocative situation

It is an old saying that what stimulates one person may sedate another. It is also true that a group of people who know one another well will know each other's tender spots.

In a potentially explosive situation the provocation leading to violence can be very slight. A look, a gesture, a bodily touch or a word may be enough for those who wish to think ill of it. If the situation is as explosive as this it may be too late for prevention; but prevention is certainly best.

Preventive means

The simmering group or the irritable man or woman may have been thus all morning. Before they find an outlet for their feelings, it should be possible to scatter or divert them. The potential protagonist may be in a complaining mood, objecting to his chair, his clothing, his food or the weather. It may be that he dislikes the look on a person's face. By himself, without too many other people around, it is usually possible to avoid the chance provocative gesture which may trigger him off. If those surrounding him are cheery his attention may be diverted. If his interest is gained so that he can be helped to laugh with somebody about something emotionally neutral it may be possible to lower the rising head of steam within him. Obviously, one should never laugh at such a person: one has to work hard at trying carefully to laugh with him. Since a great deal of time may need to be spent with such a person, the organizer of the group in which the situation is building up may need to detail one or two people to take this as their task for a while.

Lack of communication between resident and resident or between resident and care staff is a common background to a rise in tension. The brooding person may be unable to communicate his resentment; it may be that others are unwilling to hear him. The care staff member who recognizes this problem has gone half-way to solving it because he is clearly using his powers of perception to receive non-verbal signals from his residents.

Non-verbal communication is more important than verbal; it has been called the primary signalling system among animals, including humans. Humans hardly have the raised fur of the dog, or tense tail of the rabbit to signify fight or fright, but the same hormone, adrenaline, circulates in humans, causing eye change, 'goose pimples' on the skin, blanching of the face and tension in the muscles of the body – all signs which can be identified by perceptive staff. Non-verbal replies could be to sit with the resident, smile with him, hold his hand, place a hand on the shoulder or walk with him.

Verbal communication, which has been called man's second signalling system, is the route which comes easiest to staff. Yet there may be six ways of saying the same thing, even a simple word like 'yes', and the perceptive staff member will use the sensit-

ive instrument of voice, like music, to soothe the savage breast.

The domineering or provocative staff member is another part of the equation which may build up to violence. There are some staff with a loud voice, a hectoring manner, an abusive style and a flow of expletive more appropriate on a parade ground. Such staff may be well-meaning but if they cannot adjust their manner it is better for senior staff to intervene rather than to allow matters to proceed to the point of an enquiry.

Certain environmental conditions tend to increase the probability of aggressive responses. Amongst these are heat, crowding and noise (Cleland, 1978). Comparative psychological studies suggest that when feeding areas become crowded individuals eat more and faster, and frequently become more hostile to their peers. With the proviso that the results of animal studies cannot always be extrapolated to account for human behaviour, it may be that the crowded canteens often found in institutions such as schools and hospitals, together with the rapid eating necessitated by trying to feed large numbers of individuals in a short time, encourages the manifestation of aggression. Cleland concludes that neglect, however unintentional, is a precipitator of aggressive behaviour.

'Neglect' implies a lack of stimulation, and it is self-evident that when opportunities for occupation and recreation of a meaningful and varied kind are made available then aggression is less likely to occur. There are studies which indicate that other forms of stimulation can be effective. Small amounts of alcohol, for instance, can lead to a reduction in overt aggression. However, large amounts do seem to weaken inhibition and increase the possibility of outburst. Exposure to mild types of erotica and the very mild levels of sexual arousal that are induced have a similar effect (Frodi, 1977), but, again, stronger sexual arousal induced by explicit and vivid erotica seems to increase aggression. The latter may occur particularly when there are few opportunities to reduce the arousal. Sexual tension is in fact a prime cause of violence at any age after puberty. Many people become resentful at their own tension, unrequited need for love, company or sex release, and furious if others indulge in front of them. Non-verbal displays of fury result, because at any ability level these needs are difficult to describe in words. Preventive methods are made more difficult by having to decide what comprises a 'small amount' of alcohol or a 'mildly arousing' piece of erotica when it is possible that a mentally handicapped person may not be able to make that judgement for himself. Other preventive methods depend on forecasting need, providing opportunities for mixing with the opposite sex, socials, dances and outings and fostering companionship.

Edgerton and Dingman (1964) found that when mentally handicapped people in institutions were allowed to mix freely with members of the opposite sex and were encouraged to engage in 'dating' with minimal direct supervision, the residents showed an increased understanding and internalization of the rules for acceptable conduct.

Psychodynamic theory suggests that anger can be prevented through 'catharsis'. In this instance, catharsis means encouraging potentially aggressive people to blow off steam by, for example, encouraging them to do physical exercise or compete in team games. The evidence seems to suggest that such cathartic activity does cause people to feel better, but that it does not necessarily reduce the tendency to engage in harmful acts of aggression.

Many of the strategies and techniques described below can be used in prevention as well as in the control of aggression.

THE MANAGEMENT OF AGGRESSION

Personal resources

Drugs and quiet side-rooms are very much secondary resources in the treatment of the violent. They are undeniably important as back-ups, but the primary resource is the staff member whose work gives him responsibility for the care of the susceptible groups discussed above. The ward sister portrayed in the film 'One Flew over the Cuckoo's Nest' is a prime example of the destructive use of a human resource. Not too far outside the field of psychiatry, Makarenko, the Russian educationalist, used his own personality to inspire thieving and murderous juveniles orphaned by the Soviet civil war to build an enthusiastic farm commune. In the United Kingdom, the first governor of Lowdham Grange Borstal selected some of the most violent and aggressive delinquents in the English borstal system to march north to Lowdham and camp with him while they built a new Borstal on the ruins of a derelict farm. He so inspired them that there were few runaways and many asked to stay informally after their sentence ended. These are extreme examples of the force of personality, but they serve as reminders that it is possible to inspire, exhort and cajole the most unlikely people and constructively channel their energies.

In the treatment setting the person caring for an unruly group must appreciate that the best tools he has for handling them are his own will and body. Both verbal and non-verbal signals are sent and received. Both must match up. Negative signals should not be given by the staff member. If by one's face and with one's body one shows fury, tension or annoyance, it is quite possible that these signals will be interpreted by the violent person as provocation to fresh mischief. Equally if by one's face and with one's body, one shows fear, anxiety or tremulousness then the violent person may feel it safe to proceed to an exhibition of greater fury.

Positive signals have to be taught to, and displayed by, care staff. The naturally self-confident caring person may feel that he has sufficient control over the situation to reach with, turn aside or play down the violence exhibited so far. He marches in firmly, with cheerful smile, firm voice and experience gained from years of successful evaluation of such emergencies and takes the violent person away from the provoking situation, to lead him to a quieter or more constructive place to chat to him. At this stage a cup of tea is often regarded as a panacea. A quiet room away from noise and the distractions of other people may be useful in which to talk calmly, steadily and stolidly to show that all may be accepted, if not forgiven. Such evaluation and experience in the caring person is not an inborn flair: it is learnt.

It is crucial for the caring person to decide correctly if he still has control of a changing situation. It is possible that the violent person has sufficient remaining control, so that after breaking, smashing or hitting, he will have 'blown his top', and be ready to accept direction, even reproof. If so, then the sooner his interest is diverted to a fresh area of activity, the better. If violence is escalating it is important to know at what level one should call for help. It is an old adage that it takes one to start a fight but three to impose peace. Better that these three are called early, rather than so late in the day that much destruction is caused, or many join in.

Discipline and love are both needed to raise children to successful adulthood; both are needed with violent humans for long-term success. A firm face and clear eye looking straight at the protagonist aid with one; a loving smile and a soft caressing hand may help with the other. One cannot be certain which recipe of firmness or love is best for a particular broth which is boiling – this is the art of diagnosis and treatment of a particular human situation. In any case each recipe can be argued at length by staff at the interminable conferences so much a feature of residential units, but when all is said and done at such meetings, most who talk will not have been present to assess the non-verbal signals which passed at the time between group members, potential protagonists and staff.

Reference has been made to violence and alcoholism before, for the use of alcohol by people with a grudge is well known. Unfortunately, alcohol is a slowly absorbed drug and first removes the self-restraint people commonly feel and may even give false courage before stupor occurs. Thus in a hospital for the mentally handicapped or residential home, where the potentially violent customer arrives after visiting the bar it may be necessary to identify the situation, and, make a discreet retreat to summon help, rather than attempting to deal unaided with the situation once violence escalates. Alcohol is not the only agent which may release violent behaviour and it is as well to remember that one cannot always go by the smell of a person's breath in identifying how drugged he might be.

Drug addiction units illustrate how much experience helps in containing the violent. These units treat aggressive and immature personalities who depend on alcohol, as well as other drugs, and build up special techniques and experience in dealing with such people. Much rests on knowing the individuals well enough to refer in companionable terms to their families and items of shared background experience. Staff get to know the people who matter to a resident and those who have an influence, so as to build up a special relationship, which at times of stress can be used constructively.

Client and staff signals

One must remember that the person who has initially damaged property, and may have progressed to arson or assault on other humans may become very guilty about the severity of his feelings. He may go from anger to weeping, from elation to depression. The calm interval here may be a sign of danger. He is best presented with a pair of staff eyes that reflect calmness and understanding, which are unwavering and never leave his face. If these eyes show that their owner is understanding and compassionate, and is a good listener to tales of woe as well as tales of hostility, all may be well. It is best not to leave the violent person alone in a situation where he can cause harm to himself as well as material damage, for self-destruction is always a possible end-point to the extremely violent. Equally, when those in a violent state have recovered to some extent, it is even less wise to leave them alone, in case

the swings of mood lead to another outburst of destruction.

BEHAVIOURAL MANAGEMENT TECHNIQUES

The above guidelines may well be sufficient to curb or avoid aggressive behaviour. However, if such approaches fail or if it is felt by the aggressor himself or those who are involved in his care or education that a more structured and detailed management strategy is needed, then certain techniques derived from learning theory may be considered appropriate. The techniques which have been found to be useful in modifying aggressive behaviour include:

1 changing the environment;
2 reinforcement of other behaviours;
3 extinction;
4 punishment.

There is, in addition, a technique called 'stress-inoculation' training, which is derived from the work of cognitive behaviour therapists.

These techniques are often used in combinations. It is impossible to say which technique or which combination of techniques is best. A fine observational analysis of the behaviour of each aggressive individual is the only way to decide how to set about managing his particular pattern of aggression. The first step in implementing any behaviour modification programme is to define the aggressive behaviour in objective, observable and measurable terms. For example, 'John hurts people' is too 'fuzzy' a statement. What specific forms does his 'hurting people' take? Does he pinch, punch, bite, scratch, kick or hit people with objects? Once the behaviours have been defined precisely then the next step is to find out under what circumstances these behaviours occur, how often, and how long. The best way of solving this problem is to observe the client in his natural setting and note the antecedents (A) of any of the defined behaviours (B) and the consequences (C) of those behaviours. This 'ABC' analysis is the cornerstone of any programme. It will help identify how the aggression is being reinforced and maintained, and will go a long way towards helping select an appropriate technique for decreasing the behaviours. Further observations of this nature will have to be taken throughout the implementation of any programme so that its effectiveness (or otherwise) can be assessed objectively.

Positive reinforcement

Observations should not be limited to the details of a person's aggressive behaviours. It is essential to establish also what events, objects and people are reinforcers for the person's positive and valuable behaviours. It may be observed, for example, that the frequency of positive verbal contacts with other people increases when these contacts are responded to with questions about the person's well-being, or that the duration of 'on-task' work behaviour increases if tokens, which can be exchanged for goods in a shop, are used as rewards for the 'on-task' behaviour. It is essential to establish such connections for two main reasons. Firstly, people with mental handicap have a relatively limited repertoire of behaviours. To attempt to reduce the duration, frequency or intensity even of aggressive behaviours without actively encouraging socially appropriate and personally valuable behaviours is morally and ethically unacceptable. Secondly, if carers or teachers are encouraged to attend to negative behaviours (such as aggression) alone, then there is a tendency for their own behaviour to become increasingly negative and even punitive. Moreover, if over-attention to aggressive behaviour leads to the sharp reduction or withdrawal of well-established positive reinforcers then further aggression may occur (Feldman, 1977).

Changing the environment

The ABC analysis may suggest that some or all the aggressive behaviours are controlled by a specific stimulus, for instance a particular person, a particular room or a particular event. For example, if a hostel resident is violent when standing in a queue for his dinner, it may be that the aggression occurs when one other resident in particular is near him in the queue. Other stimuli may be controlling this behaviour as well; for example, the aggression may occur under these conditions only when there is a several-minute delay before collecting his dinner or when a particular staff member is visible. The solution in this sort of case may seem obvious. That is, ensure that there is less of a delay, that the other resident is further away in the queue, and that the staff member remains in an unobtrusive position. However, any such rearrangement of environmental stimuli will have a greater chance of being successful if any appropriate behaviours are clearly and consistently reinforced as well.

Sometimes it is not necessary or possible to eliminate a behaviour completely: it may be suf-ficient to get the behaviour to occur under limited, prescribed circumstances. For example, an active large severely handicapped person may of necessity be in the company of smaller physically handicapped and more delicate people. The vigour and power of the former's unpredictable movements could intentionally or otherwise cause pain or damage to the others. Setting up a special place and time when vigorous activity is positively encouraged (e.g. half an hour per day in a soft-play area or a gymnasium) could help reduce the problem. This is another instance of getting a behaviour under stimulus control.

Reinforcement of other behaviours

It is possible to use reinforcement of other behaviours without any additional programmes to reduce aggressive behaviour. Realistically, such an approach is only likely to be appropriate in cases of mild or occasional aggression. Reinforcing *any* other behaviour will not do. It is advisable to look for behaviours which are incompatible with the particular sorts of aggression manifested. For example, a child who occasionally approaches and pushes other children may be reinforced for any approach to children which is not followed by pushing. In addition, any cooperative interaction with other children may be reinforced.

It is worth noting here that some success has been claimed for the technique of reinforcing low rates of undesirable behaviour, but studies so far have been limited to schools and children. A person producing lengthy or very frequent aggressive behaviours could have any low-rate periods of aggression reinforced. If these low-rate periods subsequently extended then more time would be available to intervene and to try to substitute incompatible behaviours.

Extinction

Extinction occurs when reinforcement (for example attention) which has been maintaining a behaviour is withdrawn. Considering the complexity of the determinants of aggressive behaviour described earlier, it is often difficult to identify exactly what the reinforcers are. When the contingencies can be identified then extinction may be a suitable technique, but usually only for mild or verbal aggression, as most physical attacks cannot be ignored. If, for example, adult attention following verbal aggression is the identified reinforcer then withdrawing the attention would result in a decrease in the behaviour. However, serious physical attacks may be reinforced by the cries or cowering of the victim, in which case the reinforcer cannot be withdrawn.

Another problem arising in using extinction is the effect of the so-called 'extinction burst'. It is known that the immediate consequence of withdrawing a reinforcer is often that the target behaviour increases in intensity, frequency or duration, before it begins to reduce. Where the aggressive behaviour being modified is already dangerous and painful then the extinction programme could lead to an intolerable, if temporary, escalation of physical harm. The possible consequences of introducing such a programme need to be considered very carefully indeed.

Punishment

Punishment is an emotive word which connotes retribution and suffering. In behaviour modification punishment has a somewhat different meaning: it refers to the arrangement of consequences of a behaviour in such a way as to reduce the probability of that behaviour occurring. This definition makes it clear that the only justification for the introduction of aversive consequences is the planned reduction of, in this instance, aggressive behaviour. There have been reports of cases where 'behaviour modification' has been used to condone and to attempt to justify retaliatory and sometimes brutal actions. To avoid such abuses it is essential that use of aversive consequences is subject to rigorous and systematic monitoring and review. Any institution (hospital, special unit, school, adult training centre, hostel, community support service, or whatever) which allows the use of aversive consequences should have adequate safeguards against abuse, including a written code of practice for use of behaviour modification procedures (see, for example, the report of the working party on behaviour modification of the British Psychological Society Professional Affairs Board, 1978).

Time-out

'Time-out' is an abbreviation of 'time-out from positive reinforcement'. This involves arranging for positive reinforcement to become unavailable for a short period and usually entails the individual being removed from a situation. Success in using this technique depends upon a number of factors. Firstly, the removal should be immediate so that it is clearly contingent upon the aggressive behaviour; secondly, the business of removing the aggressor

should not become positively reinforcing. To avoid this possibility the person or people involved should not speak to the aggressor, should not make eye-contact and should use the absolute minimum of force in the process of removal. The room used for 'time-out' should be close at hand and should be devoid of opportunities for positive reinforcement. There is little point in taking the aggressor to a room in which there is furniture and a TV, for example, where opportunities exist for further violent behaviour or for entertainment. Consequently, the room used is usually bare. It should also be possible to observe the person so that when the undesirable behaviour stops he can be allowed out. The release from time-out should not occur immediately after cessation of aggression, but after a brief period of calm, acceptable behaviour. Evidence from the literature suggests that short periods of time-out (one to five minutes) are more effective than longer periods.

Obviously, such a technique will only be effective with children and adults for whom physical removal with the minimum of fuss is feasible. Finally, as the phrase 'time-out from positive reinforcement' suggests, there must be plenty of alternative positive reinforcement available, perhaps for incompatible behaviours (see above).

Response-cost

Where tokens are in use as part of a programme of positive reinforcement, either with groups or individuals, then 'fines' can be used to counter aggression. Response-cost will be effective only if not used excessively. As a general rule, the individual should have more opportunities of earning tokens than of losing them (Gathercole et al., 1980). However, those in charge of planning the programme and delivering the tokens have to find the right balance between enabling the individual to earn so many tokens that a fine is of no consequence and allowing him so few tokens that he has a constant 'overdraft' and rejects the token system altogether.

Restraint

A recent review (Murphy, 1980) comments upon the scarcity of literature on the use of restraint with mentally handicapped people. In some instances, restraint amounts to 'time-out', but the prevention of movement is additionally aversive.

Restraint contingent upon the self-injurious behaviour of eye-poking was used with a mentally handicapped partially-sighted girl. The restraint took the form of sitting the girl in a chair, placing her arms across her body, and holding her wrists from behind for 30 seconds. The programme reduced, but did not eliminate, eye-poking. Careful recording was necessary to ensure that the restraint was not positively reinforcing (in other words, that eye-poking did not increase following the restraint).

Over-correction

This was introduced by Foxx and Azrin (1972) as a way of reducing aggressive disruptive behaviour in mentally handicapped people. As an example of the use of over-correction (OC), a person who throws furniture may be required to replace it in its original position and then to straighten *all* the furniture in the room. This is called restitutional over-correction. Positive-practice over-correction might involve teaching the person the proper use of the furniture, for example, sitting on a chair at a table or setting the table. Restitutional OC depends upon it being (a) directly related to the aggressive behaviour, (b) applied immediately following the aggression, (c) extended in duration to ensure that it continues long enough to be aversive and (d) applied in an active and effortful manner (Marholin et al., 1980). The paper by Marholin et al. describes a study by Sumner in which it was found that when aggressive and disruptive behaviours in schizophrenic patients were treated by OC, a reduction in these behaviours of 91 % was observed in the group receiving restitutional OC, and there was a reduction of 55 % in an untreated group. Sumner suggested that the latter figure resulted from the untreated group modelling the behaviour of the OC group.

Aversive shock

This technique should not be confused with electro-convulsive therapy (ECT). Aversive shock refers to the delivery of shock contingent upon the manifestation of certain extreme behaviours.

Most writers now hold that shock should only be used when all other management strategies have failed and the behaviour of the individual is so extreme that his life is threatened (Corbett, 1975). Consequently, electric shock should be considered only when the individual's behaviour is excessive self-aggression (e.g., severe head-banging or self-biting). Even in such cases it has been found difficult to arrange for the effects of the shock treatment to generalize over time and to other environments. It is most improbable that electric shock would be selected as a treatment for inter-personal aggression.

Generalization and maintenance

In all punishment procedures, generalization may prove to be a problem. There is a tendency for the person on the receiving end of the aversive programme to associate the unpleasant consequences with the trainer or with the environment in which the programme is carried out. Consequently, the frequency of aggressive acts may increase in other settings or in the absence of the 'punisher'. An integral part of any plan to use aversive consequences is to teach generalization. This may take the form of varying the person carrying out the programme and varying the preferably natural settings in which it is carried out. There is also evidence to suggest that once the punishment is discontinued, the target behaviour may reappear at original strength. The reasons for this are not clear but it could be due to the lack of opportunities to produce positive behaviours and have them reinforced whilst the aversive regime is in operation. Some studies suggest that the reappearance of aggressive behaviours seems to be a function of the powerful reinforcement of such behaviour. For example, a group of mildly handicapped aggressive people placed together in a special unit may provide extensive positive reinforcement for each other's aggression. If negative sanctions applied by staff are strong enough to counteract peer influences then conforming behaviour may be achieved so long as the sanctions are in operation. But when the aversive consequences are removed peer reinforcement quickly reinstates the aggressive behaviour. Bandura (1969) suggests that it is only by rearranging the contingencies, perhaps by allowing a greater degree of self-determination to such a group so that anti-social and anti-authority behaviour has limited pay-off, that such maintenance might be avoided.

Aggression against oneself or others is frightening and every effort should be made to redirect or reduce it by means which encourage positive behaviour. However, as those faced by aggression and other forms of violence are aware, punishment in the forms defined above may be the only way of helping an aggressive mentally handicapped person. To quote Tharp and Wetzel (1969), 'it is more degrading to be removed from responsibility for one's behaviour than to be punished for it'.

Stress inoculation training

Stress inoculation training as a strategy for coping with aggression has purposely been left to last. The success of such training depends to a degree on the verbal ability of the trainee and entirely on his desire to learn how to control his anger and avoid aggression. The stages of the training are as follows:

1 A stage in which clients are taught to examine their feelings and thoughts and, in particular, to identify what they feel and think when they become angry.
2 Relaxation training to help control the physiological effects of emotional arousal. Training involves practice in thinking about images and instructions to oneself which will help reduce anger (a little like the well-known strategy of counting to ten when feeling angry).
3 An applied stage in which a client is asked to 're-run' or 're-live' in his own mind a number of recent anger-producing experiences and to re-hearse the controls he has been taught.

Such an approach has been used successfully with neurotic patients and with people of a variety of ages and intelligence levels whose aggressive be-haviours included public fighting, kicking in a plate-glass door and hurling a brick through a car window; one client decorated objects with blood from his fists after having intentionally hit a wall (Meichenbaum, 1977). To date no studies have specifically included people with mental handicap, but there is no reason to suppose that the approach would not be effective with mildly mentally handi-capped aggressive clients who may be more pre-pared to respond to this kind of treatment than to the other techniques described above.

PHYSICAL MANAGEMENT

Action

If two residents are fighting, a staff member first estimates his chances of success in stopping them, and then plans his intervention, including the way his face, his body and his arrival are seen by the participants.

Surprises and noise level are useful. A sudden arrival may daunt fighters, a quiet voice or sudden shout of 'What's this?' may surprise them. With children or underdeveloped handicapped people, two forceful hands may part fighters easily, whilst women fighters may respond with shame to a male nurse and vice versa. It is said that Newcastle pub landlords always call their wives to part drunken males!

One axiom for care staff is to use only that little bit more force that is necessary to subdue violence in progress; this might be termed 'approved esca-lation'. Thus two staff separating two patients fighting with teeth and nails are justified in dragging each back by his coat arms. A charge nurse who first knocked to the ground a severely physically handi-capped male who threatened to bite him, and then kicked his face and ribs, in temper at the end of a long day, was asked by the subsequent enquiry to resign, being judged guilty of 'gross escalation'.

A second staff axiom is to avoid damage to the patient. One should part fighters from behind, holding the clothes of the upper arm or upper leg to avoid fractures. A sitting patient can be similarly pinioned in his chair.

In the past physical methods of restraint such as strong garments or the use of chains or ropes were used, but these are now outmoded. Sometimes a side-room or quiet room is necessary for peace, quiet and segregation and discussion with a staff member. If there are very few staff, or many helpless persons about, it is on rare occasions necessary to seclude or isolate the violent person in a locked room. Most residential units require this event to be recorded and reported to avoid later charges of improper incarceration.

The law

Common law recognizes a duty on the ordinary citizen to prevent someone else wilfully damaging himself or a weaker citizen, but prosecutions are rare. The duty on paid care staff, parents or teachers to prevent damage to their charges is higher; for example, some are convicted each year in the United Kingdom for being drunk in charge of a child.

The law lays a duty on police, staff and parents to use only that force just necessary to subdue continu-ing violence – 'approved escalation'. A person is also entitled to defend himself and his charges, so for example in extremis it is a valid defence to manslaughter if a citizen kills believing himself to be about to be murdered.

The case of Poutney *v.* Griffiths (1975) has clarified the position on 'control' of potentially violent patients. This case stemmed from a Broadmoor patient, detained during Her Majesty's pleasure, alleging that at the end of visiting time a nurse had punched him on the shoulder, which was denied. The magistrates convicted the nurse. The nurse appealed and the conviction was quashed on a technicality, as the patient had failed to obtain the permission of the High Court to proceed as required by Section 141 of the 1959 Mental Health Act. More importantly the House of Lords dismissed the patient's counter appeal, Lord Edmund Davies laying down case law: 'The conception of detention and treatment necessarily implies that the staff of the hospital, including the male nurses, can and on occasion must, use reasonable force in order to ensure that control is exercised over the patient.'

The 1959 Act has now been replaced by the 1983 Mental Health Act, but there is still a requirement to obtain permission of the High Court (Section 139) before proceeding with legal action. There is, as yet, no reason to suppose that the above judgement is now inapplicable.

Whilst this appears to apply to those detained under the Mental Health Act, and common law would include restraining patients from harming others, it is wise for staff needing to restrain the habitually violent informal patient, to ask their Responsible Medical Officer to use compulsory powers (under Sections 3, 4 & 5 of the 1983 Act) to cover those in need.

Drugs

Drugs are commonly used to impose quietness, and most require medical prescription. Alcohol is the oldest sedative, and the most common drug to be self-prescribed by those who feel violent. It is noted here because, like other sedatives, in the early stages of sedation it causes loss of self-control and possible escalation of violence. Owing to the variable and erratic uptake from the stomach there follows a lengthy period of failing coordination, during which injury to the head may compound the sedation. It is not recommended.

Diazepam (Valium) 10 mg by intramuscular or slow intravenous injection is most effective for the violent. Orally, 10–20 mg by tablet or syrup is effective. It needs a medical prescription and is recommended.

Chlorpromazine (Largactil) 50 mg by intramuscular injection or 100–300 mg by tablet or syrup is hallowed by long usage in patients who are violent. It is safe, can be repeated two or three times in the day for the extremely violent and has been standard medication in casualty departments for drunkards for many years. It has to be given as a result of medical prescription and is recommended.

Haloperidol (Serenace) 3 mg orally is now often used. It probably has fewer side-effects than chlorpromazine and is more slowly absorbed and metabolized. Side-effects are rare. A medical prescription is necessary. It is recommended. Doses of up of to 30 mg in a day are used in general psychiatric hospitals to control manic or highly aggressive schizophrenic patients.

Paraldehyde 5 ml by intramuscular injection or up to 15 ml in divided injections, has been used for many years. Whilst sterile, these injections are painful and have to be given by an experienced person; since the violent person may dislike injections, its use requires that there are plenty of staff to aid the therapist. It is therefore of limited use.

Lithium (e.g. Priadel sustained release) in a dose of 400–1200 mg daily has also been found very effective in stabilizing some severely aggressive severely mentally handicapped people. The normal precautions for use must be observed.

AFTER-CARE

Following a violent incident, it is essential that the person concerned should be advised how he might better handle himself in future, Strong emotional feelings are not forgotten; indeed, they provide some of the longest lasting memory traces of all. It is never wise to ignore studiously an aggressive incident afterwards. Once it has died down the person in charge can often suggest better ways of displaying feeling than the way the aggressor chose. After the incident is over, it is a good time to try to redress any grievances possible, to offer work or activity which better deploys energy felt, to rearrange sitting, sleeping or living arrangements between people who cannot understand each other and even to allow restitution of damage done by willing work offered.

We live in a litigious age. It is therefore essential to have a proper record of the circumstances of the incident, the people concerned and what actually happened written down as soon as possible after the event has closed. Because strong memories may remain of emotion felt, those involved may well describe the incident in more lurid terms elsewhere. It therefore behoves one to show the record to those in authority who are therefore better prepared to avoid a recurrence. More staff, a redeployment of personnel, more opportunities for work and informed discussion of what was done and what could better be done may well all be indicated.

CONCLUSION

The prevention and management of aggression are important to those working with mentally handicapped people. Few staff are born to success: it comes with experience, training and the careful recognition and evaluation of signals or signs shown by clients. The art of constructing an effective care team is in staff building up expertise, and thus confidence, so that they can predict crises, take preventive measures and manage aggression as constructively as possible.

FURTHER READING

Theories of aggression

Bandura (1969) gives a brief but useful account of learning theorists' approach to aggression (pp. 378–385). Tajfel's (1978) account of the way in which aggression occurs and is maintained between groups is both fascinating and readable (pp. 401–422). Meichenbaum (1977) describes the role of cognitive factors in anger and aggression (pp. 143–182). This is particularly useful for those working with the mildly handicapped. Feldman (1977) gives an excellent coverage of the whole range of criminal behaviour. Although not strictly about mental handicap, Chapter 3, on aggression, and some of the subsequent chapters contain a wealth of information and relevant advice.

Between them, these four books give a reasonably comprehensive account of differing psychological areas of aggression.

Treatment of aggression

Bandura, Meichenbaum and Feldman cover treatment approaches, but one of the best books currently available on behaviour modification with mentally handicapped people is that by Yule and Carr (1980). Detailed information is given on how to set about functional analysis of behaviour and about the strengths and weaknesses of different management techniques.

For those who wish for a simple introduction to the business of behaviour modification, Neisworth and Smith's (1973) book (about children) is clear and easy to read.

BIBLIOGRAPHY

Bandura A (1969) *Principles of Behaviour Modification.* New York: Holt, Rinehart & Winston.

Bandura A (1973) *Aggression: A Social Learning Analysis.* Englewood Cliffs, New Jersey: Prentice-Hall.

British Psychological Society Professional Affairs Board (1978) Report of the Working Party on Behaviour Modification.

Cleland CC (1978) *Mental Retardation: A Developmental Approach.* Englewood Cliffs, New Jersey: Prentice-Hall.

Corbett J (1975) Aversion for the treatment of self-injurious behaviour. *Journal of Mental Deficiency Research 19:* 79–96.

Craft M & Mathews J (1984) Lithium and the mentally handicapped: a review. *Journal of the British Institute of Mental Handicap* (in press).

Department of Health and Social Security (1976) *The Management of Violent or Potentially Violent Hospital Patients.* London: HMSO.

Edgerton RB & Dingman HF (1964) Good reasons for bad supervision: 'dating' in a hospital for the mentally retarded. *Psychiatric Quarterly Supplement, Part 2:* 1–13.

Feldman MP (1977) *Criminal Behaviour: A Psychological Analysis.* London: Wiley.

Foxx RM & Azrin NH (1972) Restitution: a method of eliminating aggressive–disruptive behaviour of retarded and brain-damaged patients. *Behaviour Research and Therapy 10:* 15–27.

Frodi A (1977) Sexual arousal, situational restrictiveness and aggressive behaviour. *Journal of Research in Personality 11:* 48–58.

Gathercole C & Carr J (1980) The use of tokens with individuals and groups. In Yule W and Carr J (eds) *Behaviour Modification for the Mentally Handicapped.* London: Croom Helm.

Goldstein JH, Davis RW & Herman D (1975) Escalation of aggression: experimental studies. *Journal of Personality and Social Psychology 31:* 162–170.

Home Office and Department of Health and Social Security (1975) *Report of the Committee on Mentally Abnormal Offenders (Butler Committee).* Cmnd 6244. London: HMSO.

Lorenz K (1967) *On Aggression.* New York: Harcourt Brace and World.

Marholin D, Luiselli JK & Townsend NH (1980) Overcorrection: an examination of its rationale and treatment effectiveness. In Hersen M, Eiser RM & Miller PM (eds) *Progress in Behaviour Modification 9.* London: Academic Press.

Meichenbaum D (1977) *Cognitive Behaviour Modification.* New York: Plenum Press.

Milgram S (1974) *Obedience to Authority.* New York: Harper and Row; London: Tavistock.

Murphy G (1980) Decreasing undesirable behaviours. In Yule W & Carr J (eds) *Behaviour Modification for the Mentally Handicapped.* London: Croom Helm.

Neisworth JT & Smith RM (1973) *Modifying Retarded Behaviour.* Boston: Houghton Mifflin.

Parke RD, Berkowitz L, Leyens JP, West SG & Sebastian RJ (1977) Some effects of violent and non-violent movies on the behaviour of juvenile delinquents. In Berkowitz L (ed) *Advances in Experimental Social Psychology 10.* New York: Academic Press.

Poutney v. *Griffiths* [1975] 2 All E.R. 881 H.L.

Royal College of Nursing (1972) *Care of the Violent Patient.* London: RCN.

South East Thames Regional Health Authority (1977) *Guidelines to the Nursing Management of Violence.* (20-minute film, may be hired).

Tajfel H (1978) Intergroup behaviour: I, individual perspectives. In Tajfel H & Fraser C (eds) *Introducing Social Psychology.* pp 401–422. Harmondsworth: Penguin.

Tharp RG & Wetzel RJ (1969) *Behaviour Modification in the Natural Environment.* New York: Academic Press.

Yule W & Carr J (eds) (1980) *Behaviour Modification for the Mentally Handicapped.* London: Croom Helm.

Index